ACCA

Paper P3

Business Analysis

Complete Text

British library cataloguing-in-publication data

A catalogue record for this book is available from the British Library.

Published by:
Kaplan Publishing UK
Unit 2 The Business Centre
Molly Millars Lane
Wokingham
Berkshire
RG41 2QZ

ISBN 978-1-78415-684-8

© Kaplan Financial Limited, 2016

Printed and bound in Great Britain

Acknowledgements

We are grateful to the Association of Chartered Certified Accountants and the Chartered Institute of Management Accountants for permission to reproduce past examination questions. The answers have been prepared by Kaplan Publishing.

Contents

Paper Introduction

How to Use the Materials

These Kaplan Publishing learning materials have been carefully designed to make your learning experience as easy as possible and to give you the best chances of success in your examinations.

The product range contains a number of features to help you in the study process. They include:

(1) Detailed study guide and syllabus objectives

(2) Description of the examination

(3) Study skills and revision guidance

(4) Complete text or essential text

(5) Question practice

The sections on the study guide, the syllabus objectives, the examination and study skills should all be read before you commence your studies. They are designed to familiarise you with the nature and content of the examination and give you tips on how to best to approach your learning.

The **complete text or essential text** comprises the main learning materials and gives guidance as to the importance of topics and where other related resources can be found. Each chapter includes:

- The **learning objectives** contained in each chapter, which have been carefully mapped to the examining body's own syllabus learning objectives or outcomes. You should use these to check you have a clear understanding of all the topics on which you might be assessed in the examination.

- The **chapter diagram** provides a visual reference for the content in the chapter, giving an overview of the topics and how they link together.

- The **content** for each topic area commences with a brief explanation or definition to put the topic into context before covering the topic in detail. You should follow your studying of the content with a review of the illustration/s. These are worked examples which will help you to understand better how to apply the content for the topic.

- **Test your understanding** sections provide an opportunity to assess your understanding of the key topics by applying what you have learned to short questions. Answers can be found at the back of each chapter.

KAPLAN PUBLISHING

- **Summary diagrams** complete each chapter to show the important links between topics and the overall content of the paper. These diagrams should be used to check that you have covered and understood the core topics before moving on.

- **Question practice** is provided at the back of each text.

Quality and accuracy are of the utmost importance to us so if you spot an error in any of our products, please send an email to mykaplanreporting@kaplan.com with full details, or follow the link to the feedback form in MyKaplan.

Our Quality Coordinator will work with our technical team to verify the error and take action to ensure it is corrected in future editions.

Icon Explanations

 Definition – Key definitions that you will need to learn from the core content.

 Key Point – Identifies topics which are key to success and are often examined.

 Expandable Text – Expandable text provides you with additional information about a topic area and may help you gain a better understanding of the core content. Essential text users can access this additional content online (read it where you need further guidance or skip over when you are happy with the topic).

 Test Your Understanding – Exercises for you to complete to ensure that you have understood the topics just learned.

 Illustration – Worked examples help you understand the core content better.

 **Tricky topic** – When reviewing these areas care should be taken and all illustrations and test your understanding exercises should be completed to ensure that the topic is understood.

On-line subscribers

Our on-line resources are designed to increase the flexibility of your learning materials and provide you with immediate feedback on how your studies are progressing.

If you are subscribed to our on-line resources you will find:

(1) On-line referenceware: reproduces your Complete or Essential Text on-line, giving you anytime, anywhere access.

(2) On-line testing: provides you with additional on-line objective testing so you can practice what you have learned further.

(3) On-line performance management: immediate access to your on-line testing results. Review your performance by key topics and chart your achievement through the course relative to your peer group.

Ask your local customer services staff if you are not already a subscriber and wish to join.

Syllabus

Paper background

The aim of ACCA Paper P3, **Business analysis**, is to apply relevant knowledge and skills and to exercise professional judgement in assessing strategic position, determining strategic choice and implementing strategic action through beneficial business process and structural change; coordinating knowledge systems and information technology and by effectively managing quality processes, projects and people within financial and other resource constraints.

Objectives of the Syllabus

*   Assess the strategic position of an organisation.

*   Evaluate the strategic choices available to an organisation.

*   Discuss how an organisation might go about its strategic implementation.

*   Evaluate and redesign business processes and structures to implement and support the organisation's strategy taking account of customer and other major stakeholder requirements.

*   Integrate appropriate information technology solutions to support the organisation's strategy.

*   Apply appropriate quality initiatives to implement and support the organisation's strategy.

*   Advise on the principles of project management to enable the implementation of aspects of the organisation's strategy with the twin objectives of managing risk and ensuring benefits realisation.

*   Analyse and evaluate the effectiveness of a company's strategy and the financial consequences of implementing strategic decisions.

*   The role of leadership and people management in formulating and implementing business strategy.

Core areas of the syllabus

The syllabus for Paper P3, Business Analysis, is primarily concerned with two issues. The first is the external forces (the behaviour of customers, the initiatives of competitors, the emergence of new laws and regulations) that shape the environment of an organisation. The second is the internal ambitions and concerns (desire for growth, the design of processes, the competences of employees, the financial resources) that exist within an organisation. This syllabus looks at both of these perspectives, from assessing strategic position and choice to identifying and formulating strategy and strategic action. It identifies opportunities for beneficial change that involve people, finance and information technology. It examines how these opportunities may be implemented through the appropriate management of programmes and projects.

The syllabus begins with the assessment of strategic position in the present and in the future using relevant forecasting techniques, and is primarily concerned with the impact of the external environment on the business, its internal capabilities and expectations and how the organisation positions itself under these constraints. It examines how factors such as culture, leadership and stakeholder expectations shape organisational purpose. Strategic choice is concerned with decisions which have to be made about an organisation's future and the way in which it can respond to the influences and pressures identified in the assessment of its current and future strategic position.

Strategic action concerns the implementation of strategic choices and the transformation of these choices into organisational action. Such action takes place in day-to-day processes and organisational relationships and these processes and relationships need to be managed in line with the intended strategy, involving the effective coordination of information technology, people, finance and other business resources.

Companies that undertake successful business process redesign claim significant organisational improvements. This simply reflects the fact that many existing processes are less efficient than they could be and that new technology makes it possible to design more efficient processes. Strategic planning and strategy implementation has to be subject to financial benchmarks. Financial analysis explicitly recognises this, reminding candidates of the importance of focusing on the key management accounting techniques that help to determine strategic action and the financial ratios and measures that may be used to assess the viability of a strategy and to monitor and measure its success. Throughout, the syllabus recognises that successful strategic planning and implementation requires the effective recruitment, leadership, organisation and training, and development of people.

Syllabus objectives

We have reproduced the ACCA's syllabus below, showing where the objectives are explored within this book. Within the chapters, we have broken down the extensive information found in the syllabus into easily digestible and relevant sections, called Content Objectives. These correspond to the objectives at the beginning of each chapter.

Syllabus learning objectives and chapter references:

A THE STRATEGIC POSITION OF AN ORGANISATION

1 The need for, and purpose of, strategic and business analysis

(a) Recognise the fundamental nature and vocabulary of strategy and strategic decisions.[2] **Ch. 1**

(b) Discuss how strategy may be formulated at different levels (corporate business level, operational) of an organisation.[2] **Ch. 1**

(c) Explore the Johnson & Scholes and Whittington model for defining elements of strategic management – the strategic position, strategic choices and strategy into action.[3] **Ch. 1**

(d) Analyse how strategic management is affected by different organisational contexts.[3] **Ch. 1**

(e) Compare three different strategy lenses (Johnson & Scholes) for viewing and understanding strategy and strategic management.[3] **Ch. 1**

(f) Explore the scope of business analysis and its relationship to strategy and strategic management in the context of the relational diagram of this course.[3] **Ch. 1**

2 Environmental issues affecting the strategic position of, and future outlook for, an organisation

(a) Assess the macro-environment of an organisation using PESTEL. [3] **Ch. 2**

(b) Highlight the external key drivers of change likely to affect the structure of a sector or market.[3] **Ch. 2**

(c) Explore, using Porter's Diamond, the influence of national competitiveness on the strategic position of an organisation.[2] **Ch. 2**

(d) Prepare scenarios reflecting different assumptions about the future environment of an organisation.[3] **Ch. 2**

(e) Evaluate methods of business forecasting used when quantitatively assessing the likely outcome of different business strategies.[3] **Ch. 2**

3 Competitive forces affecting an organisation

(a) Discuss the significance of industry, sector and convergence.[3] **Ch. 2**

(b) Evaluate the sources of competition in an industry or sector using Porter's five forces framework.[3] **Ch. 2**

(c) Assess the contribution of the lifecycle model, the cycle of competition and associated costing implications to understanding competitive behaviour.[3] **Ch. 3**

(d) Analyse the influence of strategic groups and market segmentation. [3] **Ch. 2**

(e) Determine the opportunities and threats posed by the environment of an organisation.[2] **Ch. 2**

4 Marketing and the value of goods and services

(a) Analyse customers and markets.[2] **Ch. 11**

(b) Establish appropriate critical success factors (CSFs) and key performance indicators (KPIs) for products and services.[2] **Ch. 3**

(c) Explore the role of the value chain in creating and sustaining competitive advantage.[2] **Ch. 5**

(d) Advise on the role and influence of value networks.[3] **Ch. 5**

(e) Assess different approaches to benchmarking an organisation's performance.[3] **Ch. 5**

5 The internal resources, capabilities and competences of an organisation

(a) Discriminate between strategic capability, threshold resources, threshold competences, unique resources and core competences. [3] **Ch. 3**

(b) Discuss from a strategic perspective, the continuing need for effective cost management and control systems within organisations.[3] **Ch. 5**

(c) Discuss the capabilities required to sustain competitive advantage. [2] **Ch. 5**

(d) Explain the impact of new product, process, and service developments and innovation in supporting business strategy.[2] **Ch. 5**

(e) Discuss the contribution of organisational knowledge to the strategic capability of an organisation.[2] **Ch. 5**

(f) Determine the strengths and weaknesses of an organisation and formulate an appropriate SWOT analysis.[2] **Ch. 3**

6 The expectations of stakeholders and the influence of ethics and culture

(a) Advise on the implications of corporate governance on organisational purpose and strategy.[2] **Ch. 4**

(b) Evaluate, through stakeholder mapping, the relative influence of stakeholders on organisational purpose and strategy.[3] **Ch. 4**

(c) Assess ethical influences on organisational purpose and strategy. [3] **Ch. 4**

(d) Explore the scope of corporate social responsibility.[3] **Ch. 4**

(e) Assess the impact of culture on organisational purpose and strategy. [3] **Ch. 16**

(f) Prepare and evaluate a cultural web of an organisation.[2] **Ch. 16**

(g) Advise on how organisations can communicate their core values and mission.[3] **Ch. 4**

(h) Explain the role of integrated reporting in communicating strategy and strategic performance.[2] **Ch. 4**

B THE STRATEGIC CHOICES AVAILABLE TO AN ORGANISATION

1 The influence of corporate strategy on an organisation

(a) Explore the relationship between a corporate parent and its business units.[2] **Ch. 7**

(b) Assess the opportunities and potential problems of pursuing different corporate strategies of product/market diversification from a national, international and global perspective.[3] **Ch. 8**

(c) Assess the opportunities and potential problems of pursuing a corporate strategy of international diversity, international scale operations and globalisation.[3] **Ch. 8**

(d) Discuss a range of ways that the corporate parent can create and destroy organisational value.[2] **Ch. 7**

(e) Explain three corporate rationales for adding value – portfolio managers, synergy managers and parental developers.[3] **Ch. 7**

(f) Explain and apply a range of the following portfolio models (the BCG growth/share matrix, public sector matrix, the parenting matrix or Ashridge Portfolio display) to assist corporate parents in managing their business portfolios.[3] **Ch. 7**

2 Alternative approaches to achieving competitive advantage

(a) Evaluate, through the strategy clock, generic strategy options available to an organisation.[3] **Ch. 5**

(b) Advise on how price-based strategies, differentiation and lock-in can help an organisation sustain its competitive advantage.[3] **Ch. 5**

(c) Assess opportunities for improving competitiveness through collaboration.[3] **Ch. 5**

3 Alternative directions and methods of development

(a) Determine generic development directions (employing an adapted Ansoff matrix and a TOWS matrix) available to an organisation.[2] **Ch. 6**

(b) Assess how internal development, mergers, acquisitions and strategic alliances can be used as different methods of pursuing a chosen strategic direction.[3] **Ch. 7**

(c) Establish success criteria to assist in the choice of a strategic direction and method (strategic options).[2] **Ch. 7**

(d) Assess the suitability of different strategic options to an organisation. [3] **Ch. 6**

(e) Assess the feasibility of different strategic options to an organisation. [3] **Ch. 6**

(f) Establish the acceptability of strategic options to an organisation through analysing risk and return on investment.[3] **Ch. 6**

C STRATEGIC ACTION

1 Organising and enabling success

(a) Advise on how the organisation can be structured to deliver a selected strategy.[3] **Ch. 8**

(b) Explore generic processes that take place within the structure, with particular emphasis on the planning process.[3] **Ch. 8**

(c) Discuss how internal relationships can be organised to deliver a selected strategy.[2] **Ch. 7**

(d) Discuss how organisational structure and external relationships (boundary-less organisations; hollow, modular and virtual) and strategic alliances (joint ventures, networks, franchising, licensing) and the supporting concepts of outsourcing, offshoring and shared services, can be used to deliver a selected strategy.[2] **Ch. 8**

(e) Discuss how big data can be used to inform and implement business strategy.[2] **Ch. 8**

(f)   Explore (through Mintzberg's organisational configurations) the design of structure, processes and relationships.[3] **Ch. 8**

2 Managing strategic change

(a)   Explore different types of strategic change and their implications.[2] **Ch. 16**

(b)   Determine and diagnose the organisational context of change using Balogun and Hope Hailey's contextual features model and the cultural web.[3] **Ch. 16**

(c)   Establish potential blockages and levers of change.[2] **Ch. 16**

(d)   Advise on the style of leadership appropriate to manage strategic change.[2] **Ch. 16**

3 Understanding strategy development

(a)   Discriminate between the concepts of intended and emergent strategies.[3] **Ch. 16**

(b)   Explain how organisations attempt to put an intended strategy into place.[2] **Ch. 16**

(c)   Highlight how emergent strategies appear from within an organisation. [3] **Ch. 16**

(d)   Discuss how process redesign, quality initiatives and e-business can contribute to emergent strategies.[2] **Ch. 16**

(e)   Assess the implications of strategic drift and the demand for multiple processes of strategy development.[3] **Ch. 16**

D BUSINESS AND PROCESS CHANGE

1 Business change

(a)   Explain that business change projects are initiated to address strategic alignment.[2] **Ch. 16**

(b)   Apply the stages of the business change lifecycle (alignment, definition, design, implementation and realisation).[3] **Ch.16**

(c)   Assess the value of the four view (POPIT – people, organisation, processes and information technology) model to the successful implementation of business change.[3] **Ch. 15**

2 The role of process and process change initiatives

(a) Advise on how an organisation can reconsider the design of its processes to deliver a selected strategy.[3] **Ch. 9**

(b) Appraise business process change initiatives previously adopted by organisations.[3] **Ch. 9**

(c) Establish an appropriate scope and focus for business process change using Harmon's process-strategy matrix.[3] **Ch. 9**

(d) Explore the commoditisation of business processes.[3] **Ch. 9**

(e) Advise on the implications of business process outsourcing.[3] **Ch. 9**

(f) Recommend a business process redesign methodology for an organisation.[2] **Ch. 9**

3 Improving the processes of the organisation

(a) Evaluate the effectiveness of a current organisational process.[3] **Ch. 9**

(b) Describe a range of process redesign patterns.[2] **Ch. 9**

(c) Establish possible redesign options for improving the current processes of an organisation.[2] **Ch. 9**

(d) Assess the feasibility of possible redesign options.[3] **Ch. 9**

(e) Assess the relationship between process redesign and strategy.[3] **Ch. 9**

4 Software solutions

(a) Establish information system requirements required by business users.[2] **Ch. 9**

(b) Assess the advantages and disadvantages of using a generic software solution to fulfil those requirements.[2] **Ch. 9**

(c) Establish a process for evaluating, selecting and implementing a generic software solution.[2] **Ch. 9**

(d) Explore the relationship between generic software solutions and business process redesign.[2] **Ch. 9**

E INFORMATION TECHNOLOGY SOLUTIONS

1 Principles of information technology

(a) Advise on the basic hardware and software infrastructure required to support business information systems.[2] **Ch. 10**

(b) Identify and analyse general information technology controls and application controls required for effective accounting information systems.[2] **Ch. 10**

(c) Analyse the adequacy of general information technology controls and application controls for relevant application systems.[3] **Ch. 10**

(d) Evaluate controls over the safeguarding of information technology assets to ensure the organizational ability to meet business objectives. [3] **Ch. 10**

2 Principles of e-business

(a) Discuss the meaning and scope of e-business.[2] **Ch. 10**

(b) Advise on the reasons for the adoption of e-business and recognise barriers to its adoption.[3] **Ch. 10**

(c) Evaluate how e-business changes the relationships between organisations and their customers.[3] **Ch. 10**

(d) Discuss and evaluate the main business and marketplace models for delivering e-business.[3] **Ch. 10**

3 E-business application: upstream supply chain management

(a) Analyse the main elements of both the push and pull models of the supply chain.[2] **Ch. 10**

(b) Discuss the relationship of the supply chain to the value chain and the value network.[2] **Ch. 10**

(c) Assess the potential application of information technology to support and restructure the supply chain.[3] **Ch. 10**

(d) Advise on how external relationships with suppliers and distributors can be structured to deliver a restructured supply chain.[3] **Ch. 10**

(e) Discuss the methods, benefits and risks of e-procurement.[2] **Ch. 10**

(f) Assess different options and models for implementing e-procurement. [2] **Ch. 10**

4 E-business application: downstream supply chain management

(a) Define the scope and media of e-marketing.[2] **Ch. 11**

(b) Highlight how the media of e-marketing can be used when developing an effective e-marketing plan.[2] **Ch. 11**

(c) Explore the characteristics of the media of e-marketing using the '6I's of Interactivity, Intelligence, Individualisation, integration, Industry structure and Independence of location.[2] **Ch. 11**

(d) Evaluate the effect of the media of e-marketing on the traditional marketing mix of product, promotion, price, place, people, processes and physical evidence.[3] **Ch. 11**

(e) Describe a process for establishing a pricing strategy for products and services that recognises both economic and non-economic factors. [2] **Ch. 11**

(f) Assess the importance of, on-line branding in e-marketing and compare it with traditional branding. **Ch. 11**

5 E-business application: customer relationship management

(a) Define the meaning and scope of customer relationship management. [2] **Ch. 11**

(b) Explore different methods of acquiring customers through exploiting electronic media.[2] **Ch. 11**

(c) Evaluate different buyer behaviour amongst on-line customers.[3] **Ch. 11**

(d) Recommend techniques for retaining customers using electronic media.[2] **Ch. 11**

(e) Recommend how electronic media may be used to increase the activity and value of established, retained customers.[2] **Ch. 11**

(f) Discuss the scope of a representative software package solution designed to support customer relationship management.[2] **Ch. 11**

F PROJECT MANAGEMENT

1 Identifying and initiating projects

(a) Determine the distinguishing features of projects and the constraints they operate in.[2] **Ch. 12**

(b) Discuss the implications of the triple constraint of scope, time, and cost. [2] **Ch. 12**

(c) Discuss the relationship between organisational strategy and project management.[2] **Ch. 12**

(d) Identify and plan to manage risks.[2] **Ch. 12**

(e) Advise on the structures and information that have to be in place to successfully initiate a project.[3] **Ch. 12**

(f) Explain the relevance of projects to process re-design and e-business systems development.[2] **Ch. 12**

2 Building the business case

(a) Describe the structure and content of a business case document.[2] **Ch. 12**

(b) Analyse, describe, assess and classify the benefits of a project investment.[2] **Ch. 12**

(c) Analyse, describe, assess and classify the costs of a project investment.[2] **Ch. 12**

(d) Evaluate the costs and benefits of a business case using standard techniques.[2] **Ch. 12**

(e) Establish responsibility for the delivery of benefits.[2] **Ch. 12**

(f) Explain the role of a benefits realisation plan.[2] **Ch. 12**

3 Managing and leading projects

(a) Discuss the organisation and implications of project-based team structures.[2] **Ch. 13**

(b) Establish the role and responsibilities of the project manager and the project sponsor.[2] **Ch. 13**

(c) Identify and describe typical problems encountered by a project manager when leading a project.[2] **Ch. 13**

(d) Advise on how these typical problems might be addressed and overcome.[3] **Ch. 13**

4 Planning, monitoring and controlling projects

(a) Discuss the principles of a product break down structure.[2] **Ch. 13**

(b) Assess the importance of developing a project plan and discuss the work required to produce this plan.[3] **Ch. 13**

(c) Monitor the status of a project and identify project risks, issues, slippage and changes.[2] **Ch. 13**

(d) Formulate responses for dealing with project risks, issues, slippage and changes.[2] **Ch. 13**

(e) Discuss the role of benefits management and project gateways in project monitoring.[2] **Ch. 13**

5 Concluding a project

(a) Establish mechanisms for successfully concluding a project.[2] **Ch. 13**

(b) Discuss the relative meaning and benefits of a post-implementation and a post-project review.[2] **Ch. 13**

(c) Discuss the meaning and value of benefits realisation.[2] **Ch. 13**

(d) Evaluate how project management software may support the planning and monitoring of a project.[3] **Ch. 13**

(e) Apply 'lessons learned' to future business case validation and to capital allocation decisions.[3] **Ch. 13**

G THE ROLE OF FINANCE IN FORMULATING AND IMPLEMENTING BUSINESS STRATEGY

1 The link between strategy and finance

(a) Explain the relationship between strategy and finance.[3] **Ch. 14**
   (i)   managing for value
   (ii) financial expectations of stakeholders
   (iii) funding strategies.

(b) Discuss how the finance function has transformed to enabling an accountant to have a key role in the decision making process from strategy formulation and implementation to its impact on business performance.[2] **Ch. 14**

2 Finance decisions to formulate and support business strategy

(a) Determine the overall investment requirements of the business.[2] **Ch. 14**

(b) Evaluate alternative sources of finance for these investments and their associated risks.[3] **Ch. 14**

(c) Efficiently and effectively manage the current and non-current assets of the business from a finance and risk perspective.[2] **Ch. 14**

3 The role of cost and management accounting in strategic planning and decision making

(a) Evaluate budgeting, standard costing and variance analysis in support of strategic planning and decision making.[3] **Ch. 14**

(b) Evaluate strategic and operational decisions taking into account risk and uncertainty using decision trees.[2] **Ch. 14**

(c) Evaluate the following strategic options using marginal and relevant costing techniques.[3] **Ch. 14**

   (i) Make or buy decisions

   (ii) Accepting or declining special contracts

   (iii) Closure or continuation decisions

   (iv) Effective use of scarce resources

(d) Evaluate the role and limitations of cost accounting in strategy development and implementation, specifically relating to.[2]

   (i) Direct and indirect costs in multi-product contexts

   (ii) Overhead apportionment in full costing

   (iii) Activity based costing in planning and control

4 Financial implications of making strategic choices and of implementing strategic actions

(a) Apply efficiency ratios to assess how efficiently an organisation uses its current resources.[2] **Ch. 3**

(b) Apply appropriate gearing ratios to assess the risks associated with financing and investment in the organisation.[2] **Ch. 3**

(c) Apply appropriate liquidity ratios to assess the organisation's short-term commitments to creditors and employees.[2] **Ch. 3**

(d) Apply appropriate profitability ratios to assess the viability of chosen strategies.[2] **Ch. 3**

(e) Apply appropriate investment ratios to assist investors and shareholders in evaluating organisational performance and strategy.[2] **Ch. 3** and **Ch. 12**

H PEOPLE

(Note that Section H of the syllabus is underpinned directly by knowledge gained in F1, Accountant in Business. Students are expected to be familiar with the following Study Guide subject areas from that syllabus: A1, A2, B1-B3, D1, and D4-D6)

1 Strategy and people: leadership

(a) Explain the role of visionary leadership and identify the key leadership traits effective in the successful formulation and implementation of strategy and change management.[3] **Ch. 15**

(b) Apply and compare alternative classical and modern theories of leadership in the effective implementation of strategic objectives.[3] **Ch. 15**

2 Strategy and people: job design

(a) Assess the contribution of four different approaches to job design (scientific management, job enrichment, Japanese management and re-engineering).[3] **Ch. 15**

(b) Explain the human resource implications of knowledge work and post-industrial job design.[2] **Ch. 15**

(c) Discuss the tensions and potential ethical issues related to job design.[2] **Ch. 15**

(d) Advise on the relationship of job design to quality initiatives, process re-design, project management and the harnessing of e-business opportunities.[3] **Ch. 15**

3 Strategy and people: staff development

(a) Discuss the emergence and scope of human resource development, succession planning and their relationship to the strategy of the organisation.[2] **Ch. 15**

(b) Advise and suggest different methods of establishing human resource development.[3] **Ch. 15**

(c) Advise on the contribution of competency frameworks to human resource development.[3] **Ch. 15**

(d) Discuss the meaning and contribution of workplace learning, the learning organisation, organisation learning and knowledge management.[3] **Ch. 15**

The superscript numbers in square brackets indicate the intellectual depth at which the subject area could be assessed within the examination. Level 1 (knowledge and comprehension) broadly equates with the Knowledge module, Level 2 (application and analysis) with the Skills module and Level 3 (synthesis and evaluation) to the Professional level. However, lower level skills can continue to be assessed as you progress through each module and level.

The Examination

Business analysis will be assessed by way of a three-hour and 15 minute closed book examination.

The examination paper will be structured in two sections. Section A will be based on a case study style question comprising a compulsory 50 mark question, with requirements based on several parts, with all parts relating to the same case information. The case will usually assess across a range of subject areas within the syllabus and will require the candidate to demonstrate high level capabilities in order to evaluate information available and to prepare reports and other forms of analysis such as structure and process diagrams where required.

Section B comprises three questions of 25 marks each, of which the candidate must answer two. These questions will be more likely to assess a discrete subject area from each of the main syllabus section headings.

The questions will cover all areas of the syllabus:

	Number of marks
Section A	
One 50 mark question, possibly in several parts	50
Section B	
Two out of three 25-mark questions	50
	100

Total time allowed: 3 hours and 15 minutes

Approach to the exam

Begin by assessing all four questions. Try to determine for each question:

- Is there a model/framework that can be used to provide a structure to the answer?

- How much should be written for each part of the question (use the marks available to determine this)?

- Can each part be further sub-divided into more elements (for example, you may be asked to identify problems AND to suggest solutions so you need to make sure that you split the time available between both of these elements)?

Then make your choice of option questions before focusing on getting started. Overall, this should take around 10 minutes.

Divide the time you spend on questions in proportion to the marks on offer. One suggestion **for this examination** is to allocate 1.8 minutes to each mark available, so a 25 mark question should be completed in approximately 45 minutes.

Stick to the question and **tailor your answer** to what you are asked. Pay particular attention to the verbs in the question.

If you **get completely stuck** with a question, leave space in your answer book and **return to it later**.

Spend the last five minutes reading through your answers and making any additions or corrections.

If you do not understand what a question is asking, state your assumptions. Even if you do not answer in precisely the way the examiner hoped, you should be given some credit, if your assumptions are reasonable.

You should do everything you can to make things easy for the marker. The marker will find it easier to identify the points you have made if your answers are legible.

Don't skip parts of the syllabus. Questions will usually mix chapters and syllabus areas together so you will need broad syllabus coverage in order to pass this exam.

Practice plenty of questions to improve your ability to apply the techniques and perform the calculations.

Scenario-based questions: to analyse a scenario, first identify the area in which there is a problem, very briefly outline the main principles/theories you are going to use to answer the question, and then apply the principles/theories to the case.

Essay-style questions: Some section B questions may contain essay-style requirements. Your answer should have a clear structure. It should contain a brief introduction, a main section and a conclusion. Be concise. It is better to write a little about a lot of different points than a great deal about one or two points.

Computations: It is essential to include all your workings in your answers.

Study skills and revision guidance

This section aims to give guidance on how to study for your ACCA exams and to give ideas on how to improve your existing study techniques.

Preparing to study

Set your objectives

Before starting to study decide what you want to achieve – the type of pass you wish to obtain. This will decide the level of commitment and time you need to dedicate to your studies.

Devise a study plan

Determine which times of the week you will study.

Split these times into sessions of at least one hour for study of new material. Any shorter periods could be used for revision or practice.

Put the times you plan to study onto a study plan for the weeks from now until the exam and set yourself targets for each period of study – in your sessions make sure you cover the course, course assignments and revision.

If you are studying for more than one paper at a time, try to vary your subjects as this can help you to keep interested and see subjects as part of wider knowledge.

When working through your course, compare your progress with your plan and, if necessary, re-plan your work (perhaps including extra sessions) or, if you are ahead, do some extra revision/practice questions.

Effective studying

Active reading

You are not expected to learn the text by rote, rather, you must understand what you are reading and be able to use it to pass the exam and develop good practice. A good technique to use is SQ3Rs – Survey, Question, Read, Recall, Review:

(1) **Survey the chapter** – look at the headings and read the introduction, summary and objectives, so as to get an overview of what the chapter deals with.

(2) **Question** – whilst undertaking the survey, ask yourself the questions that you hope the chapter will answer for you.

(3) **Read** through the chapter thoroughly, answering the questions and making sure you can meet the objectives. Attempt the exercises and activities in the text, and work through all the examples.

(4) **Recall** – at the end of each section and at the end of the chapter, try to recall the main ideas of the section/chapter without referring to the text. This is best done after a short break of a couple of minutes after the reading stage.

(5) **Review** – check that your recall notes are correct.

You may also find it helpful to re-read the chapter to try to see the topic(s) it deals with as a whole.

Note-taking

Taking notes is a useful way of learning, but do not simply copy out the text. The notes must:

- be in your own words
- be concise
- cover the key points
- be well-organised
- be modified as you study further chapters in this text or in related ones.

Trying to summarise a chapter without referring to the text can be a useful way of determining which areas you know and which you don't.

Three ways of taking notes:

Summarise the key points of a chapter.

Make linear notes – a list of headings, divided up with subheadings listing the key points. If you use linear notes, you can use different colours to highlight key points and keep topic areas together. Use plenty of space to make your notes easy to use.

Try a diagrammatic form – the most common of which is a mind-map. To make a mind-map, put the main heading in the centre of the paper and put a circle around it. Then draw short lines radiating from this to the main sub-headings, which again have circles around them. Then continue the process from the sub-headings to sub-sub-headings, advantages, disadvantages, etc.

Highlighting and underlining

You may find it useful to underline or highlight key points in your study text – but do be selective. You may also wish to make notes in the margins.

Revision

The best approach to revision is to revise the course as you work through it. Also try to leave four to six weeks before the exam for final revision. Make sure you cover the whole syllabus and pay special attention to those areas where your knowledge is weak. Here are some recommendations:

Read through the text and your notes again and condense your notes into key phrases. It may help to put key revision points onto index cards to look at when you have a few minutes to spare.

Review any assignments you have completed and look at where you lost marks – put more work into those areas where you were weak.

Practise exam standard questions under timed conditions. If you are short of time, list the points that you would cover in your answer and then read the model answer, but do try to complete at least a few questions under exam conditions.

Also practise producing answer plans and comparing them to the model answer.

If you are stuck on a topic find somebody (a tutor) to explain it to you.

Read good newspapers and professional journals, especially ACCA's Student Accountant – this can give you an advantage in the exam.

Ensure you know the structure of the exam – how many questions and of what type you will be expected to answer. During your revision attempt all the different styles of questions you may be asked.

Further reading

You can find further reading and technical articles under the student section of ACCA's website.

For more details about the syllabus and the format of your exam please see your Complete Text or go online.

The nature of strategic business analysis

Chapter learning objectives

Upon completion of this chapter you will be able to:

- describe the common vocabulary of strategic management and why strategic management is important

- describe the different levels of strategic planning for a profit-seeking and a not-for-profit organisation

- describe the JSW model for both profit-seeking and not-for-profit-seeking organisations

- describe the JS lenses (strategy as design, experience, ideas)

- explore the scope of business analysis and its relationship to strategic management.

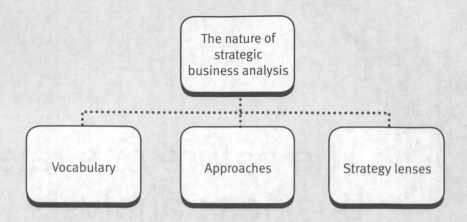

1 The nature of strategic decisions

This chapter explains what is meant by strategic planning and some of the different approaches that are taken to achieve strategic goals. By the end of the chapter you should be familiar with many of the common terms in the strategic vocabulary.

Strategic planning

'Strategic planning' can also be known as 'long-term planning' or 'corporate planning'. Those alternative names give some insight into the nature of strategic planning. It:

- considers the longer term (think of a time-horizon of about five years or beyond)
- considers the whole organisation.

Other characteristics of strategic planning are that:

- it gives direction to the whole organisation, and integrates its activities
- it considers all stakeholders
- it looks at how to gain a sustainable competitive advantage
- it relates the organisation, its resources and competences to its environment.

There is no universally accepted definition of strategy, and the word is used in different contexts to mean different things. The following definition is as useful as any.

'**Strategy** is a pattern of activities that seeks to achieve the objectives of the organisation and adapt its scope, resources and operations to environmental changes in the long term.'

Why bother?

Studies show that companies that plan are more successful than those that do not. Strategic planning can have the following potential advantages:

Advantages	Disadvantages
• forces organisations to look ahead	• can be time consuming and expensive
• improved fit with the environment	• may be difficult in rapidly changing markets
• better use of resources	• can become a straightjacket
• provides a direction/vision	• some unplanned for opportunities may be missed
• helps monitor progress	• can become bureaucratic
• ensures goal congruence	• is less relevant in a crisis

Strategic planning is particularly important when:

• there are long lead times

• the business needs to be turned around

• there is high capital expenditure

• many stakeholders are affected.

Illustration of the importance of strategic planning

Illustration – Introduction

IBM

In the 1970s IBM was one of the most successful and profitable companies in the world. It made most of its profits by selling large, main-frame computers to corporations and governments. Substantial revenues were also earned in providing maintenance and support for non-user friendly hardware and operating systems. Success continued into the early 1980s, but soon IBM reported the largest corporate loss ever made. What led to the rapid turnaround?

The following are often cited as reasons.

- Development of personal computers in the early 1980s and, in particular, how much users preferred having a computer on their desk, on which they could carry out work as and when they wanted, rather than having to submit work to the data processing department.

- Network technology that allowed PCs to be interconnected for work and data sharing.

- Simpler manufacturing. PCs are very modular, susceptible to mass production techniques, and factories could easily be established in low-cost economies.

IBM did not correctly predict the revolutionary effect that PCs would have on manufacturing and consumers. The market for main-frame computers declined rapidly and IBM was left with very high overheads and over-manning.

Why were these developments not predicted more accurately? Perhaps when a company is very dominant, it begins to think itself invincible and immune to outside developments. Long periods of success may lead to assumptions about future success. Who in management might be brave enough to say that a company might have to change radically if success is to continue in the future?

IBM has now changed from being predominantly a hardware manufacturer to being a provider of consultancy services. Recently, it sold its laptop business to Lenovo, a company based in China. IBM found that the market for PCs was a commodity market in which it was difficult to add value to enable profits to be made.

Mark-ups are better in consultancy, the provision of skilled services are more difficult for others to copy and consultancy services are almost immune from threats from cheap overseas suppliers.

Test your understanding 1

How important is strategic planning likely to be to the following organisations?

(a) A health service.

(b) A small building contractor.

KAPLAN PUBLISHING

2 The rational 'top down' approach to strategic planning

The traditional approach

This approach breaks down the process of strategic planning into three distinct steps:

- strategic analysis (examination of the current strategic position)
- strategic choice
- strategic implementation (or strategy into action).

This can be represented in the diagram on the following page. Broadly, information about the organisation and its environment is collected and rational decisions are made about future courses of action.

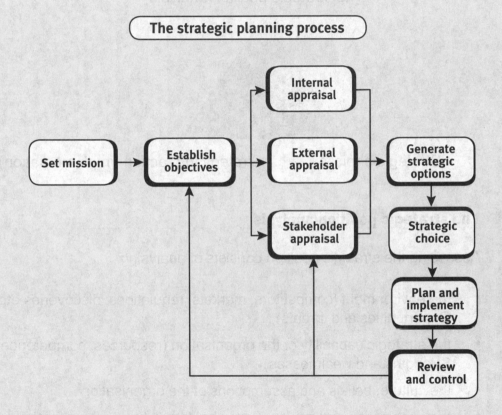

The strategic planning process

A modern adaptation

The Johnson, Scholes and Whittington (JSW) model of strategic planning is a modern development of the rational planning model. It consists of the three elements already discussed (analysis, choice, implementation) but instead of presenting these linearly, it recognises interdependencies. For example, it might only be at the strategy into action (implementation) stage that an organisation discovers something that sheds light on its strategic position. The other key difference is that Johnson, Scholes and Whittington argue that strategic planning can begin at any point. For example, firms might decide that they will launch an internet sales division without first carrying out any strategic analysis or choosing how the new strategy might compete. The examiner believes that this is a key exam model and the bulk of the syllabus is built around it.

The strategic position/analysis

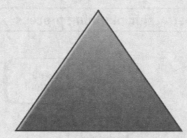

Strategic choices   Strategy into action (implementation)

The strategic position/analysis

Assessing the strategic position consists of analysing:

- the environment (competitors, markets, regulations, discoveries etc. Opportunities and threats)

- the strategic capability of the organisation (resources, competences. Strengths and weaknesses)

- the culture, beliefs and assumptions of the organisation

- the expectation and power of stakeholders (what do the shareholders want? Will employees co-operate?).

The aims of strategic analysis

The aim of strategic analysis is to form a view of the main influences on the present and future well-being of the organisation. This will obviously affect the strategy choice.

Strategic analysis would cover the following areas.

- The PESTEL environmental variables – political, economic, social, technological, environmental and legal as well as competitive factors and how they will affect the organisation and its activities.

- The resource availability and its relative strengths and weaknesses.

- The aspirations and expectations of the groups that have an interest in the organisation, e.g. shareholders, managers, owners, employees and unions.

- The beliefs and assumptions that make up the culture of the organisation will have an effect because they are the means of interpreting the environment and resource influences.

The environmental variables – Since strategy is concerned with the position a business takes in relation to its environment, an understanding of the environment's effects on an organisation is of central importance to strategic analysis. The historical and environmental effects on the business must be considered, as well as the present effects and the expected changes in environmental variables. This is a major task because the range of environmental variables is so great. Many of those variables will give rise to opportunities of some sort, and many will exert threats upon the organisation. The two main problems that have to be faced are, first, to distil out of this complexity a view of the main or overall environmental impacts for the purpose of strategic choice; and second, the fact that the range of variables is likely to be so great that it may not be possible or realistic to identify and analyse each one.

The resources of the organisation – There are internal influences as well as outside influences on the firm and its choice of strategies. One of the ways of thinking about the strategic capability of an organisation is to consider its strengths and weaknesses (what it is good or not so good at doing, or where it is at a competitive advantage or disadvantage, for example). Considering the resource areas of a business such as its physical plant, its management, its financial structure and its products may identify these strengths and weaknesses. Again, the aim is to form a view of the internal influences and constraints on strategic choice. The expectations of different stakeholders are important because they will affect what will be seen as acceptable in terms of the strategies advanced by management. However, the beliefs and assumptions that make up the culture of an organisation, though less explicit, will also have an important influence.

Expectations and influence of stakeholders – A stakeholder can be defined as someone who has an interest in the well-being of the organisation. A typical list of stakeholders for a large company would include shareholders, employees, managers, customers, locality, suppliers, government and society at large.

Strategic planning and management cannot be achieved without regard to stakeholders.

- In a profit-making organisation, management might have a choice of adopting a high risk/high return strategy or a low risk/low return strategy. It's important to know which the shareholders want.

- In a not-for-profit organisation, such as a hospital, managers need to know what the government and potential patients want. How much resource should go into heart operations, how much into hip replacement, etc.

The beliefs and assumptions within an organisation – affect the interpretation of the environmental and resource influences; so two groups of managers, perhaps working in different divisions of an organisation, may come to different conclusions about strategy, although they are faced with similar environmental and resource implications. Which influence prevails is likely to depend on which group has the greater power, and understanding this can be of great importance in recognising why an organisation follows, or is likely to follow, the strategy it does.

A consideration of all relevant features – the environment, resources, expectations and objectives within the cultural and political framework of the organisation – provides the basis for strategic analysis of that organisation. However, to understand its strategic position, it is also necessary to examine the extent to which the direction and implications of the current strategy and objectives that it is following are in line with, and can cope with, the implications of the strategic analysis.

Strategic choice

Strategic choice follows strategic analysis and is based upon the following three elements.

- Generation of strategic options, e.g. growth, acquisition, diversification or concentration.
- Evaluation of the options to assess their relative merits and feasibility.
- Selection of the strategy or option that the organisation will pursue. There could be more than one strategy chosen but there is a chance of an inherent danger or disadvantage to any choice made. Although there are techniques for evaluating specific options, the selection is often subjective and likely to be influenced by the values of managers and other groups with an interest in the organisation.

In addition to deciding the scope and direction of an organisation, choices also need to be made about how to achieve the goal. Broadly, there are two ways in which a strategy can be pursued:

- internal development (organic growth)
- external development – merger/acquisition, JV, franchising/licensing.

The generation of strategic options

Generation of strategic options

There may be several possible courses of action open to the organisation. For example, an international retailer may need to decide on areas such as:

- which areas of the world are most important to concentrate on
- whether it is possible to maintain a common basis of trading across all the different countries
- whether it is necessary to introduce variations by market focus
- what strategic directions are necessary for product development and product range
- should the company attempt to follow these strategies by internal development or joint venture activity through franchising?

All of these considerations are important and need careful consideration: indeed, in developing strategies, a potential danger is that managers do not consider any but the most obvious course of action – and the most obvious is not necessarily the best. A helpful step in strategic choice can be to generate strategic options.

Strategic options generation is the process of establishing a choice of possible future strategies. There are three main areas to consider.

Porter describes certain generic competitive strategies (lowest cost or differentiation) that an organisation may pursue for competitive advantage. They determine how you compete.

Ansoff describes product-market strategies (which markets you should enter or leave). They determine where you compete and the direction of growth.

Institutional strategies (i.e. relationships with other organisations) determine the method of growth.

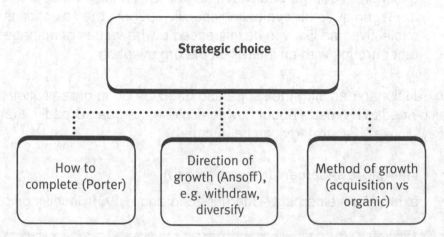

Evaluation of the options

Strategic options can be examined in the context of the strategic analysis to assess their relative merits. In deciding on any of the options that they face, the organisation might want to know whether they are suitable to the firm's existing position. They need to know which of these options builds upon strengths, overcomes weaknesses and takes advantage of opportunities, while minimising or circumventing the threats the business faces. This is called the search for strategic fit or suitability of the strategy. However, a second set of questions is important.

- To what extent could a chosen strategy be put into effect?

- Could required finance be raised, sufficient stock be made available at the right time and in the right place, staff be recruited and trained to reflect the sort of image the organisation is trying to project?

These are questions of feasibility.

Even if these criteria could be met, management would still need to know whether the choice would be acceptable to the stakeholders.

A variety of techniques are used to assess the value of strategies. Some strategies will be assessed on financial criteria (such as net present value). Where this is not possible, or where the uncertainty in the environment is great, more sophisticated models are used.

Selection of the strategy or option

This is the process of selecting those options that the organisation will pursue. There could be just one strategy chosen or several. There is unlikely to be a clear-cut 'right' or 'wrong' choice because any strategy must inevitably have some dangers or disadvantages. So in the end, choice is likely to be a matter of management judgement. It is important to understand that the selection process cannot always be viewed or understood as a purely objective, logical act. It is strongly influenced by the values of managers and other groups with interest in the organisation, and ultimately may very much reflect the power structure in the organisation.

Strategy into action/implementation

Implementing a strategy has three elements.

- Organising/structuring. For example, should the organisation be split into European, US and Asian divisions? How autonomous should divisions be?

- Enabling an organisation's resources should support the chosen strategy. For example, appropriate human resources and fixed assets need to be acquired.

- Managing change. Most strategic planning and implementation will involve change, so managing change, in particular employees' fears and resistance, is crucial.

The implementation process

Structure

It is likely that changes in organisational structure will be needed to carry through the strategy and there is also likely to be a need to adapt the systems used to manage the organisation.

Organisation structure – lines of authority and communication must be established that are appropriate to the way the strategy is broken down into detailed targets. Systems are necessary to provide the necessary strategic information, as well as essential operational procedures. Control systems are used to assess performance. The type of questions that will need answering include:

- what will different departments be held responsible for?
- what sorts of information system are needed to monitor the progress of the strategy?
- is there a need for retraining of the workforce?

Implementation involves devising sub-strategies for products and markets, human resources and so on.

Resource planning

Resource planning covers finance, human resource management and physical resources such as land and buildings. It involves assessing the key tasks to satisfy the critical success factors, and the resources to be allocated to the key tasks. It is concerned with the following questions.

- What are the key tasks that need to be carried out?
- What changes need to be made in the resource mix of the organisation?
- By when?
- Who is to be responsible for the change?

Managing change

Successful implementation will rely on the successful management of the change to the new strategy. This will involve not only the management of the systems and structures of the organisation, but also the management of its people and routines. This will involve two elements:

- overcoming resistance to change from staff
- leading staff in a manner that encourages them to make the change successfully.

Illustration 1 – The JSW model of strategic planning

Illustration – Johnson, Scholes and Whittington model of strategic planning

A full-price airline is considering setting up a 'no frills', low-fare subsidiary. The strategic planning process would include the following elements.

Strategic position: An analysis will need to be made of areas such as expected competitor actions, oil price forecasts, passenger volume forecasts, availability of cheap landing rights, public concern for environmental damage, the strength of the airlines main brand.

Strategic choices: A number of options will need to be considered such as which routes to launch? Whether to set up a service from scratch or buy an existing cheap airline? Which planes to use, what on-board services to offer?

Strategic implementation: Once a decision has been made the best way to put that decision into practice will have to be considered and this will involve an assessment of areas such as how autonomous should the new airline be? How to recruit and train staff? Implementation of the internet booking system. Acquisition of aircraft. Obtaining landing slots.

Test your understanding 2

A health provider has only large, edge of town, hospitals. It is considering setting up additional small city centre clinics capable of treating less-serious day cases.

Give examples of what the provider should consider under the headings of strategic position, strategic choices and strategic implementation.

3 Alternative approaches

Emergent strategies

The research of **Mintzberg** (1987) suggests that few of the strategies followed by organisations in the real world are as consciously planned as the approaches above suggest.

He believes this to be an unrealistic view of strategic planning, believing instead that strategies evolve over time (emerge) rather than result from an in-depth analysis of every aspect of the environment and an impartial evaluation of every possible alternative.

More details en emergent strategies

Emergent strategies

Emergent strategies do not arise out of conscious strategic planning, but result from a number of ad hoc choices, perhaps made lower down the hierarchy. In this view, the final objective of the strategy is unclear and elements still develop as the strategy proceeds, continuously adapting to human needs – the emergent strategy is evolving, incremental and continuous. Emergent strategies develop from patterns of behaviour; one idea leads to another, until a new pattern is formed and a new strategy has emerged. For example, a salesman visits a customer out in the field. The product isn't right, and together they work out some modifications. The salesman returns to the company and puts the changes through; after two or three more rounds, they finally get it right. A new product emerges, which eventually opens up a new market. The company has changed strategic course.

Incrementalism

Lindblom did not believe in the rational model to decision making as he suggested that in the real world it was not used, citing the following reasons.

- Strategic Managers do not evaluate all the possible options open to them but choose between relatively few alternatives.

- It does not normally involve an autonomous strategic planning team that impartially sifts alternative options before choosing the best solution.

- Strategy making tends to involve small-scale extensions of past policy – 'incrementals' rather than radical shifts following a comprehensive search.

Lindblom believed that strategy making involving small scale extensions of past practices would be more successful as it was likely to be more acceptable as consultation, compromise and accommodation were built into the process. He believed that comprehensive rational planning was impossible and likely to result in disaster if actively pursued.

Freewheeling opportunism

- Freewheeling opportunists do not like planning. They prefer to see and grab opportunities as they arise.

- Intellectually, this is justified by saying that planning takes too much time and is too constraining. Probably, the approach is adopted more for psychological reasons: some people simply do not like planning.

- Often such people are entrepreneurs who enjoy taking risks and the excitement of setting up new ventures. However, once the ventures are up and running, the owners lose interest in the day-to-day repetitive administration needed to run a business.

Test your understanding 3

McNamee states that 'strategic management .... is considered to be that type of management through which an organisation tries to obtain a good fit with its environment'.

Management Accounting – Strategic Planning and Marketing, McNamee

This approach has been characterised as 'proactive'.

There are many successful organisations that do not undertake strategic planning. This approach has been characterised as 'reactive' or sometimes 'freewheeling opportunism'.

Required:

Explain the essential characteristics of the two approaches (strategic planning and freewheeling opportunism) mentioned above. What are the advantages and disadvantages of the two approaches? Explain in what circumstances you would recommend an organisation to adopt each approach.

Levels of strategic planning

There are three levels of strategic planning:

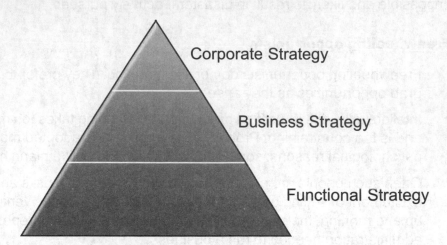

Corporate Strategy

Business Strategy

Functional Strategy

Corporate Strategy

This looks at the organisation as a whole and considers:

- the firm's orientation toward growth (also known as it's directional strategy)

- the level of diversification in the company's products and markets (also known as its portfolio strategy)

- the manner in which management coordinates activities and transfers strategic capabilities between business units (also known as its parenting strategy).

Business Strategy

This examines each individual business unit and focuses on:

- actions taken to provide value to customers and gain a competitive advantage by exploiting core competencies in specific, individual product or service markets.

- the firm's position in an industry, relative to competitors and to the five forces of competition.

Functional or Operational Strategy

Functional strategy relates to a single functional operation (such as purchasing, marketing, human resource management etc.) and the activities involved therein. Decisions at this level within the organization are often described as tactical.

They are much more detailed and specific than corporate and business level strategies and deal with areas such as:

- allocation of resources among different operations within that functional area

- coordination between functions for optimal contribution to the achievement of the SBU and corporate-level objectives

- gaining, retaining and developing resources and capabilities into ones which can give strategic advantages and support the business level strategy.

Consistency

The strategies at the different levels should be consistent. There's no point having a corporate strategy that says that the organisation should move up-market, if the business strategy is to stay in cheap markets and functions provide low-quality resources.

Strategic choices need to be made at every level, though obviously choices made at any particular level can influence choices at other levels.

Illustration – Levels of strategic planning

Gap is an international clothing retailer. Classification of different levels of strategic planning could be:

Corporate

- Should another range of shops be established (as Gap did with Banana Republic, a more up-market chain)?
- Should the company raise more share capital?

Business

- How will the company beat rivals and gain market share in Australia?

Functional/operational

- How will suitable premises be found and fitted out for the new range of shops?

Test your understanding 4

A full-service airline is making the following decisions.

(a) Should a 'no-frills', low-fare subsidiary be set up?

(b) If it is set up, how should cabin staff be recruited?

Are these likely to be corporate, business or operational decisions?

Strategic management in different contexts

Strategic management in different contexts

The different elements of the strategic planning process will vary in importance, depending on the type of organisation concerned.

Type of organisation	Characteristics	Key strategic issues
Small businesses	• Likely to operate in a single market with a limited product range • Expectations/views of founders dominate	• Dealing with pressure from larger competitors, e.g. by development of unique capabilities, niche strategies, etc. • Strategy choice may be limited by financing opportunities – relationship with banks vital
Multinationals	• Likely to operate in many diverse markets with a wide product range	• Corporate strategy – control of diverse businesses vital – e.g. relationship between head office and local subsidiaries/divisions • Business unit strategy – resource allocation to business units and co-ordination between them (e.g. logistics)

Type of organisation	Characteristics	Key strategic issues
Public sector	• Significant government influence (e.g. may have to offer a universal service) • Planning horizons driven by political rather than market conditions	• Role of ideology • Competition for resources – e.g. have to demonstrate value for money to win funding • Strategic options limited by funding (e.g. tax implications) • Strategic alliances often key (e.g. public and private partnerships)
Voluntary and not-for-profit sectors	• Key objectives non financial • Funding often not linked to recipients of service	• Role of values/ ideology – key decisions usually centralised • Competition for funds – e.g. meeting expectations of funding bodies

4 The strategy lenses

Overall, strategy is likely to come from a variety of sources and a combination of the above techniques. Johnson and Scholes suggest that strategy will be formed through the coming together of three 'strategy lenses'

- **Strategy as design** – essentially this is the same as the rational planning model discussed earlier.

- **Strategy as experience** – this is reflecting an element of incrementalism.

- **Strategy as ideas** – this reflects the emergent approach described above.

Strategies will combine all three elements – though at different times and in different environments one element might play a greater role than others.

More details

Strategy as design

The design lens views strategy as the deliberate positioning of an organisation as the result of some 'rational, analytical, structured and directive process'. Through the design lens it is the responsibility of top management to plan the destiny of the organisation. Lower levels of management carry out the operational actions required by the strategy. The design lens is associated with objective setting and a plan for moving the organisation towards these objectives. To some extent, it is outward looking and pays careful attention to changes in the environment and the objectives of external stakeholders. It is a very proactive approach to the changes that the organisation will be experiencing in its environment.

Strategy as experience

Strategy as experience provides a more adaptive approach to strategy, building on and changing the existing strategy. Changes are incremental as the organisation adapts to new opportunities and threats in the environment. The experience lens views strategy development as the combination of individual and collective experience. There is strong influence from the received wisdom and culture within an organisation about how things should be done. It therefore builds more on internal capabilities in the light of external, environmental changes for the organisation. A key assumption is that the environment will change in predictable ways based on past 'received wisdom'.

However, it has to be recognised that the assumptions and practices of the organisation may become so ingrained that it is difficult for people to question or change them. Strategy as experience is a conservative approach to strategy that works best when there are relatively few changes to the environment in which the organisation operates.

Strategy as ideas.

Strategy as ideas has a central role for innovation and new ideas. It sees strategy as emerging from the variety and diversity in an organisation. It is as likely to come from the bottom of the organisation as from the top. Consequently, the organisation should foster conditions that allow ideas to emerge and to be considered for inclusion in a 'mainstream strategy'. Certain conditions, such as a changing and unpredictable environment foster ideas and innovation. This is the view that innovation and new ideas are frequently not thought up by senior managers at the corporate planning level. Rather, new ideas will often be created throughout a diverse organisation as people try to carry out their everyday jobs and to cope with changing circumstances.

It can sometimes be more reactive than proactive which makes it very suited to unpredictable and fast-changing environments.

Using the lenses together

Johnson and Scholes suggest that viewing strategy through only one of these lenses can mean that problems that the other lenses might show up are missed. For example, too much reliance on incremental changes (strategy as experience) might overlook radical new developments that could be essential for the organisation's success (strategy as ideas).

It is worth considering the very strong influence the design and experience lenses have in large organisations and government departments. Often, the larger the organisation, the less able it is to adopt early to essential but radical changes (i.e. the strategy as ideas lense is not used at all in the development of strategies). For example, in government departments it is often the case that employees must follow established procedures (strategies as experience) and top-down directives (strategy as design) and are not encouraged or allowed to find better ways to perform tasks or to meet 'customer' needs (strategy as ideas). In this way they often lag behind commercial organisations in their operations and efficiency and are slow to react to the needs of users.

Ideally, managers should try to look at strategy through all three lenses in turn.

Illustration 2 – The strategy lenses

A university in a developing country wants to introduce new products via the medium of e-learning (where products are delivered over the internet and students study at home). The country has poor infrastructure and a cultural aversion to social mobility. But its government are planning (with the help of international investment) a major investment in technology over the next five years. This will allow over 75% of the country to have access to high speed WiMax internet at very low costs.

Let's look at how the university's strategy might develop:

Strategy as design

The environmental changes that the university is experiencing are significant and it will be important that the university react to these. Through the use of environmental analysis in combination with resource analysis etc. the design process will begin. It will then move on to strategic choices such as the decision to move onto to e-learning product development.

The design will be developed logically with carefully planned steps. Middle and lower management will play a role in the implementation of the strategy and it will have clear goals and objectives.

Strategy as experience

But the strategy is likely to be adapted over time, possibly due to the influence of all levels of management. They will have clear taken-for-granted assumptions about how strategy should proceed, based mainly on what has worked and not worked in the past. They may alter the detailed plans due to their own ideas about what will work and what won't.

But the strategy will be added to as well from these experiences. For example, the middle line managers might know from past experience that when students study at home they require a higher level of service in areas such as tutor feedback, exam marking and material delivery. This might lead to the strategy to be adapted to incorporate plans such as dedicated support staff etc. and a deliberate choice to focus on a more differentiated service from rivals who might launch low cost alternatives.

Strategy as ideas

The university's environment is not static and it will continue to evolve. A five year plan cannot therefore be static and it also should evolve as the environment evolves.

For example, if telecommunications infrastructure were to grow as other technologies grow it may well be that citizens of the country might begin to own mobile 'smartphones' (especially those in the university's target age group). This might provide an idea for providing some product aspects (such as mini exam questions) as mobile phone applications. This is unlikely to be part of the original strategic design, but as such ideas arise they will be built into the strategy over time.

Further illustration of the strategic lenses

Illustration – The strategy lenses

At the start of this chapter, a brief history of IBM was set out, describing how the rise of the personal computing and new electronics technology caused IBM to swiftly change from being one of the world's most successful companies to one that posted one of the largest ever losses.

It can be argued that IBM certainly saw strategy as a matter of design and probably one of experience. The company was large, conservative, conventionally organised and highly centralised. The main board would certainly have kept tight control of corporate strategy and the company would have progressed incrementally, based on its experience and constrained by a strong conservative corporate culture.

Perhaps if someone had been able to draw attention to the challenge to IBM arising from personal computers, and top management in the company had been willing to take this challenge more seriously, IBM might not have had the problems it had, or to the extent it had.

5 Chapter summary

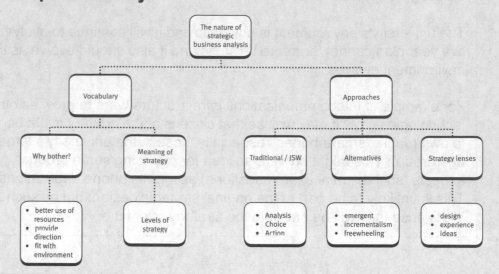

Relational diagram of the syllabus

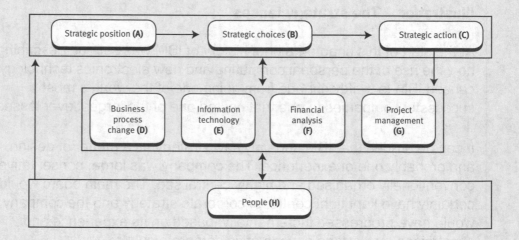

Test your understanding answers

Test your understanding 1

(a) Health service

Strategic planning is vital. Hospitals are hugely expensive and take years to plan and build and their provision must be closely aligned with population trends and treatment advances. Training medical staff is also a long-term process. If hospital and other health service facilities are inadequate, many people will be adversely affected.

(b) A small building contractor

Relatively little long-term planning is needed. If the builder buys and develops land, then some planning will be needed to ensure that land and planning permission can be acquired. Otherwise, many builders work from job to job using a high proportion of sub-contractors.

Test your understanding 2

Suggestions are:

Strategic position: likely demand. Some type of cost/benefit analysis to show that the strategy is worthwhile. Safety of patients being treated in less well-resourced environments. Acceptability to patients. Acceptability to staff.

Strategic choices: which illnesses to treat? Where should the clinics be? How should the clinics be staffed? Opening hours?

Strategic implementation: acquiring and fitting out clinics. Hiring and/or transferring staff. Publicity, so that patients know where and when to go. Liaison with general practitioners and the main hospitals.

Test your understanding 3

Strategic planning

This is a formal planning process that has clearly defined objectives, which will have been agreed by its stakeholders. Strategic planning operates within a logical set of procedures, which give it an easily understood structure.

Strategic planning is a long-term planning process with a time horizon of several years. It relates to the whole undertaking and recognises that an organisation is an open system continuously interacting with its external environment.

Strategic planning advantages:

- It sets out a clear direction for the organisation to move towards. This provides a vision for the future.

- It makes managers look ahead, think ahead and be proactive.

- Future threats and opportunities can be identified and evaluated.

- It gives a perspective of future changes so the organisation can adapt to them gradually.

- It is a structured method of planning, which employees and managers can understand and put into practice.

Some disadvantages of strategic planning include:

- It acts as a constraint on management ability to act.

- Once set, achieving the plan becomes the goal. The real objectives are lost sight of.

Freewheeling opportunism

This is the short-term identification and exploitation of opportunities. It only looks at the present and immediate future and uses an ad hoc approach to management, reacting to situations as they develop.

Freewheeling opportunism relies on the individual entrepreneurial skills of the organisation's proprietors or managers. It is informal and has no set procedures that must be followed.

Some of the advantages claimed by supporters of freewheeling opportunism are:

- It is flexible and can spontaneously adapt to a rapidly changing situation.
- It has none of the procedural constraints that formal strategic planning has.
- Decisions can be made rapidly and implemented, giving the organisation a competitive advantage.
- It supports and encourages an innovative culture in the organisation.

Some disadvantages of freewheeling opportunism are:

- There is no long-term vision for the future. Threats may not be seen in advance.
- In large undertakings, sub-optimisation will occur when it is used.
- There are no clear objectives to work towards.

Recommended approach

The method of planning used in an organisation will depend on many factors, including:

- Its size and leadership style.
- The organisation culture and structure.
- The nature of its activities.
- The skills and aspirations of its managers.

Formal strategic planning should be used in larger organisations that are established and have a degree of centralised control. It is unlikely that organisations such as government institutions and public limited companies, would survive without strategic planning in today's competitive world.

Freewheeling opportunism might be justified in very small undertakings in which responsibility for management is vested in the proprietors who have considerable entrepreneurial skills, such as a business operating in a turbulent, creative market.

Test your understanding 4

(a) There will be very high costs involved, careful planning is needed to ensure that the cheap flights do not cannibalise the expensive service. This is a decision that would be made by the main board and is a corporate level strategy.

(b) The nature of this decision is most likely to be a functional level strategy. However, it will be important that the strategy is consistent with whatever business level strategy is being followed. If the company decide to offer a low level service as part of its business level strategy, then it will be important that the recruitment of staff supports this.

2

The environment and competitive forces

Chapter learning objectives

When you have completed this chapter you will be able to:

- apply the PESTEL model in a scenario

- apply Porter's diamond in a scenario

- describe what is meant by 'convergence' in industries

- evaluate an industry sector using Porter's five forces model

- analyse the influence of strategic groups

- evaluate business forecasting techniques used to assess the likely outcome of different business strategies

- using PESTEL, Porter's five forces and other suitable models, categorise environmental effects as opportunities or threats.

- highlight how these external key drivers of change are likely to affect the structure of a sector or a market.

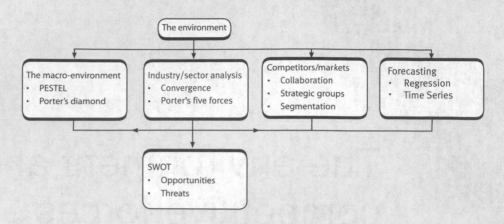

1 Introduction

If a strategic plan is going to have any chance of being useful, it has to be based on gathering and analysing information. It is not possible to plan by sitting in a darkened room, dreaming up scenarios that have no connection to reality. This chapter describes some of the planning tools that can help.

2 The PESTEL model

The **PESTEL** model looks at the macroenvironment, using the following headings:

- **Political.** The political environment includes taxation policy, government stability and foreign trade regulations.

- **Economic.** The economic environment includes interest rates, inflation, business cycles, unemployment, disposable income and energy availability and cost.

- **Social.** The social/cultural environment includes population demographics, social mobility, income distribution, lifestyle changes, attitudes to work and leisure, levels of education and consumerism.

- **Technological.** The technological environment is influenced by government spending on research, new discoveries and development, government and industry focus of technological effort, speed of technological transfer and rates of obsolescence.

- **Ecological/environmental.** The ecological environment, sometimes just referred to as 'the environment', considers ways in which the organisation can produce its goods or services with the minimum environmental damage.

- **Legal.** The legal environment covers influences such as taxation, employment law, monopoly legislation and environmental protection laws.

Overall, the model should allow a business to assess the **growth prospects** for the industry within which the organisation operates.

Further PESTEL examples

Social/cultural factors: include changes in tastes and lifestyles. They may also include changes in the demographic make-up of a population. For example in Western Europe people are living longer and in most countries the birth rate is falling, leading to an ageing population. This has obvious implications for the types of products and services which businesses and other organisations may plan to offer. Typical questions that need to be answered include:

- What are the current and emerging trends in lifestyles and fashion?
- What demographic trends will affect the size of the market or its sub-markets?
- Does the trend represent opportunities or threats?

Legal/political factors: the addition or removal of legislative or regulatory constraints can pose major strategic threats and opportunities. The organisation needs to know:

- What changes in regulations are possible and what will their impact be?
- What tax or other incentives are being developed that might affect strategy?

Economic factors: include interest rates and exchange rates, as well as the general state of the economy (e.g. entering or emerging from a recession). The organisation needs to know what the economic prospects and inflation rates are for the countries that it operates in and how will they affect strategy.

Technological factors: may include changes in retailing methods (such as direct selling via the Internet), changes in production methods (greater use of automation), and greater integration between buyers and suppliers via computer link-ups. The managers would need to know to what extent the existing technologies are maturing and what technological developments or trends are affecting or could affect the industry.

Environmental factors: include product stewardship, which considers all raw materials, components and energy sources used in the product and how more environmentally friendly substitutes could be used. They also include ways in which product and product waste could be more effectively recycled. Typical questions that need to be answered include:

- Are we adhering to the existing environmental legislation?

- Are there any new product opportunities that could be exploited that would have a favourable environmental impact on the market?

- What impact will future environmental legislation have?

Some of the **PESTEL** influences may affect every industry, but industries will vary in how much they are affected. For example, an interest rate rise is likely to affect a business selling cars (car purchase can be postponed) more than it will affect a supermarket (food purchase cannot be postponed). More detailed analysis of the environment and competitive forces will be focused on specific industries.

Illustration 1 – PESTEL for a newspaper

Illustration – The PESTEL model

A newspaper is planning for the next five years. The following would be some of the **PESTEL** factors it should consider:

- **Political influences:** tax on newspapers – many countries treat newspapers in the same way as books and have no sales tax (or value added tax) on their sales price. If government policies on the classification of newspapers were to change so that sales tax had to be charged, then sales of newspapers are likely to fall.

- **Economic influences:** exchange rates – most newspapers import their raw materials (paper, pulp etc.) and therefore they will suffer when their domestic currency weakens. Recession – in a recession buyers might move down market, so that cheap tabloids benefit, and more expensive broadsheets suffer. The opposite might apply as the economy recovers.

- **Social influences:** people want more up-to-date information – buyers are less inclined to wait for news than they were 20/30 years ago and may therefore switch to alternative sources of information. More ethnicity in countries – the increased social mobility around the world might actually open new avenues of growth for newspapers through launching, for example, different language versions.

- **Technological influences:** there are many alternative sources of information that are provided through technologies such as the internet, mobile phones and television – this is likely to adverse affect the sales of newspapers. At the same time, e-readers are becoming more popular – this might present an opportunity for newspapers to provide daily downloadable content to these devices.

- **Environmental/ecological influences:** concern about the impact of carbon emissions from the use and production of paper – newspapers may be seen as being harmful to the environment due to their use of natural resources, their high production volumes and large distribution networks. Buyers might abandon newspapers in favour of carbon neutral news via modern technologies.

- **Legal influences:** limits on what can be published – this will make it harder for newspapers to differentiate themselves from each other and therefore harm growth prospects

Overall, it would appear that growth prospects for newspapers are poor. The industry is more likely to decline than to grow. Existing rivals need to plan ahead for new products and new markets and perhaps focus on new technologies such as the provision of news via e-readers.

Note that it does not matter under which category an influence has been listed. Tax has economic, legal and political dimensions. All that matters is that tax has been considered in the environmental scan.

Test your understanding 1

Carry out a **PESTEL** analysis on a supermarket business. Try to get at least two items under each heading.

3 Porter's five forces model

Porter looked at the structure of industries. In particular, he was interested in assessing industry attractiveness, by which he meant how easy it would be to make above average **profits** (for shareholders and to fund adequate investment). He concluded that industry attractiveness depends on five factors or forces:

Force	Potential impact on attractiveness
Buyer power	Powerful buyers can demand discounted prices and extra services (which add costs to the organistion)
Supplier power	Powerful suppliers can demand higher prices for their product(s)
Competitive rivalry	High levels of competition can lead to price wars and high expenditure on marketing and innovation
New entrants	New entrants can increase the cost of resources as well as increasing the power of other forces
Substitutes	If an organisation has a lot of substitutes it will have to keep its prices low to deter customers from moving to these substitutes

As the forces become more powerful and prevalent the industry becomes less attractive (and the margins within the industry are likely to decline). The opposite applies if the forces are weak or absent.

Test your understanding 2

Consider the factors that might make each of these forces more powerful or weak.

Porter's five forces

Bargaining power of buyers

Powerful customers can force price cuts and/or quality improvements. Either way, margins are eroded. Bargaining power is high when a combination of factors arises.

Such factors could include where:

- a buyer's purchases are a high proportion of the supplier's total business or represent a high proportion of total trade in that market

- a buyer makes a low profit

- the quality of purchases is unimportant or delivery timing is irrelevant, and prices will be forced down

- there are similar alternative products available from other suppliers.

Bargaining power of suppliers

The power of suppliers to charge higher prices will be influenced by the following:

- the degree to which switching costs apply and substitutes are available

- the presence of one or two dominant suppliers controlling prices

- the extent to which products offered have a uniqueness of brand, technical performance or design not available elsewhere.

Competition/rivalry

Intensity of existing competition will depend on the following factors:

- Number and relative strength of competitors. The competition in a market can range from perfect competition through to monopoly.

- Rate of growth. Where the market is expanding, competition is low key.

- Where high fixed costs are involved companies will cut prices to marginal cost levels to protect volume, and drive weaker competitors out of the market.

- If buyers can switch easily between suppliers the competition is keen.

- If the exit barrier (i.e. the cost incurred in leaving the market) is high, companies will hang on until forced out, thereby increasing competition and depressing profit.

Threat of new entrants

New entrants into a market will bring extra capacity and intensify competition. The threat from new entrants will depend upon the strength of the barriers to entry and the likely response of existing competitors to a new entrant. Barriers to entry are factors that make it difficult for a new entrant to gain an initial foothold in a market. Major sources of barriers to entry are:

- **Economies of scale,** where the industry is one where unit costs decline significantly as volume increases, such that a new entrant will be unable to start on a comparable cost basis.

- **Product differentiation,** where established firms have good brand image and customer loyalty. The costs of overcoming this can be prohibitive.

- **Capital requirements,** where the industry requires a heavy initial investment (e.g. steel industry, rail transport).

- **Switching costs,** i.e. one-off costs in moving from one supplier to another (e.g. a garage chain switching car dealership).

- **Access to distribution channels** may be restricted (e.g. for some major toiletry brands in the UK 90% of sales go through 12 buying points, i.e. chemist multiples and major retailers). It is therefore difficult for a new toiletry product or manufacturer to gain shelf space.

- **Cost advantages of existing producers,** independent of economies of scale, e.g. patents, special knowledge, favourable access to suppliers, government subsidies.

- **Know-how.** It is much more difficult to penetrate a business where considerable know-how and skills are needed than to enter a simple, basic market.

- **Regulation.** Governments or professional bodies might supervise and limit new entrants.

Threat of substitute products

This threat is across industries (e.g. rail travel versus bus travel versus private car) or within an industry (e.g. long life milk as a substitute for delivered fresh milk). **Porter** explains that 'substitutes limit the potential returns … by placing a ceiling on the price which firms in the industry can profitably charge'. The better the price-performance alternative offered by substitutes, the more readily will customers switch.

Illustration 2 – Porter's five forces

Consider the attractiveness of the industry for a builder of commercial property:

Competitive rivalry

There are likely to be tens and perhaps hundreds of thousands of firms! But larger firms have some advantages

(1) Greater bargaining power when purchasing prime development sites.

(2) Dealing with major customers.

(3) Economies of scale (e.g. in using prefabrication building techniques).

(4) Pursuing planning applications.

(5) Better able to offset risk.

(6) Better able to use sophisticated techniques such as critical path analysis need for larger developments.

(7) More able to offer part-exchange deals to house buyers.

However, this must not be taken to extremes:

(1) The individuality of each construction project limits economies of scale – especially in respect to materials.

(2) It is difficult for firms to differentiate their product – basically make what the architect has designed.

(3) Even small firms can benefit from learning effects.

Overall, this is likely to be a highly competitive market where price wars and industry consolidation are common.

Threat of entry

There are likely to be low barriers to entry through low capital requirements (equipment can be hired if necessary) and a potential high level of available, skilled labour. Working capital may be an issue but progress payments from buyers can be used to reduce this barrier. There are also likely to be few legal barriers as no formal qualifications needed.

It will therefore be important to build a brand and a reputation (for example, based on reliability, quality, workmanship and efficiency) to ensure that a buyer chooses an existing builder over a new rival.

Threat of substitutes

The main threat is second hand property available for rent or purchase. There may be a lot of property available but high prices in some parts of the country might make new property more attractive. (However this will partly be offset by higher land prices in such areas). But as governments continue to invest in regeneration initiatives there should still be a demand for new buildings.

This factor is likely to be closely linked to the PESTEL model – for example, the threat will be highest when the economy is in decline, but it will be low when demand for housing is increasing.

Power of suppliers

There are likely to be numerous suppliers of materials selling an undifferentiated product. So suppliers should generally have low power and large builders should be able to demand bulk discounts and to achieve cost control.

Power of customers

Commercial buyers will have low switching costs, the product is undifferentiated and buyers may themselves be experiencing low profitability. This is likely to make them powerful and allow them to demand lower prices for work done.

Overall opinion

It would appear that margins in this industry are likely to be low. It is very competitive and buyers have lots of power (and lots of available substitutes). Commercial builders will have to rely on a high volume of work and will need to establish a reputation that ensures that buyers choose them over rivals.

Test your understanding 3

Apply a five forces analysis to a company that does garden maintenance for households – cutting grass, removing weeds, pruning shrubs, etc.

4 Scenario planning

PESTEL and 5 Forces analysis often focuses on the 'most likely' potential future market state. Scenario planning is therefore often employed by organisations in order to force managers to think about other potential future market positions. In scenario planning the key environmental factors are identified and the firm then considers how these might change in the future. Plans are then considered for each of these eventualities.

The number of scenarios to plan for

The most common approach to scenario planning is to create three potential future scenarios:

- The most likely scenario – this reflects the majority of managements' expectations of the future possibilities for the market.

KAPLAN PUBLISHING

- The best case scenario – this reflects a position where the key environmental factors move in a favourable direction for the organisation (for example, if the product becomes fashionable, the economy improves, competitors fail to react to changing technology etc.).

- The worst case scenario – this reflects a position where the environment turns against the organisation (for example, if there were more entrants into the market or if the economy where to suffer a period of recession).

The organisation can then evaluate how it might react to these changes. Plans should be put in place for all potential scenarios. The organisation should model how it would react to different scenarios and create key performance indicators or key risk indicators that indicate whether one scenario is becoming more likely than other expected scenarios.

However, many strategists suggest that having three alternatives, and in particular a most likely scenario, can render this analysis meaningless. They suggest that this will narrow managers' focus to this most likely scenario at the expense of the others. They therefore argue that it would be better to have only two potential future scenarios rather than distorting managers' mindsets with a 'most likely' scenario.

Also, the scenarios should be plausible alternatives rather than a consideration of every potential eventuality that can be created by managers. Scenarios are also likely to consider the culmination (and interrelation) of changes in the environment rather than plan for each one discreetly. For example, it may plan for a change which results in legislation on imports coming together with problems in achieving domestic supplier agreements occurring at the same time rather than examining these separately if separate changes are unlikely to cause business problems.

This approach is particularly useful in environments that are unpredictable or which change quickly and in unexpected ways. But that is not to say that the managers are aiming to predict the unpredictable. The aim here is to help managers become more aware of what the key environmental factors are and how they might influence the organisation in the future.

Benefits and problems of scenario planning

The key benefit of scenario planning is that it makes managers aware of what the key environmental factors for the organisation are. It also forces managers to have warning signs in place for potential scenarios that may cause problems for the organisation. Managers may also have created contingency plans for coping with different scenarios so that the organisation becomes more flexible at adapting to its environment. This last advantage may in turn lead to a strategic competitive advantage in the long term, especially in fast moving environments.

But scenario planning is time consuming and expensive to carry out. Also, care should be taken to avoid thinking of these scenarios as forecasts. These scenario plans should not be seen as a replacement for budgeting and control systems. The aim is to force management to consider and prepare for different scenarios, it is not to set these scenarios as targets as many best case scenarios, for example, will be unachievable and any target matched to this scenario is likely to be unattainable and demotivational for managers.

5 Porter's diamond

Porter tried to answer the following questions:

- Why does a nation become the home base for successful international competitors in an industry? Germany is renowned for car manufacture; Japan is prominent in consumer electronics.

- Why are firms based in a particular nation able to create and sustain competitive advantage against the world's best competitors in a particular field?

- Why is one country often the home of so many of an industry's world leaders?

KAPLAN PUBLISHING

Porter called the answers to these questions the determinants of national competitive advantage. He suggested that there are four main factors which determine national competitive advantage and expressed them in the form of a diamond.

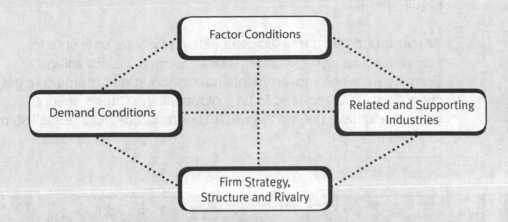

Further detail on Porter's diamond

(a) Favourable factor conditions:

   (i)   physical resources such as land, minerals and weather

   (ii) capital

   (iii) human resources such as skills, motivation, price and industrial relations

   (iv) knowledge that can be used effectively

   (v) infrastructure.

Porter also found that countries with factor disadvantages were forced to innovate to overcome these problems, e.g. Japanese firms experienced high energy costs and were forced to develop energy efficient products and processes that were subsequently demanded worldwide.

(b) Demand conditions: there must be a strong home market demand for the product or service. This determines how industries perceive and respond to buyer needs and creates the pressure to innovate. A compliant domestic market is a disadvantage because it does not force the industry to become innovative and excellent.

(c) Relating and supporting industries: the success of an industry can be due to its suppliers and related industries. Sweden's global superiority in its pulp and paper industries is supported by a network of related industries including packaging, chemicals, wood-processing, conveyor systems and truck manufacture. Many of these supporting industries have also achieved leading global positions.

(d) Firm strategy, structure and rivalry: organisational goals can be determined by ownership structure. Unquoted companies may have slightly longer time horizons to operate in because their financial performance is subject to much less scrutiny than quoted companies. They may also have different 'return on capital' requirements.

Porter found that domestic competition was vital as a spur to innovation and also enhanced global competitive advantage. Conversely, where governments have encouraged mergers to get the critical mass required to be a global player, these national monopolies have not, on the whole, been successful in establishing a global position.

Illustration 3 – Porter's diamond

Starbucks, a large American cafe chain, has been very successful when expanding overseas in areas such as Canada, Japan and the UK. To some extent this can be attributed to the following:

- **Factor conditions:** Starbucks were able to offer better looking premises which were more attractive to customers as a place to meet and mix than cafe shops previously established in these countries.

- **Demand conditions:** Starbucks had developed in a US market where customers were very demanding. Each customer wanted a bespoke/personal experience and Starbucks had to develop systems to cope with this (such as allowing customers to choose which bean to use, whether to use milk or cream, the size of the cup etc.). This allowed the company to easily adapt to new tastes and cultures in new overseas markets.

- **Structure and rivalry:** existing suppliers in these new countries were often small, local and undifferentiated. Starbucks were able to offer a branded experience with economies of scale which kept costs down. The skills it developed in achieving huge success in its domestic market were exploited to the full in these new markets.

The result is that Vancouver and London now have more Starbucks per person than New York.

But Starbucks has been slow to expand into some markets such as Germany and France (which are much larger than other markets such as the UK and Japan).

This can be put down to:

- **Factor conditions:** these countries have established cafe cultures and consumers are already experiencing high quality environments in some instances.

- **Demand conditions:** consumers often have little diversity in their tastes in these countries and there is less demand for bespoke products. Existing domestic cafes have already developed systems to cope with this when necessary.

- **Structure and rivalry:** existing cafes have a built up reputation and loyalty that Starbucks might struggle to overcome. Whereas Starbucks if often seen as a differentiator in markets such as Japan and the UK, it is likely to be perceived as a low cost alternative in markets such as Germany and France.

So Porter's diamond can be used to choose between overseas destination for expansion. It is important when choosing a country for overseas expansion that the elements of the diamond are considered and the chance of success assessed.

- **Firm strategy, structure and rivalry:** not much rivalry, so no structural advantages.

- Although factor conditions provide the right environment and home demand would be strong, the other elements of the diamond are missing.

Test your understanding 4

Apply **Porter's** diamond to the US personal computer (PC) industry.

6 Industry convergence and strategic groups

Over time industries can converge together to form one, larger industry (for example, mobile phones and PDAs have converged into the smartphone industry). This can make environmental analysis much tougher.

Industry convergence

External, environmental analysis is becoming more complicated in the real world as industries converge on one another. For example, ten years ago we could have carried out separate PESTEL and 5 Forces analysis for the mobile phone industry, the mp3 industry, the camera industry, the hand-held gaming console industry etc. But today these industries have started to converge and many products (for example, the Apple i-Phone) offer all the features that were once offered by separate products in different industries. This convergence is likely to increase as technology advances and it means that companies will be facing greater levels of substitutes than they have in the past.

In June 2008, the examiner set a question requiring 5 Forces analysis of the mobile phone industry and it was important to highlight that this would be hampered by industry convergence.

Definition:

- An **industry** is a group of firms selling the same principal product, or products which are close substitutes.

- A **sector** extends the idea of industry into the public services.

However, the boundaries of an industry or sector can change through the convergence of previously separate industries.

Convergence can be analysed in terms of whether it is supply led or demand (market) led and also whether there is convergence in substitutes or convergence in complements, e.g. products/services that complement each other.

- **Supply-led,** where producers try to see connections between separate industries or sectors, e.g. supermarkets offering retail banking.

- **Market-led,** where buyers see or want connections between separate industries or sectors, e.g. customers in a book store also wanting to browse CDs and DVDs.

- **Convergence in substitutes,** where one technology can replace another, e.g. mobile phones and landline phones.

- **Convergence in complements,** where two technologies work better together, e.g. Panasonic (electronics) and Leica (lenses) producing digital cameras.

The four influences can be shown as a matrix:

	Supply-led	Market-led
Substitutes	Mini-disc/ MP3 players	Mobiles/ landlines
Complements	Hotels/ airlines	Computer printers/digital cameras

But at the same time strategic groups might form within the industry which focus on different niches and compete on a narrower focus. For example, some mobile phones will focus on their camera ability, others will focus on their music playing ability, etc. The environmental analysis can then become a little more focused again.

Strategic groups

Strategic groups are organisations within an industry or sector with similar strategic characteristics, following similar strategies or competing on similar bases.

Strategic group analysis is a help to understanding the competitive structure of an industry:

- Against whom is an organisation directly competing?

- How possible, or likely, is it for an organisation to change strategic groups? A set of strategic groups generally includes a set of mobility barriers that inhibit or prevent organisations from moving to another group, e.g. low-cost production, brand names, low overheads or a local customer base.

- Identify potential opportunities and threats.

- Reduce the set of relevant competitors. Many industries contain many more competitors than can be analysed individually. Often it is simply not feasible to consider 30 competitors, to say nothing of hundreds. Reducing this set to a smaller number in a strategic group makes the analysis easier.

A strategic group could:

- have similar characteristics, e.g. size

- pursue similar competitive strategies over time e.g. heavy advertising and the use of the same distribution channel or

- have similar assets and skills, e.g. quality image.

The concept of strategic groups is important because one way to develop a sustainable competitive advantage is to pursue a strategy that is protected from competition by assets and skills that represent barriers to competitors. It also helps to gain a better understanding of the bases of rivalry within strategic groups and how it differs from that within other groups.

Strategic groupings can refine the strategic investment decision. Instead of determining in which industries to invest, the decision can focus on what strategic group a firm should invest in. Thus, it will be necessary to determine the current profitability and future potential profitability of the strategic group. One strategic objective is to invest in those strategic groups that will tend to be profitable over time and to disinvest or avoid strategic groups that will not be profitable.

Ultimately the selection of a strategy and its supporting assets and skills will often mean selecting or creating a strategic group.

The concept of strategic groups can also be helpful in projecting competitive strategies into the future. It is very useful for matching up groups of customers to groups of competing companies.

Test your understanding 5

What strategic groups might exist in the morning newspaper business and how are they distinguished?

It may be that some of the companies within a particular strategic group might collaborate together to improve their overall competitive or market position.

How collaboration can bring advantages

This can be looked at in terms of Porter's five forces analysis.

- Buyer pressure. This can be reduced by forming close alliances with customers. For example, collaboration on design and research and development. Once successful alliances are made, customers will be relatively reluctant to switch to another supplier.

- Supplier pressure. For example, supermarkets form close collaborations with suppliers to manage their inventories.

- Threat of new entrants. Collaboration between existing rival companies can spread marketing and research costs more thinly, making it more difficult for new companies to enter the market.

- Substitute products. The issues here are the same as for new entrants. Many trade associations exist to allow collaboration on an industry-wide level, for example by lobbying.

7 Quantitative techniques

The techniques covered so far have been **'qualitative methods'** of forecasting what might happen to future volumes, costs, revenues etc. They could be backed up by further qualitative techniques such as market research.

Businesses may also want to quantify these forecasts (for example, for budgeting, planning and evaluation purposes) and there are a number of **quantitative techniques** with which you should be familiar such as **linear regression** and **time series analysis**.

In exam scenarios students must be able to discuss the suitability, principles and uses of these techniques, but students will not be asked to perform the mathematical calculations.

Linear regression

Regression is a simple statistical tool used to model the dependence of a variable (say, costs) on one (or more) explanatory variables (say, volume). This functional relationship may then be formally stated as an equation, with associated statistical values that describe how well this equation fits the data.

Linear regression equation

The equation of a straight line is:

$$y = a + bx$$

where	y	=	dependent variable
	a	=	intercept (on y-axis)
	b	=	gradient
	x	=	independent variable

$$\text{and} \quad b = \frac{n\Sigma xy - \Sigma x \Sigma y}{n\Sigma x^2 - (\Sigma x)^2}$$

where n = number of pairs of data

and $a = \bar{y} - b\bar{x}$

Linear regression analysis can be used to make forecasts or estimates whenever a linear relationship is assumed between two variables, and historical data is available for analysis.

Example relationships

Two such relationships are:

- **A time series and trend line.** Linear regression analysis is an alternative to calculating moving averages to establish a trend line from a time series. (Time series is explained later in this chapter)
    - The independent variable (x) in a time series is time.
    - The dependent variable (y) is sales, production volume or cost etc.

- **Total costs, where costs consist of a combination of fixed costs and variable costs** (for example, total overheads, or a semi-variable cost item). Linear regression analysis is an alternative to using the high-low method of cost behaviour analysis. It should be more accurate than the high-low method, because it is based on more items of historical data, not just a 'high' and a 'low' value.
    - The independent variable (x) in total cost analysis is the volume of activity.
    - The dependent variable (y) is total cost.
    - The value of a is the amount of fixed costs.
    - The value of b is the variable cost per unit of activity.

When a linear relationship is identified and quantified using linear regression analysis, values for a and b are obtained, and these can be used to make a forecast for the budget. For example:

- a sales budget or forecast can be prepared, or

- total costs (or total overhead costs) can be estimated, for the budgeted level of activity.

Correlation

Regression analysis attempts to find the linear relationship between two variables. Correlation is concerned with establishing how strong the relationship is.

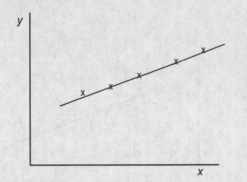 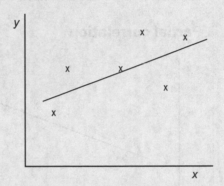

Clearly in the first diagram, the regression line would be a much more useful predictor than the regression line in the second diagram.

The correlation co-efficient

The strength of this relationship can be determined by a statistical technique (which we do not need to know for this syllabus) and expressed as a correlation co-efficient.

The main result of a correlation is called the correlation coefficient (or 'r'). It ranges from −1.0 to +1.0. The closer r is to +1 or −1, the more closely the two variables are related.

If r is close to 0, it means there is no relationship between the variables. If r is positive, it means that as one variable increases the other variable increases. If r is negative it means that as one variable increases, the other variable decreases (often called an 'inverse' correlation).

Different types of correlation explained

Perfect correlation

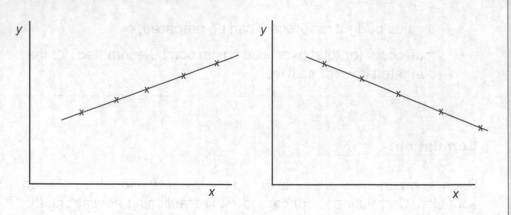

All the pairs of values lie on a straight line. There is an exact linear relationship between the two variables.

Partial correlation

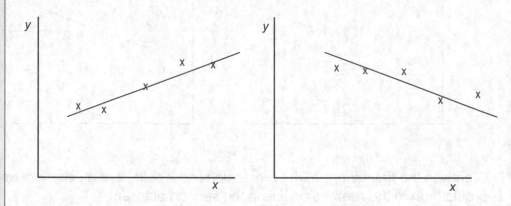

In the first diagram there is not an exact relationship, but low values of x tend to be associated with low values of y, and high values of x tend to be associated with high values of y.

In the second diagram again there is not an exact relationship, but low values of x tend to be associated with high values of y and vice versa.

No correlation

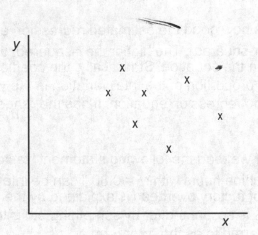

The values of the two variables seem to be completely unconnected.

Positive and negative correlation

Correlation can be positive or negative.

Positive correlation means that high values of one variable are associated with high values of the other and that low values of one are associated with low values of the other.

Negative correlation means that low values of one variable are associated with high values of the other and vice versa.

The correlation coefficient

The degree of correlation can be measured by the Pearsonian correlation coefficient, r (also known as the product moment correlation coefficient).

r must always be between −1 and +1.

If r = 1, there is perfect positive correlation
If r = 0, there is no correlation
If r = −1, there is perfect negative correlation

For other values of r, the meaning is not so clear. It is generally taken that if r > 0.8, then there is strong positive correlation and if r < −0.8, there is strong negative correlation, however more meaningful information can be gathered from calculating the coefficient of determination, r^2.

$$r = \frac{n\sum xy - \sum x \sum y}{\sqrt{\left(n\sum x^2 - \left(\sum x\right)^2\right)\left(n\sum y^2 - \left(\sum y\right)^2\right)}}$$

The coefficient of determination

This measures how good the estimated regression equation is, designated as r^2 (read as r-squared). The higher the r-squared, the more confidence one can have in the equation. Statistically, the coefficient of determination represents the proportion of the total variation in the y variable that is explained by the regression equation. It has the range of values between 0 and 1.

For example, if we read the following statement "factory overhead is a function of machine-hours with $r^2 = 0.80$," can be interpreted as "80% of the total variation of factory overhead is explained by the machine hours and the remaining 20% is accounted for by something other than machine-hours." The 20% is referred to as the error term.

Illustration on the use of linear regression

A sporting venue has used linear regression to exxamine the relationship between hot drink sales and matchday attendances as follows:

Matchday	Attendance (000) (x)	Hot drink sales ($000) (y)
1	54	54
2	48	50
3	45	49
4	60	58
5	53	49

This has created the following linear regression output:

$$y = 20.28 + 0.609x$$

$$r = 0.85$$

Matchday 6 Forecast hot drinks sales (attendance expected to be 50k)
= $51,000

Explain the meaning of this data.

Answer

The first table represents the actual data from the last 5 matchdays. For the linear regression formula, the matchday attendance has been symbolised with the letter 'x' and the sales of hot drinks is symbolised by the letter 'y'. The sporting venue believes that there is a straight line relationship between x and y, i.e. as x (matchday attendance) increases, y (sales of hot drinks) will increase (and vice versa).

KAPLAN PUBLISHING

The linear regression equation uses a mathematical formula on the data provided to formalise this relationship using the actual data provided. This data tells us two things:

- there is expected to be sales of hot drinks of 20.28k regardless of the attendance at the game (perhaps this represents regular match goers who always have a drink regardless of the weather or opponent etc.)

- sales will then increase at a rate of 0.609 for every matchgoer in attendance. This is the variable relationship that can be used in forecasting once the expected attendance is known.

The forecast uses this equation to forecast sales for the next match (where attendance is expected to be 50k) as follows:

Expected sales = 20.28 + 0.609 (50) = 50.73

This has been rounded to a forecast of $51,000.

On the face of it this assumed relationship between attendance and sales would appear to be a reasonable assumption – it is likely that if there are more visitors to the stadium then the stadium will sell more drinks. The forecast of $51,000is using the past pattern in this data to predict what might happen for the next game.

The correlation gives us some idea of how reliable this relationship might be. The correlation (r) is 0.85. This represents a relationship measured on a scale of 0 to 1, with 0 representing a very poor relationship and 1 representing a very strong relation. 0.85 is much closer to 1 than to 0 and therefore it would provide that sporting venue with some reassurance that their underlying relationship between attendance and hot drinks sales is sound.

This strength of the relationship can be further examined by calculating the coefficient of determination. This is calculated as the correlation squared

$= 0.85 \times 0.85$

$= 0.72$

This tells us that 72% of hot drinks sales can be attributed to the attendance at the match. It also means that 28% of sales can be attributed to other factors (such as the weather, the time of year or day, the quality of the opposition, or many other unknown factors not considered by the linear regression analysis). The fact that these other factors are not considered is one of the many limitations of linear regression explored in the next element of the chapter.

Limitations of simple linear regression

(1) Assumes a linear relationship between the variables.

(2) Only measures the relationship between two variables. In reality the dependent variable is affected by many independent variables.

(3) Only interpolated forecasts tend to be reliable. The equation should not be used for extrapolation.

(4) Regression assumes that the historical behaviour of the data continues into the foreseeable future.

(5) Interpolated predictions are only reliable if there is a significant correlation between the data.

Time series analysis

Time series forecasting methods are based on analysis of historical data. They make the assumption that past **patterns** in data, such as seasonality, can be used to forecast future data points. This means that it's future predictions are more curved than linear.

Trends in data can lead to curves

For example, if a business knows that, over the last 5 years, month 12 has seen volume levels that are 40% greater than typical monthly volumes, then it might be reasonable to forecast that month 12 for the forthcoming year will follow a similar pattern.

This should allow the predictions to take account of likely 'curved' performance – for example, where we don't expect sales to rise by a constant amount each period, but instead expect it to increase **and** follow past trends where some periods are above the average and some periods are below the average.

This may be best seen in the following illustration:

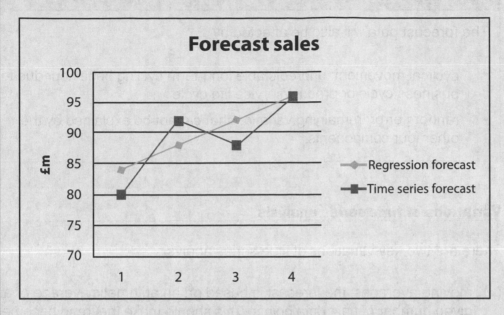

In this scenario, linear regression has predicted an increase in sales of £4m per quarter. It takes no account of any seasonality. Time series works on the same increase per quarter and reaches the same point at the end of the period. But it has taken account of past trends which suggest that quarter 1 sales are usually £4m below trend, quarter 2's are £4m above and quarter 3's are £4m below.

Be aware however that in time series analysis the trend line itself may also be curved – in fact, it would only be linear (as in this example) if the favourable and adverse seasonal affects cancel each other out.

Components of times series analysis

Time series analysis has three basic components:

- *average*: the mean of the observations over time

- *trend*: a gradual increase or decrease in the average over time

- *seasonal influence*: predictable short-term cycling behaviour due to time of day, week, month, season, year, etc.

These components can be used in different ways to produce future forecasts.

Note: Moving averages are used to identify the trend. In this way the gradual change should become more obvious as figures are 'smoothed' out.

Other elements

The forecast data will also be affected by

- cyclical movement: unpredictable long-term cycling behaviour due to business cycle or product/service life cycle

- random error: remaining variation that cannot be explained by the other four components.

Variations of time series analysis

There are two key variations of time series analysis:

(1) moving averages: the forecast is based on an arithmetic average of a given number of past data points. This should make the trend become more obvious.

(2) exponential smoothing: a type of *weighted* moving average that allows inclusion of trends, etc. This gives greater weighting to more recent data in order to reflect the more recent trend.

Example of exponential smoothing

Consider the following data set:

Period	1	2	3	4	5	6	7	8	9	10	11	12
Sales ($m)	47	50	51	48	48	52	52	49	50	52	54	50

It is difficult to immediately spot the trend as the figures appear to be constantly increasing and decreasing.

But a moving average of this data (using 4 period averaging) would show:

Moving average	49.00	49.25	49.75	50.00	50.25	50.75	50.75	51.25	51.50

It is now much easier to identify the gradual increase that is observed in the average data. (Note that the increase isn't at a constant rate so that this trend line would be slightly curved).

An exponential smoothing of the data would present a similar picture:

Exponential smoothing	49.20	48.80	49.90	50.80	50.40	50.30	50.80	52.10	51.60

Calculations:

The first moving average is calculated as the average sales from periods 1 to 4. The second is the average from periods 2 to 5 etc.

The exponential smoothing uses the same periods. But the average is calculated by taking 4 times the 4th period, 3 times the third period, 2 times the 2nd period and 1 times the first period and then dividing by a total of ten.

Advantages and disadvantages of time series analysis

Advantages	Disadvantages
• identifies seasonal variations	• complicated
• can be non-linear	• 'seasons' may change
• accurate	• based on historical data
	• less useful in the long term

Test your understanding 6

An organisation with seasonal sales has created a spreadsheet for forecasting next year's sales. The spreadsheet output provides three tables:

Table 1

A Year	B Quarter	C Units	D	E Trend	F Variation
20X1	1	220			
	2	160	765		
	3	185	775	192.5	−7.50
	4	200	780	194.4	+5.60
20X2	1	230	785	195.6	+34.40
	2	165	795	197.5	−32.50
	3	190	810	200.6	−10.60
	4	210	810	202.5	+7.50
20X3	1	245	820	203.8	+41.20
	2	165	828	206.0	−41.00
	3	200	823	206.4	−6.40
	4	218	828	206.4	+11.60
20X4	1	240	840	208.5	+31.50
	2	170	842	210.2	−40.20
	3	212			
	4	220			

Table 2

	1	2	3	4
20X1			−7.50	+5.60
20X2	+34.40	−32.50	−10.60	+7.50
20X3	+41.20	−41.00	−6.40	+11.60
20X4	+31.50	−40.20		
Total	+107.10	−113.70	−24.50	+24.70
Average	+35.70	−37.90	−8.17	+8.23
Adjustment	0.54	0.54	0.54	0.54
Seasonal variation	+36.24	−37.36	−7.63	+8.77

Table 3

20X4	3	211.70	−7.63	204.07
20X4	4	213.20	+8.77	221.97
20X5	1	214.70	+36.24	250.94
20X5	2	216.20	−37.36	178.84

> **Required:**
>
> Explain the figures in the spreadsheet used by the sales forecasting team.
>
> **Note**: No calculations need to be performed.

Conclusions on quantitative techniques

Two different forecasting techniques have been explored here (and there are many more in the real world). Linear regression is most relevant when there is a linear relationship between the variables, time series analysis is most appropriate when seasonal variations causes curved forecasts.

The reliability of a forecasting method can be established over time. If forecasts turn out to be inaccurate, management might decide that they are not worth producing, and that different methods of forecasting should be tried. On the other hand, if forecasts prove to be reasonably accurate, management are likely to continue with the same forecasting method.

8 Environmental opportunities and threats

This chapter has looked at a number of tools (or models) that can be used to help to make sense of the environment. The results of these analyses can be classified as either an:

- opportunity or a
- threat.

Once categorised as an opportunity or threat the influences first need to be:

- prioritised, e.g. some will be much more important than others.

Then the organisation has to decide how to:

- grab the best opportunities
- defend against the most serious threats.

There is absolutely no point in identifying opportunities and threats, but do nothing about them.

Explanation of opportunities and threats

Opportunities are favourable conditions that usually arise from the nature of changes in the external environment, e.g. new markets, improved economic factors or a failure of competitors. Opportunities provide the organisation with the potential to offer new or to develop existing products, facilities or services.

Threats are the opposite of opportunities and also arise from external developments. Examples include unfavourable changes in legislation, the introduction of a radically new product by a competitor, political or economic unrest, changing social conditions or the actions of a pressure group.

It may be a little simplistic to assume that blame can be apportioned exclusively to the organisation's environment when, in fact, weaknesses in (say) the management team or the organisational structure may have led to a compounding of the problems arising externally. Indeed, throughout our analysis we must bear in mind the linkages between issues and the possibility that it may have been a combination of various internal and external factors that led to the problems being experienced.

Illustration of opportunities and threats

The following might represent some of the opportunities and threats identified for a commercial television station.

Opportunities	Threats
The internet, e.g. streaming programmes as viewers want to watch them.	Competing forms of entertainment, e.g. video games, programmes streamed on the internet, podcasts.
Increased monitoring of which programmes viewers watch.	Advertisers moving to more efficient channels, e.g. advertisements triggered by internet search activity.

KAPLAN PUBLISHING

Opportunities	Threats
Highly portable computers (the equivalent of audio MP3 players) on which programmes can be watched.	Public taste changes (eventually, after the 25th series of a reality TV programme, enthusiasm for reality TV might wane).
Set of back catalogue material.	Economic downturn reducing advertising revenue.
TV acquisition by people in developing economies, e.g. China and India have high rates of economic growth. Purchasing a TV company, if permitted in those countries, could be a source of long-term growth.	Government imposing quality standards.

Many of these influences arise from **PESTEL**, but **Porter's** five forces and the other tools can be relevant also.

Remember, it doesn't matter which model is used to identify an influence. All that matters is that it has been identified.

Test your understanding 7

Perform an opportunities and threats analysis on:

(1) a passenger train service

(2) a nuclear power station.

9 Chapter summary

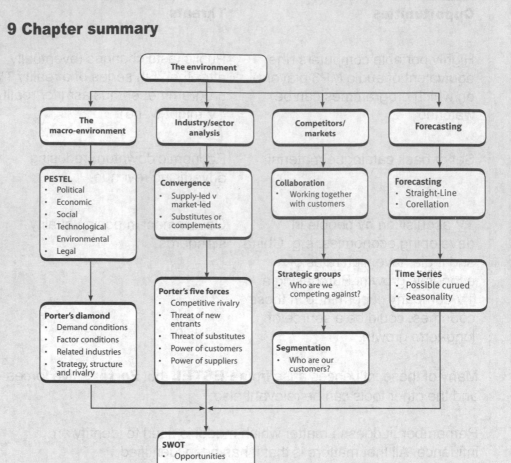

The environment

The macro-environment

Industry/sector analysis

Competitors/markets

Forecasting

PESTEL
- Political
- Economic
- Social
- Technological
- Environmental
- Legal

Convergence
- Supply-led v market-led
- Substitutes or complements

Collaboration
- Working together with customers

Forecasting
- Straight-Line
- Corellation

Porter's diamond
- Demand conditions
- Factor conditions
- Related industries
- Strategy, structure and rivalry

Porter's five forces
- Competitive rivalry
- Threat of new entrants
- Threat of substitutes
- Power of customers
- Power of suppliers

Strategic groups
- Who are we competing against?

Time Series
- Possible curued
- Seasonality

Segmentation
- Who are our customers?

SWOT
- Opportunities
- Threats

KAPLAN PUBLISHING

Test your understanding answers

Test your understanding 1

Here are our suggestions. You might have other valid ones.

Political influences: planning policy on large out-of-town sites, competition policy.

Economic influences: unemployment rate, interest rates, taxation.

Social influences: changes in population sizes, changes in consumer taste (for example, possibly more health conscious).

Technological influences: the internet (internet ordering), sophisticated Just-In-Time systems, food packaging technology.

Environmental/ecological influences: use of land for building, sustainable resources, packaging, animal welfare.

Legal influences: health and safety regulations, consumer legislation, food packaging regulations, inclusion of additives in food.

Test your understanding 2

No answer provided. The factors are considered in the expandable text which follows the Test Your Understanding question.

Test your understanding 3

A garden maintenance company

Threat of entry: high. Only modest amounts of capital and know-how are needed. No regulations, hard to differentiate, and limited scope for economies of scale.

Threat of substitute products: low, except for householders who opt for a very low-maintenance garden and for customers who choose to look after their own gardens.

Bargaining power of customers: low. There will be many small customers so individual bargaining power will be low. Quality is perhaps not a vital component of the service.

Bargaining power of suppliers: low. The supplies needed are widely available.

Competition: high. The business is very easy to get into. There are negligible switching costs.

Test your understanding 4

Factor conditions: large population of well-trained engineers.

Demand conditions: large population of individuals and businesses who need or want PCs.

Related and supporting industries: many component manufacturers close by; large and well-endowed universities.

Firm strategy, structure and rivalry: an entrepreneurial economy allowed many startups and the best survive the intense rivalry.

Test your understanding 5

Possible strategic groups are:

- the tabloids which are relatively cheap. Lots of pictures. Not much serious reporting.

- the so-called 'broadsheets' (though many are now in tabloid format). More expensive. Large amounts of reporting and editorial compared to pictures.

- the free papers. Small, chatty, enough reading to entertain you on the journey to work. No heavy editorials. High number of advertisements.

Test your understanding 6

The sales forecast can be explained as follows:

Table 1

This table records the actual past data and is used to determine past variations (seasonal upturns and downturns) from the normal trend.

The figures in each column can be explained as follows:

Column (s)	Usefulness
A – C	This is the past actual sales data for each quarter of the year over the last four years. Two general trends can easily be identified – firstly, there is a general upwards trend in sales overall over the period and, secondly, sales in quarters 2 and 3 seem to be much lower than sales achieved in quarters 1 and 4. This does therefore appear to be a seasonal business and the use of time series analysis for forecasting should be of some use to this business. The remainder of the spreadsheet applies a time series analysis technique.
D – E	The 4 quarter moving total sales in column D is used to determine the trend in column E. This is the underlying trend in sales over the four years, without any seasonal fluctuations (these have been smoothed out). The trend reflects the expectations that sales are on a general upward curve.

F	The trend has then been compared to the actual sales for each quarter to determine the seasonality in that quarter. For example, in quarter 3 20X1, the actual sales were 185 units whilst the trend was calculated at 192.5 units. This quarter was therefore deemed to be 7.50 units below trend. This variation reflects the expected variation in sales in each quarter due to seasonality.

These individual variations are then averaged out in table 2.

Table 2

The individual variations from each quarter are summarised in the first four rows of this table and then totalled. This total is then divided by three (as there are three observations from each quarter) to determine an average variation for each quarter. An adjustment is then made for rounding errors to give a final average seasonal variation for each quarter.

So, for example, on average, Quarter 2 is 37.36 units below the trend in sales. These are the average variations experienced over the last 4 years. If the business assumes that this seasonality will continue then these seasonal variations can be used to forecast sales in the following quarters. This is what is happening in Table 3.

Table 3

This table is aimed at predicating sales for the next two quarters of sales (i.e. quarters 1 and 2 of 20X5).

In the third column of the table the trend has been extrapolated. This has assumed that the trend in sales will continue upwards at its average rate of growth. The fourth column is the average seasonal variation calculated for each quarter in Table 2. The forecast trend is adjusted for this seasonal variation so that the final column provides the expected (forecast) sales. For example, the forecast sales for quarter 1 20X5 (which takes account of both the expected growth in sales and the seasonality typically experienced in that quarter) are 250.94 units.

This forecast is then likely to form the basis for all other forecasts within the business (for example, production and purchasing budgets).

KAPLAN PUBLISHING

Issues

Note that the spreadsheet highlights two of the biggest issues when using time series analysis:

- the trend is expected to follow its previous upwards pattern

- the seasonality experienced in the past is expected to be experienced to similar levels in the future.

Test your understanding 7

(1) A passenger train service

Threats

- losing the franchise or right to operate the service (if the service is provided by a private company)

- underinvestment in the network infrastructure

- terrorism

- increased affluence in some countries leading to less use of trains as people acquire cars

- competing services.

Opportunities

- increasing cost of petrol making cars more expensive to run

- environmental concerns and regulation

- building customer loyalty, e.g. perhaps a scheme similar to air miles

- innovative fares for different market segments

- new routes which are very expensive to develop but once established might be barriers to entry of competitors

- new technology, e.g. magnetic levitation; generally reduced journey times.

(2) A nuclear power station

Threats

- environmental concerns about the nuclear industry
- terrorism
- theft of nuclear material
- accidental release of radioactive material
- alternative energy sources (e.g. biotechnology might provide a very efficient way of creating fuel from sunlight)
- global warming, e.g. less fuel needed to heat homes and offices.

Opportunities

- political risks associated with reliance upon Middle Eastern and Russian supplies of fossil fuels
- environmental concerns about greenhouse gas emission from fossil fuel use
- global warming, e.g. more fuel needed to cool homes and offices
- growing world demand for power
- new technology to deal safely, and permanently, with radioactive waste.

Opportunities

- political risks associated with reliance upon Middle Eastern and Russian supplies of fossil fuels
- environmental concerns about greenhouse gas emission from fossil fuel use
- global warming, e.g. more fuel needed to cool homes and offices
- growing world demand for power
- new technology to deal safely, and permanently, with radioactive waste.

Internal resources, capabilities and competences

Chapter learning objectives

Upon completion of this chapter you will be able to:

- develop suitable CSFs (and associated KPIs) for products and services

- define and describe strategic capability, threshold resources, threshold competences, unique resources and core competences

- use the resource audit to determine organisational strengths and weakness

- apply the life cycle model and discuss how product costs can change over a product's life cycle

- perform effective quantitative analysis by using information provided in the question to devise and apply appropriate ratios to:

  - assess how efficiently an organisation is using its current resources

  - assess the risks associated with financing and investment in the organisation

  - assess the organisation's short-term commitments to creditors and employees

  - assess the viability of chosen strategies

  - assist investors and shareholders in evaluating organisational performance and strategy

- apply the SWOT model in a scenario.

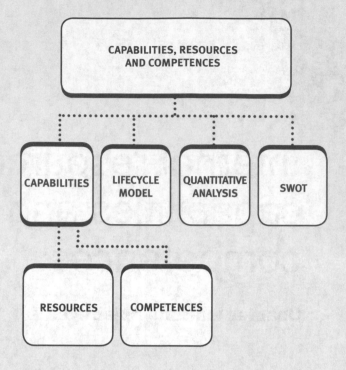

1 Introduction

This chapter looks at the internal position of an organisation. This will help determine how well the organisation can cope with the external and competitive environment which was analysed in the previous chapter. This internal analysis focuses on identifying the strengths and weaknesses that are particular to an organisation.

The chapter ends by looking at SWOT analysis, which brings together internal (strengths and weakness) and external (opportunities and threats) factors to allow organisations to assess their strategic position.

2 Critical success factors

An important strength for any organisation will be the achievement of critical success factors. This should allow the organisation to cope better than rivals with any changes in its competitive environment.

What are critical success factors?

Critical success factors (CSFs) are the essential areas of the business that must be performed well if the mission, objectives and goals of the business are to be achieved.

Critical success factors (CSFs) are performance requirements that are fundamental to an organisation's success. In this context CSFs should thus be viewed as those product features that are particularly valued by customers. This is where the organisation must outperform competition.

Examples of Critical Success Factors

The syllabus focuses on CSFs linked to customer needs. In practice CSFs can be much more general than this. An organisation will develop its CSFs when it determines its mission and objectives.

- The mission statement represents the aspirations of the organisation.

- Long-term objectives may be expressed in terms of increasing shareholder returns or shareholder value added for a profit-seeking company or to relieve poverty in developing nations or save rare animal species for a charity, i.e. a not-for-profit organisation.

- CSFs relate to how objectives can be attained and should be identified early in the strategic planning process.

- Functions and processes refer to the KPIs that help to measure the achievement of CSFs.

- Activities refer to the day-to-day functions that drive the organisation and the need to do these with excellence.

For a profit-seeking organisation, CSFs should relate to the key factors for business success, which are typically the following:

- profitability – traditionally the primary objective is growth in earnings per share

- market share

- growth

- innovation

- productivity – targets will be associated with manpower, plant, yields and costs

- customer satisfaction

- the quality of the firm's products.

Not-for-profit organisations should also provide evidence of stakeholder value and show how its activities are, or will be, able to support its aims. The CSFs for a charity should relate to the progress the organisation's work is making towards its charitable objectives. For example, for a charity aiming to save rare animal species a CSF might be to reduce demand for clothing made from rare animal fur.

Examples of CSFs for major industries include:

- in the automobile industry – styling, an efficient dealer network, organisation, performance

- in the food processing industry – new product development, good distribution channels, health aspects (e.g. low fat)

- in the life insurance industry – reputation, innovative new policies

- in the supermarket industry – the right product mix available in each store, having it actually available on the shelves, pricing it correctly.

Test your understanding 1

What might a parcel delivery service such as DHL identify as its two main critical success factors?

Key Performance Indicators (KPIs)

The achievement of CSFs will be vital to a business and it should have targets for success in these areas that are measured and monitored. Measured targets for CSFs are called key performance indicators (KPIs).

Key Performance Indicators (KPIs)

Performance measurements can relate to short-term objectives (e.g. cost control) or longer-term measures (e.g. customer satisfaction).

The objectives and goals of a business will vary depending on the type of business that is being operated. For example:

- A company's overall goal will be to maximise their shareholders wealth so they will want to monitor profitability (based on increasing sales and reducing costs) and growth or market share compared to competitors.

- A non-profit organisation, for example a government department, will want to provide the best service possible for the lowest cost so that the residents being cared for achieve value for money from the taxes they pay.

What these businesses have in common is that they will have long term (strategic) goals or objectives. These long term goals will be broken down into tactical and operational targets which will need to be monitored. To be able to do this they will identify critical success factors and key performance indicators to monitor to ensure targets are met.

Types of KPIs

KPIs in some organisations may be categorised as follows:

- quantitative – direct measures of sales, costs, ROCE and profit

- qualitative – market share, customer base; % sales growth, labour turnover, % of deliveries on time, customer returns as a % of total sales, complaints per £ of sales, reduced percentage of local population contracting HIV/AIDS or the number of countries prohibiting rare animal fur imports

- relative or absolute – relative measures are frequently more useful than measures in absolute terms, e.g. complaints per customer may be more useful than simply the number of complaints; gross profit per unit (or as a % of sales) may be more useful than total gross profit

- value for money (VFM) measures – the pursuit of economy, effectiveness and efficiency are mainly used by the public sector and other non-profit-seeking organisations.

Measures for service efforts and accomplishment fall into four categories:

- input measures – the effort expended on a programme – 'economy' is a measure of inputs to achieve a certain service

- output measures – the level of services provided – 'effectiveness' is a measure of outputs, i.e. services and facilities

- outcome measures – the effect a service has on the programme's stated objectives

- efficiency measures – a comparison of the level of inputs with outputs or outcomes – it is the optimum of economy and effectiveness, i.e. the measure of outputs over inputs.

Charities are very accustomed to measuring in this way:

- they report on the financial resources dedicated to specific programme in their financial statements and the non-financial information about the effort they expend, such as the hours spent meeting a programme goal

- output measures are often stated in non-financial terms, e.g. a homeless shelter may report the number of people housed

- outcome measures gauge how well a programme accomplished its goal, e.g. a programme designed to teach reading to adults may use the literacy rate for the area served as an outcome measure

> - a way to measure the efficiency of this programme could be to compute a cost (input) for each adult who reaches a certain reading level (output).

Although profit cannot be ignored as it is the main objective of commercial organisations, critical success factors (CSFs) and key performance indicators (KPIs) should not focus on profit alone. The view is that a range of performance indicators should be used and these should be a mix of financial and non-financial measures.

Examples of Non-financial CSFs and KPIs

The table below shows a number of non-financial performance Indicators grouped against CSFs. The organisation will formulate its own, specific KPIs which best suit its business.

CSFs	KPIs
Competitiveness	• sales growth by product or service
	• measures of customer base
	• relative market share and position
Resource utilisation	• efficiency measurements of resources planned against consume
	• measurements of resources available against those used
	• productivity measurements
Quality of service	• quality measures in every unit
	• evaluate suppliers on the basis of quality
	• number of customer complaints received
	• number of new accounts lost or gained
Customer satisfaction	• speed of response to customer needs
	• informal listening by calling a certain number of customers each week
	• number of customer visits to the factory or workplace
	• number of factory and non-factory manager visits to customers
Quality of working life	• days absence
	• labour turnover
	• overtime
	• measures of job satisfaction

KAPLAN PUBLISHING

Innovation	• proportion of new products and services to old one
	• new product or service sales levels
Responsiveness (lead time)	• order entry delays and errors
	• wrong blueprints or specifications
	• long set-up times and large lots
	• high defect count
	• machines that break down
Quality of output	• returns from customers
	• reject rates
	• reworking costs
	• warranty costs
Flexibility (ability to react to changing demand and a changing environment)	• product/service introduction flexibility
	• product/service mix flexibility
	• volume flexibility
	• delivery flexibility
	• time to respond to customer demands

Illustration 1 – Critical success factors

The following is an example of CSFs developed for a shipping terminal.

Critical success factor	Indicator	Mechanism for measurement
Health and safety	• Accident record • Industrial injuries	• Factory inspector's reports • Accidents reported
Customer satisfaction	• Complaints • Insurance claims • Stock losses	• Complaints register • Correspondence • Internal audit
Accessibility to site	• Reported delays • Quayside tidiness	• Inspection

Critical success factor	Indicator	Mechanism for measurement
Maintenance of premises	• Repair costs	• Inspection
Efficient plant use	• Down time	• Inspection • Repair bills
Traceability of documents	• Out-turn reports	• Manifest checks
Efficient use of staff	• Time standards for loading and unloading	• Training schedules

Test your understanding 2

Using the CSFs previously identified for a parcel delivery company such as DHL, explain how the company might measure their performance.

Problems with non-financial performance indicators

The use of NFPI measures is now common place, but it is not without problems:

- Setting up and operating a system involving a wide range of performance indicators can be time-consuming and costly

- It can be a complex system that managers may find difficult to understand

- There is no clear set of NFPIs that the organisation must use – it will have to select those that seem to be most appropriate

- The scope for comparison with other organisations is limited as few businesses may use precisely the same NFPIs as the organisation under review.

KAPLAN PUBLISHING

3 Strategic capabilities, resources and competences

Strategic capability is the adequacy and suitability of the resources and competences an organisation needs if it is to survive and prosper.

Another way to look at CSFs is to examine an organisation's strategic capabilities. If a business can obtain unique resources and core competences this should lead to its success. This can be explained in the following table:

	Resources	Competences
Threshold capabilities • these are necessary for any organisation to exist and compete in an industry • they are likely to be common to most rivals and easily copied • they will not lead to success or competitive advantage.	Threshold resources Example: any daily newspaper has reporters, editors, printing staff etc.	Threshold competencies Example: every consumer electronics firm will have capabilities in electrical engineering.
Strategic Capabilities • these are particular to an individual business • they will be hard to copy • they will be valued by the customer **(CSF)** • they will lead to competitive advantage.	Unique resources Example: but a particular newspaper may be able to stand out from its rivals if it has an exclusive deal with the country's top sportstar who will write a daily column on his/her sport.	Core Competences Example: Sony believe they have core competences in design and user-friendliness that their rivals can't match.

So as part of an internal analysis a business should look for any unique resources that it may own or core competences that it has created. These would be significant strengths to any business.

More on strategic capabilities

Note that capability refers to resources and competences and their relationship can be shown as:

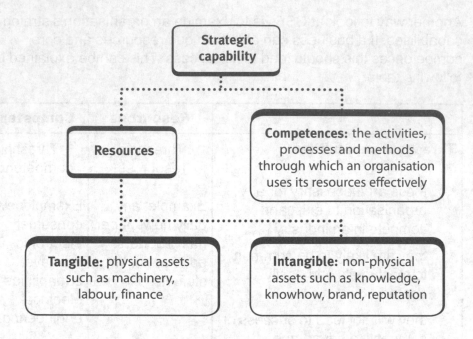

Strategic capability can also be divided into threshold capabilities and capabilities for competitive advantage.

- Threshold capabilities. These are the **minimum** capabilities needed for the organisation to be able to compete in a given market. They consist of threshold resources and threshold competences – the resources and competences needed to meet customers' minimum requirements.

- Capabilities for competitive advantage. The capabilities that allow an organisation to beat its competitors. These capabilities must meet the needs and expectations of its customers. Unique capabilities are not enough – they must be valued by the customers.

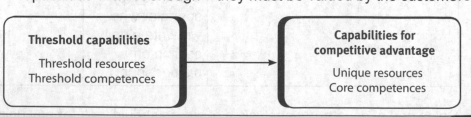

- Unique resources are those resources that create competitive advantage and that others **cannot imitate or obtain**. Examples of unique resources are:

  - brand

  - situation, for example, near a source of raw material or a source of cheap labour

  - sunk costs. Competitors have to cover depreciation costs

  - right to use a patented process.

Note that if the unique resource is people-based, the people can move to competitors or start their own business.

- Core competences are the activities, processes and methods through which an organisation uses its resources effectively, in ways that others cannot imitate or obtain. Examples of core competences are:

  - sophisticated IT that, for example, enables complex and accurate demand forecasting

  - a corporate culture that fosters innovation

  - the ability to share and lever knowledge throughout the organisation.

Illustration 2 – Capabilities, resources and competences

The Coca-Cola Corporation has, for many years, maintained a very strong position in the soft drinks market. Consider its flagship product, Coca-Cola. This has largely survived competition from supermarkets' own-label colas. There is no great secret in how to make a reasonable imitation (though purists would maintain the imitations are not as good) and the resources needed are not demanding. The own-label colas sell at much lower prices, so high-volume production resources, capable of producing flavoured carbonated water do not seem to be important in keeping production prices down. So how has Coca-Cola managed to keep its dominant position?

It has been argued above that physical resources do not seem to be important. Therefore, the answer must lie in non-physical resources (such as a very powerful brand) and core competences. The core competences lie in managing the brand by producing memorable global advertising, global recognition, careful sponsorship, responding to customer requirements (diet/light products).

The resource audit

Resources are a vital element of strategic capabilities. An organisation's resource **strengths and weaknesses** can be evaluated using a resource audit. This summarises resources into categories (using words beginning with 'M'), such as:

- money
- management
- manpower
- manufacturing
- markets
- materials
- make-up

Resource	Considerations	How to make good resource deficits
Money	Cash flow, safety margin, gearing, investment plans, dividends.	Issue shares, borrow, sale and leaseback, overdraft, instalment credit, factoring.
Management	Often a key resource issue in small companies, especially family companies, planning to expand. Family members are not guaranteed to have the required skills and entrepreneurs often do not like managing more mature organisations.	Hire good managers, training, take over another organisation to acquire management expertise, sell out to a larger company that can impose good management.
Manpower (i.e. human resources)	Number of employees with the correct skills. Particularly an issue in service industries where employees often have direct contact with customers and therefore the potential of doing instant harm to the organisation's reputation is high.	Recruitment, training, takeover, sub-contracting.

Resource	Considerations	How to make good resource deficits
Recruitment, training, takeover, sub-contracting.	Quality, flexibility, volume, cost. Age of machinery.	New machinery, training, quality initiatives, IT systems, sub-contracting, computer-aided manufacturing, relocation of production facilities to a cheap-labour area.
Markets	Volume, location, product/service requirements.	Market growth, new market development, new product development.
Materials	Price, volume, quality, location.	Locate other suppliers, enter long-term supply contracts, take-over material producer, electronic data interchange for ordering goods.
Make-up: Brand	Recognition, connotations, tainting premium brands with cheaper products.	Advertising, rebranding, new brand names, take-over of a strong brand.
Make-up: IS/IT	IS/IT and the provision of detailed information for sales, manufacturing and customers is becoming vital to many organisations. IS/IT can directly affect an organisation's competences as information is often the tool used to deploy and organise resources effectively.	Write own system, buy-in a package system, sub-contract design and/or running the IS/IT system.

Resource based view of strategy

Many theorists of strategic planning argue that strategy should be about developing and extending competences across markets, rather than focusing on one industry and trying to guess what resources and capabilities will be needed some years hence. Such thoughts have come from the study of companies such as Marriott, that one normally associates with hotels. However, most of the company's profits come from activities that they learned in the hotel business, but have managed to transfer across the organisation – facilities management, hospitality, conference organisation and very many others. The point is that their experience of competing in hotels has helped them develop a range of competences in which they are world-class – known as core competences.

These core competences are complex harmonisations of knowledge, organisational routines and the integration of production, design and marketing skills. This is a wider use of the term than simply the competences one needs to be effective in a particular market. The term 'threshold competence' is reserved for these skills that the firm must have to put a saleable product in front of a customer.

Hamel and Prahalad have argued that thinking of businesses as a portfolio of products and markets, rather than a bundle of competences, is a critical mistake. In their view, strategic management is about identifying, developing and harmonising the core competences across the organisation. They use the term 'strategic architecture' to discuss the way that information and skills are moved around the organisation. Sony and Honda, in particular, have a routine of moving experts away from their expertise into different projects and technologies. Consequently, they have a large number of expert generalists working on projects, and can bring technologies together in unexpected ways and find innovative applications for even relatively straightforward ideas.

Although firms can use all the market research techniques available to any firm, they can also rely rather more on the strategic architecture to bring them into contact with customers and partners. Resource-based firms can then diversify on the basis of superior competences and may shatter the existing patterns of competitive behaviour. For example, Canon entered the photocopier business against Xerox, a company many times its size. However, it had had superior skills in optics from its experience in cameras and had developed technologies that did not infringe Xerox's patents. Marriott moved into many of its new areas by simply noting what went on in its hotels, and thinking about the value added of the various activities.

KAPLAN PUBLISHING

Test your understanding 3

Manchester United Football Club are one of the biggest sporting institutions in the world. Recent research has shown that they have over 600 million fans across the world, they hold a record number of English championships and have been crowned the best team in Europe many times. They are most valued sporting franchise in the world (according to Forbes magazine) at over $3 billion and have shown revenue growth year on year for at least a decade.

Consider the strategic capabilities that contribute to the success of the football club.

Organisational knowledge as a strategic capability

Knowledge is a strategic capability. An organisation's knowledge of its environment (such as expected technological changes, changes in substitute availability etc.) can make it stand out from rivals. It can be more proactive towards its environment and also be in a position to react quicker to environmental changes when necessary.

Johnson, Scholes and Whittington define organisational knowledge as:

> 'the collective experience accumulated through systems, routines and activities of sharing across the organisation.'

Resources (such as staff skills, assets etc.) can be purchased but capabilities must be developed and grown. Organisations therefore need to work on this. It is not automatic and problems that are discovered too late can be difficult to rectify.

Organisational knowledge is cumulative in nature. It will be built up over time from past experience and actions. But it does not simply follow a learning curve effect (otherwise organisations of a similar 'mass' or history would have similar organisational knowledge – which is not often the case). Organisational knowledge can also be added to and improved. Environmental analysis, staff development, process improvement, organisational structure etc. (many of these areas are covered later in the syllabus) can all impact on and improve organisational knowledge.

Organisations must recognise that successful development of organisational knowledge can be a critical success factor. A key part of this can be knowledge management (which is explored in more detail in Chapter 5). Organisational learning is also considered later in the text (in Chapter 15).

4 The life cycle model

Strategic capabilities are likely to have to change over the life of a product.

The product life cycle model suggests that products go through four main phases in their life:

Life stage	Key characteristics	Key strategic capabilities
Introductory	Low sales, high costs	Marketing skills to stimulate demand
Growth	Improved performance, mass production	Resources and production capacity to meet demand
Maturity	Market competitiveness	Competitive skills and the support (and defense) of CSFs
Decline	Falling sales and price wars	The ability to find and exploit new growth opportunities

It is important in exam questions that you recognise the appropriate lifecycle stage and discuss the implications within the context of the scenario.

Further details on each stage

Typical characteristics of these stages are set out in the following table:

Industry features	Introduction	Growth	Maturity	Decline
Competition	Few players	Many new entrants and mergers/ takeovers. Fight for market share.	Shake-out leaves only a few large players	Heavy discounting and price wars
Demand	Usually higher-income buyers	Increasing market penetration	Growth rate falls, most purchases now replacement or repeat buying. Well informed, demanding buyers	Falling demand
Technology	Non-standard	Narrowing in the range of technologies applied	Knowledge is well understood by all players in the market	Becomes obsolete and superseded

Product characteristics	Differences in choice, inconsistent quality	Improvement in the design and quality	Standardisation of products with only small differentiations	Less emphasis on product differentiation
Production processes	Short production runs with specialised distributors	Mass production	Overcapacity begins to develop; long production runs	High incidence of overcapacity
Critical success factors	Innovative product	Products are able to be mass produced	Efficiency in operations to keep costs low	Brand loyalty Low overheads

Illustration 3 – The life cycle model

PCs

Initially, there were relatively few significant producers. The product was innovative, non-standardised, of inconsistent quality and expensive.

Once it looked as though it would be a successful product many producers were attracted into the market. Mass production lowered prices. The range of technologies used narrowed. Intense competition developed as firms fought for dominance and market share.

Maturity means that the product has become a commodity. The industry will be left with just a few large players (Dell, Hewlett Packard, etc.). Efficiency is very important to maintain margins. New entrants will be rare as there is little point in entering an old market.

Decline. Some companies will find that their exit costs are high and will be willing to manufacture so long as marginal revenue exceeds marginal costs. Price wars are likely.

Test your understanding 4

Consider where the following items might be in the product life cycle and comment on the competitive forces they might experience:

(a) mobile phone services

(b) flat screen (LCD/plasma) televisions.

As well as impacting on the strategic capabilities required for success at each stage of the life cycle, there are two further implications from each stage:

(1) Product costs are likely to change in terms of both their nature and their size over the life of a product.

Cost changes during the life cycle

As a product moves through its life cycle it is likely to find that the nature, value and importance of each of it costs will change. Every product will be different, but a typical pattern might be:

	Development	Introduction	Growth	Maturity	Decline
Product development and improvement costs	Extremely high	High	Low	Low	Zero
Marketing costs	Low	Very high	Medium	High	Low
Competition costs	Zero	Very low	Medium	High	Medium
Production cost per unit	Extremely high	High	Medium	Low	Very low
Total costs	Extremely high	Extremely high	Medium	Medium	Low

Every product will be different and there is no hard and fast rule as to what will happen to product costs. So the above table is simply an illustration of what would 'typically' happen to a product's costs over its life cycle.

If we look at 'competition costs' as an example. Competition costs represent elements such as the cost of matching competitor prices or offers, the cost of matching their services, or the cost of competing for resources such as staff and materials that become scarce when competitors enter the market.

In the early stages of product development and introduction these costs should be non-existent (if competition does not yet exist) or low (as competitors enter the market). In the growth phase they will start to rise though not yet to high levels as there should be less need to compete for existing customers as there should be plenty of new customers to attract in order to meet goals. But when the market matures then these costs can be high as customers become more discerning, it is difficult to find replacement customers for any that are lost, and rivals look for new ways to gain a competitive advantage.

In the decline phase these costs might actually ease off. The business might take a deliberate decision to 'harvest' the product and compete less aggressively, or competitors might themselves realise that further costs here creates a 'lose-lose' situation, or price stability arises, or competitors leave the market – there are many justifications for a fall in competition costs at this stage.

(2) The strategy for particular products is likely to change as it enters each stage of the life cycle.

Strategy implications of life cycle analysis

Life-cycle curves can be useful devices for explaining the relationships among sales and profit attributes of separate products, collections of products in a business, and collections of businesses in a conglomerate or holding company. Life-cycle analysis has been suggested by some of its advocates as a basis for selecting appropriate strategy characteristics at all levels. It also may be viewed as a guide for business level strategy implementation since it helps in selection of functional level strategies.

Introduction stage strategy implications

During the early stages of the life cycle, marketing strategy should focus on correcting product problems in design, features, and positioning so as to establish a competitive advantage and develop product awareness through advertising, promotion, and personal sales techniques. At the same time, personnel strategy should focus on planning and recruiting for new product human resource needs and dealing with union requirements. Also, one would expect the nature of research and development (R&D) strategy to shift from a technical research orientation during the phase prior to introduction to more of a development orientation during actual introduction.

Financial strategy would primarily address sources of funds needed to fuel R&D and marketing efforts as well as the capital requirements of later production facilities. Capital budgeting decisions would be outlined during these early stages so that capacity would be adequate to serve growth needs when sales volumes begin to accelerate.

Growth stage strategy implications

During the growth stage, strategic emphases change. Marketing strategy is concerned with quickly carving out a niche for the product or firm and for its distribution capabilities, even when doing so may involve risking overcapacity. Too often, firms have inadvisably accepted quality shortfalls as a necessary cost of rapid growth. Widening profit margins during the growth phase may even permit certain functional inefficiencies and risk taking. Communication strategy is directed toward establishing brand preference through heavy media use, sampling programmes, and promotion programmes, and strategy should emphasise resource acquisition to maintain strength and development of ways to continue growth when it begins to slow.

Personnel strategy may focus on developing loyalty, commitment, and expertise. Training and development programmes and various communication systems are established to build management and employee teams that can deal successfully with the demands of impending tight competition among firms during the maturity phase.

Maturity stage strategy implications

Efficiency and profit generating ability become major concerns as products enter the maturity stage. Competition grows as more firms enter the market and the implication is that only the most productive firms with established niches and competent people will survive. Marketing efforts concentrate on maintaining customer loyalty.

Production strategy concentrates on efficiency and, at the same time, sharpens the ability to meet delivery schedules and minimise defective products. Cost control systems are often put in place.

Personnel strategy may focus on various incentive systems to increase manufacturing efficiency. Advancements and transfers are used and some firms try to fit management positions to managers who have personalities more attuned to the belt-tightening needs associated with the maturity stage.

Decline stage strategy implications

When a product reaches the point where its markets are saturated an effort is often made to modify it so that its life cycle is either started anew or its maturity stage extended. When falling sales of a product cannot be reversed and it enters the decline stage, management's emphasis may switch to milking it dry of all profit. Advertising and promotion expenditures are reduced to a minimum. People are transferred to new positions where their experience can be brought to bear on products in earlier growth stages (if management were skilful enough to have created such products).

Various strategies have been suggested for products that have entered the decline stage. **Hofer** and **Schendel** suggest four choices when sales are less than 5% of those of the industry leaders:

- concentration on a small market segment and reduction of the firm's asset base to the minimum levels needed for survival

- acquisition of several similar firms so as to raise sales to 15% of the leaders' sales

- selling out to a buyer with sufficient cash resources and the willingness to use them to effect a turnaround liquidation

- liquidation.

5 Quantitative analysis

It is very likely in the exam that the examiner will provide tables and data in order to provide some of the information that is needed in order to properly perform the strategic analysis (both external and internal). It will be vital that students can both interpret and use this information in their answers.

This information might be provided using various methods and some of the key methods will be:

Tables of data

In order to reduce the amount of text in a scenario the examiner will often provide tables of data to provide part of the story. It will be important that a student can understand what the table is trying to explain, and that this part of the story is used in the answer to this part of the examination.

Test your understanding 5

The following data is given for sales of cinema tickets in a large country over the last two years.

Company	20X7 Sales ($bn)	20X8 Sales ($bn)
A	2.0	2.0
B	1.8	2.0
C	2.2	2.1
D	2.1	1.9
Others	1.6	1.7
Total industry sales	9.7	9.7

> Explain what the table tells us and how it might be used in a Five Forces analysis of the industry's competitive environment.

Financial statements

The examiner might provide sets of financial statements and a student must use this to pull out the key messages and issues. There will be some important technique points to this:

- choose three or four key ratios

- there is no need to illustrate the formula or the calculation

- only one comparator should be needed

- focus on the cause of any changes and what this might tell us about the organisation's position

Explanation of the financial statement analysis technique

- choose three or four key ratios

The aim is to try to pick some ratios that best tell the organisations "story". Key ratios might be its sales growth (which can be linked to the PESTEL), its margins (which can be linked to the 5 forces model), and its gearing (which will give an idea of the organisations risk profile and its ability to raise finance for future opportunities).

Ratio analysis has already been examined at the fundamentals level and we are not trying to show how well we can calculate ten or twelve different ratios. A ratio should not be included if it adds nothing to the story (for example, there is little point in calculating receivable days if it has not changed during the year and the business does not have a problem with debt collection).

- there is no need to illustrate the formula or the calculation

This has been examined at the fundamentals level and would only waste time at this level. There is also no need to explain what the ratio means (for example, comments such as "The gross profit percentage shows how much profit the business makes per $ of turnover" are unlikely to gain any marks).

- only one comparator should be needed

The examiner will often provide four or five years worth of financial statements. However, in order to get to the key messages for the company's story we do not need to calculate the ratios for every year. Normally we simply need to compare this year's results with last year's, or perhaps the this year's results to the first year's results.

- focus on the cause of any changes and what this might tell us about the organisation's position

The key to gaining any marks will be to analyse the data that has been calculated (simply performing the calculation and not discussing it will not achieve all of the marks that are available). So we need to explain why a ratio has changed (for example, is it due to changes in the external or internal environment) and what these changes mean for the business (for example, does it need to react to these changes or can the position be improved in the future).

Ratio analysis

Ratios

The mechanics of ratio analysis are repeated here for revision purposes.

Profitability ratios

• ROCE =	Operating Profit (PBIT)/Capital Employed	× 100
• Gross margin =	Gross profit/Sales	× 100
• Net margin =	Net profit/Sales	× 100
• ROE =	Profit after tax and preference dividends/Shareholders' funds	× 100

Efficiency ratios

- Asset turnover =   Sales/Capital Employed
- ROCE =   Net margin × asset turnover
- Receivables days =   Receivables balance/Credit sales   × 365
- Payables days =   Payable balance/Credit purchases   × 365
- Inventory days =   Inventory/Cost of sales   × 365
- Revenue per employee =   Sales/Number of employees

Liquidity ratios

- Current Ratio =   Current Assets/Current Liabilities
- Quick Ratio (acid test) =   Current Assets – inventory/Current liabilities

Gearing ratios

- Financial Gearing =   Debt/Equity
- Financial Gearing =   Debt/Debt + Equity

Investor ratios

Dividend Cover =   PAT/Total Dividend

Interest Cover =   PBIT/Interest

EPS =   Profit after tax and preference dividends/Number of shares   × 100

PE ratio =   Share price/EPS

Inter-firm comparisons

Inter-firm Comparisons (IFCs) – as previously noted, it is possible (through use of financial ratios) to compare and contrast the performance of one entity within an industry with that of another within the same industry. It is also possible to compare and contrast the performance of one firm with that of the whole industry, or a large sample or particular segment of that industry. However, these comparisons may suffer from one or more of the following limitations.

- Different accounting methods may be used by individual firms making up the industry sample, or by the firm being compared.

KAPLAN PUBLISHING

- The industry figures may be biased by one or a few very large firms within the sample.

- Conversely, an industry mean may be misleading for a small or large firm being compared with the mean. Ratios may vary for different sizes of firms.

- The companies within the industry sample may span across more than one industry classification.

- The industry figures may be relevant for a different financial period, and could possibly be out-of-date.

Key Performance Indicators (KPIs)

Other KPIs may also be presented in the scenario (such as customer return rates, % of repeat business, market share, age of products etc.).

It will be important to react to this data in the same way that we react to data that is presented in tables or financial statements – that is, to interpret what they are trying to tell us, and to link these in to the analysis of the organisation's position.

6 SWOT analysis

Strengths, weaknesses, opportunities and threats

A SWOT analysis can be used as an analysis tool in its own right or can be used as a summary sheet on which other results can be placed.

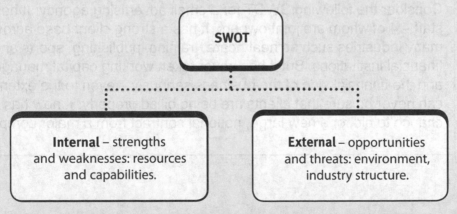

- Strengths and weaknesses relate to resources and capabilities: what is the organisation good at? What is it poor at? Where are resources in short supply? Where are resources excellent?

- Opportunities and threats relate to external factors: what will the effect on the organisation be of economic changes? Can the organisation make use of new technologies? Are new entrants likely to enter the market place? Can a powerful customer dictate terms?

The examination will feature scenarios detailing the history and current position of an organisation and possible future states. Candidates will probably have to analyse the organisation's strategic position, i.e. to carry out a corporate appraisal. It is possible to arrive at a reasonable analysis merely by producing a SWOT analysis, but it is likely to be more productive and impressive to use one or more of the other analysis tools, such as PESTEL, to help generate ideas for the SWOT analysis.

Using a SWOT analysis

The first step is to rank in order of importance the findings of the SWOT analysis.

- Strengths that match no opportunity are of little use without an opportunity.

- A distinctive competence is a strength that can be exploited.

Strategies can be developed which:

- neutralise weaknesses or convert them into strengths

- convert threats into opportunities

- match strengths with opportunities.

These are discussed in later chapters.

Illustration 4 – SWOT analysis

Consider the following SWOT for a small advertising agency: It has 12 staff – 4 of whom are joint owners. It has a strong client base across many industries such as healthcare, training, publishing, sports and financial institutions. But it has never taken working capital management and the financial side of the business seriously – even to the extent that it can never be sure that clients are being billed properly. It now has a chance to bid for a new large, national contract from a major company.

KAPLAN PUBLISHING

It's overall SWOT looks as follows:

Strengths	Weaknesses
• well diversified client portfolio • strong management team • profitable • listed on a stock exchange • low gearing • award winners • differentiated, personal service • established 60 years ago	• high work-in-progress levels • high levels of receivables • poor control of time allocation to clients • limited access to debt finance • reached overdraft limit • lacks ability to service very large clients • 40% of turnover from two clients • Recent complaint about tone of an advert
Opportunities	**Threats**
• tender for a major contract • expand overseas • launch an internet marketing advisory service • buy a rival • move into film production	• recession putting downward pressure on volume and prices • loss of bank support • loss of a major client • customers moving to e-marketing • loss of key staff • takeover by a rival

In an exam scenario, generating the SWOT should be relatively straightforward and all the necessary information would be provided in the scenario. This stage is unlikely to score many marks and is probably best considered as part of the planning phase of your answer.

Your task as a student is to then **analyse** this SWOT. This means we need to explain the importance of issues, prioritise them, spot linkages between them and consider implications for the business.

All of the issues generated by the SWOT are good, relevant points that can be explored in an exam answer. However, in an exam scenario you are unlikely to have enough time to discuss all of these. Therefore, we need to choose a selection of issues under each heading and focus on analysing these. The choice of issues to analyse is not greatly important, but you should try to focus on the more important ones.

From a time management point of view, it is important that you set yourself a deadline for these questions based on the marks available. It is very unlikely that you will not be able to analyse every point in the SWOT in the time available to you.

Let's consider an analysis of the key strengths from the above SWOT:

Analysis of key strengths

A key strength of the company is that it has a wide portfolio of clients. The company will therefore not be reliant on one industry group for its revenue. This is likely to mean that if one industry type cuts back on advertising or moves to another form of marketing, the company will be able to continue to rely on other industries for income.

The company has won marketing awards. This is likely to attract potential customers to the company. It may also mean that existing customers remain loyal and resist switching to the company's rivals.

As a listed business the company may be able to raise external equity finance on the market. This may allow it to fund new strategies and partake in the opportunities that have been identified.

Note:

Note how the points in the SWOT are not just regurgitated in the analysis. Instead, a further sentence or two is added to explain the relevance to the company, the importance of the issue, the implications for the future, links to other areas of the SWOT, etc. This is how we achieve the analysis marks in business analysis.

Test your understanding 6

Continuing on from the SWOT in the illustration just considered, analyse the weaknesses, opportunities and threats to the company.

(8 marks)

7 Chapter summary

This chapter has covered the following areas:

- defined and described strategic capability, threshold resources, threshold competences, unique resources and core competences

- explained why cost efficiency is important in all organisations

- described the capabilities needed to sustain competitive advantage

- explained, for a range of organisations, the importance of innovation in supporting business strategy

- explained the importance of knowledge management for both profit-seeking and not-for-profit organisations

- described the use of SWOT analysis.

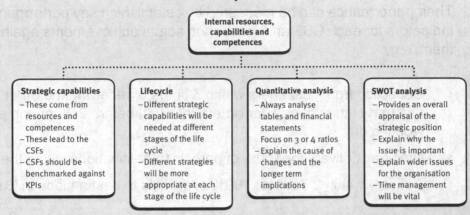

Test your understanding answers

Test your understanding 1

The two main critical success factors would probably be:

- speedy collection from customers after their request for a parcel to be delivered
- rapid and reliable delivery.

Test your understanding 2

Their performance can be measured by establishing key performance indicators for each CSF and measuring actual achievements against them, e.g.:

- Collection from customers within 3 hours of receiving the order, in any part of the country, for orders received before 2.30 pm on a working day.
- Next-day delivery for 100% of parcels to destinations within the UK.
- Delivery within 2 days for 100% of parcels to destinations in Europe.

Test your understanding 3

All football clubs will need to certain types of resources such as:

- players
- a stadium
- a manager
- a fan base
- finances.

They will also need certain competences such as:

- tactical knowledge
- training methods
- youth development
- ability to attract sponsors.

For Manchester United to be successful they must therefore develop these in ways which are unique, valued by customers and difficult to copy. Some of the ways that Manchester United have achieved this are:

Resources

Manchester United have a bigger fan base than any other sporting franchise in the world. This allows them to garner more merchandising revenue than any other franchise and also to attract better deals from sponsors.

Manchester United have the biggest stadium in England (and one of the biggest in Europe). This allows them to maximise match day revenue and be one of the leaders from this source of income in Europe.

Competences

Manchester United are the leader in acquiring and interacting with fans on social networks – they have over 65 million fans on Facebook alone. This skill allows them to keep fans informed of new product offerings as well as sell events and broaden the club's brand image.

Manchester United were one of the first clubs in the world to obtain sponsorship for their training equipment. In 2011, DHL paid the club around $60 million for the right to have their logo emblazoned on the kit. The ability to attract such sponsorships is one of the things that makes the club stand out.

Manchester United seem to have a unique ability amongst the elite teams in England in developing youth players for the first team. For example, when Manchester United were crowned champions of Europe in 2008, 5 members of their cup final squad had come through the club's ranks as youngsters. By contrast, opponents Chelsea, another English club, didn't have any players in their cup final squad that had come through the club's youth ranks. This allows the Manchester United to keep a local tradition, garner fan loyalty and reduce team development costs.

There are many other strategic capabilities at Manchester United but these examples should highlight some of the reasons why an organisation can be successful. It is not simply about having resources and competences that are necessary for existence in the industry, it is about developing and acquiring ones which can lead to competitive advantage. As can be seen in Manchester United's example, no one resource or capability might be the unique strategic capability of the club. But when they are put together, success becomes much more likely.

Test your understanding 4

(a) **Mobile phone services**

Probably a mature market. The industry went through a very rapid growth stage in many countries; most consumers who want a mobile now have one. There has been consolidation in the industry which, because of the infrastructure needed, lends itself to supporting a few large suppliers. It is relatively unlikely that new entrants will appear as they will have to fight for a share of a saturated market.

Consumers are well informed about call plans and about what competitors offer. Because a telephone number can be retained there are very low switching costs and consumers are happy to change suppliers.

No sign of decline.

(b) **Flat screen (LCD/plasma) televisions**

Internationally, this is still in the growth stage. There is a long way still to go before most conventional TVs are replaced. Prices had been very high initially, but have come down significantly as competition intensifies and manufacturing runs become longer. New entrants would remain a threat as there would still be significant market share to win. New technologies such as OLED still seem to be a few years away. Prices will continue to fall and manufacturing efficiency will become increasingly important.

Test your understanding 5

The table shows two things:

- the market overall is not growing

- no one company dominates the market.

As part of a 5 forces analysis the table is likely to indicate that this is a competitive market when we analyse competitive forces. No company has significantly better economies of scale in order to achieve cost leadership and marketing budgets and techniques are likely to be very similar which will make differentiation strategies harder. The companies will know that, in order to grow, there is unlikely to be new sales coming into the market and therefore they will have to tempt customers away from rivals – which will increase the competitive activities in the industry.

The table might also provide information on the difficulty that new entrants into the market might have in overcoming the position of the four established providers.

Test your understanding 6

Analysis of key weaknesses

Having high levels of work-in-progress and receivables will tie up a lot of cash. This will limit the company's ability to finance new opportunities.

This issue is made more important by the fact that the company is nearing its overdraft limit. Not only will this limit the company's ability to take on new work and expand the business, but it might even put the company's entire existence at risk.

The company is also reliant on only two clients for 40% of its revenue. If one of these clients were to leave the company then, again, going concern could become an issue. It will be important that the business can expand its client base in order to reduce the reliance on these clients.

Analysis of key opportunities

There is an opportunity to tender for a major new client. This would reduce the reliance on existing powerful clients. However, it is likely to put further short-term pressure on work-in-progress and the overdraft and the company also needs to consider whether it has the resources and skills to meet the needs of a large client.

The company could start to offer e-marketing services to clients. This would allow them to 'follow the customer' and meet their needs. It would need an investment in acquiring the skills and resources to provide this service, however.

A move into film production would be a move towards backward integration. It might give the company control over a key cost and a key resource. But it is likely that this might restrict the company's ability to move into other areas and customers may no longer desire filmed adverts as a source of marketing.

Analysis of weaknesses

In a recession customers are likely to cut back on discretionary expenditure such as marketing. They may also move 'downmarket' to lower cost rivals and move away from differentiated services on the basis of price.

Loss of key staff would be a major threat as staff are likely to be a key asset for the business. It will be important to tie-in staff through loyalty bonuses and strong reward schemes, as well as putting in protection clauses to contracts to stop them taking clients with them when they leave.

If customers move to e-marketing avenues and the company does not follow them it is likely to experience a steady decline in revenue. It will be important to make this switch in line with its environment and offer this service to customers.

Overall

The company is in a position where it needs to adapt to its changing environment. Its first priority needs to be to sort out its financial position and obtain the finance to secure its viability and to finance new opportunities. It then needs to consider offering e-marketing services to clients.

Note:

It is acceptable to analyse these points in other ways and to write a very different answer. The examiner will be as concerned with your style and approach as he is with your content. They key to success will be to ensure that you are not simply regurgitating points.

Stakeholders, governance and ethics

Chapter learning objectives

Upon completion of this chapter you will be able to:

- explain the importance for an organisation of communicating core values and mission

- evaluate, in a scenario, stakeholder influence using stakeholder mapping

- analyse the implications of corporate governance for a given organisation with respect to its purpose and strategy

- analyse the ethical influences on an organisation with respect to its purpose and strategy

- explain the cases for and against businesses pursuing Corporate Social Responsibility (CSR)

- explain how integrated reporting might play a role in better communicating corporate mission, values and strategies.

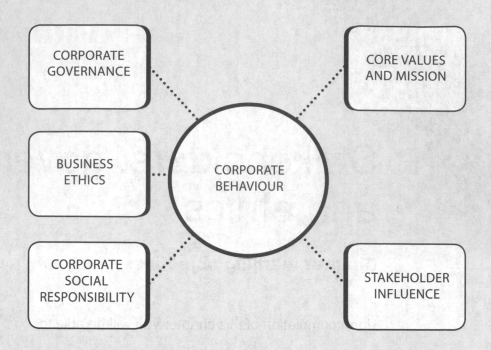

1 Introduction

This chapter looks at how organisations determine their objectives and policies. This will play a vital role in the chapters that follow when we consider choosing between different strategies that are available to an organisation. Objectives will be set by considering an organisation's mission statement, its stakeholders, corporate governance and its attitudes towards ethics. A fundamental theme in this chapter is whether an organisation's purpose should be set solely by its key stakeholders (which might, in a profit seeking business, be its shareholders, for example), or whether its purpose should include wider aspects and the viewpoints of other stakeholders.

2 Core values and mission

Introduction

Mission statements exist in order to establish the primary reason for an organisation's existence and to define core values. This should be the overriding objective from which all other objectives are set. A mission statement should consider all stakeholders of an organisation and aim to satisfy their needs.

Johnson, Scholes and Whittington refer to an organisation's mission as 'the most generalised type of objective (that) can be thought of as an expression of its raison d'être'.

Core values are the principles that guide an organisation's behaviour.

The mission indicates to both the world at large and to those making the strategic decisions, the broad ground rules that the organisation will adhere to when conducting its business.

Contents of a mission statement

A mission statement should contain the following:

- purpose
- strategy
- policies and Standards of Behaviour
- values.

Also:

- mission statements should be short – typically half a page
- note that mission statements can have a valuable role in setting ethical standards and organisational culture.

Further explanation of contents

Purpose

Why is the company in business? What is the organisation for?

Some organisations and companies do not attempt to reach a conclusion about the nature of their overall purpose. However, where companies do have an idea of their purpose, research by Campbell, Devine and Young shows that the companies fall into the following types.

- Companies that just exist for the benefit of the shareholders. Their main purpose is to maximise shareholder wealth and all decisions are assessed against a benchmark of shareholder value.

- Companies that believe that the satisfaction of shareholders is not the only reason for existence and believe it to be important to satisfy all stakeholders. In their mission they address how they are to satisfy the needs of customers, the community, the employees as well as the shareholders.

Strategy

This component of the mission statement then addresses how it is going to achieve its purpose. This could involve a statement of industrial domain (where to compete) and the nature of competitive advantage sought.

Policies and standards of behaviour

Without policy and behaviour guidelines that help staff to make decisions on a day-to-day basis the strategy and purpose has little value.

Values

Values are the feelings and moral principle that lie behind the company's culture.

Advantages and disadvantages of mission statements

The claimed advantages:

- help resolve stakeholder conflict
- set the direction of the organisation and so help formulate strategy
- help communicate values and culture to employees
- help the marketing process by communicating with customers.

The criticisms of mission statements:

- often full of meaningless terms like 'the best', which give staff little idea of what to aim at
- often written retrospectively to justify past actions
- often ignored by managers
- might simply be a public relations exercise.

KAPLAN PUBLISHING

Illustration 1 – Core values and mission

Below is the philosophy or mission of Nissan Motors (UK) (NMUK).

As a company we aim to build profitably the highest quality car sold in Europe. We want to achieve the maximum possible customer satisfaction and ensure the prosperity of the company and its staff.

To assist in this we aim to achieve mutual trust and co-operation between all people within the company and make NMUK a place where long-term job satisfaction can be achieved. We recognise that people are our most valued resource and in line with this spirit believe that the following principles will be of value to all.

People

We will develop and expand the contribution of all staff by strongly emphasising training and the expansion of everyone's capabilities.

We seek to delegate and involve each staff member in discussion and decision-making, particularly in those areas in which each of us can contribute effectively so that all may participate in the efficient running of NMUK.

Teamworking

We recognise that all staff have a valuable contribution to make as individuals but in addition believe that this contribution can be most effective within a teamworking environment.

Our aim is to build a company with which people can identify and to which we all feel commitment.

Communication

Within the bounds of commercial confidentiality we will encourage open channels of communication. We would like everyone to know what is happening in our company, how we are performing and what we plan.

We want information and views to flow freely upward, downward and across our company.

Objectives

We will agree clear and achievable objectives and provide meaningful feedback on performance.

Flexibility

We will not be restricted by the existing way of doing things. We will continuously seek improvements in all our actions.

These are tough targets and we aim high. With hard work and goodwill we can get there.

Test your understanding 1

Consider the usefulness, or otherwise, of the following mission statements:

(1) Courses for careers, research for results. (A university)

(2) To be a pioneer in graphite communications. (A manufacturer of lead pencils)

(3) To be excellent in our chosen field, and provide the best in customer service and quality that resources permit.

(4) Kill Caterpillar. (Komatsu)

3 Stakeholders

Introduction

A stakeholder of an organisation is anyone affected by the organisation.

In the chapters that follow we will explore the strategic choices that are available to an organisation in order to improve its position. In order to be able to choose between the various options that are open to organisations it will be important that an organisation has clear objectives. The objectives will help prioritise some strategies and eliminate others.

Illustration of stakeholders and their objectives

Illustration – Stakeholders

For example, a large company may have the following stakeholders.

Stakeholders		Objectives
Internal stakeholders	• Managers • Employees	Career development, pay, security, enjoyable jobs
External stakeholders	• Government • Pressure groups	Compliance with the law, tax revenue Protecting the environment
Connected stakeholders	• Shareholders • Customers • Suppliers • Financiers	Profit, growth in share price, dividend payments Low prices, quality High prices, assured demand Interest payments, security

Examples of conflicts are:

- shareholders want higher profits, employees want better working conditions

- customers want 24/7 service, employees want 9 – 5 jobs, 5 days a week

- customers want higher quality and lower prices, shareholders want higher profits

- suppliers want prompt payment, lenders want overdraft limits adhered to.

The objectives of an organisation will be governed by its key stakeholders. These key stakeholders be determined using stakeholder mapping.

Stakeholder mapping

Stakeholder mapping can help deal with stakeholders' conflicting demands. It identifies stakeholder expectations and power and helps in establishing political priorities. The process involves making decisions on the following two issues.

- How **interested** the stakeholder is to impress their expectations on the organisation's choice of strategies, i.e. how likely is the stakeholder to exercise power?
- To what extent the stakeholder has **power** to impose its wants?

Mendelow proposed a matrix to help analyse stakeholders.

		Level of interest	
		Low	**High**
Power	**Low**	A	B
	High	C	D

Understanding the matrix

The matrix is normally completed with regard to the stakeholder impact of a particular strategy.

The purpose is to assess:

- whether stakeholder resistance is likely to inhibit the success of the strategy
- what policies may ease the acceptance of the strategy?

The following strategies might be applicable to each quadrant:

Box A – Minimum effort

Their lack of interest and power makes them open to influence. They are more likely than others to accept what they are told and follow instructions.

Box B – Keep informed

These stakeholders are interested in the strategy but lack the power to do anything. Management needs to convince opponents to the strategy that the plans are justified; otherwise they will try to gain power by joining with parties in boxes C and D.

Box C – Keep satisfied

The key here is to keep these stakeholders satisfied to avoid them gaining interest and moving to box D. This could involve reassuring them of the outcomes of the strategy well in advance.

Box D – Key players/participation

These stakeholders are the major drivers of change and could stop management plans if not satisfied. Management, therefore, needs to communicate plans to them and then discuss implementation issues.

How to determine interest and power

How interested are they?

The 'level of interest' can usefully be described as how likely it is that a stakeholder will take some sort of action to exercise his or her power.

Not all stakeholders have the time or inclination to follow management's decisions closely. Again some generalisations are possible about what will lead to interest, e.g.:

- high personal financial or career investment in what the business does

- absence of alternative (e.g. alternative job, customer, supplier or employer)

- potential to be called to account for failing to monitor (e.g. local councils or government bodies such as regulators)

- high social impact of firm (e.g. well known, visible product association with particular issues).

Power

Resignation, withdrawing labour, cancelling orders, refusing to sell, calling in an overdraft, dismissing directors, legal action, granting contracts, setting remuneration.

Note that legislation tends to move power away from shareholders to other stakeholders.

- Employee protection legislation (dismissal, redundancy, health and safety) moves power to employees and away from management and shareholders.

- Environmental protection legislation moves power to the local community and other interested parties.

- Consumer legislation moves power to customers.

Test your understanding 2

Where should the following probably be mapped on the Mendelow matrix?

(1) Nurses in a hospital

(2) An airline's check-in staff

(3) Small-value customers

4 Governance and ethics

Corporate governance

Introduction

Corporate governance is about the way in which organisations are run and who should control them – the chairman, the chief executive, and the board of directors, shareholders or other stakeholders such as employees.

The need for corporate governance

The need for corporate governance arises because in all but the smallest organisations there is a separation between:

- ownership, and

- management control.

The principal-agent model is useful in explaining how the system should work: agents should work on behalf of their principals.

However.

- The gap between ultimate beneficiaries and those making day-to-day decisions can be large and agents might not know what the beneficiaries want.

- Self-interest can cause agents to work for their own benefit at the expense of their principals (remuneration packages, share options, budget padding, short-termism to make current results look good at the expense of long-term performance).

Principles of good corporate governance

Laws and principles have been developed to enhance corporate governance. These include:

- company law – for example, giving shareholders the right to dismiss directors and auditors

- the audit function – an independent review of the accounts

- accounting standards – increased and more uniform disclosure

- various codes on corporate governance. For example, all companies quoted on the London Stock Exchange are expected to comply with the Combined Code of Corporate Governance (though not forced to). If a company does not comply it must explain why.

Typical features of codes, such as the Combined Code include:

- boards should have non-executive directors – to advise and warn the executive directors. Executive and non-executive directors (NEDs) should be in balance so that neither group dominates

- there should be a separation of the roles of chairman and chief executive

- executive remuneration should be decided by a remuneration committee, consisting of non-executive directors

- an audit committee, comprising non-executive directors should look after the appointment and supervision of auditors.

Political aims of corporate governance

The broad aims of corporate governance at a political level include the following:

- Creating a framework for the control of large, powerful companies whose interests may not coincide with the national interest.

- Controlling multinationals, which can dominate the local economy.

- Ensuring that companies are answerable to all stakeholders, not just to shareholders.

- Ensuring that companies are run according to the laws and standards of the country and are not in effect states within states.

- Protecting investors who buy shares in the same way as investors are protected who buy any other financial investment product, such as insurance or a pension.

Principles of good corporate governance

Countries with high standards of corporate governance practices are more likely to attract international capital.

The OECD (Organisation of Economic Co-operation and Development) has carried out work among member countries, and identified some common elements, which underlie good corporate governance. The OECD Principles of Corporate Governance cover five sections.

- The rights of shareholders – the corporate governance framework should protect and facilitate the exercise of shareholders' rights. By raising capital from shareholders, companies commit themselves to earning an investment return on that capital. The board of that company must, therefore, be accountable to shareholders for the use of their money.

- The equitable treatment of shareholders – the corporate governance framework should ensure the equitable treatment of all shareholders, including minority and foreign shareholders. All shareholders should have the opportunity to obtain effective redress for violation of their rights.

- The role of stakeholders – the corporate governance framework should recognise the rights of stakeholders as established by law and encourage active co-operation between corporations and stakeholders in creating wealth, jobs and the sustainability of financially sound enterprises.

- Disclosure and transparency – the corporate governance framework should ensure that timely and accurate disclosure is made on all material matters regarding the corporation, including the financial situation, performance, ownership and governance of the company.

- The responsibility of the board – the corporate governance framework should ensure the strategic guidance of the company, the effective monitoring of management by the board, and the board's accountability to the company and the shareholders.

Non-executive directors

NEDs play an important role in corporate governance. These directors have no managerial responsibility, but they are full board members and therefore have access to and can influence the highest level of corporate decision making. Their functions include.

- Bringing additional experience and knowledge to the board.

- Warning executive directors about high-risk areas, ethical problems or inappropriate behaviour.

- Providing confidence to other parties as NEDs can provide independent, high-level supervision. For example, NEDs are not allowed to have share options in a company so their remuneration is independent of company performance.

- Determining executive remuneration (as mentioned earlier).

- Appointing and liaising with auditors.

- Providing confidential advice to both the board and individual directors.

The implications of governance for strategy

The results of the increasing focus on governance issues are as follows:

- Increasing power of governance bodies.

- Increasing shareholder power, ensuring that companies are run with shareholders' interests prioritised.

- Greater pressure on boards to formulate strategy and be seen to control the businesses concerned.

- Greater scrutiny of quoted businesses, resulting in more short-termism.

- Greater emphasis on risk assessments, so directors may feel pressured to undertake lower risk (and hence lower return) projects.

- Greater scrutiny of mergers and acquisitions in particular.

Ethical stances

Ethics is not just a matter of being righteous: if an organisation has a reputation for making unethical decisions it will be perceived as being a high-risk organisation that it might be better not to deal with, whether as an employee, lender, investor, supplier or partner.

Ethical stances

Johnson, Scholes and Whittington define ethical stance as:

'The extent to which an organisation will exceed its minimum obligations to stakeholders.'

There are four possible ethical stances:

Short-term shareholder interest	Longer-term shareholder interest	Multiple stakeholder obligation	Shaper of society

In effect, acting ethically means expanding the idea of stakeholder mapping so that, rather than simply focusing on key stakeholders, an organisation expands its viewpoint to consider the impact on other stakeholders.

Short-term shareholder interest (STSI)

This ethical stance has a short-term focus in that it aims to maximise profits in the financial year. Organisations with this ethical stance believe that it is the role of governments to set the legal minimum standard, and anything delivered above this would be to the detriment of their shareholders.

Longer-term shareholder interest (LTSI)

This ethical stance takes broadly the same approach as the short-term shareholder interest except that it takes a longer-term view. Hence it may be appropriate to incur additional cost now so as to achieve higher returns in the future. An example could be a public service donating some funds to a charity in the belief that it will save the taxpayer the costs associated with providing the entire service should the charity cease to work. Hence this ethical stance is aware of other stakeholders and their impact on long-term profit or cost.

Multiple stakeholder obligation (MSO)

This ethical stance accepts that the organisation exists for more than simply making a profit, or providing services at a minimal cost to taxpayers. It takes the view that all organisations have a role to play in society and so they must take account of all the stakeholders' interests. Hence they explicitly involve other stakeholders, and believe that they have a purpose beyond the financial.

Shaper of society

This ethical stance is ideologically driven and sees its vision as being the focus for all its actions. Financial and other stakeholders' interests are secondary to the overriding purpose of the organisation.

Corporate Social Responsibility (CSR)

Corporate responsibility is concerned with the ways in which an organisation **exceeds** the minimum obligations to stakeholders specified through regulation and corporate governance.

Although there might be differences of opinion about what is and is not ethical, few people would argue that business ethics, for example honesty, are voluntary. However, the case for corporate social responsibility is not so clear cut, and there are a number of different views relating to social responsibility.

The different views

The shareholder view

Friedman argues that, 'the social responsibility of business is to make a profit'. The justifications for this are:

- pursuing profit will result in increased employment, generate economic growth, stimulate innovation, increase the tax take and generally raise living standards. Making profits is therefore itself a public good and is a sufficient purpose of business

- directors should be acting on behalf of the shareholders. CSR too often means that directors are being charitable with other people's money

- shareholders are free to use their dividends to contribute towards CSR if they wish

- business is not competent to decide moral and ethical matters. Where is the democratic connection between what a business decides to spend money and effort on and where that money and effort are actually needed or wanted by society? Are CSR projects chosen simply because they are areas where directors, or their spouses, are personally interested?

The longer-term self-interest view

Drucker argues that it is in the long-term economic self-interest of business to act in a reasonably responsible manner.

- Failure to do so will prompt legislation.

- Failure to do so will damage the business and even the industry.

- The public relations and enhancement of reputation arising from CSR will increase profits in the long term. CSR is therefore seen and justified as expenditure that helps to generate long term profits.

The stakeholder view

This view assumes that shareholders are simply one stakeholder among many, and that their interests are not necessarily paramount. There may be circumstances where shareholder interest has to be sacrificed for the greater good of other stakeholders.

Quite how it is decided which stakeholders deserve generosity at any particular time is not clear. There is a danger that the stakeholders that benefit are those with most power – which is not necessarily the same as the stakeholders who might deserve attention.

Common areas for CSR issues

The following are common areas where businesses get involved in CSR issues:

- work creation and training programmes

- sponsorship of the arts and sport

- employee welfare programmes

- community welfare programmes.

- support for educational institutions and links with business

- contributions to overseas aid

- environmental programmes.

Benefits of an organisation being ethical

Apart from an ethical organisation being, perhaps, 'morally correct', there are more quantifiable business benefits:

- lower risk that, for example, should create more stable earnings and should make cheaper finance available
- attractive to customers
- attractive to potential employees
- attractive to potential collaborators and partners
- less time and cost spent dealing with investigations by regulatory bodies
- less spent on paying damages and fines.

On the other hand, acting ethically can bring the following problems:

- as a differentiating strategy it is easily copied by rivals
- it typically adds costs to activities
- success often relies on trial and error
- international businesses may have to adopt different ethical approaches in different markets which may give a lack of global consistency.

5 Integrated reporting

Typically in the past an organisation has communicated its purpose, core values and vision via its mission statement. However, integrated reporting offers a further, regular approach to communicating values and vision.

Integrated reporting recognises that an organisation is now evaluated not only from financial perspective (in terms of its ability to generate a profit), but that a wider spectrum of stakeholders need to be considered for organisational reports. These stakeholders are increasing concerned about areas such as governance and the organisation's impact on society as a whole.

Integrated reporting defined

The International Integrated Reporting Council (IIRC) defines integrated reporting <IR> as:

> <IR> is a process founded on integrated thinking that results in a periodic integrated report by an organization about value creation over time and related communications regarding aspects of value creation.

> An integrated report is a concise communication about how an organization's strategy, governance, performance and prospects, in the context of its external environment, lead to the creation of value in the short, medium and long term.

More precisely:

> An integrated report tells the overall story of the organization. It is a report to stakeholders on the strategy, performance, and activities of the organization in a manner that allows stakeholders to assess the ability of the organization to create and sustain value over the short, medium, and long term. An effective integrated report reflects an appreciation that the organization's ability to create and sustain value is based on financial, social, economic, and environmental systems and by the quality of its relationships with its stakeholders. The integrated report should be written in clear and understandable language in order for it to be a useful resource for stakeholders. Integrated Reporting demonstrates the linkages between an organisation's strategy, governance and financial performance and the social, environmental and economic context within which it operates.

Integrated reporting therefore aims to marry up this information by providing a much more comprehensive view of performance than that provided by traditional financial reports.

Contents of an integrated report

The IIRC suggest that an integrated report should have the following elements:

(1) An organisational overview, business model, and governance structure – this should explain how decisions are made and how the business aims to create value for stakeholders. This will be an opportunity for organisations to highlight their vision and long term strategic goals and mission.

(2) The operating context – this should explain the circumstances in which the organisation operates. It will effectively be an environmental analysis of the organisation's current strategic position.

(3) Strategic objectives, competencies, key performance indicators (KPIs) and key risk indicators (KRIs) – this will explain how the organisation aims to create value for stakeholders and the competencies needed to achieve this. It will also set out how progress towards these objectives will be objectively measured and monitored.

(4) An account of the organisation's performance – an evaluation of performance against the KPIs and KRIs as well as whether objectives have been achieved, competencies have been protected and improved etc. This will demonstrate links between financial performance and wider social, environmental and economic performance.

(5) consideration of future performance objectives – these will be new (potentially adjusted) objectives for future periods which react to changes in the environment, move existing performance forward and move the organisation closer to achieving its longer term strategic goals. It will also highlight areas of possible future concerns to stakeholders.

(6) Remuneration policies – the organisation's approach towards remuneration

(7) An analytical commentary – the leadership's views on how the organisation is performing and where it is with respect to achieving its mission

The report provides an opportunity for re-emphasising mission and values as well as providing an insight into progress made towards strategic goals. Thus the integrated report provides an opportunity for the organisation to communicate or reinforce its strategy to its stakeholders, including any changes made to that strategy.

The relationship to critical success factors and key performance indicators

The integrated report also provides a vehicle for illustrating progress through relevant measures of strategic performance. Failure to meet set targets can be commented upon and remedial actions, if appropriate, can be outlined. Central to this will be a discussion of the CSFs and the KPIs which have been identified to measure business performance. KPIs will have associated performance objectives which can be reported in the integrated report.

Thus, the report not only restates the KPI and its associated performance objective, it also reports on whether that performance objective has been met and, if it has not, discusses reasons for failure and the actions which are being taken to ensure that this objective is met in the next reporting period.

6 Chapter summary

```
                    ┌─────────────────────┐
                    │    Stakeholders,    │
                    │ governance and ethics│
                    └─────────────────────┘
```

The mission statement	Stakeholders	Governance and ethics	Integrated reporting
– Should be all inclusive – Should set out the vision – Should help guide strategy – But is often used as a simple PR exercise	– Can be mapped using Mendelow's matrix – Considers power and interest – This can help determine how each group should be managed	– The implications are more important	– Brings mission, strategy and performance together into one report – Recognises the needs of a wider group of stakeholders

Test your understanding answers

Test your understanding 1

(1) This is the mission statement of a British University. It identifies that the range of courses offered will be restricted to those that lead to an obvious career path, and research will be developed in partnership with those who have a commercial interest in discovery, rather than simply a sense of curiosity. As you might expect, this is a University with great ambition but relative few resources, which therefore focuses its activity into areas where it may compete effectively against its more august rivals. Note that the mission statement here implicitly describes both the customers it seeks and the services it wishes to offer.

(2) This is the mission statement of a manufacturer of lead pencils. The important point is that it suggests innovation in a field more usually noted for cost-based competition. Part of the company's business is providing jokey, amusing slogans on its pencils, and the mission statement was chosen to reflect this. Note that this mission is directed at the customers; any message for employees is rather too subtle to operate effectively.

(3) It has been argued that any mission statement containing the word 'excellent' should not be taken seriously – who wouldn't want to be 'excellent', even at providing cheap goods. Excellence subject to resource constraints also appears rather qualified. However, this particular firm embarked on a rapacious programme of takeovers in a field where this was comparatively unknown. The resource base expanded, but very little of these extra resources found their way into product quality and customer service, leading to great cynicism from staff.

(4) The final statement is a translation of the mission of Komatsu, who set their sight on taking Caterpillar's domination of the tracked vehicle market. They picked out the weaker points of their rival's operation, its softest markets and poorest products, and spent two decades building up the competences and driving them out.

Test your understanding 2

(1) Theoretically, nurses have a lot of power. If they withdrew labour, a hospital would soon have to stop admitting and treating patients. However, the ethical, professional and humanitarian standards of nurses means that industrial action is extremely rare.

(2) Airline staff have, in the past been very willing to take industrial action, which quickly cripples the airline.

(3) If a small-value customer feels aggrieved, he or she can usually easily take their business to another supplier. However, this is likely to have little effect on the supplier. Only if many small customers banded together would they achieve power.

KAPLAN PUBLISHING

5

Strategies for competitive advantage

Chapter learning objectives

Upon completion of this chapter you will be able to:

- apply the value chain in a scenario

- describe the meaning of value networks in a commercial setting

- explain, in a scenario, through the strategic clock, the generic strategy options of: cost leadership, differentiation, focus

- explain the competitive advantages that might develop from cost efficiency

- explain, for a range of organisations, the importance of innovation in supporting business strategy

- explain the importance of knowledge management for both profit-seeking and not-for-profit organisations

- discuss how big data can be used to inform and implement business strategy

- explain strategies (such as lock-in) for sustaining competitive advantage

- describe the three different types of benchmarking (historical, industry/sector, best-in-class).

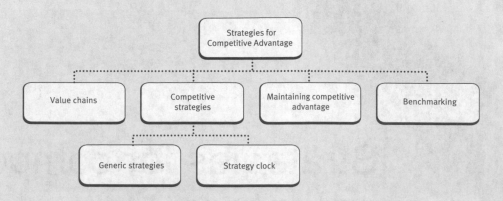

1 Value chain analysis

The best way to assess whether an organisation has achieved a competitive advantage is by examining its value chain.

The value chain

Porter developed the value chain to help identify which activities within the firm were contributing to a competitive advantage and which were not.

The approach involves breaking down the firm into five 'primary' and four 'support' activities, and then looking at each to see if they give a cost advantage or quality advantage.

Porter's value chain

Support or secondary value activities:
- Firm infrastructure
- Human resource management
- Technology development
- Procurement

Primary value activities:

Inbound logistics	Operations	Outbound logistics	Marketing and sales	Service

Explanation of the value chain activities

Primary activities:

- Inbound logistics – receiving, storing and handling raw material inputs. For example, a just-in-time stock system could give a cost advantage.

- Operations – transformation of the raw materials into finished goods and services. For example, using skilled craftsmen could give a quality advantage.

- Outbound logistics – storing, distributing and delivering finished goods to customers. For example, outsourcing delivering could give a cost advantage.

- Marketing and sales – for example, sponsorship of a sports celebrity could enhance the image of the product.

- Service – all activities that occur after the point of sale, such as installation, training and repair, e.g. Marks & Spencer's friendly approach to returns gives it a perceived quality advantage.

Secondary activities:

- Firm infrastructure – how the firm is organised. For example, centralised buying could result in cost savings due to bulk discounts.

- Technology development – how the firm uses technology. For example, the latest computer-controlled machinery gives greater flexibility to tailor products to individual customer specifications.

- Human resources development – how people contribute to competitive advantage. For example, employing expert buyers could enable a supermarket to purchase better wines than competitors.

- Procurement – purchasing, but not just limited to materials. For example, buying a building out of town could give a cost advantage over high street competitors.

All organisations in a particular industry will have a similar value chain, which will include activities such as:

- obtaining raw materials

- designing products

- building manufacturing facilities

- developing co-operative agreements

- providing customer service.

It is vital that the linkages between the different elements of a value chain are considered. Firstly this is to ensure consistency – for example, a differentiator will want to ensure that any cost advantages within the value chain do not compromise overall quality. Secondly it may be that through linking separate activities more effectively than competitors, a firm can gain a competitive advantage.

Apply the value chain in a scenario

To gain a competitive advantage over its rivals a company must either:

- perform value creation functions at a lower cost than its rivals or
- perform them in a way that leads to differentiation and a premium price.

Illustration 1 – Linking the value chain to competitive advantage

The value chain is a way of explaining and examining how and why an organisation has a competitive advantage. The value chain will differ depending on how the organisation chooses to compete.

For example, a manufacturing organisation that aims to beat rivals on price will need to keep its costs low. Therefore, in its primary activities it might have operations that have little flexibility and are geared towards bulk production. It is also likely to minimise the level of after-sales service provided. In support activities it might use low skilled labour, high levels of technology and have bulk procurement agreements with suppliers.

An organisation in the same industry which is looking to compete at the top end of the market might have operations that are more focused on producing a higher quality product with more variety and offer a more extensive service with, say, free installations and money back guarantees. In support activities it might use higher skilled labour and a wider range of quality suppliers. Note: as will be seen later in this chapter, these types of organisations are usually referred to as differentiators.

The competitive advantage will permeate all elements of the value chain:

Nature of competitive strategy:	Low cost, low selling price	High end (differentiator)
Primary activities		
Inbound logistics	Standardised components and materials with little customisation	Premium materials Selective sourcing
Operations	Bulk production Focus on efficiency High levels of standardisation	Flexible production Focus on quality Facilitation of customisation
Outbound logistics	Few outlets used Bulk delivery and careful management of delivery loads Minimal packaging	Use of premium distributors and retailers Flexible (possibly free) delivery Premium packaging
Marketing and sales	Minimal levels of marketing Sales focus is on quantity Standardised	High levels of promotion Lots of market research High levels of customer management and personalisation
Service	Very little	Extensive

Support activities		
HRM	Use low skilled staff	Use higher skilled staff
	Reduced training and staff development	Encourage staff development
		See staff as a key resource
TD	Use e-procurement to reduce costs of procurement	Less use of technology in operations
	High use of technology to improve efficiencies and cut costs	Greater use of technology in marketing in sales to facilitate high promotion levels
		High R&D
		Regular process redesign
Procurement	Seek out cheapest and most efficient supplies	Seek premium suppliers
	Use outsourcing when it reduces costs	
Infrastructure	Functional structure	Flexible structures
	Many centralised services	Small span of authority
	A more global approach	Tall structures
	Produce in cheapest locations	National independence

Note: These are simply examples to illustrate how companies with different competitive strategies will have different value chains. It does not mean that all low cost manufacturers or differentiators will have the characteristics illustrated above.

 In an exam situation you might use Porter's value chain analysis to decide how individual activities might be changed to reduce costs of operation or to improve the value of the organisation's offerings.

Test your understanding 1

Nicole has inherited a restaurant from her uncle. The restaurant had been underperforming and was closed six months ago. Nicole wants to begin a new restaurant in the premises, with a new name and a new cuisine.

She has performed some market research in the area and determined that there is a demand for a restaurant offering Mediterranean cuisine. There is little local competition for such cuisine but there are many other local restaurants offering a wide range of cuisines.

Nicole has decided to follow a differentiation strategy for her restaurant and to charge premium prices.

Requirement:

Consider how the activities in a value chain for the proposed restaurant could be used to create such a competitive position.

Value chain analysis

Value chain analysis looks at each of the processes that make up the chain of activity and:

- rates how important it is in a given company's production or service activity
- rates how the company compares to its competitors
- helps to decide how individual activities might be changed to reduce costs of operation
- helps to improve the value of the organisation's offerings.

Value networks

The organisation's value chain does not exist in isolation. There will be direct links between the inbound logistics of the firm and the outbound logistics of its suppliers, for example. An understanding of the value system and how the organisation's value chain fits in to it will therefore aid in the strategic planning process.

Illustration of value chain analysis

A value network is a web of relationships that generates economic value and other benefits through complex dynamic exchanges between two or more individuals, groups or organisations.

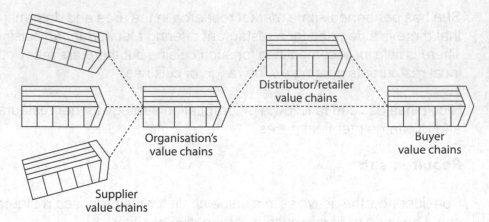

- Tangible value exchanges – involve all exchanges of goods, services or revenue, including all transactions involving contracts and invoices, return receipt of orders, request for proposals, confirmations or payment.

- Intangible knowledge exchanges – include strategic information, planning knowledge, process knowledge, technical know-how, collaborative design, policy development, etc.

Illustration

Amazon, for example, not only revolutionised the business model for selling books, but also formed an entire new value network of suppliers and buyers that redefined the value chain for acquiring books and music. Replacing the retail bookstore with a website and the 'over the counter' delivery process with FedEx and UPS delivery created a new value network that delivered customer convenience and an entirely different and lower-cost business model.

2 Competitive strategy options

Generic strategies: cost leadership, differentiation and focus

Professor Michael Porter identified three generic strategies through which an organisation could achieve competitive advantage.

	Cost Leadership	Differentiation	Focus
Aim	To cut costs of production/ purchasing/ service and in turn cut selling prices	To offer a product that can't be matched by rivals and charge a premium for this "difference"	Position the business in one particular niche in the market
How (examples)	<ul><li>economies of scale</li><li>use of learning effects</li><li>large production runs</li><li>using cheaper labour and materials</li><li>moving to cheaper premises</li></ul>	<ul><li>branding</li><li>quality & design</li><li>innovation</li><li>knowledge management</li><li>control over suppliers</li><li>support</li></ul>	1 find a segment where the cost leader or differentiators have little or no presence and build business here 2 reduction in product range

	Cost Leadership	Differentiation	Focus
Benefits	• high volumes • creates a barrier to entry • can operate in unattractive segments • win price wars • reduced power of substitutes	• builds brand loyalty and repeat purchases • higher margins • reduction in power of customers	• develops brand loyalty • little competition • often a first step towards the other generic strategies
Threats	• no fallback position if leadership is lost • larger (possibly from overseas) rivals may enter the market • strong currency makes imports cheaper	• perform badly in a recession • often easily copied in the long run • need to constantly innovate • needs much higher marketing than cost leadership • fewer barriers to entry • smaller volumes	• low volumes • if successful, it attracts cost leaders and differentiators • few barriers to entry
Suitability	Large organisations with economies of scale	Innovative companies with large marketing budgets	Small business with entrepreneurial flair, strong market knowledge and a risk taking attitude (often new starts)

A business that fails to achieve one of these generic positions will be **stuck in the middle** – it will lose some customers who will move downmarket to the cost leader, other customers who will move upmarket to differentiators, and others will move to rivals who focus on their specialist needs.

Porter's generic strategies

Cost leadership

Set out to be the lowest cost producer in an industry. By producing at the lowest possible cost the manufacturer can compete on price with every other producer in the industry and earn the highest unit profits.

How does one become a cost leader?

- Decide whom you are competing against (e.g. Tesco, M&S or Harrods food hall)?
- Perform value analysis to determine why customers value the product – what are key features that have to be matched and which product attributes could be dropped or reduced?
- Understand your own costs and cost drivers.
- Try to make a product of comparable quality for a lower cost – this may involve a full analysis of the value chain.

Advantages

- Better margins through lower costs.
- Ability to undercut competitors on price, thus reducing competitive rivalry.
- Low costs act as a barrier to entry deterring new entrants.
- Low prices make substitutes less attractive.
- Better margins give more scope to absorb pressure from powerful buyers/suppliers.
- Low costs give a platform for expansion – both gaining market share and moving into new markets.

Drawbacks of such a strategy

- In industries that only require a low critical mass of production output to achieve economies of scale, cost leadership would be difficult to achieve, because many other firms would be able to match the costs. It is only when the critical mass of production is high that a cost leadership strategy is likely to be effective.

Other drawbacks

- Only room for one cost leader – no fallback position if the cost advantage is eroded.

- Cost advantage may be lost because of inflation, movements in exchange rates, competitors using more modern manufacturing technology or cheap overseas labour, etc.

- Customers may prefer to pay extra for a better product.

Differentiation

Here the firm creates a product that is perceived to be unique in the market.

Consider the following case.

Suppose you wanted to develop a better coffee percolator. To decide what makes it 'better' you need to ask why people need a percolator rather than making instant coffee; the answer is taste.

The key issue is therefore to discover how the design of a percolator affects the taste.

(1) The most important issue is the water quality. A 'better' percolator thus needs to remove chlorine in the water and ensure it is at the correct temperature when meeting the coffee.

(2) Another key factor is the time between grinding the beans and pouring on the water. A 'better' percolator should thus grind the beans and control when the water is applied.

Ways of achieving differentiation

Quality differentiation

This has to do with the features of the product that make it better – not fundamentally different but just better.

Design differentiation

Differentiate on the basis of design and offer the customer something that is truly different as it breaks away from the dominant design if there is one.

Image differentiation

Marketing is used to feign differentiation where it otherwise does not exist, i.e. an image is created for the product. This can also include cosmetic differences to a product that do not enhance its performance in any serious way (e.g. packaging).

Support differentiation

More substantial but still has no effect on the product itself, is to differentiate on the basis of something that goes alongside the product, some basis of support, such as after-sales service.

Rewards of a differentiation strategy:

- better margins through being able to charge higher prices
- higher quality offsets competitive rivalry
- product uniqueness reduces customer power
- quality acts as a barrier to entry
- quality reduces the attractiveness of substitutes.

Risks of such a strategy:

- cheap copies
- being out-differentiated
- customers unwilling to pay the extra (e.g. in a recession)
- differentiating factors no longer valued by customers (e.g. due to changes in fashion).

Focus

Position oneself to uniquely serve one particular niche in the market. A focus strategy is based on fragmenting the market and focusing on particular market segments. The firm will not market its products industry-wide but will concentrate on a particular type of buyer or geographical area.

Cost focus

This involves selecting a particular niche in the market and focusing on providing products for that niche. By concentrating on a limited range of products or a small geographical area the costs can be kept low.

Differentiation focus

Select a particular niche and concentrate on competing in that niche on the basis of differentiation.

Reward

You become an expert in your field and understand the marketplace more.

Risks

The segment is not sustainable enough to provide the firm with a profitable basis for its operations.

Test your understanding 2

What types of generic strategies are the following companies adopting?

(1) Walmart

(2) Saga Holidays (specialises in holidays for those over 55)

(3) Bang and Olufson

The strategy clock

An alternative way of identifying strategies that might lead to competitive advantage is to look at 'market facing' generic strategies.

- This approach is based on the assumption that competitive advantage is achieved if a firm supplies what customers want better or more effectively than its competitors.

- Better could mean a more suitable product or service, or could mean a cheaper one of adequate quality.

- In effect, customers are looking for what they perceive as best 'value for money'.

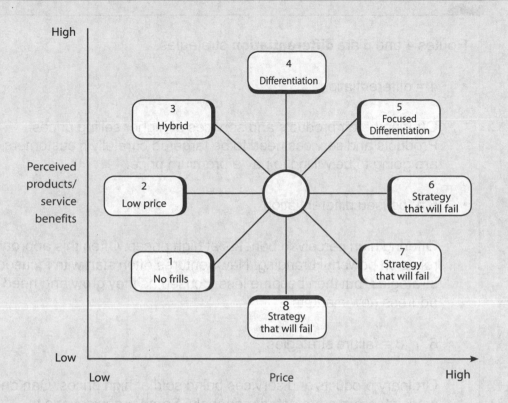

Explanation of the strategy clock strategies

(Adapted from the work of C. **Bowman** and D. Faulkner 'Competitive and Corporate Strategy – Irwin – 1996)

Routes 1 and 2 are **price-based** strategies.

- 1 = no frills

  Commodity-like products and services. Very price-sensitive customers. Simple products and services where innovation is quickly imitated – price is a key competitive weapon. Costs are kept low because the product/service is very basic.

- 2 = low price

  Aim for a low price without sacrificing perceived quality or benefits. In the long-run, the low price strategy must be supported by a low cost base.

- 3 = hybrid strategy

  Achieves differentiation, but also keeps prices down. This implies high volumes or some other way in which costs can be kept low despite the inherent costs of differentiation.

Routes 4 and 5 are **differentiation** strategies.

- 4 = differentiation

  Offering better products and services at higher selling prices. Products and services need to be targeted carefully if customers are going to be willing to pay a premium price.

- 5 = focused differentiation

  Offering high perceived benefits at high prices. Often this approach relies on powerful branding. New ventures often start with focused strategies, but then become less focused as they grow and need to address new markets.

- 6, 7, 8 = failure strategies

  Ordinary products and services being sold at high prices. Can only work if there is a protected monopoly. Some organisations try option 8 by sneakily reducing benefits while maintaining prices.

Note that an organisation can have identified several strategic business units (SBUs).

A SBU is a part of an organisation for which there is a distinct external market. Different strategies can be adopted for different SBUs. For example, Toyota and Lexus (part of Toyota) operate as separate SBUs with different strategies. Some fashion businesses successfully separate their exclusive ranges of clothing from their diffusion lines.

Illustration on the strategic clock

Illustration – Competitive strategy options – strategic clock

No frills

RyanAir (a very successful, no-frills airline). Ferocious attention to keeping costs down: non-reclining seats (break, extra weight); no back-of-seat pockets (extra cleaning); discouraging checked-baggage (airport charges for loading/unloading baggage); use of cheap airports.

Low price

Dell computers. Good quality computers at low prices. Relies on very efficient production techniques to keep costs low to preserve a reasonable margin.

Hybrid

IKEA. Cheap furnishings, but smart design and large range of inventories. Costs are kept low by self-service, efficient production, high volumes and excellent logistics.

Differentiation

Full service airlines such as British Airways. Prices are usually higher, but there is in-flight service, more leg-room and customers are better looked after if there are scheduling problems.

Focused differentiation

Business/first class on full service airlines. Another example would be couture fashion – small markets, high prices, sustained by brand names.

Failing strategy

Consider the Apple iPad. This is typically sold at a premium price as a differentiated product – it has excellent features, market leading software and strong branding. Apple is effectively placing the product in position 4 of the strategy clock. There may also be companies who position themselves in, say, position two (low cost) on the clock by selling refurbished iPads. These have not got the quality of a new iPad but they are available at a lower price. Now consider a company who decides to place itself in position 8 on the clock. It does this by attempting to sell refurbished iPads at the same price as new iPads. This strategy should fail – it can either be beaten on price by those rivals in position two who offer the same product at a lower price, or it will be beaten by Apple (in position 4) who offer a better product at the same price.

Test your understanding 3

Where on the strategy clock should the following companies or products be placed?

(1) MacDonalds

(2) Apple's i-Pad

3 Further examples of competitive strategies

Cost Efficiency

Managing costs needs both resources and competences. For example, modern, flexible machinery can cut production time and costs; having the competence to organise an efficient just-in-time inventory system will save inventory costs.

Illustration on cost efficiency (Dell)

Dell Computers is widely admired for its inventory and production system that has enabled the company to become one of the most successful and resilient computer manufacturers in the world. It sells good quality computers at very competitive prices. There is great emphasis on cost efficiency.

Broadly, their system is as follows.

(1) Orders are received by phone and over the web. The orders are consolidated every 15 minutes and orders for the parts needed are automatically transmitted to suppliers.

(2) The suppliers supply the components within an hour and a half. Suppliers all have to have their own plants close to Dell's so that supplies can be made quickly. (Note that if orders are consolidated every quarter of an hour, there will be four deliveries per hour.)

(3) The suppliers' lorries wait at the Dell factory. When an assembly line runs low of components, a forklift takes a pallet from the appropriate lorry. Only when the forklift crosses a specific white line in the factory does Dell take ownership of the goods. That's where the brief life on inventory starts.

(4) The ordered goods are assembled, tested and dispatched. The only inventory is the work-in-progress, the units being tested and the units being shipped.

(5) Every member of staff is involved in at least one Business Process Improvement project, which are all aimed at squeezing out costs. Typically, parts snap into position rather than needing screws, thus shaving 20 seconds or so from assembly time.

(6) The time between receiving an order and dispatch is between four and eight hours.

(7) Dell's manufacturing in the USA is no more expensive than manufacturing in a low labour-cost country.

KAPLAN PUBLISHING

Note that IBM decided it could not make sufficient profits making laptops and sold its business to Lenovo, a company based in China. The Dell TMC plant in Texas and its sister plant in Nashville are the only major computer manufacturing plants still left in the USA. HP, Gateway and Apple all manufacture outside the USA where costs are lower.

Illustration on cost efficiency (General Motors)

General Motors and Ford Motor Company are both having difficulties making profits in the USA. Toyota is very profitable there. Of course, there are two sides to the profit equation (revenue and costs) but it's worth looking just at one element of the General Motors' cost side to see the difficulties facing it.

General Motors is long established in the US and has many retirees who were promised generous pensions and healthcare provision. Toyota is a much more recent company in the US and has relatively few retirees. For 2004, General Motors' healthcare and pension costs amounted to around $2,200 per vehicle produced. Toyota's comparable costs were around $300 per vehicle produced. That's a large cost gap to cover with increased selling prices. In fact, GM's prices are lower than Toyota's.

Test your understanding 4

Consider how the following technologies could improve cost efficiency:

(1) the internet

(2) computer-aided design

(3) sub-contracting

(4) takeovers.

Differentiation through innovation

Innovation is increasingly seen as important for strategic success. The reasons are:

* increased rate of technical advances

* increased competition

* increased customer expectations.

In all functions that serve to produce goods and services, achieving superior innovativeness, relative to that of competitors, can help the firm to acquire new customers. Superior innovation gives a company something unique, something that its competitors lack until they are able to imitate the innovation. By the time competitors succeed in imitating the innovator, the innovating company has already built up such brand loyalty that its imitating competitors will find it difficult to attack their position.

Innovation can apply to:

- the nature of the product or service being supplied
- how the product or service is produced and delivered
- operating the firm in a new or novel way.

Research and development

Research and development (R&D) can be defined as 'the organisation of innovation at the level of the firm'. R&D aims to satisfy a market need by developing new products and by improved methods of production. It must also find applications for scientific and technical developments. However, an R&D (innovation) strategy cannot sensibly be pursued in isolation from the rest of the organisation. The business strategy will concentrate on the broad range of products that the organisation wishes to have and the broad markets in which it wishes to compete. This strategy will be supported by the organisation's competence strategy, focused on the technologies the organisation needs if it is to pursue its business strategy successfully.

The R&D function should have a major innovative role in all organisations. The pressures to introduce new ways of doing things may be 'demand pulled', that is the innovation filling a market need, or it may be 'technology pushed', the innovation coming from the application of discoveries. In many organisations, there is a group of people, not necessarily called R&D, whose responsibilities include the creation of new business ideas and techniques.

An innovation strategy calls for a management policy of giving encouragement to innovative ideas. This has a number of aspects.

- Financial backing must be given to innovation, by spending on R&D and market research and risking capital on new ideas.

- Employees must be given the opportunity to work in an environment where the exchange of ideas for innovation can take place. Appropriate management style and organisation structure are needed.

- Management can actively encourage employees and customers to put forward new ideas. Participation by subordinates in development decisions might encourage them to become more involved with development projects and committed to their success.

- Development teams can be set up and an organisation built up on project teamwork.

- Where appropriate, recruitment policy should be directed towards appointing employees with the necessary skills for doing innovative work. Employees should be trained and kept up to date.

- Certain managers should be made responsible for obtaining information about innovative ideas from the environment, and for communicating it throughout the organisation.

The importance of innovation in strategy is one of the most hotly disputed questions in the subject. In many cases, the most innovative companies in an industry consistently fail to be among the most profitable. This creates a divergence of opinion over the role of innovation-based strategy.

A company that chooses not to be innovative is still influenced by the effect of innovation. It is innovation that frequently undermines the basis of competition in existing markets, and creates new markets that may supersede old ones. Firms must learn to innovate with greater commercial effectiveness than is the case at present, or learn to replicate innovations more quickly than they would choose to. The rate of innovation is often too quick for a balanced assessment of it to be carried out in a sensible time period.

Richard Lynch identifies three distinctive roles for innovation within a business level strategy:

- achieving new growth through entry into new products and markets

- retaining competitive advantage by strengthening the product offering

- achieving competitive advantage through jumping ahead of existing rivals.

The indications are that organisations with high market share develop strategies of higher price and/or higher quality than low-share competition. These organisations tend to be more profitable, thus providing the cash to invest in R&D to improve and differentiate products, enhancing their market position and also justifying higher prices.

Acquiring new technologies

New technologies often emerge in one of two ways. Technology-push is based upon an understanding of the technology, but a less well-developed idea of market pull has important applications. A technology push-based innovator always has difficulty in finding product/market applications for the discoveries he or she makes. Consequently, a firm using technology push may frequently develop strategies by emergent processes to exploit the latest discoveries. The danger is that the new innovation might be ahead of complementary applications, and the advantage lost by the time other technologies catch up. It is possible to see this in the information technology business where hardware runs in excess of the specifications for existing software, and sellers find it increasingly difficult to justify margins at the high performance end of the market. On the other hand, breakthrough technologies are almost invariably of the technology push kind.

New ideas frequently emerge through market-pull. In this case, new technologies are developed based upon a good understanding of customer requirements, or close collaboration with a customer. In such cases, finding a market for a new product is less problematic, but may still be fraught with difficulty.

Naturally, these two approaches are not mutually exclusive, and frequently support each other. For example, an attempt to store films on a compact disc was an example of market-led innovation, but the technology was more effectively applied to data storage for computers after the failure of the original product. It is far better to think of these as the two complementary drivers to innovative activity.

Exploitation of existing technologies

An organisation that develops an advantage in a particular technology should consider a strategy of market development. That is, that the knowledge and competences can be applied to new markets. An illustration of switching from entertainment to data storage based upon knowledge of a particular technology is one such example. Where the company has a diversified product range, discoveries in one area can be readily applied to another.

Innovation and existing products

In certain stages of the product life cycle, innovation may be a threshold competence. For example, in mobile telephones and software it is vitally important to maintain product features at least as good as those of competing products. Technology-driven strategies tend to be more effective than market ones because many users will be unaware of the possibilities of the technology or the uses to which it might be put. Innovation plus good sales skills are threshold competences.

Overall

A successful company is one that:

- is outward-looking, has accepted the reality of constant change and reviews its product-market policy continuously

- is always looking to the future towards new markets, innovative products, better designs, new processes, improved quality, increased productivity

- has a structure designed for innovation in which management and staff are stimulated to think and act innovatively, which recognises potential 'intrapreneurs' and ensures that everyone (particularly senior people) welcome changes for the better

- stimulates creativity, and rewards ideas and supports individual and team abilities.

Illustration 2 – The importance of innovation

Amazon first appeared on the internet in 1995 selling books. It was a major innovator in the business of internet retailing and soon CDs and DVDs were added to its product lists. The website allowed customers to search a very extensive database and to order goods, which would normally be delivered by post in a few days. The website also allowed customers to write reviews about products, and informs customers about how consumers of a particular product also bought other products. Consumer goods such as electronics are now available from Amazon.

Although Amazon is pre-eminent in internet-based sales of books, CDs and DVDs, innovation cannot stop and the company is spending heavily on technology that will allow customers to download books, music and video over the internet rather than having them delivered by post. The company is being forced to innovate because competitors, such as Apple's iTunes, have been very successful in selling audio downloads, and have recently made movies available for downloading.

On-demand printing of books is particularly suitable for lower-volume books and those that would normally be regarded as out of print.

The development of the Kindle and Kindle fire were therefore essential to Amazon. Without these Amazon it risked losing business to those who could offer an innovative alternative method of delivery for its products – rather like a decade ago when Amazon itself attacked conventional book and music shops.

Test your understanding 5

Consider the importance of innovation in the following businesses and suggest areas that might benefit from innovation:

(1) a car manufacturer

(2) a supermarket

(3) a commercial television company.

Differentiation through knowledge management

Knowledge management involves the processes of:

- uncovering, or discovering, knowledge
- capturing knowledge
- sharing knowledge
- distributing knowledge
- levering knowledge
- maintaining knowledge.

What is knowledge?

Before the importance of knowledge management is discussed, an attempt has to be made to define 'knowledge'. This can only be done by comparing knowledge with data and information.

- Data is raw fact. For example, a list in ascending order of all outstanding invoices is data.

- Information is data that has meaning. For example, a list of all outstanding invoices sorted by customer and with subtotals calculated for each customer. Now the data has meaning and has become useful.

- Knowledge is information in someone's mind. A printout of the sales ledger contains information, but if it is never read by someone, it will never become knowledge and remains useless until it is read.

Knowledge is of two types.

- Explicit knowledge. This is generally written down and organisations know that it exists.

- Tacit knowledge. Not written, often existing only in employees' minds. Organisations are unlikely to know that it exists, or the extent to which it exists.

Illustration

Members of a sales team will have information available about the sales made to key customers and the sales trends of the company's major products. This information and knowledge is explicit as it exists in reports that are widely distributed.

A sales representative may have personal knowledge about the character, interests and background of the buyers in major customers. This helps the sales person get on with the buyers and this should help to generate sales. If the sales representative keeps this knowledge to himself, or herself, this would be an example of tacit knowledge and the organisation will not usually be aware of it. Indeed, the sales representative might not be actively aware about the importance of this knowledge and about how it is used in the sales process.

Another sales representative has read an article in a scientific journal that implies that one of the company's major products may have long-term health implications for customers. However, that knowledge remains tacit unless passed on to others and formalised.

The growing importance of knowledge management

Knowledge management has become an important part of gaining and maintaining competitive advantage. Reasons for this are as follows.

- Both business and not-for-profit organisations are more complex so there is more knowledge to manage. For example, there are many more government regulations that have to be followed for health and safety. The government sets many more targets to monitor the performance of hospitals and schools.

- The environment, technology, competitors and markets are changing rapidly. Look at the pace of change in the broadcast/internet industry.

- The move from manufacturing to service industries means that a greater proportion of an organisation's knowledge is likely to be tacit. It is relatively easy to formally specify a product, but harder to specify everything that should happen in the successful delivery of a service.

- Greater job mobility means that, unless captured and recorded, valuable knowledge can be lost as staff move on.

Test your understanding 6

A barrier to knowledge management is that many people believe that keeping knowledge secret gives them unique power. Knowledge management, however, requires that knowledge is uncovered and shared.

What arguments could be used to encourage individuals freely to give up and share knowledge?

Using Big Data to inform and implement business strategy

The ability of organisations to extract valuable information from Big Data is becoming a strategic capability. Like any capability, it requires investments in technologies, processes and governance.

Laney suggested that Big Data has the following characteristics, known as the 3V's:

- Volume – there is lots of it

- Velocity – it is generated very quickly

- Variety – it can take many varied forms

What is Big Data?

Traditionally, organisations collected data that was mainly of a transactional nature. They stored data in a database that recorded details such as customer and supplier transaction history, identifying information and they may occasionally have asked customers the question 'How did you hear about us?' This data was used primarily to keep track of operations or forecast needs.

But more recently, both the sources and volume of data collected have exploded. Much of the information will be non-transactional such as collecting data from social networks (who likes your Facebook page? who follows you on Twitter? who else do they follow on Twitter? what videos do they like on YouTube?), examining reviews that people leave about your products (on either your own site or on someone else's site), exploring internet forums to discover what people are discussing and what they want to see, examining where people are, what they are doing, where they are checking in, what they are buying elsewhere etc. Most of this data is out there. These sources of data have created modern-day treasure troves that can be mined to glean insights into products, services and customers. While this is conceptually possible, it requires the implementation of new processes, technology and governance mechanisms that are collectively being referred to as Big Data.

Characterisics of Big Data

The 3V's are commonly used to describe Big Data:

Volume

Big Data is characterised by its sheer volume. IBM believe that we create over 2.5 quintillion bytes of data every day. If the average PC can hold 100 gigabytes of data on its hard drive, there is enough Big Data created every day to completely fill 25 million PCs. Per day. For example, there are over 5 billion Facebook status likes per day. Facebook has to store this data on servers, and businesses would like to use and interpret these links to find patterns.

So there is already a large volume of Big Data out there and it's only going to get bigger. The University of London's (UCL) Big Data Institute believes that Big Data will double in size every two years. On top of that, UCL believes that currently less than 0.5% of the data that exists is ever analysed.

But this volume of Big Data causes problems for businesses. In order to perform meaningful analysis of this volume of data organisations will require new skill sets, large investments and a deliberate focus on Big Data. It is also likely that organisations will have to collaborate and share databases on Big Data. For example, the World Health Organisation has used mobile phone data held by service providers in Kenya to match human travel patterns to the spread of malaria (which it holds on its own database).

Velocity

The problem is worsened by the speed at which Big Data is created. The UK magazine, Baseline, reports that there are over 570 new websites created every minute. It also reports the commonly held belief that 90% of the world's data that is in existence has been created in the last two years.

Big Data is created quickly and moves around quickly. There are 300 hours of new content uploaded and shared to YouTube every minute, for example. For businesses wishing to exploit Big Data, they will have to obtain the information quickly, analyse it quickly and exploit it quickly. If, for example, there is a road crash or traffic build up on a particular major road, providers of satellite navigation systems for roads will want to get that information as quickly as possible (by, for example, measuring the average road speed for vehicles on a particular road), assess whether the cause is a temporary one, and then suggest an alternative route for road users. The more quickly that this can be done then the better the navigation system, and users of the system will be much more satisfied with its use.

Software systems will play a great role in dealing with the volume and velocity of Big Data. New systems such as in-memory analytics mean that the analysis can happen in real time without the need to even store the data onto disks on computer servers.

Variety

Big Data is also characterised by its variety. Consider the data that might exist and be stored about yourself, for example. You might have banking transactions, you might be following particular organisations on Twitter, you may have recorded your interests on LinkedIn, you might have a store card or loyalty card that has recorded your past transactions, you might have saved photographs in the cloud, you might have given a thumbs up to a music video on YouTube etc. The types and sources of Big Data are many fold.

These types are often subdivided into two categories:

- Structured data

  Structured data resides in a fixed field within a record or file (such as a database or spreadsheet). Your banking transactions, your contact list or your past store purchases are therefore likely to be stored as structured data. This type of data is easier to access and analyse, as long as the model is well designed (for example, past store purchases on a store card may be less useful if the file does not record quantity, timing and value).

- Unstructured data

  The vast majority of Big Data is unstructured. It does not have set fields or sizes and includes data such as your personal interests, your photographs and videos, your likes and dislikes etc. Organisations need to find ways to make the most use of this type of data. For example, an organisation might attempt to monitor and react to user actions so that if, say, you upload lots of holiday photographs then you could be presented with holiday promotions on your next visit to a website. Or an organisation might ask employees to record their skills and interests in a central database in order to best use these to exploit opportunities in future projects.

Big data is unlocking the ability of businesses to understand and act on what are typically their biggest environmental impacts – the ones outside their control. Organisations that previously had limited information on consumers now have many opportunities to collect and leverage data.

Using Big Data strategically

There are many ways that Big Data can be used strategically, based on common data analysis techniques.

Predictive modelling can predict user behaviour based on their previous business transactions and preferences. This can facilitate new product or new market development.

Cluster analysis can be used to segment customers into groups based on similar attributes. Once these groups are discovered, managers can perform targeted actions such as customising marketing messages and cross-selling to each unique group. Another popular use case is to predict what group of users may "drop out." Armed with this information, managers can proactively devise strategies to retain this user segment and lower the churn rate.

Social analytics often involves metrics such as the number of video views and the number of followers or community members. This can allow content to be updated, removed or promoted depending on changes in these metrics.

Engagement measures the level of activity and interaction among platform members, such as the frequency of user-generated content. For example, Foursquare have begun to provide 'rewards' (such as a free coffee) to those users who check in and have the greatest number of connections (number of Twitter followers, for example). This can spread brand awareness and possibly cut marketing costs so that they are better aimed at the most influential users.

Reach measures the extent to which content is disseminated to other users across social platforms. Reach can be measured with variables such as the number of retweets on Twitter and shared likes on Facebook. Products or marketing campaigns with a poor reach can be changed or removed from the business portfolio.

Decision scientists explore Big Data as a way to conduct "field research" and to test hypotheses. Big Data is therefore used prior to strategy implementation and will influence strategic choice.

There is now a general consensus that data is a most valuable asset that, when farmed in the right way, will deliver organisations increased opportunities and insights to provide a stronger competitive advantage in existing markets, and to find and develop new products and markets.

Real world examples

Financial services

Morgan Stanley uses Hadoop to analyse investments and claims to see better results in doing portfolio analysis compared to when using traditional databases and traditional grid computing due to the scale and complexity of data involved. This allows the company to identify and understand the most appropriate investments for clients.

Supply Chain, Logistics, and Industrial Engineering

UPS uses telematics to improve performance. Delivery vehicles are equipped with sensors which monitor data on speed, direction, braking performance, drive train performance and other mechanical aspects of the vehicle. This information is then used to optimise maintenance schedules and improve efficiency of delivery routes saving time, money and reducing wastage.

Data from the vehicles is combined with customer data, GPS information and data concerning the normal behaviour of delivery drivers. Using this data to optimise vehicle performance and routes has resulted in several significant improvements:

- Over 15 million minutes of idling time were eliminated in one year. This saved 103,000 gallons of fuel.

- During the same year 1.7 million miles of driving was eliminated, saving 183,000 gallons of fuel.

Retail

It is widely reported that Walmart tracks data on over 60% of adults in the US. Data gathered includes online and instore purchasing pattern, Twitter interactions and trends, weather reports and major events. This data, according to the company, ensures a highly personalised customer experience. Walmart detractors criticise the company's data collection as a breach of human rights and believe the company uses the data to make judgements and conclusions on personal information such as sexual orientation, political view and even intelligence levels.

Entertainment

Time Warner are using big data to track which types of media customers are watching and when. This can help to manage bandwidth and therefore optimise customer experience. The company also uses sophisticated systems to integrate public data such as voter registration and property records with local viewing figures. This enables targeted advertising campaigns by Time Warner's advertising clients.

Netflix has 44 million users worldwide who watch 2 billion hours of programmes a month. The company uses information gathered from analysis of viewing habits to inform decisions on which shows to invest in. Analysing past viewing figures and understanding viewer populations and the shows they are likely to watch allows the analysts to predict likely viewing figures before a show has even aired. This can help to determine if the show is a viable investment.

Test your understanding 7

MC is a mobile (cellular) phone network provider, offering mobile phones and services on a range of different tariffs to customers. The company enjoyed financial success until three years ago but increasing competitive pressure has lead to a recent decline in sales. There has also been an increase in the level of complaints regarding the customer service provided and the company's churn rate (number of customers leaving the company within a given time frame) is at an all time high.

Discuss how an understanding of Big Data can drive the strategic direction of MC company.

4 Sustaining competitive advantage

Once a competitive advantage is achieved it will be important that it is sustained. Competitive advantage can best be sustained by strategic capabilities which are:

- valued,
- rare, and
- robust.

Further details

- **Value of strategic capabilities.** The strategic capability must be one that is of value to the customer. A distinctive capability is not enough: the strategic capability must be able to generate what customers value in terms of products or services.

- **Rarity of strategic capabilities.** Competitive advantage will not be attained if competitors have identical strategic capabilities. Unique or rare resources or competences are needed to allow the organisation to outperform its rivals.

- **Robustness of strategic capabilities.** Capabilities for competitive advantage should be robust, meaning that they are hard to imitate. Therefore, competitive advantage is not so often sustained through physical/tangible resources as these can be copied/acquired over time. More important is the way in which the resources are organised and deployed as these competences are, in general, more difficult to identify and imitate.

Test your understanding 8

In the early part of this century, companies from the US and UK flocked to India to outsource their call centre operations. This was due to the presence of cheap labour, a common language, cheap property prices and development of technology which facilitated the service. Also, domestic providers had often reached capacity and couldn't facilitate further growth or expansion.

However, in recent years this trend has been reversed. Consider reasons why US and UK companies may be repatriating their call centre services.

However, organisations can also take strategic steps to protect their competitive position through:

- price based strategies,
- further differentiation, or
- lock-in.

Price based strategies

An organisation that is pursuing a price-based strategy (such as a no-frills position on the strategy clock) may be able to sustain this position as follows:

- further cost efficiencies,
- winning price wars, or
- accepting lower margins.

Further details

- further cost efficiencies – as rivals try to catch up with the organisation's cost savings, the organisation should be looking for further ways to cut costs. For example, Ryanair are a leading no-frills airline in Europe. But they are constantly looking for new ways to cut costs such as putting pressure on governments to allow them to operate flights without a co-pilot and even going to the extreme of using less ice in drinks in order to slightly reduce the weight of the craft (and subsequently the fuel usage). Ryanair are so focused on cost reductions that they have stated that one of their missions is to be able to offer customers free flights in the future.

- winning price wars – reacting aggressively to new entrants by under-cutting their prices can force them to leave the market and allow the cost leader to restore margins again in the future. For example, News Corp is a multi-national media company selling products such as daily newspapers. One newspaper in one market was attacked by a new rival who wanted to provide better news analysis at the same selling price. So News Corp (who had lower production costs per unit due to its economies of scales) reduced their selling price by two-thirds for one month. This deterred their existing readers from trying out or moving to the new rival. By the end of the month the new rival had abandoned production as it had incurred unsustainable losses in the period.

- accepting lower margins – ultimately, low cost providers may have to reduce selling prices and lower margins in the light of new competition. They would hope however that this would be compensated by higher volumes. For example, the French company Societe Bic produced the Bic pen (known as the Biro or the Cristal) and achieved a low cost position in the 1960s. Over the last 50 years there have been many rivals who have been able to match the company's cost of production so that the margin per unit on the product has steadily eroded. However, Bic have still managed to make very large profits on the product overall on the basis that they continue to be the market leader in disposable pens and sell the product in large volumes (over 100 billion of the pens have been produced). So although margin per unit has fallen, Bic continue to make profits which are larger than all of their rivals.

Differentiation based strategies

These can be sustained through:

- creating difficulties in imitation,
- achieving imperfect mobility of resources, and
- re-investing margins.

Further details

- creating difficulties in imitation – this is about ensuring that strategic capabilities cannot be copied by rivals. Examples would be patent protection, unique production methods, ownership of technology, tying in suppliers etc.

- achieving imperfect mobility of resources – this is about ensuring that the capabilities that create the difference cannot be traded to rivals. Examples would be to tie in key staff to long-term and non-competition contracts, protecting insider knowledge, creating intangible assets such as brand names etc.

- re-investing margins – as seen in earlier segments, investing profits in areas such as innovation and knowledge management can sustain a competitive advantage. For example, Apple ensure that whilst rivals try to catch up with the latest innovations that Apple have made to the iPhone or iPad, Apple are busy working on the next innovation. It means that, by the time rivals have caught up with one innovation, Apple can still be differentiated by launching an updated phone or tablet with a new innovation.

Lock-in

This approach can work for both price-based and differentiation-based strategies. It happens where a business' products become the industry standards. Examples are:

- Microsoft Windows
- Dolby
- Internet explorer

These are not necessarily the best or cheapest products but have such market-dominance that competitors find it very difficult to break into the market because users are often locked in to the product and would find it expensive or inconvenient to switch to rivals. The major threat to such businesses is likely to be attention from anti-monopoly regulators.

Hyper Competition

Hyper-competition: where the frequency, audacity, innovation and aggressiveness of competitors creates an environment of constant movement and change. Examples are seen in:

- the impact of the internet on the music business
- technological developments in telephony
- bio-engineering/pharmaceuticals.

Hyper-competition means that sustaining competitive advantage through adopting a stable price-based strategy or differentiation-based strategy becomes more difficult as products and markets change quickly and radically.

For example, traditional land-line telephone companies were in very dominant positions because of the cost of installing the infrastructure. Mobile phone technology allowed competitors to overcome this barrier much more easily. VOIP (Voice Over Internet Protocol) suppliers, such as Skype, are now able to establish fierce competition in the telecoms market.

Strategies for hyper-competitive environments

- Repositioning on the strategy clock

  For example, an organisation that was a differentiator could cut prices so that its former, relatively exclusive products, have price cuts and the products are perceived as being 'no-frills'.

- Competing successfully

  Do not be satisfied with current products; be unpredictable and radical; be a leader not a follower. It is, of course, difficult for an organisation to make the case for abandoning a currently successful formula so as to keep ahead of competition.

- Fight and overcome competitors' strategies

  For example, act to prevent lock-in by fighting a competitors' plan to gain market dominance with a new product. Imitate competitors and go one better.

- Barriers to entry may be easier to overcome in hyper-competition. If technology is changing, the competitors one-time safe, dominant position can become tenuous.

5 Benchmarking

Why benchmark?

Benchmarking is the process of systematic comparison of a service, practice or process. Its use is to provide a target for action in order to improve competitive position.

The strategic role of benchmarking

Benchmarking permeates the entire strategic planning process.

- In *strategic analysis* in can be used in value chain analysis to compare one company's values to another. Company's strengths can be garnered by comparing strategic capabilities to those of rivals, and the same can be said of rivals. For example, a company that recognises that staff are a key asset might examine their level of staff turnover and sick days to industry averages to determine whether a problem or weakness exists in this area.

- In making *strategic choices* we have seen in this chapter that a competitive advantage can be gained if a company has rarer strategic capabilities in areas such innovation, cost effiency, knowledge management. So a company might, for example, benchmark their production cost per unit if they are seeking a low cost strategy through cost efficiency.

- In putting *strategy into action (explored in detail later in the text)* benchmarking can be used in many ways to determine, for example, which processes need to be redesigned, whether staff are being utilised in the best way, setting budgets and targets, assessing the efficiency and effectiveness of IT solutions etc.

There will be links between benchmarking, critical success factors (CSFs) and key performance indicators (KPIs). Benchmarking can help decide which areas to measure and also in setting a target against which KPIs are measured.

Illustration 3 – Benchmarking

Xerox used process benchmarking in the early 1980s to help correct a serious cost deficiency. To obtain cost-reducing ideas, they attempted to identify organisations in other industries that were particularly good in functional areas similar to those at Xerox. For example, LL Bean, a sportswear retailer and mail order house, became one of the models for the warehouse operations because they also dealt with products that were diverse in shape, size and weight. Altogether Xerox made six warehouse benchmark studies, which helped it improve its annual productivity gains in the logistics and distribution area. Company-wide efforts of this type meant that Xerox overcame a cost gap with respect to Japanese manufacturers.

Types of benchmarking

There are various types of benchmarking such as:

- internal
- competitive/industry
- activity
- generic

Types of benchmarks explained

Internal benchmarking

This method examined past performance over a period of time to determine trends and best performance. Alternatively, a range of processes might be assessed in order to determine internal best practice, which can then be used as the benchmark for other processes. There is a danger however that this will result in the continuance of poor bad habits and that competitors are ignored.

Competitive benchmarking

This method compares performance of the process against other firms in the same industry or sector. Major automakers, for example, will buy cars made by their competitors then reverse engineer those cars to see how to improve their own product. However, there is a danger that, if this is only carried out on a local level, it may not promote performance that is good enough to match wider (e.g. international) rivals.

Activity benchmarking

This method looks at other organisations, not necessarily competitors, who are performing similar activities. For example, if a firm wanted to improve its delivery times to customers it might benchmark this activity against the delivery times of specialist delivery companies such as DHL. In this way, commercial best practice is identified.

Generic benchmarking

For some activities, the process might be so unique that there may not be competitive or activity benchmarks available. In these cases, a conceptually similar process is sought as a benchmark.

For example, when building a rail tunnel connecting Aomori Prefecture on the Japanese island of Honshū and the island of Hokkaidō which travels under sea, the construction company would have had no similar activities against which to benchmark (the under-sea tunnel between England and France was yet to be built). However, the tunneling was conceptually similar to explorations into volcanic crusts and this process was used as the benchmark.

Test your understanding 9

Outline the advantages of internal benchmarking compared with the other types.

Benefits and dangers of benchmarking

The main benefits include:

- improved performance and added value – benchmarking identifies methods of improving operational efficiency and product design and helps companies focus on capabilities critical to building strategic advantage

- improved understanding of environmental pressures

- improved competitive position – benchmarking reveals a company's relative cost position and identifies opportunities for improvement

- a creative process of change

- a target to motivate and improve operations

- increased rate of organisational learning – benchmarking brings new ideas into the company and facilitates experience sharing.

Dangers of benchmarking

- 'you get what you measure' – managers may learn to direct attention at what gets benchmarked rather than at what is important strategically

- Benchmarking does not always reveal the reasons for good/poor performance

- Managers need to be aware that a benchmarking exercise can appear to threaten staff where it appears that benchmarking is designed to identify weaknesses in individual performance rather than how the process itself can be improved. To alleviate this fear, managers need to be involved in the benchmarking exercise and provide reassurance to staff regarding the aims and objectives of benchmarking.

- In today's environment, the more innovative companies are less concerned with benchmarking numbers (for example, costs or productivity) than they are with focusing on the processes. If a company focuses on the **processes**, the numbers will eventually self correct.

6 Chapter summary

```
                        ┌──────────────────────┐
                        │     Strategies for    │
                        │ Competitive Advantage │
                        └──────────────────────┘
```

Value chains	Competitive strategies	Maintaining competitive advantage	Benchmarking
– Explain where existing competitive (dis)advantage comes from – Splits activities between primary and support – Primary are valued by customers – Support facilitate the primary	– We need to understand the terminology, benefits and CSFs	– Cut costs further – Differentiate in new ways – Innovate – knowledge management	– Another useful technique for comparing competitive position to rivals – Can also be used internally to assess business units

Test your understanding answers

Test your understanding 1

Note: The aim here is not to come to one, definitive solution. Instead it is testing your understanding of the elements of the value chain. You may have very different ideas to those suggested in the solution but it is important that you have considered all of the activities in the value chain and that you have considered ways that these activities can be used to stand out from the activities of rivals. You are not looking for ways to cut costs - that would be a very different type of competitive strategy and the activities are likely to look very different.

A differentiation strategy for a restaurant will be about creating a premium dining experience which allows the restaurant to charge premium prices. The strategy should be reflected in all of the primary activities of the supply chain and be supported by a differentiated approach to support activities.

Primary activities

Inbound logistics could be differentiated by the use of local, high quality produce for ingredients. This is likely to add costs and possibly bring diseconomies of scale, but it could be attractive to customers who want to know where their food has come from and who demand fresh ingredients.

Operations will concern the cooking and presentation of the food. Food should follow traditional Mediterranean recipes, be cooked on the premises and be cooked to the highest standard. It should be presented in surroundings that are upmarket, with a high investment in premium fixtures and fittings, expensive cutlery and tableware and well spaced furniture.

Outbound logistics will consider the delivery of the food to tables. This should be efficient, staff should be pleasant and tables should only be served when all meals are ready.

Marketing should highlight the premium location and surroundings as well as the high quality cooking and presentation of meals. The restaurant should seek out positive reviews from local press. The menu should be kept simple and seasonal, and the restaurant could consider offering both an a la carte and fixed price option. A fixed price could be available as a business lunch option which might spread awareness and create some repeat business. Customers should have the opportunity to book tables in advance, either by phone or via the internet.

The service could be enhanced by the use of a sommelier who could recommend wines to match particular dishes. Waiters should be knowledgeable about both the menu and the source of ingredients. The restaurant should also offer a cloakroom service and parking and/or taxi ordering services.

Support activities

From a human resource perspective, an experienced, and ideally award winning, chef should be used to ensure food is cooked to the highest standard. Staff should be trained in the highest levels of service and uniforms provided that are clean and ironed. Ideally, both the chef and the staff should have Mediterranean backgrounds in order to support the focus and marketing of the restaurant's cuisine.

Procurment of produce should happen locally and a dedicated responsibility should be created for letting suppliers. Suppliers should be carefully assessed and regular audits carried out. The restaurant should look to grow many of its ingredients itself if possible in order to ensure that ingredients are as fresh as possible.

Technology can be simple in the restaurant. There may be advanced cooking equipment required in order to create some dishes, but sales technology can be bought off-the-shelf and electronic procurement can be kept to a minimum due to the need to vet suppliers and maintain supplier flexibility.

The restaurant should be supported by an infrastructure that allows for different responsibilities to be performed efficiently. Separate roles should be created for procuring marketing, supplier vetting, staff training and appraisal etc. Some power should be decentralised so that, for example, the chef can determine the menu and ingredients and the sommelier can influence the wines purchased.

Test your understanding 2

(1) Walmart – cost leadership. Legendary attention to keeping costs low.

(2) Saga Holidays – focus.

(3) Bang and Olufson – differentiation. Upmarket, very stylish, home entertainment equipment.

Test your understanding 3

(1) MacDonalds

Probably no-frills. Prices are low, products are standardised and not perceived to be of huge value.

(2) Apple's i-Pad

Very stylish tablet computers with market leading software supported by the iTunes market and the company's excellent support and service give the product a differentiated position. But the product has also achieved market leading volumes – selling over 5 times as many units as its nearest equivalent rival. This has given it economies of scale which have driven down production costs to a level that rivals can't match.

The position would therefore to be a hybrid strategy.

Test your understanding 4

(1) The internet. The internet can be used for very cost-effective marketing, distribution of information, support, sales ordering.

(2) Computer-aided design. CAD can reduce the cost and length of time it takes to design a new product, can help designing a product that is faster and cheaper to make and might increase the chance of using components shared by several products.

(3) Sub-contracting. It might be cheaper for an organisation to buy-in goods or services from a specialist rather than supplying these itself. The specialist will have efficient large-scale manufacturing plant of its own and its research and development expense can be divided over many units. Sub-contracting gets rid of some of the fixed costs. Sub-contracting can make use of manufacturing based in low-cost economies.

(4) Takeovers. Consolidation within an industry can lead to economies of scale from greater buying power, R&D and marketing costs being spread over more units, faster progression along the learning curve.

Note, you might have suggested other valid areas for innovation.

(1)   Innovation is very important in the car industry and car manufacturers launch new models periodically. Sometimes, the innovation is limited mainly to style, but sometimes it is more fundamental. For example, petrol/electric hybrid cars such as the Toyota Prius have received very favourable publicity. Innovation has long been important in safety, for example the development of ABS braking and airbags. With increasing oil prices, fuel economy is becoming very important. New materials offer better strength-to-weight ratios and new engine design offers lower fuel consumption and less pollution. Improved design of components and automation of the production line can make production faster and cheaper.

(2)   Supermarkets can carry out both product innovation and process innovation. For example, many supermarkets developed and stock a wide range of oven-ready meals, which are a relatively new phenomenon. Genetically modified foods would, in theory, present great opportunities for new products, but there is considerable consumer resistance to this technology.

Process innovation has concentrated in supply chain management, data warehousing and data mining. Many supermarkets now carry no back-room inventories and expect their suppliers to make deliveries several times a day. Some supermarkets give suppliers access to the supermarket's inventory records and shift the onus of supplying goods at the right time onto the supplier, rather than the supermarket issuing purchase orders. In data warehousing an organisation keeps vast quantities of historical data, for example, about customers' purchases. Purchases are related to specific customers when the customer uses his or her loyalty card. This data can be 'mined' to discover associations, patterns and trends. This information can be used for demand forecasting and for addressing very tailored marketing to customers.

Many supermarkets have launched internet shopping services and deliver the goods to the customer. Supermarkets are currently investigating ways in which checkouts can be made more efficient and faster.

(3) Commercial television companies are all feeling commercial pressure from the internet, because the internet allows very targeted advertising that is very attractive to marketing departments. In Google, for example, sponsored links are paid for by the advertiser only if the user clicks on the link. Obviously, TV companies are always on the lookout to innovate by launching new programme formats and gripping series. However, this does not seem to be enough to stop the shift from TV to on-line services. High-definition television will attract viewers back for some programmes; interactive digital television might have had the same effect. However, commercial television might have to innovate more radically. For example, why are cable viewers of a new series typically allowed to watch only one episode per week? Why are episodes rationed out at the TV company's convenience? Why aren't viewers allowed to watch all episodes at one sitting (as one might do with a DVD)? Perhaps commercial TV will have to become more like an on-line service where the consumer has greater choice of what to download and when.

The use of social media is an innovation that television are keen to make the most of. They want to encourage viewers to use facebook and twitter to post comments on programmes that they are watching. This works best if friends are watching the same programme at the same time which might be a defensive use of new technology by commercial television companies.

Test your understanding 6

The following arguments could be used to encourage individuals to share knowledge.

- If everyone shares their knowledge, each person should gain more than they give up.

- Organisations are often so complex that it is rare that one person can achieve much alone. Teamwork and sharing knowledge is the best way of assuring a safe future.

- Knowledge is perishable – and increasingly so as the pace of change increases. If knowledge is not used quickly it is wasted. If knowledge is not shared the chances are that it becomes worthless before it can be used.

- Knowledge management is vital to the success of many businesses. If an organisation uses knowledge creatively the chances are that it will beat an organisation with poor knowledge management. Organisations compete with rivals; people within organisations should not be competing with each other at the organisation's expense.

Test your understanding 7

Big Data management involves using sophisticated systems to gather, store and analyse large volumes of data in a variety of structured and unstructured formats. Companies are collecting increasing volumes of data through everyday transactions and marketing activity. If managed effectively this can lead to many business benefits although there are risks involved.

A company like MC will already collect a relatively large amount of data regarding its customers, their transactions and call history. It is likely that a significant proportion of their customers are also fairly digitally engaged and therefore data can be gathered regarding preferences and complaints from social media networks. This will be particularly useful to MC as they have seen an increase in complaints and have a high churn rate so engaging with customers will be highly beneficial.

Recent competitive pressure has led to a decline in sales and so MC need to consider the strategic direction which is most appropriate for them to improve performance.

Analysing the large amounts of data available to them will inform decisions on areas such as:

- The type of handsets currently most in demand and therefore the prices required when bundling with tariffs.

- Main areas of complaint and therefore the areas of weakness which need to be resolved.

- Which types of communication are most popular (e.g data, call minutes, text messages) to ensure the tariffs have the right combinations.

- Usage statistics for pay as you go customers to drive the most appropriate offers and marketing activity.

- Most popular competitor offerings with reasons.

Test your understanding 8

Indian call service providers are struggling to sustain their international competitive advantage for the following reasons:

Robustness

The demand for call centre staff in India has made it a scarce resource. This in turn has pushed up wage rates – with annual wage inflation running at around 13% per annum in 2011. In contrast, wage inflation in the US and UK is falling and due to the economic recession call centre staff are no longer a scarce resource in these countries. Some companies are finding that domestic wage rates are coming to a par with rates in India.

Property and rent prices in India have also risen sharply in India over the past decade as call centres fight for an ever diminishing resource. This again has threatened the cost effectiveness of these centres.

Rarity

Domestic call centres had reached capacity by the late 1990's as demand for call centres grew beyond what they could cope with. However, over the last 10 years these companies have invested in extra capacity which has allowed them to satisfy the needs of domestic customers. The Indian service is now not as rare as it was ten years ago.

Value

Domestic consumers have started to complain about the quality of service from Indian call centres and this in turn leading to US and UK companies valuing the service less. In the US there has also been a political backlash against using foreign labour instead of domestic labour.

On top of this, staff turnover in Indian call centres has risen to epidemic levels as staff move on to seek higher salaries in a market where good staff are difficult to retain (recent reports show attrition rates of between 25 and 35% per annum). It is typically the better staff who are leaving and this is harming the value of the service provided.

The future

Already many small Indian call centres have closed down as they can no longer sustain their competitive advantage. Larger companies have so far managed to maintain the bulk of their customers. But they will need to focus on building value, rare and robust new strategic capabilities if they are to maintain this position in the future.

Test your understanding 9

The main advantages of internal benchmarking are that access to sensitive data and information are easier; standardised data is often readily available; and, usually less time and resources are needed. There may be fewer barriers to implementation as practices may be relatively easy to transfer across the same organisation. However, real innovation may be lacking and best in class performance is more likely to be found through external benchmarking.

6

Other elements of strategic choice

Chapter learning objectives

Upon completion of this chapter you will be able to:

- analyse, in a scenario, the development directions available to an organisation using Ansoff Matrix and a TOWS matrix

- use the Ansoff matrix to develop growth strategies for a business

- explain the use of the success criteria of suitability, acceptability and feasibility in appraising a chosen strategy.

1 Introduction

This chapter examines other ways in which organisations can grow. This will extend strategic choice beyond competitive strategies and will often mean looking at new products and markets.

The chapter closes with a discussion on how strategies should be evaluated – this is a key exam area.

2 SWOT (TOWS) analysis and strategic direction

Introduction

Strategic direction should 'fit' the results of the swot analysis. Used in this way a SWOT analysis is sometimes referred to as a TOWS matrix.

Internal factors			
External factors		Strengths (S)	Weaknesses (W)
	Opportunities (O)	Examine strategies that use strengths to make use of opportunities (SO).	Examine strategies that take advantage of opportunities by overcoming or avoiding weaknesses (WO).
	Threats (T)	Examine strategies that use strengths to overcome or avoid threats (ST).	Examine strategies that minimise the effect of weaknesses and avoid or overcome threats (WT).

Examples of the use of the TOWS matrix

Illustration – SWOT (TOWS) analysis & strategic direction

(1) A company has a prestigious brand name and is wondering whether or not to enter a new emerging foreign market.

Suggestion: (SO) the prestigious brand name is a strength and the emerging market is an opportunity. The company could make use of the brand name by adopting a differentiation or focused differentiation strategy.

(2) A company has a poor distribution network, but wants to start exporting to lucrative overseas markets.

Suggestion: (WO) Collaboration with a company that has a good distribution network might overcome the weakness so as to make use of the opportunity.

(3) A company is facing new competition from cheap overseas manufacturers. The company has a long-standing reputation for good quality products.

Suggestions: (ST) The company could move towards a differentiation strategy to try to make use of its reputation for quality to counter the competitive threat. This might not work if the imports were also of good quality and cheaper. Perhaps relocating manufacturing abroad would give a low cost-base but retain the strength of the company's reputation.

(4) A company has old product lines and is facing dynamic competition from new producers.

Suggestion: (WT) The most difficult scenario to deal with as nothing is going right – weaknesses and threats combined. Repositioning itself might help so that the company was seen as a seller of more traditional goods. Spending on new design and products would help to eradicate the weakness.

Test your understanding 1

Mobius Ltd is an engineering company and has a reputation for high-quality production of complex metal pieces to strict deadlines. It has recently been suffering falling sales because composite materials, such as carbon fibre, have been able to replace many metal components.

Required:

Using a TOWS/SWOT analysis, what are the firm's options?

3 Ansoff's matrix

Introduction

The previous chapter examined competitive strategies and these are typically used when a market is still growing. As a market matures, now **growth strategies** are required and Ansoff suggested that these can fall into 4 categories (explained on the next page).

Generally, risk increases from quadrant A to quadrant D as you work through the matrix (risk in quadrants B and C probably about equal).

The matrix

	Existing Products	New Products
Existing Markets	**Market penetration/growth.** • This typically involves the use of a new/improved competitive strategy. Key risks: • competitor reaction • can lead to stagnation	**Product development** • New products could arise from R&D, joint ventures, buying in other peoples' products, copying innovations of rivals or licensing. • It might also come from product augmentation (for example, by upgrading software capabilities). Key risks: • market size and demand are unknown • can lead to cannibalisation of existing products
New Markets	**Market development** • This involves finding new markets for existing products. • These could be new segments in current markets (e.g. new age groups) or overseas markets. Key risks: • needs a new external analysis • puts a strain on existing strategic capabilities	**Diversification** • This involves moving away from existing core activities and offer a new product to a new customer. • More details are available elsewhere in this chapter. Key risks: • combines the risks of product and market development • need good corporate parenting skills (covered in detail in the next chapter)

More details on market penetration

Market penetration – existing markets and products

Market penetration involves some of the following:

- increasing the average spend per visit for existing customers
- increasing the frequency of visits for existing customers
- winning customers away from rivals
- encouraging non-users to buy.

Strategies used to penetrate a market include:

- Changes to the marketing mix. For example, spending more on sales promotion, changing the selling price of products or redesigning the product. the marketing mix is explored in more detail in a later chapter.

- Pursuing a new competitive strategy. This would involve moving positions on the strategy clock.

- Increasing the sales force.

The ease with which a business can pursue a policy of market penetration will depend on the nature of the market and the position of competitors. When the overall market is growing it may be easier for companies with a small market share to improve quality or productivity and increase market activity rather than in static markets, where it can be much more difficult to achieve. The lessons of the experience curve stress the difficulty of market penetration in mature markets where the cost structure of the market leaders should prevent the entry of competitors with lower market share.

A market penetration strategy would be contemplated for the following reasons.

- When the overall market is growing, or can be induced to grow, it may be relatively easy for companies entering the market, or those wishing to gain market share, to do so relatively quickly. (Some companies established in the market may be unable or unwilling to invest resources in an attempt to grow to meet the new demand.) In contrast, market penetration in static, or declining, markets can be much more difficult to achieve.

- Market penetration strategy would be forced on a company that is determined to confine its interests to its existing product/market area but is unwilling to permit a decline in sales, even though the overall market is declining.

- If other companies are leaving the market for whatever reasons, penetration could prove easy – although the good sense of the strategy may be in doubt.

- An organisation that holds a strong market position, and is able to use its experience and competences to obtain strong distinctive competitive advantages, may find it relatively easy to penetrate the market.

- A market penetration strategy requires a relatively lower level of investment with a corresponding reduction in risk and senior management involvement.

Even though market penetration is seen as the least risky of Ansoff's options, it should not be assumed that risk is always low. When Yamaha attempted to gain share over Honda, it provoked a retaliation that left Yamaha in a worse position than before. The example should serve to remind us that Ansoff's strategies still require a competitive advantage to be effective (a point Ansoff made many times, but one that is frequently forgotten). Also, if a company focuses purely on market penetration and rarely develops new products, then it runs the risk of stagnation and falling behind rivals who have better more innovative products. A good example of this would be Kodak. The company focused on building market share in traditional, high-end cameras. Rivals started to leave the market and move into digital photography. So when the traditional market went into decline, Kodak were too far behind rivals to catch up on digital photography which led the company to sue for bankruptcy in 2012.

Where a company believes that the product is not performing as well as it could do, Ansoff suggests that, if penetration through an improved competitive strategy cannot be achieved, the organisation could instead consider:

- consolidation – acquire or merge with rivals in order to increase market share or obtain economies of scale

- efficiency gains – it will be important to reduce costs as much as possible and to improve processes to make them quicker, more effective and more attractive to customers

- withdrawal – if no obvious route for improvement is available it may be best to withdraw from the market entirely (for example, by selling out to rivals).

More details on product development

Product development – existing markets and new product

This strategy has the aim of increasing sales by developing products for a company's existing market. For our purposes, new-product development is a generic term that encompasses the development of innovative new products and the modification and improvement of existing products. By adopting this strategy the company could:

- develop new product features through attempting to adapt, modify, magnify, substitute, rearrange, reverse or combine existing features

- create different quality versions of the product

- develop additional models and sizes.

A company might show a preference for product development strategy for the following reasons:

(a) it holds a high relative share of the market, has a strong brand presence and enjoys distinctive competitive advantages in the market

(b) there is growth potential in the market

(c) the changing needs of its customers demand new products. Continuous product innovation is often the only way to prevent product obsolescence

(d) it needs to react to technological developments

(e) the company is particularly strong in R&D

(f) the company has a strong organisation structure based on product divisions

(g) for offensive or defensive motives, for example responding to competitive innovations in the market.

However, product development strategy does have its downside and there are strong reasons why it might not be appropriate for a company. For example, the process of creating a broad product line is expensive and potentially unprofitable, and it carries considerable investment risk. Empirical research reveals that companies enjoying high market share may benefit in profit terms from relatively high levels of R&D expenditure, while companies in weak market positions with high R&D expenditure fare badly.

There are reasons why new-product development is becoming increasingly difficult to achieve:

(a) in some industries there is a shortage of new product ideas

(b) increasing market differentiation causes market segments to narrow with the effect that low volumes reduce profit potential that in turn increases the risk of the investment involved

(c) a company typically has to develop many product ideas in order to produce one good one. This makes new product development very costly

(d) even when a product is successful it might still suffer a short life cycle with rivals quick to 'copycat' in the market but with their own innovations and improvements

(e) there is a high chance of product failure.

Success frequently depends upon stretching a brand further than the market is willing to take it. Also, there is a risk that this product will adversely affect the sales of existing products. For example, as Apple announced the launch of the third generation of its iPad, sales of second generation pads fell dramatically. This is known as sales cannibalisation.

More details on market development

Market development – existing products and new markets

Market development strategy has the aim of increasing sales by repositioning present products to new markets. (Note: this strategy is also referred to as '**market creation**'.)

Kotler suggests that there are two possibilities:

(a) the company can open additional geographical markets through regional, national or international expansion

(b) the company can try to attract other market segments through developing product versions that appeal to these segments, entering new channels of distribution, or advertising in other media.

For example, during 1992 Kellogg undertook a major television and promotion campaign to reposition Kellogg's Cornflakes (traditionally regarded as a breakfast cereal) to provide afternoon and evening meals. In the same way, the malt drink Horlicks had previously repositioned from a once-a-day product ('a night meal') to become a through-the-day 'relaxing drink' for young professionals. This was not successful. On the other hand, Lucozade has successfully moved its brand from a product associated with infirmity to a sports-related product.

Market development strategy would be contemplated for the following reasons:

(a) the company identifies potential opportunities for market development including the possibilities of repositioning, exploiting new uses for the product or spreading into new geographical areas

(b) the company's resources are structured to produce a particular product or product line and it would be very costly to switch technologies

(c) the company's distinctive competence lies with the product and it also has strong marketing competence (Coca-Cola provides a good example of a company that pursues market development strategies, as does the fast-food restaurant chain of McDonalds.)

The new market will need a new external analysis. The company will be coming up against new cultures, legal rules, competitors etc. so a new PESTEL and 5 Forces will be essential. It will also need to ensure it has the knowledge, expertise and resources to cope with the demands from a new market.

Often the risk of failure is perceived to be high and therefore strategic alliance (such as joint ventures, franchises and licensing agreements) are commonly used to reduce the risks from market development. These ideas are explored more in the next chapter.

More details on diversification

Growth by diversification – new products and new markets

Diversification is the deployment of a company's resources into new products and new markets. The company thus becomes involved in activities that differ from those in which it is currently involved. Diversification strategy means the company selectively changes the product lines, customer targets and perhaps its manufacturing and distribution arrangements.

The term 'diversification' actually covers a range of different techniques.

- **Conglomerate diversification** – a firm moves into markets that are unrelated to its existing technologies and products to build up a portfolio of businesses. Sometimes this is because the company has developed skills in turnaround or brand management, and can buy an ailing company very cheaply and quickly create value. Hanson have achieved great things in this way, based upon a nucleus of around 500 people. On other occasions, a company might use conglomerate diversification if it believes it has no real future in its existing product market domain. Finally, many entrepreneurial leaders move in and out of markets simply because of opportunities – Virgin being a good example.

- **Horizontal diversification** – synergy is highest in the case of horizontal diversification, especially if the technology is related, but the disadvantage is that little additional flexibility is provided. This type of strategy affects all parts of the value chain since fixed costs can be spread over an increased number of units. Most diversification strategies are of this type. The strategy is undertaken when a company extends its activities into products and markets in which it already possesses necessary expertise. For example, a manufacturer of televisions branching into the manufacture of DVD recorders, camcorders and hi-fi equipment.

- **Vertical integration** – this can take the form of forward or backward integration
    - **Forward integration** – moving towards the consumer – control of distribution, e.g. drinks manufacturers buying public houses.

    - **Backward integration** – moving away from the consumer – control of supplier, e.g. beer brewers buying hop growers.

    Suppose that a company currently manufactures cars. If the company were to buy a chain of car dealers, this would represent forward integration since it is moving towards the final consumer. If the company were to buy a manufacturer of car components (headlights, windscreens, etc.), this would represent backward integration.

Let's look at some of these strategies in more detail:

Unrelated/conglomerate diversification

- Diversifying into completely unrelated businesses.

- Not clear where added value comes from – except if an ailing business is turned round.

- Often leads to loss of shareholder value.

Advantages	Disadvantages
• Increased flexibility	• No synergies
• Increased profitability	• No additional benefit for shareholders
• Ability to grow quickly	• No advantage over small firms
• Better access to capital markets	• Lack of management focus
• Avoidance of anti-monopoly legislation	
• Diversification of risk	

Vertical integration

Advantages	Disadvantages
Cost	**Cost**
• Economies of combined operations.	• It may not be cheaper to do it oneself – especially if suppliers have economies of scale.
• Economies of internal control.	• Increased operating gearing.
• Economies of avoiding the market.	• Dulled incentives.
	• Capital investment.
Quality	• Reduced flexibility to switch to cheaper suppliers.
• Tap into technology – enhanced ability to differentiate.	**Quality**
Barriers	• Cut off from suppliers/customers.
• Assured supply/demand.	• Reduced flexibility to switch to better suppliers.
• Defence against lock-out.	• Differing managerial requirements.
• Create barriers by controlling supplies/distribution/retail outlets.	**Barriers**
	• Much more difficult to exit the industry.

Horizontal diversification

Horizontal diversification refers to development into activities that are competitive with, or directly complementary to, a company's present activities. There are three cases.

(a) Competitive products. Taking over a competitor can have obvious benefits, leading eventually towards achieving a monopoly. Apart from active competition, a competitor may offer advantages such as completing geographical coverage.

(b) Complementary products. For example, a manufacturer of household vacuum cleaners could make commercial cleaners. A full product range can be presented to the market and there may well be benefits to be reaped from having many of the components common between the different ranges.

(c) By-products. For example, a butter manufacturer discovering increased demand for skimmed milk. Generally, income from by-products is a windfall: any you get is counted, at least initially, as a bonus.

Advantages	Disadvantages
• Likely to be more synergies. For example, when Coca Cola moved into the production of other types of drinks such as bottled water and bottled tea, they could share bottling plants, staff and distribution networks. • This can offer a defence against substitutes. • This can widen the company's product portfolio and reduce reliance on one product or on powerful customers. • There is likely to be less risk than with vertical integration or conglomeratisation as some existing strategic capabilities can still be used.	• Selling to different customers against different rivals will require an understanding of the market. • Some new strategic capabilities will be needed. • Synergies are not automatic and will need to be worked on. • It can be more difficult to manage a diversified business. Many of these problems can be overcome by the use of strategic alliances and good corporate parenting and these ideas are explored in more detail in the next chapter.

Test your understanding 2

Tesco plc has grown from a position where 30 years ago it had revenue in excess of $3 billion p.a. to a position today where revenue exceeds $90 billion p.a. and profits exceed $3 billion p.a. and it is the third biggest retailer in the world (behind Walmart and Carrefour).

A history of the company is available for www.tescoplc.com. Consider the company's strategies over the last 30 years and where they might fit into the Ansoff matrix.

Test your understanding 3

M Company, a clothes manufacturer, is considering vertical integration.

Discuss the advantages and disadvantages for the M Company in integrating forward by buying up a chain of retail outlets and integrating backwards by buying a company that manufactures cloth.

4 Strategy evaluation

Introduction

Johnson, Scholes and Whittington argue that for a strategy to be successful it must satisfy three criteria:

- **Suitability** – whether the options are adequate responses to the firm's assessment of its strategic position.

- **Acceptability** – considers whether the options meet and are consistent with the firm's objectives and are acceptable to the stakeholders.

- **Feasibility** – assesses whether the organisation has the resources it needs to carry out the strategy.

This criteria can be applied to any strategy decision such as the competitive strategies assessed in the previous chapter, the growth strategies assessed in this chapter, or even the methods of development considered in the next chapter.

Further explanation on each test

Suitability

Suitability considers whether the new strategy fits in with the organisation's environment and addresses its key issues. It means that in this test we should consider factors that may have arisen in the PESTEL and 5 Forces analysis (covered in chapter 2), for example. Suitability would therefore consider whether the strategy takes account of

- changes in technology
- the threat from substitutes
- the reaction of competitors
- where the business is in its life cycle
- support for overseas expansion
- the timing of the strategy

So the key focus is on whether the strategy solves the problems that the company is facing (and which you are likely to have identified from previous strategic analysis).

Suitability will also examine the 'cultural fit' of the strategy – this examines whether there would be resistance to change from staff, whether the organisational structure can incorporate the new strategy, whether suitable controls are in place etc. Culture is explored in detail in a later chapter.

Feasibility

Assesses whether the organisation has the resources it needs to carry out the strategy. It could be linked back to the resource audit and strategic capabilities covered in chapter 3. This would involve ensuring that

- the organisation has the right number of staff
- staff have the right skills
- adequate finance is available
- technology is suitable

- the organisation has appropriate skills in areas such as marketing and design
- the organisation has experience with this market and/or product.

Feasibility may also consider barriers to entry to ensure that the market can be accessed.

Acceptability

Acceptability concerns assessing risk, return and stakeholders' expectations.

Risk

Risk can be assessed through using:

- financial ratios to identify any problems. For example, a low operating margin and long cash operating cycle for the strategy might highlight that there will be a risk to the organisation's cash flows and that the project will put extra burdens on finances. Assessing the impact on capital structure through using gearing ratios could be equally important.

- sensitivity analysis. You should be aware from previous studies how sensitivity (or 'what if?') analysis can identify key assumptions and provide an indication of the margin of safety in assumptions.

A strategy that is deemed to be too risky may be rejected regardless of whether it is suitable and acceptable.

Risk (and how to evaluate it) is covered in more detail in chapter 14 when we revise areas such as expected value and decision tree techniques.

Return

A project will only be acceptable if meets the returns expected by key stakeholders. These returns may be both financial and non-financial and could include areas such as:

- the change in shareholder wealth (i.e. NPV)
- the accounting return (in terms of profits)
- impact on KPI's (such as customer satisfaction, market share gains etc.)

In Chapter 3, we considered how financial ratios should be calculated and analysed and we also considered what KPIs might be important to an organisation. Later in the syllabus we will look at project appraisal techniques such as payback and NPV methods which would be appropriate here.

For non-profit organisations non-financial KPIs may take preference. But there would still be a need to assess the financial performance of any proposed strategy and techniques such as cost-benefit analysis are commonly used to achieve this.

Risk and return are typically linked together so that if one increases the other increases (i.e. taking more risks can often lead to greater returns). It will therefore be important to determine the risk attitude of key stakeholders. Risk averse stakeholders will be willing to sacrifice returns in order to keep risk low, whereas risk seekers will aim to maximise returns irrespective of risk.

Stakeholder expectations

It will be important to consider the reactions to the strategy of all stakeholders (not just shareholders). We should consider areas such as:

- stakeholder attitudes to risk (as explained above)

- how customers will react (for example, how will the new strategy affect brand and reputation)

- whether there will be any resistance from staff and whether staff will continue to be motivated by any new strategic direction (this will be particularly important when staff are a key asset)

- whether the policy is ethical and how the wider community will react

- whether the strategy fits in with the overall vision, mission and objectives of the organisation

- whether the strategy meets any known goals set out by stakeholders (for example, if industry bodies are demanding that the organisation becomes less aggressive towards competition etc.)

Stakeholder mapping and analysis (examined in chapter 4) can be of great value here.

Test your understanding 4

Sarah Wu has set up and run her own bookstore for five years. She faces little local competition and has made strong financial returns from the store. She now has $15,000 available for investment and plans to open up a second store in a nearby town which currently does not have a bookstore.

Her friend, Misah, has just returned from completing a university course and has suggested that Sarah should instead invest in a website for her store. He has said that this will allow Sarah to sell her books worldwide and make a much quicker return on her investment that the new store opening.

Required:

Evaluate Misah's strategy.

5 Chapter summary

```
┌─────────────────┐
│   Strategic     │
│     choice      │
└────────┬────────┘
         │
         ▼
┌─────────────────────────┐
│ Directions for growth   │
│ • TOWS matrix           │
│ • Ansoff's matrix       │
│    – Market             │
│      penetration        │
│    – Product            │
│      development        │
│    – Market             │
│      development        │
│    – Diversification    │
│      (vertical,         │
│      horizontal,        │
│      conglomerate)      │
└────────┬────────────────┘
         │
         ▼
┌─────────────────────────┐
│ Strategy evaluation     │
│ • Suitability           │
│ • Feasibility           │
│ • Acceptability         │
└─────────────────────────┘
```

Test your understanding answers

Test your understanding 1

The company's strengths are:

- good quality control
- good project management (strict deadlines are met)
- competence with metalwork
- high engineering ability.

The threat arises from metal components being replaced by composite ones.

The company is in the ST segment and needs to examine strategies that use strengths to overcome or avoid threats. Possible strategies for Mobius Ltd are:

- become even better known for metalwork. Some competitors will withdraw from the market as sales fall leaving more scope for Mobius Ltd. Presumably not all metal components will be replaced by composites

- capitalise on its engineering, quality control and project management strengths – possibly by branching into consultancy

- develop competence in manufacturing from composites – the engineering, quality control and project management abilities that Mobius Ltd has should make this easier.

Test your understanding 2

Ansoff matrix for Tesco plc

	Existing Products	**New Products**
Existing Markets	24 hour opening Move from a differentiation to a hybrid strategy	Expansion into petrol sales Expansion into clothing and electrical sales
New Markets	Overseas expansion Tesco Express	Launch of financial services Tesco Direct

There are many other strategies that could be added to the matrix, but even in this simple form it can be seen that companies who grow successfully will often employ the full range of the Ansoff growth strategies.

Test your understanding 3

There are several reasons why M might pursue forward integration. It will be easier for a chain of retail outlets to differentiate its clothes from those of its competitors through branding. This gives an opportunity for higher margins to be earned. The M Company can produce clothes as the shops demand them (JIT), leading to reductions in inventory levels. They will also have a guaranteed customer for its output.

There are also reasons against this course of action. The reaction of the customers that the M Company presently supplies may be hostile. If they stop stocking M Company's products, will the chain of retail outlets be able to sell enough to cover this fall in demand? What is the likely effect of the increased costs of distributing clothes to the shops, rather than to the depots of current customers?

A strategy of backward integration into the supply chain would give the M Company a dedicated supplier with both guaranteed quality and price. The material could be manufactured when required by M Company, leading to lower inventory levels.

The downside to this course of action is that, if alternative cheaper suppliers become available, the M Company will not be able to use them, since it will be committed.

There are also arguments against integration generally, whether forwards or backwards.

Being successful may require different skills from those presently possessed by the company. For example, M Company may know little about retailing or material manufacturing. To be successful, it will have to stretch its current competencies to cover these areas.

In addition, there may be a very different focus for each of the businesses. For example, the chain of retail outlets may well be successful if it can differentiate its products from those of its competitors using innovative colours and material, while the cloth manufacturer is likely to be successful by keeping its costs low by using basic materials and standardised colours. It will be difficult for the M Company to maintain both of these at the same time.

Test your understanding 4

Johnson, Scholes and Whittington's tests will be used to evaluate the strategy:

Feasibility

A website may be cheap to set up and gaining a web presence is relatively easy. But designing the site and maintaining it will need technical expertise which Sarah is unlikely to possess.

Selling internationally will also require international distribution networks that Sarah will not possess. She may be able to outsource distribution, but the costs of this are likely to outweigh any benefits.

Therefore, this strategy may not be a feasible one for Sarah.

Acceptability

As a small, owner-managed business, Sarah is likely to be risk averse and may well want to focus on the area that she is comfortable with. She may decide that international expansion is too risky and difficult to control and lack the confidence necessary to run the business successfully.

She is therefore unlikely to find the strategy to be acceptable.

Suitability

There are already worldwide book selling companies on the internet such as Amazon. They are likely to have built up a reputation and supply chain that Sarah cannot overcome. They will also have economies of scale which enable them to sell books at a lower price than Sarah would find possible and therefore Sarah's website would struggle to gain any competitive advantage against these rivals.

Therefore the strategy is also unsuitable.

Overall

This is not a valid strategy for Sarah to pursue and she should instead evaluate the market development opportunity further.

Methods of strategic development

Chapter learning objectives

Upon completion of this chapter you will be able to:

- assess how internal development, mergers, acquisitions, strategic alliances and franchising can be used as different methods of pursuing a chosen strategic direction

- describe, for a range of businesses, the relationship between corporate parents and business units and how the corporate parent can create or destroy value

- explain in the context of a business, three corporate rationales for adding value – portfolio managers, synergy managers and parental developers

- evaluate, in a scenario, the use of a BCG matrix

- evaluate, in a scenario, the public sector portfolio matrix

- evaluate, in a scenario, the Ashridge Portfolio display (or parenting matrix).

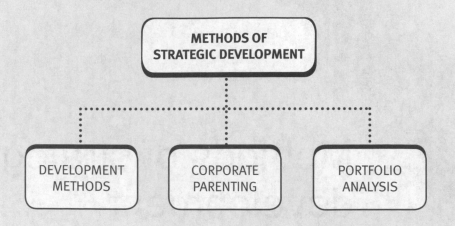

1 Introduction

This chapter looks at how some of the strategies discussed in the last two chapters might be developed. It looks at various types of business combinations. If the chosen method is to develop a strategy through acquisition, then an organisation must consider corporate parenting and portfolio analysis.

2 Alternative development options

There are many ways in which a strategy can be developed. Some of the key methods are explored in this section.

Acquisition

Advantages	Disadvantages
• it is a quick way to grow	• can be very expensive
• there can be synergistic gains	• synergies are not automatic
• acquire the necessary strategic capabilities	• can lead to cultural clashes
• overcomes barriers to entry	• there may be legal barriers to overcome (e.g. competition law)
• can choose a target that fits best (see portfolio analysis later)	• all parts of the target are acquired (including its problems)
• enhances reputation with finance providers	• requires good change management skills

Potential sources of synergy

Synergistic gains refers to a position where the combined entity is worth more than the sum of the value of the companies prior to acquisition. This can come from areas such as improved combined profitability, a better financial position or better market position.

Improved profitability

Combined profits can be higher due to:

- Sales synergies. These can come from sharing databases, selling products which are complementary, sharing distribution channels etc.
- Cost synergies. Combined costs may be lower through sharing staff (and making excess staff redundant), gaining economies of scale, sharing premises, sharing central services (such as accounting) etc.

Improved financial position

The financial position of the combined company may be better due to:

- sharing assets (and selling off excess assets)
- using assets better
- shared working capital management
- finding cheaper financing
- stabilising cash flows (e.g. removing seasonality).

Improved market position

This can come from:

- sharing skills or knowledge
- risk reduction from a portfolio effect
- improved management/better corporate parenting
- better focus.

Test your understanding 1

Blueberry is a quoted resort hotel chain based in Europe.

The industry

The hotel industry is a truly global business characterised by the following:

- Increasing competition

- An increasing emphasis on customer service with higher standards being demanded.

- In particular the range of facilities, especially spas, is becoming more important as a differentiating factor.

Performance

- Blueberry offers services at the luxury end of the market only, based on a strong brand and prestigious hotels – although its reputation has become tarnished over the last five years due to variable customer satisfaction levels.

- Despite a reputation for having the most prestigious coastal resort hotels along the Mediterranean in 20X0, Blueberry was loss-making in the financial years 20X4/5 and 20X5/6.

- To some extent this situation has been turned around in 20X6/7 with an operating profit of $11 million. However shareholders are putting the board under pressure to increase profits and dividends further.

- Management have responded to this by setting out an ambitious plan to upgrade hotel facilities throughout the company and move more upmarket. The bulk of the finance is planned to come from retained profits as Blueberry has historically kept its financial gearing low.

Acquisition opportunity

The management of Blueberry have been approached by the owner of 'The Villa d'Oeste', a luxury hotel on the shores of Lake Como in Italy, who is considering selling it. The hotel has an international reputation with world-class spa facilities and generates revenue throughout most of the year due to Lake Como's mild micro-climate. The asking price will be approximately $50m.

Required:

Outline the issues to be considered when assessing the acquisition.

Organic growth

Advantages	Disadvantages
• can spread the cost	• lack of experience in new areas
• no cultural clashes or control issues	• less attractive to finance providers
• can be set up in any way	• there may be barriers to organic entry
• may get access to government grants	• it may be too slow
• easier to terminate	• no access to skills, reputation etc. or other strategic capabilities required for success
• can be developed slowly (less risk)	• managers may be spread too thinly

Joint venture

Advantages	Disadvantages
• can share the set-up and running costs	• can often lead to disputes
• can learn from each other	• may give access to strategic capabilities and eventually allow the partner to compete in core areas
• can focus on relative strengths	• there may be a lack of commitment from each party
• may reduce political or cultural risks	• requires strong central support which may not be provided
• it is better than going it alone and then competing	• transfer pricing issues may arise and performance appraisal can be complicated

Characteristics of a well structured strategic alliance

A strategic alliance can be defined as a co-operative business activity, formed by two or more separate organisations for strategic purposes, that allocates ownership, operational responsibilities, financial risks, and rewards to each member, while preserving their separate identity/autonomy.

- Alliances can allow participants to achieve critical mass, benefit from other participants' skills and can allow skill transfer between participants.

- The technical difference between a strategic alliance and a joint venture is whether or not a new, independent business entity is formed.

- A strategic alliance is often a preliminary step to a joint venture or an acquisition. A strategic alliance can take many forms, from a loose informal agreement to a formal joint venture.

- Alliances include partnerships, joint ventures and contracting out services to outside suppliers.

Seven characteristics of a well-structured alliance have been identified.

- **Strategic synergy** – more strength when combined than they have independently.

- **Positioning opportunity** – at least one of the companies should be able to gain a leadership position (i.e. to sell a new product or service; to secure access to raw material or technology).

- **Limited resource availability** – a potentially good partner will have strengths that complement weaknesses of the other partner. One of the partners could not do this alone.

- **Less risk** – forming the alliance reduces the risk of the venture.

- **Co-operative spirit** – both companies must want to do this and be willing to co-operate fully.

- **Clarity of purpose** – results, milestones, methods and resource commitments must be clearly understood.

- **Win-win** – the structure, risks, operations and rewards must be fairly apportioned among members.

Some organisations are trying to retain some of the innovation and flexibility that is characteristic of small companies by forming strategic alliances (closer working relationships) with other organisations. They also play an important role in global strategies, where the organisation lacks a key success factor for some markets.

Franchising

Advantages	Disadvantages
• receive an initial capital injection	• share profits
• can spread brand quickly	• may give access to strategic capabilities and eventually allow the partner to compete in core areas
• easy to terminate	• there may be a lack of goal congruence
• a good way to test the market before full investment	• there is a loss of control over quality, recruitment etc.
• franchisee may provide better local knowledge	• there may be a lack of consistency across franchises
• franchisor management can focus on strategic rather than operational issues	• it may be difficult to attract franchisees

Further detail on franchising

Franchising

The mechanism

- The franchiser grants a licence to the franchisee allowing the franchisee to use the franchiser's name, goodwill and systems.
- The franchisee pays the franchiser for these rights and also for subsequent support services the franchiser may supply.
- The franchisee is responsible for the day to day running of the franchise. The franchiser may impose quality control measures on the franchisee to ensure the goodwill of the franchiser is not damaged.
- Capital for setting up the franchise is normally supplied by both parties.
- The franchiser will typically provide support services including: national advertising, market research, research and development, technical expertise, management support.

The advantages for the franchiser are as follows:

- Rapid expansion and increasing market share with relatively little equity capital.

- The franchisee provides local knowledge and unit supervision. The franchiser specialises in providing a central marketing and control function, limiting the range of management skills needed.

- The franchiser has limited capital in any one unit and therefore has low financial risk.

- Economies of scale are quickly available to the franchiser as the network increases. For example, with the supply of branded goods, extensive advertising spend are justifiable.

The advantages for the franchisee are as follows.

These are mainly in the set-up stages where many new businesses often fail.

- The franchisee will adopt a brand name, trading format and product specification that has been tested and practised.

- The learning curve and attendant risks are minimised.

- The franchisee usually undertakes training, organised by the franchiser, which should provide a running start, further reducing risk.

Disadvantages

- A franchisee is largely independent and makes personal decisions about how to run his operation. In addition, the quality of product, customer satisfaction and goodwill is under his control. The franchiser will seek to maintain some control or influence over quality and service from the centre but this will be difficult if the local unit sees opportunities to increase profit by deviating from the standards which the franchiser has established.

- There can be a clash between local needs or opportunities and the strategy of the franchiser, for example, with respect to location.

- The franchiser may seek to update/amend the products/services on offer whilst some franchisees may be slow to accept change or may find it necessary to write off existing stock holdings.

- The most successful franchisees may break away and set up as independents, thereby becoming competitors.

Test your understanding 2

Which of licensing, joint venture, strategic alliance and franchising might be the most suitable for the following circumstances?

(1) A company has invented a uniquely good ice cream and wants to set up an international chain of strongly branded outlets.

(2) Oil companies are under political pressure to develop alternative, renewable energy sources.

(3) A beer manufacturer wants to move from their existing domestic market into international sales.

3 Corporate parenting

Corporate parenting looks at the relationship between head office and individual business units. This will become more important if a business follows the route of growth through acquisitions – the aim will be to become a good "parent" to new subsidiaries.

Goold and Campbell

Goold and Campbell (1991) identified three broad approaches or 'parenting' styles reflecting the degree to which staff at corporate headquarters become involved in the process of business strategy development. The approach will have a significant impact on the role of central departments such as the accounting function. The different styles are:

- strategic planning
- financial control
- strategic control.

Different parenting styles

Strategic planning companies

In strategic planning companies such as Cadbury Schweppes and BP.

- There is a focus on a limited number of businesses where significant synergies exist leading to a concentration on a few core areas where it is possible to have a degree of expertise.

- Corporate management play a major role in setting the strategies for each of the SBUs (Strategic Business Units).

- The approach is based on the belief that strategic decisions occur relatively infrequently and that when they do, it is important for corporate headquarters to frame and control the strategic planning and decision-making process.

- There is good integration across the units, which is particularly useful when resources such as distribution may be shared.

- Decisions are made at a senior level and hence there is less likelihood of short-term views predominating.

- There may be a number of disadvantages:
    - difficulties in communication and co-ordination may slow down development

    - there may be less 'ownership' of the strategies by the operating unit managers. There is strong empirical evidence that there are fewer low-risk strategies pursued, which might otherwise be the case if strategy was centred on the unit managers

    - there is also a likelihood that this strategy formulation from the centre might result in getting 'locked into' failing businesses. There may be a resistance to the closing down of poorly performing units if the strategies have been sanctioned at the centre.

Financial control companies

In financial control companies such as Marconi (GEC).

- Timescales tend to be shorter.

- The head office takes a 'hands-off' approach but sets stringent short-term financial targets that have to be met to ensure continued funding of capital investment plans.

- Failure to meet financial targets will lead to the possibility of divestment.

- This type of strategy allows for diversity and companies generally have a wide corporate portfolio with limited links between divisions and acquisition/divestment is a continuing process as opposed to an exceptional event.

- Empirical evidence suggests that lower risk strategies are pursued but with resultant higher profitability ratios.

- Much of the growth in this scenario comes from acquisition as distinct from internal growth.

- There may be a number of disadvantages:

  - there is a propensity to be risk averse and possibly to 'milk' the business

  - this type of decentralisation may make it difficult to exploit any potential synergies

  - the control framework set up by the head office might constrain flexibility.

Strategic control companies

In strategic control companies such as ICI.

- Corporate management take a middle course, accepting that subsidiaries must develop and be responsible for their own strategies, while being able to draw on headquarters' expertise.

- Evaluation of performance extends beyond short-term financial targets to embrace strategic objectives such as growth in market share and technology development, that are seen to support long-term financial and operational effectiveness.

- Diversity is coped with more readily than the 'strategic planning' style.

- There is also a danger of greater ambiguity.

Test your understanding 3

Comment on the implications of each of Goold and Campbell's approaches for innovation.

4 Adding value

Corporate parenting

Corporate parents do not generally have direct contact with customers or suppliers but instead their main function is to manage the business units within the organisation. The issue for corporate parents whether they:

- add value to the organisation and give business units advantages that they would not otherwise have

- add cost and so destroy the value that the business units have created.

Ways of adding value

There are a number of ways in which the corporate parent can add value.

- By providing resources which the business units would not otherwise have access to, such as investment and expertise in different markets.

- By providing access to central services such as information technology and human resources that can be made available more cheaply on an organisation-wide basis due to economies of scale.

- By providing access to markets, suppliers and sources of finance that would not be available to individual units.

- By improving performance through monitoring performance against targets and taking corrective action.

- Sharing expertise, knowledge and training across business units.

- Facilitating co-operation and collaboration between business units.

- Providing strategic direction to the business and clarity of purpose to business units and external stakeholders such as shareholders.

- By helping business units to develop either through assisting with specific strategic developments or by enhancing the management expertise.

KAPLAN PUBLISHING

Destroying value

It is not uncommon for corporate parents to be criticised for destroying value such that business units would fare better on their own. There are a number of ways in which this can happen.

- The high administrative cost of the centre may exceed the benefits provided to business units.

- The added bureaucracy resulting from the organisational structure may slow decision making and limit the organisation's flexibility and speed of response to customers and environmental changes.

- If organisations become very complex, this can prevent clarity and make it difficult for managers within the organisation and external stakeholders to understand the strategic direction.

Rationales for adding value

A well-managed corporate parent should be able to add value. Johnson, Scholes and Whittington identify three corporate rationales or roles adopted by parents in order to do this:

- portfolio managers
- synergy managers
- parental developers.

Different roles adopted by good corporate parents

The portfolio manager

Portfolio managers:

- are corporate parents effectively acting as agents for financial markets and shareholders to enhance the value from individual businesses more effectively than the financial markets could

- identify and acquire under-valued businesses and improve them, perhaps by divesting low-performance businesses or improving the performance of others

- keep the costs of the centre low by minimising the provision of central services and allowing business units autonomy whilst using targets and incentives to encourage high performance

- may manage a large number of businesses, which may be unrelated.

The synergy manager

Synergy managers:

- enhance value by sharing resources and activity, such as distribution systems offices or brand names

- may however bring substantial costs as managing integration across businesses can be expensive

- may have difficulty in bringing synergy as cultures and systems in different business units may not be compatible

- may need to be very hands-on and intervene at the business unit level to ensure that synergy is actually achieved.

The parental developer

Parental developers:

- use their own central competences to add value to the businesses by applying specific skills required by business units for a particular purpose, such as financial management or research and development

- need to have a clear understanding of the value-adding capabilities of the parent and the needs of the business units in order to identify how these can be used to add value to business units

- need to ensure that they are able to add value to all businesses or be prepared to divest those to which they can offer no advantages.

Test your understanding 4

Philip Morris used strong generation of cash from its cigarette sales to purchase a large-scale food business. The management believed they had good expertise in developing strong global brand management and they could apply this to their acquisitions.

What would be their corporate rationale for adding value?

KAPLAN PUBLISHING

5 Portfolio analysis tools

The use of portfolio analysis

An organisation may have to make investment decisions such as whether to add a company to its existing portfolio or whether to divest of an existing subsidiary. One technique that can be used to perform this task is portfolio analysis which determines the fit between the business unit and other business units held by the organisation.

> **More on portfolio analysis**
>
> Portfolio analysis:
>
> - is designed to reveal whether the organisation has:
>   - too many declining products or services
>   - too few products or services with growth potential
>   - insufficient product or service profit generators to maintain present organisation performance or to provide investment funds for the nurturing of tomorrow's successful ventures
>
> - portfolio analysis can be very valuable in assessing how the balance of activities contributes to the strategic capability of the organisation
>
> - should be applied to SBUs, that is units dealing with particular market segments not whole markets
>
> - will result in different targets and expectations for different parts of the organisation, which will impact on the resource allocation processes – both capital and revenue budgets
>
> - in this section the BCG matrix is discussed in detail and alternatives in outline. The examiner has stated that he will not explicitly ask for a specific portfolio tool but will expect you to use whichever models are most useful in the scenario given.

The Boston Consulting Group (BCG) growth share matrix

- The two-by-two matrix classifies businesses, divisions or products according to the present market share and the future growth of that market.

- Growth is seen as the best measure of market attractiveness.

- Market share is seen to be a good indicator of competitive strength.

BCG measurement issues

Assessing the rate of market growth as high or low is difficult because it depends on the market. A useful tool for assessing growth is the PESTEL model studied in chapter 2. In an exam scenario, this would be a good tool to use alongside the BCG in order to assess whether a market has got good growth prospects.

Relative market share is defined by the ratio of market share to the market of the largest competitor. The log scale is used so that the midpoint of the axis is 1.0, the point at which an organisation's market share is exactly equal to that of its largest competitor. Anything to the left of the midpoint indicates that the organisation has the leading market share position.

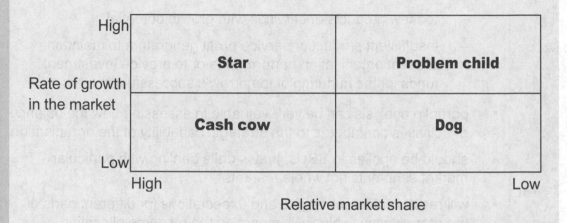

An organisation would want to have in a balanced portfolio:

- cash cows of sufficient size and/or number that can support other products in the portfolio

- stars of sufficient size and/or number which will provide sufficient cash generation when the current cash cows can no longer do so

- problem children that have reasonable prospects of becoming future stars

- no dogs or – if there are any – there would need to be good reasons for retaining them.

BCG decision making aspects

Decision-making implications for different quadrants in the matrix

A **cash cow** has a high relative market share in a low-growth market and should be generating substantial cash inflows. The period of high growth in the market has ended (the product life cycle is in the maturity or decline stage), and consequently the market is less attractive to new entrants and existing competitors. Cash cow products tend to generate cash in excess of what is needed to sustain their market positions. Profits support the growth of other company products. The firm's strategy is oriented towards maintaining the product's strong position in the market.

A **star** has a high relative market share in a high-growth market. This type of product may be in a later stage of its product life cycle. A star may be only cash-neutral despite its strong position, as large amounts of cash may need to be spent to defend an organisation's position against competitors. Competitors will be attracted to the market by the high growth rates. Failure to support a star sufficiently strongly may lead to the product losing its leading market share position, slipping eastwards in the matrix and becoming a problem child. A star, however, represents the best future prospects for an organisation. Market share can be maintained or increased through price reductions, product modifications, and/or greater distribution. As industry growth slows, stars become cash cows.

A **problem child** (sometimes called 'question mark') is characterised by a low market share in a high-growth market. Substantial net cash input is required to maintain or increase market share. The company must decide whether to do nothing – but cash continues to be absorbed – or market more intensively or get out of this market. The questions are whether this product can compete successfully with adequate support and what that support will cost.

The **dog** product has a low relative market share in a low-growth market. Such a product tends to have a negative cash flow, that is likely to continue. It is unlikely that a dog can wrest market share from competitors. Competitors, who have the advantage of having larger market shares, are likely to fiercely resist any attempts to reduce their share of a low-growth or static market. An organisation with such a product can attempt to appeal to a specialised market, delete the product or harvest profits by cutting back support services to a minimum.

Options for the future can be plotted onto a BCG matrix and the long-term rationale of business development can be highlighted by the matrix. Using the original matrix a strategist could address the following issues.

- Which strategies are most suitable to ensure a move from question marks through to stars and eventually to cash cows? In other words, will the strategy move the organisation to a dominant position in its market?

- Will there be sufficient funds from cash cows to provide the necessary investment in stars? Many bankruptcies have occurred because firms have invested heavily in the promotion of products in rapid growth without profitable and well-established products from which it can fund these new ventures.

- Does the portfolio have a balance of activities that matches the range of skills within the organisation? Unless a balance is achieved certain groups are overstretched while others remain underemployed. In general, question marks and stars can be very demanding on the time of management.

- Is the organisation thinking about an acquisition strategy? Firms that embark on acquisition programmes often forget that the most likely targets for acquisition are not the cash cows and stars of the business world but the question marks and dogs. There may be logic in acquiring a question mark for an organisation with the resources to move it towards stardom.

Strategic movements on the BCG matrix

A product's place in the matrix is not fixed for ever as the rate of growth of the market should be taken into account in determining strategy.

- Stars tend to move vertically downwards as the market growth rate slows, to become cash cows.

- The cash that they then generate can be used to turn problem children into stars, and eventually cash cows.

The ideal progression is illustrated below:

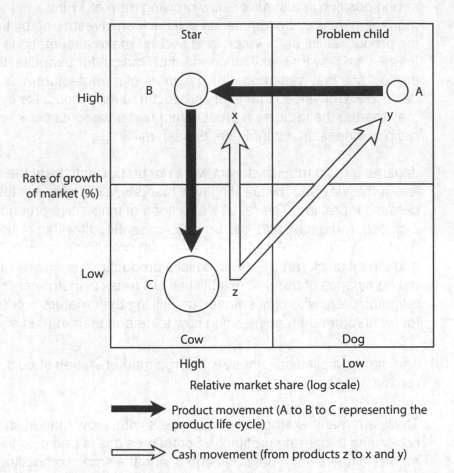

Star — Problem child

High — B — x — y — A

Rate of growth of market (%)

Low — C — z

Cow — Dog

High — Low

Relative market share (log scale)

➡ Product movement (A to B to C representing the product life cycle)

⇨ Cash movement (from products z to x and y)

Criticisms of the BCG matrix

(1) The matrix uses only two measures

The only two measures used in the BCG matrix are growth and market share. These may be too limited as a basis for policy decisions. Other portfolio tools , explained later in this chapter, look at expanding the matrix to consider other important strategic issues.

(2) The matrix encourages companies to adopt holding strategies

The strategic principles involved advocate that companies with large market shares in static or low-growth markets (i.e. cash cows) adopt holding or harvesting strategies rather than encouraging them to try to increase the total demand of the markets in which their products are selling. Compliance with these strategic tenets has led to devastating results for some companies.

There are a number of dangers in assuming that a product is a 'cash cow'. (BCG defines a cash cow as a product occupying a strong position in a static or slow growing market.) First, management may be tempted to pull back on investment, by treating the product as in 'safe-water', and second make assumptions about future cash flow that may be unrealistic. Radios, for example, form a product line that was treated by a number of manufacturers as a cash cow. Convinced that every product had its 'product life cycle' they treated the radio as a product that had passed its peak and the radio business as a candidate for cash milking.

Japanese radio manufacturers were not prepared to treat the radio-line in this way and, by creating new markets, expanded the total demand for radios. The result was a flood of innovative products that included: radio-cassette, stereo radio-cassette, ultra-thin radio, 'Walkman with radio', radio-in-pocket with calculator, radio-in-TV and digital clock radio – all successful products. Yamaha destroyed the dominance of the well-established US musical instrument manufacturers who concentrated on milking their mature products for profit rather than on planning how to defend their market shares.

(3) The matrix implies only those with large market shares should remain

There are many examples of businesses with a low market share continuing to operate profitably. Sometimes this is because the market is not unitary, but fragmented, and the small competitor has found itself a particular market niche; on other occasions large companies may prefer smaller competitors to preserve the impression of competition.

The link between profitability and market share may be weak because:

- low share competitors entering the market late may be on the steepest experience curve

- low share competitors may have some in-built cost advantage

- not all products have costs related to experience

- large competitors may receive more government attention and regulation.

(4) The matrix implies that the most profitable markets are those with high growth

Again this is not always so, due to:

- high entry barriers, especially in high-technology industries
- high price competition.

Both of these problems are typified by the microcomputer business. Despite impressive rates of growth, a number of companies have been unable to make profits because of the high levels of initial investment followed by extreme price competition from low-cost late entrants.

(5) Not all dogs should be condemned

A very large number of small but successful businesses are 'dogs', and according to the BCG concept are ripe for reinvestment or liquidation. However, this would not always be the case. Dog products are often used not with the primary aim of maximising the profit from the product itself, but to provide economies of scale in manufacturing, marketing and administration to sustain the overall business. Furthermore, the BCG portfolio theory does not seem to take into account the need for competitive strategy. A company might, for example, launch a product to act as a 'second front' to support the thrust of its main offering, although the product, by definition, is a dog.

When the Clorox company (the market leader in the US for bleach) introduced a new product, 'Wave', the purpose was to try to deflect Procter & Gamble's attack by creating a 'second front', rather than to generate substantial profits from Wave.

Despite these criticisms, in certain circumstances the model provides a useful method by which a company can (a) attempt to achieve overall cost leadership in its market(s) through aggressive use of directed efficiency; (b) focus its expenditures and capital investment programmes; and (c) plan for an appropriate balance of resources between conflicting product-market claims. Also the information and analysis required to construct the matrix will provide meaningful indicators. It should, however, not be used in a rigid, stereotype manner. The model ought to be used as a means to an end, not as representing the end objective in itself.

The evidence

Several studies have been carried out into the use of the BCG, and on the whole these would not encourage uncritical use of the model. In particular, the link between quadrant and cash flow is not particularly strong, and there are many exceptions. Fortune once described this model as the worst business model ever devised.

Test your understanding 5

The marketing manager of Fruity Drinks Ltd has invited you in for a chat. Fruity Drinks Ltd provides fruit juices to a number of supermarket chains, that sell them under their own label. 'We've got a large number of products, of course. Our freshly squeezed orange juice is doing fine – it sells in huge quantities. Although margins are low, we have sufficient economies of scale to do very nicely in this market. We've got advanced production and bottling equipment and long-term contracts with some major growers. No problems there. We also sell freshly squeezed pomegranate juice: customers loved it in the tests, but producing the stuff at the right price is a major hassle – all the seeds get in the way. We hope it will be a winner, once we get the production right and start converting customers to it. After all, the market for exotic fruit juices generally is expanding fast.'

What sort of products, according to the BCG classification, are described here?

The public sector portfolio matrix

The BCG is aimed primarily at commercial, private sector organisations. The public sector portfolio matrix adapts the BCG idea to public sector organisations and the axis are "public need and funding effectiveness" and "value for money"

Public sector portfolio matrix

The dimensions of the matrix are:

- value for money – this considers whether the service can be provided effectively

- the desirability of the service – public support and funding attractiveness.

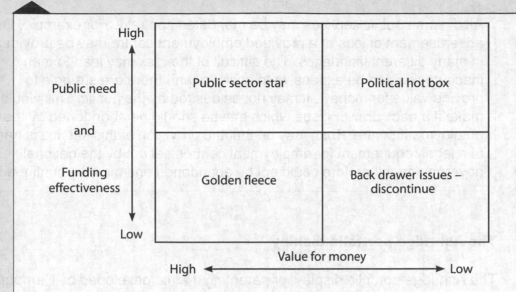

The four potential positions for services can lead to the following strategies for each service:

Position	Characteristics	Strategy
Public sector star	Attractive the public and well funded. Funds are used well and the service goals are achieved.	Continue at current funding levels.
Golden fleece	Very effective, but the public believe that it is over-funded.	Move funds to other services, aim to reduce the service or cut staff numbers.
Back drawer issues	Not effective and not desired by the public.	Remove this service.
Political hot box	Very popular but not very effective. Putting a drain on funding that could be used elsewhere.	Either aim to change the public's perceptions and change it into a back drawer issue, or try to improve effectiveness (for example, by providing extra resources) and turn it into a star. Lobby for more funding.

The major problem with the application of the public sector portfolio matrix is that its dimensions (the organisation's ability to serve effectively by providing value for money, and the public's need and support and the funding attractiveness) are all subjective, and largely dependent on the user's own perceptions as to what the body should be doing, and what the public sector body is good at.

Also, some public services may be mandated centrally. For example, the advertisement of jobs at a provided employment centre may be provided in many different languages. The difficult of the task may lead to many inaccuracies and be expensive to achieve (and therefore struggle to provide value for money . It may not be desired by the public. This would make it a back drawer issue which maybe should be abandoned by the employment centre. But it may be that the provision of this service is part of a legal requirement for employment centres set out by the national government. It therefore could not be abandoned and must be continued.

The Ashridge portfolio display

The Ashridge portfolio display, or parenting matrix, developed by Campbell, Goold and Alexander, focuses on the benefits that corporate parents can bring to business units and whether they are likely to add or destroy value (as discussed earlier in this chapter).

The matrix considers two particular questions.

- How good is the match between perceived parenting opportunities and the parent's skills?

- How good is the match between the CSFs of the business units and the skills and resources that the parent can bring?

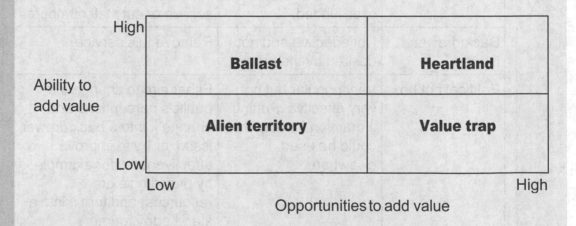

KAPLAN PUBLISHING

Explanation of the matrix

Heartland business units

- These are where there is a high degree of match and the parent company has the capabilities and experience to add value by providing the support required by the business unit.

- These businesses should be central to future strategy.

Ballast businesses

- These are those where the parent understands the business well but there are limited opportunities to offer help, sometimes because the business has been owned for a long time and has no further support needs.

- These businesses would do better if left alone or indeed divested.

Value trap businesses

- These are those where there appear to be many parenting opportunities but there is a poor fit with the critical success factors of the business.

- There appears to be good potential but in practice because of the lack of fit with the strategy there is a high possibility of destruction of value.

Alien businesses

- These are those where there is a complete mismatch.

- These should not remain part of the corporate portfolio.

Using the Ashridge portfolio display indicates which types of companies should be divested and why. Businesses that may be candidates for disinvestment are:

- alien businesses – the parent can do good to these organisations and they would achieve more in another group

- value trap businesses – despite potential a lack of fit leads to a high possibility of a loss of value

- ballast businesses – may do better as the parent has little to offer.

The matrix can be expanded to introduce what are called 'edge of heartland' business units:

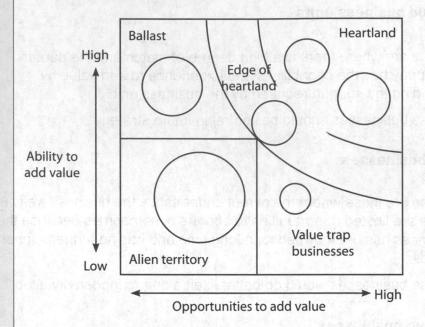

Edge of heartland business units

- These are those where there is a good fit in some areas where the parent can bring particular skills that add value to the business unit, but not in others, where the parent may destroy value.

- However, if the parent develops sufficient understanding of the business to avoid this, then the business may move into the heartland.

Test your understanding 6

Anudir Inc started as a single restaurant and has since developed to a large quoted fast food provider. Over the last ten years it has diversified as follows:

- trendy hotels
- commercial property development – a depressed market at present
- jeans manufacture.

The main skills of the parent holding company lie in identifying consumer trends regarding food and designing menus to match those trends.

From the above information – label the different business units using the Ashridge portfolio display.

6 Chapter summary

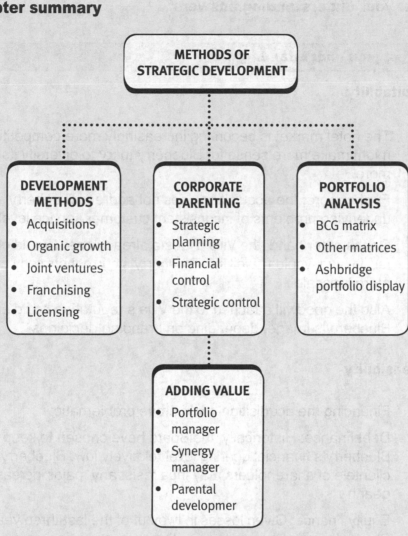

METHODS OF STRATEGIC DEVELOPMENT

DEVELOPMENT METHODS
- Acquisitions
- Organic growth
- Joint ventures
- Franchising
- Licensing

CORPORATE PARENTING
- Strategic planning
- Financial control
- Strategic control

PORTFOLIO ANALYSIS
- BCG matrix
- Other matrices
- Ashbridge portfolio display

ADDING VALUE
- Portfolio manager
- Synergy manager
- Parental developmer

Test your understanding answers

Test your understanding 1

Suitability

- The hotel market is becoming increasingly more competitive, so it might make more sense for Blueberry to try to diversify its activities more.

- Furthermore, the acquisition does not address Blueberry's underlying problems of inconsistent customer service levels.

- On the other hand, the Villa d'Oesta already has a world class spa facility and would fit well into Blueberry's current strategy of moving more 'upscale'.

- Also the goodwill attached to the Villa's reputation could enhance Blueberry's image, depending on branding decisions.

Feasibility

- Financing the acquisition could prove problematic:

- Debt finance: Historically, the Board have chosen to keep Blueberry's financial gearing level relatively low. Blueberry's existing clientele of shareholders may thus resist any major increase in gearing.

- Equity finance: Given losses in two out of the last three years, Blueberry may struggle to raise the purchase price via a rights issue.

Acceptability

- Growth by acquisition is generally quicker than organic growth, thus satisfying institutional shareholders' desire to see growth in revenues and dividends.

- Further work is needed to assess whether the $50m asking price is acceptable.

- Buying another hotel should enable Blueberry to gain additional economies of scale with respect to insurance, staff costs such as pensions and purchasing economies on drinks. This should boost margins and profitability further.

- The new hotel would fit well into Blueberry's existing portfolio of hotels, for example, by having significant cash inflows throughout the year in contrast to Blueberry's highly seasonal business, thus reducing the overall level of risk.

Preliminary Recommendations

- The opportunity to acquire the Villa d'Oeste should be rejected on the grounds that financing the acquisition would be problematic at present.

- Blueberry should instead focus on improving facilities and quality in existing hotels before looking to expand through acquisition.

Test your understanding 2

(1) A franchise arrangement would work well here. There is more than just manufacturing involved – there is the whole retail offering, and entering into franchise agreements would be a quick, effective way of expanding.

(2) Unless the oil companies felt that, because of their size, there was no need for joint research, development, marketing and lobbying, a strategic alliance of some sort could be useful. Research costs and findings could be shared. Together they could bring powerful pressure to bear on governments to, for example, allow more generous time scales for implementation of the new technology. Alternatively, the new energy technology could be developed within a joint venture organisation.

(3) Almost certainly, this company would expand by licensing local brewing companies to make and distribute its product.

Test your understanding 3

Strategic planning

- Senior management can encourage innovation. It may even be the case that innovation happens centrally (through, for example, a central research and development division that can share developments across the SBUs).

- With closely related SBUs, central management will understand the market better and are likely to be aware of changes in competitor products and consumer attributes which might force innovation onto the business.

- Where innovation does arise, it is more likely to be transferred between different SBUs who share similar CSFs. (**Note:** Only if senior management see the potential for this!)

Financial control

- Inherent risk aversion may prevent innovative ideas being adopted.

- Emphasis on financial performance and short-termism may stifle radical innovations that take time to emerge.

Strategic control

- Head office can still encourage innovation.

- Local ownership of strategy may see some managers trying to drive the business forward through innovation without the short-term financial constraints of the financial control model.

Test your understanding 4

They would consider themselves a parental developer – using their own competences to add value to the businesses by applying the specific skills (in this case marketing) required by the business units.

Test your understanding 5

Orange juice is a cash cow.

Pomegranate juice is a question-mark, which the company wants to turn into a star.

Test your understanding 6

Solution

While in practice you would have more detail on which to base your findings – the model could be applied as:

- fast food outlets – heartland (or ballast as it is debatable whether further opportunities exist for value to be added)

- jeans – alien (possibly edge of heartland if you believe that skills can be transferred to identifying consumer trends in clothing as well)

- hotels – value trap. Head office may believe that it has the skills to add value on the food side but in reality CSFs are more concerned with marketing, staffing, cost control

- property development – alien.

Organisational structure

Chapter learning objectives

Upon completion of this chapter you will be able to:

- advise on how organisations can be structured to deliver a selected strategy

- describe Mintzberg's six organisational configurations

- describe the types of control processes that can be used (input/output and direct/indirect), emphasising the planning process

- describe how responsibility and authority for operational and strategic decisions can be vested inside organisations in general

- describe from national, international and global perspectives the opportunities and problems arising from diversification and international scale

- discuss how external relationships, boundaryless structures and strategic alliances can be used to deliver an organisation's strategy.

```
┌─────────────────────────────────────────┐
│        ORGANISATIONAL STRUCTURE          │
└─────────────────────────────────────────┘
```

Types of structure
- Factors influencing structure
- Mintzberg
- Planning and control
- Responsibility and authority

Strategic solutions
- Managing international companies
- External relationships

1 Factors affecting organisational structure

The links between strategy and structure

The influences that have a bearing on organisational structure and design include:

- strategic objectives
- nature of the environment
- diversity
- future strategy
- technology
- people.

Explanation of these influences

- The organisation's strategic objectives – if co-ordination between specific parts of the organisation is of key importance then the structure should facilitate relationships between them.

- The nature of the environment in which the organisation is operating, now and in the future. Generally, product-based structures are more flexible and are more suitable in a dynamic or complex environment where organisations have to be adaptable.

- The diversity of the organisation – the needs of a multinational are different from those of a small company.

- The future strategy – for example, if a company may be making acquisitions in the future, then adopting a divisional structure now will make the acquired companies easier to assimilate.

- The technology available – IT has a significant impact on the structure, management and functioning of the organisation because of the effect it has on patterns of work, the formation and structure of groups, the nature of supervision and managerial roles. New technology has resulted in fewer management levels because it allows employees at clerical/operator level to take on a wider range of functions.

- The people within the organisation and their managerial skills.

Different structural types (functional, divisional, matrix) were studied in detail in paper F1 (or old syllabus 1.3). The key emphasis in P3 is matching structure with strategy.

TYPE	ADVANTAGES	DISADVANTAGES
Entrepreneurial	<ul><li>Quick flexible decisions</li><li>Goal congruence</li></ul>	<ul><li>Too slow for large companies</li><li>Lack of career structure for staff (demotivation)</li><li>Too many decisions for one person</li><li>Lack of specialism/ expertise in some areas</li></ul>
Functional (Bureaucratic)	<ul><li>Specialisation is efficient</li><li>Good career opportunities and extra responsibilities</li><li>Can cope with more products than entrepreneurial structure</li></ul>	<ul><li>Empire building</li><li>Conflict between functions (i.e. lack of goal congruence)</li><li>Problems if product base expands (people are too specialised)</li><li>Bureaucratic/ inflexible/slow to adapt</li><li>Lack of communication between functions</li></ul>

TYPE	ADVANTAGES	DISADVANTAGES
Divisional	• Decisions taken at point of action (so quicker/better) • Increased staff motivation • Senior management concentrate on overall strategy • Training ground for future top management • Flexible • Aids responsibility accounting (e.g. can separately appraise each division) • Can cope better with diversification than a functional structure	• Top management's level of control • Conflict between divisions e.g. transfer prices • Extra costs through repetition of functions e.g. marketing • Conflict over shared costs e.g. personnel • Lack of goal congruence • Can be harder to have consistent generic strategy
Matrix	• Customer has single point of contact • Customer can have bespoke service or product • Interfunctional communication enhanced • Staff motivation can be improved through variety of work and challenges • Very flexible (can easily react to changes in both the internal and external environments)	• Functional managers' expertise is 'diluted' – spread over many projects • Staff are serving two masters; conflict, role ambiguity, role overload • Time-consuming meetings and higher administrative costs

KAPLAN PUBLISHING

Functional advantages and disadvantages

Functional structure

Functional structures are usually found in smaller organisations, or within individual divisions in a larger organisation with a divisional structure.

Advantages

- Pooling of expertise, through the grouping of specialised tasks and staff.

- No duplication of functions and economies of scale.

- Senior managers are close to the operation of all functions.

- The facilitation of management and control of functional specialists (suited to centralised organisations).

Disadvantages

- 'Vertical' barriers between functions, that may affect work flow (creating co-ordination problems) and information flow (creating communication problems).

- Focuses on internal processes/inputs rather than outputs such as quality and customer satisfaction through a horizontal value chain.

- Struggles to cope with change, growth and diversification.

- Senior management may not have time to address strategic planning issues.

Illustration 1 – Example of a functional structure

An example of a functional structure.

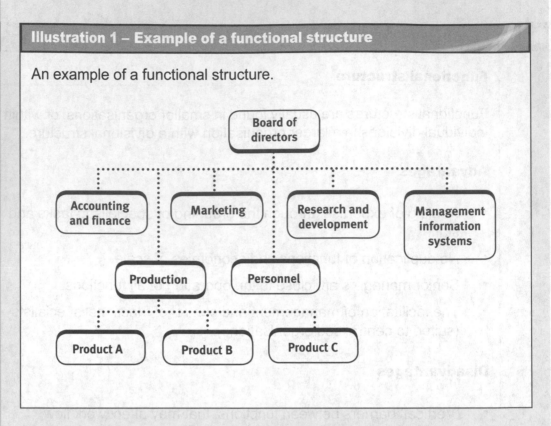

Divisional advantages and disadvantages

Divisional structures

Where the functionally structured business grows by diversification, a functional structure will be inappropriate, and the divisional structure based on products, services or geographical areas is likely to be adopted.

Advantages

- Flexibility – divisions can be closed or created to respond to changes in organisational strategy.

- Specialist expertise is built up relating to a particular product or market segment.

- Managers of divisions have a greater personal interest in the strategy for their own division.

- The enabling of performance management (and hence control) of businesses by head office from a distance.

Disadvantages

- High central management costs.
- Duplication of effort with all functions represented within divisions.
- Vertical barriers between divisions that may prevent information sharing and co-operation between divisions.
- Strategic management can be a complex hierarchical process.

Illustration 2 – Illustration of a divisional structure

Factors affecting organisational structure

Each division is responsible for its own functions in relation to a related group of products. Thus, each division may be regarded as a Strategic Business Unit (SBU). In this organisation:

- corporate strategic planning takes place at central board level
- divisional planning is concerned with developing a portfolio of products
- operational planning is at the functional level within divisions.

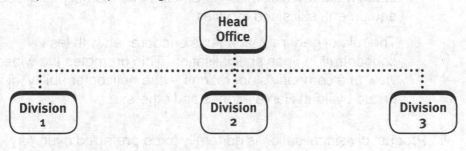

Different types of divisional structure

(1) Product divisions

In a multi-product organisation, such as Heinz (the food processing company), a product orientation is used as a modification of the functional structure. This structure establishes each product, or group of products, as an integrated unit within the framework of the company. The main functions of production, sales, people and finance are apportioned to the relative products, so that each product group could have its own specialist accounting personnel, technical, etc. Such an organisation allows considerable delegation by top management and clear profit accountability by division heads.

The advantages of product divisionalisation are as follows.

–   The focus of attention is on product performance and profitability. By placing the responsibility for product profitability at the division level, they are able to react and make decisions quickly on a day-to-day basis.

–   It encourages growth and diversity of products, for example, by adding additional flavours, sizes, etc. to capture other segments of the market. This, in turn, promotes the use of specialised equipment, skills and facilities.

–   The role of general manager is encouraged with less concentration upon specialisation. This promotes the wider view of a company's operations – 'the helicopter ability' highly prized by John Harvey-Jones and others.

Product divisionalisation is generally to be preferred over, say, geographic divisionalisation when the product is relatively complex and requires high-cost capital equipment, skilled operators and significant administrative costs. This is the situation in the car industry, farm machinery manufacture and electronics industry.

(2) **Geographical divisions**

With geographic divisionalisation, the enterprise is organised by regions or countries. The major international accountancy firms tend to follow this structure. A possible road transport company structure is outlined below:

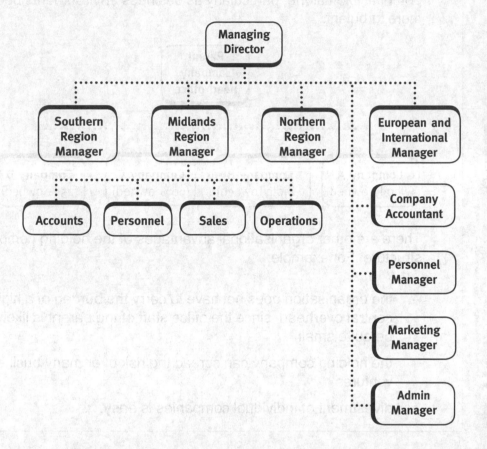

Carried to completion, the geographic division becomes a relatively complete administrative unit in itself. The geographic unit can itself be organised by function or product. The effect of the geographic division at company level is to draw a territorial boundary around these basic components.

(3) **Holding company structure**

The holding company (group) structure is a radical form of divisionalisation. Subsidiaries are separate legal entities. The holding company can be an organisation with a permanent investment or one that buys and sells businesses. In its most extreme form, a holding company is really an investment company. It may simply consist of shareholdings in a variety of individual, unconnected business operations over which it exercises little or no control.

An example of a holding company structure is shown below. Central corporate staff and services may be very limited. The essential differentiating feature for a holding company is the extent of the autonomy of the business units, particularly over strategic decisions. The advantages that a holding company can offer are based on the idea that the constituent businesses will operate to their best potential if left alone, particularly as business environments become more turbulent.

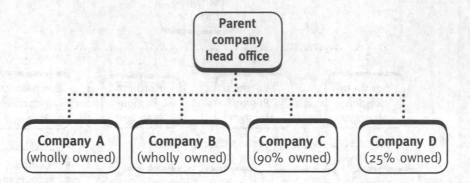

There are other organisational advantages of the holding company structure. For example:

- the organisation does not have to carry the burden of a high central overhead, since the office staff of the parent is likely to be quite small

- the holding company can spread the risk over many business ventures

- divestment of individual companies is easy.

Illustration 3 – Illustration of a matrix structure

Example of a matrix organisation

A multinational company produces three sets of product ranges (Product A, Product B and Product C) and sells the product in three geographical areas (Europe, USA and South America). The management of each product range is equally important, as is the responsiveness to the needs of the different geographical areas. The product managers and area managers have equal weight. Thus the manager of the USA area must liaise with the managers of Product A, B and C but does not have authority over them or vice versa.

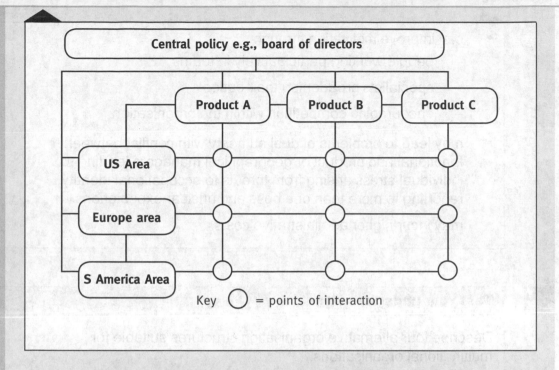

Key $\bigcirc$ = points of interaction

Matrix advantages and disadvantages

Matrix organisations

The matrix structure is a two-dimensional structure combining both a functional and divisional structure, for example product, service or geographical divisions and functional areas, in order to capitalise on combinations of expertise that exist in the organisation, but which are stifled by normal hierarchical structures. Matrix structures:

- organise horizontal groupings of individuals or units into teams that operationally deal with the strategic matter at hand

- are organic with open communications and flexible goals

- may be established as a permanent structure or be temporary to address a particular strategic commitment, such as an export research group to study international markets in a multi-product trading company might establish, or a unique product group for a limited-duration contract

- can creatively serve the needs of strategic change that otherwise might be constrained by more traditional structures

- retain functional economies and product, service or geographical co-ordination

- can improve motivation through:
  - people working participatively in teams
  - specialists broadening their outlook
  - encouraging competition within the organisation
- may lead to problems of dual authority with conflict between functional and product or geographical managers leading to individual stress arising from threats to occupational identity, reporting to more than one boss and unclear expectations
- may incur higher administrative costs.

Test your understanding 1

Describe four alternative organisation structures suitable for multinational organisations.

Centralisation v decentralisation

One factor in determining the flexibility of a structure is the level at which decisions are made. In centralised organisations the upper levels of an organisation's hierarchy retain the authority to take most decisions. The choice of organisation will depend to a certain extent on the size of the organisation and the scale of its activities, such that the functional structure is likely to be centralised, and the divisional structure is likely to be decentralised. Decentralisation:

- is more likely in large-scale organisations
- gives authority to make specific decisions to units and people at lower levels in the organisation's hierarchy
- allows front-line staff to respond flexibly to customer demands without reference upwards to senior management
- allows local management (of dispersed units) to respond flexibly to local market conditions without reference upwards to head office.

Advantages and disadvantages

Research shows that centralisation of strategic decisions and delegation of tactical and operating decisions can be very effective. Advantages of centralisation are:

- co-ordinated decisions and better management control, therefore less sub-optimising

- conformity with overall objectives – goal congruence is more likely to be achieved

- standardisation, e.g. variety reduction and rationalisation

- balance between functions, divisions, etc. – increased flexibility in use of resources

- economies of scale – general management, finance, purchasing, production, etc.

- top managers become better decision makers, because they have proven ability and they are more experienced

- speedier central decisions may be made in a crisis – delegation can be time-consuming.

There are a number of disadvantages.

- Those of lower rank experience reduced job satisfaction.

- Frequently, senior management do not possess sufficient knowledge of all organisational activities. Therefore, their ability to make decisions is narrowed and delegation becomes essential.

- Centralisation places stress and responsibility onto senior management.

- Subordinates experience restricted opportunity for career development toward senior management positions.

- Decisions often take considerable time. This restricts the flexibility of the organisation, as well as using valuable time. In addition, slower decision making impairs effective communication. Such communication problems may affect industrial relations.

2 Mintzberg's structural configurations

Building blocks and co-ordinating mechanisms

Mintzberg argues that the organisation structure exists to co-ordinate the activities of different individuals and work processes and that the nature of co-ordination changes with the increasing size of an organisation. He suggests that there are six main types of structure with configurations based on the following building blocks

- strategic apex – higher levels of management

- technostructure – provides technical input that is not part of the core activities

- operating core – members involved in producing goods and services

- middle line – middle and lower-level management

- support staff – support that is not part of the operating core

- ideology – beliefs and values.

Linking mechanisms

The detailed configuration of the organisation is also made up of linking (co-ordinating) mechanisms:

- a formally determined hierarchy of decision levels, power and responsibility

- a formal flow of information around the organisation

- an informal communication network, the 'grapevine'

- formal work constellations whereby sections of the organisation set up and operate formal co-ordinating mechanisms such as working parties and committees

- a system of ad hoc decision processes whereby the organisation responds in a particular manner when it faces a problem.

Mintzberg's configurations

	Environment	Internal factors	Key building block	Key co-ordinating mechanism
Simple structure	Simple/ dynamic	Small Young Simple tasks	Strategic apex	Direct supervision
Machine bureaucracy	Simple/static	Large Old Regulated tasks	Techno-structure	Standardisation of work
Professional bureaucracy	Complex/ static	Professional control Simple systems	Operating core	Standardisation of skills
Divisionalised	Simple/static Diverse	Very large Old Divisible tasks	Middle line	Standardisation of outputs
Adhocracy	Complex/ dynamic	Young Complex tasks	Operating core Support staff	Mutual adjustment
Missionary	Simple/static	Middle-aged Simple systems	Ideology	Standardisation of norms

Explanation

The importance and relative size of these building blocks will vary with organisations and the configuration chosen to support the organisation's strategies will depend of the mix of building block and co-ordinating mechanism. Mintzberg discusses six possible configurations, related to the environment, the type of work and the complexity of tasks facing the organisation. These are outlined below.

- Simple structure. The strategic apex, possibly consisting of a single owner-manager in a small business, exercises direct control over the operating core, and other functions are pared down to a minimum. There is little or no middle line, and technostructure and support staff are also absent. Co-ordination is achieved by direct supervision, so that this structure is flexible, and suited to dynamic environments.

- Machine bureaucracy, which arises from the power of the technostructure. The emphasis is on regulation: bureaucratic processes govern all activities within the organisation. This means that speedy reaction to change is impracticable, and this arrangement is best suited to simple, static environments.

- Professional bureaucracy, which arises from the predominance of the operating core. This type of structure commonly arises in organisations where many members of staff have a high degree of professional qualification (for example the medical staff in a hospital or the analysts and programmers in a software developer).

- Divisionalised form, which is characterised by a powerful middle line in which a large class of middle managers each takes charge of a more or less autonomous division. Depending on the extent of their autonomy, managers will be able to restrict interference from the strategic apex to a minimum.

- The 'adhocracy', a complex and disorderly structure in which procedures and processes are not formalised and core activities are carried out by project teams. This structure is suited to a complex and dynamic environment. There are two types of adhocracy:
  - operating adhocracy – innovates and solves problems directly on behalf of its clients. Admin work and operating work are blended together (consultancy firm, advertising agency)
  - administrative adhocracy – undertakes projects to serve itself, so it has its own operating core (research department, hi-tech companies)

- Missionary organisations, organisations formed on a basis of a common set of beliefs and values shared by all workers in the organisation. Firm belief in such norms implies an unwillingness to compromise or change, and this means that such organisations are only likely to prosper in simple, static environments.

Link between the structures and the building blocks

As the business and its structure grows, different building blocks develop and can become more important:

Building block	What they want	What they provide	Structure in which they dominate
Strategic apex	Direction	Supervision	Simple
Technostructure	Efficiency	Procedures and standards	Machine bureaucracy
Operating core	Proficiency	Expertise and skills	Professional bureaucracy
Middle line	Concentration	Focus and control	Divisional
Support staff	Learning	Help and training	

Example of the development of the blocks

In a simple structure there is unlikely to be any other blocks other than the strategic apex (probably a single entrepreneur or small management team) and the operating core. There will be little decentralisation and all of the power will focus on the strategic apex. The strategic apex will provide quick decision making and the operating core will have little power or involvement. There will be very few rules or controls on the strategic apex.

However, as the organisation grows it will require greater rules and controls. Standardised practices will appear. This will develop the technostructure. The technostructure might, for example, be the accounting function. They will create standard cost cards for production, they will impose limits on spending, they will implement checks and internal controls etc. This will be done in order to achieve standardisation of performance and output and to improve the efficiency of operations as tasks become repetitive. The strategic apex will delegate power to the technostructure who in turn will impose controls and limits of the strategic apex. In this way the technostructure becomes the key building block as the firm becomes a machine bureaucracy.

> As the business continues to grow and develop, further blocks will develop and some will begin to exert more control over the business than others.

Combining structures

Care should be taken when combining structures or imposing structures on new business units, as conflicts might arise between the different building blocks. For example, if a business with a machine bureaucracy (and therefore lots of rules, standardisation and controls) were to acquire an adhocracy (where the balance between the blocks is more even, and there is flexibility in the application of rules and controls), there may be difficulties both in achieving business objectives and in motivating staff.

3 Planning and control processes

Classification of control processes

Organisations and their strategies are managed and controlled by the formal and informal processes at work within them. There are a number of different possible processes, any or all of which may operate alongside one another. These processes may be:

- formal or informal
- focused on inputs or on outputs
- direct or indirect processes.

Classification of control processes

These processes may be:

- formal processes that are structured and documented
- informal
- focused on the control of resources, or inputs, such as finance or staff
- result-oriented, based on meeting targets or objectives, that is on outputs
- direct processes, formally monitoring and controlling inputs or outputs
- indirect processes, where the organisation's infrastructure such as hierarchies, relationships and culture are designed to produce certain behaviour in the organisation.

Illustration 4 – Planning and control processes

Formal control process

Examples of control processes include:

- 'all enquiries are to be processed within 48 hours of receipt'
- quality sampling to ensure process meets specification
- the budgeting process.

Generic control processes

A number of generic processes are used within organisations to ensure the strategy is delivered.

- **Direct supervision** – hands-on control of inputs by a small number of senior managers. This is typically found in small organisations, and is not possible in large or complex organisations.

- **Planning processes**, that also control inputs by monitoring their utilisation. This could include the standardisation of work processes, for example.

- Performance management using **targets based on key performance indicators**. In large organisations these targets are usually set by the centre based on required outputs. Management of business units is hands-off, or indirect, with business units allowed to achieve the targets in their own way.

- **Internal market processes** such as transfer pricing and the use of service level agreements between individual business units. This method is particularly common with services such as information technology.

- The **culture** of the organisation, where a culture is deliberately developed by means such as training and personal development in order to indirectly encourage behaviour required by the strategy. This may have an impact both on the use of inputs and the results. While this can be very effective, once established the culture may be difficult to change if new behaviour is required at a later date.

- **Self-control** by individual employees – where leadership and support frameworks are used to encourage individuals to work independently and use their initiative to produce particular results.

Planning processes

Organisations commonly manage strategy implementation through formal processes, using plans to control the deployment of resources. A particularly important process is the use of budgets to develop plans for the allocation and use of financial resources against which actual use is monitored.

Although they are designed to be fixed and clearly laid down, it is important that planning systems are flexible enough to allow for variations in the needs of different parts of the business and changing demands on departments and business units due to external or internal developments. For this reason bottom-up planning is used to allow business units to have an impact on the plans, generally by a process of negotiation with the centre, to reach a balance between the needs of individual units and those of the organisation as a whole.

There are several possible approaches to the development of plans and budgets.

- Centralised, top-down allocation of resources based on a particular formula, which may be combined with bottom-up planning to finalised resource plans.

- The use of computerised planning systems such as enterprise resource planning (ERP) systems that enable integrated management of all parts of the business.

- The implementation of standardised work processes such as quality management systems or through the use of IT systems designed to ensure processes are carried out in a particular way.

Illustration on planning and control processes

Production control processes

Control processes involved in production include:

- cost recording
- variance analysis
- lead times monitoring
- quality control inspections
- monitoring of rejection levels
- achievement of delivery times.

KAPLAN PUBLISHING

4 Managing international companies

Ansoff's matrix was discussed in Chapter 6 as a model for exploring directions for growth. In this section global strategies are considered and their implications for structure.

Reasons why companies pursue a strategy of international diversification

- There are increasing opportunities from global markets, either where products themselves are becoming global or where the organisation's customers operate on a global basis.

- If local markets are saturated or limited, it may be possible to sell products into new locations using existing skills and infrastructure.

- Risks may be spread as poor results in one market due to local economic conditions can be balanced against good conditions in another.

- It may be possible to take advantage of particular aspects of different locations and markets such as low labour costs.

Driving and restraining forces for international expansion

Driving forces:

- Technology
- Culture
- Market needs
- Cost
- Free markets
- Economic integration
- Peace/political stability
- Management vision
- Strategic intent
- Global strategy and action.

Restraining factors:

- Culture
- Market differences
- Cost
- National controls
- Nationalism
- War
- Management myopia/short-sightedness
- Organisation history
- Domestic focus.

Possible strategies for geographical diversification

- A multi-domestic strategy where products and services are tailored to individual countries and markets, with many activities specific to particular countries.

- A global strategy, where standard products are sold in different countries.

- A balance between the two above strategies, where products are largely global but have minor modifications to suit the requirements of individual countries. There will generally be a trade-off between scale economies and the need to tailor products or services to local markets.

The concept of globalisation

Globalisation, if it can be seen as a single concept at all, is a very complex one. The term provides a collective label for a whole series of trends and changes related to the significance of geography in shaping organisations and the interactions between them. For example, many local markets are globalising as their governments reduce import restrictions and tariffs, or as other countries re-open trade relationships. This not only means that goods and services become available from other parts of the world, but that the nature of competition changes from local to global, in turn affecting the way that local firms must operate in order to survive and thrive.

A somewhat different type of globalisation concerns the homogenising of tastes across geographies. Food, once highly local in style, has become more global in many respects. This is not simply what has been called the culinary imperialism of America being rolled out across the world via Coca-Cola and McDonalds. The changing economics of transportation and increased experience of foreign travel have enabled consumers to break away from largely national determinants of taste, and re-segment across countries on more individual lines. It is not that everyone is moving to a single global standard, but that shared tastes transcend national borders. Some consumers are moving towards a traditional Italian diet whether they live in London, Toronto or Stockholm, while others eat increasing quantities of Chinese style stir-fries, whether in New York, Adelaide or Madrid.

In this context globalisation simply means that geographic location is no longer the key determinant of behaviour.

Other forms of globalisation can also be distinguished. More and more firms have a presence in multiple locations across the world, rather than simply exporting from a home base. But, perhaps more importantly, as such firms seek to standardise approaches or gain purchasing economies, they increasingly demand co-ordinated, multi-country support from their suppliers. This requires the suppliers not only to be present in different parts of the world, but also to manage the relationships between their local units in new ways.

Multinational and global structures

The critical issue in deciding global structure is the extent to which local independence or responsiveness should take precedence over global co-ordination.

- The different types of multinational structure are shown in the diagram.

Local independence and responsiveness

	Low	High
Low	International divisions	International subsidiaries
Global co-ordination		
	Global products companies	Transnational corporations
High		

International divisions

- Here the home-based structure may be retained at first, whether functional or divisional, but the overseas interests are managed through a special international division.

- The international subsidiaries will draw on the products of the home company and gain advantage from this technology transfer.

- The disadvantage is a lack of local tailoring of products or technology.

- Such structures tend to work best where there is a wide geographical spread but quite closely related products.

International subsidiaries

- Are geographically based and operate independently by country.

- In these companies virtually all the management functions are nationally based, allowing for higher degrees of local responsiveness.

- The control of the parent company is likely to be dependent on some form of planning and reporting system and perhaps an ultimate veto over national strategies, but the extent of global co-ordination is likely to be low.

- The main problem lies in failing to achieve synergy between business units.

Global product companies

- Represent a move away from the international divisional or subsidiary structure to an integrated structure.

- Here the multinational is split into product divisions, which are then managed on an international basis.

- The logic of such an approach is that it should promote cost efficiency (particularly of production) on an international basis, and should provide enhanced transfer of resources (particularly technology) between geographical regions.

- The international development of many Japanese companies in electronics and car manufacture has been managed in this way.

- Research has shown that the theoretical benefits of the global product structure are not always realised. Although cost efficiency is improved, it does not appear that technology transfer is necessarily enhanced. Also, while the structure is well suited to promoting defensive or consolidation strategies, it does not seem to meet the expected benefits of better strategic planning and is not suited to the promotion of aggressive or expansionist strategies.

Transnational corporations

- Are matrix-like structures that attempt to combine the local responsiveness of the international subsidiary with the advantages of co-ordination found in global product companies.

- A major strength is in transferring knowledge across borders.

- The key lies in creating an integrated network of interdependent resources and capabilities.

Potential problems for transnational corporations

- Managers must be able and willing to work hard to simultaneously improve their specific focus (e.g. region, product, function) as well as looking at the global picture.

- The same control problems as found in matrices.

5 Boundaryless organisations

Organisations are working together, often as a network, more than ever before. Organisations often find themselves working more collaboratively with suppliers and customers as well as relying more heavily on the outsourcing of many business activities.

Boundaries created in traditional structures

Traditional structures are often seen as being bureaucratic and slow to react to change. The move to more collaborative structures (often referred to as boundaryless organisations) is a move towards welcoming and thriving on change. Traditional structures have clearly roles for those involved in the organisation as well as controls on their authority. These place barriers (or boundaries) on both employees and the organisation itself in terms of working together, making changes and working with those outside the organisation such as suppliers and customers.

The aim of a boundaryless organisation is to remove barriers to growth and change and ensure that employees, the organisation, customers and suppliers can collaborate, share ideas and identify the best way forward for the organisation. Typical boundaries found in organisations are:

- Vertical boundaries
- Horizontal boundaries
- External boundaries

More details

- Vertical boundaries: these are the levels of authority that exist within an organisation and the pathway through which decision making takes places. The more levels of authority that exist then the slower and more bureaucratic decision making becomes. It also limits communication and interaction between employees at different levels within the organisation. This could, for example, limit the ability to share ideas within the organisation. A boundaryless organisation will aim to have fewer levels of authority, more communication and interaction between all employees, and create a more collaborative decision making process. It often means that rank and role become much less important within the organisation. There is often a less formal management style, a greater desire to transform and improve staff, and a move towards a culture that embraces change more readily so that the organisation is better prepared for change (these ideas are explored further in later chapters).

- Horizontal boundaries: these are the boundaries that exist between functions in an organisation. Functions may follow their own goals rather than organisational goals and it may be that there is poor communication between employees who work within each function. The communication may be driven by bureaucracy and controls such as the budgeting system. In turn these may create cultural and knowledge boundaries – there may be different working methods in each function and it may well be that there is less sharing of knowledge that could create better performance in each function. For example, the sales function may understand well what types of components that customers would like to see in a finished product, but if this knowledge is not shared with the purchasing or production team then the organisation will underperform. To overcome these boundaries, boundaryless organisations will often have cross-functional teams, encourage staff to make secondments between departments, have more regular and quicker communications (e.g. by using more digital communications) as well as having better controls in place to ensure improved goal congruence. Areas such as knowledge management and redesigned job roles, explored elsewhere in the syllabus, can play a part in overcoming these boundaries.

- External boundaries: these are boundaries that exist between the organisation and the outside world, including customers and suppliers. These boundaries can affect the two way communications that are vital for an organisation's success. For example, it may well be that customers are not informed of what the organisation is planning or what new developments are taking place. Likewise, it may also mean that the organisation is not gathering information from customers that will require the organisation to change if it is to be successful. Similar problems can accrue if communications with suppliers are poor. Boundaryless organisations aim to collaborate with their customers and suppliers. For example, communications with customers can be improved through user contributions (reviews, expertise, feedback) and crowdsourcing (for example, asking motorists to phone in with reports of traffic hold ups). Information is provided through internet forums and regular electronic communications. Supplier collaboration is improved through systems such as e-procurement (explored later in the syllabus), strategic alliances and outsourcing.

There are three main types of boundaryless organisation:

- The hollow structure – where non-core activities are outsourced

- The modular structure – where some parts of product production are outsourced

- The virtual structure – where the organisation is made up of a collaboration of other organisational parts

Details in the types of structure

- Hollow structure: hollow organisations focus on their core competencies and outsource all other activities. Typically, processes such as human relations, information technology and event management are outsourced to a specialist provider. This leaves the company free to focus on what it considers to be its core value-adding activities. Critical to the success of this structure is the ability of the organisations to identify which core processes are critical to its mission, create a current or future competitive advantage and drive growth. It will also be important to align the suppliers' incentives and the company's strategic goals. The choice of supplier will be vital to the structure's success. As some processes become commoditised, these decisions become easier to take.

- Modular structure: modular organisations divide their product into manageable chunks and then order different parts from internal and external providers which the organisation then assembles into an overall finished product. For example, a cellular phone company might design the product and build the chip, the software and the built-in apps themselves, but then outsource the production of the glass, the chassis, the gyroscope etc. This can lead to a faster and improve production process as well as using market forces to drive down the production cost of each module of the product. It can also force internal production functions to become more efficient. Ultimately, it may well be that internal production can in turn production elements be sold externally. Samsung, for example, have made screens for other companies such as Apple and Sony.

- Virtual structure: virtual organisations rely heavily on information technology to link people, assets and ideas to form an (often temporary) organisation. Links are formed with external partners (which may be whole organisations, a part of an organisation or simply a team of experts) where each partner brings their own domain of expertise. This expertise is combined together to achieve common goals. A virtual organisation appears as a single entity from outside to its customers, but it is in fact a network of different organisational nodes created to respond to an exceptional, and often temporary, market opportunity. Over time, the parts (or members) of the virtual organisation might change. Once the market opportunity evaporates or is fully exploited, the virtual organisation either disbands or is absorbed into the larger organization.

  This is a way of responding quickly to the market without having to develop new areas of expertise or new production capacity, say. It makes use of valuable expertise that may exist outside the organisation.

As well as suffering from similar problems seen in other strategic alliances such as joint ventures (for example, in terms of the giving away of core knowledge or in the ability to find a common goal and agreement), virtual organisations require intensive communication to avoid duplicating effort. This is why information technology plays such an important role in these organisations.

Illustration 5 – A boundaryless organisation

Example of a successful network – Amazon

Amazon is now one of the best known on-line retailers. Amazon operates its website but relies on external book publishers and other suppliers, book warehouses, couriers and credit card companies to deliver the rest of the customer experience. These partners are also expected to provide Amazon with information on, for example, stock availability, delivery times, promotional material, etc. The customer feels that they are dealing with one organisation, not many. In addition, the Amazon Marketplace allows other organisations and individuals to sell their goods through the Amazon website, and its Associates system provides a means for others to earn referral fees by directing customers from their own website to Amazon products.

Test your understanding 2

What are likely to be the key advantages and disadvantages of a boundaryless organisation?

Outsourcing, offshoring, strategic alliances and the use of shared services can play a vital role in the success of a boundaryless organisation.

Outsourcing, strategic alliances and other types of networks

Outsourcing

Outsourcing plays a key role in the boundaryless organisation. It can be typically have the following advantages and disadvantages:

Advantages

- The main perceived benefit of outsourcing is reduced cost. Using external services can be much cheaper than employing in-house IT staff and not using them fully or efficiently.

- It is used to overcome skills shortages. For example, the IT function of the organisation may not have all the resources necessary to carry out the full range of activities required, or requirements of the organisation might not justify an in-house IT department, particularly in the areas of systems development. Facilities management specialists will have a larger pool of technical staff than the organisation.

- Outsourcing can bring flexibility. Using external providers allows an organisation to be flexible in its choice of services and it can buy in services as and when it needs them.

- It is argued that outsourcing allows organisations to focus on their core skills and activities where they have a clear competitive advantage, and sub-contract non-core activities. Outsourcing frees up management time, and allows management to concentrate on those areas of the business that are most critical. However, defining core activities can be problematic. Different definitions include the following activities:

  – activities critical to the performance of the organisation

  – activities that create current potential for profits and returns (or non-financial benefits, in the case of public sector organisations)

  – activities that will drive the future growth, innovation or rejuvenation of the organisation.

- Outsourcing is not without risks as there is no direct management control over the organisation providing the services.

Disadvantages

- Dependency on supplier for the quality of service provision. When a company cedes control to a single supplier, it becomes dependent on the quality of the supplier's skills, management, technology and service know-how.

- A risk of loss of confidentiality, particularly if the external supplier performs similar services for rival companies.

- Difficulties in agreeing and enforcing contract terms.

- The length of contract (the risk of being 'locked in').

- Lost in-house expertise and knowledge.

- A loss of competitive advantage (if the function being outsourced is a core competence, they must not be outsourced).

- Outsourcing might be seen by management as a way of off-loading problems onto someone else, rather than as a way of managing them constructively.

The notion of working 'in partnership', which is encouraged by vendors, is problematic. Firstly, it should be remembered that client organisations and vendors are usually both commercial organisations with separate statements of profit or loss and balance sheets, and different goals and objectives. While each organisation may wish for an effective and successful partnership, problems arise when the outsourcing company fails to realise the expectations of the client. A common example is the situation whereby the vendor imposes additional fees for work that was not in the original contract.

The client organisation should have a management team with responsibility for the oversight of the contract, to ensure that service levels are met and that any problems are resolved. Outsourcing can be a risky option, and it is essential that the risks should be properly controlled. Equally, the internal controls should be as effective with outsourcing as they would be if the function operated in-house.

Off-shoring is the outsourcing of a business process to another country. For example, Apple offshore the assembly of the iPhone to China because, even with transport delays, production is still quicker than having the unit assembled in the US. Off-shoring is another form of outsourcing. It is made easier when the destination country has the same language and skill base as the domestic country. But many organisations are reversing the trend (moving to in-shoring) as political and social pressure is building to protect domestic jobs.

Strategic alliances

Strategic alliances can take many forms, from loose informal agreements, partnerships and formal joint ventures to contracting out services to outside suppliers within a boundaryless organisation.

- Strategic alliances are co-operative business activities, formed by two or more separate organisations for strategic purposes.

- Ownership, operational responsibilities, financial risks and rewards are allocated to each member, while preserving their separate identity and autonomy.

- Strategic alliances are long-term collaborations bringing together the strengths of two or more organisations to achieve strategic goals.

- For example, IBM formed links with Ricoh for distribution of low-end computers. This allowed them to move into the Japanese market quickly, inexpensively and with a relatively high prospect for success.

- Alliances can also help result in improved access to information and technology.

- Some organisations form alliances to retain some of the innovation and flexibility that is characteristic of small companies. They are balancing bureaucracy and entrepreneurship by forming closer working relationships with other organisations.

- Strategic alliances may be used to extend an organisation's reach without increasing its size.

- Other alliances are motivated by the benefits associated with a global strategy, especially where the organisation lacks a key success factor for some market. This may be distribution, a brand name, a selling organisation, technology, R&D or manufacturing capability. To remedy this deficiency internally would often require excessive time and money.

Networks

Outsourcing and strategic alliances are examples of ways in which an organisation depends on relationships with other external organisations. There are a number of other important forms of networks:

- Networks of experts which come together for a particular project or purpose, either on a short or long-term basis.

- Teleworking, where individuals are based in different locations but work together through the use of information technology.

- One-stop-shops, where a group of organisations are co-ordinated centrally so that there is one contact point for the customer with the aim of providing a comprehensive and seamless service.

- Service networks, where the members of the network provide services to customers through any other members of the network.

Shared services

A shared service refers to the centralisation of a service (or services) that has previously been carried out remotely at each business unit. Common examples happen in areas of IT and accounting, but more recently organisations have created shared services for functions such as marketing, process redesign, property management and even content management (which simplifies the storage and security of company information).

Unlike systems such as outsourcing, shared services will still be carried out within the organisation and will not require the use of a third party external organisation. But the provision of the service will typically be moved to one location with fewer staff and a consolidated IT system.

Shared services go beyond a simple 'back officing' of common services. The shared service is typically treated as a separate and discrete business unit and its services are charged to other business units at arm's length prices. It will have its own targets to achieve and will be expected to produce continuous improvements.

Advantages

- There should be economies of scale on cost.

- The service can be benchmarked against external service providers.

- Efficiency can be improved (for example, a single IT system can be used and reduce the need for multiple systems that may have difficulty in communicating with each other).

- All talent and expertise in the service can be gathered in one place so that knowledge management within the organisation is improved.

- Shared services can also help remove organisational boundaries between business units. For example, there may be significant boundaries between one business unit that is a manufacturing company and another that is, say, another business unit that provides consultancy services. But these boundaries can be reduced and removed if the business units are sharing services such as marketing, management information systems, email systems, training etc.

Disadvantages

- There is likely to be initial resistance to change, especially as the move will often lead to redundancies across business units. But also because local business managers will lose control of a service that they may consider vital to their success.

- Creating appropriate targets for the service can be time consuming and difficult.

- There may be issues in determining the price that should be charged to business units for the use of the service.

The POPIT model (covered later in the syllabus) will play a key role in moving to a shared service system. Processes will have to change, there will be new consolidated technology required, the organisation will have to be re-organised and there will be a fundamental shift in the way that people work and manage.rt

Test your understanding 3

How important do you feel IT is to developing a virtual organisation?

6 Chapter summary

```
                          ┌─────────────────┐
                          │  Organisational │
                          │    structure    │
                          └─────────────────┘
```

Structures
- Entrepreneurial
- Machine bureaucracy
- Functional
  (Professional
  bureaucracy)
- Divisional
- Matrix/innovative
  adhocracy

**Mintzberg's
building blocks**
- Operating Core
- Strategic Apex
- Techno-structure
- Support Staff
- Ideology

**International
expansion**
- Provides growth
- Spreads risk
- Provides access to
  new resources
But:
- Hard to control
- Can dilute focus
- Must overcome
  barriers

**Boundaryless
organisation**
- Hollow structure:
  non core activities
  outsourced
- Modular structure:
  outsource parts of
  product production
- Virtual structure: all
  activities outsourced

Test your understanding answers

Test your understanding 1

The following organisational structures would be suitable for a multinational company.

- International divisional structure – this structure consists of a centralised parent company in one country and functions such as sales and marketing, production, distribution and research and development are established in the various countries where the company has divisions.

- Geographical structure – this structure follows on from the international divisional. In this instance the company is divided up into regions. The long-term strategic plan is formulated by headquarters; the short-term decisions/strategic plan are taken care of in the region. If the region is large, further sub-division may take place (e.g. by product).

- Product-based structure – here, the regions will not be based on geographical area but on products. The divisions are given responsibility for profits. The regions, although defined by products, may be split down into more manageable sub-divisions by geographical area.

- Matrix structure – this structure aims to balance product needs and geographical needs. Functional reporting may also be introduced making the structure more complicated.

Test your understanding 2

The key advantages of a boundaryless organisation are:

- Increased flexibility and ability to cope with change.

- Removes geographical barriers to productivity.

- Collaboration can bring specialisation and comparative and absolute advantages.

- More efficient communication between functions.

The key problems are:

- The organisation is only as strong as the weakest collaborator.

- Employee management and goal congruence can become more complex and difficult.

- Some boundary-spanning activities are still required (e.g. marketing).

Test your understanding 3

The idea of the virtual organisation emphasises:

- the decentralisation of control

- the creation of more flexible patterns of working

- a greater empowerment of the workforce

- the displacement of hierarchy by teamworking

- the development of a greater sense of collective responsibility

- the creation of more collaborative relationships among co-workers.

A key element in supporting the transformation is IT.

- This is mainly through the systems that facilitate co-ordination and communication, decision-making and the sharing of knowledge, skills and resources.

- Information systems can reduce the number of levels in an organisation by providing managers with information to manage and control larger numbers of workers spread over greater distances and by giving lower-level employees more decision-making authority. It is no longer necessary for these employees to work standard hours every day, nor work in an office or even the same country as their manager.

- With the emergence of global networks, team members can collaborate closely even from distant locations. Information technology permits tight co-ordination of geographically dispersed workers across time zones and cultures.

- Different companies can join together to provide goods and services.

Business process change

Chapter learning objectives

Upon completion of this chapter you will be able to:

- explain, for a given organisation, the part business process design can play/did play in an organisation's strategy

- apply Harmon's process-strategy matrix to a given organisation

- explain the commoditisation of business processes and the role of outsourcing

- recommend a business process redesign methodology for an organisation

- evaluate the effectiveness of a current organisational process and past attempts at redesign

- select, from a range of process redesign patterns, feasible options for improving an organisation's processes

- analyse information system requirements

- assess the advantages and disadvantages of package software

- describe how generic solutions can be selected, evaluated and implemented

- describe the relationship between business process redesign and generic software solutions.

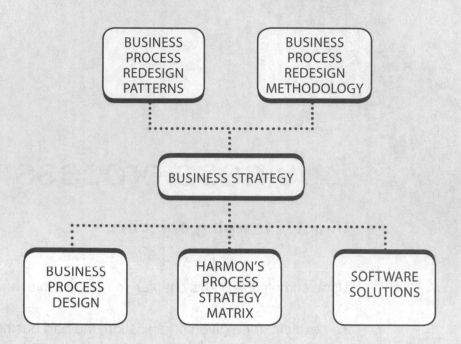

1 The role of process and process change initiatives

What is a business process?

At its most generic, a business process is any set of activities performed by a business that is initiated by an event, transforms information, materials or business commitments, and produces an output.

- Value chains and large-scale business processes produce outputs that are valued by external customers.

- Other processes generate outputs that are valued by 'internal' customers and other users.

More details

Processes typically:

- have customers, internal and external

- are independent of formal organisational structure

- may cross organisational boundaries

- should be linked to strategic objectives

- exist in a hierarchy.

Organisations rely on a range of core and support processes to create value for their customers.

- Every business has unique characteristics embedded in its core processes that help it achieve its goals and create competitive advantage.

- Strategic business processes, such as new product design or high-sensitivity customer care, provide unique and durable business advantages to organisations.

- Those processes that depend on people's intelligence, experience, knowledge, judgement and creativity are the hardest for rivals to duplicate.

Business process design and strategy

Every organisation wants to improve the way it does business in order to produce things more efficiently and/or to make greater profits. A change to a business process might lead to a competitive advantage or remove existing competitive disadvantages by either reducing costs or differentiating the business.

For example, if a bank can reduce its mortgage approval period from 10 days to 1 day, then this could allow the mortgage activity to stand out from rivals. In order to achieve this change the bank will have to redesign the approval process (for example, by changing job roles, using more efficient IT systems etc.).

In order to determine which processes should be redesigned for a potential competitive advantage we can use Harmon's process-strategy matrix.

More details on the link to strategy

Processes should contribute to the overall strategy of an organisation and the individual process goals should align with the strategic goals. For example, if the overall goal of the organisation is to become a quality leader in its respective market, process goals such as 'shortest execution time' may lead to counter-productive behaviour by process participants who receive incentives for finishing work fast – even if it does not meet the highest quality standards.

Alternatively, the investigation and potential re-design of the way processes take place within an organisation supports the lenses that Johnson, Scholes and Whittington termed, respectively, experience and ideas. An investigation of current processes might suggest that process goals and measures may not be aligned with strategy. This may be because the processes have diverged from their original specification or it may be because the strategy is not operationally feasible and the people undertaking the processes to implement it know this. Consequently, processes are often modified by employees and managers to make them workable and eventually, strategy is modified to accept this.

The re-design of processes may lead to incremental changes or it may lead to a significant strategic shift. Opportunities discovered while focusing on specific processes may have very significant repercussions for strategy.

Illustration 1 – Henry Ford

The role of process and change initiatives

In 1903 Henry Ford started the Ford Motor Company. He encouraged simplification, time studies and experimentation to identify the best way to perform a task. By organising the process as he did, Ford was able to sell cars at a modest price and pay his workers more than any other car workers. Ford's success is a great example of the power of business process change to revolutionise the economics of an industry.

Harmon's process-strategy matrix

According to Paul Harmon a process-strategy matrix is a matrix formed by an estimate of:

- the **strategic importance** of a process on the horizontal axis
- the process **complexity** and dynamics on the vertical axis.

This matrix can be used to determined how to manage individual processes.

	Strategic importance	
	Low	**High**
High	Outsource	Undertake process improvement
Low	Minimum effort	Automate

(Complexity — row axis label)

Further explanation on Harmon's matrix

	Strategic importance	
	Low	High
High	Complex processes but not part of company's core competency • outsource	Complex dynamic processes of high value and strategic importance. They provide competitive advantage • undertake process improvement effort that focuses on people
Low	Straightforward, static commodity processes • use automated ERP type of application and/or outsource • use minimum resources necessary for efficient functioning	Straightforward, static and valuable • automate to gain efficiency
	Must be done but adds little value to products or services	Very important to success, high value added to products or services

(Process complexity dynamics — row axis label)

Assuming that 'low' is positioned at the bottom left corner:

- processes that fall in the lower-left are of little complexity, do not change very often and do not have much strategic importance. They should be automated if possible and given the minimum resources necessary for efficient functioning

- processes that lie at the upper-right are complex, dynamic and of high strategic importance. These are usually the processes that provide the organisation with its competitive advantage and should be nurtured accordingly.

Illustration 2 – The role of process and change initiatives

Applying Harmon's process-strategy matrix to a children's bicycle manufacturer – Wheelies Co. The company manufactures bicycles which are then sold on to retailers for sale in their retail outlets. The management at Wheelies have identified the processes that need to be done.

- New product design.
- Negotiating partnership deals with other organisations.
- On-line purchasing.
- Stock control.
- Credit card approval.
- Bicycle assembly.
- Delivery – international.
- Funds investment.

Now they need to place them on the matrix by deciding how important and how complex the processes are:

		Strategic importance	
		Low	High
Process complexity	High	Delivery – international Funds investment	Negotiating partnership deals New product designs
	Low	Stock control Credit card approval	Bicycle assembly On-line purchasing

- New product designs and negotiating partnership deals are really important and complex – these are the likely candidates for analysing and redesigning.

- Bicycle assembly is not quite as important – the company should attempt to automate this as much as possible in order to speed up assembly time and reduce costs.

- On-line purchasing is important but routine – bespoke software could be used to ensure that this process is automated in a way that best suits the company's needs. Wheelies could perhaps look at linking the process to the IT systems of key customers in order to offer e-procurement opportunities (e-procurement is explored in detail in the next chapter).

- Stock control and credit approval both lack importance. They are likely to be routine and well understood – these processes can be left alone at present and no process improvements are likely to be needed in these areas.

- International delivery is complex but does not add much value, and funds investment is important but no one in the company has any expertise in that field – outsourcing these processes is a popular solution.

The commoditisation of business processes and outsourcing

Commoditisation is the evolutionary process that reduces all products and services to their lowest common denominator

- There is **comparability** between the firm's processes and the competences of outside suppliers.

- There is **standardisation** of processes making it easy to assess whether the process will be improved by outsourcing and to find appropriate outsource agents.

- The **costs** of outsourcing these services can be lower than the cost of providing them internally.

Advantages and disadvantages of BPO

Claimed advantages of business process outsourcing (BPO) include:

- Cost savings (currently the main decision-making factor).
- Improved customer care.
- Allows management to focus on core activities.

Problems seen to date include:

- as more processes become commoditised, it is more difficult for organisations to differentiate themselves from rivals
- problems finding a single supplier for complex processes, resulting in fragmentation
- firms are unwilling to outsource whole processes due to the strategic significance or security implications of certain elements
- inflexible contracts and other problems managing suppliers
- problems measuring performance
- data security.

Note: The "usual" pros/cons of outsourcing discussed under corporate strategy (explored in the previous chapter) – cost, quality, control, risk – still apply here.

Test your understanding 1

Assess which of the following processes is most suitable for outsourcing.

- Environmental reporting.
- Processing online customers' credit card purchases.
- Customer queries and complaints.

2 Improving the processes of an organisation

Process redesign, often called Business Process Re-engineering or Redesign (BPR), Business Process Management (BPM) or Business Process Improvement (BPI) takes a 'clean sheet' approach to the process, which is usually either broken, or so slow that it is no longer competitive in delivering the company's value to its customer.

Process redesign levels

When we analyse a process or redesign a process we ask:

- what the activity is contributing to the overall sub process or value chain to which it belongs?
- how can we determine whether the activity is actually achieving its purpose?

Looking at the business in terms of activities and processes opens up scope for challenging the ways in which things are done, and coming up with improvements, or sometimes more radical changes. The approach is often termed business process improvement or re-engineering, the latter referring to more radical rethinking. The term 'Business process redesign' is sometimes used as well.

The range (or levels) of opportunities includes the following:

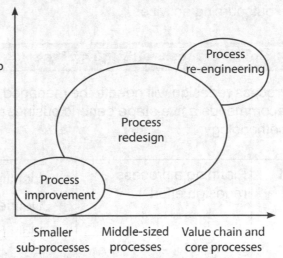

- if a process is relatively stable and the goal is to make incremental improvements, then the term 'process improvement' is used.

- at the other extreme if a major (core) process needs radical redesigning, then the term 'process re-engineering' is used.

- the term 'process redesign' is used for any processes that fall between these two extremes.

Typical problems and solutions

The key stages in a process redesign are to firstly identify problems in the process before then coming up with some relevant solutions. There are some typical issues to look out for:

Typical causes of problems in processes

- activities are unnecessary
- activities are in the wrong order
- activities are in the wrong swim lane
- activities are missing
- activities take too long.

Typical solutions in processes

- removing swim lanes
- removing unnecessary activities
- combining job roles
- combining activities

- reducing handovers between swim lanes
- changing the order of activities
- outsourcing activities.

Business process redesign methodology

Process redesign will need to be managed as a formal project. Harmon recommends a five-stage generic business process redesign methodology:

1	Planning a process redesign effort	<ul><li>Identify goals</li><li>Define scope</li><li>Identify personnel</li><li>Develop plan and schedule</li></ul>
2	Analysis of an existing process	<ul><li>Document workflow</li><li>Identify problems</li><li>Devise a general plan for the redesign</li></ul>
3	Design of a new or improved process	<ul><li>Explore alternatives and choose best redesign to achieve goals</li></ul>
4	Development of resources for an improved process	<ul><li>Make products better, easier to manufacture and maintain</li><li>Redesign managerial and supervisory jobs and develop measurement system to monitor new process</li><li>Redesign jobs, work environment and incentive systems; develop training; hire new employees if necessary</li></ul>
5	Managing the implementation of the new process	<ul><li>Integrate and test</li><li>Train employees, arrange management</li><li>Maintain process and modify as needed</li></ul>

This process can be summarised through the following diagram:

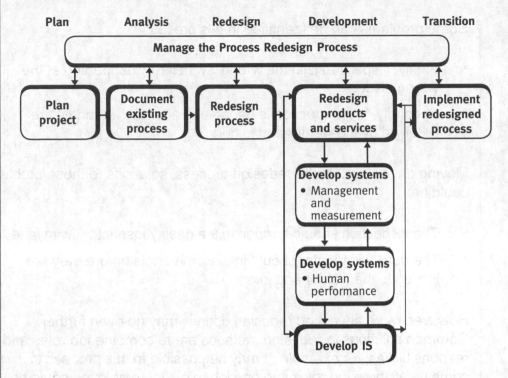

Major redesign projects are usually managed by a steering committee and undertaken by a team that represents all the functional managers involved in the change. Other key aspects of project management covered later in the syllabus will also be relevant here.

Illustration 3 – Business Process Redesign

Going back to our bicycle manufacturer – Wheelies Co.

Performing step 2 of the redesign process on one of the manufacturing processes shows the following existing process:

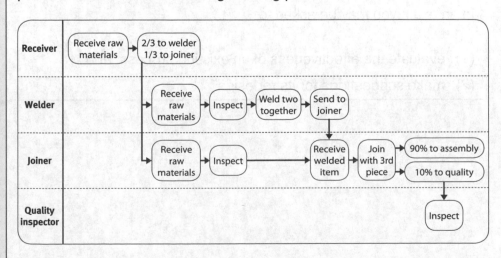

The process starts with three pieces of metal, two of which are welded together and then joined with the third.

Some problems can be identified in this process:

- Firstly, inspection is in the wrong 'swim lane'. happening at the wrong place.
- Secondly, the inspection is happening after the materials are received by the welder and joiner.

Moving on to step 3 in the redesign process, solutions to these problems could be:

- The inspection should happen in the quality inspector swim lane.
- The quality inspector should inspect materials before they are issued to the welder and joiner.

However, more advanced redesign options may go even further. Common solutions in redesign methods are to combine job roles and responsibilities, for example. It may be possible in this process to combine all three job roles into one job role. One employee could be trained to perform the welding, joining and inspecting of the parts. The receiving might also be made part of their role. In this way:

- staff costs are produced
- the process becomes more efficient
- there are less handovers between swim lanes – reducing time taken and the likelihood of errors.

Evaluating effectiveness of a business process

In an exam you may be asked to:

(1) evaluate the effectiveness of an existing process, and

(2) make suggestions for its redesign.

(1) Evaluating the effectiveness of an existing process

You may be given a diagram to analyse for this part of the question.

Diagrams are particularly useful to see who is responsible for what and it is also easy to start identifying potential inefficiencies and potential areas of improvement.

- Are there any gaps or steps missing?

- Is there duplication?

- Are there overlaps, where several people or teams perform the same task or activity?

- Are there activities that add no value?

(2) Process redesign solutions

Once the potential areas for improvement have been identified, the next step is to decide how to address the issues and make changes.

- Diagrams can also be used at this stage to map out the proposed process changes. In an exam, however, you will not be asked to create such diagrams.

- As with any proposed changes in the organisation, the pros and cons need to be analysed, and any changes that follow must be carefully planned.

Range of process redesign patterns

A process redesign pattern is an approach or solution that has often worked in the past. There are several patterns that have proved popular in redesign efforts. For example:

- Re-engineering – start with a clean sheet of paper and question all assumptions.

- Value-added analysis – try to eliminate all non-value-adding activities. Porter's value chain model covered in chapter 5 may be particularly useful here.

- Simplification – try to simplify the flow of the process, eliminating duplication and redundancy.

- Gaps and disconnects – a process redesign pattern that focuses on checking the handoffs between departments and functional groups in order to assure that flows across departmental lines are smooth and effective.

These options can be summarised in the following diagram.

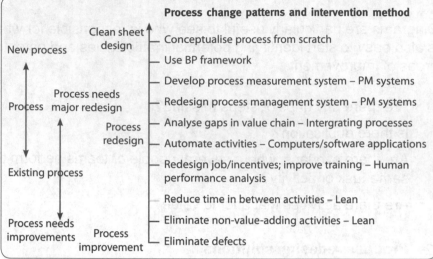

- Towards the left side, the kinds of problems companies face are outlined.

- In the middle, we show a continuum that ranges from Process Improvement to Clean Sheet Design.

- On the right, the ten popular patterns and interventions are shown, roughly aligned to the types of problems they are most commonly used to solve.

In a similar manner to strategy evaluation covered in chapter 6 (suitability, feasibility, acceptability), these redesign options need to be evaluated. Options are likely to have varying degrees of feasibility due to such factors as money, culture, effect of change, etc.

Project management

There are very strong links between process redesign and project management (covered in detail later in the syllabus). A process redesign is a type of project and many of the areas covered in project management such as developing the business case for the redesign, control the process when it is out of control and reviewing the success or failure of the redesign effort.

3 Software solutions

New software plays a key role in many redesign efforts. There are a number of areas to consider when buying new software:

- establishing what we need the software to do
- deciding between generic and bespoke solutions
- choosing a supplier of our chosen solution
- implementing the software solution

Establishing business information needs

Various methods are available for establishing business information needs, including the following:

Technique	Suitability
• Interviewing	• Standard technique for most scenarios.
• Written questions	• Where people are not available for interview.
• Questionnaires	• Where the user population is too large to interview • Generally unsuitable due to superficial nature of questions and lack of interaction.
• Observation	• Particularly useful if carried out before interviewing.
• Document analysis of existing processes	• Good source of design and analysis material.
• Workshops	• Useful for resolving conflicts and for new processes where high uncertainty exists.
• Protocol analysis – a mixture of interview and observation	• Ensures all aspects of the process are considered and none 'taken for granted' by users.
• Prototyping	• Where requirements are unclear. • Helps users reassess their desired functionality.

Using generic software solutions

There are various ways to produce a software solution.

- Purchase a standard ('generic') software package and:
  - use this without any modification
  - make suitable amendments to customise this for the organisation's specific requirements
  - add company specific modules as necessary.
- Pay for a bespoke system to be developed using existing hardware.

The advantages and disadvantages of generic solutions are as follows:

Advantages	Disadvantages
• They are generally cheaper to buy than bespoke solutions are to develop. • They are likely to be available almost immediately. • Any system bugs should have been discovered by the vendors before sale. • Good packages are likely to come with good training programs and excellent documentation and on-screen help facilities. • New updated versions of the software are likely to be available on a regular basis. • The experience of a great number of users with similar needs to those in the organisation has been incorporated into the design of the package. • Different packages will be available for different operating systems or data structures.	• They do not fit precisely the needs of the organisation – the users may need to compromise what they want with what is available. • The organisation is dependent upon an outside supplier for the maintenance of the software; many software suppliers are larger than most of their customers, and are therefore difficult to influence. • Different packages used by the organisation may have incompatible data structures. • Using the same packages as rival organisations removes the opportunity of using IS for competitive advantage.

Application packages can be altered and tailored to a buyer's requirements, but amendments to an existing package have to be paid for, and so add to the purchase cost of the software. In addition, an altered package may not accept the standard updates provided by the supplier.

Evaluating and selecting a generic software solution

In evaluating different options, both the software and the supplier need to be assessed.

Choosing software

In evaluating the software the following factors should be assessed as a minimum:

- whether the software will match the expected organisational and user **requirements**
- the level of **flexibility** in adapting the software as these requirements change
- the **competencies** of the organisation in using and exploiting the software
- the availability of **future** updates and ongoing support and maintenance
- the **compatibility** with existing hardware and software
- the provision of **training**, user manuals and/or online help
- the interface design and **user-friendliness** (referred to as the non-functional requirements)
- the **cost** of the software and the ease of implementation/transfer
- security and **controls** over access to the software

Choosing a supplier

Before tying the organisation into a particular supplier, the procurement manager should consider the following (as a minimum) for each prospective supplier:

- long-term **viability** (this could include obtaining records of financial performance and position)
- length of **time in business**
- **references** from previous customers
- **ethical** standards (this might include an assessment of the directors and any potential links to our own organisation)
- availability of **demonstrations**
- the ability to provide guarantees and **warranties** for non-compliance, later delivery, failure to meet functional and non-functional requirements etc.
- security and **controls**
- **copyright** (for bespoke solutions)

- **user base** (for generic solutions)

- **maintenance** and after-sales support

Evaluating a software purchase

There are many points to consider when evaluating possible purchases of application software. It is often useful to make out a checklist of the points that are most salient to the user. Some of the points that may be included on the checklist are:

How well the software fits the needs of the organisation.	This does not necessarily imply that every single requirement is satisfied – the users may be able to compromise, or to satisfy their information needs in some other way.
Can the software be tailored to fit the organisation's needs?	Sometimes packages can be modified by the supplier (at a cost) and, on other occasions, a package may have sufficient flexibility to allow the users to adapt it as required.
Other facilities.	Has the software any extra facilities that can be exploited by the organisation?
How well does the organisational structure fit in with the demands placed on it by the software?	The users should only acquire the software if no changes in structure are needed, or if any such changes will increase efficiency. A centralised system to help the sales force plan its calls efficiently would not be suitable where the sales people do not regularly visit the head office.
Will existing hardware need to be upgraded or replaced?	Many modern PC applications are very hungry for internal memory or hard disk space, and may not be capable of running on older machinery.
Is the software compatible with existing software and file structures?	A change to a new word processing package, for example, may require all existing documents to be converted to the new format. A supplier that is eager for business may well agree to carry out the conversion process.
Is the software compatible with the organisation's future requirements?	The users may be planning to migrate to a new operating system, which would make it necessary to acquire software compatible with the new operating environment.
Under what conditions is the software being supplied?	Extra payments may be payable each year; use of the software may be restricted to single machines; a site licence may be needed for use on more than one machine; use may be restricted to machines at a single location.

What protective measures has the supplier taken against unauthorised duplication?	Although suppliers are justified in protecting their software, the measures they take can sometimes cause operational problems. The user may be unable to take a back-up copy of the original disk that the software was supplied on. If the system becomes corrupted the user may have to obtain a replacement from the supplier. There may be a delay of several days before the system can be used again.
How fast does the system run?	The user will need to be assured that the system can cope with the volumes of data that will need to be processed and stored – some software that can look satisfactory when demonstrated by a salesperson can be unusable when asked to deal with volumes of data that are greater than it was designed for.
Can the software be adequately demonstrated?	The supplier is often able to show a special demonstration version of the software running. Sometimes a restricted version (or even a full version) of the software can be lent to the user for a period of time. Many suppliers make lists of existing customers. These can be visited to see the system running in a real situation. Seeing software running can give the user a 'feel' for how it works and can provide reassurance as to its suitability.
How user friendly is the software?	It must be both easy to use and tolerant to user error. Menus, graphical interfaces and clear prompts make the software easier to use, and attractive and uncluttered screen designs make the system enjoyable to use. One strategy used by software designers to make their products user-friendly is to mimic the look and feel of more familiar software. Microsoft Excel, for example, is often used as a pattern for other software – both spreadsheets and other types of software.
Documentation must be both comprehensive and comprehensible.	Documentation can be at several levels, ranging from brief reference cards, through easily understood user guides to system manuals that can act as a technical reference to specialist and experienced users.
How will the user acquire the expertise to run the system?	Most suppliers offer training, and both internal and external courses may be appropriate ways for users to learn how to operate the system. Well-known packages often have many experienced users who may already be employed or who can be hired in. On-screen and written tutorials allow users to learn at their own speed.

How wide is the customer base of the software?	The existence of a large number of customers provides several benefits. Most of the bugs in the software will have been identified and corrected. There is likely to be a reservoir of expertise that can be exploited by the user, and books may have been written and training courses developed. The user can be assured that they will get what they expect from the software.
Does the software have any security features?	User numbers, passwords and encryption are useful for protecting confidential data on all types of software, and are absolutely vital in multi-user and networked systems.
What sort of maintenance and after-sales service is offered?	Maintenance and after-sales service is just as important for software as it is for hardware. A maintenance fee will usually be payable for bespoke software just as it is for hardware. The availability of a help desk is very helpful to an organisation. Many suppliers charge a subscription for access to a help desk, and some suppliers charge for each call asking for advice. The existence of this kind of charge may be a disincentive towards buying a particular software package.
Are future versions of the software likely to become available?	Many software suppliers allow users to obtain updated versions of packages at advantageous rates. If an updated version is not bought, the users must assure themselves that the supplier will continue to support the older versions. The user can suffer disastrous problems if support is not kept up.
What is the cost of the software?	All aspects of cost must be included in the user's calculations – purchase price, site licences, maintenance, the cost of access to help, training costs, etc.

Procedure for choosing a supplier

Buying a software package leads to a long-term relationship between the supplier and the customer, so the latter must be comfortable with the supplier's credentials. The long-term commitment to an external supplier is very problematic in software supply, where moving formerly in-house applications to a new supplier can be technically difficult, expensive and disruptive. In general, there are significant risks associated with the long-term viability of software suppliers and the maintenance of software applications that are critical to the company. Companies go out of business and companies are sold. It is feasible that a software supplier might be bought by a competitor threatening long-term supply.

Therefore, a formal procedure should be in place for choosing a supplier and include elements such as:

- Produce a requirements listing and send this with an invitation to tender to a number of suppliers.

- Review the tender documents and make an initial selection of, say, three software packages.

- Obtain copies of those packages and test on the organisation's own computer system. Alternatively, the supplier may be asked to make a presentation to show why the purchasing company should use their particular package.

- Obtain user input and evaluation of each package.

- Obtain technical input and evaluation of each package to ensure it is compatible where applicable with existing hardware and software and provides the necessary processing capability.

- Test the package with test data from the organisation, paying particular reference to unusual items.

- Provide a final purchase recommendation, taking into account other factors such as after-sales service.

Solving problems in purchased software

If software is not fit for purpose then an organisation will often attempt to have the supplier of the software rectify the problems. This is often easier with bespoke solutions than for off-the-shelf packages, but even with off-the-shelf packages problems can be solved through:

- the provision of future updates,

- obtaining a tailored version of the software, or

- seeking a manual work-around.

Solving software problems with the supplier

It will be important that the software that is purchased meets the requirements defined by the organisation. As already explained there are some vital elements that must be achieved in order to obtain software that is fit for purpose:

- the 'purpose'; must be clear. It will be important that organisational and user requirements and competencies are clearly understood.

- the supplier must be carefully selected. It will be important to ensure competency from the supplier and that the purpose is clearly explained and understood.

- the product delivered must satisfy both functional and non-functional requirements of the organisation and the software users. Functional requirements relate to areas such as the ability to perform certain tasks, whereas non-functional requirements relate to elements such as user-friendliness.

When buying a bespoke package of software there should be contingencies (and possibly penalties) for the supplier to solve any problems in the software failing to meet communicated requirements. Note also that the long-term supplier risks are less with bespoke software, particularly if this development is undertaken in-house. The software program code belongs to the company (not the supplier) and its long-term development is under its control.

But this can be much more difficult to achieve with off-the-shelf software. If the off-the-shelf software fails to fulfil requirements there are at least three potential solutions to the problem, but each of these has disadvantages:

- to ask the software vendor to integrate these requirements into the next release of the package. However, even if the software vendor agrees, it may be a costly solution as well as allowing such innovations to become available to all users of the package.

- to ask the software vendor to build a tailored version of the application to fulfil specific requirements. This is likely to be expensive (so reducing the cost advantages of buying a package) and cause long-term maintenance problems and costs as the tailored version has to be integrated with new releases of the standard software package.

- to seek a manual work-around for the missing requirements. However, this may also be costly as well as reducing the business benefits which should have been obtained. Whichever approach is taken, it is likely to either reduce the benefits or increase the costs of adopting a software package solution.

Systems development risks

The development of new computer systems, designed and written for a specific user organisation, is a high-risk venture. It is widely recognised that many new purpose-written systems fail, for several reasons:

- They fail to satisfy the user's real requirements: the system was specified incorrectly.

- They do not provide the data processing or information for which they were designed, or to the quality expected.

- The system was therefore designed and programmed incorrectly.

- They cost much more to develop and run than expected. The system is therefore less efficient than expected.

Systems development controls

Controls should be built into the system development process to reduce these risks. These controls should be implemented at all stages of the systems development life cycle (SDLC). Examples of system development controls that can be put in place are as follows:

Control	Comments
Approval of an outline system specification by the user/IT steering committee.	The proposed system must be specified in terms of what it is expected to provide to the user, in terms of data processing and information quality, and should evaluate the expected costs and benefits. A system should not progress to detailed system design without formal authorisation. By giving formal approval to the system design, the user confirms the objectives of the system.
System designed in detail, using system design standards. The system is fully documented. A detailed system design is produced.	The documentation provides a source for checking in the event of problems with the system. By giving approval to the detailed system design, the user confirms that the programming work should begin.
Programs written using programming standards. All programs fully documented.	The documentation provides a source for checking in the event of problems with the system.
Systems and program testing.	The systems analysts and programmers should carry out their own tests on the programs and the system as a whole, to satisfy themselves that the system objectives have been met.
User testing.	Before the system 'goes live', it should be tested by the user. Before accepting the system for implementation, the user must be satisfied that it meets the planned objectives.

Development timetable and cost control.	The project development should be completed on time and within the budgeted cost. A management/project team should be given the responsibility for monitoring the progress of the project (e.g. using critical path analysis techniques) and its costs.
Control over implementation.	The implementation of the new system should be carefully planned and monitored. There are three methods of implementing a new system: • To introduce the system initially in one area or department, as a pilot test. Implement the system universally if the pilot test is successful, and after initial 'teething troubles' have been identified and resolved. • To introduce the new system by running it in parallel with the old system, until the new system is operating successfully. Parallel running can be expensive, because it involves running two systems at the same time. However, it should be less risky than an immediate changeover. • To make the changeover from old system to new system immediately and in full, without pilot testing or parallel running.
Monitoring the new system: audit of new systems.	A new system should be monitored, with a view to checking that it has been successful and has achieved its objectives. The success of a system should also be assessed in terms of: • user satisfaction levels and level of system use • actual costs and benefits.

Implementation

Implementing software solutions involves three key elements:

- data migration – transferring data from the old system to the new
- training – training staff on the new system
- changeover – introducing the new system to the business operations.

Data migration

It is vital to consider the stages that will be addressed during the migration process. Some of the stages include:

- Planning
- Data mapping
- Manual input
- Testing the solution
- Implementing the solution.

Stages in data migration

It is vital to consider the stages that will be addressed during the migration process. Some of the stages include:

- **Planning –** the organisation may need to create a Steering Committee that has representatives from a number of areas of the organisation including payroll, personnel, etc.; they may be from various levels, e.g. operational, tactical and strategic.

- **Data mapping –** this is the stage when the data is moved from one system into the field heading and file structures of the new system. An evaluation will need to take place of the structures within the new system and the existing computer system to ensure that the allocation for field headings is consistent.

- **Manual input –** there may be a requirement to enter some of the data manually from the old format to the new. This will require the organisation to consider the method of manual input as there are many issues with this type of transfer such as the type of input method, e.g. keyboard or scanner. The use of a keyboard, for example, greatly increases the chances of transposition errors that will reduce the quality of the input made.

- **Testing the solution –** there will need to be a period of testing after the conversion process to ensure that all of the data is accurate and that the system is running properly. A test environment will have to be created by the team to ensure that all the outputs from the tests made are accurate; this may include test plans and scripts for the conversion software.

- **Implementing the solution –** once the file conversion has been tested and accepted it can be run on the live data. Procedures will have to be specified to test that records are accurately converted.

Training

Training and a strategy for training are crucial. In order for this to be successful and resources not to be wasted it is vital that there is clarity about a number of issues. These are:

- Who needs to be trained and why.

- Whether training takes place on or off the job.

- Who will provide the training.

- If training should occur in a short period or be ongoing.

- What the line management involvement will be.

Methods of training

The chosen approach will depend on organisational structure, company policy and ethos. However, it is important that the approach is clear to the users.

The nature of training that users will require will vary dependent upon:

- User backgrounds.

- Purposes of the system.

- Features of the system.

- The kind of user interfaces – menus, graphics, speech, etc.

Methods of training

A number of alternative training methods are available to the organisation, but the most important factor to consider is that the type of training used is matched to the level of experience of the user. For example, it would not help an inexperienced user to be presented with a manual; to ensure success the user would need to receive first-hand information, probably in the form of a taught course. This will also help to improve the acceptance of the new system by the users.

- **External courses** – this is when the users go to the providers' premises to enable them to obtain the knowledge and the skills to use the new information system.

- **Internal courses** – the organisation runs a course in-house relating to the use of the information system. The course can be conducted by the internal training or IS department or an external provider may come into the company to teach the course.

- **Computer-based training** – as an alternative the staff may be trained using a software tutorial that is often supplied with the original software purchase. The tutorial can be quickly installed onto the PC.

Changeover techniques

- Parallel running.
- Direct changeover.
- Phased.

 Changeover techniques

- **Parallel running**

  This is when the new and the old system run side by side for a period of time, e.g. several weeks, until the analyst is satisfied with the operations of the new information system. It is known as the high-cost low-risk approach.

- **Direct changeover**

  This approach is when the old system immediately finishes and the new takes over; confidence will be high in the new information system. For example, the old finishes at 8.59.59 seconds and the new starts at 9.00.00 seconds. It is known as the high-risk low-cost approach.

- **Phased**

  This is when the new information system can be introduced part by part or stage by stage. This may be useful if the organisation is implementing an information system in a number of departments, as it will help to limit the impacts of the new system. It must be remembered that the phase can be either direct or parallel in each of the stages.

Test your understanding 2

You are responsible for implementing a payroll system for weekly paid employees, using a bought-in package on a stand-alone microcomputer system. There are 3,000 records (one for each employee) in the current manual system. Each record is held on a card. The information about each employee comprises personal details (personnel number, name, date of birth, grade, section, rate of pay, allowances, deductions from pay, etc.), held in the top section of the card. In the body of the card are held a series of line entries, one for each week of the year. As each week is worked the details are entered in the appropriate line: gross pay; tax and national insurance, by reference to the relevant tables; and net pay.

(a) Describe a procedure for transferring data from the manual to the computer to create the master file prior to going live on the new system.

(b) Specify the checks and controls to be incorporated into the process to ensure that the computerised master file is accurate, complete, up to date and suitable for running the live system.

Generic software solutions and business process redesign

Competitive advantage

Firms seek to redesign processes to increase their competitive edge. By using generic software packages they may be able to match the best practice of competitors who also use the software, but are less likely to outperform them.

Note: that there is a tension in the academic texts between those who believe that software packages define best practice (e.g. Davenport) and others (e.g. Harmon) who feel they represent average practice.

ERP-driven redesign

As opposed to the BPR approach explained in this chapter, the ERP (Enterprise Resource Planning) driven approach to software solutions occur in reverse order. In effect, businesses start with the solution and then modify processes.

Illustration 4

SAP, the main ERP vendor, provides comprehensive business maps (or 'process architectures') for different industries offering a wide range of modules covering the processes involved in that industry. For example, the insurance business map includes modules for claims notification, claims handling, claims accounting, etc. Clients can choose the modules they require and then specify how they wish to link them together and how they wish to control them. The ERP vendor will provide the underlying workflow engine that passes control from one process to the next.

It is still possible to follow traditional redesign efforts (for example, by applying Harmon's 5 step process), but, generally, companies tend to accommodate the way that they work around the application rather than the other way around.

It can be argued therefore that this approach may be more appropriate to processes that are not complex. When processes are complex, a fundamental redesign process (such as that illustrated in this chapter) should be used.

Illustration 5 – Nestlé USA

In 1997 Nestlé USA saw that its decentralised approach was causing problems. Operating companies were functioning independently of each other with little coordination. For example, companies were paying the same vendor 29 different prices for vanilla, with each company having a different coding and name for the vanilla.

Nestlé USA took the decision to standardise software systems using five SAP modules – purchasing, financials, sales and distribution, accounts payable and accounts receivable. In addition it would use a SAP supply-chain management module.

It was found that it was relatively easy to install the SAP modules but much harder to change business processes and to win the acceptance of staff.

Despite costing an estimated $200 million on the transition, Nestlé claims that the project has already paid for itself through:

- More accurate forecasting.
- Lower inventory and distribution costs.
- Other supply chain improvements.

Despite the success of the process, Jeri Dunn (Vice president and CIO of Nestlé USA) commented that if she had to do it again, she would reorder the project:

(1) Focus first on changing business processes.

(2) Achieve universal buy-in.

(3) Install software.

This feedback is typical of firms that rely on ERP applications to drive change. Organisations often see ERP applications the solution to their problems, rather than seeing them as tools which should be used in a wider project of process improvement or redesign.

4 Chapter summary

Redesign patterns
- Process improvement, e.g. eliminate defects
- Process redesign, e.g. automate activities
- Process re-engineering create process from scratch

Business process redesign
Five stages:
Plan, Analyse, Redesign, Development and Transition

BUSINESS STRATEGY

Business process design
- Process mapping
- Representation of who does what and in what order

Harmon's process-strategy matrix
Organises processes according to:
- process complexity dynamics
- strategic importance

SOFTWARE SOLUTIONS

Test your understanding answers

Test your understanding 1

Environmental reporting is likely to be complex and require great specialisation and depth of knowledge so would be difficult to outsource (except to an environmental reporting specialist?)

Processing credit card purchases is high-volume and repetitive so would appear to be ideal for outsourcing. However, issues of confidentiality and data security would need to be met first.

Dealing with customer queries requires detailed product knowledge, which might be lacking. Also there is a high risk of damaging the firm's reputation and goodwill if complaints are not handled sensitively. Many firms who used off-shore call centres to manage customer queries and complaints in the 1990s have since brought these services back in-house.

Test your understanding 2

(a) File conversion takes place during the last stages of systems development. Once the new system is in place then all data has to be transferred onto it. This process can take a considerable time when converting from a manual to a computerised system.

The way in which files are converted depends, to some extent, upon their size and complexity. In this case, there are 3,000 records for input onto a stand-alone microcomputer.

Assuming that there is only one input device, presumably a keyboard, the following sequence of events is likely to occur.

- The changeover will be thoroughly planned and a suitable time identified. In the scenario given, it would not be feasible to run any sort of parallel system and as the package being used is a bought-in package, then it will have been tried and tested and will be free from 'bugs'.

- Once a time has been chosen it is necessary to ensure that all the data held within the present system is accurate and up to date. Dead records should be removed from the system.

- The records will be in continuous use, therefore they will have to be entered in batches. Alternatively, all the cards could be photocopied and then entered onto the system.

- Initially, only the static data will be entered on the computer. This includes such data as name, address, personnel record number, etc. A record will be created for each employee containing all his or her personal static data.

- Once the static data has been entered then it will be a relatively easier task to enter the up-to-date variable information. This method avoids data becoming out of date before the system is in operation.

- Once all the data has been transferred to the computer, tests will be carried out using test data to ensure that the system is working correctly.

- Hard copies of all records would be printed out in order for employees to verify their record and also in order to comply with the terms of relevant Data Protection legislation.

- Amendments will be necessary from time to time, as in the case of changes in tax tables and national insurance rates. However, there should be standard programs within the package to facilitate amendment.

(b) Controls that would be incorporated into the process to ensure that the computerised master file is accurate, complete, up to date and suitable for running the live system would include the following.

- The controls exercised to check the completeness and accuracy of the existing manual system.

- The controls over the total number of records and the values imposed on certain key fields. Data entry should be controlled by use of a batch register to ensure that all records have been entered.

- Data should be validated by input programs to check correctness of input.

- Strict control should be exercised over any rejected records.

- Notes and records should be kept of any changes to the manual system prior to conversion.

- A check should be made by record once the data has been entered and this should be compared with the manual records.

- A full test run should be initiated in order to check the system's and operator's accuracy.

The role of information technology

Chapter learning objectives

Upon completion of this chapter you will be able to:

- describe, with examples, the meaning and use of e-business

- analyse how e-business can be delivered for organisations in general and describe what an organisation needs to deliver e-business and how this might help it to deliver a selected strategy

- advise on the hardware and software required by organisations who wish to follow and e-business strategy

- identify risks that exist from the increasing use of IT

- identify and assess controls that may be placed on an IT or accounting information system

- explain how It can be secured by businesses

- analyse, for a given business, the main elements of both the push and pull models of the supply chain

- describe the relationships between the supply chain, value chain and value network for both product-based and service-based organisations and discuss the use of IT and e-procurement in managing the supply chain

- assess the benefits and risks of an e-procurement process as well as attempts to redesign the downstream supply chain.

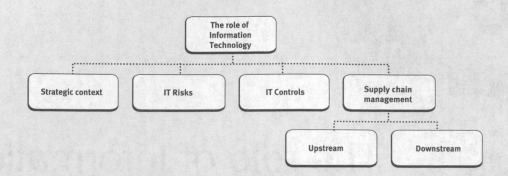

1 Information technology – the strategic context

Business strategy and information strategy

This section looks at information technology (IT) strategy in the context of the strategic planning tools met in earlier chapters.

IT is likely to permeate all elements of the strategic planning process. For example,

- as part of **strategic analysis** it can help provide strengths and strategic capabilities for a business or help it reduce the impact of threats coming, for example, from its competitive forces

Illustration 1 – Information technology – the strategic context

MP3 sound compression, the internet and fast broadband connections have forced companies like Sony and EMI to reassess their music retailing strategies. Technology is a threat to these companies.

IT and Porter's five forces

Management could use Porter's 5 Forces model to determine which of the forces poses a threat to the future success of the organisation. By ranking these threats in terms of intensity and immediacy, the most critical can then be considered in terms of how information technology or systems can be used to gain advantage or avoid disadvantage.

Threat of entry – new entrants into a market will bring extra capacity and intensify competition. The strength of the threat from new entrants will depend upon the strength of the barriers to entry and the likely response of existing competition to a new entrant. IT can have two possible roles to counteract the threat.

KAPLAN PUBLISHING

- *Defensively*, by creating barriers that new entrants to the market find difficult to overcome. IT can increase economies of scale by using computer-controlled production methods, requiring a similar investment in the technology of new entrants. Another defensive move is to colonise the distribution channels by tying customers and suppliers into the supply chain or the distribution chain. The harder the service is to emulate, the higher the barrier is for new entrants.

- *Offensively*, by breaking down the barriers to entry. An example is the use of telephone banking, which reduces the need to establish a branch network. Automated teller machines (ATMs) created new distribution channels enabling 'bank branches' to be set up in airports, out-of-town supermarkets and other areas where there are many potential customers. These machines provided not only expansion of the total market, but also a low-cost method of overcoming the barriers to entry in the areas where the cost of entry was high and space was at a premium.

Intensity of competitive rivalry – this is rivalry between firms making similar products, or offering the same services, and selling them in the same market. The most intense rivalry is where the business is more mature and the growth has slowed down.

IT can be used to compete. Cost leadership can be exploited by IT, for example, where IT is used to support just-in-time (JIT) systems. Alternatively, IT can be used as a collaborative venture, changing the basis of competition by setting up new communications networks and forming alliances with complementary organisations for the purpose of information sharing. When Thomson Holidays introduced its on-line reservation system into travel agents' offices, it changed the basis of competition, allowing customers to ask about holiday availability and special deals and book a holiday in one visit to the travel agent.

Threat of substitute products – this threat applies both between industries (e.g. rail travel with bus travel and private car) and within an industry (e.g. long-life milk as substitute for delivered fresh milk). In many cases IS themselves are the substitute product. Word-processing packages are a substitute for typewriters.

IT-based products can be used to imitate existing goods as in electronic keyboards and organs. In the case of computer games, IT has formed the basis of a new leisure industry.

Computer-aided design and computer-assisted manufacture (CAD/CAM) have helped competitors to bring innovative products to the market more quickly than in the past.

Interactive information systems add value by providing an extra service to an existing product. An example of this is provided by ICI's 'Counsellor', an expert system that advises farmers on disease control. It analyses data input by the farmer on areas such as crop varieties grown, soil type and previous history of disease and recommends fungicides or other suitable ICI products to solve the farmer's problems.

The threat from substitutes can be minimised by ensuring that an organisation develops a product before its rivals and then protects that product for a number of years by means of patents. This approach is widely used in the pharmaceutical and biotech industries where specialist software is now widely used in the drug discovery process, enabling drugs to be developed that target specific human and animal diseases.

Bargaining power of customers – the bargaining power of customers can be affected by using IT to create switching costs and 'lock' the buyer into products and services. The switching costs may be in both cash terms and operational inconvenience terms. For example, PCs run under Microsoft operating systems are not very efficient when using non-Microsoft application software.

Another form of locking customers in is to develop customer information systems that inform the organisation about the customer's behaviour, purchases and characteristics. This information enables the organisation to target customers in terms of direct marketing and other forms of incentive such as loyalty schemes, where methods of rewarding customer loyalty by giving them 'preferred customer' status are used. If a clothing retailer is launching a new collection it can offer its loyal customers a private viewing. Some airlines have deals such as frequent flyers and air miles as incentives.

The IT techniques at play here include 'data warehousing' – the collection and storage of large volumes of customer information on spending and purchasing patterns, social group, family make-up, etc. This then allows for 'data mining' – the extraction of relevant data from the warehouse as the source for target marketing drives. It was reported recently that Tesco, the UK's largest supermarket group, was mining its customer data to identify customers over the age of 60 who regularly purchased children's clothes, food and toys – possibly leading to a marketing push aimed at grandparents.

Bargaining power of suppliers – the bargaining power of suppliers, and hence their ability to charge higher prices, will be influenced by:

- the degree to which switching costs apply and substitutes are available

- the presence of one or two dominant suppliers controlling prices

- the products offered having a uniqueness of brand, technical performance or design not available elsewhere.

Reducing the suppliers' power to control the supply can erode this power. Where an organisation is dependent on components of a certain standard in a certain time, IT can provide a purchases database that enables easy scanning of prices from a number of suppliers. Suppliers' data can be shared so that the supplier and the organisation both benefit from performance improvements. The Ford Motor Company set up CAD links with its suppliers with the intention of reducing the costs of design specification and change. Both the time taken and the error rate were reduced because specifications did not have to be re-keyed into the suppliers' manufacturing tools.

Link to strategic analysis

Porter suggested three ways in which IT in general can affect the competitive environment and an organisation's ability to compete. Though these points apply to IT in general, they are particularly important when considering e-business.

- New businesses might become possible. For example, auction sites and photo-album sites.

- The industry structure can be changed. For example, in the music business it can be argued that the large CD publishers have less power because music can be self-published on the internet.

- IT can provide an organisation with competitive advantage by providing new ways of operating. For example, airlines save money by encouraging internet bookings.

- this in turn could lead to new **strategic choices**, and IT can, for example, support new competitive strategies

How IT can play a role in generic strategies

Porter identified three generic strategies for dealing with the competitive forces. The two basic strategies are overall cost leadership and differentiation. The third strategy – a focus strategy – concentrates on a particular segment of a product line or geographical market – a niche. If it is known which strategy an organisation is currently using to promote their products and/or services, it should be possible to define a role for IS to enhance that strategy.

- **Overall cost leadership** is about competing by offering products or services at low cost and value for money. The emphasis is on cost reduction. For example, driving down inventory levels, with the assistance of IT for supply chain planning and scheduling, can reduce costs. Sales forecasting software that can be fed into manufacturing resources planning applications can be used in shop floor planning and scheduling applications to increase efficiency.

- **Differentiation** is about showing that your product or service is different from those of your competitors through, e.g. brand image, customer service or design. A way of differentiating may be to make the ordering process as easy and flexible as possible. This can be done by providing on-line information services to identify the most appropriate product or service, followed up by a simple on-line ordering process. Where the differentiation is by customisation, CAD (computer-aided design) can reduce costs effectively.

- **Focus.** This strategy concentrates on a niche market, e.g. a particular buyer group, market, geographic area, segment or product line. The opportunities for IS/IT include providing access to customer information, trends and competitors so as to maximise competitive thrust and exclude competitors.

- finally, IT can play a role it putting **strategy into action**. For example, we have already seen in the previous chapter how IT can play a vital role in process redesign efforts.

Test your understanding 1

Foxtrot are a commercial property realtor who sell commercial properties on behalf of other businesses. Five years ago they experienced their fifth consecutive year of declining sales.

Analysis showed that one of the key reasons for this was the growth of rivals offering internet based alternative services. These services allowed prospective customers to choose a property that was for sale and view floor plans, planning authority permissions, internal videos and pictures etc. before having to visit the actual site. This was different to Foxtrot's business model which required prospective buyers to visit Foxtrot's office and the site that was for sale. At the other end of the market, Foxtrot lacked the economies of scale and cost efficiencies to provide a no frills service that had been successfully employed by some companies in the market.

Foxtrot took the decision that they needed to react to this changed environment. The company decided to do this by differentiating its service and focusing on executive properties. It aimed to introduce services that were not available from rivals. It aimed to have a website which allowed prospective buyers to not only do the things that they could do on rivals' sites, but they could also use elements of Computer Aided Design (CAD) to redesign interiors, try out different layouts and colour schemes and even add or remove virtual walls, doorways and non-supporting pillars.

In order to make this possible a significant investment was made in a new software system and a new e-business website. This investment allowed the business to differentiate itself from rivals. It turned out to be a very worthwhile investment for the business and over the last five years growth has returned and Foxtrot are in a position near the top of the market.

The company has now decided to move into the non-commercial market. It believes that the software that it has available to users on its website will help it stand out from other rivals selling or renting property to non-commercial customers.

Required:

Analyse the relationship between information technology and strategic planning using the context of Foxtrot to illustrate your analysis.

2 E-Business

The meaning and use of e-business

E-business has been defined as the transformation of key business processes through the use of internet technologies.

E-commerce is a subset of e-business. The most generic description of e-commerce is trading on the internet, buying and selling products and services online.

Categories of e-business

The categories of e-business functions are shown below:

		Delivery by	
		Business	Consumer
Exchange initiated by:	Business	B2B Business models, e.g. VerticalNet	B2C Business models, e.g. Amazon.com
	Consumer	C2B Business models, e.g. Priceline.com	C2C Business models, e.g. eBay.com

- B2B (business to business). For example, a supermarket IS system automatically placing orders into suppliers' IS systems.

- B2C (business to consumer). Selling over the internet – books, flights, music, etc.

- C2B (consumer to business). Some internet sites display a selection of suppliers' offerings from which the user can choose. A model that largely depends on the internet.

- C2C (consumer to consumer). Auction sites, such as ebay, putting consumers in touch with each other. Amazon does the same by offering second-hand books. This model largely depends on the internet.

- 'Buy side' e-commerce focuses on transactions between a purchasing organisation and its suppliers.

- 'Sell side' e-commerce focuses on transactions between a purchasing organisation and its customers.

The stages of e-business

The stages of e-business can be described as:

Stage		Characteristics
1	Web presence	Static or dynamic web-pages but no transactions are carried out. Would show information about the organisation, products, contact details, FAQs (Frequently Asked Questions). Faster updates are possible than with paper-based information and could be cheaper than paper-based catalogues.

2	E-commerce	Buying and selling transactions using e-commerce. Might cut out middlemen, but there is probably no fundamental change in the nature of the business.
3	Integrated e-commerce	Integrated e-commerce. For example, information can be gathered about each customer's buying habits. This can allow the organisation to target customers very precisely and to begin to predict demand.
4	E-business	E-business is now fundamental to the business strategy and may well determine the business strategy

This model helps businesses to understand where they are in the process of e-business, and this will help them to decide where to go next with further development.

Illustration 2 – E-business

In the book selling industry, small, independent second-hand or antiquarian book sellers might simply place themselves at stage 1 of the e-business cycle. They may simply use an internet site to explain the services they provide, the types of book they sell, their location etc. They are unlikely to use the site to actually buy or sell books (though they may do so as they get larger and therefore move onto stage 2 in the cycle).

Large national retailers, such as Barnes and Noble, WHSmth, Empik, Page One etc., have moved on to stage 2. They replicate offline sales via internet sites where customers can buy books at the same price as they can in stores and have these books delivered straight to their homes.

It is predicted that over the next few years some of these businesses might then move to stage 3 in the cycle. They will offer additional online content to supplement their offline or e-commerce sales. So there might be author interviews, deleted chapters, previews of new books etc. to provide a much rounder product and service. They also hope to capture more information about their customers so they can use this in e-marketing and Customer Relationship Management (both of these are explored in detail in the next chapter).

A business such as Amazon is at stage 4 of the cycle. The use of internet, e-commerce, e-marketing etc. are fundamental to how it operates and are the sole focus of its strategic plans for book selling.

Benefits of e-business

Most companies employ e-business to achieve the following:

- Cost reduction – e.g. lower overheads, cheaper procurement
- Increased revenue – e.g. online sales, better CRM
- Better information for control – e.g. monitoring website sales
- Increased visibility
- Enhanced customer service – e.g. via extranets
- Improved marketing – e.g. e-mailing customers with special offers
- Market penetration – e.g. even small suppliers can gain a global presence via the internet
- The combination of the above should be to enhance the company's competitive advantage

Barriers to e-business

Barriers to e-business can be seen in both the organisation itself and in its suppliers and customers. They include:

- technophobia
- security concerns
- set-up costs
- running costs
- limited opportunities to exploit e-business
- limited IT resources in house
- customers not likely to be interested in e-business.

Explanation of the barriers to e-business

- Technophobia. Senior managers are distrustful and sceptical about the alleged benefits of e-business
- Security concerns about hackers and electronic fraud
- Set-up costs. Simple, static pages are cheap to set up, but dynamic pages, linking to e-commerce systems and databases, with impressive design values are expensive to set up
- Running costs. Renting space on a web-server. Also, maintenance of websites is very important as most users are very unforgiving about out-of-date sites. Updating, say with special offers, is also needed to encourage return visits, perhaps linked to email campaigns

- Limited opportunities to exploit e-business. Some businesses (such as selling books) are more suitable for e-business than others (such as selling carpets)

- Limited IT resources in house (e.g. a lack of staff skills creating staff resistance) so recruitment is needed or all development and maintenance has to be sub-contracted

- Customers not likely to be interested in e-business (e.g. firms targeting retired pensioners).

E-business hardware

E-business infrastructure is the combination of hardware, software and content used to deliver e-business to both employees and customers. The quality of the hardware will have a direct link to the quality of the e-business offered. The hardware decisions that an organisation will face include areas such as:

- computers
- networks
- servers
- back-up

Alongside these decisions the organisation will also have to consider:

- the degree of outsourcing: the location and management of the hardware in terms of whether the hardware is located and managed internally or whether it is outsourced to third parties, and

- the degree of flexibility: whether the system will be able to cope as technology improves and employee and customer needs change.

More details on the hardware in an IT system

Some of the key elements of the hardware used in e-business is examined below.

Computers

There are three key elements of a computer that determine its speed and capability:

- the speed of the central processing unit (CPU),

- the amount of random access memory (RAM), and

- the ability of the graphics processing unit (GPU).

The CPU is the brains of the computer. The faster the CPU the quicker the computer can perform tasks and exchange signals with the RAM.

The more RAM that the computer has then the more tasks it can complete at once. This may be important, for example, if employees need to have more than one software application open at once such as a customer enquiry portal and an inventory portal.

The GPU are designed to rapidly manipulate and alter memory to accelerate the creation of images. The better the GPU then the quicker that the outcome of tasks can be displayed visually, for example.

Networks

In e-business, computers cannot stand alone. They need to be connected together so that users can share data and more easily and quickly communicate with each other. For internal, employee-only communication then a local area network (LAN) might suffice. This is where the computers are physically linked via wiring to each other. However, this will restrict access to those who are physically wired into the system and will make it very difficult to connect users over large distances.

Therefore, it is more common to use a wide area network (WAN) using internets, intranets and extranets that are connected through infrastructure provided by internet service providers (ISPs). These WANs allow very fast communication and transfer of data over large distances.

Servers

Servers are used to manage network traffic, share data in applications and store data (if necessary). The more CPU speed and RAM that the server has the greater number of users who can access the network at once and the quicker the network will work.

Because servers are providing and storing data for many users and applications they will need lots of RAM and physical storage space. They are typically the most powerful computer in the system. Many organisations will use what is known as a client-server model - this means that some data processing is performed locally (on the users computer, or client), but the most demanding tasks are handled by the more powerful server.

Back-up

The server holds a lot of vital information that is accessed and created by users. It will therefore be vital that this data is backed up regularly (and later in the chapter we consider how the data can be made physically secure and access to the data can be limited to the correct users).

Data will be stored on a hard disk and a typically server will have 5 hard disks working together in what is known as a RAID system. 2 disks hold and share the data with users and these 2 disks are then copied (or mirrored) regularly to 2 back-up disks. A fifth disk is ready to step into action if one of the other disks fail.

When users download data to their own client hard disk it can be used and changed. But it will only be backed up when it is copied back to the server so that the RAID system can mirror it. It is therefore better to store as much data as possible on the server than on local hard drives.

Intranets and extranets

Intranets are internal internets. They exist inside the organisation only, using website and browser technology to display information.

Commonly they contain:

- information about customers
- information about products
- information about competitors
- news/updates
- procedure manuals.

However, there's no reason why accounting information cannot be delivered over intranets.

Extranets are intranets that are connected to external intranets.

For example, a supplier could give customers access to their order processing system so that orders can be placed and tracked. It is when these types of external connection are made that e-business can begin to produce spectacular results.

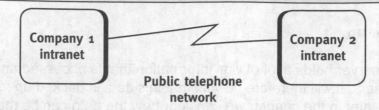

Other requirements needed to deliver an e-business strategy

Connection to the internet will not, of itself, deliver e-business. Suitable hardware, software and business processes have to be in place. Here are some examples of how e-business could affect various business areas.

Business area	Where e-business could impact	Strategic aim
Research and development	• Internet used for research purposes. • Access to research databases. • Access to patent databases.	To be a leader in innovation. To develop unique, differentiated products.
Design	Computer-aided design	Fast production of new designs and products. CAD will make designs cheaper (cost leading) and faster (differentiation)
Manufacturing/ service provision	Computer-aided manufacturing Just-in-time inventories	Flexible, low cost, but tailored to customers' requirements
Communication with customers	Website and email	
Inbound logistics	Organisation of the supply chain	Low cost, low inventory balances, flexible manufacturing
The buy side e-commerce transactions	Automating the purchases cycle	Low cost as less human intervention
Outbound logistics	Organisation of the distribution chain	Low cost, low inventory balances, fast delivery to customers.

| The sell side e-commerce transactions | Automating the sales cycle | Low cost as less human intervention. Greater accuracy |

Risks and benefits of internet and intranet use

Many organisations have intranet systems or use the Internet directly. Using an intranet or the Internet has obvious advantages, but also creates substantial risks.

The advantages of intranets and the Internet

- Employees have ready access to vast sources of external data that would not otherwise be available. Using external information can help to improve the quality of decision making.

- Organisations can advertise their goods and services on a website, and provide other information that helps to promote their image.

- Organisations can use the Internet to purchase goods or supplies, saving time and money. For example, the Internet is used regularly by businesses to purchase standard items such as stationery, and to reserve hotel rooms and purchase travel tickets.

- The Internet/intranet provides a means of operating an e-mail system. Communication by e-mail is fast and should remove the requirement for excessive quantities of paper. Using e-mails might also reduce the non-productive time spent by employees on the telephone.

- Intranets create the opportunity for more flexible organisation of work. For example, employees who are away from the office can access the organisation's IT systems and files through the Internet. Similarly, employees can work from their home but have full access to the organisation's systems.

The disadvantages of intranets and the internet

There are disadvantages with using intranets and the Internet.

- E-mail systems can become inefficient if too many messages are sent and users have to look through large amounts of 'junk mail' to find messages of value.

- E-mails can be disruptive, especially if a prompt appears on an individual's computer screen whenever a new message is received.

- Senders of e-mails often expect an immediate reply to their messages, and a delay in responding can create bad feelings and ill-will.

- Employees might waste too much time looking for information on the Internet, when the value of the information is not worth the time spent looking for it.

- Without suitable controls, employees might spend large amounts of time on the Internet or exchanging e-mails for their personal benefit, rather than in carrying out their work responsibilities.

The greatest problem with using intranets and the Internet, however, is the vulnerability of the organisation's IT systems to:

- unauthorised access by hackers, including industrial spies

- the import of viruses in attachments to e-mail messages and other malicious software.

Test your understanding 2

RBT manufactures tractors, harvesting machinery and similar farm equipment. It operates from one integrated office and factory near the capital of the country in which it is based. Due to restricted demand and the cost of manufacture of individual items, all equipment is manufactured to specific orders from clients. No inventories of finished goods are maintained although inventories of spare parts are available for sale.

The farm equipment is sold to farm owners by one of 20 sales representatives. The general procedure for making a sale is for the representative to visit the farm owner to discuss the owner's requirements. Basic price and model specification information are obtained from printed manuals that the representative carries. The representative then telephones the RBT office and confirms with production staff that the order can be made, checks the price and receives an estimated delivery date. An order confirmation is written out and the representative moves on to the next appointment. The farmer pays for the equipment on receipt.

As the country in which RBT operates is large, representatives cannot often visit RBT's office, so their price and model specification manuals may be out of date. The Board of RBT is considering the introduction of a new information system. Each representative will be given a portable PC. Information on such things as products and prices will be kept on an Intranet and downloaded by telephone line when needed by the representative. Access to production managers and sales representatives will also be made via the Intranet. The voice telephone system will be discontinued and e-mail is thought to be unnecessary.

KAPLAN PUBLISHING

Required:

(a) Evaluate the proposed use of the Intranet within the RBT Company showing whether it would provide an appropriate communication channel for the sales representatives. Suggest ways in which any problems you have identified with the new systems may be resolved.

(b) Identify and evaluate any information systems that can be used to provide clients with information on the progress of their orders with RBT while they are being manufactured.

Making websites interactive

One of the most effective things you can do with your website is to give users power over it. Give them choices, tools and features that encourage them to interact with the site and provide them with a sense of control over it.

- Search – Provide users with the ability to search your website for words, phrases and/or provide them with key topics from which to choose. Consider in what format the results are to be presented.

- Online forms – How many, number of fields in each, what needs to be verified before the user submits the form – e.g. have they completed the field for email address?

- 'Members only' section to the site – Is there a section that can only be accessed via a user name and password? Where are the user names and passwords to be stored? How will you handle people who forget their password?

- Interactive questionnaires/surveys/polls – How many, how long, how presented? What will you do with the information provided by the users?

- Animations – How can you (should you) use Flash or other programming devices to bring life into your site and illustrate products and services?

- Subscription email lists – What can users subscribe to by way of email lists, such as e-newsletters?

- Links to other sites – How many and what tools are to be employed during maintenance to check automatically on the veracity of the link?

- Downloadable files – PDFs, images, audio files – how many, in what format, with what restrictions?

- Contact Us – What contact details should be on the site – e.g. email, telephone, street address?

- Site map – What is the site map of the website to look like? Just text as links or is a diagram preferred?

- Text-only version of the site – Will you need a text-only version of the website for customers who are visually impaired or with a slow/expensive connection?

- Multilingual requirements – How many languages? How much of the site is to be multilingual? At what point are users to nominate which language they want to view the site in – e.g. home page, a splash page?

- Provision for printing and bookmarking (i.e. allowing users to store the website address in their browser's memory or 'favourites' section) – Are users to be able to bookmark specific pages or is the home page sufficient? Do you want any special print function other than the default function supplied by the browser?

3 Information Technology risks

Computer systems have unique risk and control issues that need to be addressed by business. As with any risk factor the company needs to make an assessment of the risks and decide on the appropriate level of control to reduce the risks to an acceptable level.

Risks to a computer system

A risk to a computer system could be anything that prevents the managers getting the information they need from the system at the time that they need it.

Risks to information processing facilities may arise from:

- Dissatisfied employees might deliberately modify or destroy information in the system.

- A hacker or industrial spy might break into the system.

- Viruses or malicious software could be introduced.

- Accidental mistakes could be made on input to the system.

- Inadequate security of the hardware or data.

- Faults in the hardware system.

Such risks result in the loss of information (or the loss of its integrity or confidentiality), business disruption and a loss of time and money.

Further detail on risks

Information security

Risks to information security can be categorised as follows:

Risks	Description
Risk of hardware theft	This risk might seem fairly obvious, but the theft of computer hardware is common.
Physical damage to hardware and computer media (disks, etc)	Physical damage can be caused by: • malicious damage • poor operating conditions causing damage to equipment and files • natural disasters, such as fire and flooding.
Damage to data	Data can be damaged by hackers into the system, viruses, program faults in the software and faults in the hardware or data storage media. Software, particularly purpose-written software, can become corrupted. Programs might be altered by a hacker or computer fraudster. Alternatively, a new version of a program might be written and introduced, but contain a serious error that results in the corruption or loss of data on file.
Operational mistakes	Unintentional mistakes can cause damage to data or loss of data; for example, using the wrong version of computer program, or the wrong version of a data file, or deleting data that is still of value.
Fraud and industrial espionage	This can lead to the loss of confidentiality of sensitive information, or the criminal creation of false data and false transactions, or the manipulation of data for personal gain.

Data protection legislation

Some countries give individuals the right to seek compensation against an organisation that holds personal data about them, if they suffer loss through the improper use of that data. In the UK, for example, rights are given to 'data subjects' by the Data Protection Act. There could be a risk that an organisation will improperly use or communicate personal data about individuals, in breach of the legislation.

Erroneous input

Many information systems, especially those based on transaction processing systems and with large volumes of input transactions, are vulnerable to mistakes in the input data.

- Some input items might be overlooked and omitted. Other transactions might be entered twice.

- There might be errors in the input data, particularly where the data is input by humans rather than by electronic data transfer. For example, in a system relying on input via keyboard and mouse, data accuracy depends on the ability of the operator to input the data without making a mistake.

Where input errors are high, the integrity of the data and information becomes doubtful.

Hacking

Hacking is the gaining of unauthorised access to a computer system. It might be a deliberate attempt to gain access to an organisation's systems and files, to obtain information or to alter data (perhaps fraudulently).

Once hackers have gained access to the system, there are several damaging options available to them. For example, they may:

- gain access to the file that holds all the user ID codes, passwords and authorisations

- discover the method used for generating/authorising passwords

- interfere with the access control system, to provide the hacker with open access to the system

- obtain information which is of potential use to a competitor organisation

- obtain, enter or alter data for a fraudulent purpose

- cause data corruption by the introduction of unauthorised computer programs and processing on to the system (computer viruses)

- alter or delete files.

Viruses

A virus is a piece of software that seeks to infest a computer system, hiding and automatically spreading to other systems if given the opportunity. Most computer viruses have three functions – avoiding detection, reproducing themselves and causing damage. Viruses might be introduced into a computer system directly, or by disk or e-mail attachment.

Viruses include:

- trojans – whilst carrying on one program, secretly carry on another
- worms – these replicate themselves within the systems
- trap doors – undocumented entry points to systems allowing normal controls to be by-passed
- logic bombs – triggered on the occurrence of a certain event
- time bombs – which are triggered on a certain date.

4 Controls in an information systems environment

To combat the types of risks discussed above companies will put in place control procedures. These must be assessed for cost effectiveness and should reduce risk to an acceptable level.

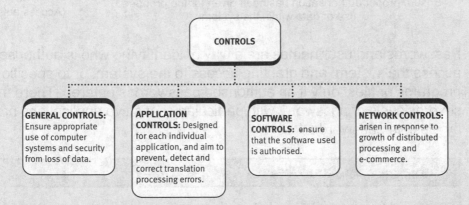

Alternative control classification

There are a number of different ways in which controls can be classified in an IT environment.

An alternative to the classification described above is:

- **Security controls:** controls designed to ensure the prevention of unauthorised access, modification or destruction of stored data.

- **Integrity controls:** controls to ensure that the data are accurate, consistent and free from accidental corruption.

- **Contingency controls:** in the event that security or integrity controls fail there must be a back-up facility and a contingency plan to restore business operations as quickly as possible.

General controls

Personnel controls

Recruitment, training and supervision needs to be in place to ensure the competency of those responsible for programming and data entry.

Logical access controls

Security over access is often based on a logical access system. This is illustrated by the following diagram:

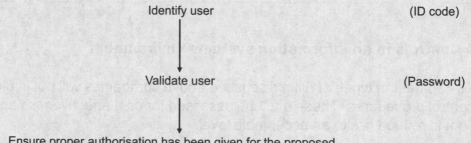

Passwords and user names are a way of identifying who is authorised to access the system, and granting access to the system, or to specific programs or files, only if an authorised password is entered. There may be several levels of password, with particularly sensitive applications protected by multiple passwords.

Problems with passwords

Password systems can only be effective if users use them conscientiously. There are several inherent problems with a password system:

- Authorised users may divulge their password to a colleague.

- Many passwords may have associations with the user so that a hacker can discover them by experimentation.

- Passwords are often written down close to the computer (e.g. pinned to the notice board inside the office) and so easily discovered.

KAPLAN PUBLISHING

To protect passwords and user numbers against discovery, a number of precautions should be adopted:

- Users should be required to change their passwords regularly.

- Passwords should be memorable but not obviously related to a user's private life.

- Users should be encouraged never to write down their passwords.

- There should be strict controls over passwords – they should never be 'lent' or written down where they can be easily seen.

- There should be automatic sentinel or watchdog programs to identify when a password has been keyed incorrectly.

Access logging

The system will produce regular reports including a system access report and various pre-determined exception reports. The effectiveness of these reports is determined by:

- The frequency of report production.
- The follow up of detected breaches in security.

Audit trail

An audit trail consists of a record or series of records that allows the processing of a transaction or an amendment by a computer or clerical system to be identified accurately, as well as verifying the authenticity of the transaction or amendment, including the identity of the individuals who initiated and authorised it.

Audit trails are also used to record customer activity in e-commerce on a company's website. The audit trail records the customer's initial access to the website, and then each subsequent activity (purchasing and payment, confirmation of order and delivery of the product). The audit trail can be used to deal with any subsequent enquiry or complaint from the customer. In some cases, 'audit trails' can be used to track down hackers into a system. A hacker might sometimes unknowingly leave a trail of where he came from, for example through records in the activity log of the hacker's Internet service provider.

Facility controls

Physical access

There are various basic categories of controlling access to sensitive areas. These include:

- security guards in buildings

- working areas to which access is through a locked door or a door with an ID card entry system or entry system requiring the user to enter a personal identification code (PIN number)

- using safes and lockable filing cabinets

- closed circuit TV used to monitor what is happening in a particular part of a building – this may be backed up by security video cameras

- doors automatically locked in the event of a security alarm.

Additionally, procedural controls to protect files and output include:

- disks should not be left lying around on desks and working surfaces

- computer printout and disks should be shredded or otherwise destroyed before being thrown away.

Location of IT facilities

It is imperative that the location of the system is considered, and hence all equipment is located so as to protect against:

- Fire

- Flood

- Smoke

- Food

- Drinks

- Power failure

- Environment.

Business continuity

Business continuity planning (**disaster recovery planning**) takes place in order to recover information systems from business critical events after they have happened. It involves:

- Making a risk assessment
- Developing a contingency plan to address those risks.

More on disaster recovery plans

An unexpected disaster can put an entire computer system out of action. For large organisations, a disaster might involve damage from a terrorist attack. There could also be threats from fire and flood damage. A disaster might simply be a software or hardware breakdown within a system.

Disaster recovery planning involves assessing what disasters might occur that would pose a serious threat to the organisation, and trying to ensure that alternative arrangements are available in the event that a disaster occurs.

In the case of a computer system for a clearing bank, this would mean having an entire back-up computer system in place that could be brought into operation if a disaster puts the main system out of action.

Not all organisations have extensive disaster recovery plans. Certainly, however, back-up copies of major data files should be kept, so that in the event that the main files are destroyed, the data can be re-created with the back-up files.

System back-ups

All files containing important information should be backed up on a regular basis. Backing up provides protection against the loss or corruption of data due to:

- faults in the hardware (e.g. hard disk)
- the accidental deletion of a file by a computer operator
- damage to a data file by a hacker.

A back-up is simply a copy of the file. If the original file is lost or becomes corrupt, the back-up can be substituted in its place, and the master file can be re-created.

There will be some loss of data if the input to the system since the most recent back-up copy of the file was made.

- However, if back-ups are made regularly, the loss of data should be limited. If there are paper records of input transactions since the most recent back-up copy was made, the file can be brought up to date by re-inputting the data.

- Some systems provide back-up copies of both master files and transaction data files, and copies of these files can be used to re-create an up-to-date master file if the original master file is lost or corrupted.

Back-up copies might be stored on the same physical computer file as the original file, but this is risky, since damage to the physical file will result in the loss of the back-up as well as the main file.

Back-up files might be created by copying them on to a disk or tape. Where security is important, any such back-up copies should be held in a secure place, such as a safe.

To counter the risk of damage to a file due to a fire or similar disaster at the premises where the IT system is located, a back-up copy might be taken off-site and held somewhere else.

Application controls

These are controls to ensure that data are correctly input, processed and correctly maintained, and only distributed to authorised personnel.

Application controls are specific to each application, but can be grouped as follows:

Input controls:

- Checking and authorising source documents manually.
- The use of batch controls.
- Pre-numbered forms.

Processing controls:

- Computer verification and validation checks.
- Error detection controls such as
  - control totals
  - balancing.

Output controls:

- Monitoring of control logs.
- Physical checking of output.

More on input controls

Some controls over the completeness and accuracy of the data to the system can be written into the system design as controls by the program.

Software controls might be applied to:

- ensure the completeness of input data
- improve the accuracy/correctness of input data.

Controls over the completeness of input. This is only possible if there is a way of checking how many transactions should be processed, or whether a transaction has been omitted. Within accounting systems, examples of completeness checks might be:

- in a payroll system, checking that the number of payroll transactions processed is exactly equal to the number of employees on the payroll file

- in a sales invoicing system, where all invoices are numbered sequentially, to ensure that no invoices have been omitted from processing. (Altering an invoice should be dealt with by raising a credit note to reverse the original invoice and issuing a new invoice.)

Controls over the accuracy of data input:

Controls over the accuracy of data. In computer systems, a combination of two techniques are used to ensure that data is accurate:

Data validation checks

Software validation checks might be written into the software to identify logical errors in the input. Commonly used checks are:

- Presence checks: this will ensure that there is data inputted into the correct area. For example, it may check that a name has been entered into the authorisation area and flag up when no area has been left blank. User websites will often do this by flagging up missing areas with a red warning signs and placing an asterisk beside elements that cannot be left blank. This is often referred to as form level validation, where fields marked as mandatory on, say, a web form must be filled in before a user can proceed to the next or final part of the form.

- Existence checks: if a particular item of data must have a code 1, 2 or 3, a data validation check can be carried out on the input to make sure that the value entered is 1, 2 or 3, and if any other value is entered, the input will not be accepted.

- Length checks: this checks the data isn't too short or too long For example, when asked to enter a password into the system it will ensure that it is, say, eight characters long.

- Format checks: this checks that the data is in the correct format. For example, it will check that a password has at least one number and one capital, or check that sales invoices have, say, three letters followed by six numbers if that is the format normally prescribed for sales invoices.

- Type checks: this checks that data is of the correct type. For example, it will ensure that only numbers are entered for sales invoice values and provide a warning if letters are entered instead.

- Reasonableness check or range check: this is a logical check to ensure that the value of an item input to the system is a reasonable value. For example, a system might carry out a reasonableness check that the value of a sales order is not in excess of, say, $50,000.

- Check digit verification: some codes used in a computer system, such as customer identity codes or inventory codes, include a check digit. A check digit allows the program to check that the entire code is valid, and that there is no error in the input digits for the code.

- Spell checks: words are checked against a dictionary. This may be used in word processed variance reports, say, to ensure that there are no spelling errors. Unusual but regularly used words (such as client or manager names) can be added to the dictionary so that misspellings can be highlighted.

- Matching or look-up checks: this ensures that data matches previously entered data or data from an approved acceptable list. For example, a matching test is often applied on user websites when creating a new account; users are often asked to input a new password twice and the software checks that the two passwords match. Or when entering the name of an authoriser of a transaction, the software might look up the name entered against a list of people who can validly authorise this transaction.

KAPLAN PUBLISHING

- Controls over the authorisation of input: manual controls include requiring the signature of an authorised individual on the authorisation document (e.g. a document giving approval to make a payment). Within a computer system, authorisation is granted by the input of an appropriate user name/password.

It is important to understand that some checks are more powerful than others. For example, presence checks or length checks will simply ensure that the data is present or is of the correct length. But they will not check that the data makes any sense or is consistent with expectations. Likewise, a range check is likely to be more powerful than a type check or format check. A type check will ensure that, say, an inputted credit limit only contains numbers, but a range check will ensure that these numbers are within a reasonable range of acceptable organisational values.

For this reason checks will often be used in conjunction with each other. For example, when asked to create a new password checks will often be made to ensure that a password is present, that it exceeds a certain length, that it has the correct format, that there is the existence of, say, numbers and letters and that it has been matched by being entered twice.

Data verification

Validation checks will ensure that data is valid but it may still contain errors. For example, if a sale was made for $300 but was recorded in the computer system as $200, many of the validation checks above would spot this error (the figure entered is still of the correct format and length and is likely to still be within a valid range). A verification check ensures that data is correctly transferred into a computer from the medium that it was originally stored on. Verification checks are usually used to check that information written on a data collection form has been correctly typed into a computer by a data entry worker. Controls over the accuracy of data have increased in importance since the growth of user input into websites in order to trigger transactions.

The two most common methods of data verification are:

- Confirmation checks: In this instance the user is asked to confirm data before proceeding. Typically, after a user has entered some data into the system the data is redisplayed on the screen. The user is then prompted to read the data and confirm that it has been entered correctly before proceeding. This allows the user to identify and correct errors before any data is output. This type of check is a very common check in payment systems where buyers are asked to confirm the data before finalising an order.

- Matching checks: just as this can work as a validation test it can also be used as a verification test. Passwords entered, for example, could be checked against those stored on a database. Or, as seen earlier, the password could be verified by asking for it to be input twice. In some organisations, this check can be extended to a dual input test whereby the data to be entered is typed in twice by two different operators. The two copies of the data are then compared. Any differences are detected. The operators will be prompted to retype the sections that differ until both copies agree. When the two copies agree it is assumed by the computer that the data has been entered correctly.

Accounting system controls

For an IT system used in the management and preparation of the accounting information for the organisation, it will be important to ensure that the accounting system is following the expected rules that have been established for the business.

Example business rules

For example, the organisation may have set credit limits for particular customers, or it may require that purchase orders are approved by a pre-determined member(s) of staff. In a manual accounting system these rules are often easy to apply. But in computerised accounting system confidence needs to be gained that these rules are being applied properly.

One way to achieve this is through the use of test data. Test data can be used by

- inputting data into the system and checking whether it is processed correctly. The expected results can be calculated in advance, and checked against the actual output from the system; and

- including invalid data in the tests, which the system should reject.

Using test data on an accounting system

Some examples of test data tests are as follows:

Tests	Reason for the test
Revenue	
Input an order into the client's system that would cause a customer to exceed their credit limit.	The order should not be accepted, or should raise a query whether you are sure you wish to proceed. If this happens then the auditors will have confidence the system is working properly.
Input a negative number of items on an order.	Ensures only positive quantities are accepted.
Input incomplete customer details.	The system should not process the order unless all information is completed.
Input an excessive amount.	There are reasonable checks in the system to identify possible input errors. A warning should appear on the screen confirming the number.
Purchases	
Raise an order from a supplier not on the preferred supplier list.	A query should be raised as to whether you want to proceed with this transaction.
Process an order with an unauthorised staff ID.	The system should reject the process altogether or send the request through to an appropriate person for authorisation.
Try and make changes to the supplier standing data using the ID of someone who is not authorised to do so.	The system should reject the process altogether or send the request through to an appropriate person for authorisation.
Payroll	
Try and set up a new employee up on the payroll system using an unauthorised ID.	The system should reject the process altogether or send the request through to an appropriate person for authorisation.
Try and make employee changes of detail using an unauthorised ID.	The system should reject the process altogether or send the request through to an appropriate person for authorisation.
Make an excess change, for example increase someone's salary by $1,000,000 by someone authorised.	The system should have parameters in place to question this amount, and maybe reject it due to it being outside the normal range.

Risks with test data

Risks	Controls
Damage to the system as the system is tested to its limits.	Ensure auditors understand the system and have software support.
Corruption of the systems data if test data are not properly removed.	Ensure process for data removal.
System down time if 'dead' data used.	Establish when system can be used with minimum disruption to the business.

Live data = test data are processed during a normal production run.

Dead data = test data are processed outside the normal cycle.

Software controls

Software control prevents making or installing unauthorised copies of software. Illegal software is more likely to fail, comes without warranties or support, can place systems at risk of viruses and the use of illegal software can result in significant financial penalties.

Software can be controlled by:

- Buying only from reputable dealers.
- Ensuring that the original disks come with the software.
- Ensuring that licences are received for all software.
- Retaining all original disks and documentation.

Network controls

Risks on networks

The increase in popularity of the LAN (local area network) has brought concerns in relation to system security. A LAN allows for many more breaches of security than does a single computer.

The main areas of concern are:

- Tapping into cables
- Unauthorised log in
- Computer viruses
- File copying
- File server security.

Controls

Controls must exist to prevent unauthorised access to data transmitted over networks and to secure the integrity of data.

Methods include:

- Firewalls
- Flow
- Data encryption
- Virus protection.

More on network controls

Firewalls: A firewall will consist of a combination of hardware and software located between the company's intranet (private network) and the public network (Internet). A set of control procedures will be established to allow public access to some parts of the organisation's computer system (outside the firewall) whilst restricting access to other parts (inside the firewall).

Flow: This regulates movement of data from one file to another. Channels are specified along which information is allowed to flow, i.e. confidential/non-confidential, and these are linked by authority levels.

Data encryption: Encryption is a technique of disguising information to preserve its confidentiality. It is disguised during processing/storage. In essence it is a method of scrambling the data in a message or file so that it is unintelligible unless it is unscrambled (or decrypted).

Virus protection: It is extremely difficult to protect systems against the introduction of computer viruses. Preventative steps may include:

- control on the use of external software (e.g. checked for viruses before using new software)

- using anti-virus software, regularly updated, to detect and deal with viruses

- educating employees to be watchful for viruses being imported as attachment files to e-mail messages.

Test your understanding 3

SP plc is considering investing in the building of a new hotel in Dubai. The hotel is to be 'state of the art', and SP's management is hoping that it will be the first 6-star hotel in the world. It is expected that the richest people in the world will want to holiday here and the hotel will, therefore, command a premium price.

Many of the facilities in the hotel will involve computerisation. For example, the booking system – via the telephone or internet, the internal telephone system, and the availability of the internet in every suite. The cost of these facilities is thought to be around $7 million because the server will be housed in a separate building on the edge of the hotel grounds.

The management of SP have over 200 other hotels around the world to oversee. Over the past 10 years, their management information has become increasingly difficult to collate due to the size of the group and the diversity of activities that each hotel undertakes. The finance director is now trying to convince the other directors to invest in an Enterprise Resource Planning System (ERPS) to hopefully overcome some of these problems.

Required:

Explain the importance of information security to SP, and recommend the main controls necessary to ensure that the computer systems and the information they hold are secure.

5 Supply chain management (SCM)

Many businesses prosper or fail depending on the success of their relationship with their suppliers and with those who they supply. Businesses that rely on other businesses to this extent are in what is called a supply chain – each supplying each other right up to the final link in the chain, the consumer. The internet can help make this relationship work more effectively and efficiently.

About supply chains

A supply chain encompasses all activities and information flows necessary for the transformation of goods from the origin of the raw material to when the product is finally consumed or discarded.

This typically involves distribution of the product from the supplier to the manufacturer to the wholesaler to the retailer and to the final consumer, otherwise known as nodes in the supply chain.

It is helpful to make a distinction between upstream and downstream supply chain management. For an Internet retailer, for example, upstream SCM would involve transactions between the firm and its suppliers (equivalent to buy-side e-commerce) and downstream, customers (equivalent to sell-side e-commerce).

The transformation of product from node to node includes activities such as:

- production planning
- purchasing
- materials management
- distribution
- customer service
- forecasting.

While each firm can be competitive through improvements to its internal practices, ultimately the ability to do business effectively depends on the efficient functioning of the entire supply chain.

Illustration 3 – Supply chain management (SCM)

In the supply chain shown, ABC Manufacturing Ltd must be responsive to its customers. Direct supplier 1 and Direct supplier 2 must be responsive to ABC Manufacturing Ltd, and Indirect supplier 1 must be responsive to Direct supplier 2.

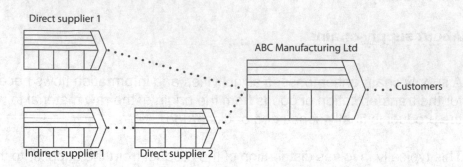

Obviously, if e-business capability is present in all members of the supply chain, management of the chain is becoming more feasible: selling, delivering, ordering, designing and manufacturing can all be linked electronically permitting:

- cost savings
- time savings
- faster innovation
- better marketing
- better quality.

Managing the chain

Active management of supply chain activities aims to maximise customer value and achieve a sustainable competitive advantage. It represents a conscious effort by the supply chain firms to develop and run supply chains in the most effective and efficient ways possible. Supply chain activities cover everything from product development, sourcing, production, and logistics, as well as the information systems needed to coordinate these activities. Managing the chain primarily therefore concentrates on managing the movement of the following three areas:

- materials/inventory
- information
- funds.

Inventory control

Amongst other things, this will include a consideration of:

- number, location and size of warehouses and distribution centres

- production scheduling (including life cycle management to ensure that new products can be successfully integrated into the chain)

- a transportation strategy (in terms of routes, timing etc.)

Information management

The key elements of information required for successful supply chain management include:

- potential levels of end-user and customer demand

- daily production and distribution plans

- resource availability and utilisation

Fund management

For the system to work it needs to be sufficiently liquid at all nodes to ensure that bottlenecks are avoided and supply can be sustained. There also needs to be a strong relationship of trust between each party in the chain.

Importance of Information Technology

IT plays an obvious role in providing, storing, managing and interrogating the information management part of supply chain management. But IT can provide aid for all of the areas that require consideration through systems such as e-procurement and customer relationship management (covered in the next chapter), and there will also be links to other areas of the syllabus such as BPR, project management, organisational structure etc.

Illustration 4 – Supply chain management (SCM)

For example, a wholesaler's inability to adequately maintain inventory control or respond to sudden changes in demand for stock may mean that a retailer cannot meet final consumer demand. Conversely, poor sales data from retailers may result in inadequate forecasting of manufacturing requirements.

Push and pull supply chain models

One key element in supply chain management is choosing between having a 'push' or a 'pull' model.

Push model

- Products are built, distributed, and ready for the customer demand.
- Product design is led by the manufacturer.
- Product quality is often determined by raw material suppliers and component manufacturers.
- There is little product personalisation to customers.
- Low set-up costs and economies of scale are possible.
- Inventories are built up waiting for customers to demand them (a push system is sometimes referred to as a Make to Stock (MTS system)).

Pull model

- Planning for a product starts when the customer places the order and creates firm demand.
- Product design is often customer led (a pull system is sometimes referred to as a Make to Order (MTO system)).
- Personalisation of the product by the customer is possible.
- Inventory levels are minimised (systems such as JIT and TQM can be used).
- Lead times can be much higher.
- Set-up costs are higher and economies of scale are not always possible.

The pull business model is less product-centric and more directly focused on the individual consumer – a more marketing-oriented approach.

- In the pull model, customers use electronic connections to pull whatever they need out of the system.
- Electronic supply chain connectivity gives end customers the opportunity to give direction to suppliers, for example, about the precise specifications of the products they want.
- Ultimately, customers have a direct voice in the functioning of the supply chain.

Driven by e-commerce's capabilities to empower clients, many companies are moving from the traditional 'push' business model, where manufacturers, suppliers, distributors and marketers have most of the power, to a customer-driven 'pull' model. E-commerce creates a much more efficient supply chain that benefits both customers and manufacturers. Companies can better serve customer needs, carry fewer inventories, and send products to market more quickly.

Today, many companies have introduced elements of the pull model so that their systems use a combination of push and pull. Nike iD is a good example of this.

Illustration 5 – Adding pull systems to a supply chain

The running shoe industry has traditionally used a push model for the supply chain. Products were built to a standardised form and consumers had to wait to find out what would be in the stores this year.

However Nike took a decision to allow customers to create their own designs for shoes and have them made to order. This product was known as Nike iD. It initially allowed consumers to create bespoke designs on the Nike website, but from 2009 this was extended so that consumers could even use an iPhone app to do this.

Nike iD allows customers to (amongst other things):

- choose colour schemes (customers can choose from a predetermined list or even take a picture with their mobile phone of the colour they want and Nike will make a shoe of that colour)

- choose the firmness of the sole

- choose lace colours

- add personal names to the running shoe

Delivery is promised in less than 4 weeks.

The system will not be a full pull system however. Nike has continued to build inventory of the common components for the shoes (such as laces, rubber, insoles, logos etc.). These inventories are built up in order to achieve economies of scale and to keep the cost of personalised Nike iD products as low as possible.

There is therefore a combination of push and pull elements within the system.

What factors should a company consider when choosing between a push and pull supply chain model?

Revisiting the value chain

Porter's value chain revisited

The theory behind the value chain is that somewhere the organisation carries out activities that customers value, are willing to pay for, and that result in profits being made. The activities could be skill and knowhow related, organisational or manufacturing.

The traditional value chain has been criticised because it:

- is designed primarily to describe manufacturing businesses

- does not emphasise the importance of the customer enough. It is product led rather than market led.

Deise proposed an alternative value chain that places more emphasis on the customer:

Market research	New product development	Market products	Purchase materials	Produce products	Manage selling, delivery, etc.

In terms of this model, e-business enables companies to:

- carry out continuous market research as products are ordered and sold

- use the results of continuous monitoring to order goods, design new products and design special offers

- allow great flexibility and speed of response, provided members of the up-stream supply chain (suppliers) also embrace e-business.

Note the last point carefully: the whole supply chain must be flexible and efficient if any one member of it is to benefit from better market information. There's no point one company knowing what its customers want if its suppliers and distributors cannot respond adequately.

KAPLAN PUBLISHING

6 Upstream SCM

The key activity of upstream SCM is e-procurement.

What is e-procurement?

The term 'procurement' covers all the activities needed to obtain items from a supplier: the whole purchases cycle.

Electronic Procurement (also known as e-procurement) is the business-to-business purchase and sale of supplies and services over the internet. It is a way of using the internet to make it easier, faster, and less expensive for businesses to purchase the goods and services they require. While e-procurement is a general term that covers a wide assortment of techniques, its overall goal is to streamline the purchasing process in order to reduce costs, increase speed and allow managers to focus on other strategic matters. An important part of many B2B sites, e-procurement is also sometimes referred to by other terms, such as supplier exchange.

The purchases cycle

- Identifying when items are needed, how many are needed and gaining authority to acquire them.
- Finding suitable suppliers.
- Choosing which supplier to order from.
- Agreeing the price or perhaps a range of prices depending on volumes.
- Ordering the goods with the chosen supplier(s).
- Receiving goods into the organisation.
- Checking the goods are as ordered and handling queries.
- Recording the goods in inventory or the fixed asset register as appropriate.
- Storing of goods.
- Receiving, checking and processing the supplier's invoice.
- Paying the supplier according to cash flow/cash discount priorities.

E-procurement is the term used to describe the electronic methods used in every stage of the procurement process, from identification of requirement through to payment. It can be broken down into the stages of e-sourcing, e-purchasing and e-payment.

E-sourcing covers electronic methods for finding new suppliers and establishing contracts.

Not only can e-sourcing save administrative time and money, it can enable companies to discover new suppliers and to source more easily from other countries.

Issuing electronic invitations to tender and requests for quotations reduces:

- administration overheads
- potentially costly errors, as the re-keying of information is minimised
- the time to respond.

E-purchasing covers product selection and ordering.

Buying and selling online streamlines procurement and reduces overheads through spending less on administration time and cutting down on bureaucracy. E-purchasing transfers effort from a central ordering department to those who need the products. Features of an e-purchasing system include:

- electronic catalogues for core/standard items
- recurring requisitions/shopping lists for regularly purchased items. The standard shopping lists form the basis of regular orders and the lists can have items added or deleted for each specific order
- electronic purchase orders despatched automatically through an extranet to suppliers
- detailed management information reporting capabilities.

Improvements in customer service can result from being able to place and track orders at any time of day. An e-catalogue is an electronic version of a supplier's paper catalogue including product name, description, an illustration, balance in hand and so on. User expectations have increased dramatically in recent years as a result of their personal experiences of shopping on the internet. Well-designed websites and web interfaces are essential to offer good functionality so as to maintain user satisfaction.

E-payment includes tools such as electronic invoicing and electronic funds transfers. Again, e-payment can make the payment processes more efficient for both the purchaser and supplier, reducing costs and errors that can occur as a result of information being transferred manually from and into their respective accounting systems. These efficiency savings can result in cost reductions to be shared by both parties.

Illustration 6 – E-procurement

ITAB Interiors is a company which specialises in shop refits. When a new tenant takes over a shop lease it will usually refit the shop with new fixtures and fittings etc. in order to meet its own particular needs. ITAB's clients include HSBC, Warehouse, Benetton and Bellway and it has many projects in operation at one time.

On each project, purchasing of required materials and fittings typically occurred in a manual manner with the following being typical stages in the process:

- Identify or anticipate material needs.
- Evaluate potential suppliers.
- Select suppliers and confirm price.
- Submit a purchase order form to management for approval
- On receiving approval, place the order.

Evaluating and selecting suppliers could, at times, take several days as could the confirmation of management approval. This made the process time consuming and expensive.

ITAB's switch to e-procurement involved the following:

- Having pre-approved suppliers for the most commonly purchased parts.
- Having an electronic system that could link inventory requests to the appropriate supplier.
- In the event that no existing supplier for the part was available, the system could perform a search of a number of suppliers and provide a range of prices and delivery estimates.

It means that the purchasing process can now take minutes instead of days. Requirements can be entered into the system and generally the system does the rest of the work. On the rare occasion when a non-approved supplier is necessary, manager approval can take place electronically and is now much more efficient than in the past.

Many organisations have expanded e-procurement beyond production-related procurement (which is directly related to the core activities of the organisation) into non-production procurement (which looks at ancillary services such as meeting administrative and distribution needs). For example, Kaplan have an e-procurement system that staff use for obtaining rail travel tickets for journeys to clients and meetings.

Benefits	Risks
• savings in labour and procurement costs	• become over reliant on the technology
• better inventory control	• there may be staff resistance
• better control over suppliers (may even be able to influence their design and production)	• cost savings may fail to materialise
• reduction in errors	• prices may become out of date or uncompetitive

Benefits and risks of e-procurement

The benefits of e-procurement

The more of the procurement process that can be automated, the better as there will be considerable financial benefits.

- Labour costs will be greatly reduced.

- Inventory holding costs will be reduced. Not only should overstocking be less likely, but if orders are cheap to place and process, they can be placed much more frequently, so average inventories can be lower.

- Production and sales should be higher as there will be fewer stock-outs because of more accurate monitoring of demand and greater ordering accuracy.

Other benefits include the following:

- The firm may benefit from a much wider choice of suppliers rather than relying on local ones.

- Greater financial transparency and accountability

- Greater control over inventories

- Quicker ordering, making it easier to operate lean or JiT manufacturing systems

- Fewer errors in terms of ordering unnecessary items, mispricing items, overpaying for items, using an incorrect supplier etc.

- There are also considerable benefits to the suppliers concerned, such as reduced ordering costs, reduced paperwork and improved cash flow, that should strengthen the relationship between the firm and its suppliers.

- Staff time is freed up to focus on other operational and managerial duties.

Potential risks of e-procurement

There are some risks associated with e-procurement. These are:

- Technology risks. There is a risk that the system (whether software or hardware) will not function correctly. There are risks that it might not interface properly with the organisation's system. There are very high risks that it will not communicate properly with a wide range of supplier systems. There are also increased risks over areas such as data security.

- Organisational risks. Staff might be reluctant to accept the new procurement methods and may become concerned over possible redundancies.

- No cost savings realised. As with all IS/IT projects, it is very difficult to predict all the benefits that can arise. Tangible benefits (such as might arise if fewer staff have to be employed) are relatively easy to forecast. However, intangible benefits (such as better customer service giving rise to an improved reputation) are very difficult to estimate with any accuracy .

- The buying company can become entrenched with existing, approved suppliers and there may be disincentives to find alternative, cheaper sources of supplies.

Illustration 7 – The growth of e-procurement

In April 2012, Amazon announced the launch of Amazon Supply:

"a new website dedicated to offering a broad selection of parts and supplies to business, industrial, scientific and commercial customers at competitive prices."

This is a move away from its typical B2C model to a B2B model. The hope is that businesses may find it more attractive to implement an e-procurement strategy if they can link systems to a business as large and valued as Amazon.

Amazon Supply "offers more than 500,000 items from leading brands" across a range of categories, including: lab & scientific, test, measure & inspect, occupational health & safety, janitorial & sanitation, office, fleet & vehicle maintenance, power & hand tools, cutting tools, abrasives & finishing, materials handling, materials (e.g., metals), hydraulics pneumatics & plumbing, fasteners and power transmission.

As Amazon adds basic buying controls, workflow, compliance and analytics capability that are commonly featured in e-procurement technologies and allow procurement to be automated (and therefore cheaper and more efficient), it is likely to become a vital part of the value chain of many businesses in the future.

Test your understanding 5

XL Travel are a tour operator based in the country's capital. They run weekly trips to the seaside resort of Black Rock (around 140 km away) for four day visits (typically Friday to Monday).

The tours are very popular – especially with people aged over 65 (who make up over 90% of XL's customers). The company has traded profitably for many years on the back of premium pricing. But recently profits have started to fall, coinciding with a minority of complaints from regular users. Some users feel that the quality of the trips have fallen and are not up to previous high standards. Other users feel that, whilst XL itself has invested (with plush new offices, better marketing, more staff, easier booking systems etc.), this investment has gone on the wrong areas.

XL has built up a large cash surplus for further investment. One of the ways that it is considering using this cash is to invest and improve its supply chain.

Required:

(a) What are likely to be the elements of XL's upstream supply chain?

(b) What areas could XL aim to change?

(c) How might IT play a role in facilitating this change?

Restructuring the supply chain

In an earlier chapter we looked at strategic choices of outsourcing, vertical integration and strategic alliances, where the key issues of cost, quality and control were highlighted.

These are still relevant for online businesses as much as for conventional 'bricks and mortar' organisations. All organisations must decide between:

- vertical integration – manufacturing in-house

- virtual integration – the majority of supply chain activities are undertaken by third parties

- virtual disintegration (disaggregation) – in between these two extremes.

However, internet technology allows more efficient and cheaper communications within the chosen structure and may make virtual integration preferred to vertical integration.

7 Downstream SCM

Downstream supply change management is about managing relationships with both customers and consumers, as well as any other intermediaries along the way.

Examples of downstream supply chain management actions are:

- providing displays for retailers

- creating a website for end users

- creating user forums on websites

- determining which retailers and distributors to use

- use of different logistical methods/providers

- changes to finished goods inventory policies

- setting recommended retail prices

- giving retail exclusivity rights

- forward integration.

Advantages	Disadvantages
• can tie in customers/increase switching costs	• can be expensive to implement
• can improve customer loyalty and retention	• as a differentiation strategy it is easily copied
• can increase market visibility	• it relies on suppliers willingness to adapt to customer needs (often needs corresponding upstream management)
• provides better information on customer needs, tastes etc.	• the organisation might become reactive rather than proactive to customer needs
• product failure rates can be reduced	• forward integration can increase business risk and exit barriers
• can facilitate pull supply chain management	• must ensure that forum/website users are representative of all users
• more regular and better communication with customers (e.g. can provide software/product updates etc.)	• requires skills and experience for the benefits to be fully realised
• gives users a voice	• there is a risk of loss of focus on core competences and activities

Dealing with intermediaries

A typical downstream for a manufacturer might involve selling to distributors, who then sell on to retailers, who in turn sell on to end users. Distributors and retailers are therefore intermediaries between the manufacturer and the consumer of the product. One element of supply chain management is to manage intermediaries.

- E-commerce can lead to **disintermediation**. In this process intermediate organisations (middlemen) can be taken out of the supply chain.

- The process of **reintermediation** is also found, i.e. new intermediaries are introduced to the value chain, or at least to some aspects of it.

- **Countermediation** is where established firms create their own new intermediaries to compete with established intermediaries.

Examples

An example of disintermediation is seen in the travel industry where travel agents have been cut out of many transactions as the public can book directly with hotels, airlines and rail companies.

The travel industry also gives an example of reintermediation. Companies like lastminute.com and expedia.com are like new travel agents, presenting a wide choice of products and services.

An example of countermediation is Opodo.com, set up by a collaboration of European airlines to encourage customers to book flights directly with them rather than using cost-comparison intermediaries such as lastminute.com.

Test your understanding 6

Following on from TYU 3, would you recommend downstream supply chain management for XL Travel?

8 Chapter summary

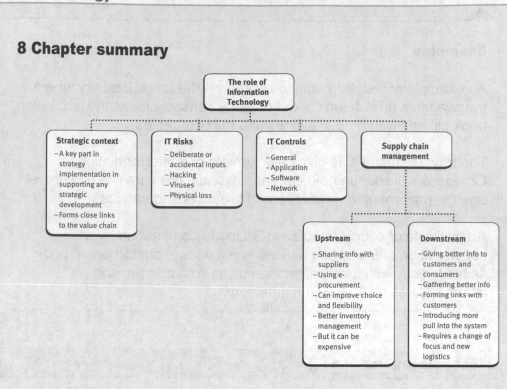

The role of Information Technology

Strategic context
- A key part in strategy implementation in supporting any strategic development
- Forms close links to the value chain

IT Risks
- Deliberate or accidental inputs
- Hacking
- Viruses
- Physical loss

IT Controls
- General
- Application
- Software
- Network

Supply chain management

Upstream
- Sharing info with suppliers
- Using e-procurement
- Can improve choice and flexibility
- Better inventory management
- But it can be expensive

Downstream
- Giving better info to customers and consumers
- Gathering better info
- Forming links with customers
- Introducing more pull into the system
- Requires a change of focus and new logistics

Test your understanding answers

The choice and use of information technology can be seen as part of the implementation stage of strategic planning. Johnson, Scholes and Whittington suggest that strategic planning has three elements:

- strategic analysis – this involves an analysis of the organisation's environment and assessing the organisation's fit to that environment

- strategic choice – this involves designing corporate and business level strategies to take account of the organisation's environment and improving the organisation's position in that environment

- strategy into action (or implementation) – this involves facilitating strategic choices through making changes to business processes, staffing, marketing, etc.

Johnson, Scholes and Whittington suggest that the three elements are inter-related. In that manner, strategy into action will be affected by strategic analysis and choice.

For example, Foxtrot analysed their environment and spotted both weaknesses and threats. This in turn affected its strategic choice. It choose to move to a new position on the strategy clock and compete in a new way. The strategic analysis and choice in turn affected its IT strategy – a new system was needed and it had to provide services that were not available elsewhere in the market in order to differentiate the company's service. The choice to differentiate meant that bespoke systems would have been needed with the ability to incorporate elements of online CAD.

So part of the relationship between IT and strategic planning can be seen here: IT decisions are clearly impacted by strategic analysis and strategic choices.

But because these elements are inter-related, Johnson, Scholes and Whittington suggested that the strategic planning process can effectively begin at any stage.

For example, it would appear that the new strategic direction is being driven by the IT investment. The investment in the new software appears to have not only given the company strengths in terms of a competitive advantage over existing rivals, but it also appears to have provided an opportunity to move into the non-commercial market. This strategic analysis has in turn impacted on the strategic choice to develop this new market and the IT system in place is likely to support a focused differentiation in this new market development.

In this way, we can see that IT strategies can impact on strategic plans. Overall, therefore, IT strategies and strategic planning are closely related. We have seen how strategic planning can impact on IT strategies, but also how IT strategies can impact on the strategic plans of an organisation.

Test your understanding 2

Key answer tips

The requirement "evaluate" is a high level verb requiring you to look at the value of something. It is often helpful to consider advantages and disadvantages of an idea when tackling this requirement. Your answers to both parts (a) and (b) of this question need to utilise information from the scenario to score high marks. Points that do not relate to RBT will not be rewarded, particularly if they are inappropriate suggestions for this type of organisation.

(a) **Intranet**

An intranet is an internal company information system where a wide variety of internal information can be posted for access by staff members. Internal information often includes company news, telephone directories, standard forms, copies of rules and procedures, and so on. In this case of the system under consideration by RBT, the intranet would hold up-to-date information on products and prices, so that sales representatives can download this information to their laptops from a customer's premises and other remote locations.

Advantages

The proposed new system has the following advantages over the old system:

– More regularly updated information

An intranet site is very easy and cheap to update, and product and price information can be kept fully up-to-date by head office. The downloaded product information will therefore be much more up-to-date than the old printed materials, and a better customer service can be provided. All the latest products would be made available to customers and customers would always be given the correct prices.

– Reduced costs of producing price lists/brochures

Regular price lists and brochures will no longer be required, and the production and printing costs of paper-based products should be reduced.

Disadvantages

The intranet site has the following disadvantages compared with the old system:

– Slower communication with the production department

Since the telephone system will be discontinued, the sales people will not have access to production staff to resolve any queries or difficulties with customers. This would be a serious weakness in the system. Good communications between sales and production staff must be maintained.

Solutions

Possible solutions to this problem include:

(i) E-mail system

E-mail might provide an efficient way for sales representatives to communicate directly with the production staff, although controls would need to be in place to ensure that the production staff responds promptly to e-mail queries they receive.

(ii) Maintain telephone access

Voice telephone access offers immediate communication. A salesperson can get in contact with a member of the production staff and get an immediate reply. Maintaining telephone access for certain queries would be a useful way of ensuring very quick communication where needed.

(iii) Access to production scheduling system

Allowing salespeople access to the production scheduling system over the intranet would allow them to estimate a delivery date themselves thus reducing the need for direct contact between production and sales.

– Less personal communication with production department

The intranet is a very impersonal way to communicate with people. It does not allow for two-way conversation, whereas personal contact may be required to resolve difficult issues.

Solution

Both e-mail and a voice telephone system are more personal forms of communication than the intranet. The voice telephone system in particular allows a two-way conversation to take place so that more difficult issues can easily be resolved.

– Rejection of new technology

The sales people may dislike the new technology that they are required to use. At present they do not use IT significantly in their work, and so new skills may be required. Many new systems also have 'teething problems' on implementation, which may also make users dislike the new system.

Solutions

(i) Training

Training will be required so people know how the system works and can get the best use from it.

(ii) Consultation

Consulting users early in the development process is an excellent way of getting user buy-in to the new system. It will also ensure the system is practical from a day-to-day usage point of view.

(iii) Testing

Testing systems well prior to implementation will help avoid the teething problems which may be encountered, particularly if the end users are involved since they know better than anyone else the way the system will be used in practice.

– Up-front costs

The proposed new system will require significant up-front costs both in terms of developing the new systems and training staff. Given the relatively small number of sales representatives (just 20) the investment may not be financially justified.

Solution

A cost-benefit analysis can be undertaken to ascertain whether the costs of the investment are justified.

(b) **Information systems – order progress**

Manufacturing system – order tracking

As part of the manufacturing process, progress on orders will need to be recorded. The information recorded will include work done, work still to do and the expected completion date. This information might already exist within the current system or it may need to be input into a database which can be accessed by clients.

EDI or extranet

Using electronic data interchange the customer would be able to log on to RBT's systems to directly access the production data.

An extranet is an extension of an intranet. External parties are allowed to log onto the intranet site and use it to access sections of the intranet. The intranet site would need to be connected to the manufacturing system/database so that up-to-date information was available.

Advantages

(1) Clients could access information themselves. This could save staff time and resources in RBT, since there will be fewer customer queries to deal with.

(2) An extranet would be relatively easy to provide if the manufacturing system is already linked to the intranet for the benefit of the salespeople.

(3) Other information could also be provided to customers (such as past order information, account balances and so on).

Disadvantages

(1) There would be a loss of personal contact with customers. The salesperson would not have as many opportunities to make contact with customers in order to build an ongoing relationship. As a consequence, they might identify fewer sales opportunities or find it harder to make a sale because they are less trusted by the customer.

(2) External parties would be accessing internal systems. There is a danger that hackers will get into parts of the system that are confidential, and a risk that important information is stolen or damaged. It could also increase the possibility of viruses being brought in which could damage internal systems.

Internet

Alternatively the RBT could put tracking information on a database which is connected to the company's web site. Clients would then be able to access their information through this site.

Advantages

(1) Labour cost savings, as described for an extranet.

(2) Customers will be familiar with the internet and so find it easier to use than an extranet or internal system accessed via EDI. It also means they will not have to dial in directly to the company's internal network, saving them time and effort.

(3) There is less opportunity for hackers or viruses to enter the internal systems using a web site on the internet, since they are not directly accessing internal systems.

(4) Other information could also be provided to customers on the internet site.

Disadvantage

The company may not currently have an internet site. This could be a significant extra expense, in terms of designing, creating and maintaining the site.

Test your understanding 3

Information security is about protecting the systems and data of an organisation from loss caused by human error, fraud, theft or hacking. Information security needs to be based on a risk assessment, and controls should be put in place to mitigate those risks.

The main elements of information security are that SP should have:

- a security policy to allocate responsibility for the information and systems in the hotel.

- a management structure with roles defined and documented, covering authorisation of purchases of software and hardware, and systems to prevent unauthorised access to data. In particular, the staff using the booking system would have access to clients' details and credit card information. This needs to be protected by employing reputable staff and by having supervision at all times.

- an asset register of all hardware and software owned by the hotel.

- systems in place and monitored to minimise risks from error, fraud, theft or hacking. All staff should be fully trained to be able to use the systems, reducing the number of errors that might occur. Systems should be protected against attack from viruses and malicious software, and should have anti-virus software, intruder detection systems and firewalls in place. This is particularly relevant since bookings will be taken over the internet and there is an internet connection in every suite. Customers may unwittingly cause a virus problem.

- controls to restrict access and provide physical security against fire and theft, e.g. passwords, locks on doors, security cameras and fire extinguishers. There should be systems access controls over physical access, passwords and authentication of remote users.

All systems should be developed in accordance with standards, tested and documented.

Change control systems should be in place to control all development and maintenance work thereafter.

SP should develop a continuity/disaster-recovery plan to cover all information systems, including backup, offsite fireproof storage of data and alternative hardware, software and building site requirements for recovery.

Adequate insurance should be taken out.

Test your understanding 4

The factors to consider are:

- Variability and knowledge of demand. A pull system will require knowledge of what customers want and when they want it. Alternatively, it will rely on customers being willing to wait for production. For example, luxury yacht supply chains typically use a pull system because buyers are willing to wait for up to two months for delivery of the product.

- The competitive strategy pursued. Low cost and no-frills companies will often follow a push supply chain as this can provide economies of scale. A differentiator might follow a pull system as product personalisation might be a way to differentiate a product.

- Inventory costs. Inventory costs and risks are higher in a pull system, so companies that have high inventory costs (such as luxury cars) may prefer a pull system.

- Manufacturing set up costs. Set ups are more frequent in a pull system so that if set up costs are high a pull system may be too expensive to operate successfully.

- Rivals' systems. If rivals are all using one model then a competitive advantage might be achieved by using an alternative model. For example, the detergent industry typically uses a push system. But some companies have found a focused differentiation model by allowing users to suggest ingredients and smells for soaps and detergents before they are then made to order. This allows these companies to charge a premium price for these services.

- IT systems. Strong IT systems will be necessary to support a pull model. The growth in e-commerce has been a major reason for the recent high growth in the creation of pull supply chain systems. E-procurement plays a vital role in pull systems.

KAPLAN PUBLISHING

Test your understanding 5

(a) The key elements of XL's upstream supply chain is likely to include:

 – travel providers (such as bus, train or airline companies)

 – accommodation providers

 – local food producers and suppliers (some of these will actually be the suppliers to the accommodation providers)

 – attractions, activity and excursion providers.

But it could be widened further to include:

 – laundry providers

 – waste disposal companies

 – energy and water suppliers

 – sports events

 – bars and clubs

 – local infrastructure providers.

However, any initial step in supply chain management is likely to focus on the management of the first group of key elements.

(b) There is an opinion amongst a minority of customers that the quality of the service as deteriorated due to a lack of investment. One element of supply chain management is to ensure that the chain contains the correct value system to support the firm's competitive advantage. XL should therefore consider whether they are using the correct travel companies, accommodation providers, attractions etc.

If existing suppliers are deemed to be appropriate then XL should look to introduce a move towards elements of a 'pull' system. XL should communicate with a selection of customers (not just those who are complaining) to determine what they would like from their tour, what their expectations are, how things could be improved etc.

This will allow them to have a better idea of what is needed from suppliers. It will allow XL to compete thorough inspections of suppliers and also to provide suppliers with information on potential changes that might be required. So focusing on the key elements of XL's supply chain, the following gives some ideas of the areas that XL could look to improve, change, redesign or remove:

– accommodation
  – location
  – ease of access
  – furniture used
  – bedding used
  – staffing
  – facilities

– travel providers
  – capacity
  – safety measures
  – check-in facilities
  – age of transport
  – in-journey refreshments, facilities and entertainment (where appropriate)
  – luggage capacity, security and safety

– food suppliers
  – ingredients used
  – range of menus
  – facilities
  – capacity
  – waiting times
  – service

- attractions etc.
  - availability
  - ease of access
  - waiting times
  - safety record
  - facilities
  - range of products

Supply chain management will require a consideration and possible investment in all of these areas and many more.

(c) Information Technology can play a very important role in supply chain management. Firstly it can gather information. Initially, in a pull system, this should be customer focused. So, for example, Customer Relationship Management (CRM - see next chapter) software can be used to determine customer needs, buying patterns, likes/dislikes etc.

The next set of information can be on elements of the upstream supply chain. For example, in part (b) some suggestions were given on what needs to be considered for each of the four key elements of XL's upstream supply chain, XL can obtain information on current performance using software to record and interrogate the data.

IT can also be used to provide and share data. Customer feedback and suggestions can be provided to suppliers. Also, suppliers can more easily access information on the potential number, age, requirements etc. of potential visitors. For example, the software might flag in advance that one of the visitors has a physical disability so that suppliers can prepare for this.

The IT system might also be able to cope with and alleviate potential 'bottlenecks' in the system. If, for example, a particular accommodation supplier hasn't got the capacity to cope with the number of visitors who are arriving on a particular date, the system should allow for alternative accommodation for the excess to be found quickly and easily.

The system could even be expanded for advance planning of elements of the system such as meals and entertainment. Customers could perhaps pre-book tickets for events or particular items on the menus of food providers.

Overall, the system is likely to provide benefits for all parties in the chain. XL can retain its competitive advantage, customers can receive a better and more personalised service, and suppliers will get better information for planning.

Test your understanding 6

There would be some definite benefits from introducing downstream management to XL Travel such as:

- e-marketing might be more easily used to give more up-to-date and personalised information to customers.

- updates to schedules, events etc. might be more easily communicated to customers,

- customers might feel more obliged to rebook with XL Travel if IT systems improve the convenience of making a booking.

However, for XL, downstream supply chain management may not be attractive for a number of reasons. Firstly, they already deal directly with their customers so there would be no 'dis-intermediation' benefits.

Also, given the age of their typical customer base, there may be little take-up of e-marketing and on-line booking systems. This is an age group that are typically low users of technology and the cost of investment in these downstream systems is unlikely to be recovered by the benefits highlighted above.

In fact, moving away from its existing personal levels of service might actually further alienate its client base and be seen as a further example of investment happening in the wrong areas.

Overall, XL Travel should focus on upstream supply chain management and avoid downstream management until a time when customers are ready for it and demanding it.

Marketing

Chapter learning objectives

Upon completion of this chapter you will be able to:

- analyse customers and markets in a commercial setting

- analyse the effect of e-business (internet and customer extranets) on the relationship with customers

- describe the common different buyer behaviours among on-line customers

- explain the use of e-marketing and how its use might affect the marketing mix

- describe a process for establishing a pricing strategy for products and services that recognises both economic and non-economic factors

- explain the characteristics of the media of e-marketing using the '6Is'

- explain, with examples, how electronic media can be used to acquire customers, retain customers and to increase income from them

- explain the importance to a business of e-branding

- explain, with examples, what is meant by the term 'customer relationship management' and how a suitable software package could support this.

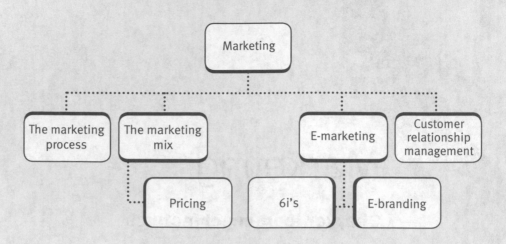

1 Stages in the marketing process

There are a number of techniques for marketing a product, but they generally follow a number of distinct stages:

(1) **Market analysis** – used to identify gaps and opportunities in a business' environment (as explored in chapter 2).

(2) **Customer analysis** – examining customers so that potential customers can be divided into segments with similar purchasing characteristics.

(3) **Market research** – determining characteristics of each segment such as size, potential, level of competition, unmet needs etc.

(4) **Targeting** – deciding which segments to target (again, chapter 2 techniques such as PESTEL, 5 forces and forecasting would be used here).

(5) **Marketing mix strategies** – developing a unique marketing mix for each segment in order to exploit it properly.

Marketing mix strategies are an important element of downstream supply chain management (explored in the previous chapter). This chapter focuses primarily on this element of marketing, though you should have an awareness of all 5 stages.

KAPLAN PUBLISHING

Market and customer analysis

Market analysis

Market analysis helps identify the appropriate marketing strategy. This analysis will include the following:

- appraisal and understanding of the present situation – this would include an analysis for each product showing its stage in the product life cycle, strength of competition, market segmentation, anticipated threats and opportunities, customer profile

- definition of objectives of profit, turnover, product image, market share and market position by segment

- evaluation of the marketing strategies available to meet these objectives, e.g. pricing policy, distribution policy, product differentiation, advertising plans, sales promotions, etc.

- definition of control methods to check progress against objectives and provide early warning, thereby enabling the marketing strategies to be adjusted.

There are two purposes of the analysis:

- to identify gaps in the market where consumer needs are not being satisfied

- to look for opportunities that the organisation can benefit from, in terms of sales or development of new products or services.

Customer analysis

There are three sets of strategic questions that are used to analyse customers – segmentation, motivation and unmet needs.

Segmentation – sets of strategic questions include the following.

- Who are the biggest, most profitable existing customers and who are the most attractive potential customers?

- Do the customers fall into any logical groups on the basis of characteristics, needs or motivations?

- Can the market be segmented into groups requiring a unique business strategy?

Traditional segmentation focuses on identifying customer groups based on a number of variables that include:

- geographic variables, such as region of the world or country, country size, or climate

- demographic variables, such as age, gender, sexual orientation, family size, income, occupation, education, socioeconomic status, religion, nationality/race, and others

- psychographic variables, such as personality, life-style, values and attitudes

- behavioural variables, such as benefit sought (quality, low price, convenience), product usage rates, brand loyalty, product end use, readiness-to-buy stage, decision-making unit, and others.

Value-based segmentation looks at groups of customers in terms of the revenue they generate and the costs of establishing and maintaining relationships with them.

For example, a food manufacturer will approach supermarket chains very differently to the small independent retailer, probably offering better prices, delivery terms, use different sales techniques and deliver direct to the supermarket chain. They might also supply own-label products to the large chain but they are unlikely to be able to offer the same terms to the corner shop. The benefit of segmentation to the company adopting this policy is that it enables them to get close to their intended customer and really find out what that customer wants (and is willing to pay for). This should make the customer happier with the product offered and, hence, lead to repeat sales and endorsements.

Motivation – concerns the customers' selection and use of their favourite brands, the elements of the product or service that they value most, the customers' objectives and the changes that are occurring in customer motivation.

Unmet needs – considers why some customers are dissatisfied and some are changing brands or suppliers. The analysis looks at the needs not being met that the customer is aware of.

Customer lifecycle segmentation model

This is another method for segmenting customers – as visitors use online services they pass through seven stages:

(1) First-time visitor

(2) Return visitor

(3) Newly registered visitor

(4) Registered visitor

(5) Have made one or more purchases

(6) Have purchased before but now inactive

(7) Have purchased before and are still active and e-responsive.

Illustration 1 – Customers and markets

The market for package holidays can be split up into a variety of different sub-markets – the family market, the elderly market, the young singles market, the activity holiday market, the budget holiday market, etc.

Because it would be virtually impossible to provide one single product that would satisfy all people in all markets, an organisation can tailor its marketing approach with a specific product and go for:

- undifferentiated marketing – one product and one market with no attempt to segment the market, e.g. sugar is a product that is marketed in a relatively undifferentiated way

- differentiated marketing – the market is segmented with products being developed to appeal to the needs of buyers in the different segments, e.g. Toyota offers a wide range of different types of vehicle (sports car, 4x4, estate) in response to differing customer needs

- niche or target marketing – specialising in one or two of the identified markets only, e.g. Ferrari only make expensive luxury sports cars.

2 Marketing mix strategies

The marketing mix is the set of controllable variables that the firm can use to influence the buyers' responses (Kotler). The variables are commonly grouped into four classes that McCarthy refers to as 'the four Ps' – product, price, promotion and place (or distribution).

The original 4Ps model

- Price – pricing strategies include price skimming, when a premium price is charged because the product has a technological advantage or brand loyalty that outweighs a price difference and market penetration, a deliberately low price to dominate the market and block competition entry.

- Promotion – the promotion mix consists of four elements: advertising, sales promotion, public relations and personal selling.

- Place – the design of a channel of distribution will be influenced by the type of product, the abilities of the intermediaries and the expectations of the consumer.

- Product – the product needs to be augmented if it is to stand out from rivals' products. This can be done by changing its brand name, its aesthetics, its quality, its packaging, or by widening the product mix or increasing/improving the services that the product comes with.

Product	Price	Promotion	Place
• Brand name	• Level	• Sales promotion	• Distribution channels
• Packaging	• Discounts	• Personal selling	• Distribution coverage
• Features	• Allowances	• Publicity	• Outlet locations
• Options	• Payment terms	• Advertising	• Sales territories
• Quality	• Delivery options		• Inventory levels
• Warranty			• Inventory locations
• Service			
• Style appeal			

Test your understanding 1

Suggest how the marketing mix might differ for a consumer product in the first two stages of the product's life cycle.

E-marketing: the 7Ps

E-marketing is marketing carried out using electronic technology.

Opportunities for e-marketing can be examined using the traditional 4Ps of

- product
- price
- promotion and
- place,

plus an additional 3Ps

- people/participants (for example, having adequately trained staff and support services)
- process (for example, payment and delivery processes) and
- physical evidence (for example, website layout and navigation).

The additional 3Ps are particularly relevant to the marketing of services.

Test your understanding 2

Hartley's Books is a firm who specialise in selling antiquarian books. Antiquarian books are usually in excess of 50 years old and often out of print, and collectors pay a premium price for books which are likely to increase in value over time, such as first editions signed by the author.

Hartley's have 6 stores spread across the company. James Hartley, the grandson of the original founder, has recently taken over the role of Managing Director of the company. He is concerned with the downturn in sales that has been experienced in the recent tough economic climate and he believes that the stores need to be better marketed if they are to take advantage of the likely upturn in the economy that he believes is 'just around the corner'.

One of the areas where he is considering investing is in launching an e-commerce website to run alongside the existing business.

Required:

Consider how Hartley's Books could be marketed, paying particular attention to the e-commerce aspect of James's plans.

The effects of electronic methods on marketing

Here are examples of the effects of electronic methods on marketing:

Product	• Retailers often offer a wider range of products through on-line websites compared with traditional catalogues.
	• Customisation. e.g. Holidays no longer have to be for the precise seven days a tour company dictates.
	• Many companies use the internet to vary the extended product. e.g. online assistance.
Price	• Prices can be lower because of e-business techniques automating processing.
	• From customers' perspectives, prices are easy to compare on the internet (greater transparency) so there is more pressure on retailers to be competitive.
	• Prices can be changed to reflect demand e.g. car rental firms in the USA will continually monitor demand and rival's prices and change their prices accordingly. This is known as "dynamic pricing".
	• New pricing approaches become feasible, such as auctions.
Promotion	• Websites
	• Search engine results (influenced by search engine marketing – see customer acquisition below under CRM).
	• emails (but not spam we hope!).
Place	• Disintermediation, reintermediation, countermediation.
	• Direct sales (manufacturer – consumer).
	• Delivery over the internet (e.g. music, software, video).
People/ participants	• Service businesses usually have high person-to-person contact. It is important that these contacts are conducted well as there is often no quality control step that can intervene between employee and customer.
	• A simple example of the use of electronics is to provide employees with an on-screen script for dealing with queries. Depending on customers' answers, the script branches to different options.

KAPLAN PUBLISHING

Processes	•	Again, in a service business, a customer is often exposed to more business processes. For example, a lot of information has to be provided if a customer is buying on-line insurance. The process has to be made high quality and easy to use.
	•	Many people become frustrated with e-commerce sites because a small error is only reported at the end of the process, and then the customer has to start from the beginning again.
Physical evidence	•	Is the website well designed? Does it look good?
	•	The website frequently gives potential customers their first impressions of the organisation.

3 More on pricing

An accountant can play an important role in determining a pricing strategy – for example, in determining product costs, value analysis, likely market volumes, market conditions, competitor reactions etc. For this reason pricing may be explored in more detail in exam scenarios.

Pricing should be determined with reference to four factors:

- **Cost** (i.e. we should ensure that all costs are covered).
- **Customers** (we should consider how much customers are willing to pay).
- **Competitors** (we should consider how much competitors are/will be charging).
- **Corporate objectives** (we should consider what we are aiming to achieve – for example, a low price might be necessary when we are trying to break into a market).

Further discussion of pricing objectives

Dibb, Simkin, Pride and Ferrell, in their book *Marketing Concepts and Strategies*, identify a number of different objectives that a business may be aiming to achieve with its pricing strategy:

- **survival** – this is a break even requirement. Companies might accept a price that just covers costs in the short-term in order to cope with a short-term crisis (e.g. a recession).

- **profit** – in the longer-term, businesses will hope to achieve a level of profit that satisfies their longer-term objectives.

- **return on investment** – a business may have a ROI target that it needs to satisfy and this could be used to determine the price.

- **market share** – often with new products and markets the initial objective is to achieve a level of market share. This may mean that prices are set below those of rivals' in order to win customers away from rivals.

- **cash flow** – if a business has cash flow problems it might price products in order to bring in cash to the business more quickly (e.g. by offering settlement discounts).

- **status quo** – the business may pursue a strategy of non-price competition (e.g. cola companies generally use this approach) in order to maintain an existing (often mature) position.

- **product quality** – price is often used as an indicator of quality. So a business who want to promote the quality of their product might use a higher selling than that of rivals.

Further discussion of competitor prices

It is important to analyse competitor prices as part of a business' own pricing strategy. Often the position on the strategy clock will determine where prices must be set in relation to competitors. For example, a low cost provider will have to ensure that prices are below that of competitors whilst a differentiator might want to have higher prices to reflect the extra product features or services offered.

A key problem in achieving this in the real world is in obtaining accurate, up-to-date information on how much competitors are charging. In some industries (such as publishing) it may appear to be straight forward as prices are often openly advertised, listed on websites or even printed on products. However, this might not disclose bulk discounts given to larger customers or special rates given to contracted customers. There may even be 'hidden extras' that are not disclosed as clearly as the advertised price.

Therefore businesses will often outsource the monitoring of competitor prices to specialist agencies.

Practical pricing methods

- Penetration pricing – a low price is set to gain market share.

- Perceived quality (or prestige) pricing – a high price is set to reflect/create an image of high quality.

- Periodic discounting – this is a temporary reduction in prices for a limited period such as a 'Holiday Sale'.

- Price discrimination – different prices are set for the same product in different markets, e.g. peak/offpeak rail fares.

- Going rate pricing – prices are set to match competitors.

- Price skimming – high prices are set when a new product is launched. Later the price is dropped to increase demand once the customers who are willing to pay more have been 'skimmed off'.

- Negotiated pricing – the price is established through bargaining between the seller and the customer.

- Loss leaders – one product may be sold at a loss with the expectation that customers will then go on and buy other more profitable products.

- Captive product pricing – this is used where customers must buy two products. The first is cheap to attract customers but the second is expensive, once they are captive.

- Bait pricing – this is also used by companies with wide product ranges, but often the lowest priced model is advertised in the hope to attract customers to the line and hope that they will actually decide to buy a higher priced item from the range.

- Bundle pricing – two or more products, usually complementary, are packaged together and sold for one price.

- Cost plus pricing – the cost per unit is calculated and then a mark-up added.

Initiating price increases

A major circumstance provoking price increases is cost inflation. Companies often raise their prices by more than the cost increase in anticipation of further inflation or government price controls in a practice called anticipatory pricing.

Another factor leading to price increases is over-demand. When a company cannot supply all of its customers, it can raise prices, ration supplies to customers or both.

A company needs to decide whether to raise its prices sharply on a one-time basis or to raise it by small amounts several times. In passing price increases on to customers, the company must avoid the image of being a price gouger. Customers memories are long.

There are techniques for avoiding this image. A sense of fairness must surround any price increase and customers must be given advance notice so they can do some forward buying or shop around. Sharp price increases need to be explained in understandable terms. Companies can also respond to higher costs or over-demand without raising prices. Possibilities include:

- Shrinking the amount of product instead of raising the price.

- Substituting less expensive materials or ingredients.

- Reducing or removing features to reduce cost.

- Removing or reducing product services such as free delivery and installation.

- Reducing the number of sizes and models used.

- Creating new, economy brands.

Test your understanding 3

Consider an appropriate pricing strategy for each of the following products:

(1) An international consumer electronics company who are launching a personal (MP4) video player which can take even 'normal', two-dimensional video material and display it as 3D images.

(2) A company launching a new magazine on practical plastic surgery.

(3) 'Robin Hood Stickers' are launching a sticker album to tie in with the popular children's character. The album comes with blank spaces where children can attach sticky pictures (sold separately) with pictures of scenes and characters from the stories. The company want children to firstly buy their sticker album and then go on to buy the stickers regularly for the album.

(4) A high-end automobile manufacturer are introducing a new model with a range of high-end features such as monitors in the front head rests for passengers in the rear to use on journeys. The monitors will be able to accept games consoles, dvds and blu-rays. The car will cost around $18,000 each to produce.

(5) James Gower who has just qualified as a plumber in a local town that is already serviced by 12 other individual plumbers (though due to the size of the community he should be able to find plenty of willing customers). All plumbers in the area advertise their services and prices in a local business directory which the community use when choosing service providers.

(6) An airline company who are introducing a new service between two neighbouring towns. The service will have 5 minute check-ins and only a 10 minute journey. Many business customers are looking forward to the service as the roads between the towns are of poor quality and over-congested.

(7) A building firm who are putting on a new roof to a building in a capital city. There is a lot of competition but the potential client owns 12 other buildings in the city which may also need new roofs due to potential damage caused by recent adverse weather conditions.

Pricing and e-businesses

It is a common misconception that internet shoppers are only concerned with price. Because they expect goods to be cheaper and can quickly compare prices between sites (there are even specialist websites that will perform this task for shoppers such as Kelkoo), there is a feeling that shoppers place 'price' at the forefront of their decision making process.

In reality, shoppers still consider the other elements of the marketing mix. They expect to achieve some savings when shopping on the internet but they do not necessarily compare prices or perform extensive price checks. Research shows that shoppers are e-loyal and will often return to familiar and trusted sites for their purchases. They often buy from the first site that they visit as long as prices are perceived to be within a reasonable or expected range.

This emphasises that the other elements of the 7P's model such as the security processes, the ease-of-use etc. for a website are equally important. CRM (covered later in the chapter) will also play a vital role in creating the site loyalty in the first place.

Cost based pricing

Cost based pricing is often inappropriate for businesses – it ignores customers, competitors, and corporate objectives. However, it may occasional prove useful for businesses – for example, in times of rapid inflation or when demanded by a particular, powerful customer.

In previous studies you will have explored cost based strategies such as full cost plus, marginal cost plus and target ROI.

More details on cost based pricing methods

The following should serve as a reminder of cost based pricing strategies that will have been studied in previous papers:

Full cost plus

In this method the total cost associated with the product is determined (i.e. all fixed and variable costs) and a net margin is added.

Advantages	*Disadvantages*
• easy to calculate	• less incentive to control costs
• ensures that a profit is generated	• relies on arbitrary overhead apportionments
• can justify price rises	

Retailers use a similar approach to this which is known as mark-up pricing – a 'mark-up' percentage is added to the purchase price of the product in order to cover operating costs, risks etc. The level of the mark can vary from industry to industry.

Marginal cost plus

In this method only the variable costs are associated with the product and a contribution margin is added.

Advantages	*Disadvantages*
• better for short-term decision making	• does not ensure that all costs are covered
• avoids overhead apportionment	• shouldn't be used for long run pricing

Target ROI (Return on Investment)

In this method a full cost for the product is determined and then an amount necessary to give a predetermined ROI is added in order to get the selling price. The predetermined ROI is calculated as the product investment multiplied by the target ROI.

KAPLAN PUBLISHING

Advantages	Disadvantages
• often used by new products or market leaders	• difficult to determine volume required to determine a price per unit
• consistent with performance appraisal techniques (so it will be liked by managers)	• if investment is shared between products arbitrary allocations are made

As seen above, relevant cost pricing can sometimes be valid (for example, in tendering processes). In calculating which costs are relevant, three criteria must be satisfied:

- the cost(s) must be incurred in the **future**,

- only the **incremental** cost(s) should be included, and

- the **cash** impact only of the cost(s) should be included.

4 Pricing in economics

Pricing in economics is based on assumptions about demand and supply and the interaction between these two factors. From a marketing perspective demand will be more important than supply.

Determining demand

The normal assumption about demand is that it will fall as the price of a product increases.

Illustration 2 – Pricing in economics

Consider the following simple example:

A company knows that if it sets its selling price to $1,000 it will only sell one unit. Market research has also shown that each time it reduces its selling price by $100 it will sell an extra unit. The product costs $600 to produce per unit (variable).

The company has produced the following summary table:

Selling price	Demand	Total revenue	Marginal revenue	Marginal cost	Profit on this unit
$1,000	1	$1,000	$1,000	$600	$400
$900	2	$1,800	$800	$600	$200
$800	3	$2,400	$600	$600	$0
$700	4	$2,800	$400	$600	($200)
$600	5	$3,000	$200	$600	($400)
$500	6	$3,000	$0	$600	($600)
$400	7	$2,800	($200)	$600	($800)
$300	8	$2,400	($400)	$600	($1000)

Notice that one of the implications of the economic assumption is that there is a gradual reduction in marginal revenue (i.e. the extra revenue gained from selling one more unit).

Profit maximisation in economics

(1) In order to maximise profits

set the price which achieves a position of

marginal revenue = marginal cost

It can be seen from the table above that, from a profit position, there is little point in producing the 4th unit. It costs $600 to produce but only brings in $400 in extra revenue. Therefore profits are maximised with production is at 3 units. To achieve this position the selling price should be set at $800 per unit.

(2) In order to maximise revenue

set the price which achieves a position of

marginal revenue = 0

If the objective is instead to maximise revenue (say, if this is a new product and the company is looking to initially establish product reputation and create a barrier to entry) then the maximum possible revenue figure occurs when 6 units are produced. This corresponds to the point where the marginal revenue is zero. To achieve this position the selling price should be set to $500.

Again, it can be seen how different objectives can lead to different pricing decisions.

Economic assumptions

As with demand, in economics some assumptions are made about costs (for example, that they can be easily split between variable and fixed elements, and that they don't change in the short-term). In reality economic assumptions rarely hold and it is important that economic pricing is therefore not seen as a precise science – as the assumptions change our analysis and pricing must also change.

However, this assumes that a number of variables remain unchanged:

- the business environment
- the buyer's needs
- the buyer's ability to pay
- the marketing mix.

Different demand curves

A change in any of these variables can lead to a shift in the position, shape or slope of the demand curve for a product.

For example, you may remember from previous studies that in an oligopolistic market – such as international accounting which is dominated by 4 large firms – the demand curve is kinked and price competition rarely arises. Firms know that price increases will lose a lot of customers, but price drops will win very few extra clients.

Demand-based pricing is a variable pricing mechanism that changes the price in order to fit the demand. It results in a high price when demand is high, and low prices when demand is low. For example, it is used at leisure amenities such as gymnasiums where prices for using facilities might be higher at 'peak times' (such as early mornings) and lower when the club typically has less visitors (such as mid-afternoon).

The elasticity of demand

The relationship price and demand is also affected by the elasticity of demand for the product.

Formula for price elasticity of demand

This is calculated as follows:

$$\text{Price elasticity of demand} = \frac{\text{\% change in quantity demanded}}{\text{\% change in price}}$$

For products with a low elasticity (i.e. where a large change in price only creates a small increase in volume) the normal strategy is to increase prices slightly so that overall revenue and profits increase. (The opposite applies when elasticity is high).

Inelastic products are usually ones where there are few substitutes and customer needs are high (such as utilities and petrol).

Further details on price elasticity

More than ever, companies need to understand the price sensitivity of their customers (existing & potential), and the trade-offs people are willing to make between price and product characteristics. Marketers also need to know how responsive, or elastic, demand is to changes in price. If demand hardly changes with a small change in price, demand is then inelastic. If demand changes considerably, demand is deemed to be elastic.

Demand is likely to be less elastic when:

- There are few or no substitutes or competitors.

- Buyers do not readily notice the high price.

- Buyers are slow to change their buying habits and search for lower prices.

- Buyers think the higher prices are justified by quality differences and/or normal inflation.

Price elasticity depends on the magnitude and direction of the contemplated price change. It may be negligible with a small price change and substantial with a large price change. Price elasticity may differ for a price cut versus a price increase.

Long-run price elasticity may differ from short-run elasticity. Buyers may continue to buy from their current supplier after a price increase because they do not notice the increase, or the increase is small, or they are distracted by other concerns, or they do not wish to incur switching costs. But, over time, they may switch suppliers on the basis of price. Here demand is seen to be more elastic in the long run than in the short run. Or the opposite may happen, buyers drop a supplier after being notified of a price increase, but return to the supplier later.

5 E-marketing: the 6Is

The 6Is of marketing is a summary of the differences between the new media and traditional media. By considering each of these aspects of the new media, marketing managers can develop plans to accommodate the characteristics of the new media.

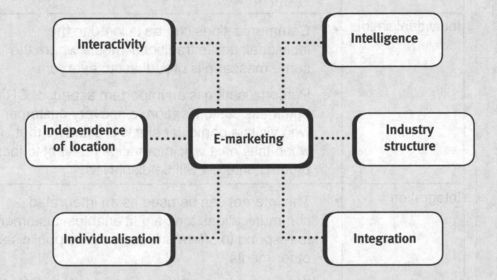

Explanation of the 6Is

Interactivity	• Traditional media are mainly 'push' media – the marketing message is broadcast from company to customer – with limited interaction.
	• On the internet it is usually a customer who seeks information on a web – it is a 'pull' mechanism.
Intelligence	• The internet can be used as a low-cost method of collecting marketing information about customer perceptions of products and services.
	• The website also records information every time a user clicks on a link. Log file analysers will identify the type of promotions or products customers are responding to and how patterns vary over time.
Individualisation	• Communications can be tailored to the individual, unlike traditional media where the same message is broadcast to everyone.
	• Personalisation is an important aspect of CRM and mass customisation, e.g. every customer who visits a particular site is profiled so that when they next visit information relevant to their product, interest will be displayed.
Integration	• The internet can be used as an integrated communications tool, e.g. it enables customers to respond to offers and promotions publicised in other media;
	• It can have a direct response or call back facility built in;
	• It can be used to support the buying decision, even if the purchase does not go through the internet – with web-specific phone numbers on websites.
Industry structure	• The relationship between a company and its channel partners can be dramatically altered by the opportunities available on the internet. For example, disintermediation and reintermediation.
Independence of location	• Electronic media gives the possibility of communicating globally – giving opportunities of selling into markets that may not have been previously accessible.

6 E-branding

A brand is a name, symbol, term, mark or design that enables customers to identify and distinguish the products of one supplier from those offered by competitors.

E-branding has become more and more important as companies decide to offer their services and products online. Website design, corporate branding, e-commerce and search engine optimisation are critical components in building a company's e-branding.

E-branding strategies

Organisations have a number of choices about how to handle e-branding.

- Carry out exactly the same branding on the website as in other places. The organisation has to be careful to ensure that the website style, quality and commercial offers are consistent with the existing brand.

- Offer a slightly amended product or service, still connected to the original brand. The slight differentiation is often signalled by putting the word 'On-line' after the original brand name. For example 'Timesonline.co.uk'. This site describes itself as 'The best of The Times and The Sunday Times in real time'. So the products are slightly different from the paper-based products, so are differentiated but still strongly linked. The 'on-line' description also promises interactivity and might suggest a free service.

- Form a partnership with an existing brand.

- Create an entirely new brand, perhaps to emphasise a more modern, flexible approach. This has been common with financial institutions such as HBOS and IF. HBOS runs a conventional banking operation and IF is its direct finance operations that makes high use of the internet.

Illustration

Aspirin's land-based brand positioning statement was 'Aspirin – provides instant pain relief'. This does not hold true for a meaningful web presence, you can't get instant pain relief on the web. So the management utilised their new e-branding creative strategies to develop a website for Aspirin that made sense to a consumer in the disintermediated world of brands on the web. The result was 'Aspirin – your self help brand', which offered visitors meaningful health-oriented intelligence and self help, over the web.

7 Customer relationship management (CRM)

Introduction

The objective of CRM is to increase customer loyalty in order to increase profitability and is thus a key aspect of e-business.

Definitions

- CRM is an approach to building and sustaining long-term business with customers.

- e-CRM is the use of digital communications technology to maximise sales to existing customers and encourage continued usage of online services.

Research

Research into e-businesses suggests the following:

- It is 20 – 30% more expensive to acquire new online customers than for traditional businesses.

- Retaining an extra 5% of customers can boost online company profits by between 25 and 95%.

The customer lifecycle

CRM involves four key marketing activities (the 'customer lifecycle').

(1) Customer **selection** – defining what type of customer is being targeted.

- Who are we targeting?

- What is their value?

- Where do we reach them?

(2) Customer **acquisition** – forming relationships with new customers.

- Need to target the right segments.

- Try to minimise acquisition costs. Methods include traditional off-line techniques (e.g. advertising, direct mail) and online techniques (e.g. search engine marketing, online PR, online partnerships, interactive adverts, opt-in e-mail and viral marketing).

- Service quality is key here.

- Choice of distribution channel also very important.

(3) Customer **retention** – keeping existing customers.

– Emphasis on understanding customer needs better to ensure better customer satisfaction.

– Use offers to reward extended website usage.

– Ensure ongoing service quality right by focusing on tangibles, reliability, responsiveness, assurance and empathy.

(4) Customer **extension** (or 'customer development') – increasing the range of products bought by the customer.

– "Re-sell" similar products to previous sales.

– "Cross-sell" closely related products.

– "Up-sell" more expensive products.

Customer acquisition

Methods of acquiring customers can be split between traditional off-line techniques (e.g. advertising, direct mail, sponsorship, etc) and rapidly-evolving on-line techniques:

Search engine marketing

- Search engine optimisation – improving the position of a company in search engine listings for key terms or phrases. For example, increasing the number of inbound links to a page through 'link building' can improve the ranking with Google.

- Pay per click (PPC) – an advert is displayed by search engines as a 'sponsored link' when particular phrases are entered. The advertiser typically pays a fee to the search engine each time the advert is clicked.

- Trusted feed – database-driven sites such as travel, shopping and auctions are very difficult to optimise for search engines and consequently haven't enjoyed much visibility in the free listings. Trusted Feed works by allowing a 'trusted' third party, usually a search engine marketing company, to 'feed' a website's entire online inventory directly into the search engine's own database, bypassing the usual submission process.

Online PR

- Media alerting services – using online media and journalists for press releases.

- Portal representation – portals are websites that act as gateways to information and services. They typically contain search engines and directories.

- Businesses blogs (effectively online journals) can be used to showcase the expertise of its employees.

- Community C2C portals (effectively the e-equivalent of a village notice board) – e.g. an oil company could set up a discussion forum on its website to facilitate discussion on issues including pollution.

Online partnerships

- Link-building – reciprocal links can be created by having quality content and linking to other sites with quality content. The objective is that they will then link to your site.

- Affiliate marketing – a commission-based arrangement where an e-retailer pays sites that link to it for sales. For example, hundreds of thousands of sites direct customers to Amazon to buy the books or CDs that they have mentioned on their pages.

- Sponsorship – web surfers are more likely to trust the integrity of a firm sponsoring a website than those who use straight ads.

- Co-branding – a lower cost form of sponsorship where products are labelled with two brand names. For example, as well as including details about their cars, the website Subaru.com also includes immediate co-branded insurance quotes with Liberty Mutual Insurance and pages devoted to outdoor lifestyles developed with LL Bean.

- Aggregators – these are comparison sites allowing customers to compare different product features and prices. For example, moneysupermarket.com allows analysis of financial services products. Clearly a mortgage lender would want their products included in such comparisons.

Interactive adverts

- Banners – banners are simply advertisements on websites with a click through facility so customers can surf to the advertiser's website.

- Rich-media – many web users have become immune to conventional banner ads so firms have tried increasingly to make their ads more noticeable through the use of animation, larger formats, overlays, etc. For example, an animated ad for Barclays banking services will appear on some business start-up sites.

- Some ads are more interactive and will change depending on user mouse movements, for example generating a slide show.

Opt-in e-mail

It is estimated that 80% of all e-mails are spam or viruses. Despite this e-mail marketing can still deliver good response rates. One survey found only 10% of e-mails were not delivered (e.g. due to spam filters), 30% were opened and 8% resulted in 'clickthroughs'. Options for e-mail include the following:

- Cold, rented lists – here the retailer buys an e-mail list from a provider such as Experian.

- Co-branded e-mail – for example, your bank sends you an e-mail advertising a mobile phone.

- 3rd party newsletters – the retailers advertises itself in a 3rd party's newsletter.

- House list e-mails – lists built up in-house from previous customers, for example.

Viral marketing

- Viral marketing is where e-mail is used to transmit a promotional message from one person to another.

- Ideally the viral ad should be a clever idea, a game or a shocking idea that is compulsive viewing so people send it to their friends.

Evaluating online customer behaviour

Recency, frequency, monetary value analysis (RFM) is the main model used to classify online buyer behaviour.

Recency

- The time since a customer completed an action – e.g. purchase, site visit, e-mail response.
- Considered to be a good indicator of potential repeat purchases.
- Allows 'vulnerable' customers to be specifically targeted.

Frequency

- The number of times an action is completed in a specified time period – e.g. five log-ins per week.
- A related concept is latency – the average time between actions – e.g. the average time between first and second purchases.
- Together these allow the firm to put in place triggers that alert them to behaviour outside the norm. For example, a customer may be taking longer than normal between first and second purchases. This could indicate that they are currently considering a purchase prompting the firm to e-mail or phone them with relevant offers.

Monetary value

- The monetary value of purchases can be measured in many different ways such as average order value, total annual purchases, etc.
- High monetary value is usually a good indicator of customer loyalty and higher future potential purchases. Such customers could be deliberately excluded from special promotions.

RFM is also known as FRAC:

- Frequency
- Recency
- Amount = monetary value
- Category = types of product purchased – not in RFM.

Customer retention

Customer retention has two goals:

* to keep customers
* to keep customers using the online channel.

Customer satisfaction

Key to retention is understanding and delivering the drivers of customer satisfaction as satisfaction drives loyalty and loyalty drives profitability.

The 'SERVQUAL' approach to service quality developed by **Parasuraman et al** focuses on the following factors.

Tangibles

* The 'tangibles' heading considers the appearance of physical facilities, equipment, personnel and communications.
* For online quality the key issue is the appearance and appeal of websites – customers will revisit websites that they find appealing.
* This can include factors such as structural and graphic design, quality of content, ease of use, speed to upload and frequency of update.

Reliability

* Reliability is the ability to provide a promised service dependably and accurately and is usually the most important of the different aspects being discussed here.
* For online service quality, reliability is mainly concerned with how easy it is to connect to the website.
* If websites are inaccessible some of the time and/or e-mails are bounced back, then customers will lose confidence in the retailer.

Responsiveness

* Responsiveness looks at the willingness of a firm to help customers and provide prompt service.
* In the context of e-business, excessive delays can cause customers to 'bail-out' of websites and/or transactions and go elsewhere.
* This could relate to how long it takes for e-mails to be answered or even how long it takes for information to be downloaded to a user's browser.

Assurance

- Assurance is the knowledge and courtesy of employees and their ability to inspire trust and confidence.

- For an online retailer, assurance looks at two issues – the quality of responses and the privacy/security of customer information.

- Quality of response includes competence, credibility and courtesy and could involve looking at whether replies to e-mails are automatic or personalised and whether questions have been answered satisfactorily.

Empathy

- Empathy considers the caring, individualised attention a firm gives its customers.

- Most people would assume that empathy can only occur through personal human contact but it can be achieved to some degree through personalising websites and e-mail.

- Key here is whether customers feel understood. For example, being recommended products that they would never dream of buying can erode empathy.

There are three stages to applying the SERVQUAL framework.

(1) Understanding customer expectations through research.

(2) Setting and communicating the service promise.

(3) Delivering the service promise to ensure that a service quality gap does not exist.

Techniques for retaining customers

Given the above consideration of service quality, firms use the following techniques to try to retain customers.

- Personalisation – delivering individualised content through web-pages or e-mail. For example, portals such as Yahoo! enable users to configure their home pages to give them the information they are most interested in.

- Mass customisation – delivering customised content to groups of users through web-pages or e-mail. For example, Amazon may recommend a particular book based on what other customers in a particular segment have been buying.

- Extranets – for example, Dell Computers uses an extranet to provide additional services to its 'Dell Premier' customers.

- Opt-in e-mail – asking customers whether they wish to receive further offers.

- Online communities – firms can set up communities where customers create the content. These could be focused on purpose (e.g. Autotrader is for people buying/selling cars), positions (e.g. the teenage chat site Doobedo), interest (e.g. Football365) or profession. Despite the potential for criticism of a company's products on a community, firms will understand where service quality can be improved, gain a better understanding of customer needs and be in a position to answer criticism.

Customer extension

Customer extension has the objective of increasing the lifetime value of a customer and typically involves the following.

- 'Re-sell' similar products to previous sales.

- 'Cross sell' closely related products.

- 'Up sell' more expensive products.

- For example, having bought a book from Amazon you could be contacted with offers of other books, DVDs or DVD players.

- Reactivate customers who have not bought anything for some time.

Key to these are propensity modelling and the 'sense, respond, adjust' model.

Propensity modelling

Propensity modelling involves evaluating customer behaviour and then making recommendations to them for future products. For example, if you have bought products from Amazon, then each time you log on there will be a recommendation of other products you may be interested in.

This can involve the following:

- Create automatic product relationships – e.g. through monitoring which products are typically bought together.

- Using trigger words or phrases – e.g. 'customers who bought …also bought…'.

- Offering related products at checkout – e.g. batteries for electronic goods.

'Sense, respond, adjust'

- Sense – monitor customer activities to classify them according to value, growth, responsiveness and defection risk. RFM analysis, discussed above, would also be relevant here.

- Respond with timely, relevant communications to encourage desired behaviours.

- Adjust – monitor responses and continue with additional communications.

Illustration 3 – E-marketing

The Amazon.com (or Amazon.co.uk) site provides the following facilities, all of which can be linked to marketing and customer service, and that help Amazon to acquire customers, retain customers and increase income from them.

- Home delivery of books/CDs, etc. (using place and independence of location to acquire customers).

- Customers can write reviews and read other people's reviews of products (using promotion and interactivity to retain customers).

- Based on previous buying habits, products are recommended (using intelligence and individualisation to extend customer purchases).

- 'Customers who bought this product also bought these products…' (using intelligence and promotion to extend customer purchases).

- Order tracking (using integration to retain customers).

- Prices of new and used items are displayed. Prices of new items are usually lower than conventional shops (using price to acquire customers).

- Very smart-looking interface (using physical evidence to acquire and retain customers).

- Search facilities (using interactivity and processes to acquire customers).

- Emails if orders are delayed (using processes and individualisation to retain customers).

Historically, marketing has focused on the first two elements in the lifecycle (selection and acquisition) at best. CRM aims to extend marketing over all four stages and build a lasting relationship with customers which creates loyalty and keeps them coming back for more.

Comparison with transactional marketing

Gordon (1998) states that there are six dimensions that illustrate how relationship marketing differs from the historical definition of marketing. These are that:

- relationship marketing seeks to create new value for customers and then share it with these customers.

- relationship marketing recognises the key role that customers have both as purchasers and in defining the value they wish to receive.

- relationship marketing businesses are seen to design and align processes, communication, technology and people in support of customer value.

- relationship marketing represents continuous cooperative effort between buyers and sellers.

- relationship marketing recognises the value of customers' purchasing lifetimes (i.e. Customer Lifetime Value).

- relationship marketing seeks to build a chain of relationships within the organisation, to create the value customers want, and between the organisation and its main stakeholders, including suppliers, distribution channels, intermediaries and shareholders.

The growing interest in relationship marketing suggests a shift in the nature of marketplace transactions from discrete to relational exchanges, from exchanges between parties with no past history and no future to interactions between parties with a history and plans for future interaction.

Transactional marketing	Relationship marketing
• Orientation to single sales	• Orientation to customer retention
• Discontinuous customer contact	• Continuous customer contact
• Focus on product features	• Focus on customer value
• Short time scale	• Long time scale
• Little emphasis on customer service	• High emphasis on customer service

• Limited commitment to meeting customer expectations	• High commitment to meeting customer expectations

Software solutions

Software plays a vital role in CRM. It can organise, automate and synchronize marketing and sales actions. For example, when a customer buys a book on Amazon's website, the software can recommend other similar books that the customer might be interested in based on both this individual customers past purchases and preferences as well as data gathered on customers who have purchased this same book in the past.

Illustration 4 – Customer relationship management (CRM)

The online aspects (there are many others) of SAP's CRM module includes the following features:

E-marketing

- Supports customer loyalty processes via the Internet.
- Personalizes customers' Web experiences.
- Generates additional revenue through a website via catalogue management, content management, customer segmentation and personalization.

E-commerce

- Runs B2B and B2C selling processes on the Internet.
- Enables a full range of online selling processes, including pricing and contracts, interactive selling, web auctions, and selling via partners.
- Streamlines sales and fulfilment with end-to-end order-to-cash processes.

E-service

- Offers customers an intuitive channel to perform service tasks, from requesting a service visit to logging a complaint or registering a product.
- Enables customers to checking order status, obtain order tracking information, manage accounts and payments, and research and resolve product problems.
- Services complex products that require sophisticated maintenance.

Web channel analytics

- Gains insight into, analyzes, and acts on e-business trends.

- Measures and optimizes the success of Web shop and online content.

- Performs analysis of marketing, sales, and service from a Web perspective.

- Tracks Web behaviour to target customers and drive future marketing activities.

Customer relationship management systems (CRMs)

CRMs do what they say: they help organisations to form and maintain relationships with customers. Customers of large organisations rarely speak to a specific named individual. This is especially so if the organisation uses a call centre approach to handle customers' calls. It is, however, important that the customer feels he or she is getting a good service, where the organisation knows about previous sales, customer preferences, previous problems and previous conversations. Typically, a CRM will show the following information on-screen to employees dealing with customers.

- The customer's name, address, telephone number, email and, if applicable, web address.

- Current debtors ledger balance.

- If the customer is an organisation, named individuals employed by the customer with whom the organisation deals, together with their job titles and authority levels.

- Some additional information about customer's employees, for example that that person is a technical expert, or previously worked for a certain company, or does not like to be contacted before 2pm.

- Summaries of previous conversations with the customer.

- Details of previous sales to the customer – description of goods/services and value.

- Diary entries to remind the organisation to carry out agreed tasks for the customer.

It is immensely valuable to have this information available when dealing with customers, both to talk intelligently to the customer, and identify sales opportunities that might arise during the conversation. CRM packages therefore allow organisations to have a much more informed, professional and, it is hoped, profitable relationship with customers.

Test your understanding 4

A top level football team want to introduce a credit card for supporters.
Explain how CRM software could help the business in the customer
selection process.

8 Chapter summary

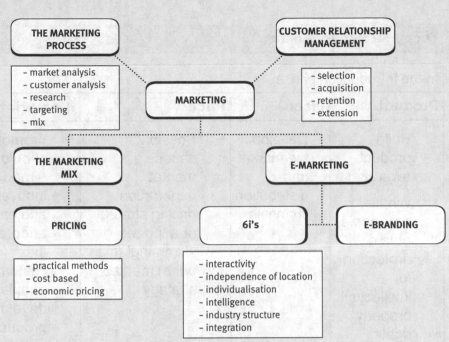

Test your understanding answers

In the introduction phase.

Product	Place	Price	Promotion
• Build product awareness • Where applicable, obtain protection for intellectual property rights (patents, etc.) • Establish the brand and the quality to be associated with the brand	• Develop the market and distribution channels	• Possibly choose a market penetration pricing strategy, or a 'price skimming' (high price) market strategy	• promotions should be aimed at innovators and early adopters in the customer population: develop product awareness

In the growth phase.

Product	Place	Price	Promotion
• Build the brand • Maintain product quality, but add additional features to create product differentiation	• Add distribution channels	• Keep prices unchanged: sales growth is rising therefore there is no need yet to change pricing strategy	• Promotion should aim now at a broader audience of potential customers

Test your understanding 2

The best way to consider how the company could be marketed is to examine the elements of the **marketing mix**:

Price

Hartley's Books are likely to use an element of perceived value pricing. There is unlikely to be a 'going rate' for such books and other strategies such as penetration or skimming are unlikely to be appropriate due to the uniqueness of the product.

Books should be valued and priced based on likely demand, uniqueness/rarity and the current economic climate. This may mean that book prices change over time – for example, they may go down as the economic climate deteriorates, but they might increase as they become older and rarer. Due to the likely low level of competition, there should be no need for discounting on the website and delivery charges could be added to the normal price that would be charged in shops.

But pricing is unlikely to be a key element of the marketing mix.

Place

It would appear that Hartley's Books have already determined the method in which books will be sold. They will have a physical presence through their six stores as well as an e-commerce website for internet sales.

Other aspects that they could consider would be some elements of integrated e-commerce. Perhaps if a book is purchased in a store extra content such as author biographies, links to author websites etc. could be available online. There might also be a 'reserve and collect' facility on the website so that a book could be reserved online and then collected in the store in order to speed up the delivery process and reduce the threats that might arise from the transport of some books.

Promotion

Techniques such as television and radio advertising, or sales promotion techniques are unlikely to be of much use to Hartley's Books due to the small size of the target market and the unlikelihood of regular purchases. There may be specialist journals or magazines in which the company could advertise but a more important avenue that may be open to the company is likely to be trade shows and exhibitions.

There may be regular events for antiquarian book collectors or even specialist author events. Hartley's Books could aim to have a physical presence at such events displaying a range of suitable books and could even aim to provide sponsorship and branding of such events. This would provide them with direct access to potential customers as well as increasing awareness of the company and more 'hits' on its website.

The lack of common promotional avenues is likely to reinforce the value of the internet venture. Hartley's Books should look to have banner adverts on author websites that link back to its own website and could even attempt to provide sponsorship in forum groups that are used by its target market. They should seek to have a high appearance rate on popular search engines and perhaps seek endorsements from authors (or their site managers) on the author's own site.

Product

The company's 'product' will be the service it provides, the shops in which sales are made and the range of books that it sells. These are the areas that it should look to differentiate from rivals.

It could improve service by perhaps offering reading or viewing facilities within its shops and by having knowledgeable staff who are experienced in understanding and meeting customer needs. Shops should reflect the nature of the product being sold and could, for example, have antique furniture such as reading chairs and indexing so that customers can find what they are looking for. The range of books should be as wide as possible in order to attract as many possible buyers as possible, and Hartley's Books could perhaps seek to offer certificates of authenticity in order to provide reassurance to buyers.

Processes

There will need to be clear security on the website for payments and if the 'reserve and collect' facility is offered it should be clear and simple to use. Due to the nature of the product the key process may be transportation and delivery as some books might be delicate and fragile in nature. This process should be may as safe and reassuring as possible and perhaps customers could be given the option of choosing or arranging their own courier as an alternative. Worldwide delivery could be offered and as many different payment methods as possible should be allowed in order to maximise potential sales. Regular customers should be given the ability to store their details for personal use and perhaps software could be used to recommend further purchases based on past buying behaviour.

People

The nature of the product undoubtedly will mean that buyers are likely to have questions when they find a book that they are interested in. It will therefore be vital that the internet site is back up with knowledgeable service staff who can answer questions on the book in question. Given the likely low numbers of sales (particularly in the early days of the site) these calls could be directed to shop floor staff, perhaps with one member of staff at each store allocated each day to answer such calls. These staff may have to work more flexible times in order to meet the times of highest demand on the internet site during the day.

This may mean that more staff need to be recruited into stores. Also, as the internet site grows, some staff could be dedicated full time to such queries.

This facility needs to be support with email support as some customers may be shopping at times when stores are closed. But most buyers may be happy to await for a call back facility as speed of delivery is unlikely to be a critical success factor in the industry.

Physical evidence

The website should be easy to navigate and well presented. One of the key elements will be to have a search facility so that buyers can find particular books that they may be interested in. There should also be a 'request' option where , if Hartley's Books do not have a copy of a particular book, a potential buyer can express and interest and be kept informed if Hartley's Books manage to source a copy.

Another aspect that may be offered could be a buying facility. Hartley's Books will not have suppliers like other bookshops. They will rely on sourcing books from individuals and estates. The internet might provide an excellent opportunity to source rare books which can be sold on at a profit through either shops or the website.

Test your understanding 3

(1) The most appropriate strategy for this product would be **price skimming**. The product should start with a high price and this price should be gradually reduced as new rivals enter the market and the technology matures. There is no need for repeat business or loyalty as consumers are only likely to buy one product and may not replace this for a number of years. These are the typical market conditions for price skimming.

(2) This product is going to need to two things from its customers in order to be successful – an initial interest and awareness, and then longer-term repeat business. These are typical conditions for **price penetration**. The magazine should start with an initial low price (possibly even as a **'loss leader'**) in order to establish an initial reader base. Then as further issues are released these could be increased to the normal issue price (when a new pricing strategy such as **perceived value pricing** might be more appropriate).

(3) The most appropriate pricing strategy here would be **captive product pricing**. The initial album should be sold at a low price (again, a **loss leader** strategy might be appropriate). Once children have the album they will demand the sticky pictures ('stickers') to fill the album. These stickers could be sold at higher prices with margins that will more than compensate for any loss incurred in the initial sale of the album.

(4) The production cost of the product will be largely irrelevant (although, obviously, the selling price must at least cover this cost). As a high-end manufacturer the company will have an image and reputation to project and protect. They are likely to use **perceived value pricing** and play on consumers perceptions of their products. Consumers will expect the price to be high to reflect perceptions on the quality of materials and the production methods used. The product is likely to be sold at 3 or 4 times its production cost.

(5) The most appropriate strategy in this scenario is likely to be to use **going rate pricing**. If James charges too high a price then customers (who are likely to price conscious) will choose James' rivals. If James charges a price below that of rivals then rivals are likely to match this price to the detriment of all plumbers in the area. In this scenario of almost perfect competition, it is likely that there will be one market price and James and his rivals will have to use other elements of the marketing mix to acquire customers.

(6) This scenario is one where **price discrimination** could be used. For example, the airline could discriminate on the basis of the timing of the booking. Those people who book their flights early could pay low prices, but those who pay later could pay progressively higher prices as the departure date of the flight approaches. For example, if a flight is booked with only one days notice, then the buyer is likely to be putting a high perceived value on the flight. This should be reflected by having a high price for the flight.

(7) Tender processes usually involve an element of **cost based pricing**. Because this contract might lead to further work in the future the builder might even forego any margin and quote at the **relevant cost** (this concept is explored in the next section) of the job to ensure an incremental break even position. The builder might consider a loss leader approach to the project but this has a number of difficulties – if no further tenders are won then the builder is left to carry the loss, and if further work is won it may be harder to justify significantly higher prices in the future.

Test your understanding 4

The CRM software is likely to hold a lot of data on supporters (customers) that could be used in the customer selection process, such as:

- Customer address and zip/post code. This might allow the company to target supporters who live in wealthy areas.

- Payment method used. Customers who have previously used a credit card as a payment method may be more likely to sign up for a new credit card.

- Missed payments. Customers who have perhaps missed payments on past transactions may be in financial difficulty and be actively seeking out credit methods.

- Items purchased. Customers who have spent large sums in the past (for example, for season tickets) might be more inclined to use credit cards.

- Age. Due to legal rules, credit cards may only be targeted at customers of a particular age.

- Contact details. If email addresses are held then these provide a route to electronic marketing.

Project management I – The business case

Chapter learning objectives

Upon completion of this chapter you will be able to:

- explain the typical distinguishing features of a project and the constraints of time, money and quality, and discuss their implications

- describe, for the strategic plan, how elements of the strategy can be broken down into a series of projects

- describe the process of identifying, assessing and dealing with risks

- advise on the structures and information that have to be in place to successfully initiate a project in organisations in general

- explain, using examples, how process redesign, e-business and systems development can be treated as projects

- describe the contents of a business case document

- analyse, describe, assess and classify the benefits and costs of a project investment

- explain the role of a benefits realisation plan

- describe and assess a benefits dependency network and explain how responsibility for the delivery of benefits can be achieved

- evaluate a project using standard project appraisal techniques.

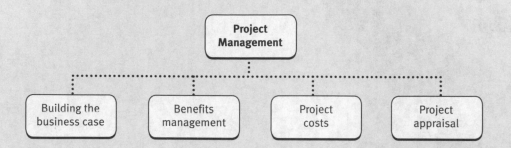

1 Project features

A project can be defined simply as an activity, which has a start, middle and end, and consumes resources. It will:

- have a specific objective

- have a defined start and end date (timescale)

- consume resources (people, equipment and finance)

- be unique (a one-time-only configuration of these elements)

- have cost constraints that must be clearly defined and understood to ensure the project remains viable

- require organisation.

2 Process redesign, e-business and systems development as projects

A project differs from 'ordinary work' that is ongoing and has a mixture of many recurring tasks and more general goals and objectives. Although some projects may be initiated on an ad-hoc basis, it is more common for them to be an implementation tool for the strategic plan of the organisation.

Projects are fundamental to other aspects of the syllabus such as business process change and IT development.

Links to other syllabus areas

Process redesign project

Business process redesign often involves specific projects linked to specific processes.

Systems development project

Developing e-business opportunities often involves specific projects. Typical steps might include:

- System Analysis
- Design
- Site Construction
- System Integration
- System Test
- Final Evaluation.

3 Stages in the project life cycle

Every project is different, but each will include at least the following five stages:

- initiation
- planning
- execution
- control
- completion.

This chapter explores the first stage of the process in more detail. The next chapter will cover the remaining elements.

Project initiation – building the business case

This chapter focuses on project initiation. It examines the contents of a business case document, it assesses what benefits might be derived from a project and how these benefits should be managed, it assesses potential project costs, and it finishes by matching up the project costs and benefits in project appraisal techniques.

Reasons for building a business case:

- to obtain funding for the project
- to compete with other projects for resources
- to improve planning
- to improve project management

The need for a business case

Not every project that managers propose can be undertaken. There may be constraints on resources which mean that, for example, there is not enough finance to fund every project, or it may simply be that in some projects the benefits do not outweigh the costs.

Therefore, a business case should be put together for any proposed project. The aim of this is to achieve approval for the project and to obtain adequate resources to achieve its goals.

4 Contents of a business case

Organisations who have performed many projects will often have developed their own method of presenting a business case. However, they are likely to have the following key elements in common:

- an assessment of the current **strategic position**
- the **constraints** that are likely to exist for any project
- the **risks** that might arise for the project and how these will be managed
- an assessment of the **benefits and costs** of performing the project and how these will be managed

These key elements will now be explored throughout the rest of this chapter.

The formal business case document

It is very unlikely that in an exam a student would be asked to create the formal business case document. Instead you are likely to be asked to focus on providing some of the key elements.

However, the formal document put together for management typically pulls the key elements together into the following sections:

(1) **Introduction**

   This sets the scene and explains the rationale behind why the project has been considered.

(2) **Executive summary**

   This is the most important part of the document as it is likely that this will be the part that is read in most detail by the senior management team. It will include the key considerations that have been made, the options considered, the rationale behind the recommendation and a summary of the key numbers (e.g. the output from a financial project appraisal).

(3) **Description of current situation**

   This will be a strategic and operational assessment of the business. It will include a SWOT analysis and aim to identify the problems that the business is facing and the opportunities available to solve those problems.

(4) **Options considered**

   This will have an assessment of each option that has been considered and provide reasons for the rejection of options that have not been recommended.

(5) **Analysis of costs and benefits**

   This will have the key elements for the project assessment. The detail will be provided in the appendices. This section will provide quantifiable benefits and costs but will also make some attempt to quantify intangible benefits and costs such as the impact on customer satisfaction and staff morale. The output from any project appraisal techniques will also be provided.

(6) Impact assessment

This will examine the impact on elements of the cultural web (studied in a later chapter) such as the organisation culture, the management style, staff roles and routines etc.

(7) Risk assessment

This section will aim to identify the risks to successful project performance and suggest how each risk should be managed. It may also contain some contingency planning to give guidance on different possible directions for the project in the face of these risks arising (though this is often left until the detailed planning stage).

(8) Recommendations

This will contain the justification for the suggested path that the project has pursued. It will pull a lot of the other sections of the business case together.

(9) Appendices

This will lay out the detailed costs and benefits and schedules for areas such as project appraisal.

Strategic analysis

The aim of the strategic analysis in the business case document will be to identify and justify the strategic reasons and drivers for the project. This will often be linked to changes in the external environment such as a new threat or major new opportunity.

The use of a SWOT analysis may be helpful to the project manager in communicating the organisation's current strategic position and the justification of the changes proposed to this position through the implementation of the project.

KAPLAN PUBLISHING

Further explanation on the use of SWOT analysis

SWOT analysis was discussed in earlier chapters as a tool for strategic position analysis. A SWOT analysis can also be used in building the business case for a project as well as being used as part of a periodic report to the project sponsor to summarise progress and raise issues.

The internal appraisal should identify:

- strengths – the organisation's strengths that the project may be able to exploit
- weaknesses – organisational weaknesses that may impact on the project.

The external appraisal should identify:

- opportunities – events or changes outside the project that can be exploited to the advantage of the project
- threats – events or changes outside the project that should be defended against.

The four parts of the SWOT analysis are shown in the diagram below.

Strengths	Weaknesses
• The things that are going well (or have gone well) in the projects • The skills that area prized • Major successes • Parts of the project that are well received by the users or where completed early	• The things that are going badly (or have gone badly) in the projects • The skills that are lacking • Major failures • Parts of the project that are poorly received by the users or were completed late

Opportunities	Threats
• Events or changes outside the project (elsewhere in the organisation or its business environment) that can be exploited to the advantage of the project • Things likely to go well in the future	• Events or changes outside the project (elsewhere in the organisation or its business environment) that should be defended against • Things likely to go badly in the future

Project constraints

There are three key project constraints:

- cost,
- time, and
- scope.

More details

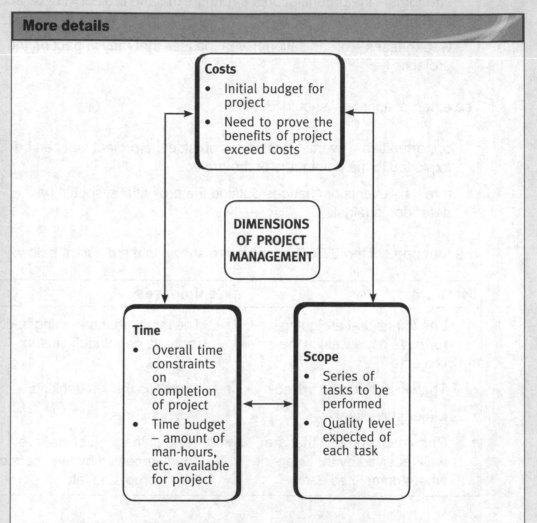

Costs
- Initial budget for project
- Need to prove the benefits of project exceed costs

DIMENSIONS OF PROJECT MANAGEMENT

Time
- Overall time constraints on completion of project
- Time budget – amount of man-hours, etc. available for project

Scope
- Series of tasks to be performed
- Quality level expected of each task

The key elements that a manager must understand are:

- the three constraints are linked together – for example, if a manager wants to increase the scope of the project then he/she is likely to have to increase both the amount of money spent on the project and the time taken to complete it.

- In building the business case, the manager should focus on the constraint that is likely to be most important to the key decision makers (or stakeholders). For example, if key decision makers are concerned primarily with the cost of projects, the project manager should ensure that the proposed project falls within this constraint.

- In project control, it will be important to understand the ranking of the constraints and to ensure that the key constraint is changed as little as possible.

Illustration 1 – Project features and constraints

It is important for project managers to determine which of the constraints (time, costs or scope/performance) is the most important and which is the least in order to focus resources in the most effective way. Additionally, when there are problems, managers should use the least important constraint (weak constraint) to aid in the solution. The most important of the constraints, the driver, should be the last to be compromised.

If scope is the key constraint, then when the project it is out of control it is best to spend more time or increase the budget rather than sacrifice quality or features. On the other hand, if scope is the weak constraint, managers might consider scaling back on features or quality to meet either time or cost constraints.

The key driver may change during a project. That is part of the dynamics of project management. However, managers have to know the initial order of the constraints before they begin the project planning step.

Risk analysis

Risk is defined as 'the chance of exposure to the adverse consequences of future events'. A risk is anything that will have a negative impact on any one or all of the primary project constraints – Time, Scope and Cost.

All projects include some risk.

- Cost over-run
- Missed deadlines
- Poor quality
- Disappointed customers
- Business disruption.

Risks can result in four types of consequences:

- benefits are delayed or reduced
- timeframes are extended
- outlays are advanced or increased
- output quality (fitness for purpose) is reduced.

In order to avoid these consequences, a project manager should add two elements to his/her business case:

- a risk assessment – explaining the type of scale of risks that might occur
- a risk management plan – explaining how these risks will be managed in order to ensure project success.

Risk assessment

Risks can be analysed and evaluated according to:

- the likelihood that they will occur, and
- the impact that they could have on the project.

Risk management

This in turn can lead to plans on how each risk should be managed:

		Likelihood	
		Low	High
Impact	**Low**	Accept	Reduce
	High	Transfer	Avoid

Reducing risk can involve the use of techniques such as internal controls. Transferring risk means moving it to another body, such as an insurance company. Risks that are high in both likelihood and impact need to be avoided in the business case, otherwise management are less likely to approve the project. The project manager might need to create contingency plans for avoiding these risks or delay the project until the likelihood is resolved.

Examples of project risks

The potential risks involved in undertaking a project can be presented in a tabular format as set out below:

Risk	Odds	Impact	Management approach – mitigating actions	Warning signs
Inability to recruit suitably qualified staff	Low	Med.	Ensure remuneration is appropriate to skill level.	Low numbers and poorly qualified applicants.
Retention of staff	Med.	Med.	Motivation via contractual terms, good job design, good working environment and personal development. Consider retention clauses in contract for key staff.	Low morale. High turnover.
Necessary premises not available	Med.	High	Accommodation available to project is currently limited. There could be implications for future of project if additional functionality is required and appropriate accommodation is not available to support it.	Delay to work plans caused by lack of facilities.
Failure to get all parties to share same understanding of purpose	Low	High	Definition of stakeholder needs and clear plan with well-defined deliverables. Use of sound project management methodology.	Differing views on forward plan. Confused messages in draft publications.

Test your understanding 1

A leisure company has just approved a large-scale investment project for the development of a new sports centre and grounds in a major city. The forecast NPV is approximately £6m, assuming five years' steady growth in business and constant returns in perpetuity thereafter. A number of specific risks have been identified:

(1) A potential lawsuit may be brought for death or injury of a member of the public using the equipment. No such event has ever occurred in the company's other centres.

(2) The loss of several weeks' revenue from pool closure for repairs following the appearance of cracks in the infrastructure. This has occurred in several of the other centres in the past few years.

(3) Income fraud as a result of high levels of cash receipts.

(4) Loss of playing field revenue from schools and colleges because of poor weather.

Required:

Suggest how these risks could best be managed.

5 Objectives and drivers for projects

The preceding elements of this chapter have covered many elements of the business case document. But so far the benefits and costs of the project have not been discussed. The remainder of the chapter focuses on these elements.

Driver analysis

The key drivers of any project will be the business strategy and the organisational objectives. Before work commences on a project, it is important that these drivers are understood and discussed. This is known as driver analysis.

Further details

A list of drivers for the project should be created. It should include drivers at all levels of the business – corporate, operational and strategic. Senior management should be involved in this process to ensure that the discussion has a strategic perspective.

> The drivers can come from the analysis carried out earlier in the syllabus – both externally and internally. They should be linked to critical success factors as well as organisational objectives. In order to fulfil all of the drivers, more than one project may be necessary.

Investment objectives

Objectives should also be personalised to the investment. These will be more detailed and operational than the overall project drivers. However, each should be directly linked to one or more of the project drivers.

The list should be short (with between three and six targets) and precise. Ideally, each objective should follow a SMART criteria.

SMART objectives

SMART is a pneumonic used to ensure that objectives are meaningful targets.

For example, a company in debt might have the following objective:

Criteria	Poor objective	Improved objective
Specific	Improve performance	Improve profit before tax
Measurable	Improve profit before tax	Improve profit before tax by 20%
Achievable	Improve profit before tax by 20%	Improve profit before tax by 5%
Relevant	Improve profit before tax by 5%	Reduce debt by 15%
Time bounded	Reduce debt by 15%	Reduce debt by 15% within 18 months

Only when an objective meets all 5 criteria is it deemed to be useful.

Linking the investment objectives to business drivers

Each project undertaken should address at least one business driver. On the other hand, any project that aims to meet all business drivers is likely to be large and complex to manage successfully to completion.

Each investment objective should be linked to at least one business driver. It will also be important to ensure that the investment objectives to not change or evolve over time and lose these links (for example, by focusing more on functional or operational objectives that have become more easily achievable).

Once investment objectives are agreed and linked to business drivers, it is then possible to consider the business benefits that can be realised and manage the process of achieving these.

6 Project benefits

There can be a wide variety of benefits from new projects such as:

- strategic benefits
- productivity gains
- management benefits
- operational benefits
- functional and support benefits
- intangible benefits
- emergent benefits.

More details on project benefits

Strategic benefits

A new project might be a way to gain a competitive advantage as already seen with areas such as business process redesign and supply chain management.

Productivity gains

A project may make operations more efficient or remove non value adding activities from the value chain in order to increase overall productivity of the business. This may be tied-in to a strategic benefit such as cost leadership.

Management benefits

A project may make the organisation more flexible and reactive to its environment. It might give more up-to-date information to managers so that they can make more agile decisions. These benefits often arise from projects which involve organisational redesign or investments in new IS/IT systems.

Operational benefits

These involve benefits seen in areas such as resources and assets. The project may lead to better management and utilisation of these areas – for example, it may simplify job roles or reduce staff turnover.

Functional and support benefits

Other areas of the value chain may also see benefits such as HRM, marketing, service etc.

Intangible benefits

These can only be measured subjectively. A benefit of a project might be to improve staff morale or customer satisfaction. These benefits should be included in the business case, and many organisations try to put some value on them regardless of how subjective that value might be.

Emergent benefits

Often referred to as secondary or unexpected benefits these benefits might not be expected at the outset of a project but they 'emerge' over time. For example, we've seen how a change to a divisional structure for a business might lead to greater focus and responsibility accounting, but it might also provide opportunities for further diversification that was not envisaged as part of the original change project. The benefits might only emerge as the organisation becomes more comfortable with its new structure. Benefits management (discussed later) aims to manage for these benefits as well as for planned benefits.

In order to make a business case on the basis of these benefits, the scale of the benefits should be assessed. The benefits can often be classified along the following scale:

(1) Observable

(2) Measureable

(3) Quantifiable

(4) Financial

In order to convince management of the business case for the project, the aim should be to have each benefit as high up the scale as possible (where level 4 is higher than level 1). However, this then brings in the scope for the project manager to upscale or overstate the project benefits in order to get project approval.

The scale of benefits

(1) Observable

Intangible benefits (such as improvements in staff morale) often fall into this category. Individuals or groups in the organisation with a level of expertise in this area will often use agreed criteria to determine whether or not this benefit has been realised.

Despite the fact that the benefits aren't measureable, they should still be included in the business case as they will be important to many stakeholders. It will also be important that they form part of the benefits management process (covered later).

(2) Measureable

A measure may exist for this type of benefit, but it may not be possible to estimate by much performance will improve when the changes are completed. This means that the business can often tell where it is at the moment but cannot specify where it will be post project.

Many strategic benefits fall into this category – for example, a project to improve product quality is likely to lead to an increase in market share, but it may not be possible to quantify by how much the increase in market share will be. But a timescale should be set for when the measure will be tested to show the benefits of this particular project (rather than being the result of other factors such as competitor actions).

If it is deemed too difficult or expensive to measure the increase in performance, then the benefit should be relegated to an observable benefit.

(3) Quantifiable

These benefits should be forecastable in terms of the benefit that should result from the changes. This means that their impact can be estimated *before* the project commences (unlike measureable benefits where the impact can only be assessed *after* the project has been completed). Often, productivity gains and operational benefits will fall into this category. For example, it may be possible to estimate that new machines will be able to produce 20% more units per hour.

(4) **Financial**

These benefits can be given a financial value – either in terms of a cost reduction or a revenue increase. The aim should be to have as many benefits as possible in this category so that a financial appraisal of the project is possible.

Test your understanding 2

In seeking to gain approval for a new project a manager has put together the following financial assessment in her business case document:

Net financial benefit from new project:

	$000
Extra revenue from increased market share	140
Savings from increased staff motivation	50
Savings from one staff redundancy	15
Extra revenue from 20% reduction in customer response times	60
Total project costs	(75)
Net benefit	$190

Consider the types of benefit included in this analysis and whether the manager's appraisal of the financial impact on the project is accurate.

7 Benefits management

'The purpose of the benefits management process is to improve the identification of achievable benefits and to ensure that decisions and actions taken over the life of the investment lead to realising all the feasible benefits.'

(Benefits Management, Ward and Daniel, 2006)

Origins of benefits management

Benefits management originally grew out of the failure of many information systems (IS) and information technology (IT) projects. Organisations started performing in-depth Post Implementation Reviews (explored in more detail in the next chapter) to determine what could be learnt from past failures.

One of the key discoveries from project failures was that perceived benefits from projects often failed to materialise or be fully realised. Organisations determined that they needed a process in order to avoid these failures in future projects.

Therefore benefits management was developed as a process for ensuring that benefits were both identified and realised. Nowadays, this process has been expanded beyond IS/IT investments into all kinds of business projects.

The suggestion here is that project benefits are not automatic – they need to be identified, planned for and actively worked on to be realised.

The benefits management process

Ward and Daniel suggest the following stages to ensure that the benefits management process realises the maximum set of benefits from the project:

(1) Identify and structure benefits

(2) Plan benefits realisation

(3) Execute benefits plan

(4) Review and evaluate results

(5) Establish potential for further benefits.

Identify and structure benefits

Potential benefits from projects have already been discussed in this chapter. The key element at this stage is to quantify the benefits, establish ownership of them, determine the impact on stakeholders and consider their impact on the business case.

It will be important that the links to the business strategy and objectives can be identified (and, ideally, quantified). The business should understand completely what it is getting from the project and where within the organisation that benefits will arise.

It is important that the benefit is linked to a particular stakeholder(s) so that an individual or group within the organisation can take ownership of delivering the benefit to the stakeholder. The likely benefit to that stakeholder should be measured (though this might not necessarily be in financial terms) and responsibility for realising that value be allocated to whoever has taken ownership of the benefit.

If sufficient benefits are not identified then the project should be abandoned at this stage.

Planning benefits realisation

This stage is a vital element of the project business case. This is what management will consider when making a decision for project approval.

It is important that all benefits are identified, responsibility is clear and the likely value of the benefit is quantified. The current level of performance should be used as a starting position (baseline), and then performance measures should be identified which can identify progress towards achieving the perceived improvement in performance/value of the benefit.

At this stage a benefit dependency network would be created (covered later in the syllabus).

Further details

The key here is that there will be an allocated responsibility for the benefit(s). This should provide better focus on achieving the benefit and the performance measures attached to each benefit should allow management to gauge performance against set parameters.

It should also identify organisational factors that will enable or frustrate the achievement of benefits. Alongside this a stakeholder analysis will enable buy-in from the stakeholders, identify which stakeholders may be resistant to change and how to overcome this resistance, and ensure that the key stakeholders for a project play a role in the project process.

Executing the benefits plan

The plan then needs to be put into action. Interim targets should be monitored and assessed and remedial action may have to be taken when these targets are not being met.

Further benefits may also be identified and a decision has to be taken on whether or not to pursue these.

> **Further details**
>
> Another problem at this stage will be that changes in the business environment (whether internal – for example, from changes of personnel – or external – for example, from changes in legislation) make intended benefits no longer feasible or relevant. In that case the benefits plan (stage 2) needs to be reassessed, and it may even be that the whole business case for the project falls apart.
>
> Change management programmes will also be important here and these are explored in more detail later in the syllabus text.

Reviewing and evaluating the results

One important element of this will involve a Post Implementation Review which is discussed in more detail in the next chapter. This allows the organisation to learn from the project so that future project decisions and actions can be improved.

The evaluation should involve all those who have responsibility for delivering benefits. It should focus on what has been achieved, identify reasons for the lack of any benefit deliveries, and identify further action needed to deliver what has not been achieved.

Establishing the potential for further benefits

Some benefits only become apparent when the project has been implemented and the associated business changes have been made. So the potential for these further benefits needs to be assessed and analysed (similar to stage 1 in this overall process).

> **Further details**
>
> This stage might actually involve a new project and a new business case for developing the newly identified further benefits. Benefits identification should be a continuous process and a benefits driven approach should applied to all projects.

KAPLAN PUBLISHING

8 A benefits dependency framework

A benefits dependency framework is aimed at ensuring that the business drivers and investment objectives are achieved by ensuring there are appropriate business changes in areas such as work methods, structure, culture etc.

The network should be established in the following order:

(1) Identify business drivers

(2) Establish investment objectives

(3) Identify business benefits

(4) Identify required business changes

(5) Associate further enabling changes.

Business and enabling changes explained

Business drivers, investment objectives and business benefits have been discussed earlier in this chapter. The changes required within the business to facilitate a successful project have been further divided into two categories:

Business changes

These are permanent changes to working methods that are required in the business in order to achieve and sustain the proposed benefits. This might include new roles and responsibilities, new performance measures, new information systems, new reward schemes etc.

Although such changes should be seen as permanent changes, they may not necessarily be long term. As further projects are introduced future business changes may be needed.

Enabling changes

These are one-off changes that are necessary to allow the business changes to be brought about. Examples include staff training, migration of data, data collection etc.

These may be further extended into enabling IS/IT changes that are required. This could include the purchase of a new IT system, for example.

It may be that each enabling change relates to more than one business change and that each business change relates to more than one business benefit (and so on). It may even be that changes within each level might relate to each other.

Illustration of a benefits dependency framework

The following is an extract from a benefits dependency framework for a business that currently finds itself in a poor competitive position on the strategy clock.

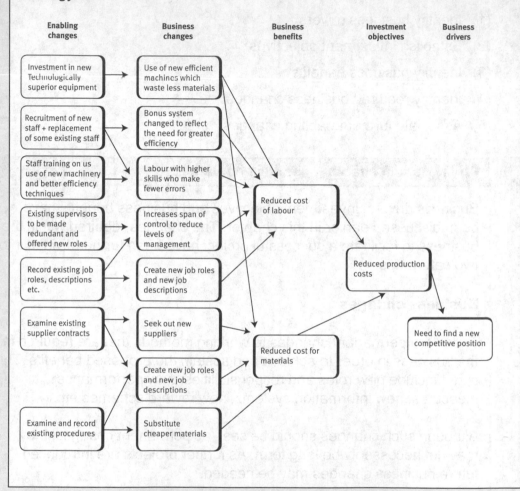

Discussion on the dependency diagram

The diagram in the preceding illustration is only an extract from the full dependency framework. The full framework would have more investment objectives (e.g. they may also want to maintain quality), business benefits (e.g. such as economies of scale and increased market share) etc. But an examination of the diagram should highlight the processes involved and how each element can link together.

> Creating the network can be a complicated process. It may be simplified by pulling benefits and changes together into benefits streams whereby linked business and enabling changes are associated to their related benefits.
>
> There should be measures in place at each stage of the network to determine when and if success has been achieved. An organisation needs to know when enabling changes have been made, when business changes have been achieved etc.
>
> Benefits dependency frameworks are often created from right to left (i.e. start with the business drivers and work back towards the enabling changes) – as has been seen in this chapter. But the work happens from left to right.

The next step in finalising the benefits dependency network is to create measures for each element so that success or failure of each element can be determined, and to then allocate responsibility or ownership for each change and benefit in the network.

Benefits ownership

A **benefit owner** should be assigned to each benefit. Ideally it should be someone who gains an advantage from the benefit and is therefore motivated to ensure that the benefit is realised.

It may occasionally be necessary to have more than one benefit owner for each benefit, but this group should be kept as small as possible.

A **change owner** will be appointed for each enabling and business change. It will be their job to ensure that the change is successfully achieved. For example, if an enabling change is to train staff in new production techniques, then perhaps an HR manager will be given ownership of this change and responsibility for its success or failure.

Benefit and change owners should have the power to effect the achievement of either benefits of change. Benefit owners might need to have the power to add extra resources to the project, whilst change owners may have to use their influence to overcome problems. Therefore, the owners will often hold senior positions in the organisation.

However, this does not always have to be the case. For simple projects where there is significant past experience, middle managers might play some ownership roles – particularly as change owners.

Example

Let's examine how the ownership might look for the changes and benefits expected in the earlier illustration.

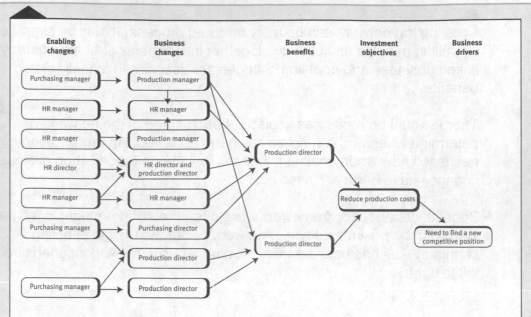

It can be seen that it is often the case that those who were responsible for making the changes also derived benefits from those changes. It can also be seen that there are a wide range of owners in the network from middle line managers to senior directors.

The role of the project team

The project team will work alongside these benefit and change owners. The team might take some responsibility for enabling changes (and therefore become respective change owners), but they are unlikely to become benefit owners.

Balancing benefit and change owners

There may be a conflict in the network if the change owner differs in goals and outlook from the benefits owner. The change owner may lack motivation if he/she enables changes but derives no benefit from those changes.

It is therefore important that change owners can understand the impact of their changes and the benefits that will be derived by the organisation as a whole. It may be important that they understand and are motivated by the business drivers. For example, in the above illustration, it will be important for HR managers to understand that without a change in competitive position the business might fail overall and put everyone's job at risk. This might make them more motivated to enable the change in workforce that is required through redundancies and new recruitment.

Therefore a balance must be sought between benefit owners and change owners. In some extremes, where there is a resistance from change owners to make the change, it may be that some project benefits have to be sacrificed for the good of the project overall.

Advantages of a benefits dependency network

- it clearly illustrates the why (business drivers), what (business benefits) and how (business and enabling changes) for the project
- linkages can be clearly identified
- enabling changes can be followed through to the business drivers
- if some business benefits require too many enabling and business changes then they may be dropped from the project
- it can feed into the project plan and improve the efficiency of that stage of project management
- it may form the basis of a project SWOT analysis
- the impact of a failure to make an enabling change, for example, can be followed through to discover the overall impact on the project.

Disadvantages of a benefits dependency framework

- it can be complicated to illustrate
- not all links from enabling changes to business changes and so forth may be identified
- it may not be complete.

9 Project costs

In order to properly assess a project the potential benefits need to be measured against the potential costs. Typical project costs might be:

- capital investment costs
- development costs
- centrally allocated costs/infrastructure costs
- external consultancy costs
- resource costs
- quality costs
- flexibility costs
- disruption costs.

Further details on project costs

- capital investment costs* – this would include the costs of IT hardware and software, project specific assets etc.

- development costs* – historic development costs may be easier to ascertain than future development costs which arise as the project is better understood and modifications are required. But an estimate of such costs should still be made.

- centrally allocated costs/infrastructure costs* – these would be costs for the use of premises and central services (such as accounting or personnel services) and may also include an allocation of charges such as depreciation. But, again, only those costs that are incurred exclusively for the project should be included as a project cost.

- external consultancy costs – these might be incurred in project design, quality management, procuring software etc.

- resource costs – these can include the ongoing staff and material costs. In the project appraisal it is normal to include only **incremental** costs here, so if staff, for example, are transferred from elsewhere in the business no cost might actually be attributed to the project.

- quality costs – this can include the cost of training staff, monitoring performance, reworks etc.

- flexibility costs – project management teams need to be as flexible as possible and there may be costs associated with achieving this. These could be costs involved in facilitating flexible working (such as providing IT equipment in staff homes) or in flexible production or servicing (such as lower batch sizes or depackaged services).

- disruption costs – an attempt should be made to quantify these (often) intangible costs from elements such as a loss of productivity during project changeover or from resource reallocations.

* these costs may be deemed to be capital costs and therefore charged to the statement of financial position (balance sheet) rather than the statement of profit or loss. From an accounting perspective, the cost would then be spread (through either depreciation or amortisation) over a number of accounting periods. This can give different results for project appraisal depending on the method of appraisal used (for example, the ARR method will use the accounting treatment whereas the NPV method will follow the timing of the cash flows and ignore the accounting treatment).

Costs are often more tangible than benefits so the important element will be to identify all costs and attempt to quantify them and determine when they will occur.

KAPLAN PUBLISHING

10 Project appraisal

Due to the large amount of time and resources that can be tied up in a project, it is important that they are screened properly. Part of that screening will involve an assessment of the financial rewards that may be derived from the project. You should be familiar from your previous studies with financial appraisal methods such as:

- accounting rate of return (ARR)

- payback period

- net present value (NPV)

- internal rate of return (IRR).

Regardless of the method used, it will be important that only **financial** costs and benefits are included in the appraisal. Often, as explained earlier, project managers will attempt to 'upscale' other benefits (such as measurable or quantifiable ones) into financial benefits and the accountant may have to remove these in order to get a true reading of the financial impact of the project.

Problems in focusing on financial returns

The project appraisal methods which follow focus purely on the financial rewards of a project. However this should not be the only decision criteria that an organisation employs. Examining only financial costs and benefits can lead to the following problems:

- non-financial costs or benefits might outweigh the financial ones. Earlier in the chapter we discussed other types of benefits such as observable and measureable benefits which are ignored in financial calculations.

- managers may be encouraged to use 'creative' calculations of benefits in order to have them classified as financial benefits.

- costs may be removed from the forecasts in order to 'overstate' the case for the project.

- managers may include slack in their forecasts in order to show enough benefit to achieve the project approval but without having onerous targets.

- projects with no financial benefits would automatically be rejected.

Accounting rate of return (ARR)

The ARR method is an accounting method that gives a percentage return that is expected from the investment.

The most common formula is:

$$ARR = \frac{\text{Average annual operating profit}}{\text{Average investment to earn that profit}} \times 100\%$$

Decision criteria

- The ARR for a project may be compared with the company's target return and if higher the project should be accepted.

- Faced with a choice of mutually-exclusive investments, the project with the highest ARR should be chosen.

Suitability

- The ARR method focuses on profitability for the project and therefore is generally only suited to organisations who have profit targets and performance measures to meet.

- This might happen most often when a financial control parenting style is employed..

Further details on ARR

Average annual profit = Net cash flow less depreciation

- The 'average annual profit' is after depreciation.
- Net cash flow is equivalent to 'profit before depreciation'.

Average investment

- The average value of the investment represents the average capital employed over the life of the project.
- That is the initial investment plus the residual value, then all divided by two.

Target return

The target return might be determined from a number of sources:

- the return from existing, similar projects
- the return on investment (ROI) of the business unit
- the return on capital employed (ROCE) from the business overall
- past returns from projects
- the company's cost of capital.

Advantages

- Simplicity – As with the payback period, it is easily understood and easily calculated.
- Link with other accounting measures – Return on capital employed, calculated annually to assess a business or sector of a business (and therefore the investment decisions made by that business), is widely used and its use for investment appraisal is consistent with that. The ARR is expressed in percentage terms with which managers and accountants are familiar. However, neither this nor the preceding point necessarily justify the use of ARR.

Disadvantages

There are a number of specific criticisms of the ARR.

- It fails to take account of either the project life or the timing of cash flows (and time value of money) within that life.
- It will vary with specific accounting policies, and the extent to which project costs are capitalised. Profit measurement is thus 'subjective', and ARR figures for identical projects would vary from business to business.
- It might ignore working capital requirements.
- Like all rate of return measures, it is not a measurement of absolute gain in wealth for the business owners.
- There is no definite investment signal. The decision to invest or not remains subjective in view of the lack of an objectively set target ARR.

It is concluded that the ARR does not provide a reliable basis for project evaluation.

The payback period

The payback period is the time a project will take to pay back the money spent on it. It is based on expected cash flows and provides a measure of liquidity.

This is the time which elapses until the invested capital is recovered. It considers cash flows only. Unlike DCF techniques, it is often assumed that the **cash flows** occur evenly during the year.

Decision criteria

- Compare the payback period to the company's maximum return time allowed and if the payback is quicker the project should be accepted.

- Faced with mutually-exclusive projects choose the project with the quickest payback.

Suitability

- Most projects will be short and therefore the time value of money will be less relevant than the payback period.

- The payback method is also very useful when there is rationing on the capital available for investment.

Further details on the payback period

Calculation – Constant annual flows

$$\text{Payback period} = \frac{\text{Initial investment}}{\text{Annual cash inflow}}$$

A payback period may not be for an exact number of years. To calculate the payback in years and months you should multiply the decimal fraction of a year by 12 to the number of months.

Calculations – Uneven annual flows

However, if cash inflows are uneven (a more likely state of affairs), the payback has to be calculated by working out the cumulative cash flow over the life of a project.

Advantages

- Simplicity

  As a concept, it is easily understood and is easily calculated.

- Rapidly changing technology

  If new plant is likely to be scrapped in a short period because of obsolescence, a quick payback is essential.

- Improving investment conditions

  When investment conditions are expected to improve in the near future, attention is directed to those projects that will release funds soonest, to take advantage of the improving climate.

  - Payback favours projects with a quick return

  It is often argued that these are to be preferred for three reasons.

  - Rapid project payback leads to rapid company growth – but in fact such a policy will lead to many profitable investment opportunities being overlooked because their payback period does not happen to be particularly swift.

  - Rapid payback minimises risk (the logic being that the shorter the payback period, the less there is that can go wrong). Not all risks are related to time, but payback is able to provide a useful means of assessing time risk (and only time risk). It is likely that earlier cash flows can be estimated with greater certainty.

  - Rapid payback maximises liquidity – but liquidity problems are best dealt with separately, through cash forecasting.

- Cash flows

  Unlike ARR it uses cash flows, rather than profits, and so is less likely to produce an unduly optimistic figure distorted by assorted accounting conventions which might permit certain costs to be carried forward and not affect profit initially.

Disadvantages

- Project returns may be ignored – In particular, cash flows arising after the payback period are totally ignored.

- Timing ignored – Cash flows are effectively categorised as pre-payback or post-payback, but no more accurate measure is made. In particular, the time value of money is ignored.

- Lack of objectivity – There is no objective measure as to what length of time should be set as the minimum payback period. Investment decisions are therefore subjective.

- Project profitability is ignored – Payback takes no account of the effects on business profits and periodic performance of the project, as evidenced in the financial statements. This is critical if the business is to be reasonably viewed by users of the accounts.

Net present value (NPV)

The net benefit or loss of benefit in present value terms from an investment opportunity.

The NPV represents the surplus funds (after funding the investment) earned on the project. This means that it tells us the impact on shareholder wealth. Therefore:

Decision criteria

- Any project with a positive NPV is viable.

- Projects with a negative NPV are not viable.

- Faced with mutually-exclusive projects, choose the project with the highest NPV.

Suitability

- NPV is only useful when the time value of money is relevant, and therefore this is only likely for projects which span a number of years.

- But NPV also relies on having a reliable cost of capital - something that would be difficult to determine for most projects and potentially be beyond the scope of the skills of most project teams.

Further details on NPV

What the NPV tells us

Suppose, in an investment problem, we calculate the NPV of certain cash flows at 12% to be – $97, and at 10% to be zero, and yet at 8% the NPV of the same cash flows is + $108. Another way of expressing this is as follows:

- If the funds were borrowed at 12% the investor would be $97 out of pocket – i.e. the investment earns a yield below the cost of capital.

- If funds were borrowed at 10% the investor would break even – i.e. the investment yields a return equal to the cost of capital.

- If funds were borrowed at 8% the investor would be $108 in pocket – i.e. the investment earns a return in excess of the cost of capital.

In other words, a positive NPV is an indication of the surplus funds available to the investor now as a result of accepting the project.

The time value of money

The required return (cost of capital) aims to take account of the time value of money. There are three main reasons for the time value of money.

Potential for earning interest

If a capital investment is to be justified, it needs to earn at least a minimum amount of profit, so that the return compensates the investor for both the amount invested and also for the length of time before the profits are made. For example, if a company could invest $80,000 now to earn revenue of $82,000 in one week's time, a profit of $2,000 in seven days would be a very good return. However, if it takes four years to earn the money, the return would be very low.

Therefore money has a time value. It can be invested to earn interest or profits, so it is better to have $1 now than in one year's time. This is because $1 now can be invested for the next year to earn a return, whereas $1 in one year's time cannot. Another way of looking at the time value of money is to say that $1 in six years' time is worth less than $1 now.

Impact of inflation

In most countries, in most years prices rise as a result of inflation. Therefore funds received today will buy more than the same amount a year later, as prices will have risen in the meantime. The funds are subject to a loss of purchasing power over time.

Risk

The earlier cash flows are due to be received, the more certain they are – there is less chance that events will prevent payment. Earlier cash flows are therefore considered to be more valuable.

Assumptions used in calculations

* All cash flows occur at the start or end of a year.

Although in practice many cash flows accrue throughout the year, for discounting purposes they are all treated as occurring at the start or end of a year. Note also that if today (T_0) is 01/01/20X0, the dates 31/12/20X1 and 01/01/20X2, although technically separate days, can be treated for discounting as occurring at the same point in time, i.e. at T_1.

* Initial investments occur at once (T_0), other cash flows start in one year's time (T_1).

In project appraisal, the investment needs to be made before the cash flows can accrue. Therefore, unless the examiner specifies otherwise, it is assumed that investments occur in advance. The first cash flows associated with running the project are therefore assumed to occur one year after the project begins, i.e. at T_1.

Advantages of NPV

When appraising projects or investments, NPV is considered to be superior (in theory) to most other methods. This is because it:

* considers the time value of money – discounting cash flows to PV takes account of the impact of interest, inflation and risk over time. These significant issues are ignored by the basic methods of payback and annual rate of return (ARR)

* is an absolute measure of return – the NPV of an investment represents the actual surplus raised by the project. This allows a business to plan more effectively

* is based on cash flows not profits – the subjectivity of profits makes them less reliable than cash flows and therefore less appropriate for decision making. Neither ARR nor payback is an absolute measure

- considers the whole life of the project – methods such as payback only consider the earlier cash flows associated with the project. NPV takes account of all relevant flows associated with the project. Discounting the flows takes account of the fact that later flows are less reliable which ARR ignores

- should lead to maximisation of shareholder wealth. If the cost of capital reflects the investors' (i.e. shareholders') required return, then the NPV reflects the theoretical increase in their wealth. For a company, this is considered to be the primary objective of the business.

Disadvantages of NPV

However, there are some potential drawbacks:

- It is difficult to explain to managers. To understand the meaning of the NPV calculated requires an understanding of discounting. The method is not as intuitive as techniques such as payback.

- It requires knowledge of the cost of capital. The calculation of the cost of capital is, in practice, more complex than identifying interest rates. It involves gathering data and making a number of calculations based on that data and some estimates. The process may be deemed too protracted for the appraisal to be carried out.

- It is relatively complex. For the reasons explained above, NPV may be rejected in favour of simpler techniques.

Internal rate of return (IRR)

This is the rate of return at which the project has a NPV of zero.

Decision criteria

- If the IRR is greater than the cost of capital the project should be accepted.

- Faced with mutually-exclusive projects choose the project with the higher IRR.

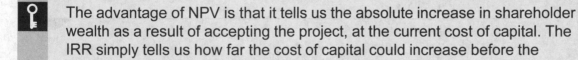

The advantage of NPV is that it tells us the absolute increase in shareholder wealth as a result of accepting the project, at the current cost of capital. The IRR simply tells us how far the cost of capital could increase before the project would not be worth accepting.

Suitability

- Like NPV, IRR is only useful when the time value of money is relevant, and therefore this is only likely for projects which span a number of years.

- IRR can provide a target, benchmark or break-even cost of capital that can be more easily understood and employed by project managers.

Further details on the IRR

Using the NPV method, PVs are calculated by discounting cash flows at a given cost of capital, and the difference between the PV of costs and the PV of benefits is the NPV. In contrast, the IRR method of DCF analysis is to calculate the exact DCF rate of return that the project is expected to achieve.

If an investment has a positive NPV, it means it is earning more than the cost of capital. If the NPV is negative, it is earning less than the cost of capital. This means that if the NPV is zero, it will be earning exactly the cost of capital.

Conversely, the percentage return on the investment must be the rate of discount or cost of capital at which the NPV equals zero. This rate of return is called the IRR, or the DCF yield and if it is higher than the target rate of return then the project is financially worth undertaking.

Calculating the IRR (using linear interpolation)

The steps in linear interpolation are:

(1) Calculate two NPVs for the project at two different costs of capital

(2) Use the following formula to find the IRR:

FORMULA FOR IRR

$$IRR = L + \frac{N_L}{N_L - N_H} \times (H - L)$$

where:

L = Lower rate of interest

H = Higher rate of interest

N_L = NPV at lower rate of interest

N_H = NPV at higher rate of interest.

Advantages

- IRR considers the time value of money. The current value earned from an investment project is therefore more accurately measured. As discussed above this is a significant improvement over the basic methods.

- IRR is a percentage and therefore easily understood. Although managers may not completely understand the detail of the IRR, the concept of a return earned is familiar and the IRR can be simply compared with the required return of the organisation.

- IRR uses cash flows not profits. These are less subjective as discussed above.

- IRR considers the whole life of the project rather than ignoring later flows (which would occur with payback for example).

- IRR a firm selecting projects where the IRR exceeds the cost of capital should increase shareholders' wealth. This holds true provided the project cash flows follow the standard pattern of an outflow followed by a series of inflows, as in the investment examples above.

- The IRR is a relative measure and is therefore a better way to compare projects of different scales. Consider the following two projects:

  Project A: Initial investment $20m   Present value of returns $20.2m   NPV $0.2m   IRR 2%

  Project B: Initial investment $0.5m   Present value of returns $0.6m   NPV $0.1m   IRR 15%

  The NPV method would suggest that Project A makes for a better investment (it simply compares the absolute value of the NPV), But this does not reflect the relative size of the investment to be made in this project – a $20m investment is likely to have higher risks and a higher return might be expected than only $200k. The IRR, on the other hand, clearly shows that Project B provides a much per return on investment and accounts for the fact that Project B involves a much smaller scale of investment.

Disadvantages

However there are a number of difficulties with the IRR approach:

- It is not a measure of absolute profitability. A project of $1,000 invested now and paying back $1,100 in a year's time has an IRR of 10%. If a company's required return is 6%, then the project is viable according to the IRR rule but most businesses would consider the absolute return too small to be worth the investment.

- Interpolation only provides an estimate (and an accurate estimate requires the use of a spreadsheet programme). The cost of capital calculation itself is also only an estimate and if the margin between required return and the IRR is small, this lack of accuracy could actually mean the wrong decision is taken.

- For example if the cost of capital is found to be 8% (but is actually 8.7%) and the project IRR is calculated as 9.2% (but is actually 8.5%) the project would be wrongly accepted. Note that where such a small margin exists, the project's success would be considered to be sensitive to the discount rate (see session 12 on risk).

- Non-conventional cash flows may give rise to no IRR or multiple IRRs. For example a project with an outflow at T0 and T2 but income at T1 could, depending on the size of the cash flows, have a number of different profiles on a graph (see below). Even where the project does have one IRR, it can be seen from the graph that the decision rule would lead to the wrong result as the project does not earn a positive NPV at any cost of capital.

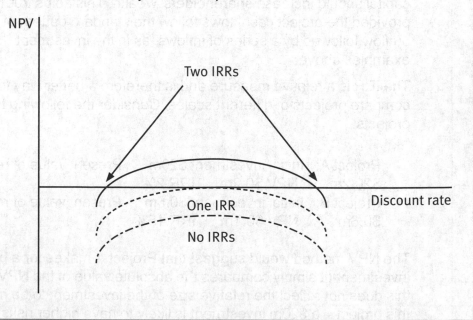

Links between project appraisal and benefits management

Project appraisal occurs before a project is undertaken. Its role is to identify the potential (mainly financial) benefits and costs of the project and provide decision making criteria.

Benefits management also wants to identify the benefits in a project, but its role is about ensuring that these benefits actually accrue. It is an ongoing process throughout the life of the project.

There is therefore some link between these processes, but benefits management extends project appraisal by scope, actions and timeframe.

11 Chapter summary

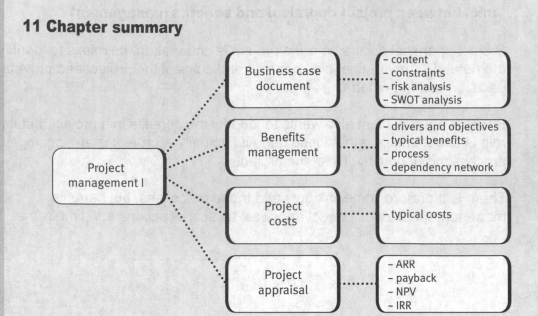

Business case document
- content
- constraints
- risk analysis
- SWOT analysis

Benefits management
- drivers and objectives
- typical benefits
- process
- dependency network

Project costs
- typical costs

Project appraisal
- ARR
- payback
- NPV
- IRR

Project management I

Test your understanding answers

Test your understanding 1

(1) The risk of a lawsuit should be dealt with my taking out indemnity insurance. The risk is then transferred to the insurance company.

(2) The risk of pool closure is serious and since a provision of a pool is clearly essential for the sports centre, the risk must be avoided instead. This would mean putting in place a series of controls over the building process to prevent later cracks from occurring – risk avoidance.

(3) The risk of fraud is exactly the type of risk that a good internal control system would be designed to prevent – risk reduction.

(4) Bad weather will always be a risk when dealing with outdoor activities and is probably best accepted and the lost revenues factored into the initial forecasts.

Test your understanding 2

In creating a business case document it is important that all potential benefits are identified and scaled. However, there is a temptation to overstate the scale of benefits in order to improve the likelihood of project appraisal. This is typically done when making a financial appraisal of the project.

In this project it would appear that many of the benefits of the project have been overstated:

- The extra returns from an increase in market share are unlikely to be quantifiable and very unlikely to be placed at the financial side of the scale. These are likely to be a *measurable* benefit only and should not be included in the financial appraisal.

- The savings from staff motivation will be very difficult to measure or quantify. These may be an *observable* benefit and should not be included as a financial one.

- The reduction in customer response times might be either measurable or even *quantifiable*. But it would be very difficult to give this a financial value, and again this should be removed from the financial appraisal.

So in the financial appraisal the project manager would only be left with the saving from the redundancy (a clearly *financial* benefit) and the project costs. This would represent a net financial cost of $60,000.

This does not mean that the project would be rejected. It simply represents the net financial cost of the project that should be measured up against other factors such as the non-financial benefits, the project risks, the project drivers etc.

Project management II – Managing the project to its conclusion

Chapter learning objectives

Upon completion of this chapter you will be able to:

- describe the contents and importance of a project plan for organisations in general

- describe, for an organisation in general, the implications of project-based teams, the roles of the main team members (project manager and sponsor) and how they might overcome typical problems preventing the project from being successful

- describe how projects can be monitored with respect to risks, issues, slippage and changes and how appropriate responses can be devised

- explain the need to integrate gateways and benefits management into formal monitoring of projects

- discuss different types of project reviews such as post-project reviews, project implementation reviews and lessons learnt reviews

- describe how projects can be successfully concluded, including the benefits of end-project and lessons learnt reviews as well as benefits realisation reviews

- explain the typical uses of project management software.

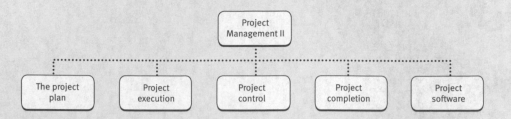

1 Introduction

The previous chapter focused on the first element of project management – project initiation. This chapter covers the remaining elements, all the way through to project completion.

2 The project plan

Alongside the benefits realisation plan and business case covered in the previous chapter, the project team will also need a detailed plan for resources, timings, interim targets etc. This will be the project plan.

Importance of a project plan

A project plan aims to ensure that the project objectives are achieved within the constraints of quality, cost and time. Planning is essential – it helps to:

- communicate what has to be done, when and by whom

- encourage forward thinking

- provide the measures of success for the project

- make clear the commitment of time, resources (people and equipment), and money required for the project

- determine if targets are achievable

- identify the activities the resources need to undertake.

The plan is likely to be recorded as an element of a Project Initiation Document (PID). This is not a one-off, pre-project document like the business case document. It will contain the business case document and project plans, but it is also likely to be constantly revised and updated throughout the project life to reflect key changes and project completion phases.

Project Initiation Document (PID)

The PID is a formal, detailed document which contains planning information extracted from other sources such as

- business case
- the dissemination plan
- the risk assessments
- Gantt charts, etc.

It contains all the information necessary for the execution of the project.

It is more operational than a business case document and its focus is very different. The business case is aimed at gaining project approval whereas the PID is aimed at ensuring that an approved project is successfully completed.

It will give guidance to the project team on what is expected from the project, when it is expected, and what level of performance is expected. It will have detailed plans (such as Gantt charts), control plans for when risks arise, responsibilities for tasks etc.

The PID is likely to be constantly revised and updated throughout the project life to reflect key changes and project completion phases. However, this can be a problem in a project as often the PID is updated and changed but it moves further away from the original business case and objectives. Benefits management becomes even more important when this occurs.

Typical contents might include:

- a purpose statement (project drivers)
- project and investment objectives
- a scope statement
- project deliverables (part of the product breakdown structure, explained later)
- cost and time estimates
- benefit and change owners
- chain of command
- team responsibilities
- project gateways, performance measures and results (updated regularly).

Contents of a project plan

For a large project the contents of the plan will be made up of several parts:

Details on the contents of a project plan

To provide an **overview of the project** the project plan will include the following.

- Background to the project – a summary of the background to the project (and how it builds on previous work) and the need for it (and why it is important).

- Aims and objectives – a list of the broad aim or purpose of the project, and the specific objectives you intend to achieve.

- Overall approach – a description of the overall approach you will take to achieve the objectives outlined above, including:
  - strategy and/or methodology and how the work will be structured
  - important issues to be addressed, e.g. interoperability
  - scope and boundaries of the work, including any issues that will not be covered
  - link to critical success factors.

- Project outputs – a list of the tangible deliverables (including reports) your project will create, and the less tangible knowledge and experience you hope to build and share.

- Project outcomes – a list of the outcomes you envisage and what change they will stimulate or enable.

- Stakeholder analysis using Mendelow's power-interest matrix – a list of the key stakeholder groups and individuals that will be interested in your project outcomes, will be affected by them, or whose support/approval is essential, both within your organisation and in the community, and assess their importance (low/medium/high).

- Risk analysis – a list of the factors that could pose a risk to the project's success and an assessment of their likelihood and severity, and how you will prevent them from happening (or manage them if they occur). Cover the types of risks listed and any others that apply.

- Standards – a list of the standards the project will use.

- Intellectual property rights – an indication of who will own the intellectual property created by the project and a list of any owned by third parties that will be incorporated into project outputs, when/how you will obtain permission to use them, and any implications for project outputs after the project ends.

The **project resources** part of the plan will contain details of the project partners and project management with a brief description of the project management framework, including:

- organisation

- reporting relationships

- decision process

- the role of any local management committee.

The **detailed part of the plan** will outline:

- the project deliverables and reports

- when they are due

- the phasing of the work and any dependencies.

It may also contain a Gantt chart, diagram, or flowchart to illustrate the phasing budget. It may alternatively include a product breakdown structure (covered later).

The **evaluation plan** will indicate how you will evaluate the quality of the project outputs and the success of the project. It will list the factors you plan to evaluate, questions the evaluation will answer, methods you will use, and how success will be measured.

The **dissemination plan** will explain how the project will share outcomes and learning with stakeholders. It will list the important dissemination activities planned throughout the project – indicating:

- purpose
- target audience
- timing
- key message.

The **exit and sustainability plans** should explain what will happen to project outputs at the end of the project (including knowledge and learning). They will focus on the work needed to ensure they are taken up by the owners and any work needed for project closedown, e.g. preservation, maintenance, documentation.

The sustainability plan will list any project outputs that may have potential to live on after the project ends, why, how they might be taken forward, and any issues involved in making them sustainable in the long term.

Product break down structure

A project is thought to produce at least one 'product' – whether that product is a physical one (such as a text book) or a more abstract one such as an improvement in a lending process of a bank. In order to ensure that each element of a project is controlled and managed, the project may be described or drawn using a product breakdown structure.

A product break down structure breaks a product down into its component points in the form of a hierarchical chart. Each product may be broken down by sub-product and then further broken down by activity.

For example, if we were to examine Kaplan's classroom based tuition courses (this would be the product), the sub-products for this would be:

- Exam text
- Class notes
- Classroom delivery
- Assessments
- Exam kit
- Mock exam.

This shows the order in which sub-products must be provided. For example, it will be important to have class notes before the classroom delivery can take place and likewise it will be important for students to attend some classroom delivery before they can attempt the assessments.

Each sub product could then be broken down by activity. For example, the activities involved in creating the exam text may be:

- Obtain the official syllabus
- Obtain the official study guides and guidance from the examiner
- Create the material
- Edit the material
- Obtain examiner/exam body approval
- Print the text
- Deliver the text.

Planning and control can then be focused on each sub-product and each activity. For example, schedules can be created, risk can be assessed, responsibility can be allocated, targets set etc.

This may therefore be a vital element of the project plan.

3 Project execution

Executing consists of the processes used to complete the work defined in the project management plan to accomplish the project's requirements. Execution process involves coordinating people and resources, as well as integrating and performing the activities of the project in accordance with the project management plan. The deliverables are produced as outputs from the processes performed as defined in the project management plan.

Managing and leading projects

Projects require people with different skills to work together in a co-ordinated way. The project team consists of individuals brought together purely for undertaking a specific project. Teams will cut across functional boundaries, giving rise to 'matrix' organisations. The size of the team and the period of their existence will be determined by the nature of the project.

Matrix structures

Projects are often interdisciplinary and cross organisational reporting lines. The project team is likely to be made up of members drawn from a variety of different functions or divisions: each individual then has a dual role, as he or she maintains functional/divisional responsibilities as well as membership of the project team.

Test your understanding 1

Consider what advantages and disadvantages a matrix structure (studied in chapter 8) might bring to project teams.

Team members

A team member is selected to join the core team because of their specialist knowledge or expertise. They are usually drawn from a functional department and therefore have a further responsibility in representing that department. Some of the roles taken on by team members in organisations include:

- Specialist or technical expert – brings specialist knowledge and advice to the team.

- Representative – as part of the core team, the member represents their 'home' department and as part of the project team communicates the project team's views and decisions when back in their 'home' department.

- Monitor – will monitor their progress against the plan appropriately and regularly.

- Change manager – as changes are identified, will ensure that the full implications have been assessed before the changes are agreed and implemented.

- Problem solver – will be faced with many problems during any project and will be required to solve them by drawing on the resources of the project team and their 'home' department and through the use of problem-solving techniques.

KAPLAN PUBLISHING

Assembling team members

There are two methods for assembling team members:

- the first approach is to use specialist project staff who are seconded to the project and removed from their existing roles. This may be backed up by external consultants who fill in any skills gaps. This approach is likely to lead to an efficient project which is completed quickly. However, there may be a lack of buy-in from line managers and staff who may resent a lack of involvement in the key project decisions.

- the second approach is to 'add on' the project to existing duties for operational staff. In this way staff would complete the project alongside their existing duties. This may mean that the project takes longer to complete but it should benefit from decision makers being closer to the decision point and from improved staff buy-in.

Project sponsor

The project sponsor or project facilitator will normally be a senior member of the management team.

- They are often chosen as the person with the most to gain from the success of the project and the most to lose from the failure of it.

- Their job is to direct the project, and allow the project manager to manage the project.

Typical roles of a project sponsor

The roles taken on by project sponsors in organisations include:

- gatekeeper – choosing the right projects for the business means ensuring that only projects that support the business strategy are started and that they are of sufficiently high priority and have clear terms of reference

- sponsor and monitor – steering the project by requesting regular meetings with the project leader and giving advice and guidance

- supporter and coach – provides practical support for the project leader, especially if they are taking on a project that is larger or more significant than they have handled before

- decision-maker – if decisions are required that are outside the scope of the project then the project sponsor will make the decision on behalf of the organisation

- champion or advocate – involves informal communication with other senior managers to ensure that they continue to have an objective view of the importance of their project in relation to other projects within the business

- problem solver – when the team faces problems that it is unable to solve or does not have the skills or experience to solve

- resource negotiator – a project's success will depend on the availability of the right resources at the right time. In cross-functional projects the sponsor may provide assistance in negotiating resources around the company.

The project manager

The project manager is the person appointed by the organisation to lead the team, and manage it on a day-to-day basis. Primarily the project manager's responsibility is to deliver the project and to ensure that effectiveness and efficiency are achieved across the entire project.

Typical roles of a project manager

Some of the roles taken on by project managers in organisations include:

- Team leader – will spend time building the team, motivating individuals and ensuring that the project has a clear purpose and that every core team member understands that purpose.

- Planner and co-ordinator – will ensure that the team creates a realistic plan and will often consolidate the individual team members' plans into a full project plan. They will then co-ordinate the activities of the team to meet that plan and deal with changes in a systematic way.

- Task manager – involves clarifying the goals of the project and ensuring that every action is moving the project towards those goals.

- Communicator and relationship manager – will take the lead in proactively communicating the project in an appropriate way to all the stakeholders and manage the relationship with key stakeholders to ensure their needs are being met.

- Problem solver – will be faced with many problems during any project and will be required to solve them through team problem-solving techniques.

- Monitor and change manager – will put controls in place to ensure the project progresses against the plan and is monitored appropriately and regularly.

- Budget manager – will involve setting up the budget and then monitoring its use to ensure the best use of resources.

- Meeting manager – most project teams only meet as a team during project meetings so it is very important that each meeting is well managed.

While there are clearly overlaps, there are some important differences between a project manager and a 'normal' line manager:

- line managers are usually specialists whereas project managers are often generalists

- line managers operate close to the technical tasks in their departments, whereas project managers may have to oversee work in many different areas

- line managers exercise direct supervisory authority, whereas project managers facilitate rather than supervise team members.

Problems faced by project managers

Typical problems faced by a project manager will include:

- managing staff who are assigned to the project part-time and have responsibilities in their 'home' departments

- managing the relationship with the departmental managers who have staff on the project team

- managing the size of the team given variable resource requirements throughout the project life cycle

- dealing with specialists in areas where the manager is not an expert.

4 Project monitoring and control

Monitoring the project

The purpose of the project monitoring, reviewing and controlling process is to track all major project variables and to ensure the team is making satisfactory progress to the project goals.

Performance measurements can include:

- Expenditure (cost).

- Schedule (time) performance – avoiding schedule slippage is a key objective.

- Scope measures – both product scope and project scope
- Functional quality
- Technical quality performance
- Issue management performance
- Client satisfaction measures.

Performance measures

Monitoring the project

Performance measurements can include.

- Expenditure (cost) – starts with the establishment of budgets and as the project progresses, decisions regarding procurement, design, development, deployment, etc., will be assessed with respect to their impact on expenditures. Actual expenditures will be compared to a baseline, and any variances will be reported to management for corrective action.

- Schedule (time) performance – refers to the timely completion of project deliverables as compared to a baseline schedule defined in the project plan. The schedules will identify all of the project's stages, phases and activities assigned to each team member, mapping them to a timeline that measures key milestones (dates) that are used to keep track of work progress. Avoiding schedule slippage is a key objective.

- Scope measures – are primarily concerned with product scope (the set of functions and features that characterise the product or service) and project scope (work that must be accomplished to deliver the product/service with the specified functions and features). Scope is measured based upon the degree of compliance of baseline product/service features and functions with proposed project deliverables (the means used for their delivery).

- Functional quality – refers to the quality or correctness of the products, and/or services, features/functions delivered as a result of the project.

- Technical quality performance – refers to the technical infrastructure that provides the foundation for product and service delivery. In the case of an IT project, such indicators as system availability, downtime, problem resolution, and response time and network utilisation would measure technical quality performance.

- Issue management performance – refers to the identification and resolution of issues or exceptions that are impacting the successful delivery of the project. Issues can be related to communications, human resources, contracts, product/service features and functions, etc. The purpose of issue management is to ensure that all matters requiring resolution, decisions or direction are addressed as soon as possible to avoid negative consequences on project objectives and deliverables (cost, schedule, scope or products/services).

- Client satisfaction measures – include client perceptions on various aspects of achieving a high degree of client satisfaction with implementation support or with operational products/services.

Monitoring and reviewing performance – a well-constructed plan with clear deliverables should make it very easy to track progress. The project manager should set up mechanisms whereby the team regularly reviews what tasks have been completed or delayed and what the impact is on the rest of the plan.

- The diagram below shows a typical review loop indicating activities that occur once only, daily, weekly and at the end of each phase.

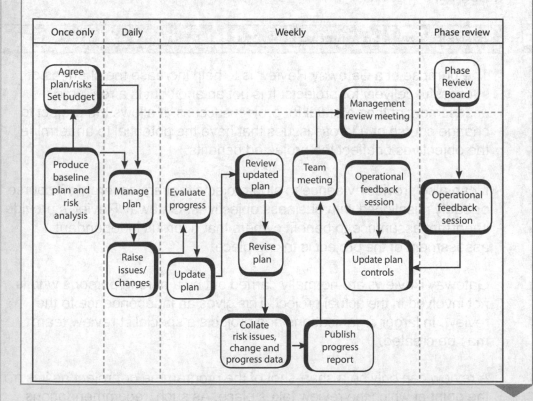

Phase boundaries are key points at which a number of aspects of the project can be reviewed.

- Is the business case for the project still valid?
- Is the project meeting its objectives?
- Has the risk situation altered?
- Should the project progress to the next phase?

Project gateways

This process is aided by specific project gateways. This will be review points that are planned for critical points in the project. The reviews will also ensure that the business case which justified the project is still valid at this stage.

If problems are identified then project control measures and corrective action will be necessary.

Further details on project gateways

The purpose of a Gateway Review is to help increase the chances of successful delivery for projects. It is not an audit but is a real-time assessment of the potential for project success. It allows the project to change course or address issues that have the potential to undermine the objectives or affect the projected benefits.

It can also provide evidence to stop projects that are severely off course or badly misaligned with business objectives. Gateway Reviews provide important assurance to benefit owners that rigorous independent assessment of the project is taking place.

Gateway Reviews are normally carried out by a person/persons who is not involved in the actual project. This gives an independence to the review. In larger organisations and projects a specialist review team may be created.

A review can only be a snap-shot of the programme or project as it is at the point at which the review takes place. As such, recommendations are based on the evidence presented and on the interviews that take place. The review process is intended to be supportive and forward looking and will take future plans into account but only as future intentions, rather than actualities.

Threat identification

The following can threaten the success of a project. Identifying these in advance can help reduce the risk of slippage and other potential problems:

- Poor management
- Poor planning
- Lack of control mechanisms
- Unrealistic deadlines
- Insufficient budget
- Moving targets.

Threat identification and slippage reduction

The following can threaten the success of a project. Suggestions are included as to how to minimise the slippage involved with those threats.

- Poor management – many project leaders will be from technical backgrounds and they may not have the proper management skills for controlling large projects. Project leaders should be properly trained so that they have managerial skills as well as technical skills. They should not be given large critically important projects until they have proved themselves on smaller exercises.

- Poor planning – managers have not made use of the various planning methods available: network analysis, PERT, Gantt charts. They have not broken the project down into its various activities and estimated a time and cost for each.

- Lack of control mechanisms – it is essential to be able to monitor the progress of projects, otherwise it is impossible to decide whether they will meet cost and time budgets. Reporting mechanisms and review dates should be set out in advance.

- Unrealistic deadlines – there is often pressure from users for projects to be completed quickly. Project teams, particularly if they have had to win the job competitively, may have suggested times that are unrealistic. Project managers must look critically at the deadlines. They should identify the critical activities of the project and ensure that these do not slip.

- Insufficient budget – too few people are employed on the project, inadequate hardware is bought, the cheapest (not the best) solutions are always sought. Of course, organisations cannot ignore costs and should try to get good value for money. However, it is important to be objective about what a given cost budget can produce by way of project outcomes. If money is tight, it might be better to do a smaller project thoroughly than a larger one poorly.

- Moving targets – the project specification keeps changing as the project progresses. This will certainly add costs and delay to the project. Users' requirements should be thoroughly examined and the analyst should check understanding before the project is started. Techniques such as structured walkthroughs and prototyping will help here.

Test your understanding 2

Printplus Inc is a printing company that has recently begun implementing a new computerised job costing system. The project manager who had started the project is now no longer with the company. You have been asked to step into the role of the project manager and complete the task of implementing the new system.

(a) Briefly describe the key factors that you will need to review in order to get to grips with the current status of the project.

(b) Identify possible threats to timely completion of the project, and state briefly how they can be minimised.

Project control

Controlling the project means:

- taking early corrective action when needed
- balancing project effort
- looking for where effort can be reduced
- making changes early rather than late.

Measurement of all relevant variables is important both for management information and also for the specification of 'what kind' and 'how much' corrective action is necessary.

Examples of corrective action include:

- 'fast tracking' – a project management technique used to ensure that projects are completed within the shortest time possible, often by doing some activities in parallel that would normally be done in sequence (such as design and construction)

- 'crashing' – project crashing is a method for shortening the project duration by reducing the time of one or more of the critical project activities to less than its normal activity time. The object of crashing is to reduce project duration while minimizing the cost of crashing

- adding additional resources (people, money, time, etc.)

- scope reduction

- adopting higher risk but potentially more efficient approaches

- employee motivation

Some corrective actions tend to be more tactical, and some more strategic.

5 Project completion

The final stages of a broadly successful project can be most rewarding. It is at this stage that people can finally see the realisation of plans and objectives.

Project success and failure

Successful project management can be defined as having achieved the project objectives and benefits:

- Within the allocated time period

- Within the budgeted cost

- At the desired performance or specification level

- While utilising the assigned resources effectively and efficiently

- With customer confirmation of expectations

- Without disturbing the main work flow of the organisation.

Reasons why projects succeed:

- Project Sponsorship at executive level
- Good PID and business case
- Strong project management
- The right mix of team players
- Good decision making structure
- Good communication
- Team members are working toward common goals.

Reasons for projects failure:

- Failure to align project with organizational objectives
- Poor scope
- Unrealistic expectations
- Lack of executive sponsorship
- Lack of true project management
- Inability to move beyond individual conflicts
- Internal politics.

The barriers to project management success are:

- Project complexity
- Customer's special requirements and scope changes
- Organisational structural and systemic resistance
- Project risks
- Changes in technology.

A Post Project Review (PPR)

This happens at the end of the project and allows the project team to move on to other projects. It can often be the last stage of the project, with the review culminating in the sign-off of the project and the formal dissolution of the project team. The focus of the post-project **review is on the conduct of the project itself**, not the product it has delivered. The aim is to identify and understand what went well and what went badly in the project and to feed lessons learned back into the project management standards with the aim of improving subsequent project management in the organisation.

It typically involves:

- disbanding the team and 'tying up loose ends'
- performance review
- determination of lessons learnt
- formal closure by the steering committee.

Contents of a post project review (PPR)

- Acceptance by client – the outputs of the project should be successfully transferred to the project's clients or users. It is important at this stage to follow the **dissemination plan**.

- Review of outputs against goals – the project team should be able to illustrate that the project has delivered its planned outputs and that outcomes can reasonably be expected to flow from them. It is important at this stage to follow the **evaluation plan**.

- Disbanding the team and 'tying up loose ends' – it is important to ensure that all project activities are satisfactorily completed and project teams should be gradually wound down. It is important at this stage to follow the **exit and sustainability plan**.

- Performance review – for large projects this may be a useful way of identifying issues and concerns that could be relevant to other projects. Key areas to review include the following:
  - Technical performance review (was scope of project achieved?).
  - Cost/budget performance.
  - Schedule performance.
  - Project planning and control.
  - Team relationships.
  - Problem identification.
  - Customer relationships.
  - Communication.
  - Risk evaluation and assessment of risk management policies.
  - Outstanding issues.

- Lessons learnt that relate to the way the project was managed should contribute to the smooth running of future projects. A starting point for any new project should be a review of the documentation of any similar projects undertaken in the past.

- Formal closure by the steering committee – the project steering committee cannot disband until the project's outcomes are seen as achieved, or the project is classed as unsuccessful.

Post Implementation Review (PIR)

A PIR is an *essential component* of the benefits management process. A post-implementation review **focuses on the product delivered** by the project. It usually takes place a specified time after the product has been delivered. This allows the actual users of the product an opportunity to use and experience the product or service and to feedback their observations into a formal review. The post-implementation review will focus on the product's fitness for purpose. The review will not only discuss strategies for fixing or addressing identified faults, but it will also make recommendations on how to avoid these faults in the future. In this instance these lessons learned are fed back into the product production process. Without a PIR, a business cannot demonstrate that its investment in the project was worthwhile.

PIRs can sometimes be an *on-going* element of project management that may be used at project gateways to examine changes implemented to date.

Comparing the PPR and PIR

For most projects, a PIR is undertaken when there has been sufficient time to demonstrate the business benefits of the new project. For a major programme of change there may be several PIRs over time. The review will normally involve the project manager, senior management representatives and, where used, internal benefits management experts.

The PPR and PIR are related but have different objectives. The PPR is a one-off exercise at the end of a project with the key objective of learning lessons and feeding them into the organisation's project management processes and procedures for the benefit of future projects.

The objective of the PIR is to ensure that the maximum benefit is obtained for the organisation through the new project, and to make recommendations if the benefits are not obtained. Every project is different, but it is typical to perform a PIR two to twelve months after completion of the project.

The PPR focuses on the performance of the project, whilst the PIR focuses on the performance of the product of the project.

A PIR would typically involve the following analysis:

- the achievement (to date) of business case objectives (effectively a gap analysis)

- costs and benefits to date against forecast

- areas for further development

- consistency of the project with the overall business strategy

- the effectiveness of revised business operations (functions, processes, staff numbers etc.)

- stakeholder satisfaction (both internal and external).

Post-implementation review of an IT system

When appraising a new IT system after changeover, comparison should be made between predicted and actual performance (variance analysis). This might include:

- Throughput speeds

- Number of errors or queries

- Cost of processing

- Amount of downtime.

The review would also need to cover whether users' needs had been met.

The review should not be performed too soon after the new system goes live, or 'teething problems' and lack of user familiarity will distort the results.

Recommendations should be made where appropriate to improve the system's future performance.

The review should also make wider recommendations on improving systems development and project planning and management processes.

Benefits realisation review

A benefits realisation review is vital because a project cannot be said to be successful until management is assured that all the benefits promised at the evaluation stage can be shown to have been subsequently realised.

Ward and Daniel identify a number of elements of a benefits review:

- to determine and confirm which planned benefits have been achieved

- to identify which expected benefits have not been achieved and to decide if remedial action can be taken to still obtain them or if they have to be foregone

- to identify any unexpected benefits that have been achieved and any unexpected 'disbenefits' that have resulted

- to understand the reasons why certain types of benefits were or were not achieved and provide lessons for future projects

- to understand how to improve the organisation's benefits management process for all projects.

A necessary part of this process will that each benefits owner should prepare a statement detailing and evidencing the extent to which the benefit was achieved or reasons for its failure.

Reasons why change fails to deliver benefits
<ul><li>vision and objectives either not clear or shared and owned</li><li>benefits/outcomes not adequately owned, tracked and reported</li><li>portfolio of programmes not all aligned to organisation's mission or strategy</li><li>business change ignored or undervalued</li><li>projects/programmes seen as delivering a capability rather than benefits</li><li>making the right investment decision; to make the right investment decision we first need a clear understanding of what needs to be done and why it needs to be done now.</li></ul>

Lessons learnt review

One important element of this stage is to perform a lessons learnt review. A formal meeting should be held to determine what can be learnt from the project. For example, it might consider the effectiveness of project control measures or the reasons for failures in business changes.

A formal action plan should be created to ensure that, in future projects, the positives can be recreated and the negatives avoided. This should feed into future benefit realisation plans. They may even be formalised into codes of practice for the organisation.

Often, for this process to be useful, and especially for long and large projects, managers need to record lessons learnt and reasons for success and failure as they go along.

6 Project management software

The planning and control of the project will be assisted through the use of appropriate software. The type of output produced by the package will vary depending upon the package being used e.g. FastPLAN and Winproject.

They may be used in a variety of ways.

Planning:

- The ability to create multiple network diagrams.
- The ability to create multiple Gantt charts.
- The ability to aid in the creation of the PID.

Estimating:

- The ability to consider alternative resource allocation.
- The ability to create and allocate project budgets.
- The ability to allocate time across multiple tasks.

Monitoring:

- Network links to all project team members.
- A central store for all project results and documentation.
- Automatic comparison to the plan, and plan revision.

Reporting:

- Access to team members.
- Ability to create technical documents.
- Ability to create end of stage reports.

Advantages:

- Improved planning and control.
- Improved communication.
- Improved quality of systems developed.

Further details on project management software

Project management software recognises that there is a sequence in which activities need to be performed.

The software package will require four items of information.

- Duration of each activity.
- Dependencies of activities.
- Resources available.
- At what stage the resource will become available.

When choosing project management software, or indeed any software package, it is important to:

- determine requirements of organisation including its current and future needs

- document requirements including the essential functions/important/wish list

- review all available packages to identify three/four products which meet the essential functions and fall within budget

- have a demonstration of the packages on a trial basis if possible

- select a package including 'roll out' strategy with installation, training, etc.

KAPLAN PUBLISHING

7 Chapter summary

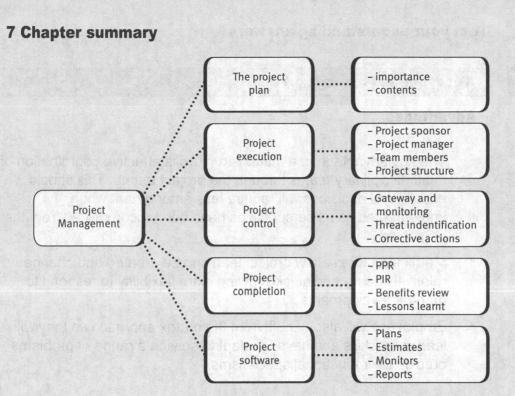

Test your understanding answers

Test your understanding 1

Advantages

- The key advantage of a matrix structure is effective coordination of multi-disciplinary teams through the project teams. This should ensure that decisions will require less amendment when implemented as all perspectives have been incorporated from the beginning.

- Matrix structures allow project teams to be created and changed relatively easily and quickly, giving extra flexibility to respond to market developments.

- Employees will also benefit from the matrix approach as they will learn new skills and have to adapt to solving a range of problems outside their functional specialisms.

Disadvantages

- The main problem with matrix structures involves clarifying responsibilities and demands made on employees. Employees may feel stressed and confused when conflicting demands are made by functional and project managers.

- This is usually resolved by having frequent meetings between functional and project heads, taking up time that could be used more effectively elsewhere. In some organisations functional heads have felt that their authority is diluted and project heads given priority.

- Linked to the above, staff appraisal becomes more difficult with a matrix structure.

Test your understanding 2

(a) The following key factors should be considered in reviewing the current status of the project.

- **Time.** The progress reports on the project should be reviewed, to determine whether or not the project is currently on target for completion within the expected time. An assessment should be made as to whether the remaining tasks can be completed by the original deadline.

- **Resources.** It will be important to identify the resources that have been allocated to the project. Resources include both human resources and computer equipment/time. Having established what resources have been made available, an assessment will have to be made of how sufficient or effective these are for achieving the project goals.

- **Cost.** The original budget for the project should be reviewed in the context of the actual costs incurred to date. A sensible estimate of the further costs that will be incurred in completing the project should then be made.

- **Quality.** The project plan should be reviewed to find out whether or not any quality standards were agreed for the intermediary stages of the project. If they were, it will be important to establish whether or not these standards are being met.

(b) The following may be identified as key threats to completion of the project on time.

Possible threat	Minimise by
Poor management of time	<ul><li>Discuss stage and completion deadline with the project team.</li><li>Stress the importance of completion targets.</li><li>Regular progress reports and progress meetings.</li></ul>
Poor planning	<ul><li>Using planning tools such as Gantt charts or CPA.</li></ul>
Lack of control mechanisms	<ul><li>Set milestones.</li><li>Ensure progress reporting throughout the project.</li></ul>
Unrealistic deadlines	<ul><li>Identify critical activities and the critical path.</li><li>Negotiate deadlines with stakeholders.</li></ul>
Insufficient budget	<ul><li>Focus cost compromises on least critical areas.</li><li>Negotiate injection of resources to complete on time.</li></ul>

Financial analysis

Chapter learning objectives

Upon completion of this chapter you will be able to:

- explain, for both profit-seeking and non-profit-seeking organisations, the relationship between strategy and finance

- determine, from information provided, the overall investment requirements of a business

- identify the advantages and disadvantages of alternative sources of finance listed in a question

- explain, for businesses in general, how their current and non-current assets should be managed with regard to finance and risk

- discuss how the role of the accountant and the finance function have been transformed within organisations

- evaluate how budgets, standard costing and variance analysis can support strategic planning and decision making

- evaluate decisions that include risk and uncertainty by using decision trees

- make decisions based on marginal and relevant costs techniques in areas such as accepting special contracts or discontinuing activities.

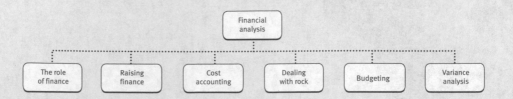

1 The relationship between strategy and finance

As with areas such as process redesign and information technology, finance can play a vital role in developing strategies and in putting them into action.

Strategic choice and financial analysis

For example, the role of finance plays a key role in making strategic choices. In applying Johnson, Scholes and Whittington's strategy evaluation tests a decision maker might have the following financial concerns and therefore carry out accompanying financial analysis:

Aspect	Key concerns	Financial analysis
Acceptability	Achieving acceptable returns to shareholders	• Cash flow forecasts to ensure dividend growth requirements can be met • NPV • ROCE • Valuation of real options • Cost-benefit analysis • Ratio analysis (e.g. dividend yield, growth)
	Risk	• Sensitivity • Breakeven • Ratio analysis (e.g. gearing, dividend cover)
Feasibility	Resources	• Cash flow forecast to identify funding needs • Ability to raise finance needed • Working capital implications • Foreign exchange implications

Suitability	Getting the best returns from alternatives	• Return on Investment • Comparison of alternatives • Profit margins

Corporate and business strategies are therefore supported and facilitated by financial strategy.

Financial strategy (in terms of how funds should be raised, where they should be allocated, how they should be managed etc.) needs to consider three key areas:

Managing for value

- It will be important that any funds available to the business are managed in a way that maximises shareholder value.

- It will also be important that the structure of funds within the business is optimised.

- Managing for value is explored in section 2 of this chapter.

Financial expectations of stakeholders

- Managing for value focuses on *shareholder* wealth. But there are financial expectations from other stakeholders which must also be considered.

Financial expectations of stakeholders

It is generally accepted that the strategic objective of a profit-seeking organisation is the long-term goal of maximising the wealth of the owners (usually shareholders) of the organisation.

- Shareholder view – the only responsibility for business is to make money for shareholders – the market is the best way to allocate scarce resources.

- Stakeholder view – the achievement of shareholder value is only possible if other stakeholders are (at least) kept satisfied.

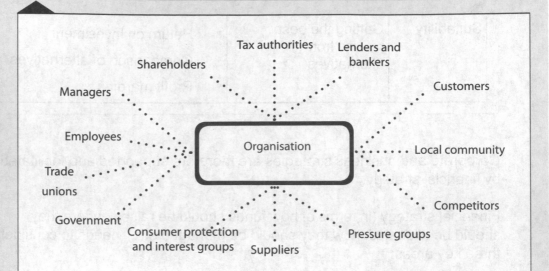

Typically:

- lenders expect profits, positive cash flow, growth and debt reduction

- employees expect increased wages and benefits as well as stable employment and growth

- creditors and suppliers expect payment within invoice terms and growth

- customers expect timely and complete delivery of services and products with increasing value and quality at appropriate pricing

- shareholders expect the continuance of the business enterprise and a fair financial return as payment of risk bearing and the use of their capital.

It is no longer enough to be profitable and have positive cash flow to be judged successful. All of the company's stakeholders require the company to perform within a narrow band of predetermined expectations. Failure to fall within the band of expected performance can, and will, result in:

- reduced access to funding both debt and equity

- loss of employee morale and de-motivation

- loss of customers and suppliers

- shareholder revolt.

Funding strategies

There are two key funding decisions for management to consider:

- where should funding be allocated?

- how should the funding be raised?

The accountant will play a role in all of elements of financial strategy, as well as playing a role in the wider decision making processes of the business.

The finance function and the role of the accountant

Over the past decade the role of the finance function, and hence the role of the accountant, has changed. Traditionally, the accountant and finance function focused on three key roles: collecting money from customers, paying suppliers, and reporting financial performance to the business. But some of those tasks have now become automated whilst business expectations of the accountant have been increased significantly.

The accountant can now be expected to be involved in areas such as:

- Gaining competitive advantage in capital markets.
- Forward-looking decision support, sensitivity and scenario planning.
- Providing quantitative and qualitative analysis.
- Finding areas for cost efficiency.
- Improving the quality of information and decision making.

In this way the value of the finance function has been transformed and it is now becoming a strategic partner to the business. New skills and practices are needed from the function. It needs to be more forward looking. It needs to be proactive rather than reactive. It needs to become a centre of excellence as a shared service for the business. The finance function needs to be focused on creating value for the business – just like any other business unit.

An organisation in which the finance function provides timely, useful information to management is likely to achieve better business performance than in others where this is not the case. Likewise, if the finance function can identify opportunities for cost savings, this can support, develop or improve an organisation's competitive position.

Organisations are recognising this value and the role of the accountant has transformed as the role of the finance function has transformed. In the past there were often organisational boundaries (and sometime physical ones too) between the accountant and the rest of the organisation. The finance function was kept apart and rarely worked with other functions or with clients.

But in modern organisations this has changed. Accountants are no longer just the counters of information but they are also the providers and analysts of information. The accountant will now typically be involved in all aspects of the strategic planning process, such as:

- Analysing the competitive position, the organisational environment, the benefits and problems from different strategic options etc. In this way, the accountant will play a key role in the strategy formulation of the organisation. For example, if an organisation is considering an overseas expansion the accountant will be expected to provide information on current and potential market sizes, the size and spending power of rivals, the expected returns from the project, the cost of the strategy, the cost of finance, and many other aspects that will help determine whether or not the strategy is pursued.

- The accountant will then be involved in the implementation of the strategy. IT systems may need to be evaluated, process redesigns will have to be costed and potential marketing channels evaluated. The accountant is likely to work in many cross-functional, matrix teams in order to aid in the implementation of strategy. So the physical and organisational barriers between the accountant and the rest of the business will disappear.

- The accountant can also add value to their organisation by measuring the performance of activities, managers and other employees within the organisation. This can help assess strategies as they progress. This can be a vital control mechanism (as seen when project management was considered) and allows the organisation to do things like take corrective action, move to contingency plans or abandon projects and strategies.

2 Managing for value

Traditionally, financial managers focused on the achievement of short-term financial targets such as profit margins, earnings per share, cost per unit etc. Managing for value aims to take a much broader, longer-term view in order to ensure that shareholder value (in terms of dividends received and increases in the capital value of shares) is maximised. There is a greater focus on value creation than there is on profits.

Value creation is achieved using three key elements of strategic management, as shown below:

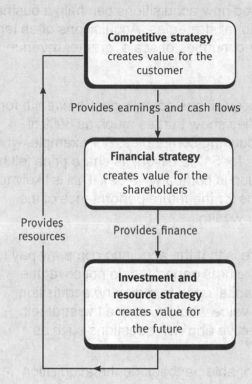

Competitive strategy creates value for the customer

Customers see value as the relationship between the benefits of using a product/service with the price they have to pay

Provides earnings and cash flows

Financial strategy creates value for the shareholders

The organisation achieves a higher return on investment than rivals and can meet all its financial obligations

Provides resources

Provides finance

Investment and resource strategy creates value for the future

For the longer term, it is necessary to create further growth and future earnings, improving the value creation for customers and shareholders

Therefore, financial strategy has three key elements with respect to value creation:

- recognising (and accounting for) a cost of capital and aiming to maximise returns against this

- managing a company's finances to ensure a minimisation of that cost of capital

- allocating capital to the areas where it is likely to generate the best return for shareholders

Illustration 1 – Managing For Value

Earlier in the syllabus we explored how acquisitions can help a business achieve its goals and organisational strategies. Acquisitions often lead to higher market shares, better economies of scale, greater revenue and profits and higher dividends.

Yet, research shows that most acquisitions actually destroy wealth for the acquiring company – some studies show that as much as 80% of acquisitions destroy value for acquiring companies. For example, when Google bought Motorola in 2012 for $12.5 billion, its share price fell by over 2% (which is around $4 billion in company value). This is likely to reflect shareholders' expectations for the future performance of the business and the impact on their wealth.

One of the key reasons for failure is that the acquiring company pay too much for their target – the extra returns generated do not cover the expected return on the cost of capital used to make the acquisition. To avoid overpaying, managing for value would examine the strategic decision from a financial perspective and ask questions such as:

- How will we achieve a reasonable payback on the acquisition price?

- What is the most we are willing to pay before we walk away?

- What investments will we need to make beyond pure purchase price?

- How dependent are we on "synergies" to make the acquisition work?

- Can we structure the deal more creatively to reduce our risk of overpaying?

So managing for value aims to ensure that the corporate or business level strategy is in line with the financial strategy and that all three work to create value for shareholders.

However, we should be aware that not-for-profit (NFP) organisations are not concerned about shareholder wealth and their financial strategy has a much different focus.

3 Not-for-profit organisations

Organisations such as charities and trade unions are not run to make profits, but to benefit prescribed groups of people.

Financial objectives of 'not-for-profit' organisations

Since the services provided are limited primarily by the funds available, their financial aim is:

- to raise the maximum possible sum each year (net of fund-raising expenses)
- to spend this sum as effectively as possible on the target group (with the minimum of administration costs).

Short term targets for NFPs

Not-for-profit organisations will normally set targets for particular aspects of each accounting period's finances, such as the following.

- Total to be raised in grants and voluntary income.
- Maximum percentage that fund-raising expenses represents of this total.
- Amounts to be spent on specified projects.
- Maximum permitted administration costs.

The actual figures achieved can then be compared with these targets and control action taken if necessary.

Value management in NFPs

An alternative strategy model developed for use with government organisations focuses the attention of managers on three key issues:

- public value to be created
- sources of legitimacy and support for the organisation
- operational capacity to deliver the value.

This focuses attention on social purpose and on the ways in which society as a whole might be mobilised to contribute to social purposes rather than on the financial objectives that can be achieved by selling products and services to markets.

Funding strategies for NFPs

What most non-profit organisations need are their core costs covered.

Core costs are the expenditure budgets that are not connected with the levels of activity undertaken by an organisation.

They are:

- the costs that will always need to be funded, regardless of the number of projects and

- are usually fundamental to the organisation's survival, even if they cannot be directly associated with any specific outcome.

Further examples of core costs

Core costs can be placed under three headings:

Management	• Costs associated with governance, board meetings, etc.
	• User engagement and consultation
	• Monitoring and evaluation
	• CEO and associated staff
Research and development	• Innovation – costs associated with developing new activities and ways of operating (before they attract funding)
	• Quality assurance
	• Staff training and development
Support services	• IT, telephone, postage and fax
	• Finance and audit
	• Income generation (including fundraising)
	• Marketing for the organisation
	• Premises
	• Travel and subsistence
	• Personnel

An organisation can only look ahead with confidence when the fundamental core costs are securely funded.

KAPLAN PUBLISHING

Creating a core funding strategy has different forms at each stage of a non-profit-seeking organisation's evolution.

- Infancy – tends to be heavily dependent on one funding source, which can limit independence.

- Growth phase – if funded by a multitude of projects and many donors it is prone to the pitfalls of mission creep (the expansion of a project or mission beyond its original goals, often after initial successes) and inefficiency.

- Maturity and maintenance – funding should be derived from a constantly changing mix of sources.

Core funding for NFPs

For a non-governmental organisation (NGO), protecting the core funding is the responsibility of the trustees. This requires more than ensuring that the annual accounts do not show an unrestricted deficit, all NGOs need to have a long-term plan as to how the core funds will be met for years ahead. A core funding strategy is a forward thinking, evolving document. It is more than a policy.

An NGO's CEO, Fundraising Director/Manager and the Finance Director/Manager will need to develop the actual strategy and manage its implementation. Each project manager will need to understand how their project budget contributes to the overall strategy.

There are five main elements to core funding.

- Strategic funding – is funding from regular, reliable donors who make an open-ended commitment to an organisation, e.g. institutional donors, wealthy individuals and faith-based communities.

- Apportioning overheads into project budgets – sometimes referred to as the business model, as it is a common formula for determining product pricing. Each project budget is expected to make a contribution towards overheads.

- Self-generated income – is where part of the core costs is funded by activities within its own control – where the donors don't specify how the funds are to be applied, e.g. an endowment, trading, fundraising events, legacy income and membership income.

- Developmental funding – donors agree to invest in the transformation of an organisation's infrastructure for a defined period. They can be described as 'second stage pump primers'.

- Cost minimisation – is astute financial management aimed at reducing core costs to an acceptable minimum. Securing gifts in kind and volunteers are excellent ways of minimising costs, as long as these gifts and the volunteers are effective in ensuring that core activities are delivered.

Test your understanding 1

A museum has previously been government funded and operated as a not-for-profit organisation. However, due to government rationalisation the museum has been forced to become a commercial company. It has achieved initial funding by listing on the company's stock exchange and issuing shares in the newly formed company.

What are the differences in strategic and operational decisions that a financial manager in the museum is likely to experience in the new business?

4 Funding strategies

As well as considering managing for value and the needs of wider stakeholders, financial decision makers must identify

- which SBUs need funding,
- how funding can support strategic decisions, and
- what type of funding they need

This will allow them to create unique funding strategies for each business unit.

Funding SBUs and strategic choices

A financial manager should recognise that funding requirements change subject to areas such as where an SBU is in its life cycle, where it lies in the organisation's portfolio (for example, within the BCG matrix) and the strategy that it is pursuing.

Funding strategies in the BCG matrix

Star	Problem child
• High growth	• High growth
• High business risk	• Very high business risk
• Use some retained earnings and new equity from investors seeking growth	• Use equity from venture capital
• High reinvestment rate so medium dividends	• Low or zero dividends in the short term.
Cash cow	**Dog**
• Low growth	• Low growth
• Medium business risk	• Low business risk
• Use retained earnings (and debt if necessary)	• Use debt until divest
• Large net cash inflows to support dividends	• Zero reinvestment rate so high dividends

Illustration 2 – Matching funding strategies to SBUs

For example, an SBU following a differentiation strategy when it currently sits in a problem child position is likely to need a high level of investment. It will need funding to improve processes, obtain better resources, innovate, market its competitive differences, and to cover short-term losses in performance.

A financial manager must also consider how best to provide this funding.

Both the need for funding and the funding strategy itself would be very different if this was a mature SBU in a cash cow position.

Alternative sources of finance

Financing was covered in detail in paper F9. A brief summary of alternatives and considerations are given here.

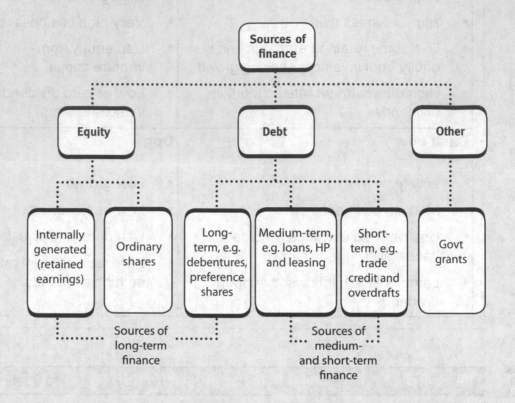

Key sources of internal finance

Internally generated finance is normally more flexible than external finance. However, it is important to remember that it still has a cost. It is an equity source of finance (and therefore will have a 'cost of equity' attached to it) and using internally generated funds instead of, say, paying a dividend to shareholders will mean that the shareholders will require a return on the investment that the organisation is effectively making on their behalf.

The key sources of internally generated finance are as follows:

(1) Using retained profits

    This is achieved by using cash generated within the business (i.e. retaining cash made from trading rather than paying it out as a dividend). This is a cheaper method of raising equity finance than issuing new shares to shareholders as issue costs are avoided, cash is raised more quickly, and it holds the advantage of retaining the existing proportional control of shareholders. It is therefore the most common source of long-term finance for an organisation.

But as a source of equity you should be aware that the cost of this finance is likely to be higher than the cost of debt that may be available to an organisation. Also, in previous studies you may have encountered what is known as the 'clientele effect'. This suggests that shareholders are attracted to particular companies by their history of either paying high dividends or, alternatively, from re-investing high levels of profits and reducing dividends. It will therefore be important that directors are aware of this when making a decision to retain a higher proportion of earnings than in the past as this may upset some shareholders who were expecting a dividend which subsequently does not arise. This may encourage such shareholders to sell their shares and adversely impact on the company's share price.

(2) Better working capital management

As explored later in this chapter, working capital policies can have a significant impact on an organisation's cash flow. Some policies will increase cash flow to the organisation and, therefore, these policies can be used to generate cash for the organisation. These often offer short-term solutions to cash flow problems and are unlikely to be sufficient to fund long term investments.

Policies that can be used can be to recover debts from receivables more quickly, reduce the investment in inventory or to increase the payment period to payables. For example, if a company with a turnover of $6m p.a. were to decrease its credit policy to customers so that they had to pay after one month instead of after two months, this is likely to increase cash inflow in the year by $500k (i.e. 1/12 × $6m).

These policies, however, may have a detrimental impact on organisational profits. For example, asking customers to pay more quickly may deter them from buying the product so that revenue is impacted as customers turn to rivals with better settlement periods. Or reducing inventory levels may mean that fewer items are available for sale so that, again, revenue is adversely impacted. There may also be business issues. For example, paying suppliers later may mean that they refuse to supply in the future or support other developments such as e-procurement.

(3) Sale of surplus assets

This is another easy source of finance for an organisation and can apply to both non-current assets and to inventories. However, it will be important to consider two elements:

– the asset must truly be surplus to requirements (sale of an asset that is not surplus to requirements may impact on the organisation's ability to operate and function efficiently and effectively),

– the long term impact must be considered (assets that are not needed now may well be needed in the medium to long term, or they may only be suffering from a seasonal effect. For example, Kaplan require less building space in January when students are awaiting results, but this is due to seasonality and does not suggest that the buildings should be sold off. It is expensive and disruptive to sell assets now that may be needed again the short to medium-term).

Factors to consider when choosing a financing package

- Cost
- Control
- Availability
- Gearing
- Security
- Cash flow
- Exit routes

Factors to consider when choosing a financing package

(1) **Cost**

– A bank loan is cheaper than an overdraft. Why? Because it is less risky from the bank's perspective. They have a repayment schedule, the loan may be secured, etc.

– Risk to the investor is the main determinant of the cost of the finance.

– Thus debt is usually cheaper than equity finance.

– Short-term loans are cheaper than long-term loans

– The issue costs of debt are also lower than for equity.

(2) Control

- Debt does not usually convey voting rights. Neither do preference shares.

- A public issue of shares may change the balance of control.

- A rights issue will not change control, provided existing shareholders take up their rights. Legally, companies must offer new shares to existing shareholders first.

(3) Availability

- Further debt may be restricted by agreements (covenants) in existing loans.

- Could shareholders afford a rights issue of the size suggested?

- Difficult to issue equity if unquoted.

(4) Gearing

- Debt is cheaper than equity but it has a hidden cost – as the level of debt increases the risk faced by the shareholders also increases. Thus their required return and hence the cost to the company will increase. Debt makes the equity more expensive

- We therefore have two effects of increased gearing – on the positive side the debt is cheap finance, on the negative side the extra risk is bad for the shareholders.

- To see the net effect of gearing we need to look at theories of gearing – general consensus is that there is an optimal level of gearing that is best not exceeded.

(5) Security

- Security is usually needed for debt.

- In a question you could look at the existing balance sheet for possible assets for security but watch for existing loans as assets may already be taken.

- Ideally assets will be land and buildings – quality assets, thus presenting a problem for service industries.

(6) Cash flow

- A general rule of thumb is to try to match the lifetimes of finance flows and project flows.

- If project cash flows are uncertain, then equity may be better as dividends may be cut if necessary.

- Fixed interest rates make budgeting easier than floating rates.

- Try to avoid loans maturing at the same time.

- In practice a cash flow forecast is essential.

(7) **Exit routes**

- Could the company repay the finance early? E.g. leases may include penalty clauses.

- Can investors get their money back early if they want to? Difficult if unquoted.

- Venture capitalists want their money back in 5 – 7 years.

Test your understanding 2

What sources of finance are available to a public sector organisation?

Managing current and non-current assets

Managing assets can either be a source of short-term finance or a burden on short-term finance that raises overall funding requirements.

Illustration 3 – The cost of asset mis-management

According to research by KPMG, UK companies alone are wasting $20 billion a year because managers have not applied proper asset management concepts. Other research indicates that companies are overspending by up to 40% because of under-utilisation, inefficient maintenance and petty theft of their assets

It has become such an issue that over the past decade, companies that typically rely on big, expensive non-current assets such as heavy manufacturers (plant and equipment) and telecom operators (infrastructure) have sought to improve their asset utilisation by outsourcing the ownership and management of these assets to other companies. Alternatively, there is asset management software available which can allow companies to improve their existing processes.

Managing non-current assets

Key internal controls (covered in earlier ACCA papers) used to manage non-current assets include:

- keeping an asset register

- ensuring proper authorisation for the purchase of assets

- measuring asset utilisation and actioning any variances from targets.

Good asset management include should lead to a reduction in costs (not just in terms of the investment needed, but also in terms of insurance premiums, security costs, reduced production costs etc.) and free up investment/finance for other purposes. It should also improve decision making when it comes to buying new assets and determining where to allocate finance.

Managing current assets

Managing current assets is also an important of financial decision making. In previous studies, you will have learnt that it is vital to manage the trade-off between profitability and liquidity. In simple terms this can be summarised as follows:

	Best for profitability	**Best for liquidity**
Receivables	Offer high settlement periods	Demand instant, cash payments
Payables	Pay instantly	Pay late
Inventories	Hold high levels	Hold low levels
Cash	Tie up cash in short-term investments	Keep cash in current accounts

A manager who tips the balance too far towards profitability is likely to put an undue burden on available finance (this is known as overtrading) whilst a manager who puts too great an emphasis on liquidity is likely to have unhappy stakeholders and is unlikely to achieve value for shareholders.

Managing cash

In the context of cash flows and liquidity, the following are risks that have to be managed:

- the risk that cash receipts will be lower than expected or that cash payments will be higher than expected, so that actual cash balances turn out to be much less than forecast

- the risk that when the business is faced with a cash shortage, it is unable to borrow the money it needs, or unable to raise more cash by selling off some of its assets

- the risk that when surplus cash is invested, the interest earned on the investment turns out to be much lower than it could have been.

The role of the cash manager is to monitor and control these risks, and to prevent them from threatening the survival of the business or having a significant impact on profitability.

The management of cash involves a trade off between:

- liquidity – having enough cash available to meet everyday demands
- profitability/cost – holding high balances of cash is costly in terms of lost investment interest; while unexpected deficits can be expensive if emergency funding is necessary.

The importance of cash forecasting

Cash forecasting is vital to ensure that sufficient funds will be available when they are needed to sustain the activities of an enterprise, at an acceptable cost. Forecasts provide an early warning of liquidity problems by estimating:

- how much cash is required
- when it is required
- how long it will be required for
- whether it will be available from anticipated sources.

Any forecast deficiency will have to be funded.

Financing assets

When financing assets there is a general rule of thumb:

- long term investments (such as those in non-current assets) should be financed through long term sources of finance
- short term investments should be financed through short term sources of finance (such as overdrafts)

Test your understanding 3

In choosing between short-term and long-term borrowing, what should the management take into consideration?

5 Ratio analysis

Ratios

Ratio analysis is particularly useful for assessing whether a strategy is achieving its desired targets. Ratio analysis has already been covered in Chapter 3.

Forecast ratios

In an examination question you may be asked to assess the implications of a proposed financing package and/or strategy.

Test your understanding 4

Explain in what ways your approach to performance appraisal would differ if you were asked to assess the performance of a not-for-profit organisation.

6 The role of cost and management accounting

Cost accounting is an approach to evaluating the overall costs that are associated with conducting business. Generally based on standard accounting practices, cost accounting is one of the tools that managers utilize to determine what type and how much expenses is involved with maintaining the current business model. At the same time, the principles of cost accounting can also be utilized to project changes to these costs in the event that specific changes are implemented.

The role of cost accounting

Cost accounting has many roles in a business, including

- Inventory valuation – the cost per unit can be used to value inventory in the statement of financial position (balance sheet).

- To record costs – the costs associated with the product need to be recorded in the statement of profit or loss.

- To price products – the business may use the cost per unit to assist in pricing the product. For example, if the cost per unit is $0.30, the business may decide to price the product at $0.50 per unit in order to make the required profit of $0.20 per unit.

- Decision making – the business may use the cost information to make important decisions regarding which products should be made and in what quantities.

From a strategic perspective, we have seen how understanding, minimising and controlling costs can link to a firm's competitive advantage such as a low cost or no-frills strategy. It may also provide a strategic capability to the organisation and create a barrier to entry through the achievement of economies of scale, for example.

Standard cost card

Much of cost accounting is based on the principles of standardisation. It assumes that businesses operate in a stable environment where, for example, a standard amount of materials will be used in the production of each product and that a standard price can be attached to the price of those materials.

The standard cost card absorption rates

A typical standard cost card for a product might look as follows:

		$
Direct materials	(4kg × $8/kg)	32
Direct labour	(3hrs × $12/hr)	36
Variable overheads	(3hrs × $4/hr)	12
Marginal production cost		80
Fixed overheads	(3hrs × $5/hr)	15
Full (absorption) production cost		95
Profit per unit		25
Selling price		120

Marginal costs are all variable.

It is relatively easy to estimate the cost per unit for direct materials and labour. In doing so we can complete the first two lines of the cost card. However, it is much more difficult to estimate the production overhead per unit. This is an indirect cost and so, by its very nature, we do not know how much is contained in each unit. Therefore, we need a method of attributing the production overheads to each unit.

Review of overhead absorption procedure

Accounting for overhead costs in an absorption costing system can be quite complex, and production overhead costs are first allocated, then apportioned and finally absorbed into production costs (or service costs).

- **Overhead allocation**. Indirect production costs are initially allocated to cost centres or cost codes. Allocation is the process of charging a cost directly and in full to the source of the expenditure. For example, the salary of a maintenance engineer would be allocated to the engineering maintenance department.

- **Overhead apportionment**. The overhead costs that have been allocated to cost centres and cost codes other than direct production departments must next be apportioned to direct production departments. Apportionment is the process of sharing on a fair basis. For example, factory rental costs might be apportioned between the production departments on the basis of the floor area occupied by each department. Similarly, the costs of the engineering maintenance department might be apportioned between production departments on the basis of the operating machine hours in each department. At the end of the apportionment process, all the production overheads have been allocated or apportioned to the direct production departments.

- **Overhead absorption**. An absorption rate is calculated for each production department. This is the rate at which production overheads will be added to the cost of production going through the department.

When the department produces a single product, production volume can be measured as the number of units produced, and the absorption rate would be a rate per unit produced.

More usually, organisations produce different products or carry out non-standard jobs for customers, and production volume is commonly measured as one of the following:

- direct labour hours worked in the department, and the absorption rate is a rate per direct labour hour worked

- machine hours worked in the department, and the absorption rate is a rate per machine hour operated

- sometimes the cost of direct labour might be used as a measure of production volume, and the absorption rate is then calculated as a percentage of direct labour cost.

Predetermined absorption rates

Although it is possible to calculate absorption rates using actual overhead costs and actual production volume, this is not the usual practice. This is because:

- It is usually inconvenient to wait until the end of an accounting period to work out what the absorption rates should be. In absorption costing systems, overhead costs are added to the cost of production as it passes through each stage in the production process, and overhead costs are absorbed when the production happens.

- A predetermined rate is required to enable a price to be estimated.

- Overhead costs may vary throughout the year. The overhead absorption rate smoothes variations in overheads by applying an average overhead cost to each unit of product throughout the year.

The normal practice is therefore to absorb production overhead costs at a predetermined rate, based on budgeted overhead expenditure and budgeted production volume.

This however can lead to an over or under-absorption of the overheads when compared to the actual overheads incurred.

This **over or under-absorption** can be calculated as follows:

= (Budgeted overhead rate per unit × actual units) – Actual overheads incurred

Problems with standard costing in modern environments

Standard product costs are associated with traditional manufacturing systems producing large quantities of standard items.

Standard costing may not be appropriate in the modern production environment because:

- Products are often non-standard
- Standards can become quickly outdated
- Production is highly automated
- Often an ideal standard is used
- Modern environments are more concerned with continuous improvement
- Modern managers need more detailed information
- More 'real time' performance measures are needed.

Further explanation

Non-standard products

Standard product costs apply to manufacturing environments in which quantities of an identical product are output from the production process. They are not suitable for manufacturing environments where products are non-standard or are customised to customer specifications.

Standard costs become outdated quickly

Shorter product life cycles in the modern business environment mean that standard costs will need to be reviewed and updated frequently. This will increase the cost of operating a standard cost system but, if the standards are not updated regularly, they will be of limited use for planning and control purposes. The extra work involved in maintaining up-to-date standards might limit the usefulness and relevance of a standard costing system.

Production is highly automated

It is doubtful whether standard costing is of much value for performance setting and control in automated manufacturing environments. There is an underlying assumption in standard costing that control can be exercised by concentrating on the efficiency of the workforce. Direct labour efficiency standards are seen as a key to management control. However, in practice, where manufacturing systems are highly automated, the rates of production output and materials consumption, are controlled by the machinery rather than the workforce.

Ideal standard used

Variances are the difference between actual performance and standard, measured in cost terms. The significance of variances for management control purposes depends on the type of standard cost used. JIT and TQM businesses often implement an ideal standard due to the emphasis on continuous improvement and high quality. Therefore, adverse variances with an ideal standard have a different meaning from adverse variances calculated with a current standard.

Emphasis on continuous improvement

Standard costing and adherence to a preset standard is inconsistent with the concept of continuous improvement, which is applied within TQM and JIT environments.

Detailed information is required

Variance analysis is often carried out on an aggregate basis (total material usage variance, total labour efficiency variance and so on) but in a complex and constantly changing business environment more detailed information is required for effective management control.

> ### Monitoring performance is important
>
> Variance analysis control reports tend to be made available to managers at the end of a reporting period. In the modern business environment managers need more 'real time' information about events as they occur.

Despite the limitations that standard costing techniques might have, the remainder of this chapter relies heavily on standard costing principles.

7 Standard costing systems

There are three main ways to produce a standard cost card:

- marginal costing – this only includes variable production costs in the cost of production

- absorption (or full) costing – as seen above this involves including all overheads (including indirect ones) in the cost of production

- activity based costing (ABC) – this is an alternative to absorption costing that provides more details on indirect costs and a better allocation between products

Marginal costing

Marginal costing is a costing method which charges products with variable costs alone. The fixed costs are treated as period costs and are written off in total against the contribution of the period.

This is useful for making short-term decisions (as will be seen later in this chapter) but the method becomes less relevant for longer term decisions where indirect and fixed overheads become more relevant.

Marginal costing advantages/disadvantages

Advantages of marginal costing

- It is the simplest costing system, because there is no requirement to apportion and absorb overhead costs.

- Marginal costing reflects the behaviour of costs in relation to activity. When sales increase, the cost of sales rise only by the additional variable costs. Since most decision-making problems involve changes to activity, marginal costing information is more relevant and appropriate for short-run decision-making than absorption costing.

- Marginal costing avoids the disadvantages of absorption costing, described later.

Disadvantages of marginal costing

- When fixed costs are high relative to variable costs, and when overheads are high relative to direct costs, the marginal cost of production and sales is only a small proportion of total costs. A costing system that focuses on marginal cost and contribution might therefore provide insufficient and inadequate information about costs and product profitability. Marginal costing is useful for short-term decision-making, but not for measuring product costs and profitability over the longer term.

- It could also be argued that the treatment of direct labour costs as a variable cost item is often unrealistic. When direct labour employees are paid a fixed wage or salary, their cost is fixed, not variable.

- 'fixed' costs might be fixed in relation to production volume, but they might vary with other activities that are not production-related. For example, factory insurance costs might vary based on the number of staff on site but stay the same regardless of the number of units produced.

Absorption costing

In absorption costing, all production overheads must be absorbed into units of production, using a suitable basis, e.g. units produced, labour hours or machine hours. The assumption underlying this method of absorption is that overhead expenditure is connected to the volume produced.

Absorption advantages/disadvantages

Advantages of absorption costing

The arguments used in favour of absorption costing are as follows:

- Fixed production costs can be a large proportion of the total production costs incurred. Unless production overheads are absorbed into product costs, a large proportion of cost would be excluded from the measurement of product costs.

- Absorption costing follows the matching concept (accruals concept) by carrying forward a proportion of the production cost in the inventory valuation to be matched against the sales value when the items are sold.

- It is necessary to include fixed production overhead in inventory values for financial statements; absorption costing produces inventory values which include a share of fixed production overhead.

- Analysis of under-/over-absorbed overhead may be useful for identifying inefficient utilisation of production resources.

- There is an argument that in the longer term, all costs are variable, and it is appropriate to try to identify overhead costs with the products or services that cause them. This argument is used as a reason for activity-based costing (ABC). ABC is a form of absorption costing, and is described later in this chapter.

Disadvantages of absorption costing

There are serious disadvantages with using absorption costing to measure costs and profits.

- **The apportionment and absorption of overhead costs is arbitrary**
  The way in which overhead costs are apportioned between cost centres and absorbed into production costs is subjective and many methods of cost allocation may be deemed appropriate. Although the process attempts to be 'fair', it is arbitrary.

  For example, suppose that a factory rental cost is apportioned between production departments on the basis of the floor area for each department. This might seem a fair way of sharing out the costs, but it is still subjective. Why not apportion the costs on the basis of the number of employees in each department? Or why not allow for the fact that some of the accommodation might be more pleasant to work in than others? In a manufacturing environment, production overheads might be absorbed on the basis of either direct labour hours or machine hours. However, choosing one instead of the other can have a significant effect on job costs or product costs, and yet it still relies on a subjective choice.

  It may be easier in some departments than others. If a department is labour intensive then allocations can be made on the basis of labour hours worked. Or if the department is machine intensive then allocations can be made on the basis of machine hours. But not every department will have this clear distinction.

- **Absorption costing can encourage over-production**
  A second criticism of absorption costing is that profits can be increased or reduced by changes in inventory levels. For example, by increasing output, more fixed overhead is absorbed into production costs, and if the extra output is not sold, the fixed overhead costs are carried forward in the closing inventory value. This can encourage managers to over-produce in order to inflate profits.

- **Overheads may not be related to the volume produced**

  Traditional absorption costing charges overhead costs to products (or services) in an arbitrary way. In product costing, overheads are absorbed on the basis of the volume of production in each production department or centre. The basis for setting an absorption rate is volume-related, such as an overhead absorption rate per unit produced, a rate per direct labour hour or a rate per machine hour.

  The assumption underlying this method of costing is that overhead expenditure is connected to the volume of production activity.

  – This assumption was probably valid many years ago, when production systems were based on labour-intensive or machine-intensive mass production of fairly standard items. Overhead costs were also fairly small relative to direct materials and direct labour costs; therefore any inaccuracy in the charging of overheads to products costs was not significant.

  – The assumption is not valid in a complex manufacturing environment, where production is based on smaller customised batches of products, indirect costs are high in relation to direct costs, and a high proportion of overhead activities – such as production scheduling, order handling and quality control – are not related to production volume.

  – For similar reasons, traditional absorption costing is not well-suited to the costing of many services.

  The criticism of absorption costing is that it cannot calculate a 'true' product cost that has any valid meaning. Overheads are charged to departments and products in an arbitrary way, and the assumption that overhead expenditure is related to direct labour hours or machine hours in the production departments is no longer realistic.

Activity based costing – a solution for modern production environments

Activity-based costing (ABC) is an alternative approach to product costing. It is a form of absorption costing, but, rather than absorbing overheads on a production volume basis it firstly allocates them to **cost pools** before absorbing them into units using **cost drivers**.

The need for ABC

Modern producers have changed they ways in which they produce so that:

- much more machinery and computerised manufacturing systems
- smaller batch sizes
- less use of 'direct' labour.

This has had the following **impact on production costs:**

- more indirect overheads (for example, insurance and depreciation of the machines and computers)
- less direct labour costs.

This means that the **traditional** methods of costing (marginal and absorption) produce **standard cost cards that are less useful** due to inaccurate product costs:

- the largest cost of production is indirect overheads but these are categorised together in one figure that lacks detail and is not useful to management
- because management does not know what the components are of the largest production cost (indirect overheads) they cannot implement proper cost control.
- the costs are often allocated between products on the basis of direct labour hours – despite the fact that direct labour is becoming a smaller proportion of product costs and does not fairly reflect the relationship between the products and the indirect overheads
- because costs are inappropriately or inaccurately shared between products it means that the total production cost can be wrong which can lead to poor pricing and production decisions

Activity based costing **(ABC) has been developed to solve some of the problems** that traditional costing methods create in these modern environments.

Cost drivers and cost pools

- A **cost pool** is an activity that consumes resources and for which overhead costs are identified and allocated. For each cost pool, there should be a cost driver.
- A **cost driver** is a unit of activity that consumes resources. An alternative definition of a cost driver is a factor influencing the level of cost.

Illustration

Imagine the machining department in a traditional absorption costing system. The Overhead Absorption Rate (OAR) would be based on machine hours because many of the overheads in the machine department would relate to the machines, e.g. power, maintenance, machine depreciation, etc., so using a machine hour basis would seem fair, however, not only does the machine department have machine related costs, but also in an absorption costing system, it would also have picked up a share of rent and rates, heating, lighting, building depreciation, canteen costs, personnel cost, etc. These costs would also be absorbed on a machine hour basis, because everything in the machine department is absorbed on machine hours and whilst this is fair for power, maintenance and machine depreciation, it is inappropriate for the other costs.

ABC overcomes this problem by not using departments as gathering points for costs, but instead using activities, and there would for example be a machine-related activity to which power would be charged, machine depreciation would be charged, and machine maintenance would be charged. It would not pick up a share of personnel costs or rent or rates or indeed anything not machine related. ABC's flexibility thus reduces the incidence of arbitrary apportionments.

When is ABC relevant?

ABC is a more expensive system to operate than traditional costing, so it should only be introduced when it is appropriate to do so. Activity-based costing could provide much more meaningful information about product costs and profits when:

- indirect costs are high relative to direct costs

- products or services are complex

- products or services are tailored to customer specifications

- some products or services are sold in large numbers but others are sold in small numbers.

In these situations, ABC will often result in significantly different product or service overhead costs, compared with traditional absorption costing.

The implications of switching to ABC

The use of ABC has potentially significant commercial implications:

- Pricing can be based on more realistic cost data.
  - Pricing decisions will be improved because the price will be based on more accurate cost data.

- Sales strategy can be more soundly based.
  - More realistic product costs as a result of the use of ABC may enable sales staff to:
    - target customers that appeared unprofitable using absorption costing but may bc profitable under ABC
    - stop targeting customers or market segments that are now shown to offer low or negative sales margins.

- Decision making can be improved.
  - Research, production and sales effort can be directed towards those products and services which ABC has identified as offering the highest sales margins.

- Performance management can be improved.
  - Performance management should be enhanced due to the focus on selling the most profitable products and through the control of cost drivers.
  - ABC can be used as the basis of budgeting and longer term forward planning of overhead costs. The more realistic budgeted overhead cost should improve the system of performance management.

Advantages and disadvantages of ABC

ABC has a number of advantages:

- It provides a more accurate cost per unit. As a result, pricing, sales strategy, performance management and decision making should be improved (see next section for detail).

- It provides much better insight into what drives overhead costs.

- ABC recognises that overhead costs are not all related to production and sales volume.

- In many businesses, overhead costs are a significant proportion of total costs, and management needs to understand the drivers of overhead costs in order to manage the business properly. Overhead costs can be controlled by managing cost drivers.

- It can be applied to derive realistic costs in a complex business environment.

- ABC can be applied to all overhead costs, not just production overheads.

- ABC can be used just as easily in service costing as in product costing.

Disadvantages of ABC:

- ABC will be of limited benefit if the overhead costs are primarily volume related or if the overhead is a small proportion of the overall cost.

- It is impossible to allocate all overhead costs to specific activities.

- The choice of both activities and cost drivers might be inappropriate.

- ABC can be more complex to explain to the stakeholders of the costing exercise.

- The benefits obtained from ABC might not justify the costs.

Test your understanding 5

Fixed overhead absorption rates are often calculated using a single measure of activity. It is suggested that fixed overhead costs should be attributed to cost units using multiple measures of activity (Activity Based Costing).

Explain Activity Based Costing and how it may provide useful information to managers.

(Your answer should refer to both the setting of cost driver rates and subsequent overhead cost control.)

8 Decision making techniques

In this section we look at two areas:

- break even analysis
- marginal analysis

Contribution to sales ratios and breakeven points

Cost-Volume-Profit (CVP) analysis

CVP analysis makes use of the contribution concept in order to assess the following measures for a single product:

- contribution to sales (C/S) ratio
- breakeven point
- margin of safety

(Contribution = selling price less **all** variable costs)

C/S ratio

The C/S ratio of a product is the proportion of the selling price that contributes to fixed overheads and profits. It is comparable to the gross profit margin. The formula for calculating the C/S ratio of a product is as follows:

$$\text{C/S ratio} = \frac{\text{Contribution per unit}}{\text{Selling price per unit}} \quad \text{or} \quad \frac{\text{Total contribution}}{\text{Total sales revenue}}$$

The C/S ratio is sometimes referred to as the P/V (Profit/Volume) ratio.

Breakeven point

The breakeven point is the point at which neither a profit nor a loss is made.

- At the breakeven point the following situations occur.

   Total sales revenue = Total costs, i.e. Profit = 0

   or

   Total contribution = Fixed costs, i.e. Profit = 0

- The following formula is used to calculate the breakeven point in terms of numbers of units sold.

$$\text{Breakeven point (in terms of numbers of units sold)} = \frac{\text{Fixed costs}}{\text{Contribution per unit}}$$

- It is also possible to calculate the breakeven point in terms of sales revenue using the C/S ratio. The equation is as follows:

Breakeven point (in terms of sales revenue) = $\dfrac{\textbf{Fixed costs}}{\textbf{C/S ratio}}$

Margin of safety

The margin of safety is the amount by which anticipated sales (in units) can fall below budget before a business makes a loss. It can be calculated in terms of numbers of units or as a percentage of budgeted sales.

The following formulae are used to calculate the margin of safety:

Margin of safety (in terms of units) = **Budgeted sales – Breakeven point sales**

Margin of safety (as a % of budgeted sales) = $\dfrac{\textbf{Budgeted sales – Breakeven sales}}{\textbf{Budgeted sales}}$ **× 100%**

Test Your Understanding 6

A break down of KP's profit in the last accounting period showed the following:

	$000
Sales	450
Variable costs	(220)
Fixed costs	(160)
Profit	70

Due to a downturn in market conditions the company is worried that next year may result in losses and would like to know the change in sales that would make this happen.

Required:

Calculate the break-even sales revenue for the business based on its current cost structure. Use this information to determine the percentage fall in sales that would be necessary before the company would begin to incur losses.

(5 marks)

Limitations of break even analysis

The assumptions of break even analysis (which also therefore become its weaknesses) are:

- We are only considering the short term.
- There is a constant contribution per unit.
- There is a constant selling price.
- There are constant variable costs per unit and constant fixed costs (so that it ignores stepped fixed costs).
- Sales = production so that there is no stock movement.
- The objective is to maximise profit.

Marginal analysis

Marginal analysis refers to situations where we use contribution to make decisions.

The key is that only costs which vary with the decision should be included in an analysis of the decision.

More details on relevant cost principles

Decision making involves making a choice between two or more alternatives. The decision will be 'rational'; profit maximising. All decisions will be made using relevant costs and revenues.

'Relevant costs are future cash flows arising as a direct consequence of the decision under consideration.'

There are three elements here:

Cash flows. To evaluate a decision actual cash flows should be considered. Non-cash items such as depreciation and interdivisional charges should be ignored.

Future costs and revenues. This means that past costs and revenues are only useful insofar as they provide a guide to the future. Costs already spent, known as sunk costs, are irrelevant for decision making.

Differential costs and revenues. Only those costs and revenues that alter as a result of a decision are relevant. Where factors are common to all the alternatives being considered they can be ignored; only the differences are relevant.

In many short run situations the fixed costs remain constant for each of the alternatives being considered and thus the marginal costing approach showing sales, marginal cost and contribution is particularly appropriate.

In the long run (and sometimes in the short run) fixed costs do change and accordingly the differential costs must include any changes in the amount of fixed costs.

Marginal analysis can be used in four key areas of decision making:

- accepting/rejecting special contracts
- determining the most efficient use of resources
- make-or-buy decisions
- closing/continuation decisions.

Each of these will now be considered in turn.

Accepting/rejecting special contracts

The basic decision rule here is that we should calculate:

Extra revenue received *less* marginal costs of meeting the special contract

This would typically mean that items such as fixed costs, contracted costs etc. would be ignored in the decision as they would not be affected by the decision.

Determining the most efficient use of resources

Businesses often operate under short-term restrictions on resources (for example, staff time may be limited during a strike). They therefore may not be able to produce all products that make a positive contribution and need to prioritise products and choose between them.

 The most profitable combination of products will occur where the contribution per usage of the scarce resource is maximised.

Detailed technique

The usual objective in questions is to maximise profit. Given that fixed costs are unaffected by the production decision in the short run, the approach should be to maximise the contribution earned.

If there is one limiting factor, then the problem is best solved using key factor analysis.

Step 1: identify the bottleneck constraint.

Step 2: calculate the contribution per unit for each product.

Step 3: calculate the contribution per unit of the bottleneck resource for each product.

Step 4: rank the products in order of the contribution per unit of the bottleneck resource.

Step 5: allocate resources using this ranking and answer the question.

Test your understanding 7

X Ltd makes three products, A, B and C, of which unit costs, machine hours and selling prices are as follows:

	Product A	Product B	Product C
Machine hours	10	12	14
	$	$	$
Direct materials @ 50c per kg	7 (14 kg)	6 (12 kg)	5 (10 kg)
Direct wages @ $7.50 per hour	9 (1.2 hours)	6 (0.8 hours)	3 (0.4 hours)
Variable overheads	3	3	3
Marginal cost	19	15	11
Selling price	25	20	15
Contribution	6	5	4

Sales demand for the period is limited as follows.

Product A	4,000
Product B	6,000
Product C	6,000

Company policy is to produce a minimum of 1,000 units of Product A.

The supply of materials in the period is unlimited, but machine hours are limited to 200,000 and direct labour hours to 5,000.

Required:

Indicate the production levels that should be adopted for the three products in order to maximise profitability, and state the maximum contribution.

Make-or-buy decisions

A product should be made in-house if the relevant cost of making the product in-house is less than the cost of buying the product externally.

Spare capacity exists

Unless stated otherwise in the question, it should be assumed that there is spare capacity.

> The relevant cost of making the product in-house = the variable cost of internal manufacture plus any fixed costs directly related to that product.

No spare capacity exists

> The relevant cost of making the product in-house = the variable cost of internal manufacture plus any fixed costs directly related to that product plus the opportunity cost of internal manufacture (e.g. lost contribution from another product).

Test your understanding 8

A factory's entire machine capacity is used to produce essential components. The production costs of using the machines are as follows.

	$
Variable	30,000
Fixed	40,000
Total	70,000

If all component production was outsourced, then the machines could be used to produce other items that would generate additional contribution of $50,000. Assume the fixed costs will still be incurred if production is outsourced.

What is the maximum price that the company should be willing to pay to the outside supplier for the components?

Closure or continuation decisions

Part of a business, for example a department or a product, may appear to be unprofitable. The business may have to make a decision as to whether or not this area should be shut down.

The quantifiable cost or benefit of closure

The relevant cash flows associated with closure should be considered. For example:

- the lost contribution from the area that is being closed (= relevant cost of closure)

- savings in specific fixed costs from closure (= relevant benefit of closure)

- known penalties and other costs resulting from the closure, e.g. redundancy, compensation to customers (= relevant cost of closure)

- any known reorganisation costs (= relevant cost of closure)

- any known additional contribution from the alternative use for resources released (= relevant benefit of closure).

If the relevant benefits are greater than the relevant costs of closure then closure may occur. However, before a final decision is made the business should also consider the non-quantifiable factors discussed below.

Other issues to consider

The decision making processes above concentrated on the financial impact of the decisions. Decision makers should also consider qualitative factors such as the impact on customers, competitive advantage and critical success factors etc.

Example of other factors to consider

For example, let's consider the qualitative factors in a make-or-buy decision.

In addition to the relative cost of buying externally compared to making in-house, management must consider a number of other issues before a final decision is made.

- **Reliability of external supplier:** can the outside company be relied upon to meet the requirements in terms of:
    - quantity required
    - quality required
    - delivering on time
    - price stability.

- **Specialist skills:** the external supplier may possess some specialist skills that are not available in-house.

- **Alternative use of resource:** outsourcing will free up resources which may be used in another part of the business.

- **Social:** will outsourcing result in a reduction of the workforce? Redundancy costs should be considered.

- **Legal:** will outsourcing affect contractual obligations with suppliers or employees?

- **Confidentiality:** is there a risk of loss of confidentiality, especially if the external supplier performs similar work for rival companies.

- **Customer reaction:** Do customers attach importance to the products being made in-house?

Non-quantifiable costs and benefits of closure

There are qualitative factors to consider in all of the above marginal decisions. For example, the closure decision might have the following qualitative factors:

- Some of the costs and benefits discussed above may be non-quantifiable at the point of making the shut-down decision:
  - penalties and other costs resulting from the closure (e.g. redundancy, compensation to customers) may not be known with certainty.
  - reorganisation costs may not be known with certainty.
  - additional contribution from the alternative use for resources released may not be known with certainty.

- Knock-on impact of the shut-down decision. For example, supermarkets often stock some goods which they sell at a loss. This is to get customers through the door, who they then hope will purchase other products which have higher profit margins for them. If the decision is taken to stop selling these products then the customers may no longer come to the store.

Test your understanding 9

KRS Ltd is considering whether to administer its own purchase ledger or to use an external accounting service. It has obtained the following cost estimates for each option:

Internal service department

	Cost	Volume
Purchase hardware/software	$320 pa	
Hardware/software maintenance	$750 pa	
Accounting stationary	$500 pa	
Part-time account clerk	$6,000 pa	

External services

	Cost	Volume
Processing of invoices/credit notes	$0.50 per document	5,000 pa
Processing of cheque payments	$0.50 per cheque	4,000 pa
Reconciling supplier accounts	$2.00 per supplier per month	150 suppliers

Determine the cost effectiveness of outsourcing the accounting activities and identify the qualitative factors involved.

9 Dealing with risk in decision making

There are many ways in which risk can be dealt with in decision making. The most common technique is to attach probabilities to the potential range of outcomes and calculate expected values from this information.

Probabilities and expected values

An expected value summarises all the different possible outcomes by calculating a single weighted average. It is the long run average (mean).

The expected value is not the most likely result. It may not even be a possible result, but instead it finds the average outcome if the same event was to take place thousands of times.

Expected value calculations

The following illustrates how calculations may be performed when using expected values.

Expected value formula

$$EV = \Sigma px$$

where   x represents the future outcome

and   p represents the probability of the outcome occurring

Example

A company expects the following monthly profits:

Monthly profit	Probability
£10,000	0.70
£20,000	0.30

Calculate the expected value of monthly profit.

Solution

Monthly profit	Probability	px
£10,000	0.70	7,000
£20,000	0.30	6,000
		13,000

Expected profit is £13,000 per month.

Test your understanding 10

A company's sales for a new product are subject to uncertainty. It has determined a range of possible outcomes over the first two years.

Year 1

Sales	$m	%
High	40	60
Low	20	40

Year 2

Sales	$m	%
High	80	90
Low	30	10

(if year 1 sales are high)

Sales	$m	%
High	30	20
Low	10	80

(if year 1 sales are low)

Required:

Calculate the expected sales for each year.

Advantages and disadvantages of EVs

Advantages:

- Takes risk into account by considering the probability of each possible outcome and using this information to calculate an expected value.

- The information is reduced to a single number resulting in easier decisions.

- Calculations are relatively simple.

Disadvantages:

- The probabilities used are usually very subjective.

- The EV is merely a weighted average and therefore has little meaning for a one-off project.

- The EV gives no indication of the dispersion of possible outcomes about the EV, i.e. the risk.

- The EV may not correspond to any of the actual possible outcomes.

Decision trees and multi-stage decision problems

A decision tree is a diagrammatic representation of a decision problem, where all possible courses of action are represented, and every possible outcome of each course of action is shown. Decision trees should be used where a problem involves a series of decisions being made and several outcomes arise during the decision-making process.

Decision trees force the decision maker to consider the logical sequence of events. A complex problem is broken down into smaller, easier-to-handle sections. The financial outcomes and probabilities are shown separately, and the decision tree is 'rolled back' by calculating expected values and making decisions. It is important that only relevant costs and revenues are considered, and that all cash is expressed in present value terms.

Drawing decision trees

In the exam it will be important that you can understand and interpret decision trees. You may also be expected to draw a simple decision tree.

Three-step method

Step 1: Draw the tree from left to right showing appropriate decisions and events/outcomes. (This is known as the forward pass).

Symbols to use:

□ A square is used to represent a decision point. At a decision point the decision maker has a choice of which course of action he wishes to undertake.

○ A circle is used at a chance outcome point. The branches from here are always subject to probabilities.

Label the tree and relevant cash inflows/outflows (discounted to present values) and probabilities associated with outcomes.

> **Step 2:** Evaluate the tree from right to left carrying out
> these two actions:
>
> Calculate an EV at each outcome point.
>
> Choose the best option at each decision point.
>
> (This is known as the backward pass.)
>
> **Step 3:** Recommend a course of action to management.

Test Your Understanding 11

A company is planning on drilling for oil. It can either drill immediately (at a cost of $50m) or carry out some preliminary tests (cost ($10m). Alternatively, the company could sell the rights to the site to another company for $40m.

If it decides to drill now there is a 55% chance that it will find oil and extract it (with a value of $150m).

If further tests are carried out first there is a 70% chance that they will indicate the presence of oil. The sales rights would then be worth $65m. Alternatively, the company could drill for oil itself at a cost of $50m. There is then an 80% chance that oil extraction (worth $150m) is successful.

If further tests are carried out and indicate that no oil is present the value of any sales rights would fall to $15m. The company could still decide to drill for oil itself- but there is only a 20% chance that it would successfully find and extract oil at that point.

Draw a decision tree of this problem and advise the company on how to proceed. Also, briefly discuss the benefits and problems of using decision trees.

10 Budgeting

A quantitative or financial plan relating to the future. It can be for the company as a whole or for departments or functions or products or for resources such as cash, materials, labour, etc. It is usually for one year or less.

As part of 'strategy in action', a business will create plans for each SBU, product, function etc. These plans are often in the form of budgets. The budget sets out the short-term plans an targets necessary to fulfil the longer-term strategic plans and objectives.

The budgets will also play a vital role in reviewing and controlling strategic plans. They will be used to identify and investigate variances and to highlight when a plan or process is 'out of control'.

Budgets are distinct from forecasts. A forecast is a prediction of a future outcome. A budget is a plan (usually in financial terms) that looks to use and/or achieve that forecast.

Purposes of budgeting

Budgets have several different purposes:

(1) Planning

(2) Control

(3) Co-ordination

(4) Communication

(5) Motivation

(6) Evaluation

(7) Authorisation

Purposes of budgets explained

Budgets have several different purposes:

(1) **Planning**

Budgets **compel** planning. The budgeting process forces management to look ahead, set targets, anticipate problems and give the organisation purpose and direction. Without the annual budgeting process the pressures of day-to-day operational problems may tempt managers not to plan for future operations. The budgeting process encourages managers to anticipate problems before they arise, and hasty decisions that are made on the spur of the moment, based on expediency rather than reasoned judgements, will be minimised. Corporate planners would regard budgeting as an important technique whereby long-term strategies are converted into shorter-term action plans.

(2) Control

The budget provides the plan against which actual results can be compared. Those results which are out-of-line with the budget can be further investigated and corrected.

(3) Co-ordination

The budget serves as a vehicle through which the actions of the different parts of an organisation can be brought together and reconciled into a common plan. Without any guidance managers may each make their own decisions believing that they are working in the best interests of the organisation. A sound budgeting system helps to co-ordinate the different activities of the business and to ensure that they are in harmony with each other.

(4) Communication

Budgets communicate targets to managers. Through the budget, top management communicates its expectations to lower-level management so that all members of the organisation may understand these expectations and can co-ordinate their activities to attain them.

(5) Motivation

The budget can be a useful device for influencing managerial behaviour and motivating managers to perform in line with the organisational objectives.

(6) Evaluation

The performance of a manager is often evaluated by measuring his success in achieving his budgets. The budget might quite possibly be the only quantitative reference point available.

(7) Authorisation

A budget may act as formal authorisation to a manager for expenditure, the hiring of staff and the pursuit of the plans contained in the budget.

Functional budgets and the master budget

A master budget for the entire organisation brings together the departmental or activity budgets for all the departments or responsibility centres within the organisation.

The structure of a budget depends on the nature of the organisation and its operations. In a manufacturing organisation, the budgeting process will probably consist of preparing several functional budgets, beginning with a sales budget.

Functional budgets

- **Sales budget**. Budget for future sales, expressed in revenue terms and possibly also in units of sale. The budget for the organisation as a whole might combine the sales budgets of several sales regions.

- **Production budget**. A production budget follows on from the sales budget, since production quantities are determined by sales volume. The production volume will differ from sales volume by the amount of any planned increase or decrease in inventories of finished goods (and work-in-progress).

In order to express the production budget in financial terms (production cost), subsidiary budgets must be prepared for materials, labour and production overheads. Several departmental managers could be involved in preparing these subsidiary budgets.

- **Direct materials usage budget**. This is a budget for the quantities and cost of the materials required for the planned production quantities.

- **Materials purchasing budget**. This is a budget for the cost of the materials to be purchased in the period. The purchase cost of direct materials will differ from the material usage budget if there is a planned increase or decrease in direct materials inventory. The purchases budget should also include the purchase costs of indirect materials.

- **Direct labour budget**. This is a budget of the direct labour costs of production. If direct labour is a variable cost, it is calculated by multiplying the production quantities (in units) by the budgeted direct labour cost per unit produced. If direct labour is a fixed cost, it can be calculated by estimating the payroll cost.

- **Production overheads**. Budgets can be produced for production overhead costs. Where a system of absorption costing is used, overheads are allocated and apportioned, and budgeted absorption rates are determined.

- **Administration and sales and distribution overheads**. Other overhead costs should be budgeted.

- **Budgeted statement of profit or loss, cash budget and balance sheet**. Having prepared budgets for sales and costs, the master budget can be summarised as a statement of profit or loss for the period, a cash budget (or cash flow forecast) and a balance sheet as at the end of the budget period.

If the budgeted profit, cash position or balance sheet are unsatisfactory, the budgets should be revised until a satisfactory planned outcome is achieved.

The stages in budget preparation are illustrated in the following diagram:

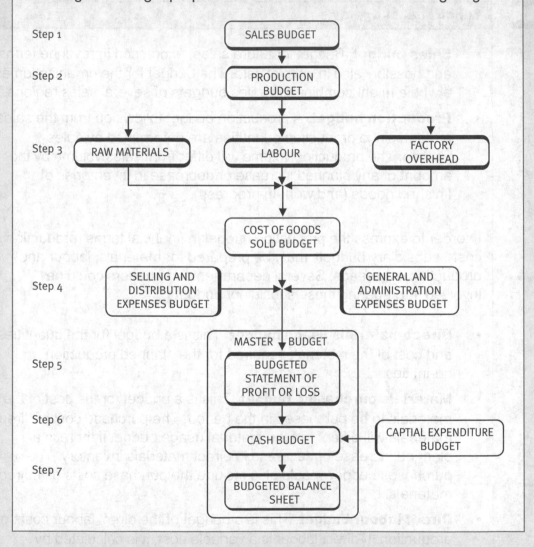

Principal budget factor

It is usually assumed in budgeting that sales demand will be the key factor setting a limit to what the organisation can expect to achieve in the budget period. Occasionally, however, there might be a shortage of a key resource, such as cash, raw material supplies, skilled labour or equipment. If a resource is in restricted supply, and the shortage cannot be overcome, the budget for the period should be determined by how to make the best use of this key budget resource, rather than be sales demand.

When a key resource is in short supply and affects the planning decisions, it is known as the **principal budget factor** or **limiting budget factor**.

Meaningful budgetary control

Budgetary control refers to not only the budget setting process but also to the monitoring of ongoing performance against these budgets. For this second process to be useful the budgets themselves must be accurate, reliable and up to date.

Why budgets may not be useful for control purposes

There are two reasons why this might not be the case. Firstly, it may well be that the organisation's environment has changed but that the budget has not been adapted to reflect this. For example, if a budget is based on a 30% forecasted increase in sales but perhaps a change in legislation means that the product is no longer as attractive and sales are now only forecasted to rise by 5%. In this case the budget should be changed in order to reflect the change in the organisation's environment. Without a change to the budget the organisation would look to be out of control and unnecessary actions and investigations would be implemented.

The second reason why the budget itself may not be useful for control purposes is due to the behavioural aspects of budgeting.

Behavioural aspects of budgets

As mentioned above, one of the purposes of budgets is to achieve motivation. There are therefore a number of factors to consider in relation to this:

- the level of difficulty in the budget,
- the links to the organisation's objectives, and
- the level of staff involvement.

Further details

- the level of difficulty in the budget. Budgets should be realistic and just tough enough so that they do not demotivate by being too difficult or present a lack of motivation by being too easy.

- the links to the organisation's objectives. As already discussed, budgets should be linked to objectives to ensure that they motivate managers and staff to achieve those objectives rather than any other objectives (such as their own).

- the level of staff involvement. Involving staff in budgets provides a responsibility that is often linked to strong motivation. On the other hand, the business must be wary of any slack that managers might want to build into budgets in which they have both an input and a responsibility.

Making budgetary control effective

Atrill and McLaney identify a number of characteristics that are common to businesses with effective budgetary control:

- a serious attitude is taken to the system
- clear demarcation between areas of managerial responsibility
- budget targets that are challenging yet achievable
- established data collection, analysis and reporting techniques
- reports aimed at individual managers
- fairly short reporting periods
- timely variance reports
- action being taken to get operations back under control if they are shown to be out of control.

11 Variance analysis

An effective part of budgetary control is to calculate and investigate variances from the budget.

Flexed budgets

Before any meaningful comparison can be made the original budget should be 'flexed' to the actual level of performance.

Example of a flexed budget

A company has a standard cost of $8 per unit for materials and expects to produce and sell 20,000 units (ignore any changes to materials stock). It sets a materials budget for the purchasing department of $160,000 in total.

During the year, because of a celebrity endorsement, the product become very popular and actual sales and production are 30,000 units (50% above what was originally expected). The purchasing department has spent $220,000 on materials and is very concerned about the massive overspend in their department.

It makes sense that the materials budget for the purchasing department should not be limited to the original $160,000 as now it will have had to buy a lot extra materials. So instead the original budget is adjusted (or flexed) to reflect the increase in actual level of activity.

	Original	Flexed budget	Actual	Total Materials Variance
Production (units)	20,000	30,000	30,000	–
Materials budget ($)	160,000	240,000	220,000	20,000 Fav

Variance groups

Variances can be divided into three main groups:

- sales variances
- variable cost variances
  - material variances
  - labour variances
  - variable overhead variances
- fixed overhead variances

Variance calculations

Sales price variance

A sales price variance shows the effect on profit of the difference between the standard sales prices for the items sold in a period and the actual sales revenue achieved. It is calculated as follows:

(a) Standard selling price multiplied by the actual number of units sold, and

(b) Actual selling price multiplied by the actual number of units sold.

Sales volume profit variance

The sales volume margin variance is the difference between actual and budgeted sales volumes valued at either standard profit, in an absorption costing system, or standard contribution in a marginal costing system.

Direct material total variance

The difference between:

(a) the standard direct material cost of the actual production and

(b) the actual cost of direct material.

Direct material price variance

The difference between:

(a) standard purchase price per kg and

(b) actual purchase price.

Multiplied by the actual quantity of material purchased or used.

Note that the material price variance can be calculated either at the time of purchase or at the time of usage. Generally, the former is preferable.

Direct material usage variance

The difference between:

(a) the standard quantity of material specified for the actual production and

(b) the actual quantity used.

multiplied by the standard purchase price.

Direct labour total cost variance

The difference between:

(a) the standard direct labour cost of the actual production and

(b) the actual cost of direct labour.

Direct labour rate variance

The difference between:

(a) standard rate per hour and the

(b) actual rate per hour.

multiplied by the actual hours that were paid for.

Direct labour efficiency variance

The difference between:

(a) the standard hours specified for the actual production and

(b) the actual hours worked.

multiplied by the standard hourly rate.

Variable production overhead total cost variance

The difference between:

(a) the standard variable overhead cost of the actual production and

(b) the actual cost of variable production overheads.

Variable production overhead cost		$
Actual quantity of output	should cost (standard)	X
	did cost	Y
Total cost variance		X–Y

Variable production overhead expenditure variance

		$
Number of hours worked	should cost/hr (standard)	X
	did cost (actual)	Y
Variable production overhead expenditure variance		X–Y

Variable production overhead efficiency variance

		Hours
Actual output produced	should take (standard hours)	X
	did take (actual hours)	Y
Efficiency variance	(in hours)	X–Y
× standard variable overhead rate per hour		$P
Variable production overhead efficiency variance		$P × (X – Y)

Fixed overhead total variance

In standard absorption costing, the total cost variance for fixed production overhead variances is the amount of over-absorbed or under-absorbed overhead. Over-absorbed overhead is a favourable variance, and under-absorbed overhead is an adverse variance.

The amount of overhead absorbed for each unit of output is the standard fixed overhead cost per unit. The total cost variance is therefore calculated as follows:

The difference between:

(a) the standard fixed overhead cost of the actual production and

(b) the actual fixed overheads incurred.

Fixed overhead expenditure variance

The difference between:

(a) Budgeted Fixed Cost and

(b) Actual Fixed Cost.

Fixed production overhead volume variance

A fixed production overhead volume variance represents the amount of fixed overhead that has been under- or over-absorbed due to the fact that actual production volume differed from the budgeted production volume.

The volume variance is calculated as the difference between:

(a) Budgeted output in units and

(b) Actual output in units.

multiplied by the Standard Fixed Overhead Cost per unit

The fixed overhead volume variance does not occur in a marginal costing system.

Test Your Understanding 12

Sam Mendes Ltd is a manufacturing company which produces a variety of products. The following information relates to one of its products – Product W:

Standard cost data		$	$
Selling Price			100
Direct Material X	5 kg	15	
Direct Material Y	4 kg	20	
Direct Labour	@ $8/hr	24	
Variable Overheads		18	
Fixed Overheads		6	
			83
Profit per unit			17

The budgeted production is 24,000 units per annum evenly spread throughout the year, with each calendar month assumed to be equal. March is a bad month in terms of sales revenue and it is expected that sales will only be 1,700 units during the month. Fixed overheads were expected to be $144,000 per year and are absorbed on a labour hour basis.

Actual results for the month of March were that sales were 2,200 units at a price of $90. There was no change in stock of finished goods or raw materials.

The purchases during the month were 11,300 kg of material X at $2.80 per kg and 8,300 kg of material Y at $5.30 per kg.

4,800 labour hours were worked at a rate of $8.10 per hour and 1,600 hours at $8.30.

The actual variable overheads for the period were $33,000 and the fixed overheads were $12,500.

The company uses an absorption costing system and maintains its raw materials account at standard.

> **Required:**
>
> Calculate appropriate variances for the month of March in as much detail as possible and present an operating statement reconciling budgeted profit with actual profit.
>
> You are not required to calculate mix or yield variances as Sam Mendes Ltd does not sub-analyse the material usage or labour efficiency variances.

Variance investigation

Variances arise naturally in standard costing because a standard cost is a long term average cost. In any period actual costs may be higher or lower than standard but in the long run these should cancel out if the process is under control.

Variances may also arise because of:

- poor budgeting
- poor recording of cost
- operational reasons (the key emphasis in exam questions)
- random factors.

It is important to identify the reason for a variance so that appropriate action can be taken, but time and effort will be wasted if all variances are investigated as many will arise as a normal part of the process.

When should a variance be investigated?

Factors to consider include the following:

- the size of the variance
- whether favourable/adverse – firms often treat adverse variances as more important than favourable
- correction costs versus benefits
- ability to correct
- past pattern
- budget reliability
- reliability of measurement/recording systems.

Variance investigation techniques

Reporting by exception

Variance reports might identify significant variances. This is a form of reporting by exception, in which particular attention is given to the aspects of performance that appear to be exceptionally good or bad.

Alternatively, a rule might be applied generally that any adverse variance or favourable variance should be investigated if it exceeds more than a given percentage amount of the standard cost. For example, a rule might be applied that all adverse variances exceeding 5% of standard cost should be investigated and all favourable variances exceeding 10% of the standard should also be investigated.

Cumulative variances and control charts

An alternative method of identifying significant variances is to investigate the cause or causes of a variance only if the cumulative total for the variance over several control periods exceeds a certain limit.

The reason for this approach is that variances each month might fluctuate, with adverse variances in some months and favourable variances in the next. Provided that over time, actual results remain close to the standard, monthly variances might be acceptable.

For example, actual fixed overhead expenditure will not be exactly the same every month. Budgeted monthly expenditure, on the other hand, might be calculated by dividing the budgeted annual expenditure by 12. Consequently, there will inevitably be favourable or adverse expenditure variances from one month to the next, although over the course of the financial year, actual and budgeted expenditure should be the same.

This approach to identifying significant variances can be illustrated by the concept of a variance control chart. Variances should only be investigated when the cumulative total of variances exceeds predetermined control limits.

Setting the control limits

The control limits used as a basis for determining whether a variance should be investigated may be set statistically based on the normal distribution.

KAPLAN PUBLISHING

Using historical data a standard can be set as an expected average cost and a standard deviation can also be established. By assuming that a cost conforms to the normal distribution a variance will be investigated if it is statistically significant and has not arisen according to chance.

- If a company has a policy to investigate variances that fall outside the range that includes 95% of outcomes, then variances which exceed 1.96 standard deviations from the standard would be investigated.

- If a company has a policy to investigate variances that fall outside the range that includes 99% of outcomes, then variances which exceed 2.58 standard deviations from the standard would be investigated.

For control purposes, management might need to establish why a particular variance has occurred. Once the reason for the variance has been established, a decision can then be taken as to what control measures, if any, might be appropriate:

- to prevent the adverse variance continuing in the future, or
- to repeat a favourable variance in the future, or
- to bring actual results back on course to achieve the budgeted targets.

Possible operational causes of variances

Possible operational causes of variances are as follows:

Material price

(1) Using a different supplier, who is either cheaper or more expensive.

(2) Buying in larger-sized orders, and getting larger bulk purchase discounts. Buying in smaller-sized orders and losing planned bulk purchase discounts.

(3) An unexpected increase in the prices charged by a supplier.

(4) Unexpected buying costs, such as high delivery charges.

(5) Efficient or inefficient buying procedures.

(6) A change in material quality, resulting in either higher or lower purchase prices.

Material usage

(1) A higher-than-expected or lower-than-expected rate of scrap or wastage.

(2) Using a different quality of material (higher or lower quality) could affect the wastage rate.

(3) Defective materials.

(4) Better quality control.

(5) More efficient work procedures, resulting in better material usage rates.

(6) Changing the materials mix to obtain a more expensive or less expensive mix than the standard.

Labour rate

(1) An unexpected increase in basic rates of pay.

(2) Payments of bonuses, where these are recorded as direct labour costs.

(3) Using labour that is more or less experienced (and so more or less expensive) than the 'standard'.

(4) A change in the composition of the work force, and so a change in average rates of pay.

Labour efficiency

(1) Taking more or less time than expected to complete work, due to efficient or inefficient working.

(2) Using labour that is more or less experienced (and so more or less efficient) than the 'standard'.

(3) A change in the composition or mix of the work force, and so a change in the level of efficiency.

(4) Improved working methods.

(5) Industrial action by the work force: 'working to rule'.

(6) Poor supervision.

(7) Improvements in efficiency due to a 'learning effect' amongst the work force.

(8) Unexpected lost time due to production bottlenecks and resource shortages.

Overhead variances

(1) Fixed overhead expenditure adverse variances are caused by spending in excess of the budget. A more detailed analysis of the expenditure variance would be needed to establish why actual expenditure has been higher or lower than budget.

(2) Variable production overhead efficiency variances: the causes are similar to those for a direct labour efficiency variance.

Sales price

(1) Higher-than-expected discounts offered to customers to persuade them to buy, or due to purchasing in bulk.

(2) Lower-than-expected discounts, perhaps due to strength of sales demand.

(3) The effect of low-price offers during a marketing campaign.

(4) Unexpected price increases.

(5) Unexpected price cuts.

Sales volume

(1) Successful or unsuccessful direct selling efforts.

(2) Successful or unsuccessful marketing efforts (for example, the effects of an advertising campaign).

(3) Unexpected changes in customer needs and buying habits.

(4) Failure to satisfy demand due to production difficulties.

(5) Higher demand due to a cut in selling prices, or lower demand due to an increase in sales prices.

Possible interdependence between variances

In many cases, the explanation for one variance might also explain one or more other variances in which case the variances are inter-related.

For control purposes, it might therefore be necessary to look at several variances together and not in isolation.

Examples of interdependent variances

Some examples of interdependence between variances are listed below.

- Using cheaper materials will result in a favourable material price variance, but using the cheaper material in production might increase the wastage rate (adverse material usage) and cause a fall in labour productivity (adverse labour and variable overhead efficiency).

  A more expensive mix of materials (adverse mix variance) might result in higher output yields (favourable yield variance).

- Using more experienced labour to do the work will result in an adverse labour rate variance, but productivity might be higher as a result (favourable labour and variable overhead efficiency).

- Changing the composition of a team might result in a cheaper labour mix (favourable mix variance) but lower productivity (adverse yield variance).

- Workers trying to improve productivity (favourable efficiency variance) in order to win a bonus (adverse rate variance) might use materials wastefully in order to save time (adverse materials usage).

- Cutting sales prices (adverse sales price variance) might result in higher sales demand from customers (favourable sales volume variance).

The controllability principle

Controllability means the extent to which a specific manager can control costs or revenues or any other item (such as output quality). The controllability principle is that a manager should only be made accountable and responsible for costs and revenues that he or she can control directly.

In variance reporting, this means that variances should be reported to the managers who are in a position to control the costs or revenues to which the variances relate.

Composite variances

Sometimes a variance might be caused by a combination of two factors. The variance is a composite variance, because it is the result of the two factors combined. To apply the controllability principle, the variance should be reported to each of the managers who are in a position to control one of the factors.

12 The strategic role of budgeting, standard costing and variances

Budgets, standard costing and variance analysis are most often seen as control mechanisms. They are used to set targets, measure performance, highlight errors, determine responsibility, and take corrective action to return the system to control.

Control mechanisms

But this does not mean that they are independent of the strategic plan. We have seen that the budgeting process will often begin with the principal budget factor. It is this factor that is often determined by the strategic plan (whether that be to increase sales, react to competitive pressure by cutting cost, improving quality etc.). Changes in the standard cost card might be determined by plans to increase efficiency, improve processes, increase quality etc.

Also, budgets etc. are not just backward looking. Many organisations implement what is known as feedforward control in order to take preventative rather than corrective action.

Feedforward is the comparison of the results that are currently expected in the light of the latest information and the desired results. If there is a difference, then it is investigated and corrected.

Feedback happens after the event and discovers that something has gone wrong (or right). It is obviously too late to affect the result that has just happened, but the idea is that if we can understand what went wrong in the previous period, then we can stop the problem from recurring.

Feedforward is more proactive and aims to anticipate problems and prevent them from occurring. Whereas feedback is based on a comparison of historical actual results with the budget for the period to date, feedforward looks ahead and compares the targets or objectives for the period (possibly determined by the strategic plan) and what actual results are now forecast.

However, budgets, standard costing and variances can also have a forward looking and strategic role in forming an important part in the strategic decision making of the organisation. They will influence decisions on whether to outsource an activity, which business units should be removed from a portfolio, which products need a new competitive strategy, whether an acquisition makes financial sense etc.

Further details

The strategic decision making process will involve identifying alternative courses of action, performing cost/benefit analysis on each course, evaluating qualitative issues and choosing a course of action. Budgeting, standard costing and variance analysis can be used alongside more traditional techniques in order to supplement each stage of this process. For example, qualitative techniques such as SWOT, PESTLE analysis and the Ansoff matrix might be used to identify different courses of action, but variance analysis might highlight trends in performance that can influence this, or changes in the standard cost card might present an opportunity for a new competitive strategy.

The performance measures inherent in these systems can be part of an organisation's big data plans. The data here will be internal. The system can provide data on churn rates, how often customers order, market share, complaint rates, changes in material usage, changes in labour efficiency, comparisons of business units etc. Much of this information can play a vital role in the formulation of future strategy and/or be important drivers for strategic change.

Key factors to consider in using budgets etc. to aid strategic planning are:

- The level of participation in budgets. Budget preparation should involve all levels of management (strategic right the way down to operational) so that there is a move away from both the top-down and bottom-up approach, and a move towards a more collaborative approach. This will ensure that strategic plans are guided and influenced by operational and tactical capabilities (and constraints), as well as gaining many of the other advantages of budgetary participation. However, this process is likely to be more time consuming than traditional budgeting techniques, and it may be difficult to obtain agreement across all levels of management.

- It will be important to ensure that standard costs remain relevant to the future strategic environment. In environments that change more rapidly and unpredictably, this will be difficult to achieve.

- A strong performance measurement system. Performance measures need to be expanded beyond traditional financial and accounting measures. Broader measures on customer performance, innovation, quality etc. need to be provided if management are to take meaningful information from the system which can be used in future strategic decisions.

- Accurate variances with clear responsibilities. Variance investigation should indicate long term patterns and fundamental changes to either operations or the environment.

Many of these elements have been explored in this chapter.

13 Chapter summary

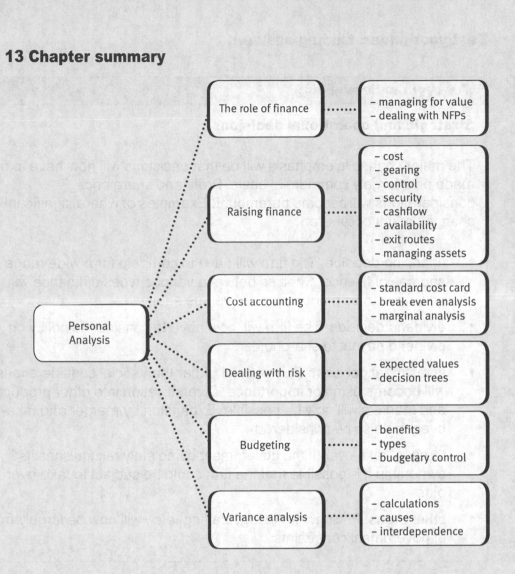

The role of finance ...... – managing for value
– dealing with NFPs

Raising finance ...... – cost
– gearing
– control
– security
– cashflow
– availability
– exit routes
– managing assets

Cost accounting ...... – standard cost card
– break even analysis
– marginal analysis

Dealing with risk ...... – expected values
– decision trees

Budgeting ...... – benefits
– types
– budgetary control

Variance analysis ...... – calculations
– causes
– interdependence

Personal
Analysis

Test your understanding answers

Test your understanding 1

Strategic and operational decisions

The major change in emphasis will be that decisions will now have to be made on a largely commercial basis. Profit and share price considerations will become paramount. Examples of where significant changes might occur are:

- financing decision: The firm will have to compete for a wide range of sources of finance. Choices between various types of finance will now have to be made, e.g. debt versus equity

- dividend decision: The firm will now have to consider its policy on dividend payout to shareholders

- investment decision: Commercial rather than social considerations will become of major importance. Diversification into other products and markets will now be possible. Expansion by merger and take-over can also be considered

- threat of take-over: If the government completely relinquishes its ownership it is possible that the firm could be subject to take-over bids

- other areas: Pricing, marketing, staffing, etc., will now be largely free of government constraints.

Test your understanding 2

- Funds from central government.

- Borrowing from external sources or long-term loan finance (such as bonds).

- User fees (e.g. charge for using a leisure facility).

- Charges to the private sector (e.g. the NHS charges for using some of its facilities, or where universities have charges for overseas students).

- Voluntary donations or legacies.

- Self generating finance through developing commercial activities (e.g. a museum which is free to enter might supplement income by offering an audio tour that visitors can pay for).

Test your understanding 3

Normally, but not invariably, long-term finance is more expensive than short-term finance. This is because lenders normally perceive the risks as being higher on long-term advances.

Long-term finance does, however, carry the advantage of security, whereas sources of short-term finance can often be withdrawn at short notice.

Short-term loans have to be regularly renewed and the company carries the risk that lenders may refuse to extend further credit. This risk is at its highest on overdraft borrowing where the bank can call in the overdraft 'on demand'.

With long-term borrowing, as long as the borrower does not breach the debt covenants involved, the finance is assured for the duration of the loan.

In choosing between short-term and long-term borrowing, the firm should consider the textbook rule of thumb for prudent financing: 'finance short-term investments with short-term funds and long-term investments with long-term funds'. Simply, this means use cheap short-term borrowing where it is safe to do so (investments that are short-term in nature and hence renewal risk is not a problem) but use long-term finance for long-lived investments.

Test your understanding 4

It is generally assumed that the objective of stock market listed companies is to maximise the wealth of their shareholders. This in turn places an emphasis on profitability and other factors that influence a company's share price. It is true that some companies have other (secondary) aims such as only engaging in ethical activities (e.g. not producing armaments) or have strong environmental considerations. Clearly by definition, not-for-profit organisations are not motivated by the need to produce profits for shareholders, but that does not mean that they should be inefficient. Many areas of assessment of profit-oriented companies are perfectly valid for not-for-profit organisations: efficient stock holdings, tight budgetary constraints, use of key performance indicators, prevention of fraud, etc.

There are a great variety of not-for-profit organisations; e.g. public sector health, education, policing and charities. It is difficult to be specific about how to assess the performance of a not-for-profit organisation without knowing what type of organisation it is. In general terms an assessment of performance must be made in the light of the stated objectives of the organisation. Thus, for example, in a public health service one could look at measures such as treatment waiting times, increasing life expectancy, etc. and although such organisations do not have a profit motive requiring efficient operation, they should nonetheless be accountable for the resources they use. Techniques such as 'value for money' and the three Es (economy, efficiency and effectiveness) have been developed and can help to assess the performance of such organisations.

Test your understanding 5

Activity Based Costing (ABC) is a system of full costing which recognises that the more traditional method of absorption costing using cost centre absorption rates may not provide accurate product costs.

ABC identifies the activities of a production process and the extent to which individual products make use of those activities. Costs are then estimated for each of these activities which are referred to as cost pools. The number of times which the activity is expected to be carried out is also estimated and a cost driver rate calculated:

$$\frac{\text{Estimated cost of pool}}{\text{Estimated number of times activity is to be performed}}$$

An individual product will probably make use of a number of different activities, and a proportion of the cost of each activity will be attributed to the product using these predetermined cost driver rates.

The actual costs of each cost pool together with the number of times the activity is performed will be collected and a comparison made with the corresponding estimated values. This is similar to the comparison of actual and budgeted costs and volumes using the traditional absorption costing approach except that there are likely to be a greater number of cost driver rates using ABC than the one per cost centre absorption rate found in traditional absorption costing.

Test Your Understanding 6

Firstly we need to calculate the break even sales revenue.

Because we haven't been given any information on units, we must have to use the contribution sales revenue technique:

$$\text{C/S ratio} = \frac{\text{Total contribution}}{\text{Total sales revenue}} = \frac{(450 - 220)}{450}$$

= 0.511 (or 51.1%)

$$\text{Breakeven point (in terms of sales revenue)} = \frac{\text{Fixed costs}}{\text{C/S ratio}}$$

$$\text{Breakeven point (in terms of sales revenue)} = \frac{\$160,000}{0.511}$$

Breakeven point
(in terms of sales revenue) = $313,000

Now that we know the break-even position we can calculate the margin of safety (this is what is required in the second element of the question).

$$\text{Margin of safety (as a \% of budgeted sales)} = \frac{\text{Budgeted sales} - \text{Breakeven sales}}{\text{Budgeted sales}} \times 100\%$$

$$\text{Margin of safety (as a \% of budgeted sales)} = \frac{450 - 313}{450} \times 100\%$$

=   0.3044 (or 30.44%)

This tells us that for the company to fall into a loss making position its sales next year would have to fall by over 30.44% from their current position.

Test your understanding 7

Step 1: Identify the bottleneck constraint.(this may be done for you in examination questions).

At potential sales level:

	Sales potential units	Total machine hours	Total labour hours
Product A	4,000	40,000	4,800
Product B	6,000	72,000	4,800
Product C	6,000	84,000	2,400
		196,000	12,000

Thus, labour hours are the limiting factor.

Step 2: calculate the contribution per unit for each product.

This has been done for us in the question.

Step 3: calculate the contribution per unit of the bottleneck resource for each product, i.e. per labour hour.

Product A $6/1.2 = $5.00

Product B $5/0.8 = $6.25

Product C $4/0.4 = $10.00

Step 4: rank the products in order of the contribution per unit of the bottleneck resource.

Thus, production should be concentrated first on C, up to the maximum available sales, then B, and finally A.

However, a minimum of 1,000 units of A must be produced.

Step 5: allocate resources using this ranking and answer the question, i.e. state the maximum contribution.

Taking these factors into account, the production schedule becomes:

	Units produced	Labour hours	Cumulative labour hours	Limiting factor
Product A	1,000	1,200	1,200	Policy to produce 1,000 units
Product C	6,000	2,400	3,600	Sales
Product B	1,750	1,400	5,000	Labour hours

The maximum contribution is therefore as follows.

	$
A (1,000 × $6)	6,000
B (1,750 × $5)	8,750
C (6,000 × $4)	24,000
	———
	38,750
	———

Test your understanding 8

	$
Variable costs saved	30,000
Contribution earned (= opportunity cost)	50,000
	———
	80,000
	———

Test your understanding 9

Annual internal processing costs

Hardware and software	$320
Hardware/software annual maintenance	$750
Accounting stationery	$500
Part time accounts clerk	$6,000
Total	$7,570

Annual outsourcing costs

Processing of invoices/credit notes	$2,500	5,000 × $0.50
Processing of cheque payments	$2,000	4,000 × $0.50
Reconciling supplier accounts	$3,600	150 × $2 × 12
Total	$8,100	

It would not be cost effective to outsource the accounting activities. The present costs of $7,570 would rise to $8,100 pa

Qualitative factors include:

- predicted volumes – higher volumes will make outsourcing more expensive

- the quality of supply – will the external supplier make more errors?

- security of information.

Test your understanding 10

Year 1

Expected value = ($40 × 60%) + ($20 × 40%) = $32m.

Year 2

Expected value = [($80 × 90%) + ($30 × 10%)] × 60% + [($30 × 20%) + ($10 × 80%)] × 40%

= [$75 × 60%] + [$14 × 40%] = $50.6m

Test Your Understanding 11

A decision tree of the problem would look as follows:

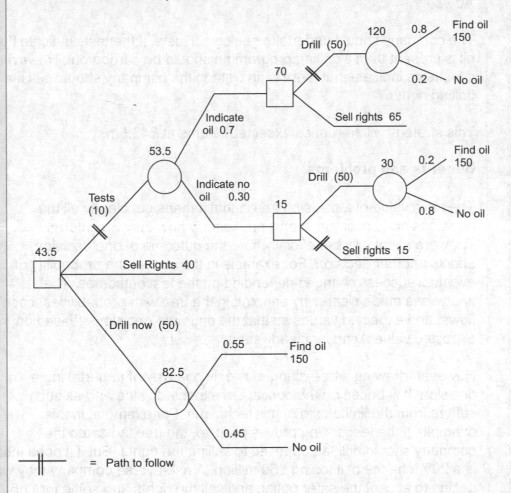

Explanation

It is easier to start at the bottom of the tree. The first box shows the first decision to be made – to test, to drill or to sell the rights. If we follow the 'drill' line/branch, we come a 'chance' point (represented by a circle). This shows that if we drill there are two possible outcomes – there is a 55% that we find oil and make a positive net return of $150m. There is also a 45% that no oil is found and that no return is made. The figure on the circle of $82.5m is the expected value calculated from these two outcomes. However, the drill line has a cost of $50m so that the overall net expected return would be $32.5m – and it is this figure that should be used to compare the drill option against the other options.

The middle branch of the tree shows the expected value from selling the rights – $40m.

The top branch shows the analysis of the testing decision. It can be seen that there are many more possible outcomes and also further decisions to made based on whether or not the tests indicate the presence of oil.

Lines that have a double cross marking on them show the best choice to be made based on expected values.

Advice

The company should undertake geological tests. If the tests indicate that oil is present then a drilling programme should be carried out. However, if the tests indicate that there is no oil then the company should sell the drilling rights.

This strategy will maximise expected returns at £43.5m.

Benefits and problems

The main value of a decision tree is that it maps out clearly all the decisions and uncertain events and exactly how they are interrelated. They are especially beneficial where the outcome of one decision affects another decision. For example in the above, the probability of eventual success changes depending on the test outcomes. The analysis is made clearer by annotating the tree with probabilities, cash flows, and expected values so that the optimum decisions (based on expected values) can be clearly seen.

However, drawing a tree diagram is only one way of undertaking a decision. It is based on the concept of expected value and as such suffers from the limitations of this technique. For example, in this example, if the test drilling proves positive, the tree indicated the company should drill, as opposed to selling the rights. But if it does there is a 20% chance of it losing £50 million. A risk-averse company may well decide to accept the safer option and sell the rights and settle for £65 million.

Test Your Understanding 12

Standard product cost

		$	$
Standard selling price			100
Material X	5 kg @ $3/kg	15	
Material Y	4 kg @ $5/kg	20	
Direct labour	3 hrs @ $8/hr	24	
Variable overheads	3 hrs @ $6/hr	18	
Fixed overheads (W1)	3 hrs @ $2/hr	6	
		——	
			83
			——
Standard profit per unit			17
			——

There are many different ways to calculate variances, of which the following is one alternative.

Material X variances

					$	
SQSP						
5 kg/unit x 2,200 units	x	$3/kg	=		33,000	Usage
AQSP						$900 A
11,300 kg	x	$3/kg	=		33,900	
AQAP						$2,260 F
11,300 kg	x	$2.8/kg	=		31,640	Price

Material Y variances

					$	
SQSP						
4 kg/unit x 2,200 units	x	$5/kg	=		44,000	Usage
AQSP						$2,500 F
8,300 kg	x	$5/kg	=		41,500	
AQAP						$2,490 A
8,300 kg	x	$5.30/kg	=		43,990	Price

Labour variances

					$	
SHSR						
3 hrs/unit x 2,200 units	x	$8/hr	=	52,800	Efficiency
AHSR						$1,600 F
6,400 hrs	x	$8/hr	=	51,200	
AHAR						$960 A
(4,800 hrs x $8.10) + (1,600 hrs x $8.30) =	52,160	Rate

Variable overhead variances

				$	
SHSR					
3 hrs/unit x 2,200 units	x	$6/hr	=	39,600	Efficiency
AHSR					$1,200 F
6,400 hrs	x	$6/hr	=	38,400	
AHAR					$5,400 F
			=	33,000	Expenditure

Fixed overhead expenditure variance

	$
Budgeted Cost	12,000
Actual Cost	12,500
	500 A

Fixed overhead volume variance

	Units
Budgeted output	2,000
Actual output	2,200
	200 F
× Std Fixed Overhead Cost per unit	× 6
	$1,200 F

KAPLAN PUBLISHING

Sales volume profit variance

	Units
Budgeted sales	1,700
Actual sales	2,200
	500 F
× Std profit per unit	× 17
	$8,500 F

Sales price variance

	$
Std selling price	100
Actual selling price	90
	10 A
× Actual No of units sold	× 2,200
	$22,000 A

Operating statement

	$
Budgeted gross profit (W2)	28,900
Sales volume profit variance	8,500 F
Standard profit on actual sales	37,400
Selling price variance	22,000 A
	15,400

		Favourable	**Adverse**	
Cost variances				
Material X	Usage		900	
	Price	2,260		
Material Y	Usage	2,500		
	Price		2,490	
Direct labour	Efficiency	1,600		
	Rate		960	
Variable Overhead	Efficiency	1,200		
	Expenditure	5,400		
Fixed Prod	Expenditure		500	
Overhead	Volume	1,200		
		14,160	4,850	9,310 F
Actual profit (W3)				24,710

Workings

(W1)

Budgeted fixed overheads are $144,000 per year and the budgeted output is 24,000 units for the year. Thus the budgeted/standard fixed cost per unit is $6.

The overheads are absorbed on direct labour hours and each unit takes 3 hours. Therefore the budgeted/standard fixed overhead is $2 per hour ($6 ÷ 3 hours).

(W2)

Budgeted profit = $17 per unit × Budgeted **sales** of 1,700 units = $28,900.

(W3)

		$	$
Sales	2,200 units × $90		198,000
Material X	11,300 kg × $2.80/kg	31,640	
Material Y	8,300 kg × $5.30/kg	43,990	
Direct labour	(4,800 hrs × $8.10) + (1,600 hrs × $8.30)	52,160	
Variable overhead		33,000	
Fixed overhead		12,500	
		–––––	
			173,290
			–––––
Actual Profit			24,710
			–––––

Strategy and people

Chapter learning objectives

Upon completion of this chapter you will be able to:

- explain, for organisations in general, how the effective recruitment, management and motivation of people is necessary for enabling strategic and operational success

- describe classical and modern leadership theories and explain, for a given scenario, how appropriate leadership can facilitate strategy formulation and implementation

- describe the contribution of four different approaches to job design (scientific management, job enrichment, Japanese management and re-engineering)

- discuss the tensions and potential ethical issues related to job design in organisations in general

- advise, for organisations in general, on the relationship of job design to process re-design, project management and the harnessing of e-business opportunities

- explain, for organisations in general, the human resource implications of knowledge work and post-industrial job design

- describe, for organisations in general, the emergence and scope of human resource development, succession planning and their relationship to the strategy of the organisation

- describe, for organisations in general, different methods of establishing human resource development

- explain, for organisations in general, the contribution of competency frameworks to human resource development

- explain, for organisations in general, the meaning and contribution of workplace learning, the learning organisation, organisation learning and knowledge management

- explain how people are only one important part of an overall business system using the POPIT model and how this model plays an important role in the implementation of business change.

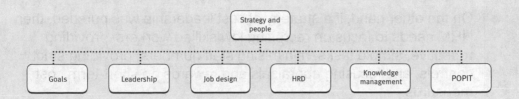

1 Human resources and organisational strategy

The strategic role of human resources

People are of central importance in most organisations and their recruitment, management and motivation forms part of the human resource management function.

HRM plays a role in all elements of the strategic planning process:

- In *strategic analysis*, HRM can generate strengths and opportunities for a business (or poor HRM might create weaknesses and threats).

- In making *strategic choices*, HRM can help a business to develop and sustain competitive advantage.

- In putting *strategy into action*, we have seen in previous chapters that HRM can play a vital role in creating good project managers, redesigning processes, achieving a flexible organisational structure etc.

HRM and competitive advantage

Human resource management (HRM) has been defined as 'a strategic and coherent approach to the management of an organisation's most valued assets: the people working there who individually and collectively contribute to the achievement of its objectives for sustainable competitive advantage' (Michael Armstrong).

The definition mentions competitive advantage and this reinforces the link between HRM and strategy.

Some examples of the link between HRM and strategy are as follows:

If a competitive advantage is sought through differentiation then HRM needs to ensure that high quality, skilled staff are recruited, that these staff are given freedom to be creative and innovative, that a culture of service and quality is prevalent, and that rewards are geared towards long-term success and beyond short-term financial measures.

On the other hand, if a strategy of cost leadership was pursued, then HRM needs to focus on recruiting low skilled workers, providing repetitive, simple tasks, minimising staff numbers, providing strict controls, and focusing appraisals and rewards on short-term cost measures.

Test your understanding 1

If an organisation planned to grow through acquisition, how might HRM contribute to the achievement of this strategy?

The relationship between strategy and HRM is not just a linear one. We have just seen how the choice of competitive strategy can influence HRM decisions, but it is equally true in the opposite direction. HRM decisions can have a massive impact on strategic decisions. For example, we will see later in this chapter that to react to changing environments a transformational approach to leadership will need to be taken, job design will have to change and staff will need to be developed in a more integrated manner. So making these HRM decisions may influence future strategic decisions and facilitate new types of strategy.

Illustration 1 – The link between HRM and strategy

The American company Automatic Data Processing Inc. is a business that offers ancillary business services such as payroll management to other companies. The company has obtained a position where it processes over 1 in 6 of all paychecks in the US.

In the early part of this century, the company took the decision to expand its services internationally. This meant that it went through a massive international recruitment drive of staff with good computer skills (most of the work is performed electronically), good client management skills and good communication skills. These were the key strategic capabilities needed from staff in this industry. So the recruitment of staff in foreign markets to support their international expansion is an example of where the strategy led the HRM decision.

However, in the last couple of years, ADP have realised that this process has created new skills and capabilities for the organisation. The experience it gained in recruitment and training of new staff was a valuable lesson for the company – and one that it realised it could leverage to clients. ADP has started to offer recruitment services to clients as it has developed the strategic capability to do this.

Its recruitment of new staff also improved its software development skill base amongst staff. The staff that it recruited to provide payroll services were actually very IT literate and had the ability to offer support to clients when necessary (not something that was actually part of their job roles). This has allowed ADP to consider moving into this new strategic area. It's all part of ADP's strategy to step out of the back office and compete head on with the largest HR software vendors in the industry such as Kronos and SAP.

So the company's HRM actions in terms of recruiting staff, empowering staff and changing job roles for staff have facilitated new strategic choices such as offering staff recruitment services and selling software.

The goals of HRM

From the above analysis it can be seen that for strategies to be successful HRM must be effective in a number of areas. These can be summarised into 4 areas (4C's):

- commitment (requires good motivation and leadership)
- competence (requires good recruitment, assessment, training and staff development)
- congruence (requires good job design)
- cost-effectiveness (this normally comes from the achievement of the others).

The goals of HRM

- **Commitment.** This means motivating staff and removing dissatisfaction. This should result in better attendance, better time-keeping and reduce staff turnover. Motivated staff are more likely to achieve targets and the organisations goals. Part of the role of HRM will be the *leadership* of staff. This will not only play a role in motivation and goal achievement, but good leadership can create loyal, committed staff who want to stay with a leader who they trust and value and who they believe can develop them in the best way.

- **Competence.** This involves having the right level of staff with the correct skills base. It includes identifying, in precise terms, the kinds of talent the organisation will need in order to achieve its strategic goals in the short, medium and long term. So careful recruitment will be important to achieve this goal.

    It also includes searching for ways of improving the performance and productivity of the most talented staff. *Training* and staff *development* will therefore play an important role.

- **Congruence.** This means that HRM need to ensure that the organisation's goals are understood and that these goals are communicated to staff.

  HRM should be represented at a senior, strategic level in order to clearly understand the organisation's goals. For example, if the goal of the company is to achieve cost leadership then the HRM function need to understand this as it will influence recruitment, training, rewards etc.

  These goals then need to be communicated to staff. This will be achieved in a number of ways. *Job design* will be important. As will be seen later, if cost leadership is the goal, for example, then a scientific approach to job design is most likely to be used.

  Reward systems and appraisals will also play a role. For example, cost leadership is likely to require strict controls and financial targets with assessments and rewards based on conformance to these controls.

- **Cost effectiveness.** It is often found that if the other goals of HRM are achieved then a natural cost effectiveness will be derived. Recruitment costs will be reduced, performance will improve, wastage will be reduced and goals will be achieved. In this way, good HRM 'pays for itself' in returns to the business.

This is useful criteria not only for improving and developing HRM, but also for assessing an organisation's existing HRM. The remainder of the chapter explores how these criteria can be met.

Human Resource Planning

Human resource (HR) planning is 'a strategy for the acquisition, utilisation, improvement and preservation of an enterprise's human resources'. It is through planning that a company can determine its recruitment and selection needs, and can assist in the planning of its training needs.

Its purpose is to reduce uncertainty in the environment and assist in shaping a company's personnel policies.

The four main phases involved in HR planning are:

- an analysis of existing staffing resources – its strengths and weaknesses, age spreads, experience and training levels, etc.

- an estimation of likely changes in resources – flows into, within, and out of, the organisation – and the ability of relevant labour markets to supply existing or future demands

- an estimation of the organisation's future HR needs in terms of numbers, type, quality and skill composition

- the identification of gaps between supply and demand and the development of policies and plans to close these.

The first step of the plan is to determine the company's long-term objectives so that the human resources can be optimally used. Corporate strategy is a reconciliation process between what an organisation might do (opportunities) and what it can do (resources). This is an impossible process without consideration of HR requirements.

The planning process serves two functions.

- It fulfils a problem-solving role by identifying HR requirements, controlling the flow of labour, developing skills and increasing adaptability.

- It also has a strategic role in contributing towards the shape of the organisation as required by external and internal changes.

In both cases, HR planning represents an important flow of information to aid decision making and the formulation of policies.

2 Leadership

Classical theories of leadership

Theories of leadership

Classical theories of leadership, which you should be familiar with from your previous studies, can be considered as falling into four main categories.

- Trait or personal characteristics, which see the individual as more important than the situation.

- Style theories, which are based on the assumption that the leadership style of a manager will affect the motivation of employees.

- Contingency (or contextual) approaches that take into account other variables such as the nature of the group in which the leader operates and the position of the leader within the group.

- Situational theories that look at situations where leaders are shown to be effective and consider the actions of leaders and the context in which they led in order to suggest the appropriate style to match the requirements of the task, the group and the individuals.

Example

Likert developed the following 'style' theory which distinguished between four key styles or 'systems' of leadership:

System 1 Exploitative autocratic

Here the leader has no confidence or trust in subordinates, imposes decisions, never delegates, motivates by threat, has little communication with subordinates and does not encourage teamwork.

System 2 Benevolent authoritative

Under this system the leader has only superficial and condescending trust in subordinates, imposes decisions, never delegates, motivates by reward and, though he sometimes will involve others in solving problems, is basically paternalistic.

System 3 Consultative

The leader has some incomplete confidence in subordinates, listens to them but controls decision making, motivates by reward and a level of involvement and will use the ideas and suggestions of subordinates constructively.

System 4 Participative

The democratic leader has complete confidence in subordinates who are allowed to make decisions for themselves. Motivation is by reward for achieving goals set by participation and there is a substantial amount of sharing of ideas and opinions and co-operation.

Likert's research shows that effective managers are those who adopt either a System 3 or a System 4 leadership style. Both are seen as being based on trust and paying attention to the needs of both the organisation and employees.

Recent approaches to leadership

More recent approaches to leadership have characterised leaders in one of two ways:

- transformational or charismatic leaders who provide a vision, inspire people to achieve it by instilling pride and gaining respect and trust. These leaders appear to be particularly effective in times of change and uncertainty

- transactional leaders who focus on managing through systems and processes. These leaders are likely to be more effective in securing improvement in stable situations.

The differences between transactional and transformational leadership are shown below:

Transactional leadership	Transformational leadership
<ul><li>Clarify goals and objectives and the focus is on short term</li><li>Focus on control mechanisms</li><li>Solving problems</li><li>Maintain status quo or improve current situation</li><li>Plan, organise and control</li><li>Guard and defend existing culture</li><li>Positional power exercised.</li></ul>	<ul><li>Establish long-term vision</li><li>Create a climate of trust</li><li>Make people solve their own problems by empowerment</li><li>Change the current situation. Every threat is seen as an opportunity</li><li>Train, coach, counsel and mentor people</li><li>Change culture</li><li>Power comes from relationships and influencing people. The pressure exerted is subtle and has greater finesse.</li></ul>
Suitability This is best suited to static, predictable environments.	*Suitability* This is best suited to environments where change is inevitable and may be unpredictable.

3 Job design

Job design and motivation

There are two major reasons for attention to job design:

(1) To enhance the personal satisfaction that people derive from their work and,

(2) To make the best use of people as a valuable resource of the organisation and to help overcome obstacles to effective performance.

Research suggests that it is primarily in the realm of job design that opportunity for constructive improvement of worker satisfaction appears to be high. The level of job satisfaction experienced is affected by a wide range of variables.

- Individual factors – personality, education, intelligence and abilities, age, marital status, and orientation to work.

- Social factors – relationships with co-workers, group working and norms, opportunities for interaction, informal organisation.

- Cultural factors – attitudes, beliefs and values.

- Organisational factors – nature and size, formal structure, personnel policies and procedures, employee relations, nature of the work, technology and work organisation, supervision and style of leadership, management systems, and working conditions.

- Environmental factors – economic, social, technical and governmental influences.

The application of motivational theories, and a greater understanding of dimensions of job satisfaction and work performance, have led to increasing interest in job design. The nature of the work organisation and the design of jobs can have a significant effect on the job satisfaction of staff and on the level of organisational performance.

Job design is concerned with the relationship between workers and the nature and content of jobs, and their task functions. It attempts to meet people's personal and social needs at work through re-organisation or restructuring of work.

Different approaches to job design

There have been a number of different approaches to job design, which have been based on different theories of behaviour of individuals in the workplace. These include:

- scientific management
- job enrichment
- Japanese management
- business process re-engineering.

Explanations

Scientific management

Frederick W Taylor is generally credited with the introduction of scientific management. He believed that workers would be motivated by obtaining the highest possible remuneration and that this could be achieved by organising work in the most efficient way, based on a true science of work whereby what constitutes a fair day's work and a fair day's pay could be determined.

The scientific management approach to job design is to have very specific job roles, strict limits and controls over employee actions, and a standardisation of job roles across staff levels: This had a huge impact on manufacturing jobs and resulted in:

- job fragmentation where individual workers focused on one single task
- the separation of planning from doing the work, and direct work from indirect
- the minimisation of requirements for skill and training time
- the minimisation of material handling
- the use of highly-specialised machinery and flow lines
- deskilling of work, with jobs becoming repetitive and boring
- low commitment from employees
- an adversarial industrial relations climate.

Job enrichment

Job enrichment developed to address some of the drawbacks of scientific management and is the process of adding tasks to a job in order to increase the amount of employee control or responsibility. The main driver behind the development of job enrichment was the belief that it could improve job satisfaction and hence performance by meeting the need for the factors identified by Herzberg as motivators (achievement, recognition, attraction of the job itself, responsibility and advancement). Job enrichment is often part of business process redesign and/or quality initiatives and:

- combines tasks vertically as employees undertake some supervisory tasks

- leads to greater responsibility for individuals, with some control delegated downwards.

Example

The enrichment of the job of a barman whose current duties only include serving drinks from a bar could involve adding further responsibilities such as:

- ordering supplies of drinks

- dealing with customer complaints

- cashing up at the end of a shift

- drawing up menus for cocktails.

Japanese management

In the 1980s, businesses around the world began to introduce management techniques based on the production methods used by large Japanese corporations. Particular characteristics of the model are:

- total quality management, with every employee taking responsibility for quality, taking part in quality improvement activities and carrying out quality control of their own work

- cellular manufacturing to improve flexibility, with assembly of complete components carried out by a team of flexible, multi-skilled workers

- just-in-time manufacture to minimise inventory and waste by having the right materials, at the right time, at the right place, and in the exact amount required

- interdependence of employees on each other, with a high degree of socialisation at work and the organisation becoming a community

- a high reliance on a skilled, flexible workforce.

Business process re-engineering (BPR)

BPR was discussed in detail in the chapter on business process change. The key implications for HRM are that BPR:

- views employees as an asset rather than a cost

- involves the establishment of a more horizontal structure with work carried out by self-managed teams with a degree of autonomy

- makes extensive use of IT to enable new forms of working and collaborating within an organisation and across organisational boundaries.

Self-managed work groups have a number of key features.

- Specific goals are set for the group but members decide the best means by which these goals are to be achieved.

- Group members have greater freedom and choice, and wider discretion over the planning, execution and control of their own work.

- Collectively, members of the group have the necessary variety of expertise and skills to undertake successfully the tasks of the group.

- The level of external supervision is reduced and the role of supervisor becomes more one of giving advice and support to the group.

- Feedback and evaluation are related to the performance of the group as a whole.

Example

Match the following characteristics to the relevant approach to job design.

(1) Total quality management.

(2) Deskilling of work, with jobs becoming repetitive and boring.

(3) The establishment of a more horizontal structure with work carried out by self-managed teams with a degree of autonomy.

(4) Greater responsibility for individuals, with some control delegated downwards.

Solution

(1) Japanese management.

(2) Scientific management.

(3) Business process re-engineering.

(4) Job enrichment.

Factors to consider when choosing a job design

These include:

- the organisation's goals

- the need for staff motivation

- the need for control over staff actions

- ethical issues

- legal issues.

It can be seen that some of these factors may lead to conflicts and tensions.

Explanation of job design issues

Job design – tensions and issues

Job design raises a number of issues for managers.

- There is a tension between the need to control cost and quality of work by the division of activities and the need to co-ordinate and integrate activities.

- Job design for a particular purpose may have unforeseen or undesired consequences that need to be addressed, as seen for example in the impact of scientific management where the sub-division of work for economic reasons led to a lack of job satisfaction and poor motivation.

- There is a conflict between the need to motivate and encourage employees by allowing them initiative and to be creative, and maintain management control.

- Whenever jobs are redesigned it is important to consider the impact on individual employees in terms of their personal satisfaction and development.

- In addition, any job design needs to be carried out in a way that is seen to be fair, consistent and complies with any legal requirements.

Test your understanding 2

Consider how job design for a chef might differ in a chain of restaurants – one which want to achieve a low cost strategy based on consistency of product and services, and another which wants to differentiate itself through a focus on high end customers wanting quality of service and a premium product offering.

Job design and strategic change

In implementing any strategic change such as quality initiatives or the implementation of e-business there are implications for the content and nature of jobs that will need to be considered as part of the implementation plan.

- The core issues of job design such as control, skill and knowledge remain the same, but need to be considered in a changing environment.

- Such initiatives should have an impact on all parts of the organisational structure. Traditional job design has focused on manual or less-skilled work, but needs to have a broader focus.

- The increasing use of information technology and e-business has a tendency to lead to more streamlined, flatter structures, which will have implications for the nature of jobs.

- Organisations and work are becoming more knowledge-intensive (this will be discussed further, later in this chapter).

- Changes to and increased complexity of relationships within the organisation and with suppliers and customers mean that staff need a broader understanding of business.

- If projects to implement change are to be successful, changes to job design need to be considered as part of the project planning phase, to ensure that the response and behaviour of individual staff supports the strategic objectives.

Cross-functional teams often drive initiatives such as quality improvement, process re-engineering and the development of e-business development. This is often through the formation of self-managed work groups who assume greater autonomy and responsibility for the effective performance of the work.

4 Human resource development

The emergence of human resource development

Human resource development encompasses the activities that are concerned with developing the skills and abilities of the people within an organisation in order to ensure its success. Today, human resource development is seen as more than just a training activity, and its scope has been extended so that:

- people are seen as a major source of competitive advantage, and their training and development is seen as an investment, not a cost

- learning is seen as essential and embedded in the organisation as a means of coping with change and ensuring that strategic objectives are met

- employees have the expectation that they will learn and change and retrain as necessary as strategy demands

- the development and training of their staff is seen as a key part of a manager's role

- changes outside the organisation are reflected in changes to training and development needs

- human resource implications are considered as part of strategic planning.

Illustration 2 – Human resource development

Many organisations have a 'fast track' whereby potential future senior managers are identified early in their careers and given work and training opportunities in an attempt to help them achieve their potential.

Succession planning

One of the most important aspects of human resource development is ensuring the management succession. Bringing in top managers from outside the company can improve the breadth of experience of the top management team, but people at the top who have come from within the business bring specialist knowledge of different aspects of the firm itself and provide an inspiration for more junior managers who can aspire to the same position.

Effective succession planning:

- identifies people with management potential early in their careers

- provides training integrated with planned career patterns including a number of development moves to widen experience. However, care must be taken that grooming the chosen few does not take precedence over everyone else's career to avoid resentment being caused and the company missing out on spotting late developers

- long-term plans based on identifying:
    - for each post, a list of perhaps three potential successors
    - for each person (at least from a certain level upwards), a list of possible development moves

- provides contingency plans for a successor for any post that becomes suddenly and unexpectedly vacant (e.g. through death).

Establishing human resource development

Most organisations establish human resource development in one of two ways:

- Systematically, according to the traditional model of training.

- Using a more integrated approach more closely linked to strategy development.

Systematic approach	Integrated approach
• Focuses on needs	• Creates a learning culture
• Often off-the-job	• Happens within the organisation itself
• Formal	• Uses coaching and mentoring
• Can be employee driven	• Uses competency frameworks
• Needs a predictable environment	• HRM closely linked with other key activities

Explanation of the HRD approaches

The systematic approach

The systematic approach has been followed by large numbers of organisations since the 1960s. This approach:

- is one in which training and development activities are planned based on needs analysis, implemented and then evaluated at the end

- includes varied training activities that are often off-the-job, and may use a variety of techniques and technologies such as e-learning and distance learning

- has contributed to the development of training as a profession

- may be less effective for organisations in a changing environment where objectives are less clear.

The integrated approach

More recently, organisations facing rapid change have begun to develop an approach that is more directly integrated with strategy, to ensure that the organisation's staff are equipped to meet the challenges required by the strategy. It is an approach in which:

- a culture of learning is created within the organisation that is reflected in its systems and processes

- close links are made between HRM and key activities within the organisation such as strategy development

- the development of staff is seen as a management responsibility

- development activities such as coaching and mentoring are established as part of HRM

- use is made of competency frameworks that are developed to identify key skills and behaviour needed to meet strategic objectives.

Test your understanding 4

The training department of a large public sector organisation uses the following model to establish its human resource development:

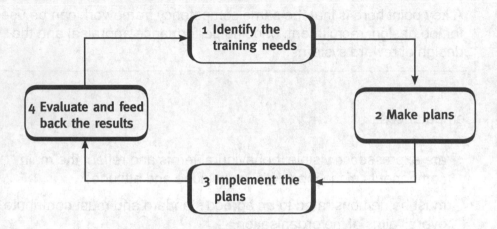

Discuss the advantages of the model used in the example above, and explain when might it not be sufficient in a fast moving environment?

Competency Frameworks

Competences are the critical skills, knowledge and attitude that a job-holder must have to perform effectively. A competent individual can perform a work role in a wide range of settings over an extended period of time.

The use of competency frameworks

Organisations are increasingly making use of competency frameworks as a way to link HRM processes to the skills and behaviour required to meet strategic objectives. Systems using competency frameworks may include many components each linking to a different aspect of human resource activity within an organisation:

- to provide an analysis of the behaviour needed to achieve a given strategy

- recruitment – as a basis for person specifications and as a basis for comparison of applicants during selection

- identifying training and development needs to develop people to a level of performance expected at work

- managing performance, focusing on what people do at work and how well they do it, often as a basis for appraisal systems such as behaviourally anchored rating scales
- benchmarking.

A key point here is that the same competency framework can be used for job design, recruitment, ongoing performance appraisal and the design of reward systems.

Competences:

- are expressed in visible, behavioural terms and reflect the main components of the job (skills, knowledge and attitude)
- must be demonstrated to an agreed standard and must contribute to the overall aims of the organisation.

Most competency frameworks cover the following categories:

- communication skills
- people management
- team skills
- customer service skills
- results-orientation
- problem-solving.

Illustration 3 – Competency frameworks

A research analyst working for the government might have the following factors within their competency framework:

Delivery skills

- Focus
- Delivery skills
- Learning and improving

Intellectual capacity

- Critical analysis and decision making
- Constructive thinking
- Professional expertise

Interpersonal skills

- Developing constructive relationships
- Communicating with impact

Leadership and management

- Leading and directing

Each of these competences will then be supported by a high level description.

For example, "Learning and improving" could be described as follows:

- Acknowledges own development needs and seeks new skills, knowledge and opportunities for learning;
- Learns from others; adapts quickly and effectively to new people, situations and task demands;
- Operates effectively in a range of roles and contexts including times and situations of uncertainty.

Test your understanding 5

List some (of the many) competences an accountant may have.

The process for assessing competencies

For any competence-based system the process is the same:

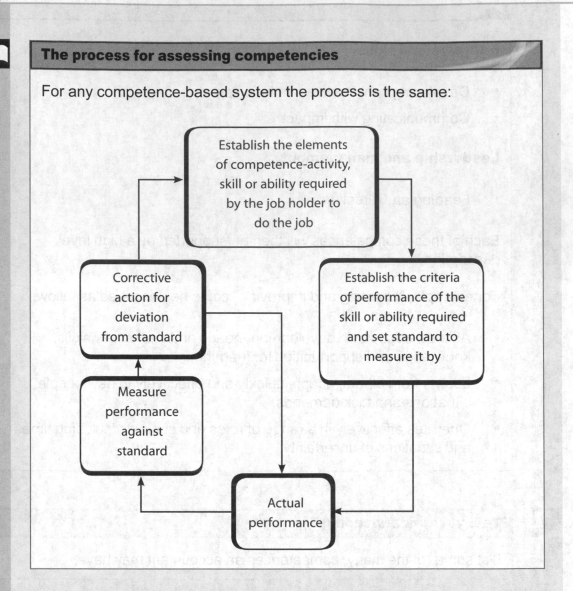

5 Workplace learning and knowledge management

Workplace learning

As has been discussed earlier, in human resource development learning is seen as key in ensuring competitive advantage. The concept of workplace learning sees the organisation as a unit of learning in which:

- learning is of strategic importance and is seen in a wider context by managers and staff

- links are made between learning and other parts of the organisation, such as training and information systems, and training and organisational development.

Some of the key elements of workplace learning are:

The learning organisation	Learning organisations are capable of adapting, changing, developing and transforming themselves in response to the needs, wishes and aspirations of people, inside and outside.
	The role of management in a learning organisation is to encourage continuous learning and acquisition of new knowledge and skills and to transform these into actual behaviour, products and processes within the organisation
Knowledge management	This is concerned with how to acquire, share, retain and use information, knowledge and experience, and how to build on and develop it
	It requires a commitment from senior management to establishing a culture where the sharing of knowledge is encouraged and supported
Knowledge workers	Knowledge workers are not involved in routine production or administrative functions but provide expertise in a defined area. Collabortion in projects is a key aspect of the knowledge worker's role.
	Management should base employee selection for these roles on the basis of skill and competences rather than application to a distinct task

The learning organisation

The idea of the 'learning organisation' emerged towards the end of the twentieth century. Pedler, Burgoyne and Boydell are the main proponents in the UK of the 'learning company', which they define as 'an organisation that facilitates the learning of all its members and continuously transforms itself'.

- In learning organisations, testing and experimentation are encouraged, because the organisation wants to find new answers, and recognises that failed answers are as important as successful ones.

- Actions have two purposes – to resolve the immediate problem and to learn from the process.

- Learning organisations are capable of adapting, changing, developing and transforming themselves in response to the needs, wishes and aspirations of people, inside and outside.

- Self-development and action-learning are also foundations of the learning organisation: as the organisation learns from the actions that it carries out, so does the individual.

The concept underlying these techniques is that learning is of strategic importance to an organisation and needs to be seen in its widest context by staff and management. It also needs to be linked to all parts of the organisation.

The role of management in a learning organisation is to encourage continuous learning and acquisition of new knowledge and skills and to transform these into actual behaviour, products and processes within the organisation.

To enable learning to take place within the organisation, the following approach should be adopted by management.

- The process of strategy formulation should be designed with learning in mind, and should incorporate experimentation and feedback.

- All members of the organisation should be encouraged, and given the opportunity, to contribute to policy making as part of the learning process.

- Information should be seen as a resource to be exploited by all members of the organisation, not as a 'power tool' reserved for a chosen few.

- Accounting systems should be designed in such a way that members of the organisation can learn how the cash resource is used.

- Employees should be encouraged to see internal users of their outputs as 'customers'.

- Employees should be encouraged to see the diversity of rewards they enjoy (not just cash), and there should be openness about why some people are paid more than others.

- The structures of the organisation – everything from office layout to managerial hierarchy – should be regarded as temporary arrangements, which can be altered in response to changing conditions.

- Employees who have contacts outside the organisation, such as salesmen, customer service staff and purchasing staff, should impart the knowledge they determine from such contacts to improve the organisation's knowledge base.

- Management must foster a climate in which workers understand that part of their task is to improve their own knowledge, and to share knowledge with other members of the organisation.

- A priority for management should be the provision of opportunities for structured learning such as courses and seminars.

Organisation learning

The idea of organisation learning is a further development of the concept of workplace learning. It is concerned not with the learning of individuals but about how learning takes place at the organisational level – that is how the organisation as an entity itself learns new ways of doing things.

- The organisation needs to be seen as organic, and learning in the same way individuals do.

- The organisation develops through collective learning from interactions within the organisation.

- Organisation learning is mainly informal and about the organisation's response to given events and circumstances. This depends on the culture of the organisation and the groups within it.

Knowledge management

Organisations are becoming more knowledge-based. As a result, success becomes more dependent on how effectively information is turned into useful knowledge that is then applied to products and processes.

- Knowledge management is concerned with how to acquire, share, retain and use information, knowledge and experience, and how to build on and develop it.

- The knowledge may be 'explicit' and formal such as the content of reports, spreadsheets or manuals, or 'tacit', which is informal, not written down, and includes knowledge, the understanding of good practice and management skills. Both types of knowledge need to be managed.

Implementing knowledge management

Effective knowledge management involves both formal and informal processes and has implications for the organisational structure if sharing of knowledge is to be achieved, with:

- commitment from senior management to establishing a culture where the sharing of knowledge is encouraged and supported

- appointment of staff to manage the process

- movement of individuals between functions and divisions to enable knowledge to be shared and to encourage the development of informal networks

- a flatter, decentralised structure so that decisions can be taken close to where key knowledge is located

- the use of technology to support knowledge management such as
  - email to facilitate the exchange of information between individuals
  - intranets to enable access to and exchange of information

- data-warehousing to store and make available large amounts of information

- decision-support systems that make use of existing knowledge.

Illustration 4 – The learning organisation

Woods Ltd provides all staff with 'works-time' to update the company's database on customers, competitors and other industry information and to allow them to keep abreast of any additions their colleagues may have made.

Knowledge workers

Recent years have seen the emergence of 'knowledge work' where work is no longer about the manufacture of products but about the development of intangible assets, and where knowledge is the main asset of organisations.

Knowledge workers are not involved in routine production or administrative functions but provide expertise in a defined area. This expertise is critical to solving complex problems and through this delivering competitive advantage.

The role of knowledge workers

Collaboration on defined projects is a key aspect to the knowledge worker's role. Other elements to the role are:

- ability to access corporate data through web-based services and corporate databases

- a roving role across departmental boundaries

- a temporary project-based role

- high levels of limited scope, massive depth expertise.

Implications for human resources management

Implications for HRM of the move towards knowledge-based organisations are:

- employee selection is on the basis of skill and competences rather than application to a distinct task

- employees require input to their own development, skills and careers

- the development of separate and relevant incentive schemes based on a variety of individual factors

- temporary, contractor-based roles

- increasing numbers of employees based in remote locations, and the emergence of flexible working schemes.

Post-industrial job design and High Performance Work Systems (HPWS)

As the nature of work has changed, new organisational structures have been proposed with a view to improving the productivity and commitment of staff. Knowledge workers are an important element in these new flexible organisations.

Other features that it is suggested are important in post-industrial organisations are:

- procedures that attempt to recruit and retain the best people

- stability in employment relationships (job security with flexibility)

- pay for performance schemes

- a minimum hierarchy

- flexible working and flexible work design

- multi-skilled employees

- empowered, involved, listened-to employees

- a commitment to training

- open, honest communication

- fair and consistent treatment of employees.

Test your understanding 6

Discuss some of the problems that might arise for traditional managers in dealing with knowledge workers.

6 Links to other syllabus areas

People play a vital role in supporting strategy, facilitating organisational change and making business systems work efficiently. However, in order to maximise business opportunities it is important that changes and opportunities are assessed across a wide range of views. The POPIT (or four-view) model provides details of the key aspects that should be considered in managing changes within any business system:

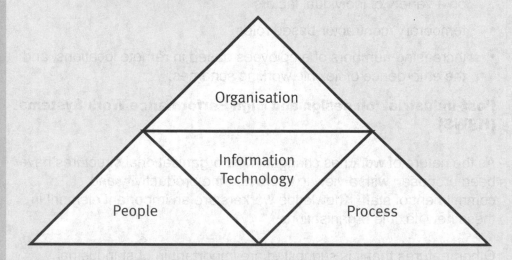

More details

The business system's success will depend upon:

- **People:** staff need to have the right skills and motivation to carry out the tasks. They need to understand tasks and their roles within the organisation. Staff need to be developed to support business changes and resistance to change has to be managed and overcome. This will involve understanding and sometimes shifting the organisational culture (covered in detail in the next chapter).

- **Organisation:** success must be organised. Job roles need to be clearly defined and understood, lines of command and communication need to be effective, the organisational structure needs to support the organisational strategy, there needs to be flexibility in changing environments and bureaucracy needs to be kept to a minimum. Organisational support will be an important link between the other elements of the business system.

- **Processes:** these must be well defined, efficient, documented and understood. Those of high strategic importance and complexity should have undergone process improvement. Opportunities for improvement in other areas must have been explored in order to maximise efficiency and support the organisational strategy

- **IT:** IT needs to support the changes that are taking place within the system. It needs to provide the relevant information at the point that it is needed. IT can replace some manual tasks and improve the efficiency of others. IT may facilitate organisational changes, process changes and staff development and it therefore binds all of the other elements together. IT must be exploited in order to maximise business benefits.

These elements must all be considered, planned and co-ordinated if business system changes (such as process redesigns) are to be successful. A failure in one area will often restrict the success in other areas. For example, organisations that are resistance to change and have bureaucratic structures often fail to make successes out of IT innovations and process redesigns.

For example, Kodak created digital photography but the senior management were reluctant to exploit it as they knew that it would destroy their film based business model. 10 years before digital photography became widespread Kodak knew of the threat. But the organisation and the people did not support the IT and processes that existed within Kodak to exploit this technology. Ultimately this meant that digital photography was exploited by rivals and Kodak failed as a business, despite the fact that Kodak was the organisation who initially created the technology.

It will be important that all four elements work together and are considered in achieving successful business changes (change management is considered in more detail in the next chapter). An organisation's capabilities are often derived from and driven from success in having these four elements working together successfully.

When to use the model

The model can be used in a number of ways:

- Identifying weaknesses in systems.

- Identifying opportunities for system improvements.

- Identifying areas that are not working well together.

- Ensuring that all aspects of business change are considered when making process redesigns.

- Ensuring that project managers do not become too blinkered and ignore all organisational consequences. For example, many project managers. become overly focused on creating an excellent process (as considered in an earlier chapter) but forget that the process will only be successful if the people in the organisation have the skills to use it properly.

In an examination, it may well be used in the review stage of a project to help identify problems that have occurred because not all consequences were considered.

The POPIT model helps to bring many syllabus areas together. You have now studied them all – you read in this chapter how people play an important role in achieving organisational change; in the chapter on organisational structure you read how a business must be structured in order to support strategies and changes; in the business process change chapter you read the role that process change can play in achieving organisational success; and in the IT chapter you read about the role that IT can play in creating opportunities for organisations and developing strategic capabilities for success. So the POPIT model allows the examiner to bring these areas together in examination questions. These chapters can easily be mixed together in examination questions and the model can be used to pull the elements together. It should also help you understand how these elements work together and fit within the Business Analysis syllabus.

Test your understanding 7

An organisation has carried out an 18 month project to redesign the way in which it manages its upstream supply chain. It has well established e-procurement systems that have been in place for over five years and which are well integrated with existing suppliers.

The project manager (formerly part of the procurement team) carried out a plan to introduce a wider variety of suppliers who were willing to provide more flexible order quantities and provide better pricing and inventory information. The procurement process was redesigned to insure that activities were in place that forced procurers to consider these suppliers and their information when making procurement decisions. All procurers were retrained and new 'super-procurers' were created as champions of the new process. These super-procurers had strong links to strategic management and were seen as a vital element in implementing, facilitating and supporting the new process. The presence of these super-procurers encouraged procurers to support the change and also gave a potential new level of employment for staff to aim at.

However, the new process has been in place for two months and has come under widespread criticism. Procurers complain that it is difficult to accumulate and assimilate the necessary information from the new system. Procurers suggest that this information is not provided via the current e-procurement system and the lack of links to these new suppliers means that the information often has to be obtained via email and subsequently becomes cumbersome and difficult to pull together. Senior management have complained that procurement costs have increased and there appears to be little or no expectation of a payback from the organisation's high initial investment. Customers have complained about low inventory levels and delayed orders and some major customers are now threatening to take their business elsewhere. It has subsequently been found that in the last few days procurement staff have reverted to the old procurement system.

Required:

Use the POPIT model to briefly consider the element(s) of the business system that appear to have been responsible for the failure of this project.

7 Chapter summary

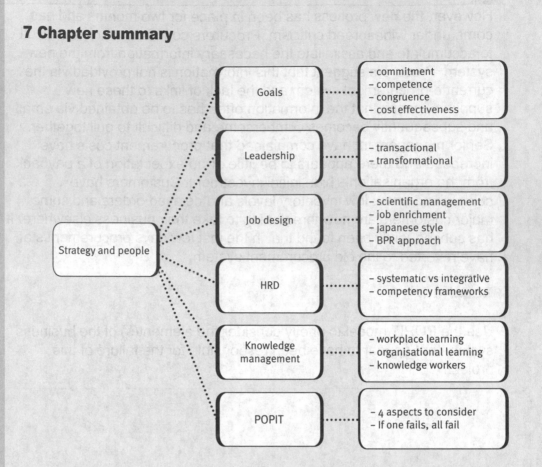

Strategy and people

Goals
- commitment
- competence
- congruence
- cost effectiveness

Leadership
- transactional
- transformational

Job design
- scientific management
- job enrichment
- japanese style
- BPR approach

HRD
- systematic vs integrative
- competency frameworks

Knowledge management
- workplace learning
- organisational learning
- knowledge workers

POPIT
- 4 aspects to consider
- If one fails, all fail

Test your understanding answers

Test your understanding 1

HRM will have to:

- plan potential redundancies when staff are measured

- to facilitate and manage the changes in culture and performance that are necessary

- to ensure that corporate goals and missions are understood and communicated

- to unify reward systems

- jobs might need to be redesigned, and

- new training might be necessary.

This is just one further example of the link between HRM and strategy, but it should illustrate how HRM plays a role in contributing to the achievement of an organisation's objectives.

Test your understanding 2

In a business aiming to achieve a low cost strategy, standardisation and efficiency are likely to be key strategic capabilities. Tasks need to become consistent, homogeneous across business units and reduced to their lowest common denominator. For example, a spaghetti dish will be defined by exactly how much spaghetti to use, how much oil to add, how long to cook it for etc.

A scientific management approach to job design is therefore likely to be used. Chefs will be given very clear instructions on how to cook, what to cook and when to cook it. There will be very little discretion given to chefs to move away from standard procedures and the focus of rewards for chefs will be on how well they followed the rules and how many hours of work they input.

On the other hand, in a business aiming for focused differentiation, a job enrichment approach might be used. Chefs will be given control over what to cook, which suppliers to use etc. and may even be given power over recruiting waiting staff and menu pricing. The focus of rewards will on output (such as number of meals served) rather than input.

Test your understanding 3

- These initiatives have an impact on all parts of the organisational structure.

- E-business has a tendency to lead to more streamlined, flatter structures, which will have implications for the nature of jobs.

- Organisations and work become more knowledge-intensive.

- The nature of the relationships within the organisation and with suppliers and customers changes.

Test your understanding 4

The model would allow a manager to:

- assess job performance

- measure performance before and after the training

- check the effectiveness of the quality

- check the quality of the training

- maintain records of job performance and training

- note areas of outstanding achievement and those of problems

- feed back to staff on their performance.

The above might not be sufficient when there is rapid change. It would be very difficult in a fast moving environment to identify training needs and to make plans for meeting these needs. In changing environments, skills and resources for success need to change alongside the environmental changes but these do not happen in predictable ways. If change is fast, training and development need to be fast and therefore it may take too long to implement new training plans.

The focus in the system explain is very systematic and formal. It will help sustain success in existing environments with existing environments. But to cope with changing environments it needs to be supplemented by an integrated approach. It will be important that staff have the skills to react to new environments, transferable abilities across environments, a willingness to accept change etc. These abilities are more likely to be developed through coaching and development on the job rather than from a systematic and formal improvement of existing skills bases.

Test your understanding 5

The competences an accountant may have include the following.

- Skills
    - Numeracy
    - Literacy
    - IT literacy
    - Bookkeeping, etc.

- Knowledge
    - FRS, IAS, etc.
    - Group accounts, partnership accounts
    - Hedges, Black-Scholes model, etc.

- Attitude
    - Contentious
    - Dynamic, etc.

Test your understanding 6

Potential problems for traditional managers in dealing with knowledge workers include:

- difficulty in measuring output and quality
- staff will require a degree of autonomy
- need for individual methods of assessment and reward
- uncertainty and change in make-up and numbers of staff
- feelings of lack of control.

Test your understanding 7

In this project it would appear that people were well organised. Procurers were retrained, the process was explained and there appeared to be a willingness for change. The new job role of super-procurer appeared to provide a potential level of motivation to the staff.

The change also appeared well organised. There was good communication as well as support from senior management. The super-procurers would help to organise staff and the project manager would organise the process. The fact that super-procurers had links to senior management would allow for any ad hoc changes required to be implemented when and if necessary.

The process was redesigned and there is no evidence in the scenario of any problems in this area. It appears that the existing process was well understood (the project manager had formerly worked as a procurer) and strong investment objectives in terms of broadening the supplier base and procurement flexibility.

But it is in the area of information technology (IT) where the business system appears to have failed. The project continued with a five year old system without any modifications for the new process. No integration appears to have been made to the system for the new suppliers and instead procurement staff are left with two incompatible systems (an integrated e-procurement system for existing suppliers and an email system for new suppliers).

The project manager has lost focus on a key element in the business systems and this appears to have been a key reason for the project failure.

Strategic development and managing strategic change

Chapter learning objectives

Upon completion of this chapter you will be able to:

- describe the concepts of intended and emergent strategy (including how these relate to unrealised and realised strategies) and how these can arise

- describe how process redesign and e-business can contribute to emergent strategies for an organisation

- describe, with the use of a diagram, what strategic drift is and how it can arise

- explain that business change is often driven by the need to address strategic alignment

- describe the types of strategic change in terms of a matrix of nature of change (incremental/big bang) and scope of change (realignment/transformation)

- determine the changes that might be needed in an organisation in terms of the cultural web (symbols, stories, rituals, control systems, structure, power) and how culture plays a part on organisational strategy

- explain the reasons for resistance to change typically found in all organisations

- advise on different leadership styles for achieving change

- explain how the leadership style applied in managing change will be affected by the contextual features of the situation faced by the organisation

- describe the main methods that can be used to manage strategic change

- explain how change management techniques play a role in all elements of the business change lifecycle.

1 Patterns of strategy development

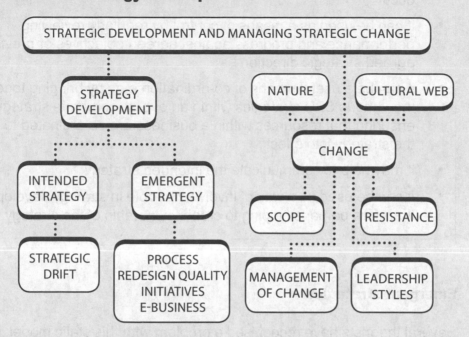

Intended and planned strategies

An intended strategy could be defined as 'a strategy whose objectives had been defined in advance and whose main elements had been developed before the strategy commenced'.

It is a formal, planned systematic approach to strategy formulation and implementation (such as the rational model of strategy making discussed in Chapter 1).

Revision of planned strategies

As discussed in chapter 1, the rational approach involves the following steps.

(1) Strategic analysis

(2) Strategic choice

(3) Strategic implementation

For intended strategies one would expect each stage to be completed before the next starts.

The benefits of a strategic planning system are as follows:

- it can provide a structured means of analysis and thinking about complex strategic problems

- managers will be required to question and challenge the received wisdom they take for granted

- it can encourage a longer-term view of strategy than might otherwise occur

- it can be used as a means of control by regularly reviewing performance and progress against agreed objectives or previously agreed strategic direction

- it can be a useful means of co-ordination e.g., by bringing together the various SBU strategies within an overall corporate strategy, or ensuring that resources within a business are co-ordinated to put the strategy into effect

- it may help to communicate the intended strategy

- it can be used as a way of involving people in strategy development, therefore perhaps helping to create ownership of the strategy.

Emergent strategies

Several theorists have recognised a problem with this static model: it is not how it is done in real life. They believe that strategy is actually a dynamic and interactive process. Henry Mintzberg made a distinction between deliberate strategy and emergent strategy.

An emergent strategy is a set of actions that is consistent over time, has not been stated in a formal plan and has developed or emerged outside the formal plan and between planning reviews.

Further details on Mintzberg's ideas

Illustration – Patterns of strategy development

Mintzberg argues that strategy emerges over time as intentions collide with and accommodate a changing reality, rather than being due to a deliberate planning process.

This emergent strategy would be one that arises from an external stimulus not envisaged in the planned strategy. For example, a supplier pursuing modern ideas on supplier/customer relationships might encourage a partnership approach to sourcing. It is easy to imagine that buyers in the customer organisation might see benefits in this, and could pursue the idea to the point where sourcing strategy took on an aspect not at all contemplated when planned strategic developments were laid down.

Mintzberg also believes that few strategies are purely deliberate or purely emergent but a mixture of the two:

- one means no control the other means no learning

- most strategies are a mixture of both to exercise control while fostering learning

- strategies have to form as well as be formulated.

Illustration – Emergent strategy

Potbelly Sandwich Works began in 1977 as a small antique store run by a young couple. Despite the fast-paced, never-a-dull-moment world of antique dealing, the couple decided to bolster their business by making sandwiches for their customers. What began as a sideline, turned out to be a stroke of genius. Soon, people who couldn't care less about vintage glass doorknobs were stopping by to enjoy special sandwiches and homemade desserts in this unusual atmosphere. As the years passed, the lines grew. Booths were added, along with ovens for toasting sandwiches to perfection, hand-dipped ice cream – even live music. The little antique shop had become the full-fledged, totally unique sandwich chain we see in America today.

Strategic innovation

Strategic innovation is the creation of growth strategies, new product categories, services or business models that change the game and generate significant new value for consumers, customers and the organisation.

Mintzberg and others are of the opinion that deliberate strategy focuses on control, while emergent strategy emphasises learning – there are many different ways that organisations can learn to add value to their product or service through areas such as process redesign and e-business.

Illustration 1 – Strategic innovation

Ford – an example of process redesign

Ford redesigned their business and manufacturing process from just manufacturing cars to manufacturing quality cars, where the number one goal is quality. This helped Ford save millions on recalls and warranty repairs. Ford has accomplished this goal by incorporating barcodes on all their parts and scanners to scan for any missing parts in a completed car coming off the assembly line. This helped them guarantee a safe and quality car.

Swatch – an example of process redesign

Swatch reduced costs with ultrasonic welding that eliminated the need for screws to close watch casings. The company also simplified the manufacturing process, fully mechanising it. The net result was the lowest price/lowest cost structure in the world for a fine watch.

Waterstones – an example of e-business

Waterstones, the booksellers, have branches all over the United Kingdom but in 2001 they formed a strategic alliance with Amazon for on-line sales, and the website for both is now http://www.amazon.co.uk.

In chapter 1 the strategy lenses explained that an organisation's strategy does not solely come from its plans and design strategy, it can also come from experience and ideas.

Illustration 2 – Strategy developed through ideas and experience

One of the more powerful examples of how operating managers can have a huge impact on the real-life strategy of the firm is Intel. While the corporate office continued to conceive of Intel as a memory chip company, an operating rule in their manufacturing organisation (to maximise gross margin per wafer of square inch) meant that the manufacturing floor was increasingly allocating more space to microprocessors. As that more profitable market grew, Intel became a microprocessor company, not a memory company. These operating-level decisions changed the de facto strategy of the firm prior to the corporate office's conception of the company strategy.

Realised and unrealised strategies

When planned strategies are not realised it is often because events develop in unexpected ways:

- the organisation's underlying assumptions turn out to be invalid
- the pace of development overtakes it
- changes in the organisation's external environment, e.g. changes in the market for the goods and services that the firm produces and in the nature of the competition facing the company
- the organisation's internal environment changes.

The rational strategic planning process has also been criticised because it ignores the effects of:

- cultural influences in maintaining strategic stability and sometimes resisting strategic change

- the power structure within the organisation

- the effect of politics and the relative influence on the decision-making of different individuals and groups.

Overall, this can mean that an organisation's actual or realised strategy can be very different from the original planned or designed strategy.

2 Strategic drift

Strategic drift describes a situation where the organisation's strategy gradually, if imperceptibly, moves away from the forces at work in its environment.

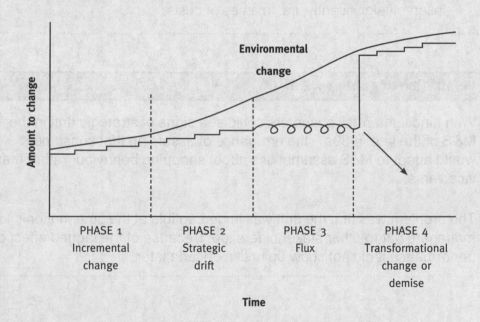

Over time, organisations will have to deal with many different types of change and it is important that these changes are managed effectively.

Explanation of the stages in strategic drift

- The organisation takes a series of logical, incremental steps that were part of its plan to change ahead of the market and develop a competitive advantage.

- The rate of change in the market place speeds up, and the firm's incrementalist approach is not enough to maintain its advantage, and it is left behind.

- Faced with a stimulus for action, managers may seek to extend the market for their business, but may assume that it will be similar to their existing market, and therefore set about managing the new venture in much the same way as they have been used to.

- If this is not successful, strategy development is likely to go into a state of flux, with no clear direction, further damaging performance.

- Eventually transformational change is required if the demise of the organisation is to be avoided.

  Transformational change tends to occur when performance has fallen off significantly, i.e. in times of crisis.

Illustration of strategic drift

With hindsight, retail observers could see signs of strategic drift in the M&S of the late 1980s – the arrogance of assuming that consumers would adapt to M&S assumptions about shopping behaviour rather than vice versa.

The problem was that the drift was imperceptible at the time, not only to managers but to other stakeholders too. Because of the lagged effect on performance it did not show up until a decade later.

3 Strategic change

Types of strategic change

Change can be classified by the extent of the change required, and the speed with which the change is to be achieved:

	Incremental	
Speed of change	Evolution	Adaptation
	Revolution	Reconstruction
Big Bang		

Transformation   Realignment

Extent   of   change

Further explanation

Explanation of the axes

Transformation	This entails changing an organisation's culture. It is a fundamental change that cannot be handled within the existing organisational paradigm.
Realignment	This does not involve a fundamental reappraisal of the central assumptions and beliefs.
Incremental change	This can take a long period of time, but results in a fundamentally different organisation once completed.
Big Bang change	This change is likely to be a forced, reactive transformation using simultaneous initiatives on many fronts, and often in a relatively short space of time.

Explanation of the types of change

Adaptation	This is the most common type of change. It is slow and gradual and is based on the existing culture, processes and competencies.
Reconstruction	This is a much quicker change, often brought about by sudden external pressures such as a new competitor innovation or a change in the regulatory environment. The change may also be motivated by a sudden downturn in financial performance. The organisation may launch many initiatives at the same time, rather than aim for the gradual approach associated with an adaptation.
Evolution	In anticipation of the need for future change an organisation will aim to change its culture over time. Johnson, Scholes and Whittington suggest that this can be the most challenging type of change as there is no immediate need for it but it will be vital to the long term success of the organisation. It might be best supported by a switch to a more learning organisation with a clear committment to sustained change.
Revolution	This involves rapid and fundamental change within an organisation. It may follow a period of strategic flux and the organisation is likely to be facing extreme external pressure for change. Culture within the organisation is likely to have to significantly adapt to new process, products , markets and objectives. Without this change in culture the change (and the organisation) will usually fail. Many new initiatives are likely to be launched simultaneously in order to reverse the organisation's direction.

Illustration 3 – Strategic change

Strategic change is by definition far-reaching. We speak of strategic change when fundamental alterations are made to the business system or the organisational system. Adding a lemon-flavoured Coke to the product portfolio is interesting, maybe important, but not a strategic change, while branching out into bottled water was – it was a major departure from Coca-Cola's traditional business system.

Selecting an approach to strategic change

Another way that evolution can be explained is by conceiving of the organisation as a learning system. However, within incremental change there may be a danger of strategic drift, because change is based on the existing paradigm and routines of the organisation, even when environmental or competitive pressure might suggest the need for more fundamental change.

In selecting an approach to strategic change, most managers struggle with the question of how bold they should be. On the one hand, they usually realise that to fundamentally transform the organisation, a break with the past is needed. To achieve strategic renewal it is essential to turn away from the firm's heritage and to start with a clean slate. On the other hand, they also recognise the value of continuity, building on past experiences, investments and loyalties. To achieve lasting strategic renewal, people in the organisation will need time to learn, adapt and grow into a new organisational reality.

The 'window of opportunity' for achieving a revolutionary strategic change can be small for a number of reasons. Some of the most common triggers are:

- competitive pressure – when a firm is under intense competitive pressure and its market position starts to erode quickly, a rapid and dramatic response might be the only approach possible. Especially when the organisation threatens to slip into a downward spiral towards insolvency, a bold turnaround can be the only option left to the firm.

- regulatory pressure – firms can also be put under pressure by the government or regulatory agencies to push through major changes within a short period of time. Such externally imposed revolutions can be witnessed among public sector organisations (e.g. hospitals and schools) and highly regulated industries (e.g. utilities and telecommunications), but in other sectors of the economy as well (e.g. public health regulations). Some larger organisations will, however, seek to influence and control regulation.

- first mover advantage – a more proactive reason for instigating revolutionary change, is to be the first firm to introduce a new product, service or technology and to build up barriers to entry for late movers.

Test your understanding 1

Briefly explain the four types of strategic change in an organisation.

4 Organisational culture

Introduction

For change to be effective an organisation will often have to change its culture. The extent of the change required will be influenced by the type of change that is planned. For example, revolution is likely to require a greater cultural change than adaptation.

Culture is the set of values, guiding beliefs, understandings and ways of thinking that are shared by the members of an organisation and is taught to new members as correct. It represents the unwritten, feeling part of the organisation.

Culture is 'the way we do things around here' (Charles Handy).

Culture is a set of 'taken-for-granted' assumptions, views of the environment, behaviours and routines (Schein).

The effect of culture

Culture, as a set of taken-for-granted assumptions, will effect:

- strategy – what should the company do? What can it do?
- approach to strategic planning. Strategy as design, experience and ideas
- perceptions about competitors
- perceptions about customers
- management style
- attitude to various stakeholders
- ethical behaviour
- attitudes towards CSR.

Cultural web

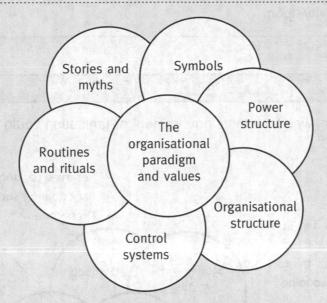

The cultural web was devised by Gerry Johnson as part of his work to attempt to explain why firms often failed to adjust to environmental change as quickly as they needed to. He concluded that firms developed a way of understanding their organisation – called a paradigm – and found it difficult to think and act outside this paradigm if it were particularly strong.

The different elements of the cultural web

It is concerned with the manifestations of culture in the organisation and has six inter-related elements.

- Routines and rituals – routines are 'the way things are done around here' and may even demonstrate a beneficial competency. They can be the written or unwritten rules of the game within the organisation.

- Stories and myths – that employees tell one another and others about the organisation, its history and personalities; used to communicate traditions, standards and role models.

- Symbols – such as logos, offices, cars, titles, type of language and terminology commonly used become a shorthand representation of the nature of the organisation.

- Power structure – formal or informal power or influence by virtue of position, control of resources, who the person knows, or history. This may be based on management position and seniority but in some organisations power can be lodged with other levels or functions.

- Organisational structure – reflects the formal and informal roles, responsibilities, and relationships and ways in which the organisation works. Structures are likely to reflect power.

- Control systems – the measurement and reward systems that emphasise what is important to monitor and to focus attention and activity upon.

Illustration 4 – The cultural web in local government

A cultural web for a local government organisation could look like the following:

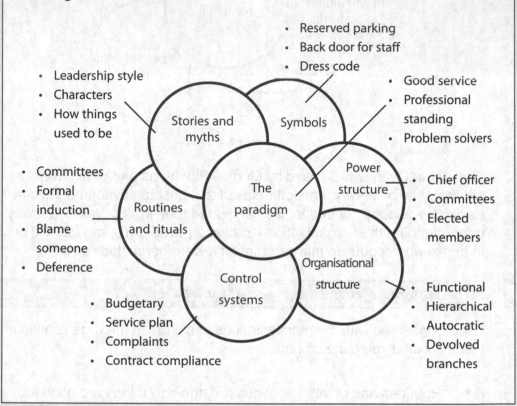

Test your understanding 2

Outline the cultural elements of a state-controlled health service provider in a cultural web.

Culture and change

Many organisations find that some elements of the cultural web are easier to change than others. For example, it may be easier to change the formal organisational structure than it is to change long established routines and habits.

Change management looks at how these changes can be achieved effectively and efficiently.

Using the cultural web to map change

The concept of the cultural web is a useful device for mapping out change but its real worth is in the fact that we can identify which elements of culture need to change. Questions to ask include:

Stories	• What core belief do the stories in my place reflect?
	• How pervasive are these beliefs (through the levels of the organisation)?
	• Do stories relate to: strengths or weaknesses, successes or failures, conformity or mavericks? Who are the heroes and villains?
	• What norms do the mavericks deviate from?
Routines and rituals	• What behaviour do routines encourage? Which would look odd if changed?
	• What are the key rituals? What core beliefs do they reflect?
	• What do training programmes emphasise?
	• How easy are the rituals/routines to change?
Organisational structures	• How mechanistic/organic are the structures in my organisation?
	• How flat/hierarchical are the structures? How formal/informal are they?
	• Do structures encourage collaboration or competition?
	• What types of power structure do they support?
Control systems	• What is most closely monitored/controlled in my organisation?
	• Is emphasis on reward or punishment? Are there many/few controls?
	• Are controls related to history or current strategies?
Power structures	• What are the core beliefs of the leadership in my organisation?
	• How strongly held are these beliefs (idealists or pragmatists)?
	• How is power distributed in the organisation?
	• What are the main blockages to change?

Symbols	• What language and jargon are used in my place of work?
	• How internal or accessible are they?
	• What aspects of strategy are highlighted in publicity?
	• What status symbols are there?
	• Are there particular symbols that denote the organisation?
Overall	• What is the dominant culture? How easy is this to change?

5 Overcoming resistance to change

Resistance to change is the action taken by individuals and groups when they perceive that a change that is occurring is a threat to them.

Resistance is 'any attitude or behaviour that reflects a person's unwillingness to make or support a desired change'.

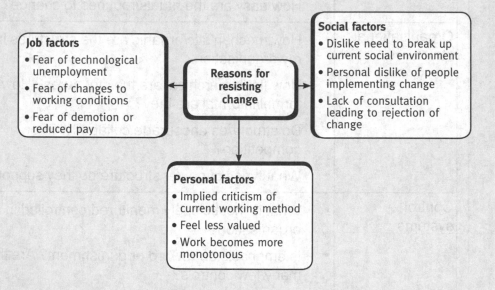

Resistance may take many forms, including active or passive, overt or covert, individual or organised, aggressive or timid. For each source of resistance, management need to provide an appropriate response.

Reasons for resisting change

According to Kotter and Schlesinger (1979) there are four reasons that explain why certain people resist change.

- Parochial self-interest (some people are concerned with the implication of the change for themselves and how it may affect their own interests, rather than considering the effects for the success of the business).

- Misunderstanding (communication problems; inadequate information).

- Low tolerance to change (certain people are very keen on security and stability in their work).

- Different assessments of the situation (some employees may disagree on the reasons for the change and on the advantages and disadvantages of the change process).

Test your understanding 3

Your organisation is going through a big upheaval and you are not very pleased – in fact you are quite worried.

What could your manager do or say to increase your resistance?

Lewin's change process

The process of change, shown in the diagram below, includes unfreezing habits or standard operating procedures, changing to new patterns and refreezing to ensure lasting effects.

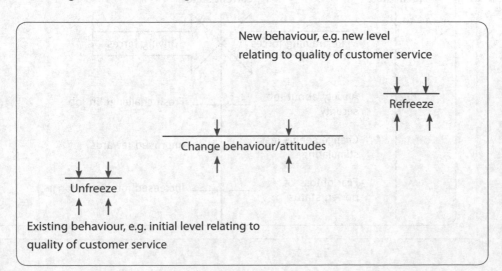

The process of change comprises three stages.

- Unfreezing – create the initial motivation to change by convincing staff of the undesirability of the present situation.

- The change process itself – mainly concerned with identifying what the new behaviour or norm should be. This stage will often involve new information being communicated and new attitudes, culture and concepts being adopted.

- Refreezing or stabilising the change – implying reinforcement of the new pattern of work or behaviour by rewards (praise, etc).

Force field analysis

Lewin also emphasised the importance of force field analysis. He argued that managers should consider any change situation in terms of:

- the factors encouraging and facilitating the change (the driving forces)

- the factors that hinder change (the restraining forces).

If we want to bring about change we must disturb the equilibrium by:

- strengthening the driving forces

- weakening the restraining forces

- or both.

The model encourages us to identify the various forces impinging on the target of change, to consider the relative strengths of these forces and to explore alternative strategies for modifying the force field.

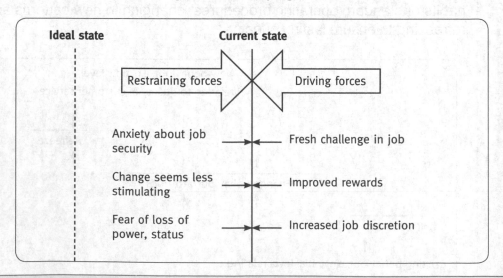

Leadership styles

Kotter and Schlesinger set out the following change approaches to deal with resistance:

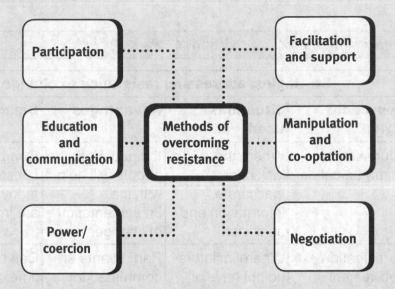

Explanation of the Kotter and Schlesinger styles

- Participation – aims to involve employees, usually by allowing some input into decision making. This could easily result in employees enjoying raised levels of autonomy, by allowing them to design their own jobs, pay structures, etc.

- Education and communication – used as a background factor to reinforce another approach. This strategy relies upon the hopeful belief that communication about the benefits of change to employees will result in their acceptance of the need to exercise the changes necessary.

- Power/coercion – involves the compulsory approach by management to implement change. This method finds its roots from the formal authority that management possesses, together with legislative support.

- Facilitation and support – employees may need to be counselled to help them overcome their fears and anxieties about change. Management may find it necessary to develop individual awareness of the need for change.

- Manipulation and co-optation – involves covert attempts to sidestep potential resistance. The information that is disseminated is selective and distorted to only emphasise the benefits of the change. Co-optation involves giving key people access to the decision-making process.

- Negotiation – is often practised in unionised companies. Simply, the process of negotiation is exercised, enabling several parties with opposing interests to bargain. This bargaining leads to a situation of compromise and agreement.

Addressing resistance to change

Strategies: addressing resistance to change			
Approach/ style	**Situations used**	**Advantages**	**Disadvantages**
Education + Communication	Where there is a lack of or inaccurate information and analysis.	If persuaded, people will help with the implementation of change.	Can be time consuming if many people are involved.
Participation + Involvement	Where initiators do not have all information to design change, and where others have power to resist.	Participants are committed to implementing change including their relevant contribution.	Can be very time consuming with possibly inappropriate changes made.
Facilitation + Support	Where resistance comes from adjustment problems.	Best approach for adjustment issues.	Can be time consuming, expensive and still fail.
Negotiation + Agreement	Where one group will lose out and has power to resist.	Can be an easy way to avoid major resistance.	Can be too expensive if it leads to general compliance.
Manipulation + Co-optation	Where other tactics won't work or are too costly.	Can be a relatively quick and inexpensive solution to resistance	Can lead to future problems if people feel they have been manipulated.
Explicit + Implicit Coercion	Where speed is essential, and the change initiators possess considerable power.	It is speedy and can overcome any kind of resistance.	Can be risky if it leaves people angry at the initiators.

KAPLAN PUBLISHING

Test your understanding 4

A manager is in charge of a team that has been given the task of introducing a new management reporting system into regional offices. There is considerable resistance to the changes from the office managers, and comments that you have heard include the following.

- I have more important work priorities to take up my time.

- I'm used to the old system.

- The new system is too complicated.

- The new system will create more paperwork.

- The new system will make me more accountable.

- My job in the new system is not clear.

How would you try to deal with this resistance to change?

6 The context for change (Balogun and Hope Hailey)

For change to be successful, implementation efforts need to fit the organisational context. There is no simple 'off the shelf' approach that will work for all organisations. Balogun and Hope Hailey suggest that there are a number of **contextual features** that should be considered before an implementation approach (for example a style of leadership) for the change is determined:

- time

- scope

- preservation

- diversity

- capability

- capacity

- readiness

- power

Explanation of the model

For the contextual features can be seen as existing within an overall change kaleidoscope. This was developed by Julia Balogun and Veronica Hope Hailey to help managers design such a 'context sensitive' approach to change.

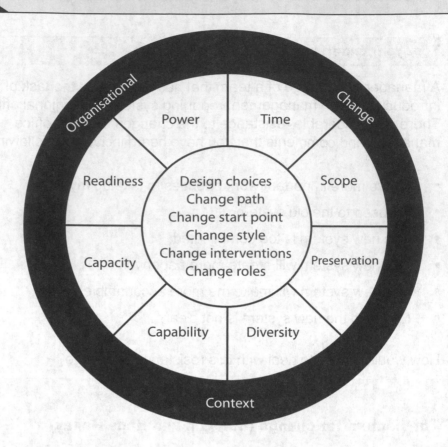

The kaleidoscope has three rings:

- The outer ring relates to the wider strategic change context.

- The middle ring relates to specific contextual factors that need to be considered when formulating a change plan.

- The inner circle gives a menu of choices and interventions ('design choices') available to change agents.

Contextual features

- **Time** – is there time for longer term strategic development or does the firm have to react quickly to a crisis?

- **Scope** – how much of the organisation will be affected? Is the change best described as realignment or transformation?

- **Preservation** – which aspects of working, culture, competences and people need to be retained?

- **Diversity** – the need to recognise that different departments (e.g., marketing and R&D) may have different sub-cultures.

- **Capability** – whether abilities exist to cope with the change. These can be on an individual, managerial or organisational level.

- **Capacity** – are resources (e.g. money, managerial time) available to invest in the change process?

- **Readiness** – are staff aware of the need for change and are they committed to that change?

- **Power** – how much authority and autonomy do change agents have to make proposed changes?

Each of these factors can be assessed as positive, negative or neutral in the context of change. Positive features facilitate change and negative ones restrict change.

Design choices

Design choices represent the key features of a change management approach:

- **Change path** – clarifying the types of change in terms of timescales, the extent of change and the desired outcomes.

- **Change start point** – where the change is initiated (e.g. top-down or bottom up).

- **Change style** – which management style should be adopted (e.g. collaborative, participative, directive or coercive)?

- **Change interventions** – which mechanisms should be deployed (e.g. education, communication, cultural interventions)?

- **Change roles** – assigning roles and responsibilities (e.g. leadership, use of consultants, role of change action teams).

7 The business change lifecycle

The overall change process can be split into five steps defined by the business change lifecycle:

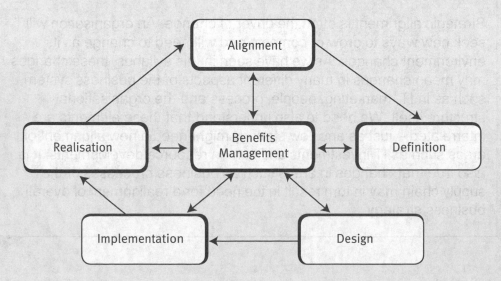

- Alignment – determining the type of change required.

- Definition – creating a project to achieve this alignment.

- Design – determining the detail changes required.

- Implementation – putting the design into action and managing its success.

- Realisation – assessing the success of the alignment.

Change management plays a role in all of these steps (for example, in identifying changes needed for alignment, in understanding the context at the definition stage, in design change actions, in implementing change and assessing the success of change actions).

More details

Alignment

This is the strategic analysis stage described earlier by Johnson, Scholes and Whittington. It concerns ensuring that the organisation's strategy is aligned with the changes that are expected in its environment. This may mean planning for changes in the external environment such as changes in the threat from substitutes or reacting to new legislation.

But organisations also need to ensure that they have the strategic capabilities in place to sustain success in the future. This means that the alignment will not just be an external alignment in terms of aligning future strategy with external environmental changes such as a change in competition or technology, but also aligning internal critical success factors to ensure that they can facilitate success and a change to a new competitive or market position. As explained elsewhere in this chapter, an alignment with organisational culture or a realignment of that culture to support a business transformation is also often required.

Strategic alignment is often the driver of change. An organisation will seek new ways to grow or compete and will need to change as its environment changes. As we have seen in this syllabus, these changes may mean changes in many different aspects of the business system, such as in IT, marketing, people, process and the organisational structure itself. We need to also understand that these elements are interrelated – just as any new strategy might need a new alignment of areas such as IT investments and human resource developments, it is also true that changes in areas such as business processes or the supply chain may in turn result in the need for a realignment of overall business strategy.

As explained in chapter 1 when we looked at the strategy lenses, these changes may be deliberately planned and designed. But they are just as likely to come from experience or ideas from within the business or emerge as better information is gathered on customer buying patterns and requirements. It may well be that the ideas come from junior management or operational staff and work their way up to senior management (a 'bottom up' approach to strategy creation). It may well mean that the aligned or actual strategy is sometimes very different from the original planned strategy.

Definition

This stage was explored in more detail in an earlier chapter when we looked at building the business case. This takes the business drivers identified in the alignment stage and formulates them into a more defined project. The key elements of this are:

- Understanding the strategic need for the project.

- Assessing different options and choosing the option that is most appropriate (there are clear links here to strategic choice, covered earlier in the syllabus).

- Having a clear project goal and project responsibilities and understanding the project constraints.

- Bringing together the costs and benefits of the project (perhaps in a financial evaluation).

- Determining benefit owners.

- Understanding project risks, assessing them and planning for how they will be managed.

It is also at this stage that the organisation should consider the context for change management and how any resistance will be overcome.

Design

This stage will design the detailed changes that need to take place in order for the change to be a success. It may consider the elements of the POPIT model considered earlier in the text in that it will make changes to areas such as:

- People: how staff will be managed, how resistance will be overcome, what elements of training will be provided, what new skills are required, allocating change ownership etc.

- Organisation: whether new job roles are required, changes to rewards systems and controls, cultural changes, changes to SBUs (strategic business units) etc.

- Processes: the removal of unnecessary activities, the avoidance of duplication, outsourcing, further automation etc.

- IT: greater use of IT, implementation of new advanced IT systems, choice of IT supplier etc.

It may also be supplemented by benefit realisation plans and thorough testing to ensure that implementation is as focused and as successful as possible.

Implementation

The detailed designs will then be put into place. The project manager will become very important at this stage and the detailed stages of project management will come into play (planning, managing and controlling).

Change and business owners will play their part and a communication plan will be necessary for all key stakeholders. The project manager might create a stakeholder map to determine how different stakeholders should be managed at this stage.

Change management will now become vital. Whether a participative, coercive or alternative approach is necessary (which will be determined at the definition and design stages), it will be important that the change is achieved. The best plans can fall apart if the people aren't onboard and managed properly. Coaching, training, mentoring, control and reward systems can all play a vital role here.

Realisation

This is effectively the review stage. It aims to ensure that the alignment has taken place. It will entail carrying out reviews such as a benefits realisation review and post implementation review as well as extending these into a lessons learnt review. Performance will be measured against pre-determined targets.

But it may also be that this stage involves looking for emergent benefits or further alignment from the project. One change may lead to the need or opportunity for new strategic changes, or changes in other parts of the organisation. In this case, the business change lifecycle is a never ending process.

Illustration 5 – Strategic change

Glaxo

Glaxo Smith Kline ('Glaxo') is often quoted as an example of a firm that has successfully managed change.

- Glaxo views change as an ongoing process rather than a series of programmes. This generally means that change timescales are thought of in years rather than months ('time' context positive).

- It also allows an emphasis on ongoing realignment rather than transformation ('scope' context positive).

- Permanent organisational development units exist at national, regional and global levels. The input of these into executive teams ensures that cash and time resources are made available ('capacity' context positive) and that directors have a high readiness for change. (Note: Some writers have commented that Glaxo's sales force were not as open to change during the Glaxo Welcome merger in the 1990s when the 'readiness' context was classified as negative overall).

8 Chapter summary

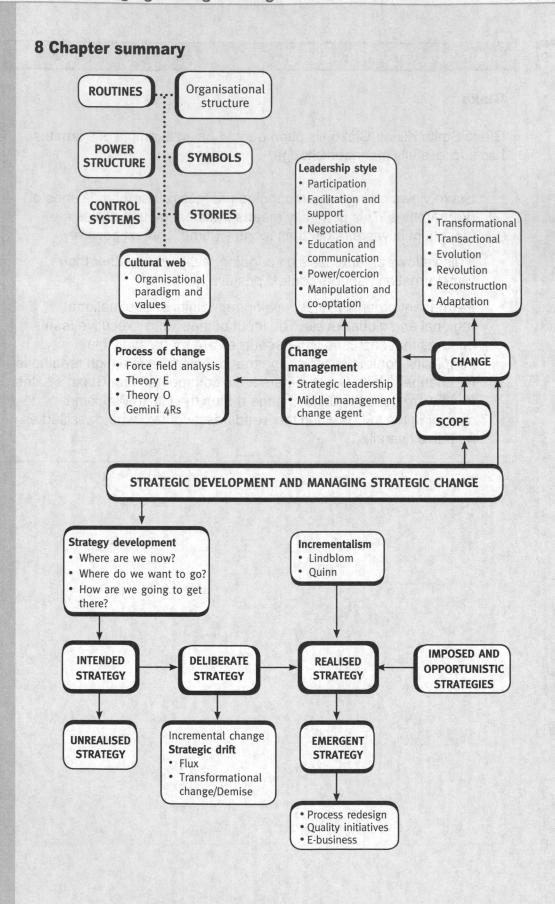

Test your understanding answers

Test your understanding 1

- Adaptation is change that can be accommodated within the current paradigm (the current organisational beliefs and assumptions) and occurs incrementally. This is the most common form of change in organisations.

- Reconstruction is the type of change that may be rapid and can involve a good deal of upheaval in an organisation, but which does not fundamentally change the paradigm.

- Evolution is a change in strategy that requires paradigm change, but over time.

- Revolution is change that requires rapid and major strategic and paradigm change, perhaps in circumstances where pressure for change is extreme, e.g. if profit decline or a take-over threatens the continued existence of the firm.

Test your understanding 2

- Stories – in many older state-controlled health providers stories and myths cover the following: cures, villains (politicians), heroes and heroism, change agents are fools, abuse of managers and the golden age.

- Symbols – include terminology, white coats/uniforms, retinues, bleepers, doctors' dining rooms and big institutions.

- Routines and rituals include clinical rituals, consultation ceremonies, blaming the next tier and treating patients like children – waiting rooms, putting to bed, waking up and ward rounds.

- Structure – is seen as hierarchical, mechanistic, tribal/functional and with a pecking order of services.

- Political systems – include professional bodies, the 'old boy' network and politicians.

- Control – is through waiting lists, financial reporting and responsibility.

- The paradigm – covers issues such as:
    - public service – it is 'ours' and a 'good thing'
    - it is free at the point of delivery
    - providers know best
    - it has superior acute sector
    - clinicians' values.

Test your understanding 3

Managers can increase resistance by:

- failing to be specific about a change
- failing to explain why change is needed
- not consulting
- keeping people in the dark
- creating excess work pressure
- expecting immediate results
- not dealing with fears and anxieties
- ignoring resistance.

Test your understanding 4

Change introduced through the use of power or manipulation is likely to add to anxiety. Education and communication will rarely succeed on their own when introducing major change. However, they are useful as a support for a negotiation or participation approach. The negotiation approach requires the existence of organised representatives and a formal procedure that is suitable for some items such as change in employment terms but would be inadvisable for other items of changing procedures, organisational changes, decentralisation, etc. In these cases, participation offers the best opportunity of allaying staff anxieties by involving them early in the change process and continuing that involvement through to completion.

Questions & Answers

1 The nature of strategic business analysis

Question 1: David Gould

David Gould set up his accounting firm, providing accounting services to small businesses, in 20X6. Within three years his fee income was in excess of £100K a year and he had nearly 100 clients most of whom had been gained through word of mouth. David recognised that these small or micro businesses, typically employing ten or fewer people, were receiving less than satisfactory service from their current accountants. These accounting firms typically had between five and ten partners and operated regionally and not nationally. Evidence of poor service included limited access to their particular accountant, poor response time to clients' enquiries and failure to identify opportunities to save clients money. In addition bad advice, lack of interest in business development opportunities for the client and poor internal communication between the partners and their staff contributed to client dissatisfaction. David has deliberately kept the costs of the business down by employing three part-time accountants and relying on his wife to run the office.

David had recently met Ian King who ran a similar sized accounting firm. The personal chemistry between the two and complementary skills led to a partnership being proposed. Gould and King Associates, subject to securing the necessary funding, is to be launched in September 20Y0. David is to focus on the business development side of the partnership and Ian on the core services provided. Indicative of their creative thinking is David's conviction that accounting services are promoted very inadequately with little attempt to communicate with clients using the Internet.

He is also convinced that there are real opportunities for the partnership to move into new areas such as providing accountancy services for property developers, both at home and abroad. Ian feels that the partnership should set up its own subsidiary in India, enjoying the benefits of much cheaper accountancy staff and avoiding the costs and complications of outsourcing their core accounting services. Ian sees fee income growing to £2 million in five years' time.

David has been asked by his bank to provide it with a business plan setting out how the partnership intends to grow and develop.

Required:

(a) Write a short report for David giving the key features that you consider to be important and that you would expect to see in the business plan for the Gould and King partnership that David has to present to his bank.

(15 marks)

There is considerable evidence that small firms are reluctant to carry out strategic planning in their businesses.

(b) What are the advantages and disadvantages for Gould and King Associates in creating and implementing a strategic plan?

(10 marks)

(Total: 25 marks)

2 The environment and competitive forces

Question 2: Dunvegan Ltd

Dunvegan Ltd is a forestry company operating in the UK, mainly in Scotland. In addition to forests at various stages of maturity, the company also owns many hectares of undeveloped land.

So far Dunvegan Ltd's timber has consisted almost exclusively of spruce trees which produce softwood used extensively in building work. Spruce sells for the equivalent of about £200 per cubic metre. However, genetic engineering has produced a remarkable new tree which has the growth characteristics of spruce, but which produces hard wood with the appearance and qualities of mahogany. This species, the Maho spruce, should grow quite happily in Scotland and produce worthwhile crops after ten years, each Maho spruce tree producing about 2 cubic metres. Currently, mahogany sells for the equivalent of £900 per cubic metre.

The company which developed the Maho spruce has ensured that the trees are sterile and has also successfully applied for worldwide patents on the genetic material. Seedlings are available only from that company at a cost of £200 each.

Dunvegan Ltd is considering whether to invest in Maho spruce. Land already owned by the company would be used (market value £1,000/hectare) and the company's planting and drainage equipment would be assigned temporarily to the project. Because the seedlings are so expensive, relatively light planting would be used at 1,500 seedlings per hectare. Annual maintenance and security would £1,000/hectare for each of the ten years of the project. Dunvegan Ltd is considering planting 1,000 hectares with Maho spruce.

In the UK Dunvegan Ltd has three main competitors; mahogany is also imported from four countries in the tropics where it is a valuable export. Some of the wood is from managed plantations, but some is from natural forest. Recently the price of mahogany has been rising as supplies become short and plantations have to be renewed. Dunvegan Ltd's accountant has read an article in a recent edition of Lumber About, the monthly trade paper of the timber business, in which the economic effects of the Maho spruce were discussed. If around 3,000 – 4,000 hectares were planted in the UK, then the price of mahogany would be £500 per cubic metre at the end of ten years. If around 2,000 hectares only were planted, then the price would be £800 per cubic metre. The breakeven price is estimated to be £639/cubic metre.

Required:

From the viewpoint of an independent consultant, write a report to the directors of Dunvegan Ltd on the proposed Maho spruce plantation. Your report should include a PESTEL analysis.

(25 marks)

Question 3: T Plc

Introduction

T plc is a well-established company providing telecommunications services both nationally and internationally. Its business has been concerned with telephone calls, the provision of telephone lines and equipment, and private telecommunication networks. T plc has supplemented these services recently by offering mobile phones, which is an expanding market worldwide.

The company maintains a diverse customer base, including residential users, multi-national companies, government agencies and public sector organisations. The company handles approximately 100 million calls each working day, and employs nearly 140,000 personnel.

Strategic development

The Chairman of T plc stated within the latest Annual Report that there are three main areas in which the company aims to develop in order to remain a world leader in the telecommunications market. He believes that the three main growth areas reflect the evolving nature of the telecommunications market and will provide scope for development. The areas in which development is planned are:

- expansion of the telecommunications business in the national and overseas markets, both by the company acting on its own and through partnership arrangements with other suppliers

- diversification into television and multi-media services, providing the hardware to permit telephone shopping from home and broadcasting services

- extension of the joint ventures and strategic alliances which have already been established with companies in North America, Europe, India and the Far East.

The Chairman explained that the company is intent on becoming a world leader in communications. This will be achieved through maintaining its focus on long-term development by improving its services to customers, developing high quality up-to-date products and being innovative, flexible and market-driven. His aim is to deliver a world-class service at competitive cost.

Financial information

Comparative statistics showing extracts from the company's financial performance in its national telecommunications market over the last two years are as follows:

	Last year $ million	Previous year $ million
Turnover	16,613	15,977
Profit before interest and tax	3,323	2,876
Capital employed	22,150	21,300

The Chairman expressed satisfaction with the increase in turnover and stated that cost efficiencies were now being generated following completion of a staff reduction programme.

Business opportunities

The Chief Executive of T plc has stated that the major opportunities for the company lie in the following areas:

- encouraging greater use of the telephone

- provision of advanced services, and research and development into new technology, including the internet and systems integration

- the increasing freedom from government control of worldwide telecommunication services.

An extensive television and poster advertising campaign has been used by the company. This was in order to penetrate further the residential market by encouraging greater use of the telephone with various charging incentives being offered to residential customers.

Markets and competition

The company is currently experiencing an erosion of its market share and faces increasingly strong competition in the mobile phone market. While T plc is the leader in its national market, with an 85% share of the telecommunications business, it has experienced a reduced demand for the supply of residential lines in the last five years as competition has increased. The market for the supply of equipment in the national telecommunications market is perceived to be static.

Industry regulation

The government has established an industry regulatory organisation to promote competition and deter anti-competitive behaviour. As a result of the activities of the regulator and aggressive pricing strategies, it is anticipated that charges to customers will remain constant for at least the next three years.

Required:

(a) Explain the nature of the political, economic, social, and technical forces which influence T plc in developing its business and increasing its market share.

(10 marks)

(b) Apply Ansoff's Product/Market matrix to assess the extent of the potential market development opportunities available to T plc.

(15 marks)

(Total: 25 marks)

Question 4: CSC Clothing

The Clothing Supply Company (CSC) is seen as a market leader in the design and manufacture of garments such as knitwear and weatherproof clothing for outdoor sports. The company is over a hundred years old and is based in rural islands of Scotland where it originally used to make and supply hill farmers with outdoor working clothes. CSC prides itself on the use of traditional fabric designs, the craftsmanship of its garment workers and the fact that it buys much of its cloth from local weavers, so supporting the local economy.

In recent years CSC has achieved a degree of dominance over other specialist Scottish clothing manufacturers. The CSC product range now enjoys an international reputation based not only on design and the quality of handmade tailoring but also on the attractive and well known brand name, which is perceived to be associated with the country lifestyle of wealthy society leaders. CSC garments are distributed to and sold at premium prices through the best department stores in London, New York and Tokyo and are especially popular with overseas tourists visiting the United Kingdom.

CSC had been a family-owned business until 1997 when it was sold to the KZ Corporation, a Pacific Rim-based multinational conglomerate involved in shipbuilding, construction and consumer electronics. The KZ Corporation is keen to maximise what it sees as the global brand potential of CSC and to justify what some KZ managers see as the excessively high price paid to the owner's family for their controlling shares in CSC.

To address these issues, the vice-president of global operations at KZ has commissioned a strategy study to identify ways in which CSC can be integrated into the KZ Corporation.

Required:

(a) Using Porter's diamond, examine the extent to which international location might determine the competitive position of the Clothing Supply Company.

(16 marks)

(b) The strategy study was concerned at the relatively high production cost of CSC clothing products and believed that costs could be substantially reduced by moving production to South East Asia. Evaluate the risks and opportunities presented by this suggestion.

(9 marks)

(Total: 25 marks)

Question 5: Scottish Holidays

A small business operating holiday homes in Scotland wishes to forecast next year's sales for the budget, using moving averages to establish a straight-line trend and seasonal variations. The accountant has assumed that sales are seasonal, with a summer season and a winter season each year.

Seasonal sales for the past seven years have been as follows:

	Sales	
	Summer	*Winter*
	$000	$000
20X4	124	70
20X5	230	180
20X6	310	270
20X7	440	360
20X8	520	470
20X9	650	

New government incentives are due to promote Winter holidays in Scotland for three years, starting in 20X9. The company hopes to be prepared for these and as a first step it has prepared the following analyses as a way of preparing a forecast for sales for Winter 20X9:

Season and year	Actual sales	Seasonal moving average	Centred moving average	Seasonal variation
	$000	$000	$000	$000
Summer 20X4	124			
		97		
Winter 20X4	70		123.5	– 53.5
		150		
Summer 20X5	230		177.5	+ 52.5
		205		
Winter 20X5	180		225.0	– 45.0
		245		
Summer 20X6	310		267.5	+ 42.5
		290		
Winter 20X6	270		322.5	– 52.5
		355		
Summer 20X7	440		377.5	+ 62.5
		400		
Winter 20X7	360		420.0	– 60.0
		440		
Summer 20X8	520		467.5	+ 52.5
		495		
Winter 20X8	470		527.5	– 57.5
		560		
Summer 20X9	650			

Seasonal variations need to add up to zero in the additive model. The seasonal variations calculated so far are:

Year	Summer $000	Winter $000
20X4		− 53.5
20X5	+ 52.5	− 45.0
20X6	+ 42.5	− 52.5
20X7	+ 62.5	− 60.0
20X8	+ 52.5	− 57.5
Total variations	+ 210.0	− 268.5

	Summer	Winter	Total
Number of measurements	4	5	
Average seasonal variation	+ 52.5	− 53.7	− 1.2
Reduce to 0 (share equally)	+ 0.6	+ 0.6	+ 1.2
Adjusted seasonal variation	+ 53.1	− 53.1	0.0

Forecast:

The average increase in sales = $50, 500 each season

Trend in Winter 20X9 = 527.5 + (2 × 50.5) = 628.5

Forecast = 628.5 − 53.1 = 575.4

Required:

Explain the forecast method used by the company and evaluate its validity.

(13 marks)

Question 6: Marcus Aurelius

Marcus Aurelius Ltd is a small supermarket chain, that has 6 shops. Each shop advertises in their local newspapers and the marketing director is interested in the relationship between the amount that they spend on advertising and the sales revenue that they achieve.

The company has just taken on 2 new stores in the same area and the predicted advertising expenditure is expected to be $150,000 for one store and $50,000 for the other.

The marketing director has collated the following information for the 6 shops for the previous year:

Shop	Advertising expenditure $000	Sales revenue $000
1	80	730
2	60	610
3	120	880
4	90	750
5	70	650
6	30	430

She has further performed some calculations to determine forecast sales revenue for the two new shops as follows:

$$b = \frac{n\Sigma xy - \Sigma x \Sigma y}{n\Sigma x^2 - (\Sigma x)^2}$$

$$= \frac{6 \times 326{,}500 - 450 \times 4{,}050}{6 \times 38{,}300 - 450^2}$$

$$= \frac{136{,}500}{27{,}300} = 5$$

$$a = \bar{y} - b\bar{x}$$

$$a = \frac{4{,}050}{6} - 5 \times \frac{450}{6} = 300$$

The regression equation is $y = 300 + 5x$

Coefficient of determination = 0.984

	$000
Expected sales revenue (Shop 7)	1,050
Expected sales revenue (Shop 8)	550

Required:

Explain the calculations and comment on the reliability of the forecasts.

(15 marks)

3 Internal resources, capabilities and competences

Question 7: MW and FS

Background

MW and FS are both supermarket chains which operate in different parts of a country. Both are listed on the country's Stock Exchange. MW operates in the north of the country while FS stores are located predominantly in the south. Recently the Chairman of FS has approached the Chairman of MW and suggested that MW may wish to present a takeover bid for FS. The Chairman of FS has indicated that such a bid would be favourably received by his Board of Directors and would pre-empt a bid being made by other less desirable predators in the industry. According to the Chairman of FS, there would need to be some staff rationalisation and about 10% of the total number of stores of the combined group would need to be sold as a result of demands which would be made by the country's competition regulatory organisation. However, he believes that there would be increased profitability for the combined group as a whole which would lead to improved shareholder value. At this stage, no public announcement of the possible takeover has been made and all the information relating to it is being treated as strictly confidential.

MW

MW was established over 100 years ago by Mr W. His son (KW), who is now over 70 years old, is the Chairman of the company. The W family has maintained strong control over the business and still owns nearly 40% of its shares. The main principle established by Mr W was that of offering quality products at a reasonable price and this principle has been rigidly maintained throughout the company's history.

Organisationally, MW stores are split into two operating areas – the North West and the North East – although it is controlled from its Head Office by KW and his management team. Each individual store is managed locally by a Store Manager and an assistant. In addition, there are supervisors, till checkout staff, store keepers and shelf stackers working in each store. Other skilled trade staff are also employed including butchers, bakers and fishmongers.

Recent results have shown that MW has increased its sales by 8% and its net profit by 15% over the previous year. MW has become a popular share as a result of the company's ability to cut its operating costs and increase its profitability each year.

KW follows the sound principles of business development established by his father. He prefers to rely on a capital structure which is low geared and has generated organic growth rather than undertaking large takeovers. The last time MW undertook a takeover was 25 years ago when it bought six supermarkets. If a bid is made for FS then it is most likely that KW will wish to offer a share exchange rather than pay any cash. He is acutely aware of competition in the industry within the country and has been advised by the Finance Director that there are two other main competitors which may put forward counter-bids if MW makes an offer for FS.

FS

FS's stores operate within the South West and South East of the country. Approximately 55% of its shares are held by ten major institutional shareholders who have been disappointed in recent performance. These institutional shareholders have been impressed by the success of MW and instructed the Chairman to begin takeover negotiations with KW.

Performance of both companies for the last financial year

For simplicity, the data supplied below represents the average for each store in the relevant area. All stores for each company are built to a standard layout. On average, FS stores are 20% smaller in terms of area than MW stores.

	MW		FS	
	North West	North East	South West	South East
	$ million	$ million	$ million	$ million
Turnover	10.0	8.0	6.0	5.0
Cost of sales (excluding wages)	4.0	3.0	2.0	1.8
Overheads				
Salaries	1.0	1.0	0.7	0.6
Non-supervisory wages	1.0	0.7	0.7	0.6
Other overheads	1.0	1.1	1.1	0.9
Local taxes	1.0	0.8	0.7	0.6
Net profit	2.0	1.4	0.8	0.5

Additional information

Per store:	MW		FS	
	North West	North East	South West	South East
Total square metres	6,000	6,000	4,800	4,800
Average number of customer visits	0.3 million	0.25 million	0.15 million	0.1 million
Managers and supervisors	15	12	14	12
Total staff	69	56	56	51

The profit attributable to ordinary shareholders in the last financial year was $225 million for MW and $200 million for FS. Inventory is held centrally by each company in its own secure warehouse. It is issued on a daily basis to each store. On average, each MW store has an inventory turnover of 2 days while each FS store has an inventory turnover of 3.5 days.

Required:

(a) (i)   Produce a SWOT analysis for MW.

(ii) Explain how such an analysis can assist the company in achieving its organisational objectives.

(13 marks)

(b) In your capacity as Management Accountant for MW, prepare an initial briefing report for the Board's consideration prior to any combination of the two businesses which compares the performance of the two businesses. Your report should include an analysis of the data provided in the scenario by making whatever calculations you think appropriate

(12 marks)

(Total: 25 marks)

Question 8: Qualispecs

Qualispecs has a reputation for quality, traditional products. It has a group of optician shops, both rented and owned, from which it sells its spectacles. Recently, it has suffered intense competition and eroding customer loyalty, but a new chief executive has joined from one of its major rivals Fastglass.

Fastglass is capturing Qualispecs' market through partnership with a high street shopping group. These shops install mini-labs in which prescriptions for spectacles are dispensed within an hour. Some competitors have successfully experimented with designer frames and sunglasses. Others have reduced costs through new computer-aided production methods.

Qualispecs has continued to operate as it always has, letting the product 'speak for itself' and failing to utilise advances in technology. Although production costs remain high, Qualispecs is financially secure and has large cash reserves. Fortunately, the country's most popular sports star recently received a prestigious international award wearing a pair of Qualispecs' spectacles.

The new chief executive has established as a priority the need for improved financial performance. Following a review she discovers that:

(i) targets are set centrally and shops report monthly. Site profitability varies enormously, and fixed costs are high in shopping malls

(ii) shops exercise no control over job roles, working conditions, and pay rates

(iii) individual staff pay is increased annually according to a pre-determined pay scale. Everyone also receives a small one-off payment based on group financial performance.

Market analysts predict a slowdown in the national economy but feel that consumer spending will continue to increase, particularly among 18 to 30 year olds.

Required:

(a) Produce a corporate appraisal of Qualispecs, taking account of internal and external factors, and discuss the key strategic challenges facing the company.

(20 marks)

(b) Corporate appraisal offers a 'snapshot' of the present. In order to focus on the future there is a need to develop realistic policies and programmes. Recommend, with reasons, strategies from your appraisal that would enable Qualispecs to build on its past success.

(5 marks)

(Total: 25 marks)

Question 9: Wargrin

Wargrin designs, develops and sells many PC games. Games have a short lifecycle lasting around three years only. Performance of the games is measured by reference to the profits made in each of the expected three years of popularity. Wargrin accepts a net profit of 35% of turnover as reasonable. A rate of contribution (sales price less variable cost) of 75% is also considered acceptable.

Wargrin has a large centralised development department which carries out all the design work before it passes the completed game to the sales and distribution department to market and distribute the product.

Wargrin has developed a brand new game called Stealth and this has the following budgeted performance figures.

The selling price of Stealth will be a constant $30 per game. Analysis of the costs show that at a volume of 10,000 units a total cost of $130,000 is expected. However at a volume of 14,000 units a total cost of $150,000 is expected. If volumes exceed 15,000 units the fixed costs will increase by 50%.

Stealth's budgeted volumes are as follows:

Year	1	2	3
Sales volume (units)	8,000	16,000	4,000

In addition, marketing costs for Stealth will be $60,000 in year one and $40,000 in year two. Design and development costs are all incurred before the game is launched and has cost $300,000 for Stealth. These costs are written off to the statement of profit or loss as incurred (i.e. before year 1 above).

Required:

(a) Explain the principles behind lifecycle costing and briefly state why Wargrin in particular should consider these lifecycle principles.

(4 marks)

(b) Produce the budgeted results for the game 'Stealth' and briefly assess the game's expected performance, taking into account the whole lifecycle of the game.

(9 marks)

(c) Explain why incremental budgeting is a common method of budgeting and outline the main problems with such an approach.

(7 marks)

(Total: 20 marks)

4 Stakeholders, governance and ethics

Question 10: Digwell Explorations

Eastborough is a large region with a rugged, beautiful coastline where rare birds have recently settled on undisturbed cliffs. Since mining ceased 150 years ago, its main industries have been agriculture and fishing. However, today, many communities in Eastborough suffer high unemployment. Government initiatives for regeneration through tourism have met with little success as the area has poor road networks, unsightly derelict buildings and dirty beaches.

Digwell Explorations, a listed company, has a reputation for maximising shareholder returns and has discovered substantial tin reserves in Eastborough. With new technology, mining could be profitable, provide jobs and boost the economy. A number of interest and pressure groups have, however, been vocal in opposing the scheme.

Digwell Explorations, after much lobbying, has just received government permission to undertake mining. It could face difficulties in proceeding because of the likely activity of a group called the Eastborough Protection Alliance. This group includes wildlife protection representatives, villagers worried about the potential increase in traffic congestion and noise, environmentalists, and anti-capitalism groups.

Required:

(a) Discuss the ethical issues that should have been considered by the government when granting permission for mining to go ahead. Explain the conflicts between the main stakeholder groups.

(12 marks)

(b) By use of some (mapping) framework, analyse how the interest and power of pressure and stakeholder groups can be understood. Based on this analysis, identify how Digwell Explorations might respond to these groups.

(13 marks)

(Total: 25 marks)

5 Strategies for competitive advantage

Question 11: A University

A University which derives most of its funds from the government provides undergraduate courses (leading to bachelors' degrees) and post-graduate courses (leading to masters' degrees). Some of its funds come from contributions from student fees, consultancy work and research. In recent years, the University has placed emphasis on recruiting lecturers who have achieved success in delivering good academic research. This has led to the University improving its reputation within its national academic community, and applications from prospective students for its courses have increased.

The University has good student support facilities in respect of a library, which is well-stocked with books and journals and up-to-date IT equipment. It also has a gymnasium and comprehensive sports facilities. Courses at the University are administered by well-qualified and trained non-teaching staff that provide non-academic (that is, not learning-related) support to the lecturers and students.

The University has had no difficulty in filling its courses to the level permitted by the government, but has experienced an increase in the numbers of students who have withdrawn from the first year of their courses after only a few months. An increasing number of students are also transferring from their three-year undergraduate courses to other courses within the University but many have left and gone to different universities. This increasing trend of student withdrawal is having a detrimental effect on the University's income as the government pays only for students who complete a full year of their study.

You are the University's management accountant and have been asked by the vice-chancellor (who is the chief executive of the University) to review the withdrawal rate of students from the University's courses.

(Candidates do not require any knowledge of University admission and withdrawal processes to answer this question.)

Required:

Apply Value Chain Analysis to the University's activities, and advise the vice-chancellor how this analysis will help to determine why the rate of student withdrawal is increasing.

(25 marks)

6 Other elements of strategic choice

Question 12: News Reel Inc

News Reel Inc was incorporated in 1958 and has been wholly owned by members of the Xiang family since that date. The board of directors consists solely of family members. The company manufactures newsprint for sale in the newspaper and magazine industry at a single site in Hoyan Province, to the north west of Eastlandia. Eastlandia is a small island, approximately 200 kilometres off the coast of the mainland continent. In terms of the paper industry, News Reel may be regarded as a small to medium-sized manufacturing company.

The company profile

Markets

The company's major customer has for many years been the Eastlandian Evening Star (EES), for which it is the sole supplier of newsprint. The contract is renewable each year and the price is determined on a cost plus basis.

Historically the EES contract has made up about 30% of the company's revenue, but during the economic recession other business has suffered significantly. As a result the EES contract made up 40% of total revenue in News Reel's last accounting year.

The remaining 60% of sales was mainly to magazines and free newspapers published and circulated across Eastlandia. Frequently orders have been won by News Reel's willingness to provide small quantities of newsprint from short production runs and its promise of prompt delivery.

Raw materials

The major raw material for News Reel is pulp. Rather than rely on the major pulp manufacturers, which import timber from Canada and Scandinavia, the company is supplied exclusively under short-term contracts from a privately-owned Eastlandian mill, Quickpulp Inc, which possess local softwoods.

In recent years News Reel Inc's purchases have accounted for 8% to 10% of Quickpulp Inc's revenue. Whilst these supplies of pulp are slightly more expensive than those that can be purchased from the larger manufacturers, they have the advantage of short and certain delivery times, enabling News Reel to carry negligible inventories of raw materials.

Production

News Reel makes a single product, reels of newsprint. The company's manufacturing operations have been built up over time; as a result a small proportion of its operating non-current assets are replaced each year. Given the scale of its activities, the business is not as capital intensive as many of its larger competitors in the industry; consequently it has a higher proportion of labour costs per tonne of output than the industry average.

In fact, News Reel struggles to compete when tendering for major orders as it uses more pulp per tonne of output than would be the case if it could operate large scale, modern machinery. In compensation however, set-up costs are much lower, and this enables small production runs to be accommodated, ensuring greater flexibility in production scheduling. Due to weak trading volumes the company has only been operating at 70% of productive capacity this year, and a similar level of 30% surplus capacity is expected next year.

KAPLAN PUBLISHING

The competitive environment

The Eastlandian paper industry is dominated by ten listed companies, whose operations are primarily based on the mainland continent. All produce both commodity newsprint and a variety of branded paper products for specialist markets.

There are also a number of smaller companies, of a similar size to News Reel, which mainly specialise in niche markets. A new phenomenon affecting all sectors has been the growth of low-cost, low-quality recycled paper, supported by subsidies from some foreign governments for their own producers.

The paper industry has been affected significantly by the recession, with most companies operating with excess capacity. This in turn has led them to cut margins when tendering for contracts. The following are the features of the competitive environment:

- Depressed pulp and paper prices (a reflection of their historic value).

- The failure of one or two small operators and downsizing by survivors as they rationalise their operations.

- An increased tendency towards diversification

A strategic dilemma

The chairman of News Reel has recently been informed that the EES has been acquired by a multinational and that when the existing commitment expires at the end of this year, the contract to supply newsprint will be put out to tender on an annual basis.

He has also been told that the terms of the new contract will be that all newsprint which the EES requires next year will be supplied by the successful bidder at a predetermined tender price per reel. The bids have to be submitted by 30 November and the successful bid will be announced a month later. The contract will not be awarded solely on the basis of price, but this is likely to be a major factor. At the board meeting to discuss these developments the following views were expressed:

The marketing director

'It has long been my view that we have been over-dependent on EES as a customer. Even if we do win the contract next year, there is no guarantee that we will be able to retain it in the future. In my view it is therefore essential that we seek out new markets and new products.

'In particular we are too small to be a commodity producer of newsprint without the EES contract. We need to develop into niche markets within the paper sector by producing differentiated branded products.

'In fact there is currently an opportunity for us. A small local firm, MedicNote Inc, is currently looking for a buyer. It has been very profitable, specialising in exploiting the growing demand in the market for pharmaceutical paper products, but it has experienced severe cash flow problems recently due to overtrading.'

The production director

'I agree with the need to diversify, but making newsprint is what we are good at. We have no experience in other markets. I have just been told that Quickpulp shareholders are looking to sell the company due to recent losses arising from weak world pulp prices. In my opinion this represents an ideal opportunity to secure pulp supplies at a low cost. I am also in favour of more modern large scale machinery in order to drive down marginal costs. This will enable us to compete in the long run in our core activity.'

The finance director

'Even if an acquisition strategy is felt to be appropriate, it is very difficult to evaluate the feasibility of the two options in precise monetary terms as much will depend on the prices of the two businesses. In my judgement News Reel is sufficiently liquid to fund one or other of the options suggested but, given current uncertainties, it would be difficult to raise finance for both of them.'

Required:

As a management consultant you have been commissioned to prepare briefing notes for the directors of News Reel covering the following areas:

(a) Analyse the company's current strategic position

(14 marks)

(b) Evaluate the future strategic options available to the company by appraising:

- the potential growth strategies that the company could pursue, and

- the particular diversification/acquisition strategies suggested.

(24 marks)

The chairman of News Reel Inc is concerned that the demand or the core product is likely to decline further as people move to digital technologies as means of getting news and information. He is keen to plan ahead for the next ten years so that he can ensure the long term viability of the company for coming generations.

(c) Johnson, Scholes and Whittington identify three strategy lenses; design, experience and ideas. Examine the different roles these lenses might play in the process of long term strategy development at News Reel Inc.

(12 marks)

(Total: 50 marks)

7 Methods of strategic development

Question 13: Pelatihan

Introduction

Pelatihan is a privately-owned training college, which specialises in providing courses in business subjects. Pelatihan was founded in 1992 by its current Chief Executive, who is a qualified lawyer. Pelatihan grew rapidly to become one of the largest and most highly regarded colleges in A, an Asian country.

The general situation in A

The last two decades have been a period of rapid social change for the residents of A. The country's economy has developed from being mainly based on subsistence agriculture (that is, agriculture carried out with the aim of feeding the farmer and his/her family), to being much more progressive in all respects. The population is now fairly well educated, with literacy levels much higher among the under-20 age group than in the older population.

This is partly as a result of government policy (introduced in the 1970s) aimed at making education to age 16 available to all citizens of A. While subsistence agriculture has declined sharply, commercial agriculture still contributes about 40% of the country's Gross National Product (GNP). The fastest developing sectors are manufacturing, food production, tourism, financial services and retail.

A is now regarded as a developed Asian economy, with a well-established business and financial community. A is home to many large industrial and commercial corporations, many of which operate globally. Recently, the economy of A has been growing at a rate of about 15% each year. This is better than the growth rates in neighbouring countries. A has a stable, democratic, political system. Its government has been in power for the last six years. A general election is expected at some time in the next two years, and the government is concerned that the main opposition party may be elected. Unlike a number of other countries in the region, A has no recent history of violent unrest or terrorist activity.

The business training market in A

The business training industry is dominated by three major colleges (of which Pelatihan is one).

There are also a number of smaller colleges. The estimated market shares are shown below.

Market shares %	Pelatihan	Koulos	Opleid	Smaller colleges
Finance & Accounting (F&A) courses	40	15	30	15
Marketing courses	15	40	15	30
Law courses	35	30	25	10
Human Resource Management (HRM) courses	20	25	40	15
Other courses	–	40	20	40

Pelatihan has grown to its current size by means of organic growth. Both Koulos and Opleid, on the other hand, have made several acquisitions of smaller colleges in the last five years. Indeed, there have been rumours of a possible merger between Koulos and Opleid, but there is no evidence to support this. Koulos was founded in 1990 by a group of academics from a university. Opleid was founded in 1994 by an ex-director of Koulos, to specialise in Finance courses. Opleid has since recruited a number of experienced tutors from elsewhere in the industry, including an ex-director of Pelatihan.

An independent survey, reported in the press in early 20X1, made the following comments about the market:

"The business training industry in A is very buoyant in most sectors. Demand for courses in Law and HRM is rising quite rapidly, while the market for Finance courses is also growing (though at a slower rate). Marketing is the only sector in decline, possibly as a result of the growth in online 'e-learning' courses provided by The Marketing Institute".

'The Marketing Institute' (mentioned in the comment) is the professional body responsible for the development of marketing professionals in A. It is not a college. Currently it is the only professional institute in A to offer its own courses, whether online or 'face-to-face'. Other institutes are known to be considering the provision of online courses. Koulos is known to be developing online courses, though Pelatihan has no plans to do so.

The structure and performance of Pelatihan

The Board of Directors of Pelatihan now consists of the Chief Executive and four other directors. They are all senior tutors. Each of the four directors is responsible for a 'faculty' of the college, each of which provides courses in a specialist professional area.

The courses provided by Pelatihan range from one day 'insight' or 'update' courses, on a theoretical or practical topic, to much longer courses leading towards exams for academic and professional qualifications. Courses for diplomas, degrees and professional qualifications require students to attend the college for up to 60 days in any one year. Pelatihan does not provide any full time courses and does not provide any student accommodation.

Almost all the students on one day courses have their courses paid for by their employers. Some students on longer courses are also funded by their employers, but approximately half pay their own tuition fees. The college does not discriminate on price between employer-funded students and those who pay their own fees on individual courses. However, some large employers receive a discount for 'bulk purchase' of places on courses.

The performance of the college during its most recent financial year is summarised in Table 1.

Table 1
Comparison of results
Year ended 30 September 20X1

	Actual	Budget
Sales revenue (A$ Million)		
Finance and Accounting (F&A) faculty	4.2	4.5
Marketing faculty	0.8	1.0
Law faculty	4.0	4.0
HRM faculty	3.1	3.5
Total for Pelatihan	12.1	13.0
Profit (before interest and tax) (A$ Million)		
Finance and Accounting (F&A) faculty	0.6	1.0
Marketing faculty	(0.1)	0.5
Law faculty	0.6	1.0
HRM faculty	0.4	1.0
Corporate and central costs	(1.4)	(1.2)
Total for Pelatihan	0.1	2.3
Staff numbers (equivalent full time employees)		
Finance and Accounting (F&A) faculty	23	*
Marketing faculty	6	*
Law faculty	26	*
HRM faculty	18	*
Corporate and central costs	14	*
Total for Pelatihan	87	*
Student day numbers **		
Finance and Accounting (F&A) faculty	2030	2000
Marketing faculty	410	450
Law faculty	2100	2000
HRM faculty	1150	1500
Total for Pelatihan	5690	5950

*   No budget was set for staff numbers

**   A student day is one student attending for one day

The recent Board meeting of Pelatihan

At a recent Board meeting, the following issues were raised:

- The directors responsible for the F&A and Marketing faculties each raised concerns about a small number of large employer organisations which represent a significant proportion of their faculty's business. These organisations are starting to demand discounts in excess of 20%. This is far higher than the discounts given to other corporate customers. The director of the Law faculty said that one of the law firms she deals with often books up to half of the places on a course, but now demands a discount of 20%.

- The director responsible for the Law faculty reported that two of her tutors had recently resigned, in order to take up positions with Koulos.

- The Chief Executive expressed concern at the poor financial performance of Pelatihan, when compared to the budget for 20X0-X1. He asked for a volunteer to take responsibility for financial planning and control for the new financial year. The director of the F&A faculty said that he could not help, as he was too busy teaching students and dealing with clients. There was no volunteer, so the Chief Executive reluctantly agreed to continue overseeing the work of the three finance staff.

Required:

(a) Using the Boston Consulting Group (BCG) matrix, evaluate the product portfolio of Pelatihan. In the light of this matrix and the information contained in Table 1, comment on the performance of the business.

(13 marks)

(b) Using a technique such as SWOT analysis, analyse the company's overall position.

(12 marks)

(Total: 25 marks)

Question 14: WG plc

Introduction

WG plc was formed four years ago following the merger of two large pharmaceutical companies. Prior to the merger the two companies had been competitors: they believed that by combining forces the shareholders of each company would benefit from increased profits arising from the rationalisation of manufacturing facilities, distribution networks, and concentration of resources towards more focused research and development.

With operating outlets in Europe, Asia, the United States of America and Africa, WG plc regards itself as a global company. It employs approximately 50,000 people worldwide and has developed a wide portfolio of products. Its profits before tax last year increased by 20% and represented approximately 35% of turnover. The company declared that its earnings and dividends per share in the same period each increased by 15% over the previous financial year.

All manufacturers of pharmaceutical products claim that their pricing policies need to be set at a level to achieve high profitability in order to attract funds from investors. They argue that this is necessary to meet their high research and development commitments. In recent years, WG plc and other pharmaceutical manufacturers have encountered public and governmental challenges to their high levels of profitability.

WG plc encounters strong competition from other world-class pharmaceutical manufacturers, but these are few in number. High research and development costs present a major obstacle to potential competitors tempted to enter the industry.

Mission and objectives

The directors of WG plc have defined their overall corporate mission as being to 'combat disease by developing innovative medicines and services and providing them to healthcare organisations for the treatment of patients worldwide'.

The directors have confirmed their main objective is to sustain profitability while achieving the company's overall mission. They have also explained that WG plc aims to work towards eliminating those diseases for which the company is engaged in providing treatments. Achievement of the profitability objective is continually threatened by patents coming to the end of their lives. Patents give the sole right to make, use and sell a new product for a limited period.

Product development

A large proportion of the company's turnover in recent years has been derived from one particular drug. The patent for this drug expires next year and it is expected that its sales at that time will represent no more than 10% of total turnover. Four years ago, the sales of this drug produced almost half the company's entire turnover.

A new product, Coffstop, has now completed its rigorous development phases and is being marketed to pharmaceutical stores throughout the world by WG plc. It is in competition with a similar drug, Peffstill, produced and marketed by a direct competitor of WG plc. Medical research and opinion has concluded that Coffstop is generally more effective than Peffstill in treating the condition for which they are intended. Both drugs are available over the counter from pharmacies. The directors of WG plc are optimistic that Coffstop will become very popular because of its improved effectiveness over other market products.

Market development

WG plc has experienced slow growth in its mature markets of Western Europe, North America and Japan. These markets contribute 80% of overall turnover but their governments have reduced expenditure on pharmaceutical products in recent years. The company has encountered a rapid sales increase in its expanding markets of Eastern Europe, South America, the Asia Pacific region, India, Africa and the Middle East. The directors of the company hold the view that increasing population growth in these markets is likely to provide substantial opportunities for the company over the next two decades.

Research and development

Almost 15% of WG plc's turnover last year was spent on research and development. WG plc has the largest research and development organisation of all pharmaceutical companies worldwide.

Much research is sponsored by national governments and world health organisations. A major piece of research which has recently been undertaken relates to new treatments for malaria as the disease is now demonstrating some resistance to existing treatments. WG plc has established a 'donation programme' for the new drug in virulent areas for the disease. This means that the company is donating batches of the drug to the health organisations in these areas. The cost of this programme is offset by the sales of the new drug in other areas of the world by making it available to people proposing to travel to the regions where malaria is widespread.

Required:

(a) Evaluate the nature and importance of the market threat which WG plc would face if it failed to provide sufficient resources for product development.

(10 marks)

(b) Discuss the practical issues which the directors of WG plc would need to consider if the company entered a strategic alliance with a competitor for the joint development of future pharmaceutical products.

(10 marks)

(Total: 20 marks)

8 Organisational structure

Question 15: Multinational company

A multinational company which makes and sells consumer durables is reviewing the future organisational structure of its European operations, which employ over 100,000 people.

Development of the company

The company has expanded rapidly in the late 1940s and 1950s. Separate marketing companies were established in all the main European countries to serve the distinctive needs of the markets in each individual country, with some manufacturing facilities in the larger countries. Some exports to other smaller European markets had also been made. A divisional structure was adopted which permitted considerable freedom to individual country managers, who were responsible for all operations in their country. They could decide what models to design, make and sell, the marketing and pricing strategy, and the sourcing.

The industry background

There has been progressive integration of European economies, making cross-border transactions easier. The consumer durable industry has also become much more competitive and cost-conscious, and is faced with considerable overcapacity. New product models can no longer be justified for one country only, but are designed for sale in all countries, and made in one or two chosen plants (possibly in Eastern Europe, with cheaper labour) to serve all markets.

The company now

Although the country-based divisional structure is still in place, most key decisions are now taken at European Head Office. These include the selection of new models to make and sell, and the plants at which these models are to be made, whether these are existing plants or new plants in cheap labour areas.

Local markets are still distinctive with different taxation, distribution costs and pricing structures. Individual country managers still set country selling prices, although comparisons of prices across Europe reveal considerable anomalies. Manufacturing facilities are still operated in major countries, even though it is difficult to justify continuing investment without government subsidy.

Required:

Discuss the potential problems of the present country-based divisional structure and its effectiveness as Europe becomes more integrated and cross-border transactions become easier.

Recommend, with reasons, whether the present divisional organisational structure should be retained, and if this is not supported, recommend an alternative.

(25 marks)

Question 16: QS Software – Part 1

QS is a small software design company, set up in May 20X0 by two graduates, John Jones and Sam Smith. Since it started, it has built a strong local reputation, working with a range of small- to medium-sized businesses to design and develop software applications. It also occasionally advises businesses on hardware installation. It also runs a retail shop, where it constructs and sells custom-made computers to individuals and undertakes repairs and maintenance in a workshop located behind the shop. The design and development team are located above the shop.

Organisation chart

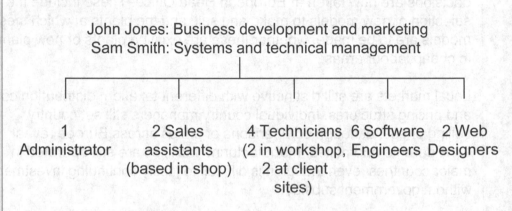

John Jones: Business development and marketing
Sam Smith: Systems and technical management

| 1 Administrator | 2 Sales assistants (based in shop) | 4 Technicians (2 in workshop, 2 at client sites) | 6 Software Engineers | 2 Web Designers |

Both owners recognise that the quality of products and services is vital in such a highly competitive market and, to date, QS has managed to maintain a high quality of customer service by focusing only upon individuals customers and small- to medium-sized businesses.

New business opportunity: Regal Global Advertising (RGA)

In August 20X6, John Jones met an old university friend who was working as the IT manager of a large local marketing company called Regal Global Advertising (RGA). It emerged that RGA was looking to invest in setting up a new customer database and website. RGA was also considering re-investing in new hardware throughout the organisation, which would require an on-going maintenance facility. The customer database and website would need to be in place and fully operational by 30 May 20X8.

On returning to the office, John began to put together an outline tender document and an outline project plan. However, Sam Smith, the other partner, was reluctant to take on such a large project as they had no previous experience of managing work on this scale and, more importantly, they already had sufficient work with existing clients for the foreseeable future. John's response to Sam's concerns of maintaining quality for existing customers was: 'Don't worry, we'll fit it in around everything else – there's plenty of time to get it all done'. As John was responsible for new business, which in the past had always been successful, Sam agreed to allow the tender to progress.

John Jones and Sam Smith both have ambitions to develop QS into a major software company, and they are already considering how they should be planning the structure of the organisation to cope with the demands of growing and succeeding in the competitive software industry.

They believe that the future success of the company will depend primarily on the initiative and ingenuity of the IT specialists that the company employs. They are hoping that within a few years, they will be able to take more of a 'back seat' role in the management and direction of the company.

Their ideas about organisation structure have been influenced by the analysis by Mintzberg of an organisation into five elements.

Required:

(a) Analyse the current organisational structure of QS and identify any advantages and disadvantages this structural form might have in the business environment in which QS operates.

(12 marks)

(b) Describe the five elements in an organisation into which Mintzberg suggested that employees can be divided and suggest how this analysis by Mintzberg might apply to the future organisation structure of QS.

(13 marks)

(Total: 25 marks)

9 Business process change

Question 17: Nikki Photocopiers

Nikki Photocopiers manufactures and sells photocopiers to businesses throughout Europe. The market is highly competitive with major global players present.

Despite earlier success, the firm has recently seen a downturn in its performance as typified by the following customer ratings in **European Business Photocopier Magazine:**

	Rating (last year's rating in brackets)
Value for money	2nd (1st)
Features	2nd (3rd)
Reliability	3rd (2nd)
Servicing and maintenance	7th (5th)

Last year the firm introduced a customer relationship management (CRM) software system so the fall in the service rating was a surprise. Before this survey had been published the directors had planned to redesign research and production processes but, based on this feedback, decided to look at the customer servicing and maintenance process first. Outsourcing was rejected as an option and the focus was placed on reengineering the process instead.

Current process

CURRENT PROCESS

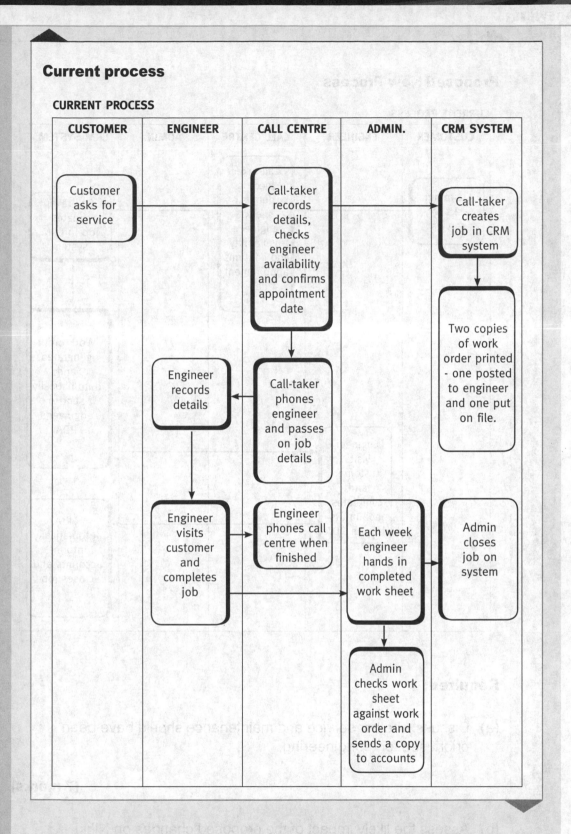

Proposed New Process

CURRENT PROCESS

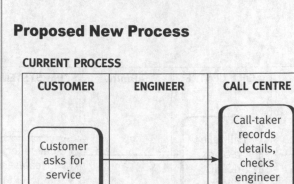

CUSTOMER	ENGINEER	CALL CENTRE	ADMIN.	CRM SYSTEM
Customer asks for service		Call-taker records details, checks engineer availability and confirms appointment date		Call-taker creates job in CRM system
				Work order generated and automatically sent to engineer's PDA
	Engineer visits customer and completes job. Inputs data on PDA			CRM automatically informs accounts and closes job

Required:

(a) Discuss whether service and maintenance should have been prioritised for reengineering.

(7 marks)

(b) Assess the likely impact of the proposed changes on Nikki Photocopiers' competitive advantage.

(6 marks)

(c) Outline the IT/IS implications of the proposal.

(5 marks)

(d) Outline the arguments for and against outsourcing maintenance.

(7 marks)

(Total: 25 marks)

Question 18: Institute of Information Systems Administrators

The Institute of Information System Administrators (IISA) holds examinations all over the world. Every six months 200,000 students in 450 centres in 75 different countries take one or more papers in the Institute's six-paper qualification. The examinations are conventional three-hour examinations with the candidates writing answers in script answer books similar to those used by ACCA. The current system (described below) is both costly and time-consuming and so the Institute has set up a project to look at the feasibility of on-line marking, where markers download images of the scripts and mark them on a Personal Computer. An outline of the proposed system is also described below.

Current System

At present the script answer books completed by the students are taken from the examination room by the invigilator and sent by secure courier to the IISA head office in London. From here, the scripts are sent by courier to examiners, who select and despatch scripts (again by secure courier) to markers. Once the scripts are marked they are returned to the IISA head office who arrange for them to be checked. This is an arithmetic check, making sure that the total for each question and script is correct. Once scripts have been checked, the marks for each question answered on the script are entered into a computer system. This system provides statistical analysis of the marks as well as printing certificates for successful candidates. A selection of the scripts is sent (again by courier) to the examiners for moderation, i.e. to check that markers have correctly applied the approved marking scheme. The examiners are also sent scripts where arithmetic errors have been found. All scripts are stored at the IISA head office. There are currently 6 examiners, 500 markers and 250 checkers.

Proposed System

The On-Line Marking Project (OLMAP) proposes that all script answer books are taken from the examination room by the invigilator and sent by secure courier to a document-imaging centre in Singapore. Here, the hand-written scripts will be scanned into a computer system. Examiners will be provided with on-line access (via the Internet) and they will be able to allocate a script to a particular marker. Once this allocation has taken place, the script is available for on-line marking. The marker is given access via the Internet and is able to download allocated scripts on the computer screen, where they may be marked using simple mouse movements. The software assists the marker by adding up the marks automatically, so no arithmetic script checking is required. At any time an examiner can download marked scripts to undertake moderation. This is made particularly effective by the system allowing the 'hiding' of marks given to the script by the original marker. Certificates will also be printed from this system.

Project Issues

The project manager for the project is Margaret Mendoza. She is impatient to progress the project and has identified a software package Emark, marketed by a multinational software company, which appears to fulfil the requirements. She believes that all examination subjects should use the package commencing with the examination session in 12 months' time. She is committed to a direct changeover/conversion approach as 'parallel running is just not a possibility in this situation'. However, the package is comparatively expensive, is untried in a world-wide application, and has received some criticism from an IT examiner, Sue Yorke, who has attended a demonstration of the Emark software.

The sponsor of the project is Mike Palmer. Mike is concerned about Margaret's enthusiasm and impatience and wants a slower and more reflective approach to the project. He would like to see the software used in a pilot run, employing it on just one or two examinations at first. One of the reasons for this is his concern about the performance of the software, as he is worried that a slow response time will make the system unusable. Sue Yorke has suggested that it could be used on her IT paper, where markers are IT literate and enthusiastic to adopt the new marking software. In contrast to Margaret, Mike is in favour of a bespoke development (either in-house or using an external software house) with the eventual goal of making the software commercially available to other examining bodies.

Required:

(a) Margaret Mendoza advocates the purchase of a software package, whilst Mike Palmer wishes to go for a bespoke application. Discuss whether a software package or a bespoke solution should be used.

(12 marks)

(b) Mike Palmer has already expressed concerns about potential performance problems with the software. Explain how the on-line marking application could be tested.

(5 marks)

(c) Discuss whether parallel running or direct changeover is more appropriate in this situation.

(8 marks)

(Total: 25 marks)

10 The role of information technology

Question 19: SDW

The SDW Company has been trading for one year. It provides rail travel services between three major cities in the country in which it operates.

Mr M, the majority shareholder and managing director, is keen to expand its operations and, in particular, to use the internet as the major selling medium. He has discovered, for example, that doubling sales on the internet usually results in no additional costs. However, doubling sales using a call centre normally results in a doubling of staff and an increase in costs.

All tickets are currently sold via the company's call centre. The company has an internet site although this is used for publicity only, not for sales or marketing. Competitors currently use a mixture of selling media, although detailed information on the success of each medium is not available to the SDW Company.

Mr M has asked you, as a qualified management accountant, to assist him in upgrading the company's internet site and, in particular, showing how this will help to reduce operating costs.

Required:

(a) Advise Mr M on how to establish and implement an appropriate internet strategy for the SDW Company.

(13 marks)

(b) Discuss the key customer-orientated features of an internet site, showing how these can be used to meet the objective of cost reduction required by Mr M.

(12 marks)

(Total: 25 marks)

Question 20: MACOMP

Introduction

MACOMP is a small manufacturer of replacement machine components for machinery used in the mining and oil exploration industries. It is based in an African country, Zedland. It was formed in 1952, as a partnership between two engineers, and incorporated in 1977.

MACOMP now employs 120 staff, and has an annual turnover equivalent to one million US dollars. MACOMP is proud to offer the very highest levels of customer service. Much of the machinery used by MACOMP's customers is quite old and, as a result, components are no longer available from the original equipment manufacturers (OEMs), most of which are large multinational companies. MACOMP mostly supplies parts directly to the end-users but also receives a small but significant proportion of its business from OEMs, who then supply the components to their customers.

The current business model

MACOMP has always run its business in a very traditional way. The sales manager receives most orders by telephone or fax. The order specifies the OEM part number that the component is to replace. If MACOMP has previously supplied that component, the sales manager checks the price list and tells the customer the price. MACOMP holds very low levels of finished goods inventory, and then only of the most commonly ordered components.

Where MACOMP needs to make a component for the first time, an MACOMP 'estimator' (a qualified engineer, responsible for producing an estimate of the material and labour involved in manufacturing the item) obtains the original drawings of the component, either from MACOMP's extensive archives or from the OEM. The estimator then produces detailed engineering drawings, a list of materials and parts required, and an estimate of the labour hours likely to be used at each stage of the manufacturing process. The estimate is passed to a costing clerk in the accounts department who calculates the likely product cost (labour, materials and overheads), adds a 'mark-up' of 50%, and advises the sales manager of the price. If the customer accepts the price, an order is passed to the production department, which schedules and completes the work. If the actual cost of production is significantly different from that estimated, the price list is amended to reflect the actual manufacturing cost.

Very occasionally, a customer sends (or brings in) an old component, which cannot be traced back to an OEM. The sales manager gives the component to an estimator, who dismantles the component and produces the necessary engineering drawings and estimate. This process is called 'reverse engineering', and is common in the component manufacturing industry. Reverse engineering currently accounts for about 5% of MACOMP's business.

When an order is fulfilled, the component is delivered to the customer, together with an invoice. Most customers pay within 30 days, by cash or cheque. MACOMP does not have a problem with bad debts. An increasing proportion of MACOMP's business is now transacted in US dollars, as African currencies tend to be unstable.

MACOMP prides itself on the personal service it provides. The close contact it has with its customers means that MACOMP receives a significant amount of repeat business. MACOMP has never advertised its services, but grew significantly until 20X9 as a result of 'word of mouth' recommendations by satisfied customers. MACOMP, however, has not experienced growth for the last two years, although turnover and profit have remained stable.

MACOMP uses only very basic Information Systems (IS), and reports its performance using a simple comparison between budget and actual, which is produced using a spreadsheet package. MACOMP's accounting system is not automated, and transactions are recorded in traditional ledgers.

Project E: Computerised accounting and e-commerce systems

The sales manager of MACOMP has noticed that customers are increasingly mentioning that they would like to be able to order online. He knows that there has been a significant growth in business-to-business (B2B) e-commerce in recent years. The sales manager has recognised that in order to grow and to make a move into e-commerce possible, MACOMP's accounting system will have to be updated to a computerised one.

Having spoken to a number of potential suppliers, the sales manager has now received a proposal from SSS, a local company, to supply tailored 'off-the-shelf' systems for both accounting and e-commerce.

The sales manager believes that, following implementation of the new systems e-commerce could lead to an increase in the company's turnover of 10% each year for the foreseeable future. However, the sales manager thinks that a cautious approach should be taken and that the system may only lead to strategic advantages for around 5 years, after which time competitors are likely to have caught up and developed similar systems.

The sales manager also thinks that any increase in indirect costs as a result of this higher volume of business will be fully offset by a reduction in administration workload as a result of the new computerised accounting system. The mark-up on products sold by e-commerce will be the same as at present (that is, 50%).

Required:

(a) Briefly explain how e-commerce has impacted on the way business is conducted and briefly discuss how a new Information Systems (IS) strategy might impact upon corporate and business strategies.

(12 marks)

(b) Using a model such as Porters value chain, explain how the e-commerce investment could benefit the activities of MACOMP.

(13 marks)

(Total: 25 marks)

Question 21: RBT

RBT manufactures tractors, harvesting machinery and similar farm equipment. It operates from one integrated office and factory near the capital of the country in which it is based. Due to restricted demand and the cost of manufacture of individual items, all equipment is manufactured to specific orders from clients. No inventories of finished goods are maintained although inventories of spare parts are available for sale.

The farm equipment is sold to farm owners by one of 20 sales representatives. The general procedure for making a sale is for the representative to visit the farm owner to discuss the owner's requirements. Basic price and model specification information are obtained from printed manuals that the representative carries. The representative then telephones the RBT office and confirms with production staff that the order can be made, checks the price and receives an estimated delivery date. An order confirmation is written out and the representative moves on to the next appointment. The farmer pays for the equipment on receipt.

As the country in which RBT operates is large, representatives cannot often visit RBT's office, so their price and model specification manuals may be out of date.

The Board of RBT is considering the introduction of a new information system. Each representative will be given a portable PC. Information on such things as products and prices will be kept on an Intranet and downloaded by telephone line when needed by the representative. Access to production managers and sales representatives will also be made via the Intranet. The voice telephone system will be discontinued and e-mail is thought to be unnecessary.

Required:

(a) Evaluate the proposed use of the Intranet within the RBT Company showing whether it would provide an appropriate communication channel for the sales representatives. Suggest ways in which any problems you have identified with the new systems may be resolved.

(b) Identify and evaluate any information systems that can be used to provide clients with information on the progress of their orders with RBT while they are being manufactured.

11 Marketing

Question 22: Marketing

Prendips is a national company which has been built up over many years primarily through an acquisition strategy. It now has three distinct subsidiaries in the UK and group head office is assessing how each subsidiary's product should be marketed. The three subsidiaries are as follows:

- ABC Inc makes and sells machine parts which are used in the manufacture of 10 pin bowling machines.

- DEF Ltd sells fridges, freezers and cookers to the general public.

- GHI Inc manufactures and sells kids jelly sweet candy.

Discuss how the marketing mix could be used to sell each of the subsidiary's products.

(25 marks)

Question 23: Motor Car Pricing

A producer of high quality executive motor cars has developed a new model which it knows to be very advanced both technically and in style compared to the competition in its market segment.

The company's reputation for high quality is well-established and its servicing network in its major markets is excellent. However, its record in timely delivery has not been so good in previous years, though this has been improving considerably.

In the past few years it has introduced annual variations/improvements in its major models. When it launched a major new vehicle some six years ago the recommended retail price was so low in relation to the excellent specification of the car that a tremendous demand built up quickly and a two-year waiting list for the car developed within six months. Within three months a second-hand model had been sold at an auction for nearly 50% more than the list price and even after a year of production a sizeable premium above list price was being obtained.

The company considers that, in relation to the competition, the proposed new model will be as attractive as was its predecessor six years ago. Control of costs is very good so that accurate cost data for the new model are to hand. For the previous model, the company assessed the long-term targeted annual production level and calculated its prices on that basis. In the first year production was 30% of that total.

For the present model the company expects that the relationship between first-year production and longer-term annual production will also be about 30%, though the absolute levels in both cases are expected to be higher than previously.

The senior management committee, of which you are a member, has been asked to recommend the pricing approach that the company should adopt for the new model.

Required:

List the major pricing approaches available in this situation and discuss some of the relative merits and disadvantages to the company of each approach in the context of the new model. Recommend which approach you would propose, giving your reasons.

(15 marks)

12 Project management I

Question 24: Risk management

(a) Explain what is meant by the term 'risk management' when applied to information systems.

(b) Explain how risks in information systems can be classified, and the various approaches that might be taken to manage information system risk.

(c) Explain four factors that could result in information system failure.

(d) Explain four measures that could be used to assess systems success.

Question 25: MN plc

MN plc has a rolling programme of investment decisions. One of these investment decisions is to consider mutually-exclusive investments A, B and C. The following information has been produced by the investment manager.

	Investment decision A £	Investment decision B £	Investment decision C £
Initial investment	105,000	187,000	245,000
Cash inflow for A: years 1 to 3	48,000		
Cash inflow for B: years 1 to 6		48,000	
Cash inflow for C: years 1 to 9			48,000
Net present value (NPV) at 10% each year	14,376	22,040	31,432
Ranking	3rd	2nd	1st
Internal rate of return (IRR)	17.5%	14%	13%
Ranking	1st	2nd	3rd

Required:

(a) Prepare a report for the management of MN plc which includes:

 – a statement of the reasons for differences between NPV and IRR rankings – use investment A to illustrate the points you make;

 – a brief summary which gives MN plc's management advice on which project should be selected.

(9 marks)

(b) One of the directors has suggested using payback to assess the investments. Explain to him the advantages and disadvantages of using payback methods over IRR and NPV. Use the figures above to illustrate your answer.

(7 marks)

(Total: 16 marks)

Question 26: Ski Runs

A landowner in an area of the country which has high mountain peaks proposes to develop a number of ski runs down the side of a mountain. The runs will be approximately 5 km long, dropping 1,000 metres from the mountain's summit to a car park. Two alternative strategies (each giving the same capacity) are being considered for the development:

Investment levels

Low investment, involving the construction of a series of tows to haul skiers from the car park to the summit: the initial cost of constructing the tows will be $250,000 and tow motors will have to be replaced after five years at a cost of $50,000; operating costs will be $90,000 per year (fixed) and $3.50 per skier (variable).

High investment, involving the construction of a cable-car system giving a non-stop ride to the summit: the initial cost of constructing the lift will be $1,200,000; operating costs will be $30,000 per year (fixed) and $1 per skier (variable).

The regional tourist board will subsidise the initial construction cost of the development (using either strategy) by providing a loan for half the value of the initial construction cost. The loan is at an interest rate of 4% repayable over six years on an annuity basis. The tourist board requires (as a condition of the loan) that a flat fee of $8 is charged for each skier towed/lifted to the summit.

Number of skiers

The number of skiers using the runs will be dependent on the quality of snow cover. The better the snow cover, then the more runs it will be possible to open and the longer will the runs be able to stay open. The landowner forecasts that in any ten-year period, and assuming an $8 fee, the seasons will be as follows:

Quality of snow cover	Number of seasons	Number of skiers
Good	3	60,000
Moderate	4	40,000
Poor	3	5,000

Business risks

The landowner has stated:

'Although the quality of snow cover is unpredictable for any one year, we can determine the expected outcome for an average year using probabilities and base our investment appraisal and business plan on that.'

A business adviser has commented on this statement as follows:

'The whole problem about winter sports in this country is the variability and unpredictability of snow cover. On average, conditions are as good as any in on the continent. However, if your first three seasons are poor then this could have a devastating effect on project viability.'

Financial returns

The landowner's cost of money is 12% per annum and in appraising investments he considers cash flows over a ten-year period only. He has ignored fixed costs from the assessment due to their nature, but included the cost of the loan repayments as a relevant cash flow.

His calculations are as follows:

Time		Cash flow Low $000	High $000	12% DF	NPV Low $000	High $000
0	Construction	(250.0)	(1,200.0)	1	(250.0)	(1,200.0)
0	Tourist Board loan	125.0	600.0	1	125.0	600.0
1–10	Fee income	284.0	284.0	5.650	1604.6	1604.6
1–10	Variable costs					
	($3.50/$1 × 35.5)	(124.3)	(35.5)	5.650	(702.3)	(200.6)
5	Replacement motors	(50.0)		0.567	(28.4)	
1–6	Loan repayments	(23.8)	(114.5)	4.111	(97.8)	(470.7)
	NPV				651.1	333.3

Note on loan repayments: 4% 6 yr annuity factor = 5.242. Annual repayments = 125/5.242 = 23.8.

On this basis the landowner has decided to make the low level of investment.

Required:

(a) Explain and briefly assess the landowners financial appraisal of the project. Your answer should include an explanation on why finance-related cash flows (loan drawdowns, interest payments and loan repayments) are normally excluded from project appraisal exercises, and identify the circumstances when such cash flows are included in the appraisal.

(13 marks)

(b) Explain the full range of risks and uncertainties involved in the project at the outset. Explain how these can be incorporated and allowed for in appraisal of the project.

(12 marks)

(Total: 25 marks)

13 Project management II

Question 27: QS Software – Part 2

(Part 1 of this question was covered in an earlier chapter and should be read before attempting this part of the scenario.)

QS was awarded the contract to undertake the project at the end of October 20X7.

Project scope

The project was to be completed by 30 May 20X8, 30 calendar weeks after the award of the contract, with the design and delivery of a customer database, which could be utilised by the customers through access to a re-designed website. In addition, there was an option to extend the contract for a further 12 months for systems maintenance. This would be negotiated and finalised only after successful project completion and systems performance evaluation.

Project resources

Sam Smith was assigned the role of project manager, with responsibility for managing the delivery of the final project to RGA. It was planned that three of the software engineers and one of the workshop technicians would work full-time on the project. However, due to QS already being committed to other jobs, Sam allowed these core staff to be released from the RGA work when necessary. Other QS staff were to be assigned temporarily to the RGA project as and when they were needed.

John Jones agreed to act as liaison between the project team and the IT manager of RGA, as he considered it to be his project, having won the contract. However, John would not be directly involved in the day-to-day activities of the project.

Sam was not happy about being responsible for team management and co-ordination. He preferred the technical work to managing people and had little experience of team leadership and delegation. No contract undertaken by QS previously had required this level of project management.

Project progress

Phase one of the project began one week late, due to one software engineer working on another job. It was agreed at this point by Sam and John that, to save time, the purchase of the hardware could be brought forward. However, the first stage payment had not yet been made and the purchases had to be made by extending the overdraft facility. John was confident that the first key payment milestone would be reached and the financial concerns would be short-lived.

The website and customer database were completed on time, but prototype construction had to be delayed, as Sam allowed the technician to work on other jobs during this time. (Sam was not fully aware of all the details of the project plan as he had not been involved at the planning stage, and he and John rarely saw each other. Sam himself was often absent visiting other clients.) The first stage deadline was missed. Although technically the project was progressing as planned, the main concern for Sam Smith was the availability of staff to complete key stages. Although other existing work being carried out by QS was small in comparison to the RGA project, these customers also required a quality service and commitment to deadlines. The second stage deadline was in danger of being missed.

In March, the IT manager from RGA contacted John Jones to demand an explanation for the project delays. He was also concerned that so few staff of QS were working on the project, in particular the lack of visibility of the project manager. The IT manager demanded a meeting with both Sam and John to review the current project status. John also spoke to QS's bank manager who was concerned about the current overdraft facility.

A small business adviser was assigned from the bank to assist QS for the remainder of the project.

Project review meeting – 2 April 20X8

John called an emergency meeting with Sam, the other key project team members and the small business adviser. The main issues which arose from the meeting were as follows.

- The designers were concerned that they did not know which work to prioritise.

- The project team members were not aware of any deadlines for the RGA project, as no one had shown them a project plan or schedule of work.

- Sam argued that he was not a trained project manager and could not be expected to manage such a large undertaking and be responsible for all of the other smaller jobs in progress.

- The cash resources of the business were in a critical state. QS could not afford to miss another stage deadline or lose the lucrative maintenance contract.

Required:

(a) Identify the problems currently being encountered by Sam in managing the project team of the RGA Project.

(13 marks)

(b) Recommend ways in which the managers of QS could improve the management of the project team.

(12 marks)

(Total: 25 marks)

14 The role of finance in formulating and implementing business strategy

Question 28: Multinational and local authority

All organisations have objectives in some form or another. The methods of setting these objectives vary depending on the nature of the organisation. After they have been set and an appropriate period of time has elapsed, organisations should assess to what extent their objectives have been achieved.

Two organisations with very different characteristics set strategic objectives and evaluate their achievement. The two organisations are:

- a publicly-funded local administrative authority which provides housing, education, social and road maintenance services for an area within a country, and

- a multinational conglomerate company (MNC).

Required:

(a) Explain the differences between how the local administrative authority and the MNC should set their strategic objectives.

(10 marks)

(b) Discuss how each organisation should assess how well it has performed in respect of the attainment of its strategic objectives.

(15 marks)

(Total: 25 marks)

Question 29: Spartan Inc.

It is easier to revise sources of finance and ratios using a question.

Spartan Inc. is a medium-sized manufacturing company that plans to increase capacity by purchasing new machinery at an initial cost of $3m. The following are the most recent financial statements of the company:

Statement of profit or loss for the years ending 31 December

	20X6	20X5
	$000	$000
Turnover	5,000	5,000
Cost of sales	3,100	3,000
Gross profit	1,900	2,000
Administration and distribution expenses	400	250
Profit before interest and tax	1,500	1,750
Interest	400	380
Profit before tax	1,100	1,370
Tax	330	400
Profit after tax	770	970
Dividends	390	390
Retained earnings	380	580

Balance sheets (statements of financial position) as at 31 December

	20X6		20X5	
	$000	$000	$000	$000
Non-current assets		6,500		6,400
Current assets				
Inventories	1,170		1,000	
Debtors	850		900	
Cash	130		100	
	2,150		2,000	
Total assets		8,650		8,400
Equity and liabilities				
Share capital				
Ordinary shares ($1 each)		3,500		3,500
Reserves		500		120
		4,000		3,620
10% Loan notes 2011		3,500		3,500
Current liabilities		1,150		1,280
Total equity and liabilities		8,650		8,400

The investment is expected to increase annual sales by 5,500 units. Investment in replacement machinery would be needed after five years. Financial data on the additional units to be sold is as follows:

Selling price per unit	$500
Production costs per unit	$200

- Variable administration and distribution expenses are expected to increase by $220,000 per year as a result of the increase in capacity.

- In addition to the initial investment in new machinery, $400,000 would need to be invested in working capital.

- The full amount of the initial investment in new machinery of $3 million will give rise to capital allowances on a 25% per year reducing balance basis. The scrap value of the machinery after five years is expected to be negligible.

- Tax liabilities are paid in the year in which they arise and Spartan Inc. pays tax at 30% of annual profits.

- The Finance Director of Spartan has proposed that the $3.4 million investment should be financed by an issue of loan notes at a fixed rate of 8% per year.

- Spartan uses an after-tax discount rate of 12% to evaluate investment proposals. In preparing its financial statements, Spartan uses straight-line depreciation over the expected life of fixed assets.

- Average data for the business sector in which Spartan operates is as follows:

    - Gearing (book value of debt/book value of equity) 100%

    - Interest cover 4 times

    - Current ratio 2:1

    - Inventory days 90 days.

Required:

(a) Suggest alternative sources of finance that Spartan could use, outlining the advantages and disadvantages of each.

(b) Analyse and comment on the recent financial performance of the company.

(c) Calculate the effect on the gearing and interest cover of Spartan Inc. of financing the proposed investment with an issue of loan notes and compare your results with the sector averages.

Question 30: Bits and Pieces

Bits and Pieces (B&P) operates a retail store selling spares and accessories for the car market. The store has previously only opened for six days per week for the 50 working weeks in the year, but B&P is now considering also opening on Sundays. The sales of the business on Monday through to Saturday averages at $10,000 per day with average gross profit of 70% earned.

B&P expects that the gross profit % earned on a Sunday will be 20 percentage points lower than the average earned on the other days in the week. This is because they plan to offer substantial discounts and promotions on a Sunday to attract customers. Given the price reduction, Sunday sales revenues are expected to be 60% more than the average daily sales revenues for the other days. These Sunday sales estimates are for new customers only, with no allowance being made for those customers that may transfer from other days.

B&P buys all its goods from one supplier. This supplier gives a 5% discount on all purchases if annual spend exceeds $1,000,000. It has been agreed to pay time and a half to sales assistants that work on Sundays. The normal hourly rate is $20 per hour. In total five sales assistants will be needed for the six hours that the store will be open on a Sunday. They will also be able to take a half-day off (four hours) during the week. Staffing levels will be allowed to reduce slightly during the week to avoid extra costs being incurred.

The staff will have to be supervised by a manager, currently employed by the company and paid an annual salary of $80,000. If he works on a Sunday he will take the equivalent time off during the week when the assistant manager is available to cover for him at no extra cost to B&P. He will also be paid a bonus of 1% of the extra sales generated on the Sunday project.

The store will have to be lit at a cost of $30 per hour and heated at a cost of $45 per hour. The heating will come on two hours before the store opens in the 25 'winter' weeks to make sure it is warm enough for customers to come in at opening time. The store is not heated in the other weeks.

The rent of the store amounts to $420,000 annum.

Required:

(a) Calculate whether the Sunday opening incremental revenue exceeds the incremental costs over a year (ignore inventory movements) and on this basis reach a conclusion as to whether Sunday opening is financially justifiable.

(12 marks)

(b) Discuss whether the manager's pay deal (time off and bonus) is likely to motivate him.

(4 marks)

(c) Briefly discuss whether offering substantial price discounts and promotions on Sunday is a good suggestion.

(4 marks)

(Total: 20 marks)

Question 31: Teemo

The holding company of Teemo, a manufacturer, have had a shake up at all levels of Teemo's organisational organisation. A new board has been appointed as well as many new senior managers. The newly-appointed Managing Director of Teemo has lots of experience in the industry but very little accounting knowledge. She has received a variance report for Month 6, which is shown below:

Month 6 Variance Report

	Favourable	Adverse	$
Expected profit on actual sales			38,000
Production variances			
	$	$	
Materials price		6,300	
Materials usage		6,000	
Labour rate	5,400		
Labour efficiency		2,400	
Variable overhead expenditure	–	–	
Variable overhead efficiency		1,200	
Fixed overhead		4,000	
	5,040	19,900	14,860
Actual profit			11,140

The previous managing director was focused on cost control and was less concerned about the performance of the sales department. The new MD has asked the new finance director to provide some idea of the performance of the sales team and to explain the variance report to her so that she can make a judgement on the performance of the company over the last month. She would like to know what the budgeted contribution was before she makes a judgement on the overall performance.

The finance director has gathered together the following information prior to preparing his report.

(1) Teemo produces one type of product. It operates a standard marginal costing system.

(2) The standard unit cost and price of the product is as follows:

	$	$
Selling price		250
Direct material (5kg at $20)	100	
Direct labour (4 hours at $10)	40	
Variable overheads	20	160
Contribution		90

(3) The variable overhead absorption rate is based on direct labour hours. The company has budgeted fixed overheads of £70,000 per month.

(4) Budgeted sales and production levels are 1,000 units per month.

(5) 1,200 units were actually produced and sold in month 6.

(6) The actual direct materials purchased and used was 6,300 kg costing £132,300 and the actual direct labour hours worked were 5,040 hours.

Required:

Prepare a report for the Managing Director of FX that explains and interprets the Month 6 variance report.

(14 marks)

Question 32: Tupik

A manufacturing company, Tupik, makes and sells two products A and B, each of which passes through the same automated production operations. The following estimated information is available for period 1:

Production unit data	A	B
Direct material cost ($)	2	40
Variable production overhead cost ($)	28	4
Overall hours per product unit (hours)	0.25	0.15

Production/sales of products A and B are 120,000 units and 45,000 units with selling prices per unit $60 and $70 respectively. Maximum demand for each product is 20% above the estimated sales levels. Total fixed production overhead cost is $1,470,000. This is absorbed at an average rate per hour based on the estimated production levels.

One of the production operations has a maximum capacity of 3,075 hours which has been identified as a bottleneck which limits the overall production/sales of products A and B. The bottleneck hours required per product unit for products A and B are 0.02 and 0.015 respectively.

The management have always been indifferent between the two products and have not managed resources to manage one over the other. The sales manager argues that each product is designed to make the same net profit per unit and that makes his job easier. He just divides his resources between the products and doesn't do anything more complicated as resource planning.

But the company's finance director believes that profits should be higher and wants to encourage the production director to consider more careful resource planning and the sales director to have a clearer idea of the company's priorities.

Required:

(a) Show why the sales manager of Tupik argues that he is indifferent on financial grounds as to the mix of products A and B which should be produced and sold.

(5 marks)

(b) Advise the company on which product(s) it *should* make and sell.

(10 marks)

(Total: 15 marks)

Question 33: Cost accounting

The following question is aimed at improving the recall of some of the brought forward cost accounting techniques which may appear in this exam.

Traditional costing

An organisation budgets to produce and sell 3,800 units of a product in the forthcoming year. The amount of capital investment attributable to the product will be $600,000 and the organisation requires a rate of return of 15% on all capital invested.

Further details concerning the product are as follows:

Direct material cost per unit	$14
Direct labour cost per unit	$19
Variable overhead cost per unit	$3
Machine hours per unit	8

Fixed overhead is absorbed at a rate of $11 per machine hour.

Required:

Determine the selling price per unit of the product which will achieve the specified return on investment.

Activity based costing

A small accountancy firm provides three services as follows:

	Statutory audit	Tax services	Other services
Budgeted services	50	100	400
Budgeted labour hours per service	18	2	4
Average number of reviews per service	3	0.5	2

Other services includes services such as pension planning, business consultancy and business valuations.

The budgeted activity cost for reviews was $55,000.

Required:

If an ABC system is used by the accountancy firm, determine how much review cost is attached to each statutory audit service. Comment briefly on the suitability of an ABC system to a firm of accountants.

Decision making

A company manufactures two models of a pocket calculator: The basic model sells for $5.50, has a direct material cost of $1.25 and requires 0.25 hours of labour time to produce. The other model, the Scientist, sells for $7.50, has a direct material cost of $1.63 and takes 0.375 hours to produce.

Labour, which is paid at the rate of $6 per hour, is currently very scarce, while demand for the company's calculators is heavy. The company is currently producing 8,000 of the basic model and 4,000 of the Scientist model per month, while fixed costs are $24,000 per month.

An overseas customer has offered the company a contract, worth $35,000, for a number of calculators made to its requirements. The estimating department has ascertained the following facts in respect of the work:

- The labour time for the contract would be 1,200 hours.

- The material cost would be $9,000 plus the cost of a particular component not normally used in the company's models.

- These components could be purchased from a supplier for $2,500 or alternatively, they could be made internally for a material cost of $1,000 and an additional labour time of 150 hours.

Required:

Determine whether the company should accept the proposed new contract.

Dealing with risk and uncertainty

A firm of consultants provides regular service work for a large client based in the east of the country. The client is now expanding to the west of the country and has asked the firm of consultants to bid for the consultancy work that would be needed for this area. The contract is referred to as the West Contract.

The consultancy firm has determined that it makes $60 contribution per labour hour from existing work for this client and it would expect this level of contribution to continue if it wins the new West Contract. The work could be carried out from the existing office (although there is likely to be around an extra $4,000 in administrative costs), but the firm believe that without a commitment to the west of the country there is only a 60% chance of winning the contract. The cost of preparing the bid from the existing office is $20,000.

If the bid is won there is an expectation of gaining 1,000 hour of consultancy work from the client for each of the next three years (when the contract is typically re-opened for tender). The cost of preparing the bid would rise to $30,000.

However, if the consultancy firm was to make a commitment to having a physical presence in the west of the country they expect to be able to gain a further 3,000 hours of work from other clients. Work for these other clients would be expected to make a contribution of $80 per hour.

The physical presence in the west would also increase the firm's chance of winning the West Contract by 20%. It would, however, involve setting up an office in the west (i.e. renting space and hiring staff etc.) which has an expected cost of $750,000 and has no expected residual value in three years' time (the time period over which the firm evaluates all new strategic proposals).

Required:

Determine the best course of action for the firm. Ignore the time value of money.

Variance analysis

The following data relates to the budget for a company producing a product in March:

Budgeted production and sales	1,750
Standard cost per unit:	units
	$
Direct materials	6.00
Direct labour	3.00
Variable production overhead	0.75
Fixed production overhead	2.50
Standard sales price	12.25
	18.25
Standard profit per unit	
	6.00
Number of units produced and sold in March	1,800
	units
Actual sales revenue	$32,300

Required:

Calculate the sales price and sales volume profit variance. What would be the sales volume contribution variance if standard marginal costing were used?

15 Strategy and people

Question 34: Jays

Jays is a former footwear manufacturer. The firm was started in Melbourne, Australia in 1900 by the grandfather of Jay, the present owner. Over the years, Jays grew into a national retail chain with hundreds of shops. In 1996, cheap imports forced the sale of the shoe retail business but Jay retained 123 outlets and developed a 'while-you-wait' shoe repair service in comfortable surroundings.

The formula proved very successful and the business has grown to 325 outlets. By 1999, the market in shoe repairs was becoming saturated, so Jay added the high-margin businesses of key-cutting and watch repair, using the same outlets as used for shoe repair and adding more as demand grew.

Though watch repair has traditionally been the preserve of high-street jewellers, Jay found that the skill barrier to this occupation was not as high as jewellers claimed it to be. In fact, he found that most watch repairs boil down to about ten simple operations and anything more complex could be dealt with by specialists at a national centre. In two years sales grew from zero to three million Australian dollars.

Employees in each of these businesses are primarily craftsmen or semi-skilled operators but, as a retailer, Jay recognises how critical excellent customer service is in this business. The outlets are typically staffed by a handful of craftsmen, though in busy centres the number rises to ten or more. Seating is provided for customers, with magazines and piped music to keep them occupied while waiting.

Required:

(a) Explain the human resource management implications of Jays' shift from shoe retailer to that of a provider of services in shoe repair, key-cutting and watch repairs.

(15 marks)

(b) Describe how Jays might go about motivating its workforce.

(10 marks)

(Total: 25 marks)

16 Strategic development and managing strategic change

Question 35: Y

Y is one of the five main high street banks in the country. Since banking deregulation in the late 1980s, Y, like other banks, has been facing increasing competition, first from other existing financial institutions but more recently from new entrants who have started to offer deposit accounts and a number of other financial services.

In seeking to respond to these competitive threats, the bank's senior management has started to implement a number of changes. These involve a significant restructuring of the organisation with the removal of a number of layers of management, and a consequent reduction in staffing levels in most divisions. The closure of a number of high street branches is also planned. The telephone-banking arm is being substantially enlarged and a major investment in IT is being undertaken. The effect on staff will be considerable. A programme of voluntary redundancy and redeployment is planned and, given the demand for new skills, a considerable amount of training will need to be carried out. Despite clear evidence of the threat of the future of the bank, the plans set forth by management are meeting resistance from the workforce. The banking unions in particular seem determined to obstruct the changes wherever possible.

Required (with reference to the above scenario)

(a) Explain why the implementation of organisational change often proves to be so difficult.

(12 marks)

(b) Advise Y's management about the ways in which change can be facilitated.

(13 marks)

(Total: 25 marks)

Question 36: BHH Clothing

The European clothing industry is a mature industry characterised by the following:

- Powerful retailers resulting in high pressure on manufacturers' margins.

- Increasing globalisation resulting in many manufacturers switching production to cheaper locations outside Europe to reduce their cost base.

- Increasing competition from Chinese manufacturers due to their lower costs, an improving reputation for quality and the relaxation of quotas.

Retailers buy on three criteria and put pressure on manufacturers to improve each of the following:

- Design/quality
- Cost/price
- Speed to market/lead times.

BHH is a clothing manufacturer based in Europe, making ladies and girls' clothing aimed at the medium/high price segments of the market. The majority are sold under retailers' own labels. BHH's competitive strategy to date has been to differentiate through close collaboration with clients, good designs and hand finishing of garments. Historically BHH has resisted the pressure to source garments from cheaper countries outside of Europe but falling margins have lead directors to question this stance.

Issues were brought to a head recently when BHH lost Forum, a major customer, despite offering a 4% price cut. Forum claimed that they could get similar garments supplied much cheaper by companies that use Chinese factories to make them. Two other large customers are also putting pressure on BHH to cut prices without compromising quality.

At a recent board meeting directors decided that the only way forward was to keep design and finishing in Europe but outsource the manufacture of the basic garment to China. Unfortunately news of this decision leaked out to the workforce before the board could make a formal announcement, causing widespread unrest amongst employees, some of whom have worked for BHH for over twenty years. There is thus now the threat of strike action to try to resist feared redundancies.

Required:

Apply the change kaleidoscope model to BHH as follows:

(a) Examine the wider strategic context for change by assessing the main environmental influences and considering the alternative strategies available to BHH.

(10 marks)

(b) Analyse, information permitting, the contextual features that the directors must consider.

(10 marks)

(c) Discuss the design choices available to manage the change process and make recommendations.

(5 marks)

(Total: 25 marks)

Test your understanding answers

Question 1: David Gould

(a) Writing a business plan is a critical stage in moving an idea for a business into a reality. The reality includes presenting a convincing case to potential financers of the business, be they banks or venture capitalists. The key ingredients include clearly saying what you plan to do and why people should want to buy your particular service. Experts warn of starting with a detailed cash flow and then working backwards to make the numbers fit. You should regard the business plan as a management tool and not simply a sales document. Again, the advice is to make credible and achievable projections; it is better to exceed low targets than fail to achieve over-ambitious ones. Many business plans are based on deeply flawed research. Key to your business success will be the size of your target market. There is much evidence to suggest that it is the make-up of the team presenting the plan and their commitment rather than the business idea itself that will determine whether the necessary financial support is made.

Clearly, you need to say how much money you require and why. Again the advice is not to be afraid to ask for large amounts if your business requires it. Linked to how much you want is a clear statement of the return the investor or lender will get – how much of the equity are you willing to give or what security can you offer the lender? Figure are important and you need projected cash flows, profit and loss accounts and balance sheets for at least three years ahead. Potential investors and/or lenders are likely to be impressed by a plan which clearly indicates where the major risks are to be found and the strategies available to handle such risks.

There needs to be a clear statement of the major steps and milestones on the way to achieving your goals. Where are you now, where do you intend to be and how are you going to get there. One expert argues there are three elements of the plan itself – an executive summary pulling together the key points in your proposal, secondly the plan itself and finally an 'elevator pitch', a one paragraph description that explains the business in the time it takes to go up in a lift.

In summary, your business plan should contain an executive summary as explained above, the objectives of the business, including key financial targets and the philosophy of the business, the target market and relevant forecasts, the range of products/services, the marketing strategy linked to the target markets, resource availability, people and organisation involved, performance measurement to measure progress towards stated objectives and a summary of financial information.

One final point is to remember that no business plan ever was carried out exactly! In many ways it is the quality of the thinking the plan includes and the actual process through which it is developed that will determine success.

(b) Clearly, there is a link between the ability to write a business plan and the willingness, or otherwise, of small firms to carry out strategic planning. Whilst writing a business plan may be a necessity in order to acquire financial support, there is much more question over the benefits to the existing small business, such as Gould and King, of carrying out strategic planning. One of the areas of greatest debate is whether carrying out strategic planning leads to improved performance. Equally contentious is whether the formal rational planning model is worthwhile or whether strategy is much more of an emergent process, with the firm responding to changes in its competitive environment.

One source argues that small firms may be reluctant to create a strategic plan because of the time involved; small firms may find day-to-day survival and crisis management prevents them having the luxury of planning where they mean to be over the next few years. Secondly, strategic plans may also be viewed as too restricting, stopping the firm responding flexibly and quickly to opportunities and threats. Thirdly, many small firms may feel that they lack the necessary skills to carry out strategic planning. Strategic planning is seen as a 'big' firm process and inappropriate for small firms. Again, there is evidence to suggest that owner-managers are much less aware of strategic management tools such as SWOT, PESTEL and mission statements than their managers. Finally, owner-managers may be reluctant to involve others in the planning process, which would necessitate giving them access to key information about the business. Here there is an issue of the lack of trust and openness preventing the owner-manager developing and sharing a strategic plan. Many owner-managers may be quite happy to limit the size of the business to one which they can personally control.

KAPLAN PUBLISHING

On the positive side there is evidence to show that a commitment to strategic planning results in speedier decision making, a better ability to introduce change and innovation and being good at managing change. This in turn results in better performance including higher rates of growth and profits, clear indicators of competitive advantage. If Gould and King are looking to grow the business as suggested, this means some strategic planning will necessarily be involved.

Question 2: Dunvegan Ltd

Report

To	The Directors of Dunvegan Ltd
From	Independent Consultant
Date	Today
Subject	Proposed Maho spruce plantation

Introduction

I have been asked to give advice on the proposal to plant 1,000 hectares of land with Maho spruce.

Political

Mahogany currently comes from four countries in the tropics. As it is a valuable export, these countries can be expected to be willing to sell mahogany irrespective of local political changes.

In the UK, however, there is growing concern about the deforestation of the tropics and suspicion about the source of many hardwoods. It is possible that the UK or EC will tighten import legislation.

Locally-grown, renewable mahogany substitute should be favoured in this ecologically-aware age.

Economic

Mahogany is principally used for building (window frames etc.) and furniture (veneers). Both of these industries are very sensitive to the health of the economy. It is difficult to predict the economic health of the country ten years hence and so the project will have considerable risk and uncertainty.

Social

If home-owning continues to grow, it is to be expected that demand for high-quality materials will also grow. As mentioned under the political paragraph, using tropical hardwoods could become socially unacceptable and it would appear that the Maho spruce should provide a politically acceptable substitute.

However, some people may object to using genetically-engineered material.

Technological

Although Maho spruce has been patented, there is no reason why other manufacturers could not develop similar products. That would drive down the cost of seedlings (a major cost of the undertaking) and hence the price that would eventually have to be achieved to make the investment pay.

The industry competitive position

The industry competitive position can be analysed in terms of rivals, buyers, suppliers, substitutes and potential new entrants to the market.

Rivals

The potential rivals are the other UK forestry companies and the suppliers from the tropics.

Whether other UK forestry companies will decide to compete is a very complex decision and is discussed below.

The foreign suppliers, which depend on their hardwood for valuable foreign currency, are likely to retaliate with price cuts when they perceive Maho spruce as a threat.

Buyers

It is likely that there are many relatively small buyers of hardwood. If so, there will be little pressure from them.

Suppliers

The main supplier to Dunvegan Ltd is the supplier of the seedlings. At the moment there is only one supplier and this would normally place that company in a very strong position.

However, the supply pattern here is unusual. Once 1,000 hectares are planted, the supplier has no power at all over this project as no further supplies are needed for it.

Future projects would need to be evaluated in the light of supplier attitudes at the time.

New entrants

New entrants into the forestry industry are unlikely, but there is some risk if the crops become more lucrative and land is set aside from normal agricultural use (EC regulations). Much will depend on the perceived economies of the industry.

Substitutes

Maho spruce is an excellent substitute for mahogany. Substitutes for Maho spruce might be other genetically-engineered trees with more attractive or cheaper timber. Substitutes maturing more quickly would be particularly serious as they would capture the market and drive down prices before Dunvegan's timber had matured.

Financial forecasts

If the present price of mahogany and mahogany substitutes is maintained, then the project will produce a positive net present value.

If the price falls by more than about 30% to below £639, then the project will produce a negative net present value.

Competitor reaction

As mentioned above, it is likely that the foreign suppliers will cut their prices so as to keep earning foreign exchange. The reaction of UK forestry companies will depend on their estimates of future prices and supplies.

If the price of mahogany is expected to fall to £500, then the plantation should not be undertaken as there would be a negative NPV. If the price is expected to fall to no less than £800 then the project would produce a positive NPV.

However, Dunvegan Ltd's competitors will have carried out similar calculations. Their break-even points must be very similar to Dunvegan Ltd's as the NPV calculation is dominated by the initial price of the seedlings and the final price of the timber.

The competitors can also be assumed to have read the economist's article in the trade journal.

All the players are faced with an investment paradox.

(a) If a player believes that the others will invest, then investing is not worthwhile as the timber price will fall to an uneconomic level. (Of course, if they all believe this, no one will invest and the price would stay high.)

(b) If a player believes that the others will not invest, then investing is worthwhile as the price would stay high. (Of course, if they all believe this, all will invest and the price would fall.)

Conventional financial analysis is of little further help here. It is crucial to try to find out the true intentions of the competition or to try to limit their scope for competition.

It is in the interests of the producers of the Maho spruce to bring stability to their market. If everyone is afraid to invest, then that company will get no revenue. An agreement with the supply company to limit the sale of seedlings each year would ensure that the prices remained higher and that investment would be worthwhile.

Size of investment

The proposed investment is large, especially as there are many important factors which could change over the project's life: the project is high risk even if not using innovative technology.

Risk could be reduced by planting over several years rather than 1,000 hectares at one time. That way the economics of the investment could be monitored and decisions taken about each slice of investment. Naturally, this approach would delay the maturity of some of the crop. There is a risk that this would reduce the final income (if mahogany prices were to fall) but prices could also rise (strong reaction against natural mahogany, economic upturn). Delaying planting could also reduce the initial price of seedlings as other bioengineering companies launch new products.

Summary

In so far as environmental factors can be judged, it would seem that Maho spruce should be a popular product. The main risk arises from technological advances which could produce similar cheaper timber. However, the economics of the project are very dependent on the future price of Maho spruce timber, its substitutes and the reactions of rivals.

Question 3: T Plc

(a) **PEST Analysis**

The following external factors are relevant to T plc:

Political factors

T plc currently dominates its national telecommunications market with an 85% share of the market. The company will be under political pressure from the national government to reduce its dominance by opening up the national telecom market to competition and reducing prices for telecom products charged to consumers.

The government has appointed an industry regulator to be directly involved in the control of the telecom industry and T plc no doubt will be under close scrutiny. Political forces will be a major factor affecting the operations and plans of T plc.

Economic factors

There are three main economic elements that T plc needs to consider. These are:

– Shareholder wealth

T plc's shareholders are a major stakeholder group who will have economic objectives of profit maximisation and rising share value.

– The contribution of the telecommunications industry to the national economy.

The telecommunications industry plays a major role in contributing towards economic growth and prosperity. T plc has a responsibility to develop new technology and to provide a reliable, value for money service to its users.

– The economies of foreign countries.

The economic conditions in each foreign country T plc operates in should be considered e.g. foreign currency exchange rates and national economic boom and slump cycles.

Social factors

Telecommunication products are social products used by people for many reasons. The company should ensure that it understands the social role of the industry and provides a reliable service. The company should also portray itself as socially responsible, have a set of social objectives and keep in close contact with the consumers e.g. by producing a range of services for elderly citizens who are more dependent on telephones for obtaining help when needed.

Technical factors

The telecommunications Industry is a high-tech industry that is currently very dynamic. T plc is the market leader in the industry and must be innovative to maintain its competitive advantage. The company must invest in research and development to ensure it has a constant supply of new products in the years ahead to replace those going into the decline stage of their product life cycle.

(b) **Ansoff matrix**

By relating products to markets, Ansoff identified four main strategies for achieving long-term growth. Using this model the potential market opportunities are as follows:

Market penetration strategies

T plc currently has 85% of its national market. There is little scope for obtaining any growth by increasing its market share. Most households and businesses will have a conventional telephone line so some of the company's products will be at the maturity stage of their life cycle offering little prospect of growth. Some market growth might be achieved by getting existing customers to use the telephone more.

A market penetration strategy only offers limited growth prospects.

Product development strategy

This strategy involves introducing new products in existing markets. T plc has already achieved a good track record for new product development and with continued investment in research and development should maintain its momentum. There is a lot of market opportunity in the industry for this strategy, for example further developments in mobile phone and Internet technology.

Market development strategy

T plc has pursued a successful strategy of expanding into foreign markets with existing products. It currently has operations in North America, Europe, India and the Far East. In T plc's latest annual report, the Chairman refers to developing these markets further. Tremendous opportunities exist in additional developing countries such as those in Africa where the company currently has operations.

Diversification strategy

This involves introducing new products to new markets and is a high-risk strategy. T plc is a large profitable company with a prospector (innovative) culture. The company should evaluate carefully the risk of any diversification strategy and if opportunities exist they should be considered e.g. digital television technology.

The company should pursue all four strategies with the main emphasis on product development and market development, as these exploit the company's main strengths of expertise in research and development, and growth in foreign markets.

Question 4: CSC Clothing

(a) The extent to which location has historically determined the competitive advantage of CSC and the extent to which it will do so in the future are issues of crucial importance to KZ. A historical analysis of location provides a deeper understanding of CSC's strategic position, and an analysis of the extent to which it is still relevant will assist KZ as it contemplates shifting CSC production and exploiting the CSC brand image.

The debate about **location and comparative advantage** is both long standing and ongoing. However, the work of **Porter (Competitive Advantage of Nations)** presents us with a useful framework in which to consider the attributes of advantage.

Porter identifies **four interlocking elements which form a 'diamond' of location-based advantage**. These four elements can be used to analyse the position of CSC as follows:

- **Factor conditions**. These are the resource inputs needed by the business and in particular the inherited factors of natural resources – climate, labour and the evolution of knowledge and skills. CSC grew out of a business which originally both made and supplied outdoor clothing to Scottish hill farmers thus reflecting the influence of a climate and a geography which demanded tough weatherproof clothing (influences – quality and fitness for purpose) and developed the knowledge and skills to design and manufacture such clothing.

- **Intense home market demand conditions**, led by sophisticated and numerous independent buyers, drive firms to innovate continually and improve their products. Over time, CSC has been required to meet the demanding product requirements of the Scottish hill farmers which means that its products have evolved features of superior weatherproofing and durability. Although the products may today be bought by people who will never venture on a mountain in winter, they are nevertheless buying into what is seen to be a product ownership image associated with the product's history and design attributes (similar to buying an off-road, four-wheel drive vehicle for use within a city environment).

- **Related and supporting local industries**, which through mutual support and collaboration enhance competitive potential, for example through design synergies achieved by close co-operation between firms operating within the value chain. CSC has enjoyed the support of local weavers which allows integration of cloth requirements such as supply and delivery, quality attributes and, in particular, the traditional pattern design used in the garment fabrics.

- **Intense local demand rivalry** which leads to the emergence of firms with strong competitive characteristics, in other words, the home market hones competitive skills which promote domination in worldwide markets. This appears to be the case within CSC's home market where CSC first emerged as the market leader among a number of competing Scottish firms within this specialist garment business.

Porter also identifies other factors, such as the **role of government**, which might assist through intervention – industry support in research and development, or more often non-intervention – creating a business environment which promotes competition. CSC has evolved through a one-hundred-year period of relative business stability and freedom from either intervention or subsidy.

Finally, there is always an element of chance within business success stories. CSC has achieved its success through a process of product development (moving from simple garments for farmers to garment-based products for sports such as shooting and fishing), and market development (using existing products in new markets – creating a fashion niche image). Both opportunities have in part been made possible by the chance adoption of its basic products by the rich and famous, which in turn has made the products prestigious and therefore ones which the not-so-rich and famous wish to acquire.

(b) CSC could reduce its product costs by moving garment production from Scotland to South East Asia. However, it is doubtful to what extent this move has a strategic fit with the competitive strategy adopted by CSC. The CSC strategy is based on **focused differentiation**, that is, creating a perception of high value to the customer and charging a high price for it – by implication such a strategy will lead to **niche market segmentation**. In this case, the niche is a global one which targets similar customers with similar aspirations world-wide (other product examples, Rolex, Gucci) and is independent of cultural differences.

This is the context within which KZ must decide its production policy for CSC. The **decision cannot be cost-based alone** and subsequently made in isolation of the values, needs and requirements of the customers of CSC and their associated patterns of buyer behaviour. CSC products are not bought on the basis of price, but on the basis of buyers seeking to acquire reflected status associated with the product.

The fact that each garment is handmade in Scotland, using traditional materials and design, is a key part of what the customer is buying into. CSC recognise this and its integrated marketing strategy reflects this – price, product concept, distribution channels (the best stores) and promotion are all in balance. Although it may be possible to maintain product quality by moving production away from Scotland KZ would run a major risk of destroying the CSC product concept and hence the differentiation element which allows the adoption of a premium pricing approach.

Question 5: Scottish Holidays

Explanation of the calculation

The business has used time series analysis to prepare its forecast as follows:

The trend

The first table has been used to calculate the underlying trend in the data and any past seasonal variations. The first two columns represent the actual recorded historic data.

The next two columns represent the trend calculation. Firstly a moving average has been calculated. A two period average has been calculated (though a longer period may have been more appropriate in order to 'iron out' any anomalies). It is moved forward by one period each time (by adding a new period and removing the oldest period) so that an underlying trend can be identified.

These moving averages are then averaged (each pair is totalled and divided by two) to give a centred moving average. This allows the moving average to tie together with actual data periods. This centred moving average is the trend line. A pattern is immediately obvious – it would appear that there is an increase in the trend each period (of around $50,000). So we can tell that over the four years sales have shown a constant underlying increase.

The seasonal variation

The final column is used to calculate the seasonal variation. This is the difference between the actual sales and the underlying trend. For example, in summer 20X8, we can see that sales were $52,500 above 'trend'. This pattern recurs through all 4 years, with summer periods shown seasonal peaks well above the trend, and winter periods showing troughs well below the trend.

The second and third tables seek to calculate an average of the seasonal variations and conclude that, on average, summer sales are $53,100 above average and winter sales are $53,100 below average (slight mathematical adjustment has been made to ensure that these averages net to zero).

The forecast

The forecast is in two parts. Firstly the trend line has been extrapolated forward to Winter 20X9. This has been done by taking the last recorded trend figure (52.7 in winter 20X8) and adding two more periods to it. An average increase in the trend has been calculated over the four years using a high low method. This gives an average increase of [($527,500 – $123,500)/8 seasons =] $50, 500 each season.

Once the underlying trend figure has been identified for winter 20X9, this trend is then adjusted for the average seasonal variation (calculated earlier) to give the forecast sales for winter 20X9.

Validity of the calculation

Advantages

There are some advantages in using this method of forecasting. Firstly, there appears to be a clear seasonal pattern to past sales and using time series analysis is a good way of identifying and using this. Secondly, the trend seems very consistent so that using past data to predict future sales would seem to be theoretically sound. Thirdly, the basis of the forecast seems sound in that the average increase in the trend and the average seasonal variation have been used to produce the forecast sales.

Disadvantages

But the method also has some disadvantages. The main disadvantage is that it ignores changes in the external environment. This is important in this scenario due to the political factors that could potentially boost sales in future periods. The government's initiatives may mean that winter sales are not as low as in the past and that therefore the underlying trend and seasonal variation may not be applicable.

The method also doesn't account for any internal changes to the organisation. It may well be that the business will carry out extra marketing or make some capital investments which might also 'buck' the trend experienced in past years.

Conclusions

The technique used by the business is accurate and theoretically sound. However, the business is likely to experience significant changes due to new government plans which may mean that past data will not be a good predictor of future sales patterns.

Question 6: Marcus Aurelius

Linear regression analysis

The marketing director has used a forecasting technique known as limiting factor analysis. This assumes that there is a linear relationship between two variables. In this instance, it will assume that as advertising expenditure increases, sales revenue will also increase at a constant rate.

Line of best fit

To determine the rate of increase (donated by the letter 'b' in forecast calculations) a mathematical formula is used to find what is known as the 'line of best fit'. This effectively calculates the average increase observed from the data that has been recorded.

It can be seen in these calculations that 'b' has been determined to be 5. This means that, on average, based on the observations from the five shops examined, for every $1 spent on advertising, sales can be expected to increase by $5.

Underlying sales

Using the average revenue and average advertising expenditure recorded an estimate is then made of underling sales (donated by the letter 'a' in forecast calculations). This has been estimated at 300. This implies that even if there was no advertising carried out by a shop, sales would still be $300,000. For example, if we believe that 5 is the best estimate of the relationship between the variables and examine shop 4, we can estimate that the effect of advertising on this shop is to generate $450,000 of sales revenue (i.e. 5 times the $90,000 that was spent on advertising). This would leave $300,000 of sales that have not been determined by any advertising expenditure.

Coefficient of determination

This tests the strength of the relationship between the variables (advertising expenditure and sales revenue in this scenario). A figure of 0.984 tells that 98.4% of any change in sales revenue can be attributed to a change in advertising expenditure. This is a high figure and should give some reassurance to the accuracy of the estimate of b.

Forecast sales revenue

The two calculated figures (5 for the line of best fit, and $300,000 for the underlying sales revenue) have then been used to forecast sales for the two new shops as follows:

			$000
Sales revenue (shop 7)	= $300k + (5 × $150k)	=	1,050
Sales revenue (shop 8)	= $300k + (5 × $50k)	=	550

Validity of the technique

As already explained, there does appear to be a strong relationship between the variables -- as is shown by the high coefficient of determination. However, it should be noted that even in this estimate it still means that 1.6% of changes in sales cannot be attributed to a change in sales revenue and therefore an element of uncertainty/error+ does exist.

The relationship does appear to hold true for the chops that have been observed and the period that has been examined. But linear regression does not take account of changes in the external environment of the business. For example, changes in popularity of the product or an economic downturn may both affect sales irrespective of what happens to advertising expenditure.

There may also be internal changes to the organisation such as the methods used for advertising the product or the outlets used. This will not be reflected in the linear regression forecast, which assumes that the past will be a good indicator of the future and therefore ignores both internal and external changes which might affect the company.

The second prediction is the more reliable as it involves interpolation. The first prediction goes beyond the original data upon which the regression line was based and thus assumes that the relationship will continue on in the same way, which may not be true. There may be a maximum level of sales that a shop can handle, for example, so that sales do not constantly rise at the same rate.

Overall

The forecasting method used is in itself sound. There appears to be a strong relationship between advertising expenditure and sales revenue. But the company should carefully consider whether the new shops will operate under the same conditions as the existing shops and whether there are other internal or external factors or changes that need to be considered.

Question 7: MW and FS

(a) (i) Production of a SWOT analysis for MW

When developing a strategic plan it is useful to undertake a SWOT analysis. At the current time MW is seeking to enhance its shareholder value, its main objective. Therefore the SWOT analysis can be used to identify how the business can build on its strengths and take corrective action for its weaknesses. This in turn will increase both profitability and market share for MW.

Strengths

– Secure financial base.

– Well established in the North.

– Increased share price and profitability.

Weaknesses

– Prior experience in takeovers is limited.

– Lack of experience in managing the takeover process itself.

– Not maximising use of capital resources.

– Not much opportunity for further organic growth in the North.

– The company cultures will be different, so will require integration.

Opportunities

– Takeover will mean improvements in both competitiveness and market share.

– An increase in gearing will mean that the company will make increased use of debt, in turn resulting in lower costs, as debt is cheaper than equity.

– Takeover of FS will mean expansion into the South.

Threats

- Staff morale may fall when stores are sold after the takeover takes place.

- The bid cost may rise if competitors are also interested in purchasing FS.

- If MW does not do the takeover, it risks stagnation in its own market.

- The family shareholding will be diluted if the takeover goes ahead.

- Another competitor could purchase FS, meaning that MW would see a reduction in its competitiveness as well as losing market share.

(ii) Usefulness of SWOT Analysis

The SWOT analysis for MW has highlighted the fact that the northern market is reaching saturation. This means that for MW to increase shareholder value it must increase both the market growth rate and its market share, so consideration should be given to the possibility of a takeover. However, care must be taken by MW to ensure that the weaknesses identified in the SWOT analysis are addressed. Therefore consideration should be given to how the takeover process will be managed, given MW's lack of experience in this area. Also, it must consider that its bid may be unsuccessful, resulting in the loss of expenses incurred prior to the decision being made.

(b) Assessment of FS

It is immediately apparent from the calculations that the FS stores do not reach the level of absolute profitability enjoyed by MW. They do, however, have better gross profit to turnover levels. This means that MW is more efficient in terms of its overhead costs. If the takeover goes ahead shareholder value will be enhanced providing MW is able to achieve overall the same ratio of gross profit to turnover that FS currently achieves. Also, in order to increase shareholder value the net profit to turnover ratio of MW will need to be achieved within the new company, by carrying out efficiency improvements within FS. Inventory turnover is a good example of where MW currently has greater efficiency than FS, as FS holds inventory for 75% longer on average, meaning there is a potential to reduce costs by putting MW's policies in place.

Looking at the sales, gross profit and net profits per customer, it is apparent that FS uses premium pricing in comparison with MW. For example, if a comparison is made between the sales of northwest MW and the southwest FS stores the following calculation can be made:

$$\text{Volume of customers} = \frac{\$10 \text{ million}}{\$6 \text{ million}} \times 0.15 = \frac{0.25 \text{ million customers}}{\text{(MW pricing policies)}}$$

This compares to 0.3 million customers of MW in the northwest, so reinforcing the fact that the higher sales and profits are a result of premium pricing.

In FS stores the gross profit to turnover is higher than in MW stores, whilst the profit per square metre of FS stores in the southwest is comparable to the northeast MW stores, but lower in the southeast. Also net profit per square metre is lower for the FS stores. This demonstrates that the increased gross profit to turnover ratio of FS is achieved by premium pricing and not efficient use of space. This means that this is another area where MW could add shareholder value, by increased efficiency in the use of floor space in FS stores.

It is also apparent from the calculations that the staff of MW generate more turnover per employee than those of FS. This again supports the fact that, if MW's efficiency can be implemented in FS stores, this will result in increased shareholder value. This lower level of turnover per employee could be caused by the fact that FS staff get paid less than MW employees doing the same job, meaning that staff morale could be low. I feel that this should also be looked at within the different geographical areas of MW, as at the present time there is a difference in salaries between those working in the northwest and the northeast.

Calculations based on data provided in the scenario

	MW		FS	
	North West	*North East*	*South West*	*South East*
Gross profit	$5 million	$6 million	$3.2 million	$4.0 million
GP %	62.5%	60%	64%	67%
NP %	17.5%	20%	10%	13.3%
GP/sq. mtr.	$833	$1,000	$667	$833
NP/sq. mtr.	$233	$333	$104	$167
Sales/customer visit	$40	$33.33	$50	$40
GP/customer visit	$25	$20	$32	$27
NP/customer visit	$7	$6.67	$5	$5.30
Turnover/employee	$143k	$145k	$98k	$107k
Salaries/supervisor	$83.3k	$66.7k	$50k	$50k
Wages/employee	$16k	$18.5k	$15k	$16.k

Question 8: Qualispecs

(a) Corporate appraisal

A corporate appraisal is an overview of an organisation's current position. It leads on from the internal and external analysis undertaken as part of the business planning process.

As the company works towards achieving its objectives, the corporate appraisal is a summary of the company's:

- strengths within the organisation relative to competitors
- weaknesses within the organisation relative to competitors
- opportunities available from the external environment
- threats from the external environment.

The company must develop a strategy which:

– capitalises on the strengths
– overcomes or mitigates the impact of weaknesses
– takes suitable opportunities
– overcomes or mitigates the threats.

In the case of Qualispecs:

Strengths

– Reputation for quality

  Quality is a major reason why people buy products, and continuing to build on this reputation will ensure customers continue to buy Qualispecs's products.

– Financially secure/large cash reserves

  Qualispecs does not need to rush into the implementation of new strategies. It can take its time to ensure strategies chosen are appropriate for the business and implemented effectively. They also have funds to invest in new ventures without having to raise external funds.

– Backing of a famous sports star

  This helps to improve the image of Qualispecs's products which in turn should result in higher sales, particularly amongst the younger market that might be influenced by the sports star.

– New Chief Executive

  The group has a new Chief Executive who has joined from a rival, Fastglass. Fastglass has been a successful and innovative company and the Chief Executive may be able to bring new ideas and provide a fresh approach.

– Established group with many stores

  The group has a good basic infrastructure including many stores and experienced staff. This allows them to implement new strategies quickly and easily.

Weaknesses

– Slower dispensing of spectacles

Customer service is worse than competitors in this respect and may be a reason for the reducing customer loyalty.

– Less trendy products than competitors

Some competitors have successfully sold designer frames. These are likely to be stylish and trendy compared to Qualispecs' traditional products. Qualispecs may need to update products more often with the latest designs.

– Smaller product range than competitors

Some competitors have a wider product range than Qualispecs. This provides more choice which may attract customers and also gives competitors the opportunity to on-sell products, i.e. selling prescription sunglasses at the same time as standard spectacles.

– Older production methods causing higher costs

This will either cause prices to be higher than competitors or margins to be less. In either case competitors have a distinct advantage.

– Varying performance around the group

Little action is being taken to improve performance of poorly performing stores causing varying performance around the group. This indicates a weakness in internal control systems and perhaps also in development and training programmes.

– Little autonomy for shops

Without autonomy there is little a shop manager can do to improve local operations. In London, for instance, pay may need to be higher to attract the right staff. With no local control over pay levels, shop managers may find it hard to employ good staff and hence improve their business.

This lack of autonomy may also be demotivating to managers. Responsibility was one of the major factors outlined by Hertzberg in his motivation theory as a way to motivate staff.

– No incentive to improve for staff

The use of group-based bonuses means that people cannot be rewarded for good individual performance. Therefore, individuals have little incentive to improve.

Opportunities

Note: Opportunities should be in relation to the market as a whole. They therefore need to be available to all competitors in the market.

– To adopt new technologies to reduce costs (see earlier)
– To stock a wide range of up-to-date products (see earlier)
– Consumer spending will continue to increase

Despite a slowdown in the economy, consumer spending is likely to increase suggesting an increasing market size in the future. There is therefore further opportunity for all competitors to increase sales.

– Targeting 18 to 30 year olds

The 18 to 30-year-old age group offers a particular opportunity since its spending is likely to increase especially quickly. There is therefore an opportunity to understand this group's needs and to target it specifically.

– Develop a partnership with a high street shopping group

Fastglass has already done this successfully and Qualispecs could follow suit. There are likely to be limited suitable partners so Qualispecs must act quickly before other firms make arrangements with the best partners.

Threats

–   Intense competition/eroding customer loyalty

Existing competitors are adopting new strategies with great success (e.g. Fastglass developed joint ventures). This has resulted in Qualispecs's customers moving to competitors, thus reducing profits. This is likely to be a continued threat to Qualispecs who needs to respond.

–   Downturn in the economy

In the long-term, if the downturn continues it will affect all industries and consumer spending will be likely to fall as people become more defensive in their spending habits.

Key strategic challenges

In summary, the key strategic challenges are to:

–   Improve the current lack of clear generic strategy ('stuck in the middle')

Examining Michael Porter's **Generic Strategies**, Qualispecs appears to have neither a cost leader differentiation nor a focus on any particular niche. While traditionally quality has been their focus, new innovations from competitors have eroded its position as the highest quality spectacle retailer. In the long run it will find it hard to compete effectively if it does not rectify this.

Note: When asked to discuss current or future strategies Porter's **Generic Strategies** is always a good model to use. It is common in the exam to present failing companies (like Qualispecs) and you usually find such companies are 'stuck in the middle' and need to clarify their generic strategy in order to compete.

– Be more innovative in product and market development

Competitors have successfully developed new strategies while Qualispecs has done very little. This has seen it lose business to competitors. To be successful in the future it needs to update their product range regularly and be more innovative in developing new strategies (e.g. joint ventures).

– Improve performance on a divisional basis by updating internal policies and procedures

Current policies and procedures are demotivating staff and causing varying divisional performance.

(b) **Strategies to move the business forward**

Note: Detailed tools for generating strategic options are discussed in chapter 6. At this stage you were expected to use your common sense.

Competitive strategy

Given the key strength of Qualispecs as having a reputation for quality spectacles, and their current weakness in the cost of products produced, it would appear logical for Qualispecs to refocus activities on quality by producing very high quality spectacles (modern design, hard-wearing, up-to-date features) with a high-quality service (fast dispensing, knowledgeable staff).

Current product/current market

Qualispecs would benefit from consolidating its current strengths and refocusing on quality. It should invest in new technology in order to reduce costs which will it to them be competitive. This also capitalises on its significant cash reserves.

It needs to improve its internal processes to ensure that staff are motivated through a good incentive scheme, quality training and by being given autonomy. This will capitalise on its skilled workforce and overcome the weakness in the way it is managed.

Current market/new products

Product development is a vital new strategy for Qualispecs to follow. Its competitors have been successful in doing this. One aspect of providing a high quality service is being able to offer a wide range of products to meet varying customer needs. Qualispecs may need to invest more in Research and Development and implement new product development programmes.

New market/current products

A joint venture strategy with a retailer who competes based on quality (e.g. Marks and Spencer) would both build on the reputation of Qualispecs and also introduce it to a new group of customers who will buy its products through association with the retail group. The retail group may also have outlets in other parts of the country (or even internationally) which would allow Qualispecs to expand its markets.

Diversification

There appears no need at present to diversify. The disadvantages of operating in new markets with new products (e.g. lack of experience and reputation) outweigh any possible advantages.

Question 9: Wargrin

(a) Lifecycle costing is a concept which traces all costs to a product over its complete lifecycle, from design through to cessation. It recognises that for many products there are significant costs to be incurred in the early stages of its lifecycle. This is probably very true for Wargrin Limited. The design and development of software is a long and complicated process and it is likely that the costs involved would be very significant.

The profitability of a product can then be assessed taking all costs in to consideration.

It is also likely that adopting lifecycle costing would improve decision-making and cost control. The early development costs would have to be seen in the context of the expected trading results therefore preventing a serious over spend at this stage or under pricing at the launch point.

(b) **Budgeted results for game**

	Year 1 ($)	Year 2 ($)	Year 3 ($)	Total ($)
Sales	240,000	480,000	120,000	840,000
Variable costs (W1)	40,000	80,000	20,000	140,000
Fixed costs (W1)	80,000	120,000	80,000	280,000
Marketing cost	60,000	40,000		100,000
Profit	60,000	240,000	20,000	320,000

On the face of it the game will generate profits in each of its three years of life. Games only have a short lifecycle as the game players are likely to become bored of the game and move on to something new.

The pattern of sales follows a classic product lifecycle with poor levels of sales towards the end of the life of the game.

The stealth product has generated $320,000 of profit over its three year life measured on a traditional basis. This represents 40% of turnover – ahead of its target. Indeed it shows a positive net profit in each of its years on existence.

The contribution level is steady at around 83% indicating reasonable control and reliability of the production processes. This figure is better than the stated target.

Considering traditional performance management concepts, Wargrin Limited is likely to be relatively happy with the game's performance.

However, the initial design and development costs were incurred and were significant at $300,000 and are ignored in the annual profit calculations. Taking these into consideration the game only just broke even making a small $20,000 profit. Whether this is enough is debatable, it represents only 2.4% of sales for example. In order to properly assess the performance of a product the whole lifecycle needs to be considered.

Workings

(W1) Split of variable and fixed cost for Stealth

	Volume (units)	Cost ($)
High	14,000	150,000
Low	10,000	130,000
Difference	4,000	20,000

(**Note:** The high-low method is unlikely to be examined in P3, but it should be a technique that students are familiar with from previous studies.)

Variable cost per unit = $20,000/4,000 unit = $5 per unit

Total cost = fixed cost + variable cost
$150,000 = fixed cost + (14,000 ÷ $5)
$150,000 = fixed cost + $70,000

Fixed cost = $80,000 (and $120,000 if volume exceeds 15,000 units in a year.)

(c) Incremental budgeting is a process whereby this year's budget is set by reference to last year's actual results after an adjustment for inflation and other incremental factors. It is commonly used because:

- It is quick to do and a relatively simple process.

- The information is readily available, so very limited quantitative analysis is needed.

- It is appropriate in some circumstances. For example in a stable business the amount of stationery spent in one year is unlikely to be significantly different in the next year, so taking the actual spend in year one and adding a little for inflation should be a reasonable target for the spend in the next year.

There are problems involved with incremental budgeting:

- It builds on wasteful spending. If the actual figures for this year include overspends caused by some form of error then the budget for the next year would potentially include this overspend again.

- It encourages organisations to spend up to the maximum allowed in the knowledge that if they don't do this then they will not have as much to spend in the following year's budget.

- Assessing the amount of the increment can be difficult.

- It is not appropriate in a rapidly changing business.

- Can ignore the true (activity based) drivers of a cost leading to poor budgeting.

Question 10: Digwell Explorations

(a) Ethics

Ethics are a code of moral principles that people follow with respect to what is right or wrong. General examples might include staying within the law, not engaging in bribery or theft or endangering other people.

Also a part of ethics is social responsibility; the duty towards the wider community or society in general which includes environmental issues, public safety, employment and exploitation of third world workers.

In this case ethical issues which the government should have considered when granting permission for mining include:

(1) Employment in the local area

The government has a duty toward people to provide them with jobs. In Eastborough there is significant unemployment so it is particularly important to the government to generate jobs in the area. The effect of the mining on employment levels should therefore be considered.

(2) **The local economy**

The government has an obligation to the people of Eastborough to improve the wealth of the people there. This largely depends on a successful economy. The local economy of Eastborough has been performing badly despite various initiatives based around tourism. The effect of mining on the local economy generally must be considered (i.e. jobs create income which is then spent in local shops, demand for property increases and prices rise for all in the area).

(3) **Environmental concerns**

Eastborough has a beautiful coastline with rare birds nesting there. The government has a debt towards society generally to preserve areas of natural beauty for all to appreciate and enjoy, and a moral obligation towards other species on the planet to protect them from extinction.

The effects of the mining operations on the rare birds, the beauty of the coastline and any pollution caused in the locality should therefore have been considered by the government.

(4) **Rights of local individuals**

Individuals have the right for their quality of life to remain high. While employment and an improved economy may improve the quality of life of many, there may also be negative effects for some local people such as increased noise and traffic congestion. These broader effects on villagers is likely to have been considered.

(5) **Right to free operation of business**

Many capitalist countries believe in free trade and removing barriers to trade. This may be seen as a right of the business, and it may be considered as part of the decision to allow Digwell to open the mining operation.

Conflicts between stakeholder groups

Stakeholders are people who are affected or interested in some way by the mining operations.

In this case stakeholders include:

- national government

- local government

- local people

- wildlife protection groups

- environmental groups

- directors of Digwell

- employees of Digwell

- shareholders of Digwell.

The conflicts which may exist include the following:

(1) **National v local government**

Local government will be interested in Eastborough and its interests. National government have to balance those needs with the needs of all people of the country. There may be a conflict over the amount of funding available to support local initiatives such as to help start up the mining operations.

(2) **Unemployed v people based near mining operations/working people**

Unemployed people of the area will notice a direct benefit from the mining operations through increased jobs and are likely to support it. Other local residents may simply view the operations as disrupting their existing life (noise/congestion) and oppose the idea.

(3) **Shareholders/directors of Digwell v environmental/wildlife protection groups**

Both shareholders and directors of Digwell wish to make profits from Digwell's operations. The mining operations will enable them to make full use of an asset they own (tin reserves) and hence increase profit. They will wish it to go ahead, and may have very little interest in the broader impact. Environmental groups aim to protect the environment and are likely to oppose any part of the mining operation which will affect the environment irrespective of profitability.

(b) **Stakeholder mapping**

A useful model that can be used to examine stakeholders and how an organisation should deal with them is Mendelow's Matrix.

Mendelow said that there are two key aspects of understanding stakeholders:

(1) **Power**

This is the degree to which the stakeholder group can exert influence over Digwell, its operations and likely profitability. The local government, for instance, have the power to grant or refuse planning applications and hence have a lot of power in the tin mining issue.

A local individual who feels strongly against the mining operations may have little power because whatever they do they are unlikely to be able to influence the decision. A large local group of people, on the other hand, have more power since they may be able to influence the local authority who must ensure the best interests of local people are met.

The greater the power a group has the more their views will be considered when decisions are being made. Digwell, for instance, will have ensured that all local government concerns are met in order to get permission to undertake mining.

(2) Interest

The level of interest which the stakeholder has in the company (or in this case the mining operations) is also important to the company. If a party is not interested then the company will not need to concern itself with communicating with them or adapting to meet their needs.

In this case, for instance, central government is likely to have little interest in the local issue even though they have significant power. As long as the issue is not seen to affect national issues they are likely to remain unconcerned.

The matrix

Stakeholders can be placed into Mendelow's Matrix according to their interest and power. Depending on where they fall, a different response will be necessary from Digwell.

	INTEREST	
	Low High	
Low	Minimal effort General public outside Eastborough	Keep informed Local people Environmental groups Wildlife protection groups Digwell employees
POWER		
High	Keep happy Central government Digwell shareholders Large customers of Digwell	Key player – keep close Local government Digwell directors

The responses required are as follows:

Key player – keep close

Key players must be kept close to the company in all major issues relating to the mining operations. For example, close relationships should be built with the local government so that they are continually kept informed of new plans. This ensures the plans are acceptable and within regulation. Any new requirements are also quickly understood and can be dealt with promptly.

Keep happy

For example, the central government should be kept happy by ensuring that the issue does not affect their main concern, national issues as a whole. So long as this is the case they are unlikely to get involved in this local issue and exert their considerable power.

Keep informed

For example, Digwell employees will be very interested in the effect of the new operations on jobs. It may, for instance, create job security for them, or mean they have to relocate. It is therefore very important to ensure they understand the impact on them and expectations of them. Without formal notification, information will spread via rumour which may be inaccurate and cause undue concern.

Minimal effort

It is important to clarify which groups have little power or interest to avoid unnecessary effort being made. An example here is the general public outside Eastborough. They are likely to have little interest or power and so no effort needs to be made to keep them happy and there is little benefit from keeping them informed.

Question 11: A University

Value activities consist of all those activities a firm undertakes, from the moment of initial purchase of raw materials and other inputs, to the moment of final receipt of payment from the customer. Value chain analysis (VCA) looks at each of the processes that make up the chain of activity and asks both how important it is in a given company's production or service activity, and how the company compares in that respect to its competitors. The value chain model divides an organisation's activities into nine generic activities, five primary activities and four support activities.

To review the withdrawal rate of students from the University's courses a clear statement of the University's objectives and what they are trying to achieve needs to be drawn up by the management team. The management accountant will then analyse the primary and support activities in the University's value chain and identify areas that are causing the greatest level of concern.

Primary activities

- **Inbound logistics** – are the activities concerned with handling the inputs. From the University's point of view the analysis will cover:
  - the intake of students, e.g. whether entry requirements have changed. A lowering of standards may lead to students being unable to cope with the work, while a raising may find students' expectations of the course is not fulfilled. An increase in the intake could lead to more revenue but less individual attention for students with short-term problems.
  - the courses offered and whether they have changed over the period of increased withdrawal.

- **Operations** – concerned with the transformation of the inputs and will look in detail at:
  - how the University compares with competitor institutions – do they have similar withdrawal rates in the first year? If not, then the University needs to determine what they are doing differently and what they must do to improve the service. A review of the students that leave might show a pattern to the transfers, e.g. students leaving to go to particular universities.

  - the calibre of staff – are the lecturers able to communicate effectively and do they show an interest in helping the students in their studies? Also, does their treatment of students vary between the first year and subsequent years?

- **Outbound logistics** – are concerned with the finished product, i.e. the skills and abilities of the graduates after completing their courses and the perception of the customers – the government and employers.

- **Marketing and sales** – are responsible for communication with the customers, e.g. advertising and promotion. The analysis should assess what attracts the students and why an increasing number believe that the course is not living up to their expectations.

- **Service** – covers all of the activities that occur after graduation and includes arranging milk rounds, job fairs and other links to potential employers. The management accountant should analyse the types of contact with the graduate and the retention rates for students moving on to other courses in the University.

Support activities

- **Procurement** – is the process of purchasing inputs. Areas that will be analysed include the efficiency and adequacy of the supplies and the level of administrative support provided to the lecturers and students.

- **Technology development** – covers not just machines and processes, but also know-how. Improved technology development may be employed in delivering course material to students. Technology may also be used in undertaking marketing research into the attractiveness of types of courses to prospective students.

- **Human resource management** transcends all primary activities. It includes all the activities involved in the recruitment, training, development and remuneration of staff.

- **Infrastructure** – which supports the entire value chain, includes the systems of planning, finance, quality control and estate management.

Managing the linkages

- **Primary-primary**. Inter-departmental co-operation between, say, inbound logistics and marketing to ensure that prospective students are given sufficient information about courses.

- **Support-primary**. Computer-based operations, involving co-operation between information technology and lecturers. For example, teaching aids and course notes made available.

- **Support-support**. Computer-based information systems automatically monitoring recruitment policies.

The VCA analysis will help to determine why the rate of student withdrawal is increasing and to decide how individual activities might be changed to improve the value of the University's offerings. Because of the linkages it is important that the organisation's activities are not dealt with in isolation. Choices will have to be made about the relationships and how they influence strategic capability e.g. the recruitment of staff with more teaching rather than research experience might have a positive effect on the students' experience but a negative effect on the University's reputation within its national academic community.

Linkages between the University's support and primary activities may also need strengthening, e.g. if some of the lecturers are lacking in communication skills it could be a direct result of management style or a failure of human resources policy. Any inadequacies in support will have a detrimental effect on lecturers, which may be a contributory factor leading to the problems of student withdrawal facing the University.

Question 12: News Reel Inc

(a) Strategic position analysis

There are a number of tools that can be used to analyse a company's position such as the value chain, PESTEL or 5 Forces analysis. The first of these models analyses the internal position of the business whereas the other models focus on its external position and prospects. The models can be brought together in a SWOT analysis and it is this model that will be used to assess News Reel's position.

Key strategic strengths

– News Reel is a focused differentiator. It stands out (differentiates) on its flexibility and delivery times. This has been arrived at by having less automated production, flexible suppliers and flexible production methods. This should allow the company to gain a competitive advantage and adapt quickly to changes in customer needs.

– Despite being a family owned business, News Reel's past performance has allowed it to accumulate cash and put itself in a strong financial position. It has created a cash reserve sufficient enough to finance an acquisition and allow the company to partake in the opportunities available to it.

– News Reel's reputation and association with EES will further enhance its competitive position and may create a barrier to entry to some foreign rivals.

Key strategic weaknesses

– News Reel is very dependent on EES who make up 40% of the company's revenue. The contract is up for renewal and the loss of such a significant proportion of income could seriously affect the company's viability.

– The company's core market is mature. There is unlikely to be further growth in sales of reels of paper. News Reel need to seek out new markets and or new products.

– In order to achieve its competitive advantage of flexibility, News Reel have had to accept higher costs of production. Unfortunately this will require higher selling prices which may be difficult to sustain in a tough economic climate.

Key strategic opportunities

Key opportunities for acquisitions have been identified by the company and these will be explored in more detail later. Other opportunities for the business might include expansion into the mainline continent or developing recycled paper. These will also be explored in more detail later. But overall there are a number of opportunities that News Reel could pursue.

Key strategic threats

- The economic downturn in Eastlandia is a threat to New Reel. During such times customers might abandon differentiators and switch to cheaper suppliers in order to cope with falling sales.

- In the longer term, technological changes such as the growth of news aggregators and ereaders might reduce the need for such large volumes of paper products that provide news and entertainment.

- New competition from the mainland may enter the market. They are likely to be bigger than News Reel and have economies of scale which can further drive down selling prices.

- Recycled paper may be more culturally acceptable and in some instances cheaper than traditional paper reels. This substitute could win customers away from News Reels traditional market.

Overall strategic position

News Reel has a strong history and a strong competitive position. But it is over-reliant on one product and one customer in a maturing market. As its market continues to change its strategic position is likely to worsen. It therefore needs to seek out new opportunities in order to secure the long term future of the business.

(b) **Future strategic options**

Appropriateness of strategic diversification

There are a number of strategic options open to News Reel, but not all of them will satisfy the three criteria of being feasible, suitable and acceptable. Ansoff summarised strategic growth options into four categories and these are explored below.

Market penetration

This involves gaining market share by enhancing a competitive advantage through competitive strategies such as cost leadership and differentiation. Cost leadership is unlikely to be feasible for News Reel due to its low economies of scale (when compared to rivals) and flexible production methods. It would also appear that News Reel have already differentiated the business well and there would be few opportunities for further differentiation. Market penetration would therefore be an unsuitable strategy.

Product development

News Reel could attempt to develop a recycled paper range. However they are likely to lack skills and experience in this area as well as sufficient supply and production facilities. They are also likely to encounter more developed and reputable competitors who will have potentially developed barriers to entry through customer tie-ups and branding. Furthermore, it would appear that the demand for recycled paper is in the low-cost, low-quality sector, which would not suit News Reel's competitive advantage.

Overall, both the feasibility and suitability of a product development strategy can be questioned.

Market development

Market development could be achieved through expansion into the mainland continent. However News Reel are likely to experience similar competitive problems as those experienced in product development as there will be established rivals with better reputations and lower costs. Also, the mainland market is likely to be experiencing similar maturity to the Eastlandian market with the same long-term threats. It would therefore appear to be neither suitable nor acceptable for the long-term future of the business.

Diversification

Feasible acquisitions have been identified by the company and these appear to be acceptable to the board. As already discussed, News Reel need to change their strategic position and diversification would appear to be the most suitable way to achieve this.

Acquisition of Quickpulp

This is a form of backward integration. News Reel would take control of a supplier and it is likely that they would source more materials from this supplier.

Quickpulp seem eager to sell and News Reel may therefore acquire the business at a favourable price. It is also appealing to the production director as this is a way to secure supplies and possibly drive down production costs in order to compete better and win more tenders.

But the suitability of this strategy must be questioned. It is likely Quickpulp are willing to sell because they are experiencing the same market maturity and downward pressure on prices that News Reel are experiencing. In effect, an acquisition of Quickpulp would only deepen News Reels problems and make the company more entrenched in an industry that is mature and that News Reel should be looking to remove itself from long-term. News Reel would still be reliant on EES and face the same competitive threats that it is currently experiencing. Buying Quickpulp would also increase the exit barriers from the industry if News Reel was to attempt an exit in the future.

Furthermore, News Reel's key competitive advantage is its flexibility. However, tying itself in with a supplier would potentially reduce flexibility and destroy News Reels competitive advantage.

Overall, it would be advised that News Reel avoids an acquisition of Quickpulp.

Acquisition of Medicnote

An acquisition of Medicnote also appears feasible and acceptable to the board. Once again they are looking for a buyer and their overtrading difficulties might again mean that News Reel can make the acquisition at a favourable price.

But Medicnote would appear to be much more suitable as an acquisition than Quickpulp. It is experiencing growing demand, is very profitable and is in a unique, specialised market position. It is also a move away from a reliance on EES and the problems that News Reel are experiencing in their current market.

This acquisition is likely to remove a number of News Reel's weaknesses (mature market, over-reliance on EES) and avoid some of the future threats (such as social and technological changes which may make newsprint obsolete). Overall it appears to be feasible, suitable and acceptable and it is recommended that News Reel pursue an acquisition of Medicnote.

(c) **Strategy lenses**

The *design lens* views strategy as the deliberate positioning of an organisation as the result of some 'rational, analytical, structured and directive process'. Through the design lens it is the responsibility of top management to plan the destiny of the organisation. Lower levels of management carry out the operational actions required by the strategy. The design lens is associated with objective setting and a plan for moving the organisation towards these objectives. In the context of the scenario, this process has already begun. News Reel has analysed its strategic position and begun to make strategic choices. It will have a deliberate 'design' to reduce dependence on news print and move towards pharmaceutical paper and other products and markets. It needs to set clear, long term objectives for the business and a mission statement of where it wants to be in ten years time.

Strategy as experience provides a more adaptive approach to strategy, building on and changing the existing strategy. Changes are incremental as the organisation adapts to new opportunities and threats in the environment. The experience lens views strategy development as the combination of individual and collective experience together with the taken-for-granted assumptions of cultural influences.

For News Reel, it will not completely abandon news print, especially not in the short run. The move towards diversification will be an incremental one and it will continue to tender for contracts and win business in news print.

It also needs to use the experience it has gained from this industry and apply it to new strategies. For example, its flexibility could be used to improve the performance and competitive advantage of MedicNote. This experience will be built into the design lens and there will be some crossover between the two. The company will have a definite design on where it wants to go, but this will be built on past experience and knowledge.

Strategy as ideas has a central role for innovation and new ideas. It sees strategy as emerging from the variety and diversity in an organisation. It is as likely to come from the bottom of the organisation as from the top. Consequently, the organisation should foster conditions that allow ideas to emerge and to be considered for inclusion in a 'mainstream strategy'. Certain conditions, such as a changing and unpredictable environment foster ideas and innovation.

News Reel cannot be expected to predict what technologies will arrive in the market place and the social changes that might arise in Eastlandia and the mainland continent. But it needs to be prepared to react to these. Staff should be encouraged to develop ideas and innovations that take account of technological and social changes. The ten year design will not predict or plan for these changes, but the strategic planning process has to ensure that, as these ideas and market needs emerge, the company are in a position to react to them.

Overall, the strategic planning process is likely to combine elements of all three lenses. The chairman can create a long term mission of where the business should be in ten years time and design strategies to get it to that position. But these strategies should build on the experiences that the company has had and be ready to accept new ideas that might emerge both internally and externally.

Question 13: Pelatihan

(a) **Assessment of the company's performance**

The product portfolio

The Boston Consulting Group Matrix (BCG) categorises products (or SBU's) according to their market growth on the one hand, and their relative market share on the other.

Finance and Accounting

According to BCG, Finance and Accounting courses would be classified as a cash cow, having a relatively high share of what is a lower growth market according to the independent survey. Since the survey states that the market is growing at a slower rate than Law and HRM this will make it less attractive to new entrants. This SBU should not therefore need cash to defend its position, but instead be able to provide funds to finance other areas of the business.

Marketing

According to BCG, Marketing would be classified as a dog product, having a relatively low share of a low growth (and hence unattractive) market. The market is actually in decline according to the survey. This would normally imply a product with few prospects which should be discontinued in the long term.

Law

According to BCG, Law would be classified as a star product, having a high share of a high growth (and hence attractive) market. A star needs to be defended since new entrants will be attracted to the market and potentially steal Pelatihan's market share.

HRM

According to BCG, HRM would be classified as a problem child having a relatively low share of a high growth (and hence attractive) market. To continue with a problem child and grow market share, cash will need to be taken from other SBU's and invested.

Overall Portfolio Evaluation

On first glance Pelatihan's portfolio appears balanced with Finance and Accounting courses generating cash to fund HRM and Law. Only Marketing has a questionable future, with competition from online courses forcing the market into decline. However, the BCG appraisal is simplistic and Pelatihan's profits are significantly below budget suggesting there are issues with the present portfolio.

Strengths and Weaknesses of Pelatihan's performance

Strengths:

Performance of law and finance

The Law SBU has achieved its sales revenue target of $4m. As a 'star' with 35% of the market in a buoyant sector, this is encouraging for Pelatihan. The competition in this market is strong, with Koulos and Opleid having 30% and 25% of the market respectively. These other colleges are likely to try to increase market share going forward and Pelatihan will need to defend their position in order to safeguard Law as a future cash cow (when demand slows.)

Student day numbers (defined as one student attending for one day) are up on budget in both the Law faculty (5% above budget) and the Finance faculty (1.5% above budget). This would suggest that Pelatihan has been successful in attracting students to these courses (despite the fact that these additional days have not translated into extra revenue.) This may be due to the fact that both Law and Finance are areas where 'update' courses will be popular as legislation or accounting standards change. All qualified personnel in country A could potentially be targeted to attend such courses.

HRM on the other hand, has seen a student day reduction of 23% against budget. Despite this, corresponding revenue is only down by 11.4% or $0.4m. Budgeted revenue per student day in this faculty was $2333 and a figure of $2696 has actually been achieved. The increasing demand for HRM courses as mentioned in the independent survey may explain why Pelatihan has been able to charge more per student day than budgeted. However, since this is a problem child SBU, requiring significant investment, Pelatihan will need to work on attracting more students on to courses to bring actual days in line with the budget.

Revenue from each faculty

Pelatihan is not overly dependent on any one sector for revenue, however Finance represents the biggest contributor at 34.7% (budget 34.6%). Since finance is the Cash Cow, the generation of extra revenue is a positive. The percentage of revenue coming from marketing (the dog SBU) has fallen to 6.6 (budget 7.7) which shows a good strategic direction is being taken in order to become less reliant on this product.

Efficiency of each faculty

The finance faculty staff are the most efficient, with 88 student days per staff member. This is a relative strength and is further borne out by the mix statistics which show that the finance faculty teaches 36% of Pelatihan's student days with only 32% of the staff. Since Pelatihan is the market leader in Finance and Accounting, building on such economies of scale is essential. Finance, as a cash cow SBU, needs to provide funding for the other faculties and the staff efficiency would seem to give good grounding for this to occur.

The law faculty, with rapidly rising demand has also been able to generate a relatively high number of student days per staff member at 81 (against an average of 75.)

Weaknesses

Overall performance

Overall sales revenue is down 6.9% or $0.9m against budget. The marketing sector is the worst performer, missing the target by 20% (which explains $0.2m of the total shortfall.)

This is disappointing since presumably the online courses offered by The Marketing Institute were considered when the budget was set and more student days would appear to have been lost than envisaged at that time (marketing student days are down 9% on budget).

The discounts being demanded by large employer organisations could be an explanation for the loss of expected marketing revenue as well as the 6.6% fall against budget of finance faculty revenue.

Budgeted profit before interest and tax ($2.3m) is all but wiped out in Pelatihan's actual results. An overall margin of 17.7% was expected but in reality only 0.8% was achieved. The weaknesses which have led to this result are explored further below.

Cost control

There are significant weaknesses in cost control in each faculty with all 4 exceeding budgeted costs despite revenue targets not being hit (this weakness can also be seen in the 16.7% increase in central costs over budget.) Overall sales revenue is down 6.9% as mentioned above but for this to translate into a 96% drop in expected profits is indicative of total inefficiency.

What is unclear from the analysis is why, in a mainly fixed cost business, such massive increases in cost should have occurred at all. The problem is compounded by the fact the CEO has been unable to find a senior member of staff willing to take responsibility for financial planning and control. An investigation into the reasons for such high costs is therefore unlikely.

Profit margins

The marketing faculty, classified as a 'dog' by the BCG is loss making despite an expected 50% PBIT margin. All other margins are significantly lower than the budgeted figures with HRM falling from 28.5% in the budget to 12.9% in the actual results. This does suggest that the problems with cost control span the entire organisation.

Revenue per staff member

Staff members are seemingly unable to generate as much revenue as expected. Despite the director of the Finance faculty spending so much time teaching students and dealing with clients, staff in his SBU are 6.6% below budget in terms of revenue per staff member.

Mix of days/staff and revenue

Inefficiencies can be seen in the marketing faculty, employing 8% of the staff to generate only 7% of Pelatihan's revenue and student days and also the Law division, using 36% of the staff to generate 33% of the revenue. Pelatihan should consider using 'multi skilled' tutors who can teach across faculties to try and increase utilisation of all staff.

Revenue and costs per student day

The finance and marketing faculties have both experienced adverse variances in terms of revenue per student day, presumably due, at least in part to the excessive discounts demanded by corporate clients. The law faculty has also seen a 5% adverse variance in pricing however, and it may be that the competition from Koulos and Opleid has been stronger than expected, driving prices down.

The cost per student day is of real concern, particularly in the marketing faculty where it is double that budgeted. The HRM faculty has also failed to control costs, with cost per student day 41% higher than expected. Action will need to be taken immediately to deal with the problems faced by this division.

Reliability of budgets

Finally, it is worth mentioning that there may be a weakness in the budget itself. With no senior member of staff willing to take on responsibility for it, it is possible that the targets set were not realistic in the current climate, or that mistakes have been made (for example the budgeted cost per student day in Marketing which does appear low compared to the other faculties and has led to the almost 100% adverse variance mentioned earlier.)

(b) Overall strategic position and performance of Pelatihan

Strengths

Pelatihan is one of the largest and most highly regarded colleges in country A. Its brand name will be a significant strength and should serve to attract students to enrol on its courses. Pelatihan has a stronger position in the Finance and Accounting and Law markets due to its superior market share.

Pelatihan is operating in country A which has a well-educated younger population and a stable government likely to continue its investment in training. The fact that many of Pelatihan's students are funded by employers gives Pelatihan some security in respect of demand levels. Employers are more likely to pay for 'block' training or see staff through to the end of a qualification despite economic conditions. They will also provide significant student numbers in many instances (as is the case in the Law faculty.)

Country A is much more stable than many of its neighbours with no history of violence or unrest. This is likely to be attractive to overseas students who cannot access training in unstable home nations.

The structure of Pelatihan is divisionalised with four senior tutors each heading up a faculty and the CEO overseeing the entire operation. This will create focus, with each 'expert' director making decisions tailored to their market. The fact that Pelatihan has grown organically (as opposed to via acquisition like Koulos and Opleid) will further add to the cohesiveness of its structure and the ability to present a uniform culture with none of the integration problems likely to be faced by other acquisitive competitors.

The economy of A is growing at 15% a year. This means increasing numbers of organisations requiring training are present. Since Pelatihan doesn't specialise in one sector, it is able to cater to the training requirements of all organisations. Companies which do not require accountancy or legal training may still take advantage of HRM courses or marketing. Pelatihan's broad product range is however, also present in its biggest competitors.

Weaknesses

Pelatihan has a major weakness in financial planning and control, with inaccurate budgets and no real understanding of why the 07/08 results are so far below budget. In such a highly competitive industry this is a serious problem, leading to poor decision making across the organisation.

Pelatihan provides similar products to its main competitors and this lack of differentiation makes it difficult for Pelatihan to compete on anything other than price. Pelatihan's pricing strategy is being threatened by a small number of employer organisations demanding discounts in excess of those usually offered. The inability to negotiate and build up ongoing relationships with clients to protect against such demands is a weakness.

Most of Pelatihan's costs will be fixed (for example, staff costs and premises) and this exposes the business to great risk if revenue falls. Any such fall (for example through discounts) will impact immediately on profit.

Pelatihan would appear to be less innovative than its main competitors. The introduction of e-learning by the Institute of Marketing has been enough to push the marketing sector which Pelatihan operates in into decline. Koulos is known to be developing on online courses but despite this, Pelatihan has no plans to do likewise.

There are staff issues within Pelatihan. Firstly, the loss of staff from the law faculty to join a main competitor signals a lack of loyalty amongst what should be, in a training organisation, the biggest asset of the business (namely tutors). Without the reputation of talented tutors, Pelatihan will find it difficult to attract students and it is also the case that students may follow tutors to their new employer further weakening Pelatihan's position.

The second staff issue is apparent from the inability of the CEO to find a volunteer amongst his senior colleagues to take over the financial planning and control of the organisation (a weakness highlighted above). The director of the finance faculty, an obvious choice for the role, claims to be too busy dealing with clients despite having a relatively large contingent of 23 staff. To leave the CEO (a lawyer) in charge of this particular area would appear to be unwise, particularly for an organisation which presumably employs many qualified accountants, the director of Finance being just one, who could take on the role.

Opportunities

Firstly, Pelatihan could choose to invest in the Law and HRM faculties in line with the findings of the BCG matrix. Demand for courses in both areas is rising rapidly and Pelatihan will need significant investment to maintain its current leading market share in Law and build up its relatively low market share in HRM.

On-line courses are a potential area for investment and have already proved successful for the Marketing Institute in country A. It is likely to be the case in the future that provision of such courses becomes 'expected' by students and moves very quickly from being a core competence to a threshold competence. Pelatihan needs to begin investing now, in all faculties to bring this kind of training into their organisation. Online courses could enable them to sell courses to overseas students, allowing market development without the costs associated with setting up new colleges.

Since Pelatihan has staff and premises, they could look to provide other courses and increase the utilisation of both. For example, there may be a demand for bespoke training courses which Pelatihan, with a talented tutor team, could easily provide. It may even be possible to carry out these courses at client premises, saving even more costs. Such courses, if successful, would impact greatly on revenue without a corresponding increase in costs. Koulos and Opleid both have a significant share of the 'other' course market (40% and 20% respectively) and Pelatihan could use its reputation as a highly regarded training provider to cross over into this market.

Pelatihan is one of the three dominant training organisations in country A, however there are smaller colleges operating in every one of Pelatihan's sectors. An opportunity may arise to purchase one or more of these smaller colleges, particularly if they have a significant share of the 'other' courses market (small colleges hold 40% market share). Although Pelatihan has never grown this way before, it would provide a quick entry into a potentially lucrative market.

Country A has a growing economy and no history of violence or terrorist attacks. Many neighbouring countries are not so stable and since Pelatihan does not currently offer full time courses or accommodation, they could attempt to attract students from neighbouring countries by offering both.

A strategy to increase the utilisation of tutors could be devised with teaching across faculties becoming part of the culture at Pelatihan. Finally, developing relationships (and contracts) with corporate clients so that they are not in a position of power to demand high discounts is an opportunity Pelatihan should try to exploit.

Threats

A is a developed Asian country whose government has been in power for 6 years and has been responsible for making education more widely available as well as supporting the development of new industries. A general election is however coming up and there are fears that the opposition party may be elected. This could change the position of training companies significantly if they no longer have the support of the ruling party, they may find that taxes increase or their market contracts.

There are threats to the Finance and Marketing faculties from a small number of corporate clients who are demanding high discounts. This is also apparent in the Law faculty where one particular client books up to half the places on a course but demands a 20% discount. If Pelatihan does not offer these discounts there is a very real chance that clients will be lost to the competition, since, as already mentioned, the product itself is unlikely to be differentiated and price will be the main bargaining tool.

As well as the potential loss of clients, more tutors could be lost to competitors. The Law faculty operates in a fast growing market and at present Pelatihan is the market leader. Koulos is however only 5% behind in terms of market share and since students will often follow popular tutors to a new training organisation, there is a possibility that Pelatihan will lose its market leader position as a result of this loss of staff.

Provision of online courses by the Marketing Institute is probably the reason why the marketing sector has gone into decline. Koulos operate in all four of Pelatihan's sectors and are already in the process of developing online training. There is a risk that the provision of online training by a competitor pushes the other 'traditional' sectors into decline, leaving Pelatihan with very little to fall back on.

In addition, there are rumours of a possible merger between Koulos and Opleid. If this were to go ahead, Pelatihan would lose their market leader position in both the law and finance faculties. The new merged operation would be able to exploit significant economies of scale and Pelatihan would find it impossible to compete.

Finally, poor financial control and ultimately, disappointing performance against budget may be enough to damage Pelatihan's reputation.

Question 14: WG plc

(a) Product development

For any company to retain its position as market leader, it must introduce a continual stream of new products, services or ideas to replace those that are declining. WG plc holds a position as one of the leaders in the global pharmaceutical industry, so it is important that it is able to introduce new products to replace existing ones when patents expire. Because the development phase in the pharmaceutical industry is very long and very risky, it is important that WG plc invests regularly in a programme of research and development (R&D). This will help to ensure that it has new products and services that will meet both its profitability objective and its aim of developing innovative medicines and services.

It has been a well-established idea for many years that products and services follow a **'life cycle'** that affects the current rate of sale and, more importantly, has significant implications for the strategic options for the future. The theory breaks the economic life of a product into a number of stages. Being aware of the fact that a product has a life cycle can become the foundation for policies and practices aimed at building up the market. The best advantage it gives is in the launching of a new product.

The **Boston Consulting Group (BCG) matrix** attempts to relate critical strategic issues to the different phases of the product life cycle. Using the rate of market growth and relative market share, the matrix classifies products as either cash cows, stars, problem children or dogs. It is likely that, at any time, companies will have products in all these categories. The position of the product or service within the matrix has implications for the cash flows of the company and it is therefore important that the managers monitor the position continuously. They must recognise that products that are currently classified as cash cows will eventually become dogs and cease to generate cash. To avoid having too many products in a low growth and low market share category, it is essential that steps are taken to ensure that the company is always developing new products that have the potential to become stars. For companies like WG plc it is imperative that adequate resources are allocated to R&D in the strategic plan.

An example of the effects of the stages in the life cycle and in the Boston matrix can be illustrated by one of WG plc's products. Four years ago one particular drug produced almost half of its turnover. Because the patent expires next year, it is expected that sales will drop to represent no more than 10% of turnover. This type of problem makes the company vulnerable to competition in the dynamic environment of the pharmaceutical industry. It is essential for WG plc to be continually developing new products, if it is to retain its dominant position in the industry.

Almost 15% of WG plc's turnover last year was spent on research and development. They have the largest research and development organisation of all pharmaceutical companies worldwide. It is clear that the managers have taken a decision to allocate resources to research activities to ensure that the company retains its competitive advantage. They are also determined to produce and develop new and innovative medicines and services worldwide to enable the company to achieve its corporate mission and objectives.

If the company did not provide the necessary resources to fund R&D, it is likely that the number of new products would not keep up with demand and the company would lose its dominant position in the pharmaceutical industry. This could lead to competitors enjoying increases in their sales, market share and, possibly, profits at WG plc's expense. R&D is evidently the source of WG plc's competitive advantage and so sufficient resources must be allocated to this activity if the company is to retain its current dominance in the pharmaceutical industry.

(b) **Strategic alliances**

Strategic alliances play an important part in global strategies where competitors lack a key success factor for some market. It may be distribution, a brand name, a selling organisation, the technology, R&D capability or manufacturing capability. The pharmaceutical industry requires large inputs of both technical expertise and resources, as R&D activities are crucial to the success of the companies. There are many practical issues that the directors of WG plc would need to consider if the company entered a strategic alliance with a competitor for the joint development of future pharmaceutical products.

If the strategic alliance is an informal arrangement it can be implemented faster and be more flexible. As conditions change and people change, the alliance can be adjusted. The problem with this type of arrangement is that with low exit barriers and commitment, there may be a low level of strategic importance and a temptation to pull out when difficulties arise.

A formal joint venture involving equity and legal documentation, on the other hand, has a different set of problems. When equity sharing is involved, there are issues about control, return on investment and achieving a fair percentage of the venture. A major concern is whether or not such a permanent relationship will be equitable in the face of uncertainty about the relative contributions of the partners and the eventual success of the venture. Before the commencement of the strategic alliance it is important that an equitable and agreed method of contributing to and sharing the venture's outputs is finalised.

Basically there are usually two sets of systems, people, cultures and structures that need to be reconciled, so it is essential that the control and management of the venture is discussed and finalised to minimise the possibility of serious disputes during the collaboration. It may be necessary to allocate special managers to the collaboration, but there will still be issues that arise in relation to the fundamental loyalty and commitment of the staff that participate in the venture. The main areas for the directors of WG plc to consider are the extent of the alliance in terms of markets and products and the sharing of costs and expenses between the two participants. It is important that these are agreed so that the position is clear to both parties.

One of the main issues facing the directors of WG plc is likely to be the input of resources, both intangible and physical. The intangible assets such as skill, expertise and patents are likely to be the cause of more disputes than the capital and machinery in an organisation. It may be necessary to share confidential and sensitive information that might prove to be difficult before trust is built up between the parties involved at both the personal and corporate levels. To enhance the chances of a successful strategic alliance, both sides must gain. They should protect and enhance the assets and skills being contributed and not let a partner take over.

The directors should also consider the effect on competitors and regulatory bodies to avoid any legislation or regulations that will affect the alliance adversely. By recognising that there may potential problems in this area, it may be possible to minimise the impact of them.

All of these practical issues will need to be agreed by the directors from the outset if the alliance is to be successful. However, if the companies are able to manage this effectively, a strategic alliance provides the potential of accomplishing a strategic objective or task quickly, inexpensively and with a high prospect for success. It should result in major benefits.

Question 15: Multinational company

The company currently operates with two different structures:

- A centralised structure with the European Head Office maintaining responsibility for product design, manufacturing and the product range.
- A decentralised structure based on national divisions within Europe, with each division's managers being responsible for setting the selling prices of each product and the distribution of products.

This organisation, using joint responsibility, has the following weaknesses:

- Conflict and resentment between head office managers and divisional managers will arise because some decisions are imposed on divisional managers whilst they must make others. It is likely that when things go wrong, managers spend a lot of time blaming each other instead of trying to solve problems.
- Divisional managers are likely to be de-motivated by the removal of their authority over the years as the European Head Office has taken over responsibility for decisions they used to have.
- As European business practice becomes more integrated and greater harmonisation between countries occurs, there will be less benefits that can be obtained from having a divisional structure based on different countries. Duplication of work will result, particularly associated with marketing. Further integration within Europe is likely to result in a single European Currency, harmonisation of taxes and pricing within Europe becoming more uniform.

Recommendation

The company should restructure and reconfigure itself as a divisional structure based on related product groups. The company is quite large with over 100,000 employees in Europe.

The company should be divided into three or four product divisions comprising about 30,000 – 35,000 employees with head office retaining responsibility for administration. Each division should be responsible for product design, production decisions and marketing for the whole of Europe. Each division can be further sub-divided into small product groups each having its own management team.

The structure will have the following benefits:

- Each division can be established as an investment centre with its own performance targets. This will enable head office to monitor each division and, at the same time, will enable divisional management to make their own decisions.

- Head Office will be less involved in all operational decisions allowing decisions to be made by divisional managers who know about their product range.

- Each division will be more involved in all operational decisions allowing decisions to be made by divisional managers, who know about their product range.

- Each division will be large enough to benefit from economies of scale. This will ensure that inefficiencies of having too many small national divisions can be eliminated.

- The managers of each division will be motivated to ensure that their division operates effectively and economically, as the performance of their division can be benchmarked against its competitors.

- It will be easier to divest a division at a later time if required or add a division should an acquisition or merger be made.

- The European Head Office can be reduced in size because some of its current responsibilities will be taken over by the divisions.

It should be emphasised that this is a strategic structural change and will take time to accomplish. It will need the support of the company's managers and employees and its success will depend upon the integration of the European business environment. If this does not take place the current structure should be retained with minor improvements.

Question 16: QS Software – Part 1

(a) **Organisational structure**

The formal structure of QS, as described in its organisation chart can be analysed as follows.

(i) (Departmentation is primarily on a functional basis, although it also reflects product categories (web, software, hardware, repairs). The management partnership is also functionally divided.

(ii) The overall configuration is what Mintzberg calls a 'simple structure'.

– The strategic apex (the partners) exercises direct control over the operating core: sales assistants, technicians, software engineers and web designers.

– Other functions are pared down to a minimum. There is no middle line or technostructure, and only a one-person support staff (the administrator).

(iii) The organisation is flat, with (as far as we know) only two levels of hierarchy.

The advantages of QS's structure for its environment may be summarised as follows.

– It has short lines of communication and authority, with direct connection between the strategic apex and operating core. This should lead to responsiveness to client demands and environmental changes (e.g. developments in web-based technologies), as decisions can swiftly be made in response to upward communication and feedback.

– Mintzberg suggested that simple structures are suited to dynamic environments, because they are able to co-ordinate by direct supervision.

– Clients requiring individual products or services are likely to benefit from the clarity of the functional departments (and their distinct locations).

The disadvantages of QS's structure for its environment may be summarised as follows.

- Direct supervision from the strategic apex may become dysfunctional where the span of control and the number of tasks to be supervised gets too large. The two owners may not be able to supervise the complex multiple tasks required if QS wins the RGA contract.

- QS does not (as far as we know) have alternative co-ordination mechanisms in place. In order to co-ordinate project work (such as the RGA contract), some element of matrix organisation will be required, with software engineers, web designers, administrators and managers working together on the project team.

- Functional organisations can create vertical barriers to the 'horizontal' expectations of customers who require multi-functional expertise on a project (Peters).

(b) **Developing the organisation**

Mintzberg identified five basic parts or elements within an organisation:

- There is a strategic apex, consisting of the managers who make the key policy decisions.

- There is an operating core, consisting of the employees who do the basic operational work of making goods or providing services for customers.

- The middle line consists of the middle managers who link the strategic apex to the operating core.

- There is a technostructure, which consists of the technical experts and analysts who plan and control the work of others in the organisation (such as accountants).

- Finally, there are support staff who provide internal services, such as building cleaning and maintenance, car fleet management and legal services.

Mintzberg suggested that the organisation structure for any organisation will depend on the extent to which one or more of these elements dominates within the organisation. For example, if the strategic apex is dominant, the organisation will tend to be entrepreneurial. If the technostructure is strong, the organisation might be a 'machine bureaucracy' focusing primarily on improving deficiency. When the middle line is strong, the organisation will tend to be diversified and conglomerate in nature. When the operating core is strong, for example in a hospital or in schools, the organisation will lean towards professional proficiency in its operations.

It would appear that the owners of the company want to allow their IT specialists a large degree of initiative, suggesting that professional proficiency will be an important feature of the company. It is not totally clear, however, whether the owners plan to create a strong middle line (consisting perhaps of IT specialists-cum-managers), or whether they expect to retain a fairly large amount of management control themselves.

If the owners intend to develop a strong middle line over time, it might be expected that the company will expand through diversification and innovation, retaining an emphasis on proficiency in developing IT software.

Question 17: Nikki Photocopiers

(a) Whether service and maintenance should have been prioritised for reengineering.

Critical success factors for Nikki should include the following:

– Production cost

– Quality control

– Value for money

– Features

– Reliability

– Servicing and maintenance.

Servicing is just one of a number of key areas that could be a candidate for reengineering.

Using Harmon's strategy/process matrix, servicing would be classified as follows:

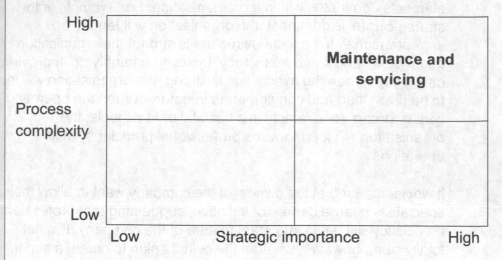

Processes that lie at the upper-right are complex, dynamic and of high strategic importance. These are usually the processes that provide the organisation with its competitive advantage and should be nurtured accordingly.

The main arguments for reengineering servicing and maintenance first are as follows:

– It has seen the largest fall in the magazine ratings.

– Nikki have their worst score in the ratings in this respect.

– The new CRM system does not appear to be generating the benefits it should have.

It could be argued, however, that value for money should have been targeted first, with its implications for pricing and production, as falling from being rated 1st to 2nd has major implications for competitive advantage. A fall from 5th to 7th in servicing is unlikely to be the main factor in Nikki Photocopiers' decline.

(b) Impact of the proposed changes on competitive advantage.

We are not given enough information in the scenario to classify the firm's competitive strategy as either differentiation or cost leadership. However, the process change can be explained in terms of its impact on cost and/or quality as follows:

Quality improvements

- By avoiding having to explain issues over the phone, there is less chance of the engineer being misinformed about the nature of the customer's problem. The likelihood of them turning up without relevant components and having to pay more than one visit is thus reduced.

- The system allows for more detailed customer requirements to be sent to the engineer than could be communicated effectively by phone.

Cost savings

- A cut in administration input and the elimination of the role of call-takers could lead to job cuts and cost-savings.

- Invoices will be able to be prepared instantly rather than at the end of each week. This should result in quicker cash receipts from customers and improved cash flow, thus reducing financing costs, for example.

- Savings in postage and printing costs as the system becomes more paper-free.

(c) IT/IS implications

The main IT/IS implications of the proposal are as follows:

Software – the CRM system

- The proposal involves the CRM system automatically generating work orders and sending details to engineers' PDAs. Furthermore, details are automatically sent to accounts once the job is done.

- While none of these are technically difficult, it is not known whether the current system has these capabilities. If not, then additional add-on applications (either off-the-shelf or bespoke) may have to be purchased.

- Even if present, new templates may have to be designed and training given to call-takers and engineers on filling them in correctly.

Hardware – using PDAs

- Presumably new PDAs (and associated software) will have to be bought and training given to engineers on their use.

- An automatic phone system where calls are made between PDAs and the CRM system may also be needed.

(d) Should maintenance be outsourced?

Arguments for outsourcing maintenance

- Photocopiers are relatively simple machines, so it is likely that external firms will have the expertise to be able to maintain them.

- External firms may have economies of scale – for example, having more engineers makes it possible to see customers sooner.

Arguments against outsourcing maintenance

- The most suitable processes for outsourcing are repetitive and transaction-intensive. Maintenance may have aspects of the former but does not fit the latter criterion.

- Dealing with customer queries is a critical success factor so should be kept in-house.

- Also there is a high risk of damaging the firm's reputation and goodwill if problems are not handled properly.

- The process of maintenance may generate useful information for designing new/improved photocopiers.

On balance, the critical nature of service and maintenance means it should be kept in-house.

Question 18: Institute of Information Systems Administrators

(a) A bespoke solution is one developed specifically for an organisation. In this instance the Institute of Information System Administrators would comprehensively specify their requirements for the **On-Line Marking Project** (OLMAP). This requirements specification would be used by the internal Information Systems (IS) department or by an external software house to produce a system that exactly matched the requirements. The software would be owned by the Institute, who could make changes to it in the future to reflect changes to the original requirements.

A software package is a generalised solution to an application area offered for sale by a software vendor. In this instance a software company has recognised that a number of educational and training organisations would benefit from on-line marking software. They have constructed their own specification of requirements and developed a software package called Emark which they now market and license throughout the world.

Advantages of the software package approach to systems development might include:

Quality

The software package is a proven product that has undergone systems testing (in development) and user acceptance testing (by the users who have already bought and used the package). Hence the product should be bug-free, as well as fulfilling most of the functional requirements of the application. The implementation should not be affected by the programming errors and misconceptions that are normally associated with bespoke systems development.

Time

The bespoke systems development needs to be tightly specified, designed, programmed and tested. These parts of the lifecycle are very time-consuming and during this period requirements may change, so complicating the process even further. The software package is a product that already exists. It can be purchased and implemented almost immediately. There is no requirement for design, programming, unit and systems testing.

Other perceived advantages include:

- High quality documentation and training available for inspection.
- Maintenance and enhancement provided at a fixed price under an agreement.
- Try before you buy, because the software is already available.

Disadvantages of the software package approach to systems development might include:

Failure to completely fit requirements

One of the most commonly claimed disadvantages of the software package approach is the inability of the product to fit all of the users' requirements. This means that either:

(1) Users have to make compromises and accept that they will not get all the functionality they require, or

(2) Tailored amendments will have to be made to the software product to deliver the required functionality.

Whichever way is chosen, it is clear that most software packages do not fulfil all the user requirements defined for a particular application. Furthermore, they often include facilities and functions not required by a particular user, which only serve to confuse when the product is implemented into the organisation. In contrast, the bespoke solution should completely fulfil all the user's requirements and, if it doesn't, will be amended until it does.

Financial stability of the supplier

Internal Information Systems (IS) departments do not go out of business. However, external software suppliers are subject to the vagaries of management and the markets. There is a risk that they may go out of business, or experience financial problems that affect the quality of their support and development services. It is possible to reduce these risks (through Escrow agreements) but the disruption likely to accompany the enactment of such an agreement should not be underestimated.

Other disadvantages include:

- Inability to generate a competitive edge because the package is also available to competitors.
- Ownership is retained by the supplier.
- Legal redress is virtually impossible because of the licence agreement.

(b) In the context of the OLMAP project, performance testing will mean

- Testing the scanning time of a batch of scripts.
- Testing the response time of the system when a specified number of examiners and markers simultaneously access scripts for marking and moderation.

Testing the scanning time of a batch of scripts.

A test can be set up where a certain number of scripts are taken from the IISA Head Office and scanned into the system. The time taken for scanning can be recorded and further tests may be undertaken to confirm this time. This time can then be scaled up to estimate the time for scanning the scripts of 200,000 students. Scanning time should scale linearly with the number of scripts scanned into the system.

Testing the response time of the system

This test is difficult to simulate. It is likely that a limited test can be arranged with markers and examiners asked to access the system and record the results. However, the use of load testing software would be more effective. This software allows the testers to simulate a large number of 'virtual' users and to diagnose any bottlenecks. Any problems can be addressed before the software is released. The point here is that the response time of the system is unlikely to scan linearly with the number of users accessing it.

(c) In **Direct Changeover/Conversion**, the new system is implemented completely and the old system is withdrawn. Thus processing of the current system may end on a Friday night and all transactions pass through the new computer system from Monday morning onwards. Where possible, direct changeovers should occur in slack periods and take advantage of natural breaks in the operations of the organisation, such as industrial holidays.

Direct Changeover/Conversion is particularly appropriate to the OLMAP application because there is a natural break in processing within the application. It is not a continual process (like order processing, invoicing and payroll) but an application that runs for a limited amount of time every six months. Direct Changeover/ Conversion demands very thorough testing, but it is the quickest and cheapest implementation strategy.

In parallel running the old and new systems are run simultaneously for an agreed period of time and results from the two systems are compared. Once the user has complete confidence in the system the old system is abandoned and transactions are only passed through the new one. Parallel running places a large administrative overhead on the user department because every transaction has to be done twice – once through the established procedures and then again through the new computer system.

Parallel running makes very little sense in the OLMAP application because the proposed and current systems are so different. The proposed application area (marking) is currently not computerised and any attempt at a parallel run would be costly (involving courier and marking costs) and time consuming. It is unlikely that the results would be very valuable (for example, what lessons could be gained from marking a paper script and its screen-based equivalent?) and they could not be achieved in the tight time constraints of the marking process. The OLMAP application will need thorough testing, but there is little to gain from parallel running. If direct changeover/conversion fails, it would be relatively easy to switch back to the current process as all the paper examination scripts will still be available in a warehouse in Singapore.

Question 19: SDW

(a) Establishing the website

Before Mr M tries to establish an internet strategy, he should look at his overall business strategy. In doing this he should find answers to a number of questions, such as:

- Is he only going to continue to operate between three domestic cities?

- How far does he want to expand both internally (in the home market as indicated) and beyond (internationally)?

- Does he have the capacity to take on more bookings should they arise?

- Is he aiming at a different market sector?

- Does he have a business plan?

Checking this strategy is essential because the IT strategy must be seen to support the overall strategy of the company and not drive it. In the case of the SDW Company, this does not appear to be an issue; the owner wishes to develop an e-commerce facility on the internet site. However, care must be taken to ensure that the site does not cause unnecessary disruption to other systems within the company.

Having determined his business strategy, he needs to look at his IT strategy. Would an internet site for bookings be part of his overall IT strategy or simply an add-on? Piecemeal implementation could affect other areas of his business systems.

The SDW Company already has an internet site, so development of any new site must take this into account along with the overall requirements of the business. Expert advice needs to be obtained as to whether or not to amend this site or design a new one. Experts in web design may have to be employed if this expertise is not available in-house.

Additional care will be required in implementing the IT, for example in ensuring that no incompatible systems are introduced. The IT systems being used in the new internet site must be able to connect to the existing call centre systems. Similarly, the initial focus of the site must be on selling seats on the company's trains; other services may be offered later, but establishing the core business first is essential.

Deciding on e-commerce may have an impact on other parts of the business. For example, setting an objective of a given percentage of business through the internet will decrease percentages of business in other areas. Within the SDW Company, there will (hopefully) be a fall in the use of the call centre. This change must be anticipated and planned for. Staff in the call centre must be kept informed concerning the setting up of the internet site, and then assurances given regarding job prospects and training, either within the call centre or other areas of the company. Where reductions in staffing are required, it is better to obtain these naturally rather than by compulsory redundancies.

Mr M should also attempt to obtain information on competitors' sites (and more broadly, sites relevant to the travel industry), to assess particularly their design and ease of use. This would be relatively easy to do – he could even visit the sites himself. This would not tell him how successful the sites were, although some companies boast about the use of their sites in published information. Some travel operators even offer discounted fares for booking this way. He should be careful that any claims are verifiable, and not just another way of attracting publicity. It may be possible to commission some survey information to obtain potential customers' views on booking through a website.

Given the need for security and the current lack of in-house knowledge, setting up an e-commerce system will require specialist assistance, either by recruitment or outsourcing the writing and monitoring of the site.

The services to be offered through e-commerce must also be determined. Decisions regarding services will have a direct impact on the writing of the website, as the authors will need to ensure that the required services can be made available. As already noted, the initial focus must be on travel bookings. Additional services and products may be made available after this core business activity has been satisfied.

Whichever method of writing the website is chosen, budgets must be set for this activity and agreed at Board level. If necessary, a cost-benefit analysis will be required, partly to justify the cost of writing the site and partly to show the potential benefits from using the website rather than a call centre.

Implementation issues

The charges (if any) for providing services to customers must also be determined. If ecommerce is to be encouraged, then some discount or other benefit can be expected to attract customers to this service. Given that this method of booking results in lower costs than when booking via a call centre, then the SDW Company can pass on these cost savings to its customers.

Prior to the e-commerce service being made available, it will have to be advertised. The Board will need to decide where to advertise and how much the advertising budget will be. Possibilities will include mail-shots to existing customers, perhaps by e-mail, and advertising on the websites of other organisations.

One of the aims of the provision of e-commerce is to try to remain competitive. A review of competitors' and other online sites is advisable to help determine the content and structure of the SDW Company site. This review may also help to identify other areas where competitors currently have an advantage so that the Board can address this.

(b) Features of internet sites focusing on cost reduction

The site must, of course, be very easy to use. SDW should specify simple instructions on a site that is easy to understand and quick to load. The omission of detailed graphics and providing an 'uncluttered' site will also decrease programming costs.

Incentives to book on-line such as obtaining loyalty benefits, cheaper prices or being able to book earlier (which may not be available on off-line bookings) could be offered. Although this may not save costs on the internet, it will provide overall cost savings by decreasing reliance on the call centre, thus limiting the number of staff employed.

Removing reliance on other more expensive selling media, such as the call centre, removes not only salary costs but also accommodation, pension, equipment and similar costs. Focusing on one booking medium becomes easier to support as only one cost structure is required.

Providing appropriate support to customers within the website which does not involve additional human contact. For example, provision of FAQs, a good help system and advice on each stage of the booking process. Customers are encouraged to resolve their own problems, which limits intervention from expensive staff.

Provision of other information on the website to attract customers to it, for example details of company performance or similar information already available within the organisation. Placing the information on the website is relatively inexpensive given that the information is already required in-house. Setting up web-specific information would be more expensive.

Innovative uses of Internet technology, for example suggesting destinations on a limited budget rather than customers specifying where they want to go. Providing these ideas as unique selling points will attract more customers to the website, again limiting reliance on other media.

Question 20: MACOMP

(a) Benefits of e-business

E-commerce refers to all transactions between an organisation and external parties using electronic media. It is more than just buying using the internet.

The main ways that e-commerce has impacted on the way business is conducted are:

(1) Sales have been made in new markets since geographical limitations have been removed by e-commerce. Orders via a website can be placed from anywhere in the world and thus organisations are able to expand their businesses cheaply and easily.

(2) Business is being conducted much more quickly, with instant orders and purchases possible via e-commerce. Next day delivery is common in many cases or at least 'estimated delivery times' from orders being placed.

(3) Costs are being reduced through e-procurement. Orders to suppliers can be directly triggered once inventory reaches a certain level. This saves time and reduces the risk of 'stock out' as well as inventory holding costs.

(4) Suppliers have been made to compete on price since e-procurement software can check prices automatically through the internet and configure purchase orders to the cheapest suppliers. This means business is conducted in a more competitive way than ever before.

(5) Business can be conducted via on line catalogues when one business is purchasing or selling from another (B2B). Quotes and estimates can be communicated via the internet which means that customer service has in many cases improved. Queries are dealt with immediately and there is an automatic 'audit trail' in terms of order information.

Information systems strategy is concerned with seeking strategic advantage from Information Technology (IT). For MACOMP, a new Information Systems strategy might impact upon corporate and business strategies in the following ways:

Impact on Corporate Strategy – IS strategy should be long term in nature and so impact on the overall strategy of the organisation. The board of directors may look at how information systems could support existing strategies, for example expansion of component manufacturing in MACOMP or how it could help develop entirely new directions for the company, for example a move into second hand component sales via the internet.

It is important that IS strategy is demand-led and so environmental analysis already carried out at a corporate level will be useful. Via PESTLE and 5 forces, the company can identify opportunities which could be exploited by a new information systems strategy.

Impact on Business Strategy – The strategy of the strategic business unit (SBU) will be affected by a new Information Systems strategy. The organisation will consider objectives at the business level, for example how the processes undertaken by managers in the OEM sales business could be speeded up in MACOMP. It will then look at what information would be needed for this to happen and how that information will need to interconnect and interact with other information in the organisation.

The reverse engineering SBU is likely to need standard order information from the customer and the ability to input measurements and 'draw' straight onto the system. Estimates can then be carried out much more efficiently.

Overall, IS strategies must be capable of delivering tangible benefits and ultimately enhanced profits.

(b) Impact on the value chain

The proposed e-commerce business will impact on every activity in MACOMP. Using Porter's value chain, the benefits to each part of the organisation can be evaluated.

Primary Activities:

Inbound Logistics – MACOMP builds components for old machinery. In order to establish which raw materials will be required for a part not made before, a qualified engineer either searches MACOMP's archives for drawings or obtains them from the Original Equipment Manufacturer (OEM). This is only the beginning of the costing process carried out by the engineer who must then pull together an estimate to be approved by the customer. An e-commerce system would allow archives to be held on the system, possibly with links to OEM archives as well. The internet would be a key resource to see if components were being supplied by competitors and at what price. MACOMP could therefore ensure a competitive quote or even access drawings from other sources.

If the parts required for each component were listed on the system, together with supplier details, it is possible that automatic orders for raw materials could be generated once a customer accepts a quotation. It would also be possible to give customers prices for components made previously by MACOMP immediately; price lists could be available via email for example.

The work the qualified engineer carries out before the price is accepted by the customer needs to be kept to a minimum to maintain competitive advantage. By transferring purchasing information onto an e-commerce system and computerising archives with links to external information via the internet, as well as making electronic price lists and on line ordering available to customers, MACOMP should be able to cut costs and so benefit strategically.

Operations – The production department is not able to schedule work until an accepted order is passed to them by a sales manager. If MACOMP had an e-commerce system in place and orders were placed electronically, these orders could interface with the production schedule which could update automatically. This would be of particular strategic benefit if the system recorded standard labour hours for each 'known component'. The customer could be given an accurate completion date electronically, improving MACOMP's core competence in customer care even further.

The small proportion of MACOMP's business which comes from the large multinational OEM's may grow once these companies are able to deal with MACOMP electronically. Since profits have been stagnant for the past 2 years, this would be hugely beneficial.

For items not made before, the estimate of the labour hours could also be built into the production schedule. One of the main strategic benefits to MACOMP would be the ability to calculate instant variances using the e-commerce system. Since the production schedule will have standard or estimated hours built in to it, any overrun can be immediately flagged and investigated. Similarly, any estimate which is not correct can be altered to produce a realistic standard cost going forward.

Outbound Logistics – MACOMP holds low levels of finished goods inventory already since goods are made to order. The main strategic benefit of an e-commerce system where outbound logistics is concerned will be the ability to give customers an accurate idea of when their components will be ready for delivery. In this way, MACOMP can maintain their competitive advantage of minimal inventory holding costs.

At present, inventories of the most commonly ordered components are kept. With an e-commerce system, MACOMP will have accurate, up to date management information as to which components should be included in this category. The system of holding such components as inventory could be replaced by a 'predictive' ordering system where MACOMP assigns each component a realistic 'life expectancy' and a repeat order to a customer is automatically generated by MACOMP's system at the end of that life. MACOMP receives a significant amount of repeat business and regular customers are likely to see this as very beneficial.

Sales and Marketing – MACOMP has not experienced growth for the last two years and this could be down to a lack of advertising and a reliance on 'word of mouth'. If MACOMP invests in an e-commerce system and has its own website, growth is likely to result from potential customers searching the internet for suppliers. At present, with no internet presence, such potential buyers do not know that MACOMP exists. A website would be advertising in itself and could be used to inform customers about MACOMP's core values and mission statement as well as answer 'frequently asked questions'.

Service – If customers are given access to a website and an email address, they will be able to submit queries to MACOMP. Dealing with customer enquiries on a timely basis will enable MACOMP to maintain the personal service they pride themselves on. In addition, it will be possible to maintain customer mailing lists on line and to communicate on a regular basis with those businesses that have purchased components from MACOMP.

Secondary Activities

Procurement – As previously mentioned MACOMP will be able to save money with e-procurement, automatically searching the internet for the cheapest supplier of raw materials and therefore forcing suppliers to compete on price.

Information Technology – MACOMP's accounting systems are not automated and transactions are recorded in manual ledgers. Investment in a computerised system means that MACOMP can implement internal controls, reduce the risk of human error and become more competitive as a result. The quality of management information produced on an IT system will far outclass anything the company has at present.

Order processing could move to being systems based so that sales staff can trace the progress of orders on the customer's behalf.

HRM – In the future, MACOMP is likely to need fewer employees since much of the manual work will be done automatically on the system. Currently, MACOMP has 120 staff who, if they are retained may find they have more time to work on growing the business as their 'manual' workload decreases.

Infrastructure – The e-commerce system may bring beneficial changes to the culture and structure of MACOMP, allowing it to be more flexible. Since far more information will be available on the system, it may be possible to alter working practices and gain competitive advantage. New roles could be created looking after overseas customers for example, who are now able to order via the internet.

The strategic and competitive benefits of the new e-commerce system to MACOMP can be seen throughout all of the businesses activities. In the long term, these benefits will enable costs to be cut and efficiencies to be exploited. Ultimately, MACOMP will be able to provide a better service to more customers.

Question 21: RBT

Intranet

An intranet is an internal company information system where a wide variety of internal information can be posted for access by staff members. Internal information often includes company news, telephone directories, standard forms, copies of rules and procedures, and so on. In this case of the system under consideration by RBT, the intranet would hold up-to-date information on products and prices, so that sales representatives can download this information to their laptops from customer's premises and other remote locations.

Advantages

The proposed new system has the following advantages over the old system:

(1) **More regularly updated information**

An intranet site is very easy and cheap to update, and product and price information can be kept fully up-to-date by head office. The downloaded product information will therefore be much more up-to-date than the old printed materials, and a better customer service can be provided. All the latest products would be made available to customers and customers would always be given the correct prices.

(2) **Reduced costs of producing price lists/brochures**

Regular price lists and brochures will no longer be required, and the production and printing costs of paper-based products should be reduced.

Disadvantages

The intranet site has the following disadvantages compared with the old system:

(1) **Slower communication with the production department**

Since the telephone system will be discontinued, the sales people will not have access to production staff to resolve any queries or difficulties with customers. This would be a serious weakness in the system. Good communications between sales and production staff must be maintained.

Solutions

Possible solutions to this problem include:

(i) *E-mail system*

E-mail might provide an efficient way for sales representatives to communicate directly with the production staff, although controls would need to be in place to ensure that the production staff respond promptly to e-mail queries they receive.

(ii) *Maintain telephone access*

Voice telephone access offers immediate communication. A salesperson can get in contact with a member of the production staff and get an immediate reply. Maintaining telephone access for certain queries would be a useful way of ensuring very quick communication where needed.

(iii) *Access to production scheduling system*

Allowing salespeople access to the production scheduling system over the intranet would allow them to estimate delivery date themselves thus reducing the need for direct contact between production and sales.

(2) **Less personal communication with production department**

The intranet is a very impersonal way to communicate with people. It does not allow for two-way conversation, whereas personal contact may be required to resolve difficult issues.

Solution

Both e-mail and a voice telephone system are more personal forms of communication than the intranet. The voice telephone system in particular allows a two-way conversation to take place so that more difficult issues can easily be resolved.

(3) **Rejection of new technology**

The sales people may dislike the new technology that they are required to use. At present they do not use IT significantly in their work, and so new skills may be required. Many new systems also have 'teething problems' on implementation, which may also make users dislike the new system.

Solutions

(i) *Training*

Training will be required so people know how the system works and can get the best use from it.

(ii) *Consultation*

Consulting users early in the development process is an excellent way of getting user buy-in to the new system. It will also ensure the system is practical from a day-to-day usage point of view.

(iii) *Testing*

Testing systems well prior to implementation will help avoid the teething problems which may be encountered, particularly if the end users are involved since they know better than anyone else the way the system will be used in practice.

(4) Up-front costs

The proposed new system will require significant up-front costs both in terms of developing the new systems and training staff. Given the relatively small number of sales representatives (just 20) the investment may not be financially justified.

Solution

A cost benefit analysis can be undertaken to ascertain whether the costs of the investment are justified.

(5) Information systems – order progress

Manufacturing system – order tracking

As part of the manufacturing process, progress on orders will need to be recorded. The information recorded will include work done, work still to do and the expected completion date. This information might already exist within the current system or it may need to be input into a database which can be accessed by clients.

EDI or extranet

Using electronic data interchange the customer would be able to log on to RBT's systems to directly access the production data.

An extranet is an extension of an intranet. External parties are allowed to log onto the intranet site and use it to access sections of the intranet. The intranet site would need to be connected to the manufacturing system/database so that up-to-date information was available.

Advantages

(1) Clients could access information themselves. This could save staff time and resources in RBT, since there will be fewer customer queries to deal with.

(2) An extranet would be relatively easy to provide if the manufacturing system is already linked to the intranet for the benefit of the salespeople.

(3) Other information could also be provided to customers (such as past order information, account balances and so on).

Disadvantages

(1) There would be a loss of personal contact with customers. The salesperson would not have as many opportunities to make contact with customers in order to build an ongoing relationship. As a consequence, they might identify fewer sales opportunities or find it harder to make a sale because they are less trusted by the customer.

(2) External parties would be accessing internal systems. There is a danger that hackers will get into parts of the system that are confidential, and a risk that important information is stolen or damaged. It could also increase the possibility of viruses being brought in which could damage internal systems.

Internet

Alternatively the RBT could put tracking information on a database which is connected to the company's web site. Clients would then be able to access their information through this site.

Advantages

(1) Labour cost savings, as described for an extranet.

(2) Customers will be familiar with the internet and so find it easier to use than an extranet or internal system accessed via EDI. It also means they will not have to dial in directly to the company's internal network, saving them time and effort.

(3) There is less opportunity for hackers or viruses to enter the internal systems using a web site on the internet, since they are not directly accessing internal systems.

(4) Other information could also be provided to customers on the internet site.

Disadvantage

The company may not currently have an internet site. This could be a significant extra expense, in terms of designing, creating and maintaining the site.

Question 22: Marketing

ABC Ltd – selling machine parts

These goods are likely to be supplied to order rather than from stock. Technical performance and reliability of the product are likely to be of primary importance. Price may be of secondary performance. There are likely to be only a small number of customers and therefore the company will only require a small sales team. Promotion and advertising are likely to be of minor importance and distribution is likely to be direct to the customer.

The company should concentrate resources in improving product performance (more regular quality controls, newer machines, well trained labour etc.) than on promotion. Economies of scale may be possible to reduce costs and selling prices.

DEF Ltd – selling consumer durables

This market is very competitive with both large national stores and local specialists competing for market share. However most products will have a manufacturer's retail price which will most companies will stick to in order to avoid price wars (even timing special sale periods to coincide with competitors). The division will sell direct to the public so place is not a vital concern for the marketing mix. The important factors are likely to be product and promotion. Consumers will be interested in areas of the product such as its efficiency, power, size etc. which the company cannot really change as it does not manufacturer the product. However DEF can augment the product with areas such as guarantees and installations. With so much competition promotion of the products will be important. Promotion should be made through adverts in newspapers, direct mailing and the use of trade in policies.

In such a competitive market, the company should concentrate its marketing on promotion and augmenting the product so that it is seen to be different from that of competitors (who are selling the same basic product).

GHI Ltd – producing and selling kids jellies

The first decision the company has to make is the place that it sells its goods. There are three possible options: through supermarkets, through independent traders (corner shops etc.) or directly to the public. There are disadvantages in all three strategies: supermarkets are powerful and will demand lower prices, independent traders are likely to give a lower volume, and selling direct to the public would involve setting up a network of retail shops which would be very expensive. It is suggested that the company aims to sell to supermarkets as this is likely to give a higher volume and agreements can be made for national coverage. If the company decides it wants to sell to supermarkets then it will have to compete for shelf space. It is therefore recommended that it follows at strategy of price penetration i.e. starts off at a low price to stimulate demand and then builds the price up as brand loyalty and awareness increase. The product should be designed to be colourful and jolly to appeal to kids.

The company should focus and place and price within its marketing mix and promotion is seen as a less important factor within the mix.

Question 23: Motor Car Pricing

The following are the major pricing approaches which may be used in this situation:

(i) *Price skimming*

This involves charging a high price relative to competitors. The advantage is that the contribution earned per unit is high. The potential disadvantage is that market share will be restricted. In this situation this restriction in market share would be beneficial in the early stages since it is expected that production in the first year is to be restricted. This would also avoid charging too low a price as happened previously. It would be necessary to advertise to promote the technological and style advantages to potential customers which would help to justify the higher price.

(ii) *Penetration pricing*

Here the aim is to charge a lower price than competitors in order to obtain a high market share at an early stage in the product life cycle. The advantage is that a lower price will encourage people to 'try out' a new product rather than keeping with a familiar 'existing' product. This incentive would appear unnecessary in this case on two counts. Firstly, the reputation of the company is well established and the car's predecessor was well received six years ago. Secondly, the car is very advanced both technically and in style compared with the competition. This 'non-price' advantage may be sufficient to encourage people to choose this vehicle.

The main advantage of penetration pricing – a high market share – would be a disadvantage for this particular car since it could result in excess demand in the first year, a waiting list and further damage to reputation regarding delivery. Another disadvantage of charging a low price is the small contribution generated on sales. It may be necessary to charge a lower price at a later stage if a superior quality competitor comes on to the market.

(iii) *Match competitor's prices*

In this case there is a further pricing option which is to charge a price at a similar level to that of competitors. The better technology and style of the car would act as selling features which could result in increased market share which would be a disadvantage in the early stages when production capacity is restricted.

Advantages are that market share may be obtained without offering a discount against competitors' prices and that a price similar to competitors' will not 'rock the boat'. A low price could start a 'price war' which could be very damaging.

Recommended pricing strategy

In this situation the approach proposed is to charge a high price relative to competitors in the first year and a price similar to that of competitors in later years because:

–   It enables a high contribution to be earned per car in the first year to compensate for the higher average cost caused by volume being lower and to aid recovery of development costs.

–   It is likely to match demand with production, i.e. low in first year and increasing thereafter.

–   High prices in the first year should prevent excess demand and waiting lists forming.

–   A high initial price may make it easier to boost market share in the second year when prices are reduced.

Care must be taken to equate demand with supply to avoid delivery delays or excess inventories. Average unit costs may be calculated for each year but this is likely to be of limited use compared with assessment of competitor prices and demand.

Question 24: Risk management

(a) Risk management when applied to an information system is the management process of ensuring that the risks to the system are removed or kept within acceptable levels. The process involves identifying and assessing the risks, deciding on appropriate controls for those risks and implementing those controls, and monitoring actual performance of the information system to ensure that the risks have been suitably controlled. Where appropriate new controls should be introduced or existing controls improved.

(b) **Classifying and managing risk**

Risks can be classified in various ways.

– Risks can be classified as risks to the achievement of strategic, financial or operational objectives.

– Alternatively, risks could be classified as risks from ineffective system design and testing, risks from inefficient operations and financial risks.

– Risks might also be categorised according to their potential severity and the probability that an adverse outcome will occur, so that they can be mapped and priorities assigned to them.

The sub-categories of risk might include:

– Ineffective system design and testing

– Delays in systems development, delaying the implantation of the system.

– Inadequate system testing, to check that the system meets user needs.

– Excessive software faults.

– Failure of the system to provide suitable information (reliable or relevant information).

– Inappropriate technology for the system, given user requirements.

Inefficient operations

- Bottlenecks in the system, resulting in processing delays.

- Frequent breakdowns.

- Inadequate use of the system.

- Inadequate security in the system, with unauthorised access from hackers, the release of confidential information or damage to data or software from viruses and worms etc.

Financial risks

- Cost over-runs on system design.

- Cost over-runs for hardware.

- Cost over-runs for system operations.

- Failure of the system to deliver the expected financial benefits.

Approaches to risk management

There are various ways in which the risk from information systems might be managed.

Risk avoidance

Risks can be avoided by not having such extensive or complex information systems. However, the risks of not having IS might be even greater than the risks of having them.

Risk transfer

Some risk can be transferred to others more able to handle it, such as a specialist supplier of software. This might reduce the risk that the system will be designed inefficiently. It might also be possible to transfer some of the financial risk by persuading a supplier to agree to a fixed price contract.

Risk reduction

Some risks can be reduced, using a variety of risk control methods.

–   Internal controls should be implemented for the operations of IS/IT systems, such as management and supervision controls, the use of anti-virus software, security controls, system design controls, and so on.

–   Some risks, particularly to hardware damage or loss, might be insurable.

–   The risks of bottlenecks on system operations, or the risks of system down-time can be reduced by investing in more hardware and communication links.

(c) **Information systems failure**

Possible reasons why systems could fail relate to the system risks described earlier. They include the following:

(1) The design of the system fails to reflect the information needs of the user, due to lack of planning, poor user involvement in the design and planning process or inappropriate hardware and software specifications. Users will be reluctant to use the system if it does not meet their specific needs or allow them to carry out their jobs effectively. User involvement is a key requirement for systems success.

(2) The data used by the system may be inaccurate or incomplete, caused by incorrect data input or incorrect processing. If data or information produced by an IS cannot be trusted by the user, it will not be used.

(3) Systems may also fail because development costs exceed budget. In some instances, development may be stopped before the system is complete because predicted future costs are considered unacceptable.

(4) The system itself may not operate particularly well, due to delays in processing or hardware and software faults.

(d) **Measures of systems success**

(1) *Level of use*

If the system is used as intended, this indicates that it is acceptable to the user. However, actual levels and frequency of use would need to be compared with the planned or expected levels of use.

(2) *User satisfaction*

Users can be asked to express their satisfaction or dissatisfaction with the system, for example by means of interviews and questionnaires.

(3) *Achievement of systems objectives*

Probably the most important measurement of systems success is whether the new system achieves or exceeds its original objectives. It is important for the project team to review the original objectives set at the planning stages of the project and compare actual operational performance and outcomes with expected performance or outcomes.

(4) *Financial benefit*

Although the actual costs of the system up to and including the actual implementation are normally quite easy to ascertain and monitor, on-going costs, in particular intangible costs and benefits are not as easy to monitor. Improved performance, increased staff morale, improved skill levels are all potential areas of benefit, but measuring their financial impact is difficult.

Question 25: MN plc

(a)

To:	The Management
From:	The Management Accountant
Subject:	Investment projects A, B and C
Date:	1 July 2006

The investment manager has analysed three mutually-exclusive investment opportunities A, B and C.

Reasons for differences between NPV and IRR rankings

There are two main reasons that NPV and IRR rankings differ:

(1) The magnitude of the cash flows.

(2) The timing of the cash flows.

Magnitude of cash flows

Imagine we were faced with a choice between the following two projects:

Project A$_1$	**Year**	**Cash flow**
		£
	0	(105,000)
	1	48,000
	2	48,000
	3	48,000

Project A$_2$	**Year**	**Cash flow**
		£
	0	(105)
	1	49
	2	49
	3	49

The cash flows in Project A_1 are approximately 1,000 times bigger than those in Project A_2. Hence the NPV of Project A_1 will be approximately 1,000 times bigger than the NPV of Project A_2. The NPV of Project A_1 is £14,376, but the NPV of A_2 will be just over £16.86. NPV would therefore suggest that Project A_1 should be preferred.

Consider the IRRs of A_1 and A_2. In project A_2 the return is £48,000 p.a., whereas project A_2 yields £49 p.a. The relative percentage return from Project A_2 is thus higher than that of Project A_1. Hence A_2 has a greater IRR than A_1.

The inconsistency in ranking has been caused by the magnitude of the figures.

Timing of cash flows

The actual time periods when the cash is generated can produce conflicting results.

Again consider two projects.

Project A_1	Year	Cash flow £
	0	(105,000)
	1	48,000
	2	48,000
	3	48,000

Project A_2	Year	Cash flow £
	0	(105,000)
	1	130,000
	2	0
	3	0

The NPV of Project A_2 is £13,170 (130 × 0.909 – 105).

This NPV is lower than the NPV of Project A_1.

The magnitude of the cash sums is very similar in both projects.

If we consider how the NPVs of the two projects reduce as the discount rate rises.

The NPV of A_1 will fall rapidly as the cash flows in the years 2 and 3 very quickly reduce in present value terms. The NPV of this project becomes zero at a 17.5% discount rate.

KAPLAN PUBLISHING

The cash in Project A_2 is all received in the first year. This cash sum is only £130,000, compared to cash in flows of £144,000 in Project A_1. However the value of the year 1 cash flow remains strong even as the discount rate rises.

Indeed, at a discount rate of 17.5% the NPV of A_2 is still positive at £5,630 (130 × 1/1.175 – 105).

Hence the IRR of Project A_2 MUST be greater than 17.5%. Again there has been a conflict in the rankings, this time because of the timing of the cash flows.

These examples should illustrate that it is just as important to consider WHEN the cash flows arise as to consider HOW MUCH the cash flows are. It is very important to obtain cash in the early years of a project whilst it holds a high present value.

Comparison of opportunities A, B and C

The capital outlay in Project C is much greater than the other two projects. Cash inflows are generated for 9 years.

At a low cost of capital this project is worth the most to the company. The cash in years 6–9 maintains a high value when discount rates are low. However, this project is very sensitive to increases in discount rates. As the cost of capital rises the NPV of Project C declines rapidly. This is illustrated in the graph at the beginning of the report.

Project A is less sensitive to increases in discount rates. All its cash is received in years 1 to 3. These maintain a strong value as the discount rate increases. Project A could be said to be the least risky of the three choices if interest rates are volatile.

Which project should be selected?

The company has a cost of capital of 10%. At this rate Project C produces an NPV of £31,432. This is of higher benefit to MN plc than either projects A or B. Hence this project should be selected.

Assumptions: cash flows are known and certain. The cost of capital is known. Taxation and inflationary aspects have been ignored. If MN plc is very risk averse, Project A may be considered as its NPV is more robust to increases in the cost of capital than projects B or C.

If you require any further information on this matter, please do not hesitate to contact me.

Signed: Management Accountant

(b) The payback period is the time that elapses before the initial cash outlay is recovered.

The paybacks in the example are:

	Assuming even cash flows	Assuming year end cash flows
Project A:	2 years 2 months	3 years
Project B:	3 years 10 months	4 years
Project C:	5 years 1 month	6 years

Advantages of payback

(1) *Exposure to risk*. It is widely recognised that long-term forecasting is less reliable than short-term forecasts. Projects with short paybacks tend to be less risky than projects with long paybacks. A project with a one-year payback is less risky than a project with a 10-year payback. Management can have very little confidence in forecasts of events ten years from now.

(2) *Liquidity*. Investment opportunities often require significant capital outlay. It may be important to recover this capital expenditure quickly for the company to maintain a strong position. Payback illustrates how quickly the capital can be recovered.

(3) *Simple measure*. The payback period is not a complicated measure. Technical expertise is not required to understand the meaning of payback.

(4) *Not subjective*. Payback period uses cash flows. Some investment appraisal methods use the rather more subjective measure of accounting profit (the accounting rate of return).

Disadvantages of payback

(1) The time value of money is ignored. Each of the projects being considered by MN plc generates £48,000. Payback period fails to recognise that as time elapses the present value of this cash diminishes. It would be possible to overcome this problem by calculating a discounted payback period.

(2) Cash flows after the payback are ignored. Option C has a payback of a little over five years. This information does not reveal that Project C continues to generate cash for four further years.

(3) Not a measure of absolute profitability. Payback fails to indicate HOW MUCH each project is worth. It seems naïve to select a project on the basis of payback without considering the amount of benefit received.

In the example Project A has a payback of just over two years, however its NPV is only £14,376.

Project C yields an NPV of £31,432 – more than double A's NPV. Payback period ignores this fact.

Question 26: Ski Runs

(a) The landowner has used a net present value (NPV) technique. This is the best technique to use for a project which is expected to last so far into the future. It means that the time value of money will be accounted for and that an estimate of the overall benefit (in current terms) of each investment can be used. The project with the highest NPV should be the project which is chosen for investment. This explains why the landowner has suggested that the low level of investment is the best decision.

The key elements of the calculation are:

(1) Fee income

This has been calculated on the basis of expected values (if 3 out of 10 seasons will be good, for example, this represents a 30% probability.

Expected number of skiers per year = [(30% × 60,000) + (40% × 40,000) + (30% × 5,000)] = 35,500

Expected fee income = 35,500 * $8 = $284,000

(2) Annual costs

The variable costs have rightly been included and calculated properly. But there is no reason to ignore fixed costs. It would be relevant to ignore fixed costs if they were not affected by the investment and were the same for each project. But that is not the case in this scenario. This is a fundamental cost for this project. It is one of the key differentiators between the investments – making the high investment might mean a higher initial lay out, but the landowner would benefit from fixed costs which are $60,000 per annum lower.

At a discount factor of 5.650 (for 10 years at 12%), the present value of the fixed costs would be $508,500 for the low investment but only $169,500 for the high investment. This would change the whole nature of the decision because the NPV of the low investment would fall to $142,600, whilst the high level investment would become $163,800. It would mean that the project decision would change and that the high investment is the better project path to follow.

(3) Loan repayments/finance cost

Discounting a project's operating flows at the investor's cost of capital allows for the meeting of finance costs of the investment (at that cost of capital) out of the inflows before giving the investor a benefit, as measured by the NPV.

An alternative approach would be to prepare a 'loan statement', showing year by year the interest clocking up, cash inflows and loan/interest payments, reaching a final net balance at the end of the project.

Including the finance cash flows with the operating cash flows in an NPV calculation would be a combination of these two approaches and would be a waste of time, if the finance cost of the investment was equal to the rate at which the flows were being discounted. This is because the NPV of the finance flows at this rate would, by definition, be 0 (see tutorial illustration below).

KAPLAN PUBLISHING

However, if the specific finance for the project is not part of the investor's general funds, with a cost at a rate differing from that used in the NPV calculation, it should be regarded as a separate set of cash flows to be included within the NPV calculation. In the case of the skiing project, half of the finance is provided by means of a subsidised loan from the Tourist Board, at 4%. Discounting these flows at the landowner's cost of capital, 12%, would actually result in a positive NPV, representing the benefit gained by receiving a loan at below average cost.

Tutorial Illustration:

For example, suppose a loan of $400,000 was taken out at an interest rate of 10%, with annual interest payments and the principal to be repaid after two years:

Time		Finance flow	10% Discount Factor	NPV
		$000		$000
0	Drawdown	400	1	400.0
1	Interest	(40)	0.909	(36.4)
2	Interest	(40)	0.826	(33.0)
2	Repaid	(400)	0.826	(330.6)
				———
	NPV			0
				———

(b) Virtually all the data used in the assessment of the project NPVs could be subject to variation, or risk. The most significant variable is probably the quality of snow cover, which in turn affects level of demand, and an attempt has been made to quantify this variability.

Other potential variables are costs, both initial and subsequent capital expenditure and annual operating costs. The discount rate (cost of capital) and fees may also be subject to variation and may have to be changed if anticipated demand levels are not realised at the original fee set.

The extent to which variability can be built into the project appraisal depends upon whether it can be expressed in quantifiable terms. If possible values for the variable can be predicted, with relative likelihoods (probabilities) then the approach may be to:

- use an expected value within one NPV calculation; or
- calculate several NPVs based upon the different values to give a range of possible outcomes.

The advantage of the first approach is that it will give a precise decision; however, that decision will be based upon a value that will often not coincide with an actual possible value. It is instead a long-run average value that may not be appropriate for a one-off situation.

The second approach will allow the investor to review all possible actual outcomes, and their likelihoods, in order that he can make a decision based upon his own risk-return preferences. This will be affected, inter alia, by the size of the investment relative to the investor's wealth and the amount he can afford to lose.

If the degree of uncertainty of an input variable cannot be reasonably quantified, the variability cannot actually be built into the NPV computation itself. However, sensitivity analysis may be used to assess the extent to which the value could change from that used in the NPV computation before it changes the decision – i.e. before it turns a positive NPV negative or vice versa.

Information about the sensitive variables in a problem will help the investor to make an informed decision.

Question 27: QS Software – Part 2

(a) Project management problems

Successful management of a project team requires:

– clarity about the project's scope and objectives, and about team member roles within it

– up-to-date awareness of (changing) project plans and feedback on current progress in regard to defined gates and milestones

– focused commitment and availability to the project (including visibility to stakeholders)

– the encouragement of multi-directional communication between team leader and members

– leadership skills: particularly in team-building, motivation and negotiation.

Sam apparently has the following key problems in these areas.

(1) He lacks clarity about the project's objectives and milestones. Not having been involved in the planning stage, and not being in direct contact with the RGA IT manager, he appears to be unaware of the project plans and crucial stage deadlines. He has therefore been unable to brief his team, who in turn have problems prioritising, co-ordinating and scheduling work.

(2) He lacks focused commitment and availability to the project, having to divide his time between RGA and other clients. This is reflected in his lack of 'visibility' to key project stakeholders (particularly the IT manager of RGA), which causes concern about the level of commitment and resource being devoted to the project. It is also likely to convey confused priorities to his team members – especially since he supports this by allowing core staff to be released from RGA work 'when necessary'.

(3) He lacks the skills and orientation for project team management. He is 'not happy' about his role as team manager/co-ordinator, as his preference is for technical work and he has little experience of people management or project management on this scale.

(4) There appears to have been little communication between team members, or between the team (as represented by Sam) and other stakeholders, either in the form of project plans or team meetings. This makes it difficult for the team to co-ordinate work, monitor progress and solve problems. It also makes it difficult for them to feel committed to the project – especially given the mixed messages from Sam.

(5) The unclear and dysfunctional project management structure exacerbates these problems. John Jones considers it to be 'his' project and therefore adopts the role of liaison between the project team and RGA – even though this is the project manager's (Sam's) role, and he himself has no day-to-day involvement in the work. John fails to communicate regularly or effectively with Sam.

(b) **Improving project management**

Recommendations for improvement in the team management, which should take effect from this point on, are as follows.

(1) Sam should be empowered to take up the project manager's role. He should be the one to be in regular contact with the client (in the person of the IT manager of RGA) – not John. Sam is already in the best position to appreciate the scheduling priorities and conflicts of the technical team, so he is in the best position to negotiate with the client. However, this requires that he also receives more information on the project scope and objectives, plans, progress and adjustments.

(2) Sam needs to dedicate his time to the RGA project and ensure that he is more 'visible' to the key project stakeholders (as a symbol of QS's commitment of resource to the project). There is genuine conflict with QS's objective of maintaining quality to other clients, but RGA must be classed as QS's key account – quite apart from the costs of continuing delays. If Sam is unwilling or unable to devote the time to RGA, QS should consider shifting the project management role to John – or to a contracted project manager.

(3) Sam needs to deploy project team members in a more focused fashion. He cannot afford to release RGA team members over the next seven or eight weeks: instead, he may have to negotiate delays with other clients. Alternatively, he may be able to sub-contract work or to hire additional specialist staff on a short-contract or freelance basis. RGA's own IT staff might also become more involved (e.g. in testing and installation).

(4) QS staff working on RGA should be regarded as a dedicated temporary project team, focusing solely on RGA work, collaborating and communicating on a regular basis. Sam should attempt, even at this stage, to do some 'team building' to enhance the team's commitment to the project, through a project re-launch (involving comprehensive briefing on the client, project scope, project plans and so on), team meetings and other techniques.

(5) Communication mechanisms should be set up to ensure regular, multi-directional flow of information about plans, adjustments and progress. Daily team review meetings might be held at QS, with regular progress reports, liaison with the IT manager of RGA and stakeholder reviews.

Question 28: Multinational and local authority

(a) The objectives of any organisation should relate to its mission. A **mission statement** is frequently formally stated, but this is not always the case. Sometimes this mission statement is informal i.e. it is not set out in unequivocal terms but is widely known and understood. The organisation's mission encapsulates the 'raison d'être' of the organisation and should focus on the demands of the principal stakeholders. Following from this, the objectives of the organisation can then be stated within the framework of the rational planning model.

Within the MNC the **main stakeholder group** would be the shareholders, whereas within the local administrative authority the main stakeholder group would probably be the local community.

It might well be that central government prescribes **objectives** for the local administrative authority, permitting some degree of freedom.

In order to determine exactly what the strategic targets should be, those responsible for the local administrative authority must make a detailed assessment of the needs of the local community. Thus there exists the need to liaise with a number of other organisations with a local presence. Whatever strategic targets are set they will be set with the over-riding need to satisfy the objective that **economic, efficient and effective** services are provided by the local administrative authority. The targets should be set in a manner that enables performance measures to be made as to the extent to which the three Es have been attained.

It is quite conceivable that the needs of the local population will vary between different areas within the overall boundaries of the authority. Statistical information should be used in order to assess the actual level of service provision against the perceived level of need; for example, in assessing whether the provision of local housing in a particular location met the demand for such accommodation. This will assist in the setting of future objectives. Perhaps it may be necessary for housing to be established as the primary objective because there is a significant under-provision of locally administered housing. If this were to be the case then it is probable that other services would be affected.

By way of contrast, an MNC is likely to find its objectives much easier to establish. The shareholders are the major stakeholder group in the business. The primary objective of an MNC will be to maximise its long-term wealth and increase the value attached to its shareholding. It is probable that the MNC has secondary objectives relating to issues such as social responsibility, ethical trading practices and the quality of goods and services. These are usually set with the attainment of the primary objective, i.e. creation of long-term wealth for its shareholders in mind.

(b) The **measurement of performance levels** achieved by an organisation must relate to the nature of the objective that has been agreed. Objectives should be capable of being measured, and thus one that is non-specific in nature is likely to prove problematic as regards its measurement. Consequently, the extent of its attainment is difficult to quantify with any degree of exactitude. It is probable that the local administrative authority will establish targets, thereby enabling measurement of the extent to which objectives have been achieved. Carefully chosen performance indicators will be monitored. For example, with reference to locally administered housing, then appropriate performance indicators would be the number of residents waiting for accommodation and the average waiting time to be housed. In the event that a reduction were to occur in the number of residents awaiting housing due to the increased provision by the authority, this would indicate that the objective of effective service provision was being achieved with regard to housing in the area.

It is also possible for performance measurement to be made utilising the **'balanced scorecard'** approach. This would be applied in respect of the financial perspective, internal business processes, learning and growth and customer perspective. In order to determine how economically the local administrative authority is providing its services, it should not only compare its results with those of previous years, but also make detailed comparisons with the results of other authorities. The authority may review its business processes for the provision of various services and state how it has made changes to these processes as a consequence of learning from experience. The conduct of customer surveys will enable the measurement of the satisfaction of local residents to be measured.

As part of the **objective setting process**, it is appropriate for the representatives of the authority to determine how objectives will be measured. The appropriateness of performance measures will need to be reviewed in order to take into account the changing nature of the service provision in respect of the dynamic business environment.

The local administrative authority should give consideration to inviting members from within the local community to contribute to the measurement of its performance. For instance the local press, charity groups and other local interest groups would invariably seek a role in measuring the performance levels achieved by the authority. It would be much more positive for them to work in conjunction with the authority towards the attainment of agreed objectives as opposed to adoption of a more combative posture.

The MNC will probably have significantly lower levels of stakeholder participation in the measurement of its primary objective. Objectives defined in terms of profitability will be set within a given timeframe. The MNC will report on the levels of its earnings and the impact upon shareholder value. The financial markets will primarily determine the extent to which the MNC is successful in achieving its objectives. In contrast, the view of the local community will be the principal determinant as to whether the objectives of the local administrative authority have been attained.

Local vested interests will inevitably be visible within a local community, whereas the shareholders of the MNC will not have interests of such a nature. The shareholders will comprise a group with disparate interests. The MNC will therefore be subject to market pressures. The market will view the worldwide activities of the MNC, and the prevailing share price of the MNC will reflect the attitude of the market to those activities.

The 'balanced scorecard' approach could be used by the MNC in order to measure its overall performance. The principal aim of this approach is the quantification of how much shareholder value has been added. In essence, the market determines this value.

Question 29: Spartan Inc.

(a) **Retained earnings** – the most important form of finance in practice for both smaller and larger businesses. However, while retained earnings may seem an easy source of finance for a company, there is a danger that if it does not achieve an adequate internal return on these retained earnings, it may become the subject of a take-over bid from another company that considers that it could manage the capital of the business more effectively. This does not apply to Spartan because they do not have sufficient funds to finance the growth.

Equity – is the net value of a company after deducting its liabilities from its assets. However, in financing language, equity is usually taken to be the share capital in the business, and a slice of equity can be sold to raise money either to invest in the business or for shareholders to realise some cash for themselves, or a mix of these. Spartan have already issued shares but could release some more. The potential benefits are:

- raise money without the burden of interest payment or compulsory capital repayment (although dividend payments will be required)

- Spartan can bring strategic partners into the company, which can help with credibility

- the new shareholders may well participate in further rounds of financing

- they can provide expertise, e.g. as non-executive directors.

Further sources of equity include:

- Personal resources, friends and family.

- Corporate venturing – where a major company invests in a smaller one, to gain access to innovation and ideas.

- Government-sponsored funds.

Grants – Grants are available for all sorts of projects, although the main targets are businesses involved in:

- innovation
- research
- export
- heritage and arts
- technology and training and
- those based in 'disadvantaged' areas.

The biggest disadvantage is identifying what grants are available, and completing the paperwork required.

Loans – there are many types.

- Regular institutional loan – from banks, etc. – money is advanced for a specific purpose and is repayable over a fixed period at a fixed or variable rate. The maximum loan amount will be based on available security (often personal) and the ability to 'service' (pay) interest and capital repayments. It may be possible to negotiate stepped payments and capital repayment holidays. The lender will want to see credible financial forecasts, especially cash flow projections.

- 'Soft' loans – from government sponsored funds – a number of loan funds have been established, financed by a mix of public and private money, to help certain defined industry sectors or regions. These loans are usually unsecured, and the terms are often easier than regular loans.

- Mezzanine funds – available from various sources including banks, venture capital firms and specialist mezzanine loan providers. This type of debt sits between equity and regular loans (hence the name). The loan is unsecured, and in return for the increased risk the interest rate will be higher and typically the lender will require the right to buy shares in the company on favourable terms (known as 'equity kicker', warrants, or share options).

The advantages and disadvantages are outlined below:

Advantages	Disadvantages
• Debt finance is usually cheaper than equity finance.	• Although debt is attractive due to its cheap cost, its disadvantage is that interest has to be paid.
• Generally, short-term borrowing (less than one year) is cheaper than longer-term borrowing.	• If too much is borrowed then the company may not be able to meet interest and principal payments and liquidation may follow.
• Debt interest is corporation tax deductible (unlike equity dividends) making it even cheaper to a taxpaying company.	• The level of a company's borrowings is usually measured by the capital gearing ratio (the ratio of debt finance to equity finance) and companies must ensure this does not become too high.
• Arrangement costs are usually lower on debt finance than equity finance and once again, unlike equity arrangement costs, they are also tax deductible.	• Many lenders will require assets to be pledged as security against loans – good quality assets such as land and buildings provide security for borrowing – intangible assets such as capitalised research and development expenditure usually do not.
• With long-term borrowing, if the borrower does not breach the debt covenants, the finance is assured for the duration of the loan.	• This risk is at its highest on overdraft borrowing where the bank can call in the overdraft 'on demand'.
	• Some types of debt finance are only available to large listed companies.

Outside of equity, loans and grants, the following sources of finance should be considered – although these will not be suitable for Spartan's investment.

Overdraft – a facility to borrow up to a prescribed amount for a defined period (usually one year renewable).

Factoring or invoice discounting – a factoring agent, usually a bank subsidiary, pays a company up to 85% of the invoice value when the invoice is originated, i.e. when the goods or services are delivered by the company. The balance is paid, less fees, when the customer settles the invoice.

Leasing, HP, contract purchase – all forms of loan where the security given is over the asset purchased.

(b) **Ratio calculations**

	Calc	20X5	Calc	20X6
ROCE	1,750/7,120	24.6%	1,500/7,500	20%
Net profit margin	1,750/5,000	35%	1,500/5	30%
Asset turnover	5,000/7,120	0.70	5,000/7,500	0.67
Current ratio	2,000/1,280	1.56	2,150/1,150	1.87
Quick ratio	1,000/1,280	0.78	980/1,150	0.85
Inventory days	365 × 1,000/3,000	122 days	365 × 1,170/3,100	138 days
Receivable days	12 × 900/5,000	2.2 months	12 × 850/5,000	2 months
Sales/working capital	5,000/720	6.9	5,000/1,000	5.0
Debt/equity	3,500/3,620	96.7%	3,500/4,000	87.5%
Interest cover	1,750/380	4.6	1,500/400	3.75

The return on capital employed of Spartan has declined as a result of both falling net profit margin and falling asset turnover: while comparable with the sector average of 25% in 20X5, it is well below the sector average in 20X6. The problem here is that turnover has remained static while both cost of sales and investment in assets have increased.

Despite the fall in profitability, both current ratio and quick ratio have improved, in the main due to the increase in inventory levels and the decline in current liabilities, the composition of which is unknown. The current ratio remains below the sector average, however. The increase in both inventory levels and inventory days, together with the fact that inventory days is now 53% above the sector average, may indicate that current products are becoming harder to sell, a conclusion supported by the failure to increase turnover and the reduced profit margin. The expected increase in sales volume is therefore likely to be associated with a new product launch, since it is unlikely that an increase in capacity alone will be able to generate increased sales. There is also the possibility that the static sales of existing products may herald a decline in sales in the future.

The decrease in receivables days is an encouraging sign, but the interpretation of the decreased sales/working capital ratio is uncertain. While the decrease could indicate less aggressive working capital management, it could also indicate that trade creditors are less willing to extend credit to Spartan, or that inventory management is poor.

The gearing of the company has fallen, but only because reserves have been increased by retained profit. The interest cover has declined since interest has increased and operating profit has fallen. Given the constant long-term debt, the increase in interest, although small, could indicate an increase in overdraft finance.

Ratio analysis offers evidence that the financial performance of Spartan Inc. has been disappointing in terms of sales, profitability and inventory management. It may be that the management of Spartan see the increase in capacity as a cure for the company's declining performance.

(c) The current gearing of Spartan Inc. = $100 \times (3.5m/4m)$ = 87.5%

Total debt after issuing $3.4m of debt = 3.5m + 3.4m = $6.9m

New level of gearing = $100 \times (6.9m/4m)$ = 172.5%

Current annual loan note interest = $350,000 ($3.5m \times 0.1$)

Current interest on overdraft = 400,000 − 350,000 = $50,000

Annual interest on new debt = $272,000 ($3.4m \times 0.08$)

Expected annual interest = 400,000 + 272,000 = $672,000

Current profit before interest and tax = $1.5m

Current interest cover = 3.75 (1.5m/0.4m)

Assuming straight line depreciation, additional depreciation = $600,000 per year

Expected profit before interest and tax = 1.5 + 1.43 – 0.6 = $2.33m

Expected interest cover = 3.47 (2.33/0.672)

This is lower than the current interest cover and also assumes no change in overdraft interest.

Thus, Spartan's gearing is expected to rise from slightly below the sector average of 100% to significantly more than the sector average. Spartan's interest cover is likely to remain at a level lower than the sector average of four times, and will be slightly reduced assuming no change in overdraft interest.

Question 30: Bits and Pieces

(a) The decision to open on Sundays is to be based on incremental revenue and incremental costs:

	Ref	$	$
Incremental revenue	(W1)		800,000
Incremental costs			
Cost of sales	(W2)	335,000	
Staff	(W3)	45,000	
Lighting	(W4)	9,000	
Heating	(W5)	9,000	
Manager's bonus	(W6)	8,000	
Total costs			(406,000)
Net incremental revenue			394,000

Conclusion

On the basis of the above it is clear that the incremental revenue exceeds the incremental costs and therefore it is financially justifiable.

(W1) Incremental revenue

Day	Sales	Gross profit	Gross profit	Cost of sales
	$	%	$	$
Average	10,000	70.0%		
Sunday (+60% of average)	16,000	50.0%	8,000	8,000
Annually (50 days)	800,000	50.0%	400,000	400,000
Current results (300 days)	3,000,000	70.0%	2,100,000	
New results	3,800,000	65.8%	2,500,000	

(W2) Purchasing and discount on purchasing

Current annual purchasing is $18,000 × 50 = $900,000
Extra purchasing from Sunday trading is $800,000 – $400,000 = $400,000
New annual purchasing is ($900,000 + $400,000) × 0.95 = $1,235,000
Incremental cost is $1,235,000 – $900,000 = $335,000 (a $65,000 discount)

(W3) Staff costs

Staff costs on a Sunday are 5 staff × 6 hours × $20 per hour × 1.5 = $900 per day Annual cost is $900 × 50 days = $45,000

(W4) Lighting costs

Lighting costs are 6 hours × $30 per hour × 50 days = $9,000

(W5) Heating costs

Heating cost in winter is 8 hours × $45 per hour × 25 days = $9,000

(W6) Manager's bonus

This is based on the incremental revenue $800,000 × 1% = $8,000 (or $160 per day)

KAPLAN PUBLISHING

Tutorial note

Only relevant cash flows should be taken into consideration when making this decision, i.e. the future incremental cash flows that occur as a result of Sunday opening. Prepare a summary of the relevant cash flows and reference in workings, where required.

(b) The manager's rewards can be summarised as follows:

Time off

This appears far from generous. The other staff are being paid time and a half and yet the manager does not appear to have this option and also is only being given time off in lieu (TOIL) at normal rates. Some managers may want their time back as TOIL so as to spend time with family or social friends; others may want the cash to spend. One would have thought some flexibility would have been sensible if the manager is to be motivated properly.

Bonus

The bonus can be calculated at $8,000 per annum (W6); on a day worked basis, this is $160 per day. This is less than that being paid to normal staff; at time and a half they earn 6 hours × $20 × 1.5 = $180 per day. It is very unlikely to be enough to keep the presumably better qualified manager happy. Indeed the bonus is dependent on the level of new sales and so there is an element of risk involved for the manager. Generally speaking higher risk for lower returns is far from motivating.

The level of sales could of course be much bigger than is currently predicted. However, given the uplift on normal average daily sales is already +60%, this is unlikely to be significant.

(c) When new products or in this case opening times are launched then some form of market stimulant is often necessary. B&P has chosen to offer substantial discounts and promotions. There are various issues here:

- *Changing buying patterns:* It is possible that customers might delay a purchase a day or two in order to buy on a Sunday. This would cost the business since the margin earned on Sunday is predicted to be 20% points lower than on other days.

- *Complaints:* Customers that have already bought an item on another day might complain when they see the same product on sale for much less when they come back in for something else on a Sunday. Businesses need to be strong in this regard in that they have to retain control over their pricing policy. Studies have shown that only a small proportion of people will actually complain in this situation. More might not, though, be caught out twice and hence will change the timing of purchases (as above).

- *Quality:* The price of an item can say something about its quality. Low prices tend to suggest poor quality and vice versa. B&P should be careful so as not to suggest that lower prices do not damage the reputation of the business as regards quality.

Question 31: Teemo

REPORT

To: The Managing Director of Teemo
From: Management Accountant
Date:
Subject: Month 6 Variance Report

This report aims to explain and interpret the Month 6 variance report.

Original planned profit

As can be seen from the original standard cost card, the original plan was to sell the product for £250. With a cost per unit of £160 (made up of material, labour and overhead costs), a contribution of £90 was planned for each unit.

Teemo budgeted to produce and sell 1,000 units so total contribution was expected to be £90,000. Budgeted fixed overheads (which could include items such as rent and insurance) were expected to be £70,000 so that a profit of £20,000 was the company's original target.

As actual profit was only £11,140 there must have been some deviation (or 'variance') away from the original plan. The variance report aims to explain why and where this has occurred.

Variances

There have been a number of deviations away from the original plan and each one is split into a different variance on the variance report.

Volume variance

Teemo sold 200 units more than was budgeted. So at a contribution of £90 per unit this should have created an extra £18,000 of profit. This is the 'volume variance' so that the expected profit on actual sales of 1,200 units was £38,000. This may have been caused by the fall in selling price (see next variance).

Sales price variance

The sales price variance is negative as it has been deducted from the expected profit – it has had an 'adverse' affect on profit. This tells us that the actual selling price of the product must have been below the original budgeted price of £250.

As 1,200 units were sold and the variance totals £12,000, the reduction in price must have been £10 per unit. So the actual selling price must have been reduced to £240 per unit. Without further investigation we do not know why the price was lowered, it could have been a deliberate marketing strategy or a reaction to similar moves by rivals.

Materials price variance

This is another adverse variance – in order to have an adverse affect on profit the price per kg of material (budgeted to be £20/kg) must have increased. The company spent £132,300 on 6,300kg of material which gives an actual price of £21/kg. This £1/kg increase for the 6,300kg purchased has caused the £6,300 adverse variance. This might have been caused by an uncontrollable change in market price or a switch of supplier.

Materials usage variance

Teemo originally planned to use 5kg of material on each unit of production. As 1,200 units were produced, 6,000kg should have been used. 6,300kg were actually used which gives an adverse variance of 300kg. At a standard cost of £20/kg, this caused the adverse usage variance of £6,000. This might have been caused by a change in the materials used causing unfamiliarity to staff.

Labour rate variance

A favourable labour rate variance means that there has been a positive effect on profits by a change in the labour rate per hour. £5,040 was saved on the 5,040 hours worked – a saving of £1 per hour. The budgeted rate per hour was £10 so the company must have paid an average rate of only £9 per hour. Perhaps a lower grade of labour was used – which might also explain the adverse materials usage variance.

Labour efficiency variance

Teemo budgeted for each unit to take 4 hours of labour. The total expected time for the 1,200 units actually produced would therefore be 4,800 units. 5,040 hours were actually worked, giving 240 extra hours of labour that weren't expected. At a standard cost of £10 per hour this creates a total adverse variance of £2,400. This would be consistent with the use of a lower grade of labour who may take longer to complete the task.

Variable overhead expenditure variance

There was no variance here which means that the planned expenditure on variable overheads per hour (£5) and the actual cost per hour must have been the same.

Variable overhead efficiency variance

Variable overhead efficiency is linked to the labour efficiency variance (and will have an identical cause). Because labour worked 240 hours more than expected, the company's machines, for example, will have had to have been operated for an extra 240 hours – this gives an extra cost to the company. At a standard cost of £5 per hour for variable overheads, the total extra cost will be £1,200.

Fixed overhead variance

The adverse fixed overhead variance tells us that Teemo spent £4,000 more than the £70,000 originally budgeted on these costs. More detailed analysis is not possible without a detailed breakdown of the individual elements of the fixed overheads, but this could be caused by extra system costs of monitoring new staff, materials wastage etc.

Overall

The variance report highlights that the main cause of the downturn in profits was the cost overruns – especially on materials. The next step should be to investigate why these variances occurred.

Question 32: Tupik

(a) The net profit for each product is calculated as follows:

	A	B
	$	$
Direct material cost	2	40
Variable production overhead cost	28	4
Fixed production overhead [$40 (W1) × hours]	10	6
Total cost	40	50
Selling price	60	70
Net profit	20	20

Overall

On the basis of profits, both products give the same net profit per unit and therefore the company would be indifferent as to which one should be produced.

(W1)

Fixed production overhead is absorbed at an average rate per hour:
Total hours (120,000 * 0.25) + (45,000 * 0.15) = 36,750
Absorption rate per hour = $1,470,000/36,750 = $40

(b) **Production plan**

Decision making should be based on contribution rather than on net profit. Also, when there is a scarce resource/bottleneck, the contribution per usage of the scarce resource should be used in order to reflect the bottleneck problem. For Tupik this would appear as follows:

	A	B
	$	$
Selling price	60	70
Less:		
Direct material cost	2	4
Variable production overhead cost	28	40
Contribution	30	26
Bottleneck hours per unit	0.02	0.015
Contribution per bottleneck hour	1,500	1,733

The company should then prioritise sales and production of the product with the highest contribution per bottleneck hour. This means that product B should take priority.

Maximum demand of product B = 45,000 * 120% = 54,000 units
Bottleneck hours required for B = 54,000 * 0.015 = 810 hours
Bottleneck hours available for A = 3,075 – 810 = 2,265 hours
Output of product A which is possible = 2,265/0.02 = 113,250 units

So the production plan should be to make 54,000 units and prioritise production resources to this product, and then to make 113,250 units of A. This is less of product A than is currently sold, but overall profits should be increased.

Existing profits

	A	B	Total
Net profit per unit	$20	$20	
Production sales	120,000	45,000 units	
Net profit in total	$2,400,000	$900,000	$3,300,000

Profits from new production plan

	A	B	Total
Contribution per unit	$30	$26	
Production sales	113,250	54,000 units	
Contribution in total	$3,397,500	$1,404,000	$4,801,500
Fixed overheads			$1,470,000
			————
Total net profit			$3,331,500

Other factors to consider

The increase in profits is marginal ($31,500) and it may well be that the cost of reorganisation and planning may outweigh this. It should be considered whether this is a one-off, short-term problem or a longer-term issue.

It may be that the bottleneck can be removed. Product A makes a contribution per unit of $30 and there is a potential unsatisfied demand of 30,750 units (maximum demand is 144,000 and only 113,250 will be produced). So there is a potential gain of almost $1m. If it would cost less than this to remove the bottleneck then that strategy should be pursued.

KAPLAN PUBLISHING

From a strategic point of view the company should consider the longer term impact on customers, rivals and shareholder returns. It a lack of product availability might harm company reputation and provide competitors with greater economies of scale and a better competitive position. It may also be that the products are at different stages of their life cycle and that it may be a better strategy to maximise production and sales of A even if it means lower profits in the short-term (for example, if this product is in decline the company may want to sell as many as possible before sales completely dry up).

Overall

There are many factors to consider in making the production decision. But the use of net profit per unit over-simplifies the situation and could lead to poor decision making.

Question 33: Cost accounting

Traditional costing

The variable cost per unit of the product is $36 per unit (direct material $14 + direct labour $19 + variable overhead $3 = $36).

The total (full) cost of the product is $124 per unit (variable cost $36 + fixed overhead (8 hours × $11) = $124)

The red return from investment in the product is

= $600,000 × 15% = $90,000

The required return per unit sold = $90,000/3,800 units = $23.68

The required selling price = $124.00 full cost + $23.68 = $147.68

Activity based costing

The most appropriate cost driver for reviews would be the number of reviews per service.

Total number of reviews = (50 × 3) + (100 × 0.5) + (400 × 2) = 1,000

Cost per review = $55,000/1,000 = $55

The review cost for statutory audit services = $55 × 3 = $165.

Activity based costing was originally developed for manufacturing industries. But it has now gained widespread use in many service organisations such as hospitals, accountancy practices, banks and insurance companies. It is just as important for these businesses to control costs, maximise the use of resources and improve pricing as it is in a manufacturing business.

An accountancy practice would seem to satisfy much of the criteria that make ABC relevant and useful to an organisation in that:

- indirect costs are high relative to direct costs (accountancy firms will have high levels of indirect overheads such as administrative costs, rent, depreciation, insurance etc. and very low direct costs such as material), and

- services are complex and are often tailored to customer specifications (and therefore, unlike in traditional costing, it would not be very useful to have one sole cost driver [such as direct labour hours] for all services).

Decision making

In view of its scarcity, labour is taken as the limiting factor.

The decision on whether to make or buy the component has to be made before it can be decided whether or not to accept the contract. In order to do this the contribution per labour hour for normal production must first be calculated, as the contract will replace some normal production.

	Basic		Scientist	
	$	$	$	$
Selling price		5.50		7.50
Materials	1.25		1.63	
Labour	1.50		2.25	
	—		—	
		2.75		3.88
	—		—	
Contribution		2.75		3.62
		—		—
Contribution per direct labour hour (@0.25/0.375 hours per unit)		11.00		9.653

Therefore, if the company is to make the component it would be better to reduce production of the 'Scientist' model, in order to accommodate the special order.

The company should now compare the costs of making or buying the component.

An opportunity cost arises due to the lost contribution on the Scientist model.

Special contract:	*Manufacture of component*
	$
Materials	1,000
Labour ($6 × 150 hours)	900
Opportunity cost (150 hours × $9.6533)	1,448
	———
Production cost	3,348
	———

Since this is higher than the bought-in price of $2,500 the company would be advised to buy the component from the supplier if they accept the contract.

The contract can now be evaluated:

	$	Contract contribution $
Sales revenue		35,000
Material cost	9,000	
Component	2,500	
Labour ($6 × 1,200)	7,200	
		18,700
Contribution		16,300
Contribution per direct labour hour		$13.58

Since the contribution is higher than either of the existing products, the company should accept the contract assuming this would not prejudice the market for existing products.

Because the contribution is higher for the 'Basic' model, it would be wise to reduce production of the Scientist model. However, the hours spent on producing the Scientist model per month are 4,000 units × 0.375 hours – 1,500, and so the contract would displace 80% of the production time of the scientist model. The recommendation assumes that this can be done without harming long-term sales of the scientist model (the scenario suggests that the demand for the product is high and therefore there would be no lost sales of the product in the long term).

As the customer is overseas, this seems a reasonable assumption. However, before finalising the decision there are many other factors that should be considered such as:

- whether all costs have been considered (for example, extra delivery costs for the overseas customer)

- the potential impact of any foreign exchange rate movements

- whether this will be a one-off contract or whether it will open the door for more profitable work with this customer

- the value of the experience and impact on overseas reputation of beginning to export the product

- the level of competition for the contract

- the extra administration involved in dealing with a foreign customer (such as dealing in a foreign language and performing reasonable credit checks etc.

- the potential impact on existing customers who buy packages of basic and scientific models

Dealing with risk and uncertainty

There are number of possible outcomes that need to be considered here and the expected value for each of these needs to be considered.

The value of the contract with the existing client is

= 3 years × 1,000 hours × $60 per hour contribution = $180,000.

If the firm remains in the east, there will be an extra $4,000 in administrative costs and a bid fee of $20,000 giving two possible net outcomes from the bid as follows:

	Probability	Net outcome
Win the bid	60%	$156,000
Lose the bid	40%	($24,000)

The expected value for this is

= (60% × 156,000) + (40% × –24,000) = $84,000

If the organisation moves to the west it will win additional work alongside the contract with a value of

= 3 years × 3,000 hours × $80 per hour contribution = $720,0000

But moving to the west would mean that there would be a required investment of $750,000 and the bid preparation cost would be $30,000. The net outcome of losing the bid would therefore be

= 720,000 – 750,000 – 30,000 = ($60,000)

This would give two possible net outcomes from the bid as follows:

	Probability	Net outcome
Win the bid	80%	$180,000
Lose the bid	20%	($60,000)

The expected value for this is

= (80% × 180,000) + (20% × –60,000) = $132,000

There is no advantage of moving to the west unless the contract bid is also made (if the firm moves to the west without bidding and winning the contract it will lose $30,000). On the basis of expected values, the best course of action is to move to the west and bid for the contract (this provides an expected value of $132,000 as opposed to only $84,000 if the bid is made from the existing eastern office).

But there are many other factors that the firm should consider before finalising its decision. Some of these are discussed below.

The expected value technique used has a number of issues. For example, it ignores the range of possible outcomes when the decisions are compared. Staying in the east has a range of –$24,000 to $156,000, but moving to the west opens the firm up to the possibility of a much higher loss of $60,000. If the firm is very risk averse then this may help decide in favour of remaining in the east. Also, the technique used is based on subjective probabilities and some sensitivity to these should be determined. Finally, the expected value technique is best used for long-term recurring decisions rather than for one-off decisions such as this.

The firm should also consider whether failing to move to the west and match the clients needs might lead to the loss of existing work with this client - especially if the door is opened to a competitor in the west to build a relationship with the client. Also, the possibility of further work from the client as it expands in the future might open up even greater opportunities for the firm.

There may also be some synergies possible from having offices in two locations such as having better access to staff or offering staff secondments between offices. It may also be that new clients won in the west may be able to provide extra work for the eastern office.

But there may also be problems with operating in the west such as the ability of the firm's organisational structure to cope with having offices in more than one location. Or it may be that the money tied up in the investment may have been better used for other strategies or opportunities.

Overall, it would appear that moving to the west has a strong financial logic. But major strategic decisions such as this should be evaluated against much wider criteria than a simple expected financial outcome.

Variance analysis

Sales price variance:

	$
Units sold should have sold for (1.800 units × $18.25 per unit	32,850
(actual sales revenue)	32,300
Sales price variance	550 (A)

Sales volume variance	**Units**
Actual sales volume	1,800
Budgeted sales volume	1,750
Sales volume variance	50
× standard profit per unit	× $6
Sales volume profit variance	$300 (F)

If marginal costing is used, the contribution per unit is $8.50 ($18.25 – 6.00 – 3.00 – 0.75)

Sales volume variance	**Units**
Actual sales volume	1,800
Budgeted sales volume	1,750
Sales volume variance	50
× standard contribution per unit	× $8.50
Sales volume contribution variance	$425 (F)

Question 34: Jays

(a) There are a number of Human Resource Management (HRM) issues that will be impacted upon by the move from retailer to services.

Recruitment

On a fundamental level, when Jays were retailing shoes they operated 123 outlets; the move into repairs meant trebling the number of outlets to over 300. This expansion will have meant a significant increase in the number of employees within the outlets. As well as this, the skills required between retailing and repair are different and so different types of employee would have been hired.

In addition, the number of outlets may require an increase in the management positions at head office analysing the data produced.

Finally, Jays is expecting that more difficult repairs will be carried out at a national centre. Specialist employees to carry out this work will need to be recruited.

Training

There are some overlaps between the retailing and repairs businesses. Retailing is very much geared towards customer service, an area that Jays has identified as important within the repairs business. There will obviously be some training involved for the watch repairers. However, it has already been identified that this can be broken down into ten easy operations. This should make the training progress quicker.

Delegation

It appears that Jays is already a decentralised organisation since much of the decision-making is already carried out at each individual outlet. Jays will need to ensure that there is consistency between outlets particularly over which repairs are passed back to the national centre.

Culture

The culture within the outlets at Jays may cause the management problems. As the company concentrated less on shoe retailing and more on shoe repair, the culture of the craftsman may have appeared. Under this, knowledge, skill and experience would be respected and passed on to more junior members of staff (almost like apprentices). The watch repair side, as noted above, has been made extremely simple with the result that the status of the 'expert' repairer may be diminished.

(b) Motivating the workforce at Jays may prove more difficult than it initially appears. A number of methods that might normally work in companies might prove difficult to implement in Jays' situation.

For example, the work at Jays might prove to be monotonous and so job rotation might be undertaken. The difficulty with this is that this would mean training all the staff in the skills of shoe repair which might prove costly. Similarly, due to the geographical area being covered, moving staff between branches may not be practical.

Another common motivation technique would be to undertake job enrichment, whereby members of staff add on new skills to their current ones. Again, in the context of Jays' large number of small (ten employees or fewer) autonomous shops there is a limit to how far this can be developed.

One suggestion would be to reward staff on the outcomes of their performance. For example, measuring customer feedback (although how useful this might prove is debatable). A broader reward based on the financial performance of the shop might be introduced. The difficulty with this is that the nature of the business is reactive, if nobody's shoes need repairing there is nothing the branch can do about it.

The likelihood is that some kind of competence-based system will be introduced. Under this, the employee would be graded by the branch manager on how well they fulfil certain competencies. These might include technical competencies such as their knowledge and the quality of their repairs and to service competencies such as how well they deal with customers.

Question 35: Y

(a) Resistance to change in organisations can be considered according to whether the resistance comes from individuals, groups or the organisations themselves.

Individual level

At the individual level, the following reasons/causes have been noted as factors involved in resistance: fear of the unknown, well-formed habits, threats to economic interest/status and the threat of inconvenience. In the case of Y, there is much for employees to fear. Several will be afraid that, in the longer term, they may lose their jobs. Some will fear that they may have to move from one job to another or from one department to another. For some, this will be quite an upheaval, although others may welcome the change. Some will fear that the change may bring a loss of status in the organisation, especially those in middle management whose jobs are to go. Redeployment to another job may include a protected salary, but delayering will inevitably result in a loss of status for some employees. Then there are the problems with learning new skills. Some employees will fear that they might not make the grade and be reluctant to take on retraining.

Group level

At group level there will be collections of individuals who see their position threatened and who will combine to resist any threats to their position. The middle management groups in Y in particular will feel threatened and will be looking to their trade union to protect their interests. There may well be calls for industrial action to attempt to prevent delayering from taking place, or at least to win for the managers affected the highest possible severance pay or redeployment terms.

Even where individuals are not members of a trade union, it is possible for groups of employees, including managers, to collude informally to resist change. This may be achieved by such measures as withholding information or by not being wholly co-operative with those seeking to implement change.

Organisational level

At the level of the organisation, a number of factors will operate to make the change process difficult. These included the existing structure and culture of the organisation, the existing investment in resources, and past contracts and agreements with various stakeholders within the organisation. For example, many state industries that have been privatised in recent years have required flatter, more organic, organisational structures; it is hard to change from a 'role' culture to a 'task' culture to cope with competition in the open market and hard to renegotiate the terms of the contracts with stakeholders, such as the trade unions.

(b) A useful way of looking at the problem of resistance to change is via the simple framework formulated by American social psychologist, Lewin.

Lewin's framework suggests that change, or lack of it, is the result of disequilibrium or equilibrium between two sets of opposing forces. One set he refers to as 'driving' forces, because they act to encourage and facilitate change, and the other as 'restraining forces' because they act in the opposite direction and seek to maintain the status quo.

Any attempt to bring about change, therefore, requires ways and means of overcoming resistance to change. This may be achieved in a variety of ways, but it is apparent that what is required is either a further strengthening of the forces for change or a reduction in the power of restraining forces.

Using this framework we can see that the major driving force for change is the increasing competition brought about by changes in the industry environment. There is little that Y can do about this except to respond to it by becoming leaner and more effective. The reduction in management levels should help to cut costs, and the strengthening of the telephone banking division should help the bank's competitiveness, as should the investment in IT and training.

The spur to change is the threat of the new competition, and management should seek to communicate the message to managers and other employees more effectively. We cannot tell from the scenario just what attempts have been made to communicate to the workforce either the seriousness of the bank's situation, or the rationale behind senior management's plans to combat this situation. To the extent that the need for the planned action has not been properly communicated it follows that this must be an early priority for the senior management team. Communication, along with other means such as education, participation, consultation, manipulation and coercion are part of typology of methods advocated by theorists such as Kotter and Schlesinger for assisting in the management of change process.

It may be that communication is not sufficient and that a process of education is required. In this day and age the senior managers should tread carefully. Bank employees generally have a high level of education and it would not help the case for change if management underestimated this. Nevertheless, in trying to persuade employees that the plans management have drawn up are in the best interests of all, there may be a place for the education of some staff members to management's point of view.

A method associated with communication and education is that of facilitation and support. Y management may be able to alleviate fears of some individuals by the use of counselling and group discussion.

Another way of reducing resistance to change is that of involving all employees from the start of the change process. By putting the problem the bank is facing to employees in a series of face-to-face meetings, and offering the possibility of participation in the decision-making and planning process, it may be possible to get more employees to buy into the planned changes. The problem in the case of Y is that senior management may already have made decisions without consultation. This kind of participation exercise is also time-consuming.

Given that the decisions have been made and that resistance has already been encountered it may well be that the best way forward now is through a process of negotiation with representatives of the workforce. In the case of Y it is probable that trade union officials will represent the employees' side. Through a process of negotiation and bargaining it may be that the union can gain sufficient concessions from management, in terms of built-in safeguards and appropriate compensation for its members. The bank could then be allowed to proceed without further hindrance.

An alternative approach is the less ethically based use of manipulation and co-optation. Manipulation involves seeking to persuade people by the use of partial and misleading information while co-optation involves 'buying people off' by the promise of some kind of reward for going along with the proposed changes. Through these methods are used, they are not the kinds of methods that professional people would involve themselves with.

If all else fails, however; senior management may find that the use of explicit and implicit coercion is the only way forward. This may involve mass redundancies without right of appeal. This method would be one of last resort since the image of the bank would suffer and the morale of the remaining workforce would be badly affected.

Question 36: BHH Clothing

(a) The strategic context

The key environmental issues are as follows:

– High customer power.

– The threat from low cost competitors.

Both of these threats are likely to increase rather than decrease.

The options available to BHH include the following:

(1) The main advantages of the current plan are that they should reduce cost without compromising quality. Furthermore BHH keeps the higher-skilled value-added finishing aspects in-house. This should help BHH manage the threat from low-cost competitors but does not address the problem of high customer power.

(2) Keep manufacturing in Europe but focus on improving production efficiency to reduce costs. This could involve implementing TQM, better use of IT, improved throughput, eliminating processes that do not add value and improving employee motivation and output. This could be planned as part of a BPR project but is likely to be just a short term fix. In the longer term the threat from lower-cost Chinese manufacturers will still need to be addressed.

(3) BHH could shift both manufacturing and finishing overseas, focusing mainly on the customer relationship and design aspects. This should reduce costs further but would lose the differentiating factor that comes from high quality finishing.

(4) BHH could seek to sell goods under its own brand name to reduce customer power. However, this will require substantial investment to develop the BHH brand in the market.

(5) BHH could seek to vertically integrate forwards and open its own retail outlets. Again, the problem for BHH would be the major investment required.

(6) BHH could manufacture higher volume garments overseas but seek to make and deliver small batches of more exclusive lines with shorter lead times. This would allow BHH to be more responsive to market trends, thus reducing the risk of "fashion miss" (i.e. producing items that consumers do not want). The offer of reduced lead times may be difficult for Chinese firms to match and so would enhance BHH's strategy of differentiation. This would also reduce the scale of redundancies facing BHH.

Summary

Given its lack of brand strength, BHH has to move at least some of its manufacturing overseas to respond to the serious environmental threats it faces. Major change is thus unavoidable. However, the directors may wish to consider option 6 above as a way of reducing the impact of the change process.

(b) **Contextual features**

The key contextual features are as follows:

- **Time** – Given the recent loss of Forum and the threat from other retailers, BHH has to act quickly to develop a response. The time context is close to being a crisis rather than allowing an incremental approach. Time must thus be viewed as a strong driver of change but as a negative aspect in terms of how easy that change will be.

- **Scope** – A significant proportion of manufacturing must be outsourced but design and finishing should continue as before without major changes. On balance the scope aspect is best described as realignment rather than transformational.

- **Preservation** – It is vital that design, customer service and finishing skills are retained, despite other production staff (presumably) being made redundant. A major threat is that current employee unrest will result in key staff looking for new jobs elsewhere. The existing culture may need to be refocused firmly on high quality and customer responsiveness.

- **Diversity** – While there is likely to be a difference in sub-culture between production and design, only the latter will really be impacted by the change. Furthermore, there is likely to be a strong sense of unity within BHH due to them all being based in the same location and the length of time many employees have worked together. Given that the change will primarily impact production workers, diversity is unlikely to be a problem. (Note: were BHH to switch to short lead-time, small-batch production, then the change would be more widespread, in which case diversity would be a more major consideration).

- **Capability** – Given that management have so far resisted the industry trend to outsource production, it is likely that BHH does not have staff who are experienced in change and change management.

- **Capacity** – Given falling margins it is probable that BHH does not have significant funds to invest in the change process. However, the move to outsourcing will not require significant funds. Instead there will be pressure on management time to locate and screen potential suppliers. There is insufficient information available to determine whether or not this will be a problem.

- **Readiness** – A major problem facing management is that staff have discovered some aspects of the change without being properly informed. The negative implications have thus been blown out of proportion, resulting in threatened strike action. Staff are thus likely to oppose any changes rather than support them.

- **Power** – There is insufficient information to determine how much authority and respect change agents have to implement proposed changes. It is clear however, that employee representatives are key players in the change process.

(c) Design choices

Key recommendations are as follows:

- **Change path** – The most pressing problem is to avoid strike action and to reassure staff about the actual changes proposed. Only then can management look to address the details of how, when and where production should be outsourced.

- **Change start point** – The crisis nature of the problem necessitates a top-down approach initially where senior management need to regain control of event.

- **Change style** – Once the immediate problem of staff unrest is addressed, management should adopt a participative approach to involve employee representatives in deciding how and where redundancies should be made, whether some staff could be retrained and what support will be offered to staff who lose their jobs.

- **Change interventions** – Initially the key mechanism is likely to be communication and education to convince employees that only production staff involved in making the basic garments might lose jobs. As stated above participation will be key to successful change management.

- **Change roles** – Given the lack of experience of change, BHH may wish to employ the services of external consultants. Either way it is vital that change action teams are set up, including designers, finishers and production staff. BHH could also consider including representatives from key customers to improve BHH's chances of keeping their accounts. Certainly consultants should be used to investigate potential Chinese suppliers.

Index

Index

KAPLAN PUBLISHING

Index

Index